Computers

Second Edition

Larry Long

Nancy Long

Prentice Hall, Englewood Cliffs, New Jersey 07632

Library of Congress Cataloging-in-Publication Data

Long, Larry E.
    Computers / Larry Long and Nancy Long.—2nd ed.

        p.   cm.
      ISBN 0–13–168626–7
      1. Computers.   2. Electronic data processing.   I. Long, Nancy.
    II. Title.
    QA76.L576   1990b
    004—dc20   89–26437
                                                          CIP

*To our children, Troy and Brady. They bring
great joy to our lives.*

Editorial/production supervision: Nancy DeWolfe
Interior design: Linda Conway and A Good Thing, Inc.
Interior illustrations: Network Graphics
Cover design: Jerry Votta
Manufacturing buyers: Laura Crossland and Mary Ann Gloriande
Page layout: Karen Noferi and Lillian Caporlingua

 © 1990 by Prentice-Hall, Inc.
A Division of Simon & Schuster
Englewood Cliffs, New Jersey 07632

Printed in the United States of America
10 9 8 7 6 5 4 3 2 1

ISBN 0-13-168626-7 01

Prentice-Hall International (UK) Limited, *London*
Prentice-Hall of Australia Pty. Limited, *Sydney*
Prentice-Hall Canada Inc., *Toronto*
Prentice-Hall Hispanoamericana, S.A., *Mexico*
Prentice-Hall of India Private Limited, *New Delhi*
Prentice-Hall of Japan, Inc., *Tokyo*
Simon & Schuster Asia Pte. Ltd., *Singapore*
Editora Prentice-Hall do Brasil, Ltda., *Rio de Janeiro*

Overview

APPENDICES

Contents

v

APPENDICES

Preface to the Student

We are in the midst of a technological revolution that is changing our way of life. The cornerstone of this revolution, the computer, is transforming the way we communicate, do business, and learn. This text provides an overview of computers—what they are, what they are doing, and what they can do. Once you have read and understood its content, you will be poised to play an active role in this revolution.

Getting the Most from This Text

The layout and organization of the text and its content are designed to be interesting, to present concepts in a logical and informative manner, and to provide a reference for the reinforcement of classroom lectures.

A good way to approach each chapter is to:

1. Look over the Student Learning Objectives in the chapter opener.
2. Turn to the end of the chapter and read the Summary and Important Terms.
3. Read over the major headings and subheadings and think of how they are related.
4. Read the chapter and note the important terms that are in **boldface** type and in *italic* type.
5. Relate photos and photo captions to the text. (A picture is worth a thousand words.)
6. Go over the Summary Outline and Important Terms again, paying particular attention to the boldface terms.
7. Take the Self-Test. Reread those sections that you do not fully understand.
8. Answer the questions in the Review Exercises.

Color is used throughout the book to add another dimension to the learning process. There are many instances where concepts can be reinforced and made easier to understand with the judicious use of color. We call this the *functional use of color.*

Computers is supported by a comprehensive learning assistance package. The package is detailed in the "Preface to the Instructor." Ask your instructor about the availability of these learning supplements.

You, Computers, and the Future

Whether you are pursuing a career as an economist, a social worker, an attorney, a dancer, an accountant, a computer specialist, a sales manager, or virtually any other career from shop supervisor to politician, the knowledge you gain from this course ultimately will prove beneficial. Keep your course notes and this book, because they will provide valuable reference material in other courses and in your career. The chapter material addresses a broad range of computer concepts that occur frequently in other classes, at work, and even at home.

The use of computers for information processing is in its infancy. By taking this course, you are getting in on the ground floor. Each class you attend and each page you turn will present a learning experience that will let you advance one step closer to an understanding of how computers are making the world a better place in which to live and work. You also will be gaining the knowledge necessary to become an active participant in what is the most exciting decade of technological innovation and change in recorded history.

Preface to the Instructor

Much has transpired since 1986 when students began using the first edition of *Computers*.

- The technology has taken yet another giant leap.
- Students are more aware of computers and information processing and of how they affect them personally, both now and in the future.
- College curriculums in all disciplines have been modified to recognize the growing importance of computers.

In this second edition of *Computers* we have retained the basic pedagogical philosophy that made the first edition a bestseller, while making revisions to reflect advances in the technology, greater student awareness, and the inevitable evolution of college curriculums.

In the late 1980s, computer knowledge has moved from the "nice-to-have" category to the "career-critical" category. What students learn (or do not learn) in the introductory computer course probably will have some bearing on how successful they are in their chosen careers. This places a tremendous responsibility on you, as instructors, and us, as authors. We were ever cognizant of this responsibility during the writing of the second edition. In that regard, we have been careful to cover from all angles the *what, why, when, where, how,* and *who*.

- *What*. All appropriate terms and concepts are discussed at a level of depth and in a manner in which they can be understood and applied to personal and business computing needs.
- *Why*. Hundreds of times throughout the book we explain why— why use this DBMS, why use this printer, why use this programming language, or why use computers.
- *When*. As needed, we describe when, or under what circumstances, a concept or tool is applied or implemented (prototyping or proprietary software, for example).
- *Where*. We feel that students should know where concepts are applied (for example, in which industry or at which level in a company).
- *How*. We address the "how" aspect of pedagogy many times in every chapter—how a compiler works; how an information sys-

tem is developed; or how data are stored on a magnetic disk. (The supplements package includes "how to" books on micro applications software and BASIC programming.)

- *Who*. *Computers* identifies who is responsible for accomplishing particular tasks (functional specifications, maintenance of operating systems) or who employs a particular aspect of automation (CASE tools or decision support systems).

Intended Audience

The target course for the second edition of *Computers* and its teaching/ learning system consists of students who have a variety of skill levels, interests, and career orientations. The course covers a broad range of introductory computer and information processing concepts, applications, issues, concerns, and trends. The teaching/learning system includes hands-on laboratory materials for MS-DOS, WordPerfect, Lotus 1-2-3, dBASE III PLUS and dBASE IV, and BASIC programming. The student completing this course will use his or her newly acquired knowledge to become an effective end user of computers or as a stepping-stone to a computer-related career.

Features

All the features that made the first edition a success remain intact, and a few have been added.

- *Applications oriented*. Throughout the book, concepts are presented within the context of computer applications.
- *Presentation style*. *Computers* is written in a style that remains pedagogically sound while conveying the energy and excitement of computers to the student. Moreover, the material is written so that it can be understood by average learners, yet challenge the more advanced students.
- *Functional use of color*. Color is used functionally to relate ideas to one another and to illustrate the text. We pioneered this pedagogical innovation in the first edition.
- *Readability*. All elements (box items, photos, figures, memory bits, and so on) are integrated with the text to create a reading and study rhythm that complements and reinforces learning. The reading level was carefully monitored to avoid the problems associated with inappropriate levels of presentation.
- *Currency plus*. The material is more than current, it's "current plus"—anticipating the emergence and implementation of computer technology. *Computers* covers connectivity, magneto-optical (read-and-write) disks, expert systems, electronic data interchange, CASE, SQL, and all the other "hot topics."
- *Flexibility*. The text and its teaching/learning system are organized to permit maximum flexibility in course design and in the selection, assignment, and presentation of material.

- *Chapter pedagogy*. Chapter organization and pedagogy is consistent throughout the text. The chapter is prefaced by *Student Learning Objectives*. In the body of the chapter, all major headings are numbered (1–1, 1–2, and so on) to facilitate selective assignment and to provide an easy cross-reference to all related material in the supplements. Important terms and phrases are highlighted in **boldface** print. Words and phrases to be emphasized appear in *italics*. Informative box items, photos, memory bits (outlines of key points), and cartoons are strategically positioned to complement the running text. Each chapter concludes with a *Summary Outline and Important Terms*, *Review Exercises* (concepts and discussion), and a *Self-Test*.

The Second Edition

It is our feeling that the second edition of any college text should reflect not only the pedagogical philosophy of its authors but its first-edition users as well. Fortunately, we had the opportunity to gather formal and informal feedback from many of the thousands of professors who used *Computers* in the classroom. The second edition of *Computers* is the result of our collective thinking. For those of you who are familiar with the first edition, the following summary of revisions may help you to better evaluate the book in relation to your college's educational needs.

1. The coverage of microcomputer productivity software is now integrated into the chapter material (from an appendix).
2. Coverage of BASIC has been rewritten and moved from the main text to a special BASIC supplement.
3. The chapters have been reorganized for better flow and to reflect changes in the technology, student awareness, and curriculums.

   - The two "Computers in Society" chapters (2 and 17) have been trimmed to one (Chapter 17).
   - The mainframe chapter now precedes the micro chapter.
   - The I/O chapter now precedes the data storage chapter.
   - Chapter 10, "The MIS and Decision Support Systems," has been added.
   - The two chapters on information system applications (12 and 13) have been combined into Chapter 11, "Applications of Information Technology."
   - Those areas in which coverage varies markedly between curriculums have been moved to appendices. These include the history of computers, numbering systems, design techniques, and programming concepts.

4. Changes have been made on virtually every page of the second edition, but the following changes from the first edition would be considered major:

- The information in the micros chapter (3) is expanded to help prepare students for the actual use and operations of micros.
- The data communications chapter (7) now includes a segment on connectivity.
- The data management chapter (9) is expanded to include coverage of all three major types of database management system software.
- Coverage of management information systems, decision support systems, and expert systems is expanded (Chapter 10).
- Coverage of prototyping is expanded, and coverage of automated applications development is added (Chapter 12).
- The material in Chapters 14 and 15 on micro productivity software has been written to reflect common business applications.

The *Computers* Teaching/Learning System

The second edition of *Computers* is the cornerstone of a comprehensive teaching/learning system. The other components of the system are:

Computers Annotated Instructor's Edition The *Computers* Annotated Instructor's Edition (AIE) is an innovation in introductory computer education. The AIE is a four-color instructor's version of *Computers* that includes lecture notes, teaching tips, interesting supplemental material, in-class discussion questions and exercises, supplemental examples, warnings, quotes, cross-references to other components of the teaching/learning system, and much more—all in the margin of the text! When you open your book, you not only see what the student sees, but you see what you need to deliver an interesting and informative lecture on the accompanying material. The AIE also contains an Instructor's Resource Manual that has teaching hints, chapter outlines with key terms and concepts, solutions to exercises, instructions on the use of all of the teaching and learning materials, and teaching notes to accompany the BASIC supplement to this text.

Instructor's Resource Manual on a Disk Most of the Lecture Notes portion of the IRM is available on disk in a generic ASCII format. Use your word processing package to customize this IRM lecture material to meet your teaching style and educational objectives.

Study Guide The student *Study Guide* is designed to support the student learning objectives. Section I, the first of four sections, contains Student Learning Objectives, Important Terms, and a Self-Test for each chapter or appendix in the main text and for each learning module in the BASIC supplement. Section II contains the Checkups for material in the text and in the BASIC supplement, which can be assigned as hand-in exercises. Section III contains the answers to the Self-Tests in Section I. Section IV is the "Guide to *The New Literacy* Videotape Series." This section provides material that enables students to make the most effective use of the 26-part videotape series *The New Literacy: An Introduction to Computers.*

CAPS (Computer-Assisted Presentation System)—Electronic Transparencies *CAPS*, a breakthrough in instructional technology, provides instructors with an integrated set of dynamic graphics, sometimes called *electronic transparencies*. Graphic displays are used in conjunction with a personal computer and a screen-image projector to enhance and facilitate classroom lectures. These computer-based "transparencies" enable the *dynamic* presentation of graphics, text, and animation. The transparencies contain key lecture points and appropriate graphics, and can be recalled from a menu and displayed as needed.

Microcomputer Software: Step by Step Many introductory computer courses have a microcomputer lab component. *Microcomputer Software: Step by Step* by Ted Kalmon, Larry Long, and Nancy Long (Prentice Hall, 1990) is written to support laboratory courses teaching word processing, electronic spreadsheet, or database software in the IBM PC environment. Specifically, this lab book contains conceptual overviews, step-by-step hands-on tutorials, exercises, and quick reference guides for MS-DOS (3.3 and 4.01), WordPerfect (5.0), Lotus 1-2-3 (releases 2.01 and 3.0), and dBASE III PLUS and IV. The step-by-step tutorials are organized in topical sessions. *Microcomputer Software: Step by Step* is written to be consistent with the pedagogy and examples in *Computers*; however, it can also be used as a stand-alone text.

BASIC for Introductory Computing *Computers* is available with or without BASIC. In the BASIC version, the booklet *BASIC for Introductory Computing* by Larry Long (1990, Prentice Hall) is packaged with the main text. The increase in cost is nominal. The BASIC supplement is a concise treatment of the BASIC programming language and is designed especially to complement introductory computer courses. The booklet, which is less than 100 pages long, is divided into five learning modules so that the student can systematically progress through increasingly sophisticated levels of understanding. If you wish only to expose the student to BASIC and assign a few simple programs, then Modules I, II, and III will suffice. Modules IV and V take the student to an intermediate skill level.

Test Item File Diskettes and Booklet The *Test Item File*, which covers material in both *Computers* and *BASIC for Introductory Computing*, comes in both diskette and booklet forms. The *Test Item File* contains over 3842 multiple-choice, true/false, and essay questions for the main text and 385 questions for the BASIC supplement. The *Test Item File* diskettes are distributed for use with *DataManager*, Prentice Hall's test preparation and classroom management software.

Prentice Hall DataManager (Computer-Based Testing and Classroom Management) The *Prentice Hall DataManager* is an integrated IBM-PC–compatible software package that provides a complete classroom management system. Broad in its scope, the package allows instructors to design and create tests, to maintain student records, and to provide practice testing for students.

The *PH DataManager* has three modules: the Test Manager, the Grade Manager, and the Study Manager. The Test Manager module allows you to interact with the *Computers Test Item File* to construct and print exams. Use this module to create your own customized exam or request that the exams be generated randomly. You can also edit *Test Item File* questions and add questions of your own. When printed, the exam is ready for duplication. Student answer sheets and the answer key are also produced. The Grade Manager module is a record-keeping system that keeps track of student performance and calculates grades. The Study Manager module is used in conjunction with a computer-based file of the questions in the *Study Guide*.

Computerized Testing Service   The Computerized Testing Service is available free of charge to all instructors who adopt *Computers*. This service eliminates the tasks associated with test preparation by providing a customized exam based on the questions in the *Test Item File*. To take advantage of this service, simply call in your test order to Prentice Hall.

Color Transparency Acetates   One hundred color transparency acetates, which support material in the text and the *Computers* Annotated Instructor's Edition, are provided to facilitate in-class explanation. Fifty percent of the acetates are taken from the text; the remainder are supplemental.

Full Function Word Processing Software   Prentice Hall has made a special arrangement with its parent company, Simon & Schuster, Inc., that will enable students using *Computers* to purchase the full function versions of Webster's NewWorld Writer and its 100,000-plus word Spelling Checker for about the cost of the diskettes! These Simon & Schuster products sell for more than $100 at computer stores. Webster's NewWorld Writer has redefined the meaning of "user-friendly" in word processing software. Its easy-to-use, menu-driven user interface is designed to display instructional prompts in windows if the user hesitates in selecting an option from a menu. A student can actually learn Webster's NewWorld Writer while using it—without a manual.

Microcomputer Software and Micro Software Support Materials   Prentice Hall is the largest and most prolific publisher of computer textbooks in the world. In many instances, full function and educational versions of commercial software are distributed with these books (WordPerfect, The TWiN [emulates Lotus 1-2-3], dBASE III PLUS, and Excel, for example). We recognize that your laboratory environment may have special needs. In that regard, your Prentice Hall representative will be happy to discuss the many options you have in the selection of lab manuals and support software.

Videotape Series—*The New Literacy: An Introduction to Computers* A 13-tape, 26-segment video series, entitled *The New Literacy: An Introduction to Computers*, sets the material in the text into motion. Each video addresses a particular facet of the use and application of computers. The videotape series is made available free of charge to qualified adopters of *Computers* and to others at discount prices. *The New Literacy*, which is produced by the Southern California Consortium, was released in 1984 and revised in 1988. The *Study Guide* contains assignments, videotape overviews, and review exercises that relate to *The New Literacy* videotapes.

Video Software Tutorials—The *Video Professor* A series of video tutorials are available to qualified adopters. For the IBM-PC–compatible environment, the series includes instructional tapes for MS-DOS, WordPerfect 4.2 and 5.0, Lotus 1-2-3, dBASE III PLUS, dBASE IV, WordStar Professional, Microsoft Word, Ventura, MultiMate Advantage II, Excel, and Microsoft Works WordProcessing. The *Video Professor* series also includes instructional tapes for the Apple II, IIe, IIc, and IIgs environment and the Macintosh environment.

SuperSoftware The dual-purpose SuperSoftware is equally effective as a stand-alone educational software package or as a vehicle for in-class demonstration of a myriad of computer-related concepts. When used as a hands-on educational package, SuperSoftware actively involves students through interactive communication with the computer. It contains 50-plus hours of hands-on lab activity for the IBM PC version (25-plus hours for the Apple version) and is designed to instruct, intrigue, and motivate. SuperSoftware provides many dynamic electronic transparencies. When used in conjunction with a screen-image projector, SuperSoftware can demonstrate dozens of important computer (configuring a micro), information processing (airline reservations), software (mail merge with word processing), and programming (sorting) concepts.

Author "Hotline" Professors and administrators of colleges adopting *Computers*, Second Edition, are encouraged to call Larry or Nancy Long (the hotline number is in the "Preface to the Annotated Instructor's Edition") to discuss specific questions relating to the use of the text and its support package or to discuss more general questions relating to course organization or curriculum planning.

Acknowledgments

Computers, Second Edition, is the continuation of a long and fruitful friendship that we have enjoyed with the people at Prentice Hall. Many of these dedicated professionals have made significant contributions to *Computers* and its accompanying teaching/learning system, and we thank them one and all. Several people embrace *Computers* with the same passion that we do, and well they should—it is their book, too. They are Gary June, Nancy DeWolfe, Ted Werthman, Linda Conway, Lori Drazien, Jenny Kletzin, Laura Crossland, Janet Schmid, Karen Noferi, and Mary Ann Gloriande. We would also like to express our gratitude to managers Dennis Hogan, Jeanne Hoeting, Caroline Ruddle, and Alison Reeves for their continued support and commitment to excellence. Also, we would like to extend our special appreciation to our colleague and friend, Ted Kalmon, for his insight and contributions to the support package.

Thousands of professors selected the first edition for use in their classrooms. We thank them, for without their confidence and encouragement, there would be no second edition. Continuing the tradition, the second edition is also a product of collective thinking. In that regard, we are deeply indebted to our colleagues:

- Michael J. Belgard, Bryant and Stratton College
- Roy Bunch, Chemeketa Community College
- Marvin Daugherty, Indiana Vocational Technical College
- Joyce Derocher, Bay de Noc Community College
- Kirk L. Gibson, City College of San Francisco
- Randy Goldberg, Marist College
- Don Hall, Manatee Community College
- Seth Hock, Columbus State Community College
- Dr. M. B. Kahn, California State University at Long Beach
- Michael A. Kelly, City College of San Francisco
- Constance A. Knapp, CSP, Pace University
- Sandra Lehmann, Moraine Park Technical College
- William McTammany, Florida Community College at Jacksonville
- Margaret J. Moore, Coastal Carolina Community College
- Thomas H. Miller, University of Idaho
- Anne L. Olsen, Wingate College
- Verale Phillips, Cincinnati Technical College
- Mark Seagroves, Wingate College
- Bari Siddique, Texas Southmost College
- Dr. Joseph Williams, University of Texas at Austin
- Larry B. Wintermeyer, Chemeketa Community College
- Floyd Jay Winters, Manatee Community College

Nancy Long, Ph.D.   Larry Long, Ph.D.

Computers

1

The World of Computers

STUDENT LEARNING OBJECTIVES

- To grasp the scope of computer understanding needed by someone living in an information society.
- To contrast the function and purpose of an information services department with that of an information center.
- To distinguish computer myth from computer reality.
- To distinguish between data and information.
- To describe the fundamental components and the operational capabilities of a computer system.
- To learn ways in which the computer can enhance our lives.

1-1 Why Study Computers?

In his book *Cultural Literacy*, E. D. Hirsch discusses a body of knowledge that is "necessary for functional literacy and effective national communication." Hirsch says, "To be culturally literate is to possess the basic information needed to thrive in the modern world."* To thrive in the business world, you need to possess both cultural literacy and **computer literacy**.

Hirsch's concept of cultural literacy does not include such terms as *network*, *data base*, *microcomputer*, or *output*. Yet these and hundreds of other computer-related terms are used in everyday conversation by those who aspire to be successful in the business world—accountants, secretaries, salespeople, hospital administrators, lawyers, newspaper reporters, financial analysts, and people in hundreds of other professions. The same can be said about the world of education and of government.

Until recently, **computers** were found only in environmentally controlled rooms behind locked doors. Only computer professionals dared enter these secured premises. In contrast, computers today are found in millions of homes and just about every office. In fact, most office workers have a computer or **video display terminal** at or near their desks. The video display terminal, or **VDT**, is a device with a televisionlike screen and a keyboard that permits communication

Just a few years ago, paperwork, dated reports, manually completed forms, and telephone tag were the norm in the business world. Today we are making a transition to an information society. Computer-based information systems enable "knowledge workers" at this insurance company to have ready access to the information they need to accomplish their jobs.

*E. D. Hirsch, *Cultural Literacy* (New York: Vintage Books, 1988).

A computer artist used a computer and 3D graphics software to create this remarkable street scene image. The chapter openers throughout the book provide a gallery for this new art form.

with a remote computer. You probably have seen people interact with VDTs at airports, banks, around your college, and in many other places. Eventually, all of us will have at least one computer, and we will use it every day in our work and leisure. That day is not too far away.

Computer Literacy

A decade ago, the term *computer literacy* had little meaning. Either you were a computer professional who had dedicated years of study to computers or you were not. Only computer professionals were computer literate. Things have changed. Now computers are for everyone!

In a few months, you will achieve computer literacy. So what does this mean to you? You will:

The precise, untiring movement of a computer-controlled industrial robot helps this reliability engineer test a new keyboard to ensure that the feel of the keys meets company standards.

The play-by-play announcer for the Washington Redskins games uses a personal computer to speed his work and add depth to his commentary. For example, when the Redskins block a punt, he enters *block* and *last time* to get an immediate display of the date, who blocked it, and against what team.

1. Feel comfortable using a computer system.
2. Be able to make the computer work for you through judicious development of *or* use of **software**. (Software refers collectively to a set of machine-readable instructions, called **programs**, that cause the computer to perform desired functions.)
3. Be able to interact with the computer—that is, generate input to the computer and interpret output from the computer.
4. Understand how computers are changing society, now and in the future.
5. Be an intelligent consumer of computer-related products and services.

Why Computer Literacy?

There are four main reasons to become computer literate:

1. To realize that the computer revolution is upon us and computers are affecting the way we live, work, and play.
2. To overcome any fear of computers.
3. To learn the jargon, called *computerese*.
4. To attain a level of computer education that will enable you to take full advantage of the opportunities afforded by the computer revolution.

The Computer Revolution   In a little more than three decades, computer technology has come a very long way. The first commercial computer was large enough to fill a gymnasium and was considered too expensive for all but the largest companies. Today the small **personal computers**, also called **PCs**, that we use for all kinds of domestic and business applications are thousands of times faster and more powerful than the first commercial computers. If the automobile industry had experienced similar progress, a new car would now cost less than a gallon of gas!

The *computer revolution* is upon us. This unprecedented technical revolution has made computers a *part of life*. With the rapid growth

COMPUTER LITERACY: REAL QUESTIONS WITH REAL ANSWERS

These questions and answers on computer literacy first appeared in Larry Long's "Turnaround Time" column, formerly a regular feature in *Computerworld*, a newsweekly for the computer community.

Q. Is computer literacy a fad or bandwagon on which people hop without thinking? The two most visible impacts on society in this century have been the automobile and the computer. I have not, however, found any reference to an "automobile literacy." I can make a few minor adjustments, such as pumping gas and changing tires, but when my car really needs attention, I take it to an expert. I know a few buzz words like *compression ratio*, and I even have a vague idea of what they mean. This knowledge neither helps nor hinders me when I drive across town.

Computer literacy is relative. I am a manager and professionally could stand to be more computer literate, but I know enough to be able to punch the keys on an automatic teller machine.

A. The analogy to automobile literacy does not hold water. Those of us who drive automobiles take full advantage of their potential. When it is cold we turn on the heater; at night, we turn on the lights; on the interstate, we drive within the speed limit. A typical auto will have about 20 user-controlled options.

Computing hardware and the associated concepts are much more sophisticated. A computer user may have thousands of control options. Computer-literate people do not have to understand synchronous communications protocols, but they should have a basic understanding of the devices and appropriate associated concepts such as data management, systems versus applications software, and so on.

Perhaps the term *computer literacy* is a fad, but the concept is not. A person achieves computer literacy at a point in time. Part of becoming computer literate is learning that there is much more to learn. Unless a computer-literate person retains some exposure to the dynamic field of computers, that knowledge is quickly lost or becomes obsolete.

Over 90% of the population between the ages of 21 and 65 are "automobile literate," but less than 5% of that same group can "drive" a computer.

Q. It is our responsibility as managers to de-emphasize computer literacy as a priority goal in our society. I would prefer that my son learns to think, feel, and understand than to find his precocity in the byways of the computer world. Likewise, I seek in a prospective employee one who can think analytically and creatively and can relate to other people in a sensitive manner.

The computer is a fine tool, but can't it be learned as needed to meet the tasks at hand?

A. You imply that computer literacy and learning to "think, feel, and understand" are mutually exclusive activities—and many agree with you. Although I agree that thinking, feeling, and understanding are worthy developmental goals, I contend that computer literacy can be a part of that development and perhaps even hasten progress toward other goals.

When you recommend that the computer be learned as needed, you are suggesting that we be reactive rather than proactive to a need for automation. I have always recommended that both computer professionals and users have a storehouse of knowledge that can be applied immediately to a variety of situations.

Q. Computer literacy happens to be one of my pet peeves. Nobody can define it but everybody is selling it. Even if a computer illiterate knew what it was, he or she still would not know how to go about becoming computer literate.

Computer literacy comes in different flavors. Computer professionals are computer literate, but this level of knowledge is not necessary for the ordinary computer user. What are the necessary conditions for computer literacy, then? I believe that a necessary condition is an understanding of how a computer "thinks," with all it implies. In general, this means an understanding of the interconnection of hardware, the functions of the operating system, and the mechanics of software application.

In essence, what every computer illiterate needs is to attend a good seminar on "computer mentality." Do you agree?

A. Perhaps *computer mentality* may someday nudge out *computer literacy* as the term of choice, but both still address the same issue—introductory computer education.

in the number and variety of computer applications, they are rapidly becoming a *way of life*.

In our private lives, computers may speed the checkout process at supermarkets, enable 24-hour home banking, provide up-to-the-minute weather information, and, of course, entertain us with video games. And if that is not enough, computers are the culprits behind our "conversations" with elevators, automobiles, and vending machines.

In our professional lives, the computer is an integral tool in the performance of many jobs. In the theater, set directors create and view sets on the computer before constructing them. Sociologists use the computer to analyze demographic patterns. Writers use word processing systems to check spelling, grammar, and style. Geologists rely on an "expert" computer system for guidance in the quest for minerals. Financial analysts examine up-to-the-minute securities information on their workstations. Computer artists have millions (yes, millions!) of colors from which to choose.

On the down side, the computer revolution has raised serious social issues. Personal information is more accessible and therefore more vulnerable to abuse. The "take" in an average "electronic heist" is a hundred times that of the more traditional bank robbery. One computer-controlled robot can replace four or more workers. These and other automation issues are discussed in Chapter 17, "Computers in Society: Today and Tomorrow," and throughout the book.

Computers and technology in general have potential for both good and bad. Numerous surveys have attempted to evaluate public opinion on computers and automation. The findings show that the overwhelming majority believe that computers enhance the quality of life. People have become committed to a better way of life through computers, and it is unlikely that the momentum toward this goal will change. It is our responsibility to ensure that this inevitable evolution of computer technology is directed to the benefit of society.

Fear of the Unknown   Computers are synonymous with change, and any type of change is usually met with some resistance. We can attribute much of this resistance to a lack of knowledge about computers and, perhaps, to a fear of the unknown. It is human nature to fear that which we don't understand, be it the Extra Terrestrial or computers.

Fear of the computer is so widespread that psychologists have created a name for it: **cyberphobia**. Cyberphobia is the irrational fear of, and aversion to, computers. In truth, computers are merely machines and don't merit being the focus of such fear. If you are cyberphobic, you will soon see that your fears are unfounded.

Computerese   A by-product of the computer revolution is a new language called **computerese**. Computerese is a mixture of English and computer jargon, which could just as well be ancient hieroglyphics to the novice. With the expanded use and acceptance of computers both at home and at work, it is becoming more and more important to be fluent in computerese. You may be happy to know that you are already well along your way to fluency in computerese. You are probably familiar with about half of its vocabulary. For example, you know:

- window
- read
- run
- bit
- menu

- block
- bug
- page
- host
- gateway

- write
- job
- word
- memory
- field

- record
- flag
- trace
- loop
- load

Your familiarity with these terms is the good news. Now for the bad news: They all mean something different in computerese. In computerese, you don't "walk through a *gateway*," "apply for a *job*," "wave a *flag*," or "*load* a truck." But, as you will learn, a parallel often exists between the computerese usage and the common definition of familiar words. Before you become fluent in computerese, you will need to learn many new vocabulary words, such as *byte* and *ROM*.

Opportunity Computers provide many opportunities for us to improve the quality of both our private and professional lives. The challenge is to take advantage of these opportunities. People like you who are willing to put forth the effort and accept the challenge will be the ones who benefit the most.

For some, this course will be a stepping-stone to more advanced topics and, perhaps, a career in information systems or computer science. For others, this course will provide a solid foundation that

The computer system at this West Coast textile warehouse helps administrative personnel keep track of orders and shipping information.

will prove helpful in the pursuit of virtually any career. In either case, you will be prepared to play an active role in the age of information.

Achieving Computer Literacy

Computer literacy is achieved through study, practice, and interest in the topic. There is no "quick fix" that will result in your becoming a computer-literate person. A magazine article, a few television shows, or a computer demonstration may serve to heighten your interest, but these are side trips on the way to computer literacy. You are about to embark on an emotional and intellectual *journey* that will stimulate your imagination, challenge your every resource from physical dexterity to intellect, and, perhaps, alter your sense of perspective. Computer literacy is more than learning—it's an adventure. Enjoy your journey into the world of computers!

1–2 Computers Are for Everyone

From Dirt to Data

Two centuries ago, 90 of every 100 people worked to produce food. As people became more efficient in food production, an *agrarian society* gave way to the growth of an *industrial society*. Today, two people produce enough food for the other 98, and the industrial society is making way for an emerging *information society*.

The trend in today's factories is paralleling that of the farm 200 years earlier. If history repeats itself (and most experts believe it will), automation will continue to reduce the number of workers needed to produce manufactured goods. And, sometime in the near future, our industrial society will mature into an information society.

In an information society, **knowledge workers** will concentrate their energy on providing a myriad of information services. The knowledge worker's job function revolves around the use, manipulation, and dissemination of information. Today it is a bit difficult to imagine a society that may become desperately dependent on certain information services. Let's put it into perspective. How would our nineteenth-century forefathers react to our need for television and hair dryers? Who among us would give up our hair dryer!

And so it will be with the inevitable information services. Grocery shopping will be done from the comfort of our own homes. When diagnosing a patient, a physician will routinely ask for a second opinion—from the computer, of course. National elections will be completed in minutes. Many factories will have no windows or light—most industrial robots don't need to see.

Computer Systems Then and Now

In "the old days," that is, during the 1950s, 1960s, and even into the 1970s, business computer systems were designed so that a computer professional served as an intermediary between the **end user** and the computer system. End users, or simply **users**, are blue- and white-

With a personal computer, you are the boss! Computing capabilities similar to those of much larger computers are within arm's reach. This man is is updating the guest list and creating an imaginative invitation for his daughter's upcoming birthday party.

collar workers who use the computer to do their jobs better. In the past, plant supervisors, financial directors, and marketing managers would relate their information needs to computer professionals, such as programmers or systems analysts, who would then work with the computer system to generate the needed information.

In "the old days," the **turnaround time**, or elapsed time between the submission of a request for information and the distribution of the results, could be at least a week or as much as a month. The resulting information was often obsolete or of little value by the time it reached the manager.

The *timeliness of information* is critical in today's fast-paced business world. Managers can't wait for the information they need. They want it now, not next week or next month. In response to managers' requests for more timely information, computer systems are now designed to be *interactive*. **Interactive computer systems** eliminate the need to interact through an intermediary (the computer professional) and permit users to communicate directly with the computer system. This interactive mode of operation gives managers the flexibility to analyze the results of one query, then make subsequent queries based on more information.

Fortunately, today's computers are for everyone. And that's good, because virtually everybody will be using them! Today computers and software are being designed to be **user friendly**. Being user friendly means that someone with a fundamental knowledge of and exposure to computers can make effective use of the computer and its software. Ten years ago, this was not the case. If you didn't have a computer science degree and the mental agility of a wizard, you were out of luck.

Hackers: Computer Enthusiasts

The majority of white-collar workers and a growing number of blue-collar workers are end users. Traditionally, users have relied on the technical expertise of professional programmers and systems analysts to write programs and select computers. But more and more users have taken a keen interest in computers and have educated themselves to the point where they can write their own programs and are comfortable with sophisticated software and hardware.

Many of these sophisticated users are **hackers**, a name given to computer enthusiasts who use the computer as a source of recreation. Hackers all over the country have formed clubs and associations to share interesting computer discoveries. Hackers are old and young, manager and laborer, ecologist and geologist, all sharing a common bond: to explore the seemingly infinite capabilities of their computers. On occasion, hackers have carried their enthusiasm for computers beyond the limits of the law. It is perfectly legal for willing hackers to share files and ideas, but it is not legal for hackers to use their computers to tap into sensitive business and government data bases. Unauthorized access to data bases is discussed in more detail in Chapter 13, "System Implementation."

1–3 Supporting a Company's Information Needs: Where to Go for Help

The Information Services Department

Most companies have a computer center and the personnel to support their **information systems**. An information system is a computer-based system that provides *data processing capability* and *information for making decisions*. This combination of computing equipment (called **hardware**), the software that tells the computers what to do,

The hub of any information services division is the central computing facility that houses the mainframe computer system.

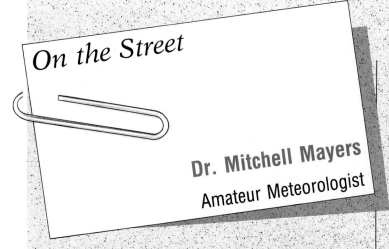

A though a dentist by profession for almost 25 years, Dr. Mitchell Mayers has another passion: predicting the weather. And this passion has turned into quite a hobby for Mayers, who founded the Rockland Climatic Station in West Nyack, New York. He has filled the spare room of his home with a menagerie of meteorological equipment, including an IBM PS/2 Model 30 (to forecast weather), a Hewlett-Packard color printer (to produce graphs and maps), and a facsimile machine hookup to the National Weather Service.

Like most weather fanatics, Mayers loves storms—especially snowstorms. When one hits their area, Mayers and his teenage son, Scott, will spend the night in their weather room tracking the storm with their computer, which is hooked up via the telephone lines to the National Weather Service's mainframe in Washington, D.C.

In fact, the National Weather Service gets most of its information from weather observers like Mayers all over the country. This is the typical scenario: As coordinator of the Rockland Climatic Station, Mayers receives nightly temperature and precipitation reports from the over 20 weather observers in the county. He then relays these findings to his station leader in Albany who, in turn, sends this information via the computer to data centers all around the country. Dr. Mayers can then retrieve any data in the system from any place in the United States—instantly.

Additionally, Mayers can print out full-color maps through his hookup to a graphics house (S.S.I. in St. Louis is one) that superimposes weather data over graphics. Mayers also has purchased software developed by Harvard Graphics that enables him to produce color charts and tables based on information the Rockland Climatic Station has collected over the past month or year (actual and normal precipitation for the month of May 1989, for example).

Mayers credits much of his success as a weather predictor to the computer. "The advent of recent technology has really opened up my ability to forecast. In seconds, I have access to data from all over the country. I can't wait to see what they'll come up with next!"

and the people who run the computers and develop the software is often referred to as the *information services department,* or the *data processing (DP) department.*

The information services department handles the organization's information needs in the same way that the finance department handles the organization's money needs. The department provides data processing and information-related services to virtually every business area. For example, programmers and systems analysts might work with plant managers and engineers to develop a computer-based production and inventory-control system. Jobs and employment opportunities in an information services department are discussed in Chapter 16, "Jobs and Career Opportunities."

The Information Center

There are managers who submit handwritten drafts for typing, secretaries who frequently refer to dictionaries, clerks who use hand calculators throughout the day, administrative personnel who assemble reports with glue and scissors, executives who would like to (but cannot) do "what if" analysis, or researchers who use pencils and graph paper to plot their results. All these people would benefit greatly from a visit to their companies' **information center**. Information centers can provide personnel with the opportunity to learn to use computers and to be more productive with their time.

An information center is a "hands-on" facility in which computing resources are made available to various user groups. Users come to an information center because they know they can find the computing resources and technical support they need to help with their personal information and computing needs. The computing resources might include:

- *Video display terminals* that enable users to interact directly with the business's central computer system and the integrated corporate **data base**. The data base is the company's central repository for data that can be accessed by computer.
- *Microcomputers* for *personal*, or stand-alone, computing. "**Micros**," as they are commonly called, are designed primarily for use by one person at a time.
- *Printers* for **hard copy**, or printed output. An information center typically will have at least one printer that produces *near typeset-quality* print.
- *Plotters* for preparing of presentation graphics.
- *Desktop publishing* equipment.

The information center would also maintain a variety of software packages for users, such as electronic spreadsheet, word processing, data management, and graphics. The center might also provide decision support software and the capability to write programs. All these hardware and software tools are discussed in detail in later chapters.

1-4 Computer Mythology

Computers are inanimate; they have only the logic capability that is programmed by human intelligence—no more, no less. As you will see in your journey toward computer literacy, the mystique surrounding computers is unwarranted. Nevertheless, certain myths have evolved about computers. Let's take time to dispel these myths.

Until recently, this composer used only one keyboard when he wrote songs; now he uses two. By relieving the tedium associated with documenting the composition, the computer allows him to focus on the creative aspects of songwriting.

Myth No. 1: "Computers stifle creativity." Polls have revealed that the majority of the population believe they will eventually end up working for computers and not using their brains creatively. Music composers, architects, economists, nurses, and people in a hundred other professions who have *used* computers could easily dispel this widely held myth.

When using a computer in composing music, a composer need not break concentration to draw each note manually on a staff. As a note is played, it is immediately displayed in music notation on a video display screen. With the laborious task of documenting the creation being handled by the computer, the composer's efforts can be devoted to the creative aspects of the composition. This is just one of many examples of how computers *enhance* creativity.

Myth No. 2: "The computer did it." Major newspapers and magazines routinely carry headlines reinforcing the myth that "the computer did it," headlines such as "Payroll Foul-up Attributed to Computer Error" or "Erroneous Tax Assessment Blamed on Computer." The computer has no feelings and is the perfect scapegoat.

Computers do fail. But, with the proper safeguards, failures are noted before they do any harm; the only thing lost is a little time. Most of the time errors can be traced to a breakdown in procedures or a human error (oops!).

Myth No. 3: "Computers cause the loss of jobs." The U.S. Department of Labor continually reminds us that computer-related job displacement is more than offset by the jobs created. The implementation of a computer system may eliminate jobs devoted to certain routine tasks, but the people holding these jobs are usually retrained and moved to positions with greater opportunities. In general, the computer industry is experiencing enormous growth. The net effect is the creation, not the loss, of jobs.

Society is in transition from an industrial to an information society. During this transition, the complexion of jobs will change dramatically.

Myth No. 4: "Computers can do anything." The Heuristic Algorithmic computer (HAL) of Arthur Clarke's *2001: A Space Odyssey* is a classic invention of this imaginative science fiction writer. HAL and other similarly conceived computers are far removed from the reality of modern computers. A timely example is George Orwell's fictionalized but very vivid portrayal of Big Brother in the novel *1984*. The year 1984 has come and gone and we still do not have an electronic dictator, nor will we ever. Big Brother is not technologically feasible or sociologically possible.

HAL could see, learn, and reason. In reality, the state of the art of computer technology in these areas is still in the embryonic stages of research. This is not to say that we will never see robots such as C-3PO of the *Star Wars* films. Perhaps we will, but not for a long while.

Myth No. 5: "You have to be good at mathematics to be good at computers." Not only engineers and mathematicians but also sociologists, teachers, and people from almost every area of interest have had success in using computers. Computers are for everyone.

The need for information exists in all fields of endeavor, not just business. These astrophysicists rely on computer-generated information to help them in their study of the formation and growth of galaxies.

Myth No. 6: "Computers are synonymous with programming." The novice tends to associate all computer-related activities with programming. Relatively few users actually write their own programs. Most rely on user-friendly software to obtain the information they need. Programming is an integral part of the development of information systems, but at least a dozen other computer-related careers do not involve programming. A knowledge of programming, however, is always an asset to those who work with computers.

1–5 Data: The Source of Information

Up to now we have talked quite a bit about information, but little about the origin of information—data. **Data** (the plural of *datum*) are the raw material from which information is derived. **Information** is data that have been collected and processed into a meaningful form.

We routinely deal with the concepts of data and information in our everyday experiences. We use data to produce information that will help us make decisions. For example, when we wake up in the morning, we collect two pieces of data. We look at the time, then recall from our memory the time when our first class begins or when we are due at work. Then we subtract the current time from the starting time of the class (or work). This mental computation provides information on how much time we have to get ready and go. Based on this information, we make a decision to hurry up or to relax and take it easy.

We produce information from data to help us make decisions for thousands of situations each day. In many ways, the contents of this book are just an extension of concepts you already understand.

1–6 Uncovering the "Mystery" of Computers

The Computer System

Technically speaking, the computer is any counting device. But in the context of modern technology, we'll define the computer as *an electronic device capable of interpreting and executing programmed commands for input, output, computation, and logic operations.*

Computers may be technically complex, but they are conceptually simple. The computer, also called a **processor**, is the "intelligence" of a **computer system**. A computer system has only four fundamental components—*input, processing, output,* and *storage*. Note that a computer system (not a computer) is made up of the four components. The actual computer is the processing component; when combined with the other three components, it forms a *computer system* (see Figures 1–1 and 1–2).

The relationship of data to a computer system is best explained by an analogy to gasoline and an automobile. Data are to a computer system as gas is to a car. Data provide the fuel for a computer system. A computer system without data is like a car with an empty gas tank: No gas, no go; no data, no information.

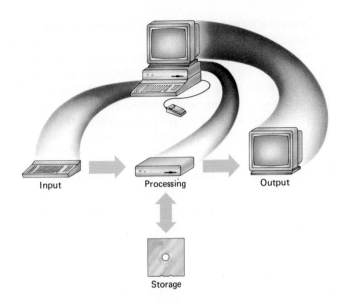

FIGURE 1–1   The Four Fundamental Components of a Microcomputer System
In a microcomputer system, the storage and processing components are often contained in the same physical unit. In the illustration, the diskette storage medium is inserted into the unit that contains the processor.

How a Computer System Works

A computer system can be likened to the biological system of the human body. Your brain is the processing component. Your eyes and ears are input components that send signals to the brain. If you see someone approaching, your brain matches the visual image of this person with others in your memory (storage component). If the visual image is matched in memory with that of a friend, your brain sends signals to your vocal chords and right arm (output components) to greet your friend with a hello and a handshake. Computer system components interact in a similar way.

FIGURE 1–2   The Four Fundamental Components of a Computer System
In larger computer systems, each of the four components is contained in a separate physical unit.

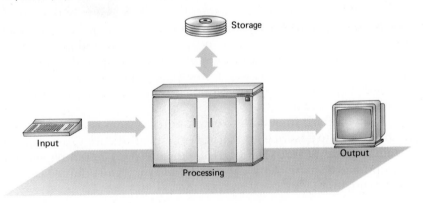

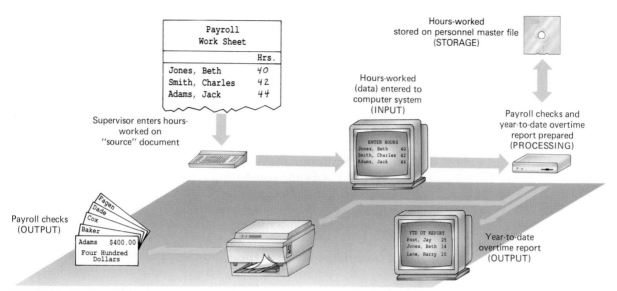

FIGURE 1–3 Payroll System
This microcomputer-based payroll system illustrates input, storage, processing, and output.

The payroll system in Figure 1–3 illustrates how data are entered and how the four computer-system components interact to produce information (a "year-to-date overtime report") and the payroll checks. The hours-worked data are *input* to the system and are *stored* on the personnel **master file**. The master file is make up of **records**, each of which contains data about a particular employee (for example: name, hours worked). Files, records, and other data management concepts are discussed in detail in Chapter 9, "Data Management."

The payroll checks are produced when the *processing* component, or the computer, executes a program. In this example, the employee records are recalled from storage, and the pay amounts are calculated. The *output* is the printed payroll checks. Other programs extract data from the personnel master file to produce a year-to-date overtime report and any other information that might help in the management decision-making process.

The Hardware

In the payroll example, data are entered (input) on a video display terminal (VDT). A video display terminal, or simply **terminal**, has a typewriterlike **keyboard** for input and a televisionlike (video) screen, called a **monitor**, for output. The payroll checks are then output on a device called a **printer**. Data are stored for later recall on **magnetic disk**. There are a wide variety of input/output (**I/O**) and storage devices. The variety of hardware devices that make up a computer system are discussed in detail in Part II, "Hardware."

The principles discussed above apply equally to microcomputers (Figure 1–1), or PCs, and **mainframe computers** (Figures 1–2 and 1–3). Each has the four components and each uses data to produce information in a similar manner. The difference is that personal computers are more limited in their capabilities and are designed primarily for use by *one person at a time*. Mainframe computers can service *many users*, perhaps every manager in the company, all at once. In Chapters 2 and 3 we discuss microcomputers and mainframe computers in detail.

What Can a Computer Do?

Remember from our previous discussion that the *input/output* and *data storage* hardware components are "configured" with the *processing* component (the computer) to make up a computer system (see Figures 1–1 and 1–2). Let's discuss the operational capabilities of a computer system just a bit further.

Input/Output Operations   The computer *reads* from input and storage devices. The computer *writes* to output and storage devices. Before data can be processed, they must be "read" from an input device or data storage device. Input data are usually entered by an operator on a video display terminal or retrieved from a data storage device, such as a magnetic disk drive. Once data have been processed, they are "written" to an output device, such as a printer, or to a data storage device.

Input/output (I/O) operations are illustrated in the payroll system example in Figure 1–3. Hours-worked data are entered and "read" into the computer system. These data are "written" to magnetic disk storage for recall at a later date.

Processing Operations   The computer is totally objective. That is, any two computers instructed to perform the same operation will arrive at the same result. This is because the computer can perform only *computation* and *logic operations*.

On the floor of the Chicago Mercantile Exchange, securities are traded in much the same way they were during the stock market crash of 1929, but with one major difference. Today all trading data is entered into, processed by, and displayed by computers.

The computational capabilities of the computer include adding, subtracting, multiplying, and dividing. Logic capability permits the computer to make comparisons between numbers and between words, then, based on the result of the comparison, perform appropriate functions. In the payroll system example of Figure 1–3, the computer calculates the gross pay in a computation operation (for example, 40 hours at $15/hour = $600). In a logic operation, the computer compares the number of hours worked to 40 to determine the number of overtime hours that an employee has worked during a given week. If the hours-worked figure is greater than or equal to 40, say 42, the difference (2 hours) is credited as overtime and paid at "time and a half."

Computer System Capabilities

In a nutshell, computers are fast, accurate, and reliable; they don't forget anything; and they don't complain. Now for the details.

Speed   The smallest unit of time in the human experience is, realistically, the second. Computer operations (the execution of an instruction, such as adding two numbers) are measured in **milliseconds**, **microseconds**, **nanoseconds**, and **picoseconds** (one thousandth, one millionth, one billionth, and one trillionth of a second, respectively). A beam of light travels down the length of this page in about 1 nanosecond!

Accuracy   Errors do occur in computer-based information systems, but precious few can be directly attributed to the computer system. The vast majority of these errors can be traced to a program logic error, a procedural error, or erroneous data. These are *human errors*.

Reliability   Computer systems are particularly adept at repetitive tasks. They don't take sick days and coffee breaks, and they seldom complain. Anything below 99.9 percent *uptime* is usually unacceptable. For some companies, any *downtime* is unacceptable. These companies provide *backup* computers that take over if the main computers fail.

Memory Capability   Computer systems have total and instant recall of data and an almost unlimited capacity to store these data. A typical mainframe computer system will have many billions of characters stored and available for instant recall. To give you a benchmark for comparison, this book contains approximately 1,500,000 characters.

1–7 Applications of the Computer: Limited Only by Our Imaginations

Twenty years ago, *space* and *distance* were formidable obstacles to what we could and could not do with the computer. But today *microminiaturization* and *data communications* have removed these obstacles. Microminiaturization of electronic circuitry has made it possible to put computers in wristwatches. Computers with capabilities similar to those of the mainframe computers of the early 1960s are about the size of a fingernail. Data communications satellites make it possible for computers in the United States to communicate with computers in Japan, France, or in any other country (see Chapter 7 on data communications).

The door is now open for applications of the computer that were only dreams or fantasies two decades ago. The number and the type of computer applications are limited only by our imaginations. This section contains a brief overview of a variety of familiar computer applications. You probably have had occasion to use, or at least appreciate, each of these information systems at one time or another. Applications in other fields of endeavor will be presented throughout the book in the textual material, in photo captions, and in the special-interest boxes.

Health Care

Several pharmacy chains are providing, free of charge, a potential life-saving information service to their customers. Each retail pharmacy location has a terminal connected to a central computer. When a customer asks a pharmacist to fill one or more prescriptions, the pharmacist enters the name of the drug or drugs prescribed and the patient's name (see Figure 1–4). If the customer does not have a record on file, he or she is asked to fill out a customer profile that includes such information as address, drugs that cause allergic reactions, and other pertinent information. The system accesses the patient's record and checks other drugs that the patient is presently taking. The possible drug interactions of the prescribed drug(s) and the drugs currently being taken are checked against the drug-interaction data base and potentially hazardous interactions are identified. This system minimizes the possibility of an adverse drug interaction and a potentially fatal accident. If the system flags an interaction that could be severe, the customer is warned and the physician involved is notified. The system also warns customers if a prescription contains a drug that may cause an allergic reaction.

A drug-interaction system helps physicians and pharmacists prepare and administer the proper drug to a patient. Literally thousands

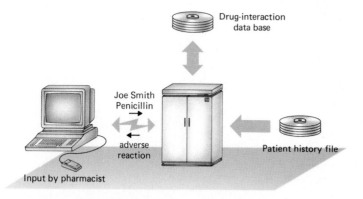

Drug-interaction
data base

Joe Smith
Penicillin
→

←
adverse
reaction

Input by pharmacist

Patient history file

FIGURE 1–4 Drug-Interaction System
Drugs currently being administered to Joe Smith are matched
against penicillin and the drug-interaction data base to check for
a possible adverse reaction.

of drugs can be prescribed by an attending physician, and a mistake
in selecting drug pairs could cause an adverse chemical reaction that
might be serious or even fatal.

Airlines

An airline reservation system is a classic example of an information
system that reflects an up-to-the-minute status. An airline reservations
agent communicates with a centralized computer via a remote terminal to update the data base the moment a seat on any flight is filled
or becomes available.

Before each flight, the pilot and copilot get a weather briefing and pick up a
"computer-produced" flight plan. Just as cars travel on highways, airplanes
travel on airways. Based on wind speed and direction, the computer selects the
best airway route and projects a flying time for each leg. The flight plan also
suggests flying altitudes that minimize fuel consumption.

When you travel by air and check your luggage through to your destination, a three-character destination tag (CHI is Chicago, OKC is Oklahoma City) is attached to each piece of luggage. At this airport, the destination code on the luggage tag is read by an optical scanner and your luggage is automatically routed, via conveyor, to the appropriate pickup station.

An airline reservation system does much more than keep track of flight reservations. Departure and arrival times are closely monitored so that ground crew activities can be coordinated. The system offers many kinds of management information needs: the number of passenger miles flown, profit per passenger on a particular flight, percent of arrivals on time, average number of empty seats on each flight for each day of the week, and so on.

The first airlines reservation system, American Airlines' Sabre System, was implemented in 1976. The Apollo System of United Airlines was installed five months later. By being first, American Airlines and United Airlines grabbed the lion's share of the reservations market, over 60 percent. Other airlines' reservations are handled by three other systems: Texas Air's System One, TWA and Northwest's PARS Service Partnership, and Delta Airlines' Datas II. To give you an idea of the size and scope of these systems, the Sabre System involves more than 100,000 terminals and printers and can process 1,450 transactions per second!

You may be interested to know that airlines routinely overbook flights; that is, they book seats they do not have. The number of extra seats sold is based on historical "no-show" statistics compiled from the reservation system data base. Although these statistics provide good guidelines, occasionally everyone does show up!

Art

The computer is an *image processor* as well as an *information processor*. Computer art is now a well-accepted art form in the artistic community. It is gaining great visibility on television and as a regular feature on the covers of magazines. All the marvelously dynamic images you see on television during the openings of sporting events and movies are creations of computer artists.

The computer gives the artist enormous flexibility in creating a piece of art. The basic reds, greens, and blues can be mixed to create up to 16.8 million colors! The artist can do just about anything with an image. For example, a square box can be elongated, stood on end, enlarged or reduced, moved, multiplied, rotated in three dimensions, distorted, and so on. Computer art can be dynamic as well as static. That is, the image can be created to change right before your eyes.

Let's say an artist would like the eyes of the clown in the photo below to be blue. The artist pushes a few keys, and the clown's eyes are "painted" blue.

Banking

Financial institutions, especially banks, have been among the most progressive users of computers. The ever-present **automatic teller machine (ATM)** is an application of **electronic funds transfer (EFT)**. ATMs are strategically placed throughout the city and linked to a central computer. ATMs enable bank customers to deposit, withdraw, and transfer funds from or to their various accounts. As each money transaction is completed, the customer's record is updated and the customer is provided with a printed receipt (see Figure 1–5). The widespread acceptance of the convenience afforded by ATMs has prompted the banking industry to expand the scope of this service. Recognizing that our society is becoming increasingly mobile, participating banks are linking their computers so that customers can complete banking transactions on ATMs anywhere in the country. Of course, ATMs provide more than customer convenience. An ATM transaction costs the bank less than half that of a transaction made with a human bank teller!

The next level of banking convenience is enabling the customer to do his or her banking at home. Some banks are hoping to gain the **competitive advantage** by offering *home banking* services. Subscribers to a home banking service use their personal computers as terminals to pay bills, to transfer funds, and to make inquiries about the status of their accounts.

This clown was created by a computer artist. Just as a writer can edit a manuscript by using word processing software, an artist can easily make changes to computer art pieces. For example, the artist could change this clown's hair from bright orange to purple. Whether the artist uses a palette and easel or a computer, it still takes a creative mind and a keen eye to produce good art.

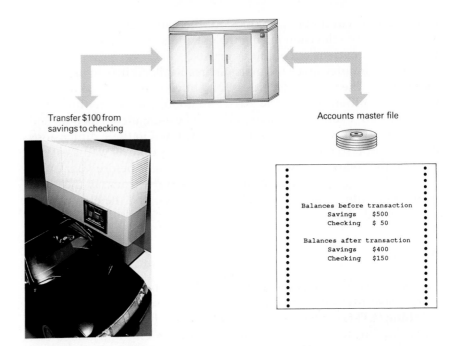

Transfer $100 from
savings to checking

Accounts master file

```
Balances before transaction
       Savings    $500
       Checking   $ 50

Balances after transaction
       Savings    $400
       Checking   $150
```

FIGURE 1–5   Banking Transactions at an Automatic Teller Machine
The electronic funds transfer (EFT) of $100 from savings to checking updates
the accounts master file.

Municipal Government

Have you ever driven an automobile through a city with an automated
traffic-control system? If so, you would soon notice how the traffic
signals are coordinated to minimize delays and optimize traffic flow.
Traffic sensors are strategically placed throughout the city to feed
data continuously to the computer on the volume and direction of
traffic flow (see Figure 1–6).

Many computer-controlled machine tools used in manufacturing are real-time
control systems that operate in a continuous feedback loop.

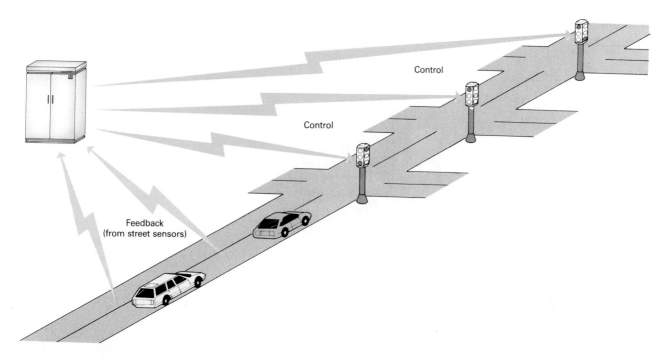

FIGURE 1–6 An Automated Traffic Control System
In a continuous feedback loop, street sensors provide input to a process-control computer system about the direction and volume of traffic flow. Based on their feedback, the system controls the traffic lights to optimize the flow of traffic.

The computer system that activates the traffic signals is programmed to plan ahead. That is, if the sensors locate a group of cars traveling together, traffic signals are then timed accordingly. An automated traffic-control system is a good example of the continuous feedback loop in a computerized **process-control system**. In a **feedback loop**, the process itself generates data that become input to the computer. As the data are received and interpreted by the computer, the computer initiates action to control the ongoing process—in this case, an automated traffic-control system.

Retail Sales

In the retail sales industry (see Figure 1–7), transactions are recorded on cash-register-like computer terminals at the **point of sale** (**POS**). Each point-of-sale terminal is linked to a central computer and a shelf-item master file. To record a sale, the sales clerk enters only the item number. The current price and item description are retrieved from the item master file. A sales ticket and customer receipt are printed automatically. The item master file is always up to date because the file is updated each time an item is sold. Without taking a physical inventory, managers know which items are moving, which are not, and when to order and restock. Companies with sophisticated POS capabilities gain the competitive advantage by being able to restock fast-selling items before their competitors realize they are out of stock.

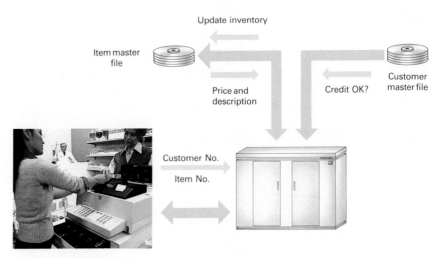

FIGURE 1–7   Point-of-Sale (POS) System
POS systems permit retailers to record each sale and update inventory on the item master file. Some systems also query the customer master file to check a customer's line of credit.

Some point-of-sale systems go one step further than this: They also handle credit transactions. When a customer purchases an item on credit, the sales clerk enters the customer number. The point-of-sale system automatically checks the amount of the purchase against the customer's credit limit. An "OK" light on the terminal is a signal to the sales clerk that the transaction can be completed.

1–8 Computers and Opportunity

Computer literacy opens the door to opportunity in many professions. Many organizations already have set computer literacy as a prerequisite for employment, and the number is growing. Others require it for promotion. Once you complete this course, the door will be open. Your marketability for employment will have improved. You will have an advantage over those of your peers who are computer illiterate. If you are or will become a self-employed professional, such as an attorney, an engineer, or a physician, this course will provide you with the prerequisite knowledge you will need to maintain a competitive edge.

Once you establish a foundation in computer understanding, the rate at which you can learn more about computers will accelerate. Your base of knowledge will grow so that you will be better equipped to keep pace with a rapidly changing technology.

If you decide to pursue a career in computers and information systems, you will find that the opportunities have never been better. These jobs have no geographic or industry restrictions. You can work in a hospital in New York, in a bank in Colorado, or on a ranch in Texas. It is inevitable that the ever-widening vistas for computer applications will create more and greater career opportunities. Today there are at least a dozen well-defined information systems jobs (that

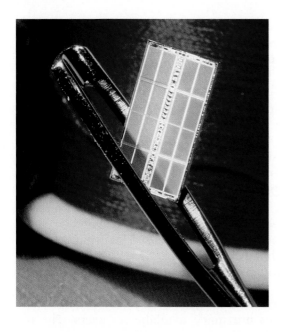

Tiny integrated circuits provide the foundation for computer technology. This memory chip can store more that a million pieces of data.

is, programmer, systems analyst, data base administrator, operator, information systems consultant, information systems auditor, and so on). Next year there will be even more. The variety of possible computer/information systems career paths is discussed in detail in Chapter 16, "Jobs and Career Opportunities."

Computers provide many opportunities for us to improve the quality of both our private and professional lives. The challenge is to take advantage of the opportunities afforded by the computer revolution and our emergence as an information society. People like you who are willing to put forth the effort and accept the challenge will be the ones who benefit the most.

Summary Outline and Important Terms

1–1 WHY STUDY COMPUTERS? Just as cultural literacy is a prerequisite of effective national communication, computer literacy is essential for those who wish to thrive in the business world. Today most office workers have a **computer** or **video display terminal** (**VDT**) at or near their desks.

Computer literacy is achieved through study, practice, and interest in the topic. Computer-literate people know how to purchase, use, and operate a computer system and how to make it work for them. They do this through judicious use of **software** (machine-readable instructions called **programs**). The computer-literate person is also aware of the computer's impact on society.

People study computers because the computer is affecting the way we live, work, and play; to overcome **cyberphobia**; to learn **computerese**; and to be in a better position to take advantage of opportunities afforded by the computer revolution. Each year computers, both in general and at a more personal level (**personal computers,** or **PCs**), are having a greater influence on our lives.

1–2 COMPUTERS ARE FOR EVERYONE. After existing for millennia as an agrarian society, the people of the world progressed to an industrial society. Today what is emerging is an information society. In an information society, computers and software are **user friendly** and, therefore, can be used by everyone—**knowledge workers** and **users** in all environments, computer professionals, and **hackers.**

1–3 SUPPORTING A COMPANY'S INFORMATION NEEDS: WHERE TO GO FOR HELP. Companies depend on **information systems** and the capabilities of computing **hardware** for their data processing and information needs. The organizational entity charged with supporting these needs is called the information services department, or data processing department.

An **information center** is a hands-on facility in which computing resources are made available to users. The resources include video display terminals, microcomputers, printers for **hard copy** output, plotters, and a variety of user-oriented software packages. These resources enable interaction with the integrated corporate **data base.**

1–4 COMPUTER MYTHOLOGY. The computer mystique has caused our society to build certain myths around computers. These myths revolve around a "thinking machine" that is threatening to society's general well-being. But, in reality, computers are inanimate and are capable of only that logic programmed by human intelligence.

1–5 DATA: THE SOURCE OF INFORMATION. **Data** are the raw material from which information is derived. **Information** is data that have been collected and processed into a meaningful form.

1–6 UNCOVERING THE "MYSTERY" OF COMPUTERS. The computer, or **processor**, is an electronic device capable of interpreting and executing programmed commands for input, output, computation, and logic operations. Computer system capabilities are defined as either input/output or processing. Processing capabilities are subdivided into computation and logic operations. A **computer system** is not as complex as we are sometimes led to believe. Personal computers, also called **microcomputers**, and **mainframe computers** are both computer systems, and each has only four fundamental components: input (for example, a **terminal** with a **keyboard**), processing (executing a program), output (for example, a **monitor** or a **printer**), and storage (for example, a **magnetic disk**). The storage component holds the **master file**, which is made up of **records**. The computer is fast, accurate, reliable, and has an enormous memory capacity.

1–7 APPLICATIONS OF THE COMPUTER: LIMITED ONLY BY OUR IMAGINATION. Recent innovations in microminiaturization of circuitry and data communications have opened the door for computer applications that were only dreams or fantasies two decades ago. Computer-based information systems can be found in diverse business and government environments including health care, transportation, art, banking (for example, **ATM** and **EFT**), municipal government, and retail sales (for example, **POS**). Some companies are using information systems to gain the **competitive advantage**.

1–8 COMPUTERS AND OPPORTUNITY. Computer literacy opens the door to opportunity in many professions.

Review Exercises

Concepts

1. What are the four fundamental components of a computer system?
2. Which component of a computer system executes the program?
3. Light travels at 186,000 miles per second. How many milliseconds does it take for a beam of light to travel across the United States, a distance of about 3000 miles?
4. Compare the information processing capabilities of human beings to that of computers with respect to speed, accuracy, reliability, and memory.
5. What are the primary functions of an organization's information services department?
6. Describe the relationship between data and information.
7. In computerese, what is meant by *read* and *write*?
8. What type of hardware and software would be appropriate for an information center?
9. How have the system design constraints of space and distance been overcome?
10. The operational capabilities of a computer system include what two types of processing operations?

Discussion

11. The computer has had far-reaching effects on our lives. How has the computer affected your life?
12. What is your concept of computer literacy? In what ways do you think achieving computer literacy will change your domestic life? Your business life?
13. At what age should computer literacy education begin?

14. Discuss how the complexion of jobs will change as we evolve from an industrial society into an information society. Give several examples.

15. The use of computers tends to stifle creativity. Argue for or against this statement.

16. Comment on how computers are changing our traditional patterns of personal communication.

17. Comment on how computers are changing our traditional patterns of recreation.

Self-Test (by section)

1–1 **a.** To be computer literate, you must be able to write computer programs. (T/F)

b. The _____ is a device with a televisionlike screen and a keyboard that permits communication with a remote computer.

c. The irrational fear of, or aversion to, computers is called _____ .

1–2 **a.** The knowledge worker's job function revolves around the use, manipulation, and dissemination of: (a) data, (b) electronic memoranda, or (c) information.

b. A computer enthusiast is: (a) user friendly, (b) a hacker, or (c) a computerist.

1–3 **a.** An information system is a computer-based system that provides _____ and information for making decisions.

b. The information services department is a company's primary resource for the development of full-scale information systems. (T/F)

1–4 A solid knowledge of upper-division mathematics is a prerequisite of becoming computer literate. (T/F)

1–5 _____ are the raw material from which _____ is derived.

1–6 **a.** A printer is an example of which of the four computer system components?

b. A master file is made up of: (a) records, (b) logic bits, or (c) data bases.

c. The computer _____ from input devices and _____ to output devices.

d. The two types of processing operations performed by computers are _____ and _____ .

1–7 **a.** In 1976, American Airlines installed the first airlines reservation system and named it the Sabre System. (T/F)

b. In a _____ , the process itself generates data that become input to the computer.

1–8 There are fewer than six well-defined computer-related jobs. (T/F)

Self-test answers. **1–1** (a) F;   (b) video display terminal (VDT);   (c) cyberphobia.   **1–2** (a) c;   (b) b.   **1–3** (a) data processing;   (b) T.   **1–4** F.   **1–5** data, information.   **1–6** (a) output;   (b) a; (c) reads, writes;   (d) computation, logic.   **1–7** (a) T;   (b) feedback loop.   **1–8** F.

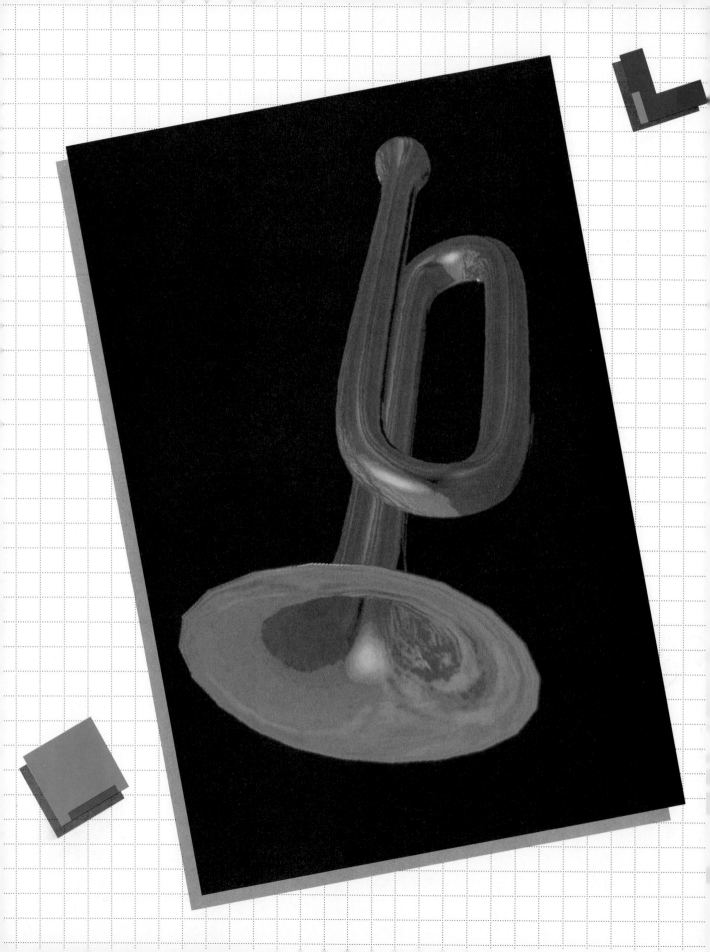

2
Minis, Mainframes, and Supercomputers

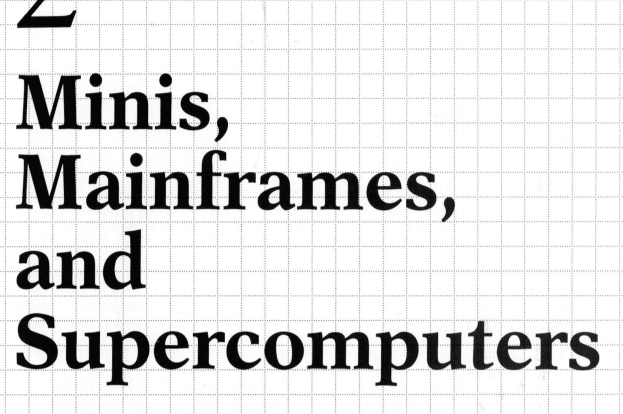

STUDENT LEARNING OBJECTIVES

- To distinguish between microcomputers, minicomputers, mainframes, and supercomputers.
- To illustrate typical hardware configurations for minicomputers and mainframes.
- To demonstrate awareness of the relative size, scope, characteristics, and variety of multiuser computer systems.
- To describe the functions and relationships of the various processors in a computer system.
- To discuss the concept of distributed processing.
- To describe applications of special-purpose computer systems.

2–1　Computers Come in All Shapes and Sizes

Categories of Computer Systems

The four main categories of computer systems are:

- Microcomputer system
- Minicomputer system
- Mainframe computer system
- Supercomputer system

In keeping with conversational computerese, we will drop the word *system* when discussing these categories. Therefore, throughout the remainder of the book, a reference to any of these categories implies a reference to the entire computer system.

Most computers are boxlike, but they can be found in a variety of shapes, from U-shaped to cylindrical. However, the most distinguishing characteristic of any computer system is its *size*—not its physical size, but its computing capacity. Loosely speaking, *size*, or computer capacity, is the amount of processing that can be accomplished by a computer system per unit of time. **Minicomputers** have greater computing capacities than *microcomputers*. *Mainframe computers* have greater computing capacities than minicomputers. And **supercomputers**, the biggest of all, have greater computing capacities than mainframe computers. Some vendors are not content with pigeonholing their products into one of the four major categories, so they have created new niches such as *supermicrocomputers*, *superminicomputers*, and *minisupercomputers*. In this chapter, we will focus on the four major categories.

Now, and even in the past, these computer classifications have defied definition. Even though it is doubtful that any two computer specialists would describe a minicomputer or a supercomputer in the same way, these terms are still frequently used. Rapid advances in computer technology have caused what used to be distinguishing characteristics (for example, physical size, cost, memory capacity, and so on) to become blurred.

All computers, no matter how small or large, have the same fundamental capabilities. Just as "a rose, is a rose, is a rose. . . ." (Gertrude Stein), "a computer, is a computer, is a computer. . . ." Keep this in mind as we discuss the minicomputers, mainframe computers, and supercomputers in this chapter and microcomputers in Chapter 3. It should be emphasized that these are relative categories, and what people call a minicomputer system today may be called a microcomputer system at some time in the future.

In all probability you have been exposed to a microcomputer or a minicomputer system. You can't walk very far into an office building or a school at any level without seeing a microcomputer. Now minicomputers about the size of a copy machine are often part of the decor in all kinds of offices, from medical clinics to accounting departments. Most students have had at least a casual exposure to com-

The clean lines of this mainframe computer system hide the thousands of integrated circuits, miles of wire, and even gold, that make up the inner workings of a computer system. This data center provides information processing support for hundreds of end users.

puters before taking this course. An increasing number of students have personal computers in their homes. Others use them at work. Don't feel left out if you were not exposed to computers in high school, college, or at work, and you don't own one. If you have used an automatic teller machine (ATM), played a video game, or programmed a VCR, then you have some experience as a user of computers.

Micros versus Minis, Mainframes, and Supercomputers

Micros are computer systems. Minicomputers, mainframes, and supercomputers are computer systems. Each offers a variety of input and output alternatives, and each is supported by a wide variety of packaged software. There are, of course, obvious differences in size and capabilities. Everything associated with minicomputers, mainframes, and supercomputers is larger in scope: Execution of programs is faster; disk storage has more capacity; printer speeds are much faster. Computers in these three categories can service many terminals, and, of course, they cost more. (Interestingly, the price–performance of computers is inversely proportional to the size of the computer. That is, it costs less to execute a million instructions on a microcomputer than than it does to execute the same number on a minicomputer.)

Besides size and capability, the single most distinguishing characteristic of minicomputers, mainframe computers, and supercomputers is the manner in which they are used. The three larger computers, with their expanded processing capabilities, provide a computing resource that can be shared by an entire company, not just a single user. For example, it is common in a company for the finance, personnel, and accounting departments to share the resources

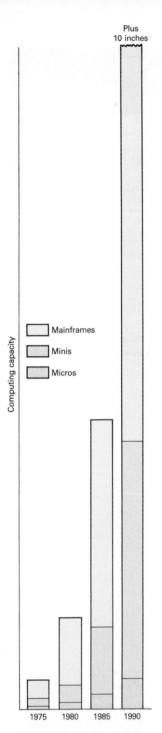

FIGURE 2–1   Micro, Mini, and Mainframe Computing Capacities
The computing capacity of a micro, mini, and mainframe increases with advancing technology. As a rule of thumb, the computing capacity of supercomputers is 10 times that of a mainframe computer.

of a mini, mainframe, or supercomputer, possibly all at the same time. Because of their functional similarities, the top three computer categories are addressed in this chapter. Because micros are designed primarily for the single user environment, they are covered separately in Chapter 3, "Microcomputers."

2–2   Minicomputers: Department-Sized Computers

Until the late 1960s, all computers were mainframe computers, and they were expensive—too expensive for all but the larger companies. About that time vendors introduced smaller, but slightly "watered down" computers that were more affordable for smaller companies. The industry dubbed these small computers *minicomputers*, or simply **minis**. The name has stuck, even though some of today's so-called minis are many times as powerful as the largest mainframes of the early 1970s (see Figure 2–1).

What Is a Mini and How Is It Used?

In the past, the minicomputer has been described in terms of physical size, processing capability, the number of people that could be serviced simultaneously, memory capacity, the type of technology used in the processor, environmental requirements (temperature and humidity), and, yes, even weight. In truth, there is no generally accepted definition of a minicomputer. Each leap in technological innovation and the passing of time have served to obscure whatever clear-cut distinctions could be made between minis and mainframe computers. Minis are now accomplishing processing tasks that traditionally have been associated with mainframes. Moreover, some of the more powerful micros permit multiple users and look very much like small minis. Minicomputers bridge the gap between micros and mainframes, but the manner in which they are used makes them more characteristic of mainframes than of micros. Creating a rigorous definition of a minicomputer is like trying to grab a speeding bullet. Since technology has created a moving target, we will describe the minicomputer simply as a small mainframe computer.

Minicomputers usually serve as stand-alone computer systems for small businesses (10 to 400 employees) and as remote **departmental computer systems**. In the latter case, these departmental systems are used both as stand-alone systems in support of a particular department and as part of a network of departmental minis, all linked to a large centralized computer. Minis are also common in research groups, engineering firms, and colleges.

Configuring a Minicomputer System

Minis have most of the operational capabilities of mainframe computers that may be 10 to 1000 times faster. They just perform their

Minicomputers are being designed to operate in a normal office environment. Most minicomputers, such as the one in this management consulting firm, do not require special accommodations for temperature and humidity control.

tasks more slowly. Minicomputer input, output, and storage devices are similar in appearance and function to those used on much larger systems. However, the printers are not quite as fast, the storage capacity is smaller, and fewer terminals can be serviced. Figure 2–2 illustrates a midsized minicomputer system configuration that pro-

FIGURE 2–2 A Minicomputer System
This system supports a mail-order sporting goods retailer with $40 million in sales and is representative of a midsized minicomputer.

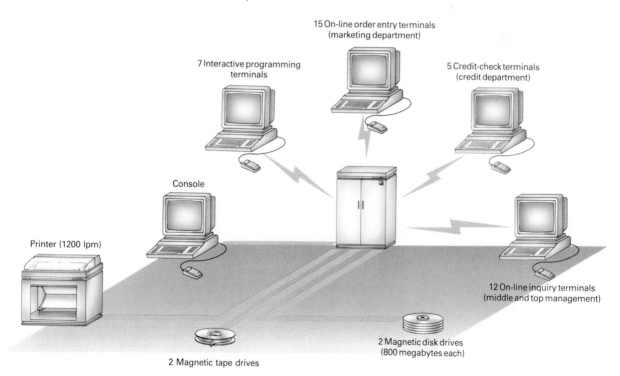

These circuit boards will ultimately provide the logic for a minicomputer, assuming they are given the okay by this robotic tester.

vides information systems support for a mail-order sporting goods retailer with $40 million in sales. The components illustrated in Figure 2–2 are described in the following discussion.

- *Processing.* It is premature to give you a technical description of processing capabilities. That will be done in Chapter 4, "Inside the Computer." We can, however, give you a feeling for the relative processing capabilities of a minicomputer by comparing it to one with which most of us have at least a casual familiarity—the microcomputer. The processor in the minicomputer system of Figure 2–2 has about 10 times the processing capability of a state-of-the-art single-user micro.

- *Storage.* An organization's storage-capacity requirements increase even faster than its processing requirements. The minicomputer system in Figure 2–2 has four *disk drives* (discussed in Chapter 6, "Data Storage Devices and Media"), each capable of storing 800 megabytes (million characters), for a total capacity of 3200 megabytes. The system also has two magnetic *tape drives*, each with a capacity of 200 megabytes of on-line sequential storage. Disk data files are periodically dumped, or loaded, to tape for backup. If, for some reason, the data on the disks are destroyed, the data on the backup tapes could be loaded to the disks so that processing could continue.

- *Input.* The primary means of data input to the system are the 20 VDTs installed in the marketing and credit departments. The **operator console** in the machine room is also used to communicate instructions to the system. Seven terminals are used by programmers to write and test their programs.

- *Output.* A 1200-line-per-minute (lpm) printer provides hard copy output. The VDTs in the marketing, credit, and programming departments, and the console in the machine room provide soft copy output. Twelve VDTs are made available to middle and top management for on-line inquiry.

It is unlikely that you would find two minicomputers configured in exactly the same way. A company that prefers to use disk rather than tape backup would not need magnetic tape drives. Another may have a substantial volume of printed output and require a 2000-line-per-minute printer and a laser printer that prints two pages of output each second. Figure 2–2 is just an example of one possible configuration.

As the definition of a minicomputer becomes more obscure, the term *minicomputer* will take its place beside *electronic brain*. But for now it remains a commonly used term, even though it lacks a commonly accepted definition. The term *supermini* is often applied to a high-end minicomputer. Superminis typically have the capability of servicing a hundred or more users simultaneously. Such systems are difficult to distinguish from small mainframe computers.

2–3 Mainframe Computers: The Corporate Workhorse

Besides the obvious difference in the speeds at which they process data, the major difference between minicomputers and other mainframe computers is in the number of remote terminals they can service. The category of computers that falls between minicomputers and supercomputers is sometimes referred to as **maxicomputers**; however, in conversational computerese, most people continue to refer to this category of computers simply as mainframes. As a rule of thumb, any computer that services more than 100 remote terminals can no longer be called a minicomputer. Some supercomputers, the fastest and most powerful of computers, provide service to over 10,000 remote terminals.

The speed at which medium-sized and large mainframe computers can perform operations allows more input, output, and storage devices with greater capabilities to be configured in the computer system. The computer system in Figure 2–3 is used by the municipal government of a city of about one million people. This example should give you an appreciation of the relative size and potential of a medium-sized mainframe computer system. The hardware devices illustrated will be explained in detail in subsequent chapters. The components are described briefly below.

- *Processing*. Mainframe computer systems, including some minis, will normally be configured with the mainframe or *host processor* and several other processors. A typical configuration would feature a host processor, a *front-end processor*, and perhaps a *back-end processor*. The host is the main computer and is substantially larger and more powerful than the other *subordinate* processors. The front-end and back-end processors control the data flow in

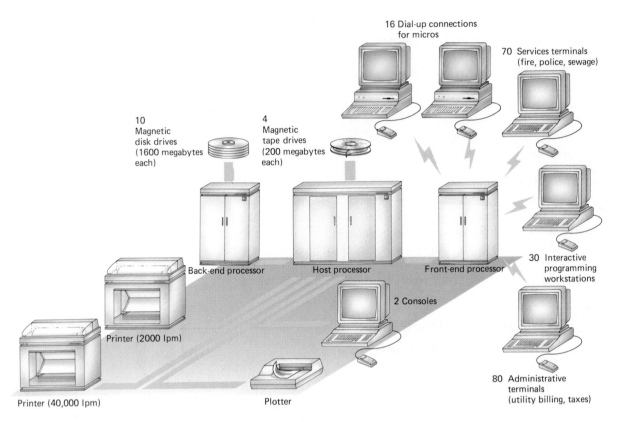

16 Dial-up connections
for micros

70 Services terminals
(fire, police, sewage)

10
Magnetic
disk drives
(1600 megabytes
each)

4
Magnetic
tape drives
(200 megabytes
each)

Back-end processor

Host processor

Front-end processor

30 Interactive
programming
workstations

2 Consoles

Printer (2000 lpm)

Printer (40,000 lpm)

Plotter

80 Administrative
terminals
(utility billing, taxes)

FIGURE 2–3 A Mainframe Computer System
This midsized mainframe computer system supports the administrative processing needs for the municipal government of a city with a population of about one million.

and out of the host processor. Although the host could handle the entire system without the assistance of the front-end and back-end processors, overall system efficiency would be drastically reduced without them. The different types of processors are described in more detail in Section 2–5.

■ *Storage.* All mainframe computer systems use similar direct and sequential storage media. The larger ones simply have more of them and they usually work faster. In Figure 2–3 there are four magnetic tape drives and 10 magnetic disk drives. The disk drives are *dual density* and can pack twice the data in the same amount of physical storage space as can the disks shown in Figure 2–2. The total data storage capacity in the example is 800 megabytes of sequential storage (tape) and 16,000 megabytes of direct-access storage (disk).

■ *Input.* The primary means of entering data to the system is the same, no matter what the size of the computer system. The only difference between a large and a small system is in the number and location of the terminals. In the example of Figure 2–3, 150 terminals are dedicated to service and administrative functions, 30 are used for programming, and 16 **ports** are available for those who might wish to use their PCs to establish a link with the mainframe computer. A port is an access point in a computer

The activity in a mainframe machine room is fast and furious. However, most of the activity is electronic. It is not unusual for one or two operators to handle all of the machine room duties for a multimillion-dollar computer system that services scores of programmers and hundreds of users.

system that permits data to be transmitted between the computer and a peripheral device.

■ *Output.* As in the minicomputer system in Figure 2–2, the hard copy is produced on high-speed printers and the soft copy on terminals. In the Figure 2–3 example, there are two printers: a line printer with a speed of 2000 lines per minute and a page printer that uses laser printing technology to achieve speeds of over 40,000 lines per minute. The plotter, also pictured in the configuration, is used by city engineers to produce hard copies of graphs, charts, and drawings.

2–4 Supercomputers: Processing Giants

During the early 1970s, administrative data processing dominated computer applications. Bankers, college administrators, and advertising executives were amazed by the blinding speed at which these million-dollar mainframes processed data. Engineers and scientists were grateful for this tremendous technological achievement, but they were far from satisfied. When business executives talked about unlimited capability, engineers and scientists knew they would have to wait for future enhancements before they could use computers to address complex problems. Automotive engineers were yet to build three-dimensional prototypes of automobiles inside a computer. Physicists could not explore the activities of an atom during a nuclear explosion. The engineering and scientific community had a desperate need for more powerful computers. In response to that need, computer designers began work on what is now known as supercomputers.

This supercomputer, which is one of the world's fastest computers, is being installed at a computer services company. It can perform over 400 million mathematical calculations per second!

The large mainframe computers are oriented to **input/output-bound operation**; that is, the amount of work that can be performed by the computer system is limited primarily by the speeds of the I/O devices. Administrative data processing jobs, such as generating monthly statements for checking accounts at a bank, require relatively little calculation and a great deal of input and output. In I/O-bound operations, the computer is often waiting for data to be entered or for an output device to complete its current task. In contrast, the types of computer applications that are helpful to engineers and scientists are **processor-bound** and require relatively little in the way of input or output: The amount of work that can be performed by the computer system is limited primarily by the speed of the computer. A typical scientific job involves the manipulation of a complex mathematical model, often requiring trillions of operations to resolve. During the early 1970s, some of the complex processor-bound scientific jobs would tie up large mainframe computers at major universities for days at a time. This, of course, was unacceptable.

During the past two decades, computer designers have employed three basic strategies for increasing the speed of computers.

1. *Use faster components.* Essentially this means employing electronic circuitry that enables the fastest possible switching between the two electronic states—on and off.

2. *Reduce the distance that an electronic signal must travel.* This means increasing the density of the electronic circuitry.

3. *Improve the computer system architecture.* The architecture of a computer refers to the manner in which it handles data and performs logic operations and calculations. The architecture of supercomputers is substantially different than that of the other three categories of computers.

The greatest obstacle facing designers of supercomputers is heat buildup. Densely packed integrated circuits produce a tremendous amount of heat. For example, imagine burning 3000 sixty-watt light bulbs in a space the size of an average clothes closet. Without some type of cooling mechanism, densely packed integrated circuits would literally melt. The air cooling systems traditionally used in mainframe computers proved inadequate, so designers have tried a variety of *supercooling* methods, from freon-based refrigeration to bathing the circuit elements in a liquid coolant. Computer designers are continually trying to increase the density of the integrated circuits while allowing for adequate cooling. At this point in the evolution of supercomputers, innovation in supercooling is just as important as innovation in electronic circuitry.

Supercomputers are known as much for their applications as they are for their speed or their computing capacity, often an order of magnitude (10 times) that of the largest mainframe computers. Supercomputers sort through and analyze mountains of seismic data gathered during oil-seeking explorations. Supercomputers enable the simulation of airflow around an airplane at different speeds and altitudes. Auto manufacturers use supercomputers to simulate auto accidents on video screens (it is less expensive, more revealing, and safer than crashing the real thing). Physicists use supercomputers to study the results of explosions of nuclear weapons. Meteorologists employ supercomputers to study the formation of tornados. Even Hollywood has found an application for supercomputers. Studios use advanced graphics to create special effects for movies and TV commercials. All these applications are impractical, if not impossible, on mainframes.

The graphics that introduce television newscasts, sports events, and movies are by-products of supercomputer technology. The processing power of supercomputers is needed to manipulate billions of picture elements into imaginative dynamic images.

The world's first automatic electronic digital computer was constructed in this building in 1939 by John Vincent Atanasoff, a mathematician and physicist on the Iowa State faculty, who conceived the idea, and by Clifford Edward Berry, a physics graduate student.

These words appear on a metal plaque in the lobby of the old physics building on the Iowa State University campus.

For years computer historians stated that the ENIAC, built at the University of Pennsylvania in 1946 by J. Presper Eckert and John W. Mauchly, was the first electronic digital computer. But history was changed by a court decision on October 19, 1973, when Judge Earl R. Larsen ruled that "Eckert and Mauchly did not themselves first invent the automatic electronic digital computer, but instead derived that subject matter from one Dr. John Vincent Atanasoff."

During the years 1935 through 1938, Dr. John V. Atanasoff had begun to think about a machine that could reduce the time it took for him and his physics students to make long, complicated mathematical calculations. The ABC was, in fact, born of frustration. Dr. Atanasoff later explained that one night in the winter of 1937, "nothing was happening" with respect to creating an electronic device that could help solve physics problems. His "despair grew," so he got in his car and drove for several hours across the state of Iowa and then across the Mississippi River. Finally he stopped at an Illinois roadhouse for a drink. It was in this roadhouse that Dr. Atanasoff overcame his creative block and conceived ideas that would lay the foundation for the evolution of the modern computer. The decisions he made on such aspects as an electronic medium with vacuum tubes, the base-2 numbering system, memory, and logic circuits set the direction for the development of the modern computer.

In 1939 Professor Atanasoff and his graduate stu-

The ABC.

dent, Clifford E. Berry, assembled a prototype of the ABC computer (Atanasoff Berry Computer), which by 1942 was a workable model. However, neither Iowa State, the business world, nor the scientific community showed much interest in the ABC. For example, the Iowa State University alumni magazine ran a short article in 1942 about two "devices" developed on the campus by the Science Division, "which, following the war, will meet important needs." The article described "an improved swivel mounting for microscopes" and "a machine that can solve linear algebraic equations involving 30 unknowns many times faster than any present device." Iowa State University patented the microscope, but not the ABC computer.

In 1984 Iowa State University presented Atanasoff with the university's highest award for an alumnus—the Distinguished Achievement Citation.

Supercomputers are seldom called upon to do I/O-bound administrative processing, such as payroll processing or accounting. To do so would waste an expensive and relatively rare resource (only a few hundred supercomputers are currently installed in the world). A supercomputer could not process the payroll any faster than a mainframe. Because of their applications, supercomputers are more likely to be configured with sophisticated graphics workstations and plotters than with rows of high-speed printers.

A "Host" of Computers

Fifteen years ago, most processors were simply called **central processing units**, or **CPUs** for short; today, however, not all processors are "central." Figure 2–3 demonstrates how a computer system can have three processors: a host, a front-end, and a back-end processor. Figure 2–4 illustrates an even greater variety of subordinate processors, each one performing a different function.

These special-function processors are strategically located throughout a computer system to increase efficiency and **throughput**, the rate at which work can be performed by a computer system. A computer system can be configured with the host plus none or all of the subordinate processors shown in Figure 2–4. Circumstances dictate which, if any, of these subordinate processors should be included.

The Need for Special-Function Processors

A processor executes only one instruction at a time, even though it appears to be handling many tasks simultaneously. A **task** is the basic unit of work for a processor. At any given time, several tasks will compete for processor time. For example, one task might involve calculating finance charges and another, the analysis of data from a research project.

Since a single processor is capable of executing only one instruction at a time, one task will be given priority; the others will have to

FIGURE 2–4   Host and Subordinate Processors

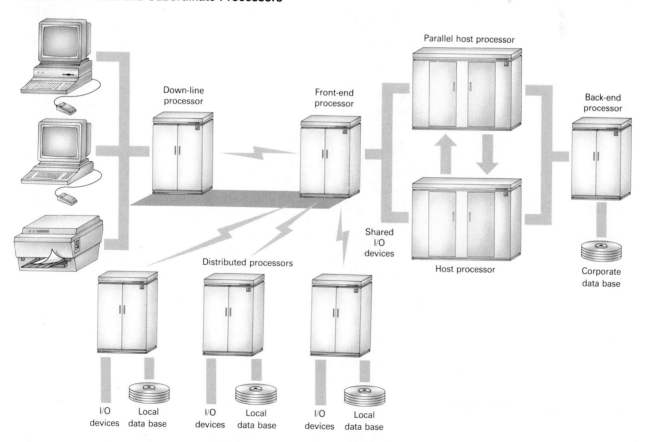

wait. The processor rotates between competing tasks so quickly, however, that it appears as if all are being executed at once. Even so, this rotation eventually takes its toll on processor efficiency. To improve the overall efficiency of a computer system, the *processing load* is *distributed* among several other special-function processors.

The *host*, or *mainframe*, processor is responsible for overall control of the computer system and for the execution of applications programs, such as payroll or accounting. Other processors in the computer system are under the control of and subordinate to the host. The function and relationship of the host and its subordinate processors are discussed here.

The Host Processor   The **host processor** has direct control over all the other processors, storage devices, and input/output devices. The other processors relieve the host of certain routine processing requirements, such as locating a particular record on a data storage device. In this way, the host can concentrate on overall system control and the execution of applications software.

Figure 2–4 includes a **parallel host**. A parallel host is necessary where **downtime** (host not operational) is unacceptable. For example, in an airline reservation system, thousands of reservations are made and cancelled each hour, 24 hours a day, seven days a week. If the host fails, the parallel host takes over and provides **backup** to keep the system in continuous operation. Most computer systems do not need a parallel host.

The Front-End Processor   A **front-end processor** relieves the host processor of communications-related processing duties (discussed in more detail in Chapter 7, "Connectivity and Data Communications"). All data transmitted *to* the host processor *from* remote locations or *from* the host processor *to* remote locations are handled by the front-end processor.

The Back-End Processor   The **back-end processor,** or **data base machine**, handles tasks associated with the retrieval and manipulation of data from storage devices, such as magnetic disk. For example, suppose a program that is executing in the host requires Sally Smith's record from the personnel master file. The host processor issues a request to the back-end processor to retrieve the record of Sally Smith. It is then the responsibility of the back-end processor to issue the commands necessary to retrieve the record from magnetic disk storage and transmit it to the host for processing. By handling the logic and the mechanics of tasks involving the data base, the back-end processor substantially reduces the processing load of the host, thereby speeding the execution of applications programs.

Down-Line Processor   The **down-line processor** is an extension of the front-end processor. Its name is derived from its physical location. It is located "down-line"—at or near a remote site. The down-line processor formats and prepares the input of several remote terminals for transmission over a *communications link* (line over which data

All the terminals and input/output devices at this bank branch office are connected to a down-line processor. The down-line processor is linked to a front-end processor at the host site.

are transmitted, often a telephone line). It then transmits the data to the front-end processor. The down-line processor also receives and distributes host output to the appropriate remote terminals.

The Distributed Processor   The **distributed processor** is an extension of the host. In effect, it is a *host* processor system that is *distributed*, or physically located, in a functional area department (such as accounting, marketing, or manufacturing). These microcomputer and minicomputer systems, also known as *departmental computer systems*, have their own input/output (I/O), terminals, and storage capabilities and can operate as a stand-alone system (independent of the host) or as a distributed system (an extension of the host). See Section 2–6 for more information on distributed systems.

Device Processors   Virtually every hardware device (printers, terminals, disk drives, and so on) will have at least one embedded processor, usually a small **microprocessor**. (Microprocessors are discussed in Chapter 3, "Microcomputers.") These device processors, which are literally "computers on a chip," are there to relieve the host and other subordinate processors of the routine tasks associated with hardware operation. For example, in a printer, a microprocessor formats and readies all text for print, then it activates the appropriate mechanisms to feed the paper and do the actual printing.

Processor Summary

As you can see, a mainframe computer system is not just one processor. And researchers are continuously seeking new ways to introduce more and more processors into a computer system. If four processors are better than one, then 50 must be better than four, and so on. Some supercomputer systems already have more than 100 processors! In fact, computer designers are thinking in terms of linking *millions* of chip-sized processors in a single computer system! This kind of *parallel processing* is expected to result in enormous improvements in throughput.

2–6 Integrated Computer Networks: Computers Working Together

Centralization versus Decentralization

Through the mid-1970s, the prevailing thought was to take advantage of the economy of scale and *centralize* all information processing in an organization. At the time, an organization could get more computing capacity for its dollar by purchasing larger and larger computer systems. This is no longer true.

Some centralized computer centers have grown so big and complex that they have lost their ability to be responsive to the organization's information needs. This lack of responsiveness was a major factor in reversing the trend from centralization to *decentralization*, or **distributed processing**. The introduction of microcomputers and reasonably priced minis into the business community in the early 1980s offered the means by which to decentralize.

Distributed Processing

Distributed processing is both a technological and an organizational concept. Its premise is that information processing can be more effective if computer *hardware* (usually micros and minis), *data*, *software*, and, in some cases, *personnel* are moved physically closer to the

One of the objectives noted in this company's strategic plan is to provide greater user accessibility to the computer and information services through distributed processing. Currently five departments, including the marketing department shown in the photo, have installed a minicomputer for local processing. The departmental minis are part of a companywide network that includes the corporate mainframe.

people who use these resources. If the public relations people need access to a computer and information, these resources are made available to them in their work area. They don't need to go to the information services department for every request. With distributed processing, users have greater control over their computing environment.

In distributed processing, computer systems are arranged in a **computer network**, with each system connected to one or more other systems. (Computer networks are described in detail in Chapter 7, "Connectivity and Data Communications.") A distributed processing network of computer systems is usually designed around a combination of geographical and functional considerations. In Figure 2–5, for example, a distributed processing network is illustrated for Zimco Enterprises. At the headquarters location in Dallas, Zimco has *functionally* distributed processing systems in the sales and marketing division, the finance and accounting division, and the home office plant/distribution center. *Geographically* distributed processing systems are located at each of three plant/distribution centers in Chicago, Atlanta, and Los Angeles.

FIGURE 2–5 A Distributed Processing Network
The distributed processing network demonstrates both geographical and functional distribution of processing.

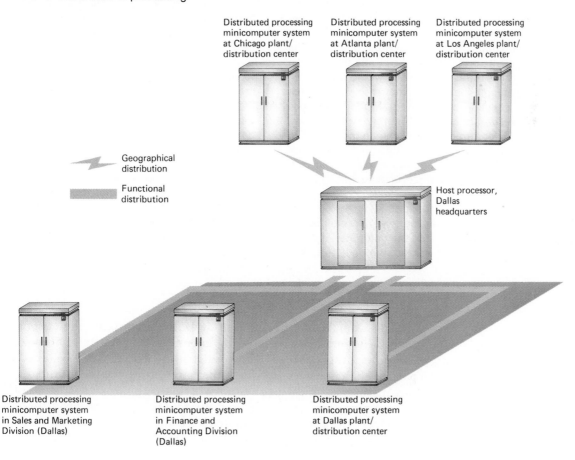

On the Street

Kathy Collins
Registered Nurse

Assistant Head Nurse Kathy Collins' general medical floor at a large metropolitan hospital recently joined the computer age. Before automation, when a doctor wanted a lab test from a blood draw—such as a complete blood count done on one of the 41 patients on the floor—he or she filled out an order. The nurse or secretary would then fill out a slip, stamp the patient's name on it, and place it in a pickup box labeled *Monday*, *Tuesday*, *Wednesday*, and so on. Then a day or so later, the lab department would call up the results to the floor. As you can see, this method left a lot of room for error. In addition to being time-consuming, slips were often misplaced or lost altogether.

Automating has changed all that. Now after the doctor writes an order, the nurse types the lab request directly into the computer, indicating the type of test wanted, the date and time, and whether it's routine or an emergency. The computer is hooked up to the blood lab and automatically prints labels for the blood tubing (leading to fewer mix-ups). After the test is complete, the lab department enters the results into the computer, where they can be easily accessed by the nurses and doctors on the floor.

"Having the results sent to us via the computer really saves us a great deal of time—especially when we have 41 patients to care for. And, when there's an abnormal value that requires immediate attention, our computer is programmed to automatically print it out for us."

The hospital has a similar system set up with the Dietary Department. All special meals (such as low sodium, clear liquid, and soft foods) are ordered through the terminals. If one of the patients asks for a ginger ale and an extra helping of Jell-O, Kathy simply plugs this information into the computer.

At press time, the hospital was beginning work on another system that would enable the medical staff to order medications directly from the pharmacy. This, too, would save the nurses the time they now spend running back and forth between their patients and the pharmacy.

Having an automated hospital benefits visitors as well as patients and staff. At the touch of a button, any hospital employee can tell a family member exactly what room his or her relative is in and what the patient's status is. For a brand-new grandmother anxiously waiting to see her new addition, this information can't come too quickly!

The host computer system at Dallas maintains the corporate data base and services those divisions that do not have their own computer system. Although the distributed processing systems are part of the computer network, they are entirely self-contained and can operate as stand-alone systems. In this example, all the distributed systems are similarly configured minicomputers. The basic configuration for the functionally distributed mini in the finance and accounting division is shown in Figure 2–6.

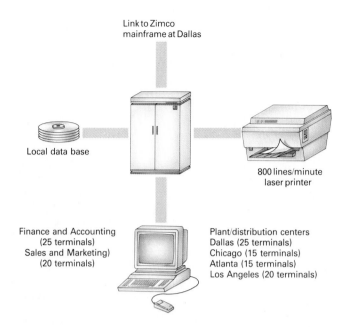

Link to Zimco
mainframe at Dallas

Local data base

800 lines/minute
laser printer

Finance and Accounting
(25 terminals)
Sales and Marketing)
(20 terminals)

Plant/distribution centers
Dallas (25 terminals)
Chicago (15 terminals)
Atlanta (15 terminals)
Los Angeles (20 terminals)

FIGURE 2–6 Configuration of a Minicomputer System in a Distributed Processing Network
The distributed minis at the Zimco plants and at the home office (see Figure 2–5) have similar configurations. Each has a disk for a local data base, a laser printer, and from 15 to 25 terminals.

2–7 Dedicated Computers: Computers with a Purpose

Computer systems have the flexibility to perform an ever-changing variety of tasks, from computer-assisted instruction and inventory processing to presentation graphics. Most of the computers you see in companies and on desk tops are referred to as **general-purpose computers**. Some computers, however, are designed to handle only one application. These are called **special-purpose computers**. A special-purpose computer is just another computer system, but it is *dedicated* to a single application and may have special requirements for input/output connections. Front-end processors and back-end processors are special-purpose computers. Special-purpose computers are installed in aircraft to aid in navigation and in general flight control. They are the violins, clarinets, and drums of music synthesizers. They are also used for materials handling in warehouses to select and move containers without human intervention. Certainly one of the most visible special-purpose uses of the computer can be observed at any video arcade. Video games are *computer* games. Special-purpose computers control the industrial robots that move, paint, weld, and inspect work in progress in a manufacturing plant. An increasingly common application of special-purpose computers is in "smart buildings." In smart buildings, a single dedicated computer can monitor and control the temperature and humidity, and it can help prevent unauthorized access to secured areas.

Perhaps the most important point to be made in this chapter is

"Well, let's see what the computer says."

this: Whether we talk about a special-purpose computer, a mainframe, a mini, or any other kind of computer system, their differences are, for the most part, in size and how they are applied.

Summary Outline and Important Terms

2–1 COMPUTERS COME IN ALL SHAPES AND SIZES. Each of the computers in the four main categories (micros, **minicomputers**, mainframes, and **supercomputers**) is a computer system, but they differ greatly in processing capabilities and in how they are used. The top three have many functional similarities, including their ability to service many users. The microcomputer, however, is designed primarily for the single-user environment.

2–2 MINICOMPUTERS: DEPARTMENT-SIZED COMPUTERS. The term *minicomputer*, or **mini**, emerged about 20 years ago as a name for small computers. The name has stuck, even though some of today's minis are more powerful than any computer of the 1960s. Minis now accomplish processing tasks that traditionally have been associated with mainframe computers. Minicomputers usually serve as stand-alone computer systems for small businesses and as remote **departmental computer systems**.

2–3 MAINFRAME COMPUTERS: THE CORPORATE WORK-HORSE. Mainframe computers, the computer category between minicomputers and supercomputers, are also called **maxicomputers**. Besides the obvious differences in processing speed, the major difference between minicomputers and mainframes is the number of remote terminals that can be serviced. A computer servicing more than 100 terminals is no longer a minicomputer.

2–4 SUPERCOMPUTERS: PROCESSING GIANTS. Mainframe computers are oriented to **input/output-bound operation**. In contrast, supercomputers handle the types of computer applications that are helpful to engineers and scientists. These applications are typically **processor-bound** and require relatively little in the way of input or output. Supercomputers are more likely to be configured with sophisticated graphics workstations and plotters than with high-speed printers.

2–5 A "HOST" OF COMPUTERS. Processors used to be called **central processing units**, or **CPUs**, but today computer systems, even micros, will normally have several processors to increase **throughput**. A typical configuration might have a **host processor** (usually a mainframe), a **front-end processor**, and perhaps a **back-end processor** (or **data base machine**). Other special-function processors include **parallel hosts**, **down-line processors**, **distributed processors**, and device processors. A parallel host is necessary where **downtime** cannot be tolerated. Virtually every hardware device has an embedded processor, usually a **microprocessor**.

2–6 INTEGRATED COMPUTER NETWORKS: COMPUTERS WORKING TOGETHER. The trend through the 1970s was toward large centralized information services departments. The current trend is toward decentralizing people, hardware, and information systems through **distributed processing**. Distributed processing is the implementation of a **computer network** of geographically and functionally distributed processors. Distributed processing can result in more effective information processing because hardware, data, software, and personnel are closer to the people who use them.

2–7 DEDICATED COMPUTERS: COMPUTERS WITH A PURPOSE. In contrast to **general-purpose computers**, **special-purpose computers** are designed for and usually dedicated to a specific application. Video games, music synthesizers, industrial robots, and "smart buildings" are a few of the hundreds of applications of special-purpose computers.

Review Exercises

Concepts

1. In distributed processing, what is distributed?
2. Under what circumstances would it be necessary to install a parallel host?
3. What are the four main categories of computer systems?
4. Give two examples of places where a device processor would be installed.

5. Contrast general-purpose computer systems with special-purpose computer systems.

6. What is the purpose of the operator console in a machine room?

7. Departmental computer systems are generally associated with which category of computer systems?

8. Contrast the processing environment of a mainframe computer with that of a microcomputer.

9. Name three subordinate processors that might be configured with a mainframe computer system.

10. What term is used to describe the basic unit of work for a processor?

Discussion

11. Ask two people who have worked with computers for at least three years to describe a minicomputer. What can you conclude from their responses?

12. Discuss centralization and decentralization as they are applied to computers and information processing.

13. Discuss how special-function processors can enhance the throughput of a mainframe computer system.

14. Explain the rationale for distributed processing.

15. Departmental computer systems are often installed in the user areas (for example, the accounting department). Who should be responsible for the ongoing operation of these computer systems?

Self-Test (by section)

2–1 **a.** The most distinguishing characteristic of any computer system is physical size. (T/F)

b. The price–performance of computers is _____ .(directly or inversely) proportional to the computing capacity of the computer.

2–2 **a.** A minicomputer has less computing capacity than a microcomputer. (T/F)

b. There is no commonly accepted definition of a minicomputer. (T/F)

2–3 **a.** Peripheral devices are connected to a mainframe computer through a: (a) base, (b) port, or (c) plug.

b. Mainframe computers are also called: (a) minicomputers, (b) midicomputers, or (c) maxicomputers.

2–4 **a.** Supercomputers are oriented to _____-bound applications.

b. One of the strategies employed by computer designers to increase the speed of computers involves reducing the distance that an electronic signal must travel. (T/F)

2–5 a. The database machine, or _____, processor handles tasks associated with the retrieval and manipulation of data stored on magnetic disk.

    b. The rate at which work can be performed by a computer system is its _____.

2–6 a. The trend in organizations is to centralize all information processing activities. (T/F)

    b. A distributed processing network of computer systems is usually designed around a combination of _____ and _____ considerations.

2–7 A special-purpose computer is dedicated to a single application and does not have any input/output connections. (T/F)

Self-test answers. **2–1** (a) F; (b) inversely. **2–2** (a) F; (b) T. **2–3** (a) b; (b) c. **2–4** (a) processor; (b) T. **2–5** (a) back-end; (b) throughput. **2–6** (a) F; (b) geographical, functional. **2–7** F.

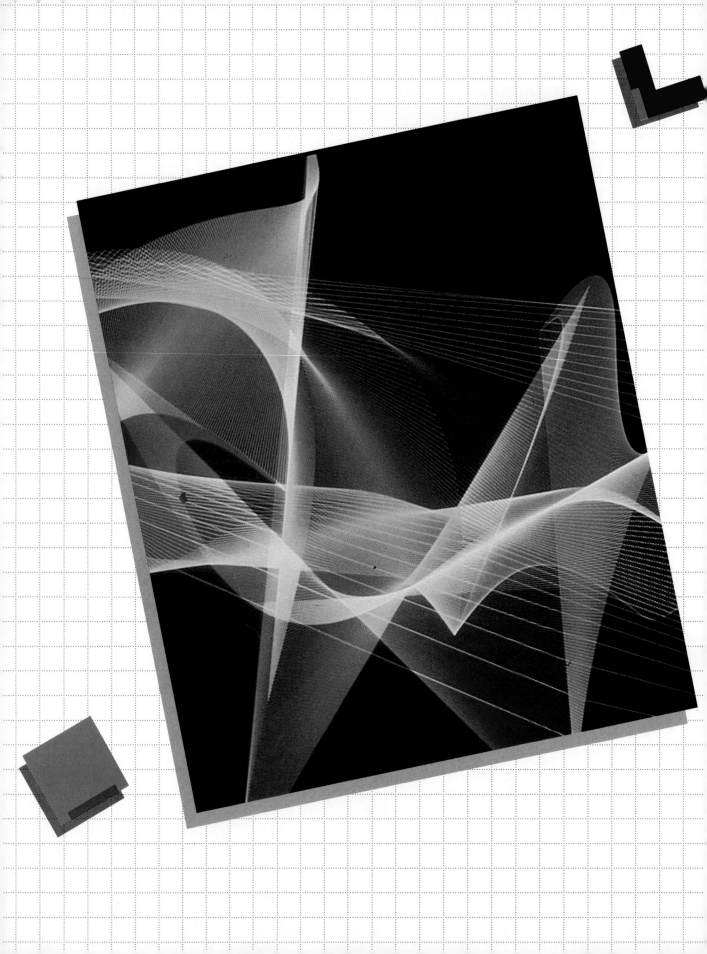

3
Microcomputers

STUDENT LEARNING OBJECTIVES

- To identify the types of microcomputers.
- To describe approaches to configuring microcomputer systems.
- To describe the proper care and maintenance of personal computers and disk storage media.
- To describe various keyboard and data entry conventions.
- To grasp concepts related to effective interaction with and use of micros and micro software.
- To describe a procedure for and considerations in the evaluation, selection, and purchase of a personal computer.

3-1 The Personal Computer Revolution

The First Personal Computer Boom

For the most part, a *microcomputer* is used by one person at a time; therefore the *micro* is also called a *personal computer*, or *PC* for short. The media attention given these desktop miracles of technology was intense during their infant years—the late 1970s and early 1980s. Fear of falling behind the competition motivated businesses to purchase personal computers by the truckload. Parents hurried to buy a personal computer so that little Johnny or Mary could march to the head of the class.

Unfortunately, businesses, parents, and others bought PCs with very little knowledge of what they do or what to do with them. In fact, the first personal computer boom was actually a bust! A great many PCs were sold, but relatively few made significant contributions to businesses, homes, or educational institutions. Because they were misunderstood and did not live up to their fanfare, the buying public cooled to PCs.

The Second Personal Computer Boom

The second personal computer boom began in the late 1980s. By then micros were easier to use and people had more realistic and informed expectations of them. The second personal computer boom, which continues today, is more deliberate. That is, people are educating themselves about the use and application of micros, then they are buying them with purpose and direction. The result is millions of micro enthusiasts.

Personal computers are everywhere, from kindergartens to corporate boardrooms. You can see them at work, at school, and possibly in your home. The most recent boom has enabled people in every walk of life to see firsthand the usefulness of personal computers. Each passing month brings more power at less expense and an expansion of the seemingly endless array of microcomputer software.

Why Are Micros So Popular?

The minimal cost and almost unlimited applications of the microcomputer have made it the darling of the computer industry. A little more than a decade ago, very few people had heard of a microcomputer. Now the number of microcomputers sold in one month exceeds the total number of operational computers in existence in the United States 12 years ago.

When you use a personal computer, the capabilities of a complete computer system are at your fingertips. Some are more powerful than the computers that once handled the data processing requirements of large banks. PCs and their support software are designed to be easy to use and understand. The wide variety of software available for microcomputers offers something for almost everyone, from video

With computers, you're never too young. First grade students use microcomputers to sharpen their reading skills.

games to word processing, to education, to home finances, to inventory control, to an on-line encyclopedia.

A personal computer is an electronic version of a scratch pad, a file cabinet, a drawing board, a typewriter, a musical instrument, and even a friend. It can help you to think logically, to improve your spelling, to select the right word, to expand your memory, to organize data, to add numbers, and much more. It can even help you assess your psychological well-being.

These reasons for the micro's popularity pale when we talk of the *real* reason for its unparalleled success: It is just plain fun to use, whether for personal, business, or scientific computing.

3–2   Microcomputers: Small but Powerful

Microprocessors

Here is a tough one. What is smaller than a dime and found in wristwatches, sewing machines, and jukeboxes? The answer: a **microprocessor**. Microprocessors play a very important role in our lives. You probably have a dozen or more of them at home and may not know it. They are used in telephones, ovens, televisions, thermostats, greeting cards, cars, and, of course, personal computers.

The microprocessor is a product of the microminiaturization of electronic circuitry; it is literally a "computer on a chip." The first fully operational microprocessor was demonstrated in March 1971. Since that time, these relatively inexpensive microprocessors have been integrated into thousands of mechanical and electronic devices, even elevators and ski-boot bindings. In a few years virtually ev-

erything mechanical or electronic will incorporate microprocessor technology into its design.

The ultra-high-performance Intel i486 microprocessor, the most recent addition to the popular Intel family of microprocessors, packs 1.2 million transistors in a 0.414-inch-by-0.619-inch die.

Microcomputers

As we learned in Chapter 2, there is no commonly accepted definition of minicomputer, mainframe computer, and supercomputer. The same can be said about a microcomputer. A microcomputer is just a small computer. However, it is a safe bet that any computer you can pick up and carry is probably a micro. But don't be misled by the *micro* prefix. You can pick up and carry some very powerful computers!

The microprocessor is sometimes confused with its famous offspring, the microcomputer. A keyboard, video monitor, and memory were attached to the microprocessor and the microcomputer was born! Suddenly owning a computer became an economic reality for individuals and small businesses.

The Motherboard In a microcomputer, the microprocessor, the electronic circuitry for handling input/output signals from the peripheral devices (keyboard, printer, and so on), and the memory chips are mounted on a single circuit board, called a **motherboard**. Before being attached to the motherboard, the microprocessor and other chips are mounted onto a *carrier*. Carriers have standard-sized pin connectors that permit the chips to be attached to the motherboard.

The motherboard, the "guts" of a microcomputer, is what distinguishes one microcomputer from another. The motherboard is simply "plugged" into one of several slots designed for circuit boards.

The processing components of most micros are sold with several empty **expansion slots** so that you can purchase and plug in optional capabilities in the form of **add-on boards**. Add-on boards are discussed in the next section.

Pocket, Lap, and Desktop PCs   Personal computers come in three different physical sizes: *pocket PCs*, *lap PCs*, and *desktop PCs*. The pocket and lap PCs are light (a few ounces to 8 pounds), compact, and can operate without an external power source, so they earn the "portable" label as well. There are also a number of "transportable" desktop PCs on the market, but they are more cumbersome to move. They fold up to about the size of a small suitcase, weigh about 25 pounds, and usually require an external power source. Desktop PCs are not designed for frequent movement and are therefore not considered portable.

The power of a PC is not necessarily in proportion to its size. A few lap PCs can run circles around some of the desktop PCs. Some user conveniences, however, must be sacrificed to achieve portability. For instance, the miniature keyboards on pocket PCs make data entry and interaction with the computer difficult and slow. The display screen on some lap PCs is small and does not hold as much text as a display screen on a desktop PC.

When searching for a personal computer, this sales representative identified portability as her primary criterion. She purchased a lap PC because it gave her the flexibility to carry her files and the power of a computer on sales calls.

This project manager carries his portable PC home on weekends to review the schedule of project activities for the coming week. This portable PC is unique in that it includes a printer. To prepare the computer to be moved, the keyboard is detached and fastened in position to cover the monitor. A handle is attached to the top of the micro.

3–3 Configuring a PC: Putting the Pieces Together

Normally computer professionals are called upon to select, configure, and install the hardware associated with minis, mainframes, and supercomputers. But the user typically selects, configures, and installs his or her own micro; therefore, it is important that you know what makes up a microcomputer system and how it fits together.

A Typical Microcomputer Configuration

The computer and its peripheral devices are called the computer system **configuration**. The configuration of a microcomputer can vary. The most typical micro configuration consists of the following:

1. A computer
2. A keyboard for input
3. A monitor for *soft copy* (temporary) output
4. A printer for *hard copy* (printed) output
5. One or two disk drives for permanent storage of data and programs

In some microcomputer systems these components are purchased as separate physical units, then linked together. Micros that give users the flexibility to configure the system with a variety of peripheral devices (input/output and storage) are said to have an **open architecture**. A good analogy to illustrate the concept of open architecture is a component stereo system to which a record turntable, an equalizer, a tape deck, a compact disk player, speakers, and so on can be attached. A microcomputer system with an open architecture is configured by linking any of the many peripheral devices discussed in Chapters 5 and 6 (I/O and data storage devices) to the processor component. In a **closed architecture**, the system is fully configured when it is sold. Except for a few pocket and lap PCs, virtually all micros placed on the market during the past couple of years have an open architecture.

Linking Micro Components

An open architecture, also called a **bus architecture**, is possible because all micro components are linked by a common electrical **bus**. In Chapter 1, we likened the processing component of a microcomputer to the human brain. Just as the brain sends and receives signals through the central nervous system, the processor sends and receives electrical signals through the bus. The bus is the path through which the processor sends data and commands to **random access memory** and all peripheral devices, such as printers and disk storage. Random access memory, which is usually called **RAM** (rhymes with *Sam*), is made up of solid state electronics components, specifically memory chips. All programs and data must reside in RAM before programs can be executed or data can be processed. RAM is discussed in detail in Chapter 4, "Inside the Computer." Data and commands are transmitted between the processor, RAM, and its peripheral devices in the

Some of the more powerful desktop microcomputers actually sit under or beside a desk. This provides more space for the keyboard, monitor, printer, and other peripheral devices. This IBM PS/2 Model 80 has an open architecture so peripherals can be added as they are needed.

form of electronic signals. In short, the bus is a vehicle for communication between the processor, RAM, and the peripheral devices.

In an open architecture, external input/output devices (that is, devices external to the processor cabinet) and some storage devices are plugged into the bus in much the same way you would plug a lamp into a electrical outlet. The receptacle, called a *port*, provides a direct link to the micro's common electrical bus.

External peripheral devices are linked, or *interfaced*, with the processor through either a **serial port** or a **parallel port**. Serial ports facilitate the *serial transmission* of data—the transmission of only one electronic signal at a time. Serial ports provide an interface for low-speed printers and other low-speed devices. The de facto standard for micro serial ports is the 25-pin (male or female) **RS-232C port**.

Parallel ports facilitate the *parallel transmission* of data, that is, the simultaneous transmission of multiple electronic signals. Parallel ports provide the interface for devices like high-speed printers (such as laser printers), magnetic tape backup units, and other computers.

Also connected to the common electrical bus are *expansion slots*, which are usually housed in the processor cabinet. These slots enable a micro owner to enhance the functionality of a basic micro configuration with a wide variety of special-function *add-on boards*, also called **add-on cards**. These "add-ons" contain the electronic circuitry for a wide variety of computer-related functions. The number of available expansion slots varies from computer to computer. Some of the more popular add-on boards are listed below.

- *RAM*. Expands random access memory, usually in increments that permit an extra 64,000 characters of RAM.
- *Color and graphics adapter*. Permits the interfacing of video monitors that have graphics and/or color capabilities. The *EGA*, or

A portable micro is configured here with all the trimmings: a printer, a power supply (in front of the carrying case), the keyboard and processor unit (which also contains one disk drive), a mouse (for input), another disk drive, a modem (under telephone) for making connections to other computers, and a joy stick (far right). These add-ons are discussed in Chapters 5, 6, and 7. The processor unit is the central focus of the system. Cables from each device are connected to the input/output ports at the rear of the processor unit.

All or parts of many traditional office fixtures can be absorbed within a PC— typewriters and opaque fluid, calculators, notepads and worksheets, drawing equipment, telephone indices, calendars, tickler files, file cabinets, important reports and memos, and reference books such as a dictionary or thesaurus. The coffee cup, however, will continue to occupy its place on the desktop.

enhanced graphic adapter board, enables the interfacing of high-resolution monitors (monitors capable of producing high-quality displays). The EGA boards usually come with dedicated RAM that is not accessible to the user.

- *Modem.* Permits communication with remote computers via a telephone line link.
- *Internal battery-powered clock/calendar.* Provides continuous and/ or on-demand display of or access to the current date and time (for example, Monday, Dec. 18, 1991, 9:35 a.m.).
- *Serial port.* Installation of the board provides access to the bus via another serial port.
- *Parallel port.* Installation of the board provides access to the bus via another parallel port.
- *Printer spooler.* Enables data to be printed while the user continues with other processing activities. The data are transferred (spooled) at high speed from RAM to a *print buffer* (an intermediate storage area) and then routed to the printer from the buffer.
- *Hard disk.* Hard disks with capacities of as much as 40M bytes can be installed in expansion slots.
- *Coprocessor.* These "extra" processors, which are under the control of the main processor, help relieve the main processor of certain tasks, such as arithmetic functions. This sharing of duties helps increase system throughput.

The capabilities of a microcomputer can be enhanced with the addition of a memory expansion add-on board (top) and/or a multifunction add-on board (bottom).

- *VCR backup*. This board enables an ordinary Beta or VHS videocassette recorder to be used as a tape backup device. One ordinary videocassette tape can hold up to 80M bytes of data.

Most of the add-on boards are *multifunctional*: That is, they include two or more of these capabilities. For example, one popular **multifunction add-on board** comes with a serial port, a modem, and an internal battery-powered clock/calendar.

Expansion slots are at a premium. To make the most efficient use of these slots, circuit board manufacturers have created half-size expansion boards that fit in a *short slot* (half an expansion slot). These half-size boards effectively double the number of expansion slots available for a given microcomputer.

Multiuser Micros

In the early 1960s, mainframe computer systems could service only one user at a time. By the mid-1960s, technological improvements had made it possible for computers to service several users simultaneously. A quarter of a century later, some mainframes service thousands of users at the same time!

We can draw a parallel between what happened to the mainframe in the 1960s and what is happening to microcomputers today. Until recently micros were "personal" computers—for individual use only. But technological improvements have been so rapid that it has become difficult for a single user to tap the full potential of state-of-the-art micros. To tap this unused potential, hardware and software vendors are marketing products that permit several people to use the system at once.

These multiuser micros are configured with up to 12 VDTs. These terminals, often located in the same office, share the microcomputer's resources and its peripheral devices. With a multiuser micro, a secretary can be transcribing dictation at one terminal, a manager can be doing financial analysis at another terminal, and a clerk can be entering data to a data base at yet another terminal. All this is taking place at the same time on the same multiuser micro.

The Dual-Purpose Micro: Two for the Price of One

A terminal is the hardware that allows you to interact with a computer system, be it a mainframe or a multiuser micro. A microcomputer can also be a terminal. With the installation of an optional data communications adapter, a micro has the flexibility to serve as a *stand-alone* computer system or as an "intelligent" terminal of a multiuser micro, a mini, a mainframe, or a supercomputer.

The term *intelligent* is applied to terminals that can also operate as stand-alone computer systems, independent of any other computer system. For example, you can dial up any one of a number of commercial information services on travel, securities, and consumer goods, link your micro to the telephone line and remote computer, then use your micro as a terminal to obtain information. Both the micro and the VDT can transmit and receive data from a remote computer, but only the micro terminal can process and store the data independently.

Care and Maintenance of a Micro

Microcomputers are very reliable. Apply the dictates of common sense to their care and maintenance, and they will give you months, even years, of maintenance-free operation. A few helpful hints are listed here.

- Avoid excessive dust and extremes in temperature and humidity.
- Avoid frequent movement of desktop micros.
- Install a *surge protector* between the power source and the micro. Micros as well as other electronic devices can be seriously damaged by a sudden surge of power caused by such things as a bolt of lightning striking a power line.

3–4 Interacting with a Personal Computer

To interact effectively with a personal computer you need to be knowledgeable in four areas.

1. The operation of microcomputer hardware (for example, the keyboard)
2. General microcomputer software concepts (such as windows and scrolling)
3. The operating system (the program that resides in RAM and controls the execution of all other software, the most popular being MS-DOS, Macintosh DOS, OS/2, and UNIX)
4. The specific applications programs you are using (for example, Lotus 1-2-3)

The first three areas of understanding are prerequisites of the fourth; that is, you will need a working knowledge of micro hardware, software concepts, and the operating system before you can make effective use of applications programs like dBASE IV (a data management program), WordPerfect (a word processing program), or any of the thousands of micro software packages. The first two areas of knowledge are discussed in this chapter. The third area, operating systems, is discussed in Chapter 8, "Programming Languages and Software Concepts." Popular applications software for micros, the fourth area of knowledge, is discussed in Chapters 14 and 15 in Part IV, "Personal Computing."

Getting Started

Once all the micro components have been installed and connected to the processor unit, the operating system has been installed, and the various components are connected to an electrical power source, you are ready to begin processing. Micros are similar to copy machines, toasters, and other electrical devices: You must activate them with electrical power. If you have a micro with a permanently installed hard disk, all you have to do is turn on the computer and, perhaps, the monitor and printer. After a short period, a beep signals the end of the *system check* and the operating system is loaded automatically from disk to RAM. If your micro does not have a hard disk and is configured with one or two diskette drives, you must insert the diskette containing the operating system software before turning on the system. Interaction with MS-DOS for the IBM PC and compatible micros and procedures for running and using an applications program are covered in detail in *Microcomputer Software*: *Step by Step*, a hands-on skills text that complements this book.

Entering Commands and Data

Micros can be very picky. A personal computer is responsive to your commands, but it does *exactly* what you tell it to do—no more, no less. If you do something wrong it tells you, and then gives you another chance.

Whether entering an operating system command or an applications program command, you must be explicit. For example, if you wish to copy a word processing document file from one disk to another, you cannot just enter "copy", or even "copy MYFILE". You must enter the command that tells the micro to copy MYFILE from disk A to disk B (for example in MS-DOS, "copy a:myfile b:"). If you omit necessary information in a command or if the format of the command is incorrect, an error message will be displayed and/or an on-screen prompt will request that you reenter the command correctly.

This personal computer has more power than some mainframes of a decade ago. This added power has opened the door for micro users to run sophisticated software that was previously restricted to mainframe computers. This architect is using computer-aided design software.

Micros are not always so picky, however. You can enter DOS commands and filenames as either uppercase or lowercase characters. For example, the system interprets the command "copy a:myfile b:" and "COPY A:MYFILE B:" to be the same command. Some software packages do not distinguish between uppercase and lowercase *commands*; but all software packages do make the distinction between uppercase and lowercase entries for *keyed-in data*.

The Keyboard

A microcomputer's *keyboard* is normally its primary input and control device. You enter data and issue commands via the keyboard. Besides the standard typewriter keyboard, most micro keyboards have **function keys**, also called **soft keys** (see Figure 3–1). When pressed, these function keys trigger the execution of software, thus the name soft key. For example, pressing a particular function key might call up a *menu* of possible activities that can be performed. Another function key might rearrange a paragraph in a word processing document for right and left justification. Some function keys are permanently labeled: copy, find, save, and so on. Others are numbered and assigned different functions for different software packages. The software packages are usually distributed with **keyboard templates** that designate which commands are assigned to which function keys. For example, "help" is often assigned to F1, or function key number 1. The templates are usually designed to fit over the keyboard or be attached with an adhesive.

Most keyboards are equipped with a *10-key pad* and *cursor control keys* (see Figure 3–1). The **cursor,** or blinking character, always indicates the location of the next input on the screen. The 10-key pad permits rapid numeric data entry. It is normally positioned to the right of the standard alphanumeric keyboard. The **cursor control keys,** or "arrow" keys, allow you to move the cursor up and down (usually a line at a time) and left and right (usually a character at a

FIGURE 3–1   A Microcomputer Keyboard
This is a representative microcomputer keyboard. In this figure, the alphanumeric characters follow the commonly used Qwerty layout. The positioning of the function keys, cursor control keys, and the 10-key pad may vary substantially from keyboard to keyboard.

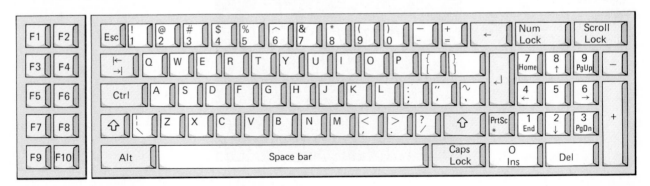

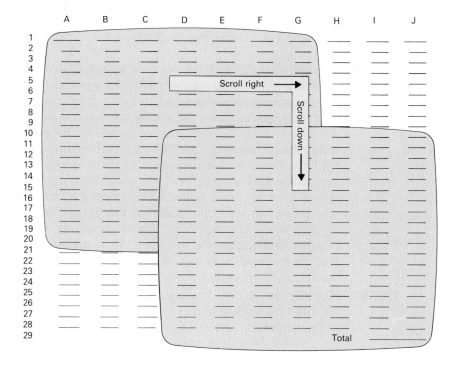

FIGURE 3–2   Scrolling

Scroll horizontally (right in the figure) and vertically (down in the figure) to view those portions of an electronic spreadsheet that do not fit on a single screen.

time). To move the cursor rapidly about the screen, simply hold down the desired cursor control key.

For many software packages, you can use the cursor control keys to view parts of a document or worksheet that extend past the bottom, top, or sides of the screen. This is known as **scrolling**. Use the up and down cursor control keys to *scroll vertically* and the left and right keys to *scroll horizontally*. For example, if you wish to scroll vertically through a word processing document, move the up or down cursor control key to the edge of the current screen and continue to press the key to view more of the document, one line at a time. Figure 3–2 illustrates vertical and horizontal scrolling.

In summary, there are three basic ways to enter a command on the keyboard:

- *Key in* the command using the alphanumeric portion of the keyboard.
- Press a *function key*.
- Use the *cursor control keys* to select a *menu option* from the display of a menu. Menus are discussed in detail in the next section.

Other important keys common to most keyboards are the *enter* or *carriage return* (ENTER or RETURN), *home* (HOME), *end* (END), *page up* and *page down* (PGUP and PGDN), *delete* (DEL), *insert-overstrike toggle* (INS), *backspace* (BKSP), *escape* (ESC), *space* (SPACE), *control* (CTRL), and *alternate* (ALT) keys (see Figure 3–1).

ENTER   Normally the ENTER key is used to send keyed-in data or a selected command to RAM for processing. For example, when you want to enter data into an electronic spreadsheet, the characters you enter are displayed in an edit area until you press ENTER, also called the *carriage return* or RETURN. When you press ENTER, the data are displayed in the appropriate area in the spreadsheet. When you highlight a menu option with a cursor control key, press ENTER to select that option. Like most of the special keys, ENTER has other meanings, depending on the type of software package you are using. In word processing, for example, you would designate the end of a paragraph by pressing the ENTER key.

HOME   Pressing the HOME key results in different actions for different packages, but often the cursor is moved to the beginning of a work area (the beginning of the screen or document in word processing, the upper left corner of the spreadsheet, or the first record in a data base).

END   With most software packages, press END to move the cursor to the end of the work area (the end of the screen or document in word processing, the lower right corner of the spreadsheet, or the last record in a data base).

PGUP, PGDN   Press PGUP (*page up*, or previous) and PGDN (*page down*, or next) to vertically scroll *a page (screen) at a time* to see parts of the document or spreadsheet that extend past the top or bottom of the screen, respectively. PGUP and PGDN are also used to position the cursor at the previous and next record, respectively, when using database software.

DEL   Press DEL to *delete* the character at the cursor position.

INS   Press INS to **toggle** (switch) between the two modes of entering data and text—*insert and replace*. Both modes are discussed and illustrated later in the word processing discussion in Chapter 14. The term *toggle* is used to describe the action of pressing a single key to alternate between two or more modes of operation (insert and replace), functions (underline on or underline off), or operational specifications (for type of database field: character, numeric, date, memo).

BKSP   Press the BKSP, or *backspace*, key to move the cursor one position to the left and delete the character in that position.

ESC	The ESC, or *escape*, key may have many functions, depending on the software package, but in most situations you can press the ESC key to negate the current command.
SPACE	Press the SPACE bar at the bottom of the keyboard to key in a space at the cursor position.
CTRL, ALT	The CTRL, or *control*, and ALT, or *alternate*, keys are used in conjunction with another key to expand the functionality of the keyboard. You hold down a CTRL or ALT key to give another key new meaning. For example, on some word processing systems you press HOME to move the cursor to the top left corner of the screen. When you press CTRL and HOME together, the cursor is positioned at the beginning of the document.

Each keystroke you enter is sent first to an intermediate *keystroke buffer* that can save from 15 to hundreds of keystrokes. Under normal processing conditions, the keystroke is sent immediately from the buffer to the processor; however, there are many instances in which you may have to wait for processing to finish (such as disk reads or preparation of a graphics display). When this happens you can key ahead. For example, if you know that the next prompt to be displayed is "Enter filename:" you can enter the desired filename in anticipation of the prompt. When the prompt appears, the filename that you entered is loaded from the keystroke buffer and displayed after the prompt. Judicious use of the keystroke buffer can make your interaction with micro software packages much more efficient.

The Mouse

Another device used for input and control is the **mouse**. The hand-held mouse is connected to the computer by an electrical cable (the mouse's "tail") and the mouse is rolled over a desktop to move the cursor. The mouse is used for quick positioning of the cursor over the

At many colleges, microcomputers are strategically located throughout campus so that students and professors can have ready access both to a wide variety of information and to the processing capability of a micro. These Apple Macintosh micros in the library are available on a first-come, first-serve basis. All Macintosh micros are configured with both a keyboard and a mouse for input.

desired menu item or a graphic image, called an **icon** (for example, a graphic rendering of a file cabinet or a diskette). Buttons on the mouse are activated to select a menu item or icon, or to perform certain tasks, such as moving blocks of data from one part of the screen to another. Also, the mouse permits the random cursor movements needed for the user to "draw" lines and create images on the screen.

Issuing Commands to Micro Software Packages

You can interact with software packages, such as electronic spreadsheet and database, at several different levels of sophistication: the *menu level*, the *macro level*, and the *programming level*. These three levels of command interaction are discussed in the following sections.

Menus

The hierarchy of menus. When using micro applications software, you issue commands and initiate operations by selecting activities to be performed from a hierarchy of **menus**. These hierarchies are sometimes called *menu trees* (see Figure 3–3). When you select an item from the **main menu**, you are often presented with another menu of activities, and so on. Depending on the items you select, you may progress through as few as one and as many as eight levels of menus before processing is initiated for the desired activity.

Let's use graphics software to illustrate how you might use a

FIGURE 3–3   A Hierarchy of Menus

This figure illustrates how a user of Lotus 1-2-3, a popular electronic spreadsheet program, progresses through a hierarchy of menus to format all numeric entries to a currency format with two decimal places (for example, the entry 1234.56 would be displayed as $1,234.56). Selecting the "Worksheet" option causes a display of the second-level menu. The "Global" option indicates that further menu options apply to all applicable spreadsheet entries. At the third and fourth levels, the user selects the "Format" and "Currency" options. Upon selecting the "Currency" option, the user is prompted to enter the desired number of decimal places.

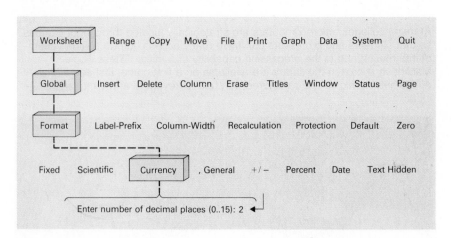

hierarchy of menus. The main menu of a graphics software package might give you the choice of what type of graph you want produced:

Bar   Pie   Line

If you select *bar graph*, another menu lets you choose whether you wish to create a new one, revise an existing one, or view an existing one.

Create   Revise   View

If you select *create*, more menus are presented that permit you to describe the appearance of the graph (using labels) and to identify what data are to be graphed.

Types of menus. A menu can appear as a **bar menu** in the *user interface* portion of the display, a **pull-down menu**, or a **pop-up menu**. The user interface is from one to six lines at the bottom and/or top of the screen. The menu options in a bar menu are displayed across the screen. To select an item in a bar menu, use the left and right cursor control keys to highlight the desired menu option and press ENTER.

The result of a menu selection from a bar menu at the top of the screen is often a pull-down menu. The subordinate menu is "pulled-down" from the selected menu option and displayed as a vertical list of menu options. The entire menu is shown in a **window** directly under the selected menu option and over whatever is currently on the screen. A window is a rectangular display that is temporarily superimposed over whatever is currently on the screen. Use the up and down cursor-control keys to highlight the desired menu option and press ENTER to select it.

Like the pull-down menu, the pop-up menu is superimposed on the current screen in a window. A pop-up menu can be called up in a variety of ways, including function keys or as the result of a selection from a higher-level pop-up menu.

Defaults. As you progress through a series of menus, you are eventually asked to enter the specifications for data to be graphed (graphics software), the size of the output paper (word processing software), and so on. As a convenience to the user, many of the specification options are already filled in for common situations. For example, word processing packages set output document size at 8 1/2 by 11 inches. If the user is satisfied with these **default options**, no further specifications are required. The user can easily revise the default options to accommodate less common situations. So, to print a document on legal-sized paper, the default paper length of 11 inches would need to be revised to 14 inches.

Menu summary. During any given point in a work session, the options available to the user of a micro software tool are displayed somewhere on the screen. For example, in word processing, the instructions for calling up the main menu or a help screen are prom-

Micros throughout this bank help loan officers provide customers with quick turnaround on loans, letters of credit, guarantees, and other customer documents.

inently displayed above or below the document work area. If you are ever confused about what to do next, the options are usually displayed on the current screen.

Macros and Programming   At the menu level of command interaction, you are initiating individual commands. At the macro and programming levels of interaction, you can string together commands and even introduce logic operations.

A handy feature available with most micro software packages is the **macro**. A macro is a sequence of frequently used operations or keystrokes that can be recalled as you need them. You create a macro by entering the sequence of operations or keystrokes and storing them on disk for later recall. To *invoke*, or execute, the macro, you either refer to it by name (perhaps in the text of a word processing file) or enter the series of keystrokes that identify the desired macro (for example, ALT-8, CTRL-F4). Three common user-supplied macros in word processing could be the commands necessary to format the first-, second-, and third-level headings in a report. For example, the user might want the first-level heading to be centered, boldface, and followed by two spaces; the second level to be flush left, boldface, and followed by an indented paragraph; and the third level to be flush left, underlined, and followed on the same line by the beginning of the first paragraph. In electronic spreadsheets, macros are commonly used to produce graphs automatically from spreadsheet data.

Some software packages allow users the flexibility to do their own *programming*. That is, micro software users can create logical sequences of instructions. For example, a database software program can be written that will retrieve records from a particular data base depending on preset criteria, process the data according to programmed instructions, and print out a report. The programming capability enables users to create microcomputer-based information systems for an endless number of applications, from payroll processing to inventory control. Programming concepts are discussed in Chapter 8.

3-5 User-Friendly Software

Virtually all vendors of micro software tout their product as being **user friendly**. Software is said to be user friendly when someone with relatively little computer experience has little difficulty using the system. User-friendly software communicates easily understood words, phrases, and **icons**, or pictographs, to the end user, thus simplifying the user's interaction with the computer system. A central focus of the design of any micro software package is user friendliness.

Help Commands

A handy feature available on most software packages is the **help command**. When you find yourself in a corner, so to speak, you can press the help key, often assigned to a numbered function key, to get a more detailed explanation or instructions on how to proceed. In most micro software packages, the help commands are *context sensitive*—the explanation provided relates to what you were doing when you issued the help command. For example, if you were entering data into a data base, the explanation would address how to enter data. When you are finished reading the help information, the system returns you to your work at the same point you left it.

Windows

Windows allow users to "look through" several windows on a single display screen; however, you can manipulate text or data in only one window at a time. This is called the *current window*. Windows can overlap one another on the display screen. For example, some integrated software packages allow users to view a spreadsheet in one window, a bar chart in another, and a word processing document

This Apple Macintosh SE display illustrates several micro software concepts—the bar menu at the top the screen, three windows, and an icon (the trash can at lower right). To delete a file, a user would move the mouse to position the arrow (currently in the center of the screen) over the trash can icon.

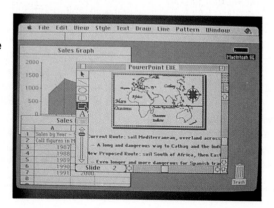

More than a million people a year go through the process of buying a microcomputer, micro peripheral devices, and related software. This sidebar contains information that will help those planning to purchase a microcomputer to spend their money wisely.

RETAIL SALES

Where to Buy. Microcomputers and related hardware and software can be purchased at thousands of convenient locations. Retail chains, such as Computer-Land, ENTRE', and MicroAge, market and service a variety of small computer systems. Radio Shack stores carry and sell their own line of computers. Micros are also sold in the computer department of most department stores. The demand for micros has encouraged major computer system manufacturers to open retail stores.

There is an alternative to buying a computer at a retail store. If you know what you want, you can call any of several mail order services, give them a credit card number, and your PC will be delivered to your doorstep.

The Perks of Employment. You might be able to acquire a micro through your employer. Many companies offer their employees a "computer perk." In cooperation with vendors, companies make volume purchases of PCs at discount rates and then offer them to employees at substantial savings. Many colleges sponsor similar programs to benefit students and professors.

STEPS TO BUYING A MICROCOMPUTER

Buying a microcomputer can be a harrowing experience, or it can be a thrilling and fulfilling one. If you approach the purchase of a micro haphazardly, expect the former. If you go about the acquisition methodically and with purpose, expect the latter. This section contains a seven-step procedure that will help you in the evaluation and selection of a microcomputer (summarized in the figure).

1. *Achieve computer literacy.* You do not buy an automobile before you learn how to drive, and you should not buy a microcomputer without a good understanding of its capabilities and how you intend to use it.

2. *Determine your information and computer usage needs.* There is an adage: "If you don't know where you are going, any road will get you there." The statement is certainly true of choosing a PC. Knowing where you are going can be translated to mean "How do you plan to use the PC?"

Do you wish to develop your own software or purchase commercially available software packages, or perhaps do both? If you want to write your own programs, you must select the programming language best suited to your application needs. The only programming language supported by all microcomputers is BASIC. If you plan on purchasing the software, determine which general application areas you wish to have supported on the proposed PC (spreadsheet, accounting, word processing, home banking, or others).

3. *Assess availability of software and information services.* Determine what software and information services are available to meet your prescribed needs. Good sources of this type of information include a wide variety of periodicals (*PC, Byte, Software, Computerworld*, and *Personal Computing*, to name a few), salespeople at computer stores, and acquaintances who have knowledge in the area.

Several hundred micro productivity software packages are available commercially and vary greatly in capabilities and price. Software with essentially the same capabilities may be priced with differences of as much as several hundred dollars. Some graphics software creates displays of graphs in seconds, while others take minutes. Some software packages are easy to learn and are accompanied by good documentation, while others are not. Considering the amount of time you might spend using micro software, any extra time you devote to evaluating the software will be time well spent.

4. *Investigate hardware options.* If you select a specific software product or an information service, your selection may dictate the general computer system configuration requirements and, in some cases, a specific microcomputer system. In all likelihood you will have several, if not a dozen, hardware alternatives available to you. Become familiar with the features and options of each system.

5. *Determine features desired.* You can go with a minimum system configuration, or you can add a few "bells and whistles." Expect to pay for each feature in convenience, quality, and speed that you add to the minimum configuration. For example, people are usually willing to pay a little extra for the added convenience of a two-disk system (usually a floppy and

a hard disk), even though one disk will suffice. On the other hand, a color monitor may be an unnecessary luxury for some applications. The peripherals you select depend on your specific needs and volume of usage. For example, the type of printer you choose will depend on the volume of hard-copy output you anticipate, whether or not you need graphics output, whether or not you need letter-quality print, and so on.

6. *"Test drive" several alternatives.* Once you have selected several software and hardware alternatives, spend enough time to gain some familiarity with them. Do you prefer one keyboard over another? Does a word processing system fully use the features of the hardware? Is one system easier to understand and use than another? Use these sessions to answer any questions you might have about the hardware or software. Salespeople at most retail stores are happy to give you a "test drive"—just ask.

7. *Select and buy.* Apply your criteria, select, and then buy your hardware and software.

FACTORS TO CONSIDER WHEN BUYING A MICRO

- *Future computing needs.* What will your computer and information processing needs be in the future? Make sure the system you select can grow with your needs.

- *Who will use the system?* Plan not only for yourself but for others in your home or office who will also use the system. Get their input and consider their needs along with yours.

- *Availability of software.* Software is developed for one or several microcomputers, but not for all microcomputers. As you might expect, a more extensive array of software is available for the more popular micros. However, do not overlook some of the less visible vendors if their products, in your mind, are superior to the alternatives.

- *Service.* Computing hardware is very reliable. Even so, the possibility exists that one or several of the components will eventually malfunction and have to be repaired. Before purchasing a micro, identify a reliable source of hardware maintenance. Most retailers service what they sell. If a retailer says that the hardware must be returned to the manufacturer for repair, choose another retailer or another system.

Most retailers or vendors will offer a variety of maintenance contracts. Maintenance contract options range from on-site repair that covers all parts and service to carry-in service that does not include parts. Most domestic users elect to treat their micros like their televisions and cars: When the warranty runs out, they pay for repairs as they are needed. Under normal circumstances, this strategy will prove the least expensive.

Service extends beyond hardware maintenance. Service is also an organization's willingness to respond to your inquiries, before *and* after the sale. Some retailers and vendors offer classes in programming and in the use of the hardware and software that they sell.

- *Hardware obsolescence.* "I'm going to buy one as soon as the price goes down a little more." If you adopt this strategy, you may never purchase a computer. If you wait another six months, you will probably be able to get a more powerful micro for less money. But what about the lost opportunity?

  There is, however, a danger in purchasing a micro that is near or at the end of its life cycle. Focus your search on micros with state-of-the-art technology. Even though you may get a substantial discount on the older micro, you will normally get more for your money with the newer one.

- *Software obsolescence.* Software can become obsolete as well. Software vendors are continually improving their software packages. Each package is assigned a *version number.* The first *release* might be identified as 1.0 (referred to as "one point zero"). Subsequent updates to version 1.0 become version 1.1, version 1.2, and so on. The next major revision to the package is released as version number 2.0. Make sure that you are buying the most recent release of a particular software package.

- *Other costs.* The cost of the actual microcomputer system is the major expense, but there are numerous incidental expenses that can mount up that may influence your selection of a micro. If you have a spending limit, consider these costs (the cost ranges listed are for a first-time user) when purchasing the hardware: software ($100–$1500); maintenance ($0–$500 a year); diskettes and tape cassettes ($50–$200); furniture ($0–$350); insurance ($0–$40); and printer ribbons or cartridges, paper, and other supplies ($40–$400).

in a third window. With windows, you can work the way you think and think the way you work. Several projects are at the tips of your fingers and you can switch between them with relative ease.

You can perform work in one of several windows on a display screen or you can **zoom** in on a particular window—that is, the window you select expands to fill the entire screen. Press a key and you can return to a multiwindow display. A multiwindow display permits you to see how a change in one window affects another window. For example, as you change the data in a spreadsheet, you can see how an accompanying pie graph is revised to reflect the new data.

You can even create **window panes**! As you might expect, a window is divided into panes so you can view several parts of the same window subarea at a time. For example, if you are writing a long report in a word processing window, you might wish to write the conclusions to the report in one window pane while viewing portions of the report in another window pane.

Summary Outline and Important Terms

3–1 THE PERSONAL COMPUTER REVOLUTION.   Typically, a micro is used by one person at a time. The first personal-computer, or PC, boom was actually a bust because people were not prepared to cope with these new technological marvels. Today a better educated and more deliberate buying public have spawned a very successful second personal computer boom. The powerful micro and the availability of a seemingly endless array of microcomputer software (computer programs) have encouraged people in every endeavor to jump on the PC bandwagon.

3–2 MICROCOMPUTERS: SMALL BUT POWERFUL. **Microprocessors** not only set the stage for microcomputers, but they are found in dozens of devices about the home. The **motherboard** in a microcomputer contains the electronic circuitry for processing, input/output operations, and some memory. The processing components of most micros have several empty **expansion slots** so you can purchase and plug in optional capabilities in the form of **add-on boards**. The micro comes in pocket, lap, and desktop sizes.

3–3 CONFIGURING A PC: PUTTING THE PIECES TOGETHER. The computer and its peripheral devices are called the computer system **configuration**. A typical micro configuration would be a computer, a keyboard, a monitor, a printer, and one or two disk drives. Micros that give users the flexibility to configure the system with a variety of peripheral devices are said to have an **open architecture**, or **bus architecture**. In a **closed architecture**, the system is fully configured when it is sold.

The electrical **bus** is the path through which the processor sends and receives data and commands to **RAM** (**random**

access memory) and all peripheral devices. A port provides a direct link to the micro's bus. External peripheral devices are interfaced with the processor through either a **serial port** or a **parallel port**. The de facto standard for micro serial ports is the **RS-232C port**.

Expansion slots can house a wide variety of special-function add-on boards, or **add-on cards**. The add-ons can include one or more of the following functions: RAM, color/graphics adapter, modem, internal battery-powered clock/calendar, serial port, parallel port, printer spooler, hard disk, coprocessor, and VCR backup. Most are **multifunction add-on boards**.

Multiuser micros are configured with several terminals. Micros can be used as stand-alone computer systems or they can serve as "intelligent" terminals to mainframe computers.

Apply the dictates of common sense to the care and maintenance of micros, peripheral devices, and storage media. For example, avoid excessive dust; avoid extremes in temperature and humidity; and don't fold, spindle, or mutilate the diskettes.

3–4 INTERACTING WITH A PERSONAL COMPUTER. To interact effectively with a personal computer, you need to understand the operation of microcomputer hardware, general microcomputer software concepts, the operating system (for example, MS-DOS), and the specific applications programs you are using. The first three areas of understanding are prerequisites of the fourth.

A personal computer is responsive to your commands, but it does exactly what you tell it to do. A micro's keyboard is the primary input and control device. Most micro keyboards have a 10-key pad, **cursor control keys**, and **function keys**, or **soft keys**. **Keyboard templates** show you which commands are assigned to which function keys. Use the cursor control keys for vertical and horizontal **scrolling** and for menu selection. The mouse is another device used for input and control.

You can interact with software packages at several different levels of sophistication: the menu level, the macro level, and the programming level. You issue individual commands and initiate operations by selecting activities from a hierarchy of **menus**, starting with the **main menu**. A menu can appear as a **bar menu** in the user interface portion of the display, a **pull-down menu**, or a **pop-up menu**. Menus are sometimes displayed in a **window**.

As a convenience to the user, many of the specification options are already filled in to reflect common situations. These are called **default options**.

At the menu level of interaction, you are initiating individual commands. At the macro and programming levels of of interaction, you can string together commands and even introduce logic operations. A **macro** is a sequence of frequently used operations or keystrokes that can be recalled as you need them. Micro software users can create logical sequences of instructions called programs.

3–5 USER-FRIENDLY SOFTWARE. Software is said to be **user friendly** when someone with relatively little computer experience has little difficulty using the system. Some software packages use **icons**, or pictographs, to communicate with the end user. You issue the **help command** to get a more detailed explanation or instructions on how to proceed. You can perform work in one of several windows on a display screen, or you can **zoom** in on a particular window or create **window panes**.

 Review Exercises

Concepts

1. What is the purpose of soft keys? Of cursor control keys?
2. Describe the attributes of user-friendly software.
3. Contrast a bar menu and a pull-down menu.
4. Most word processing packages have a default document size. What other defaults might a word processing package have?
5. Briefly describe a typical configuration of a microcomputer system.
6. List five functional enhancements that can be made to a microcomputer by inserting one or more optional add-on boards into expansion slots.
7. What is a printer spooler?
8. Briefly describe three ways in which you can use a keyboard to enter commands into a microcomputer.
9. During a micro software session, what key would you commonly press to move to the beginning of the work area? To negate the current command?
10. When would you use the zoom feature of a microcomputer software package?
11. How is a pop-up menu displayed?
12. Why are some microcomputers sold with empty expansion slots?
13. What is a macro, and how can using one save time?
14. What is the relationship between a microprocessor and a microcomputer?
15. What is the software capability that enables the viewing of electronic spreadsheet data and a bar graph at the same time?
16. In terms of physical size, how are PCs categorized?

Discussion

17. Home banking services are available only to those who have personal computers. To encourage customer participation,

some banks offer this service at a price below their cost. The difference is then passed on to all customers. Is this fair? Explain.

18. List at least 10 products that are smaller than a breadbox and use microprocessors. Select one of the 10 and describe the function of its microprocessor.

19. What options would you like to have on your own personal micro that are not included in a minimum configuration? Why?

20. Discuss at least five domestic applications of personal computers.

21. How might a microcomputer help in the day-to-day administration of an academic department at a college (for example, the Psychology Department, the Nursing Department)?

Self-Test (by section)

3–1 References to a microcomputer or a personal computer are often abbreviated to _____ and _____, respectively.

3–2 **a.** The processing component of a microcomputer is a _____.

b. The three size categories of personal computers are miniature, portable, and business. (T/F)

3–3 **a.** A microcomputer cannot be linked to a mainframe computer. (T/F)

b. The computer and its peripheral devices are called the computer system _____.

c. The RS-232C connector provides the interface to a parallel port. (T/F)

3–4 **a.** Use the _____ for rapid numeric data entry.

b. When interacting with microcomputers, you must wait until one command is executed before issuing another. (T/F)

c. A sequence of frequently used operations or keystrokes that can be activated by the user is called a: (a) menu, (b) macro, or (c) program.

d. Use the _____ and _____ cursor control keys to scroll vertically.

3–5 **a.** Pictographs, called _____, are often associated with user-friendly software.

b. Window panes enable users to view several parts of the same window subarea at a time. (T/F)

Self-test answers. **3–1** micro, PC. **3–2** (a) microprocessor; (b) F. **3–3** (a) F; (b) configuration; (c) F. **3–4** (a) 10-key pad; (b) F; (c) b; (d) up, down. **3–5** (a) icons; (b) T.

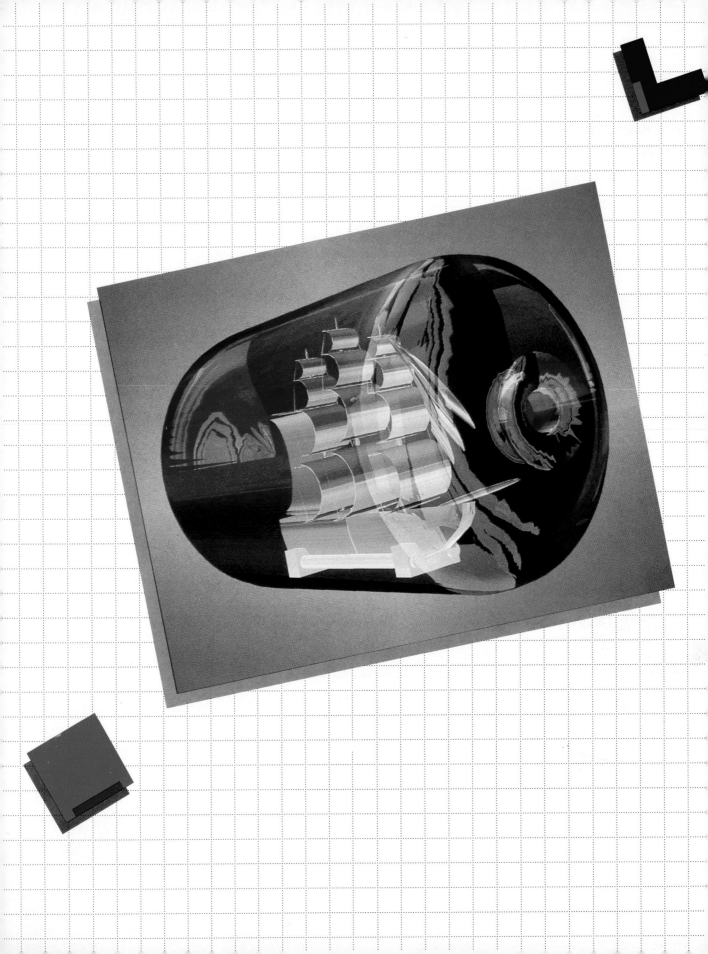

4

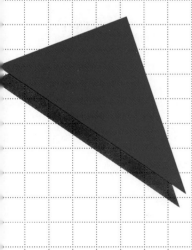

Inside
the Computer

STUDENT LEARNING OBJECTIVES

- To describe how data are stored in a computer system.
- To demonstrate the relationships between bits, bytes, characters, and encoding systems.
- To understand the translation of alphanumeric data into a format for internal computer representation.
- To explain and illustrate the principles of computer operations.
- To identify and describe the relationships between the internal components of a computer.
- To distinguish processors by their speed, memory capacity, and word length.

4–1 Data Storage: Data in the Computer

In Chapter 1 we learned that *data*, not *information*, are stored in a computer system. *Data are the raw material from which information is derived*, and *information is data that have been collected and manipulated into a meaningful form*. To manipulate data, we must have a way to store and retrieve this raw material.

It is easy to understand data storage in a manual system. For example, when a customer's address changes, we pull the folder, erase the old address, and write in the new one. We can see and easily interpret data that are kept manually. We cannot see or easily interpret data stored in a computer. Data are represented and stored in a computer system to take advantage of the physical characteristics of electronics and computer hardware, not human beings.

Data are stored *temporarily* during processing in a section of the computer system called **primary storage**. Primary storage is also called **main memory**, or random-access memory (RAM). If you will remember, RAM was introduced and discussed briefly in Chapter 3, "Microcomputers." Data are stored *permanently* in **secondary storage** devices, such as magnetic tape and disk drives. We discuss primary storage in detail later in this chapter. Secondary storage is covered in Chapter 6, "Data Storage Devices and Media." In this chapter we focus on the details of how data are represented internally in both primary and secondary storage, and on the internal workings of a computer.

4–2 A Bit about the Bit

The computer's seemingly endless potential is, in fact, based on only two electrical states—*on* and *off*. The physical characteristics of the computer make it possible to combine these two electronic states to

Programs and data are stored temporarily in these solid-state RAM chips (primary storage) during processing. Permanent storage is on magnetic disk (secondary storage).

In the first generation of computers (1951–59), each bit was represented by a vacuum tube. Today computers use fingernail-sized chips that can store over one million bits.

represent letters and numbers. An "on" or "off" electronic state is represented by a **bit**. *Bit* is short for *b*inary dig*it*. The presence or absence of a bit is referred to as *on-bit* and *off-bit*, respectively. In the **binary** numbering system (base 2) and in written text, the on-bit is a 1 and the off-bit is a 0.

The vacuum tubes, transistors, and integrated circuits (see Appendix A, "An Abbreviated History of Computers") that characterize the generations of computers enable them to distinguish between on and off and, therefore, to use binary logic.

Physically, these states are achieved in a variety of ways. In primary storage the two electronic states are represented by the direction of current flow. Another approach is to turn the circuit on or off. In secondary storage the two states are made possible by the magnetic arrangement of the surface coating on magnetic tapes and disks. The coating is usually an alloy of easily magnetized elements, such as iron, cobalt, chromium, and nickel.

Bits may be fine for computers, but human beings are more comfortable with letters and decimal numbers (the base-10 numerals 0 through 9). Therefore, the letters and decimal numbers that we input to a computer system must be translated to 1s and 0s for processing and storage. The computer translates the bits back to letters and decimal numbers on output. This translation is performed so we can recognize and understand the output. It is made possible by encoding systems.

4–3 Encoding Systems: Combining Bits to Form Bytes

EBCDIC and ASCII

Computers do not talk to each other in English, Spanish, or French. They have their own languages, which are better suited to electronic communication. In these languages, bits are combined according to an **encoding system** to represent letters (**alpha** characters), numbers (**numeric** characters), and special characters (such as *, $, +, and &). For example, in the eight-bit **EBCDIC** encoding system (*E*xtended *B*inary-*C*oded *D*ecimal *I*nterchange *C*ode—pronounced *IB-see-dik*), which is used primarily in mainframe computers, 11000010 represents the letter *B*, and 11110011 represents a decimal number 3. In the seven-bit **ASCII** encoding system (*American Standard Code for Information Interchange*—pronounced *AS-key*), which is used primarily in micros and data communications, a *B* and a 3 are represented by 1000010 and 0110011, respectively. There is also an eight-bit version of ASCII, called **ASCII-8**.

Letters, numbers, and special characters are collectively referred to as **alphanumeric** characters. Alphanumeric characters are *encoded* to a bit configuration on input so that the computer can interpret them. When you press the letter *B* on a PC keyboard, the *B* is transmitted to the processor as a coded string of binary digits (for example, 1000010 in ASCII). The characters are *decoded* on output so that we can interpret them. For example, a monitor's device controller will interpret an ASCII 0110011 as a 3 and display a 3 on the screen.

Character	ASCII Code		
	Binary Value		Decimal Value
A	100	0001	65
B	100	0010	66
C	100	0011	67
D	100	0100	68
E	100	0101	69
F	100	0110	70
G	100	0111	71
H	100	1000	72
I	100	1001	73
J	100	1010	74
K	100	1011	75
L	100	1100	76
M	100	1101	77
N	100	1110	78
O	100	1111	79
P	101	0000	80
Q	101	0001	81
R	101	0010	82
S	101	0011	83
T	101	0100	84
U	101	0101	85
V	101	0110	86
W	101	0111	87
X	101	1000	88
Y	101	1001	89
Z	101	1010	90
a	110	0001	97
b	110	0010	98
c	110	0011	99
d	110	0100	100
e	110	0101	101
f	110	0110	102
g	110	0111	103
h	110	1000	104
i	110	1001	105
j	110	1010	106
k	110	1011	107
l	110	1100	108
m	110	1101	109
n	110	1110	110
o	110	1111	111
p	111	0000	112
q	111	0001	113
r	111	0010	114
s	111	0011	115
t	111	0100	116
u	111	0101	117
v	111	0110	118
w	111	0111	119
x	111	1000	120
y	111	1001	121
z	111	1010	122

Character	ASCII Code		
	Binary Value		Decimal Value
0	011	0000	48
1	011	0001	49
2	011	0010	50
3	011	0011	51
4	011	0100	52
5	011	0101	53
6	011	0110	54
7	011	0111	55
8	011	1000	56
9	011	1001	57
Space	010	0000	32
.	010	1110	46
<	011	1100	60
(	010	1000	40
+	010	1011	43
&	010	0110	38
!	010	0001	33
$	010	0100	36
*	010	1010	42
)	010	1001	41
;	011	1011	59
,	010	1100	44
%	010	0101	37
—	101	1111	95
>	011	1110	62
?	011	1111	63
:	011	1010	58
#	010	0011	35
@	100	0000	64
'	010	0111	39
=	011	1101	61
"	010	0010	34
½	1010	1011	171
¼	1010	1100	172
▒	1011	0010	178
■	1101	1011	219
▬	1101	1100	220
▌	1101	1101	221
▐	1101	1110	222
▬	1101	1111	223
√	1111	1011	251
n	1111	1100	252
2	1111	1101	253
■	1111	1110	254
(blank)	1111	1111	255

FIGURE 4–1 ASCII Codes

This figure contains the binary and decimal values for commonly used ASCII characters.

This coding, which is based on a particular encoding system, equates a unique series of bits and no-bits with a specific character. Just as the words *mother* and *father* are arbitrary English-language character strings that refer to our parents, 11000010 is an arbitrary EBCDIC code that refers to the letter *B*. The combination of bits used to represent a character is called a **byte** (pronounced *bite*). Figure 4–1 shows the binary value (the actual bit configuration) and the decimal equivalent of commonly used characters in ASCII.

The seven-bit ASCII can represent up to 128 characters (2^7). EBCDIC and ASCII-8 can represent up to 256 characters (2^8). Even though the English language has considerably fewer than 128 *printable* characters, the extra bit configurations are needed to communicate a variety of activities, from ringing a bell to signaling the computer to accept a piece of datum.

The Nibble

The eight-bit EBCDIC and ASCII-8 encoding systems are endowed with an interesting and useful quality. Only four bit positions are needed to represent the 10 decimal digits. Therefore, a single numeric digit can be stored in a half-byte, or a **nibble**, as it is sometimes called. This enables us to store data more efficiently by "packing" *two* decimal digits into one eight-bit byte (see Figure 4–2).

Since two decimal digits can be packed into one byte, a byte is not always the same as a character. Even so, the terms *byte* and *character* are often used interchangeably, with an implied understanding that some bytes may contain two numeric characters.

Parity Checking

Within a computer system, data in the form of coded characters are continuously transferred at high rates of speed between the computer, the input/output (I/O) and storage devices, and the remote workstations. Each device uses a built-in checking procedure to help ensure that the transmission is complete and accurate. This procedure is called **parity checking**.

Logically, an ASCII character may have seven bits, but physically there are actually *eight* bits transmitted between hardware devices. Confused? Don't be. The extra **parity bit**, which is not part of the character code, is used in the parity-checking procedure to detect

FIGURE 4–2 Decimal 29 in ASCII-8
Because all numeric codes in ASCII-8 have 0011 in the first four positions, the 1s can be eliminated and two numeric digits can be "packed" into one byte. EBCDIC numbers are packed in a similar manner.

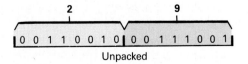

Unpacked

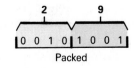

Packed

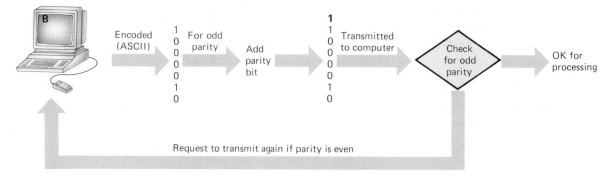

FIGURE 4–3 Parity Checking
The letter *B* is entered and transmitted to the computer for processing. Since the ASCII *B* has an even number of bits, an on-bit must be added to maintain odd parity.

whether a bit has been accidentally changed, or "dropped," during transmission. A dropped bit results in a **parity error**.

To maintain *odd parity* (see Figure 4–3), the extra parity bit is turned *on* when the seven-bit ASCII byte has an *even* number of on-bits. When the ASCII byte has an *odd* number of on-bits, the parity bit is turned *off*. The receiving device checks for this condition. A parity error occurs when an even number of on-bits is encountered. Some computer systems are designed to maintain *even parity*, but odd and even parity work in a similar manner.

4–4 Numbering Systems and Computers

We humans use a **decimal**, or base-10, numbering system, presumably because people have 10 fingers. If we had three fingers and a thumb on each hand, as does the Extra Terrestrial (E.T.) from the popular movie, then in all probability we would be using the **octal** numbering system, which has a base of 8.

Early computers were designed around the decimal numbering system, which made the design of computer logic capabilities unnecessarily complex and inefficient. For example, 10 vacuum tubes were needed to represent one decimal digit. In 1945, as computer pioneers were struggling to improve this cumbersome approach, John von Neumann suggested that the numbering system used by computers should take advantage of the physical characteristics of electronic circuitry. To deal with the basic electronic states of *on* and *off*, von Neumann suggested using the *binary* numbering system. His insight has vastly simplified the way computers handle data.

Computers *operate* in binary and *communicate* to us in decimal. A special program translates decimal into binary on input, and binary into decimal on output. Under normal circumstances, a programmer would see only decimal input and output. On occasion, though, we must deal with long and confusing strings of 1s and 0s in the form of a **dump**. A dump is like a snapshot of the contents of primary stor-

```
38C070   29306294 4580623F D20DD0AA 62A29640   8CECCC04 88F00010 80000004 88100010   41110003 5010D064 94FCD067 D703D06C
38C0A0   D06E0610 12114770 6202D203 D09F629D   4120D121 45B06236 5820D120 413062C4   477061A6 4810D06E 41110001 4010D06E
38C0D0   1A2C44E0 60701A1E 41818001 44F06076   9640D112 455062DA 94BFD112 4810D06C   02FF1302 FFC3C9D5 C5E240E2 C1D4C540
38C100   FF0098E0 D08012EE 47806310 D27CF000   48A0D06A 4BA0D06C 88A00002 45B0f23E   D12094FC D1235B00 D1201A10 5800D120
```

FIGURE 4–4   A Hexadecimal Dump

Each of the lines contains a hexadecimal representation of the contents of primary storage. The column of numbers farthest to the left consists of storage addresses. Each pair of hexadecimal digits represents the eight bits of an EBCDIC byte. The address of the first byte in the dump (29) is 0038C070 in hexadecimal, or 00000000001110001100000001110000 in binary. You can see how much space is saved by displaying dumps in "hex" rather than binary.

age (on-bits and off-bits) at a moment in time. To reduce at least part of the confusion of seeing only 1s and 0s on the output, the **hexadecimal** (base-16) numbering system is used as a shorthand to display the binary contents of both primary and secondary storage (see Figure 4–4).

The decimal equivalents for binary, decimal, and hexadecimal numbers are shown in Figure 4–5. We know that in decimal, any number greater than 9 is represented by a sequence of digits. When you count in decimal, you "carry" to the next position in groups of 10. As you examine Figure 4–5, notice that you carry in groups of 2 in binary and in groups of 16 in hexadecimal. Also, note that *four* binary digits can be represented by one "hex" digit.

The hexadecimal numbering system is used only for the convenience of the programmer when reading and reviewing the binary output of a dump (see Figure 4–4). Computers *do not operate or process* in hex. During the 1960s and early 1970s, programmers often had to examine the contents of primary storage to debug their programs (that is, to eliminate program errors). Today's programming languages have sophisticated **diagnostics** (called *error messages*) and computer-assisted tools that help programmers during program development. These diagnostics and development aids have minimized

Binary (base a)	Decimal (base 10)	Hexadecimal (base 16)
0	0	0
1	1	1
10	2	2
11	3	3
100	4	4
101	5	5
110	6	6
111	7	7
1000	8	8
1001	9	9
1010	10	A
1011	11	B
1100	12	C
1101	13	D
1110	14	E
1111	15	F
10000	16	10

FIGURE 4–5   Numbering-System Equivalence Table

the need for applications programmers to convert binary and hexadecimal numbers to their more familiar decimal equivalents. However, if you become familiar with these numbering systems, you should achieve a better overall understanding of computers.

Appendix B, "Working with Numbering Systems," presents the principles of numbering systems, discusses numbering-system arithmetic, and illustrates how to convert a value in one numbering system to its equivalent in another.

4–5 Components of a Computer System: A Closer Look at the Processor and Primary Storage

Let's review. We have learned that all computers have similar capabilities and perform essentially the same functions, although some might be faster than others. We have also learned that a computer system has input, output, storage, and processing components; that the *processor* is the "intelligence" of a computer system; and that a single computer system may have several processors. We have discussed how data are represented inside a computer system in electronic states called bits. We are now ready to expose the inner workings of the nucleus of the computer system—the processor.

The internal operation of a computer is interesting, but there really is no mystery about it. The mystery is in the minds of those who listen to hearsay and believe science fiction writers. The computer is a nonthinking electronic device that has to be plugged into an electrical power source, just like a toaster or a lamp.

Literally hundreds of different types of computers are marketed by scores of manufacturers. The complexity of each type may vary considerably, but in the end each processor, sometimes called the **central processing unit** or **CPU**, has only two fundamental sections: the *control unit* and the *arithmetic and logic unit. Primary storage* also plays an integral part in the internal operation of a processor. These

Modern technology has taken away some of the romance associated with the computer mystique. Today's computers don't have hundreds of multicolored blinking lights and swirling tapes. The processing component of this mainframe computer system (behind the operator) has only one switch—on/off.

three—primary storage, the control unit, and the arithmetic and logic unit—work together. Let's look at their functions and the relationships between them.

Primary Storage

The Technology   Unlike magnetic secondary storage devices, such as tape and disk, primary storage has no moving parts. With no mechanical movement, data can be accessed from primary storage at electronic speeds, or close to the speed of light. Most of today's computers use CMOS (*Complementary Metal-Oxide Semiconductor*) technology for primary storage. A state-of-the-art CMOS memory chip that is about one-eighth the size of a postage stamp can store about 4,000,000 bits, or over 400,000 characters of data!

But there is one major problem with semiconductor storage. When the electrical current is turned off or interrupted, the data are lost. Researchers are working to perfect a primary storage that will retain its contents after an electrical interruption. Several "nonvolatile" technologies, such as **bubble memory**, have emerged, but none has exhibited the qualities necessary for widespread application. However, bubble memory is superior to CMOS for use in certain computers. It is highly reliable, it is not susceptible to environmental fluctuations, and it can operate on battery power for a considerable length of time. These qualities make bubble memory well suited for use with industrial robots and in portable computers.

Function   Primary storage, or main memory, provides the processor with *temporary* storage for programs and data. *All programs and data must be transferred to primary storage from an input device (such as a VDT) or from secondary storage (such as a disk) before programs can be executed or data can be processed.* Primary storage space is always at a premium; therefore, after a program has been executed, the storage space it occupied is reallocated to another program awaiting execution.

Figure 4–6 illustrates how all input/output (I/O) is "read to" or "written from" primary storage. In the figure, an inquiry (input) is made on a VDT. The inquiry, in the form of a message, is routed to primary storage over a **channel** (such as a coaxial cable). The message is interpreted, and the processor initiates action to retrieve the appropriate program and data from secondary storage. The program and data are "loaded," or moved, to primary storage from secondary storage. This is a *nondestructive read* process. That is, the program and data that are read reside in both primary storage (temporarily) and secondary storage (permanently). The data are manipulated according to program instructions, and a report is written from primary storage to a printer.

A program instruction or a piece of data is stored in a specific primary storage location called an **address**. Addresses permit program instructions and data to be located, accessed, and processed. The content of each address is constantly changing as different programs are executed and new data are processed.

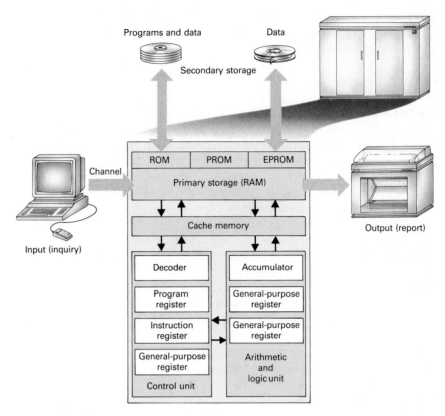

Programs and data   Data

Secondary storage

Channel

| ROM | PROM | EPROM |

Primary storage (RAM)

Cache memory

Decoder   Accumulator

Program register   General-purpose register

Instruction register   General-purpose register

General-purpose register   Arithmetic and logic unit

Control unit

Input (inquiry)   Output (report)

FIGURE 4–6 Interaction Between Primary Storage and Computer System Components
All programs and data must be transferred from an input device or from secondary storage before programs can be executed and data can be processed. During processing, instructions and data are passed between the various types of internal memories, the control unit, and the arithmetic and logic unit. Output is transferred to the printer from primary storage.

RAM, ROM, PROM, and EPROM   Another name for primary storage is random-access memory, or RAM. A special type of primary storage, called **read-only memory (ROM)**, cannot be altered by the programmer. The contents of ROM are "hard-wired" (designed into the logic of the memory chip) by the manufacturer and can be "read only." When you turn on a microcomputer system, a program in ROM automatically readies the computer system for use. Then the ROM program produces the initial display screen prompt.

A variation of ROM is **programmable read-only memory (PROM)**. PROM is ROM into which you, the user, can load "read-only" programs and data. Some microcomputer software packages, such as electronic spreadsheets, are available as PROM units as well as on diskette. Once a program is loaded to PROM, it is seldom, if ever, changed. However, if you need to be able to revise the contents of PROM, there is **EPROM**, erasable PROM.

Cache Memory   Programs and data are loaded to primary storage, or RAM, from secondary storage because the time required to access a program instruction or piece of data from primary storage is significantly less than for secondary storage. Thousands of instructions or pieces of data can be accessed from primary storage in the time it would take to access a single piece of data from disk storage. RAM is essentially a high-speed holding area for data and programs. In fact, nothing really happens in a computer system until the program instructions and data are moved to the processor. This transfer of instructions and data to the processor can be time-consuming, even at microsecond speeds. To facilitate an even faster transfer of instructions and data to the processor, some computers are designed with **cache memory** (see Figure 4–6). Cache memory is employed by computer designers to increase the computer system throughput (the rate at which work is performed).

Like RAM, cache is a high-speed holding area for program instructions and data. However, cache memory uses a technology that is about 10 times faster than RAM and about 100 times more expensive. With only a fraction of the capacity of RAM, cache memory holds only those instructions and data that are likely to be needed next by the processor.

The Control Unit

Just as the processor is the nucleus of a computer system, the **control unit** is the nucleus of the processor. If you will recall from an earlier discussion, the control unit and the arithmetic and logic unit are the two fundamental sections of a processor. The control unit has three primary functions:

1. To read and interpret program instructions
2. To direct the operation of internal processor components
3. To control the flow of programs and data in and out of primary storage

A program must first be loaded to primary storage before it can be executed. During execution, the first in a sequence of program instructions is moved from primary storage to the control unit, where it is decoded and interpreted by the **decoder**. The control unit then directs other processor components to carry out the operations necessary to execute the instruction.

The control unit contains high-speed working storage areas called **registers** that can store no more than a few bytes (see Figure 4–6). The speed at which registers handle instructions and data is about 10 times faster than that of cache memory. They are used for a variety of processing functions. One register, called the **instruction register**, contains the instruction being executed. Other general-purpose registers store data needed for immediate processing. Registers also store status information. For example, the **program register** contains the address of the next instruction to be executed. Registers facilitate the movement of data and instructions between primary storage, the control unit, and the arithmetic and logic unit.

Memory Bits

INTERNAL STORAGE
- Primary storage (or main memory, RAM)
- ROM, PROM, and EPROM
- Cache
- Registers

The Arithmetic and Logic Unit

The **arithmetic and logic unit** performs all computations (addition, subtraction, multiplication, and division) and all logic operations (comparisons).

Examples of *computations* include the payroll deduction for social security, the day-end inventory, the balance on a bank statement, and the like. A *logic* operation compares two pieces of data. Then, based on the result of the comparison, the program "branches" to one of several alternative sets of program instructions. Let's use an inventory system to illustrate the logic operation. At the end of each day the inventory level of each item in stock is compared to a reorder point. For each comparison indicating an inventory level that falls below (<) the reorder point, a sequence of program instructions is executed that produces a purchase order. For each comparison indicating an inventory level at or above (= or >) the reorder point, another sequence of instructions is executed.

The arithmetic and logic unit also does alphabetic comparisons. For example, when comparing Smyth and Smith, Smyth is evaluated as being alphabetically greater, so it is positioned after Smith.

The Machine Cycle

You have probably heard of computer programming languages such as COBOL, BASIC, and RPG. There are dozens of programming languages in common usage. However, in the end, COBOL, BASIC, and the other languages are translated into the only language that a computer understands—machine language. Machine language instructions are represented inside the computer as strings of binary digits, up to 64 digits in length. An overview of machine languages and of some of the more popular "higher level" programming languages is provided in Chapter 8, "Programming Languages and Software Concepts."

Every machine language has a predefined format for each type of instruction. The relative position within the instruction designates whether a sequence of characters is an **operation code**, an **operand**, or irrelevant. The typical machine language will have from 50 to 200 separate operation codes. The operation code, or **op-code**, is that portion of the fundamental computer instruction that designates the operation to be performed (add, compare, retrieve data from RAM, and so on). The operand is that portion of the instruction that designates data or refers to one or more addresses in RAM in which data can be found or placed. The op-code determines whether the operand is data, addresses, or both.

Every computer has a **machine cycle**. The following actions take place during the machine cycle (see Figure 4–7):

- The next instruction to be executed (op-code and operand) is retrieved, or "fetched," from RAM or cache memory and loaded into the instruction register in the control unit (see Figure 4–6).
- The instruction is decoded and interpreted.

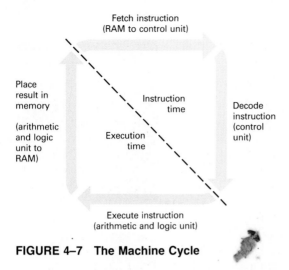

Fetch instruction
(RAM to control unit)

Place result in memory

(arithmetic and logic unit to RAM)

Instruction time

Decode instruction (control unit)

Execution time

Execute instruction
(arithmetic and logic unit)

FIGURE 4–7 The Machine Cycle

■ Using whatever processor resources are needed (general-purpose registers, arithmetic and logic unit, and so on), the instruction is executed.

■ The results are placed in the appropriate memory position (usually RAM or a register in the arithmetic and logic unit called the **accumulator**). (See Figure 4–6.)

The speed of a processor is sometimes measured by how long it takes to complete a machine cycle. The timed interval that comprises the machine cycle is the summation of the **instruction time**, or **I-time**, and the **execution time**, or **E-time** (see Figure 4–7). The I-time is made up of the first two activities of the machine cycle—fetch and decode the instruction. The E-time comprises the last two activities of the machine cycle—execute the instruction and store the results.

Parallel Processing: An Alternative Design Architecture

Computer manufacturers have relied on the single processor design architecture presented in this section since the late 1940s. In this environment, the processor addresses the programming problem sequentially, from beginning to end. Today designers are doing research on computers that will be able to break a programming problem into pieces. Work on each of these pieces will then be executed simultaneously in separate processors, all of which are part of the same computer. The concept of using multiple processors in the same computer system is known as **parallel processing**.

In Chapter 2, "Minis, Mainframes, and Supercomputer," the point was made that a computer system may be made up of several special-function processors. For example, a single computer system may have a host, a front-end processor, and a backup processor. By sharing the workload among several special-function processors, the system throughput is increased. Computer designers began asking themselves, "If three or four processors can enhance throughput, what could be accomplished with 20 or even a thousand processors?"

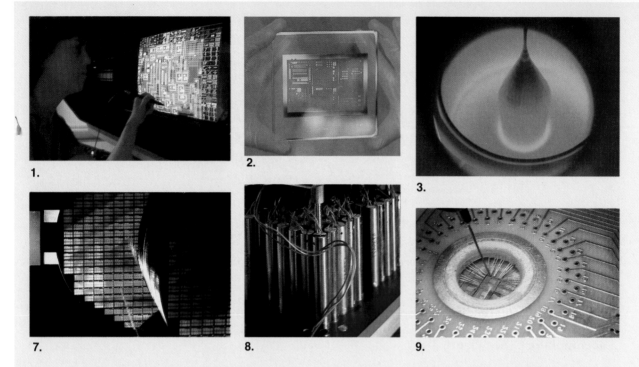

1.

2.

3.

7.

8.

9.

The 1879 invention of the light bulb symbolized the beginning of electronics. Electronics then evolved into the use of vacuum tubes, then to transistors, then to the integrated circuits now used. Today's microminiaturization of electronic circuitry is continuing to have a profound effect on the way we live and work.

These relatively inexpensive "computers on a chip" have thousands of uses, many of which we now take for granted. They are found in almost every type of modern machine from computers to robots, from "smart" home appliances to "talking" cash registers, from automobile dashboards to high-flying spaceships.

Current technology permits the placement of hundreds of thousands of transistors and electronic switches on a single chip. Chips already fit into wristwatches and credit cards, but electrical and computer engineers want them even smaller. In electronics, smaller is better. The ENIAC, the first full-scale digital electronic computer, weighed 50 tons and occupied an entire room. Today a complete computer is fabricated within a single piece of silicon the size of a child's fingernail.

Chip designers think in terms of nanoseconds (1/1,000,000,000 of a second) and microns (1/1,000,000 of a meter). They want to pack as many circuit elements as they can into the structure of a chip. High-density packing reduces the time required for an electrical signal to travel from one circuit element to the next—and the result is faster computers. Current research indicates that chips eventually will be produced that contain millions of circuit elements!

The fabrication of integrated circuits involves a multistep process using various photochemical etching and metallurgical techniques. This complex and interesting process is illustrated here with photos, from silicon to the finished product.

DESIGN

1. Chips are designed and made to accomplish a particular function. One chip might be a microprocessor for a personal computer. Another might be primary storage. Another might be the logic for a talking vending machine. Chip designers use computer-aided design (CAD) systems to create the logic for individual circuits. A chip will contain from one to 30 layers of circuits. In this multilayer circuit design, each layer is color-coded so the designer can distinguish between the various layers.

2. An electron-beam exposure system etches the circuitry into a glass stencil called a *mask*. A mask, such as this one, is produced for each circuit layer. The number of layers depends on the complexity of the chip's logic.

FABRICATION

3. Molten silicon is spun into cylindrical ingots. Because silicon, the second most abundant substance, is used in the fabrication of inte-

4.

6.

5.

10.

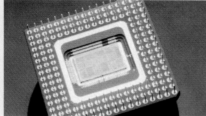

11.

12.

grated circuits, chips are sometimes referred to as "intelligent grains of sand."

4. The ingot is shaped and prepared prior to being cut into silicon wafers. Once the wafers are cut, they are polished to a perfect finish.

5. Silicon wafers that will eventually contain several hundred chips are placed in an oxygen furnace at 1200 degrees Centigrade. In the furnace the wafer is coated with other minerals to create the physical properties needed to produce transistors and electronic switches on the surface of the wafer.

6. The mask is placed over the wafer and both are exposed to ultraviolet light. In this way the circuit pattern is transferred onto the wafer. Plasma technology (superhot gases) is used to etch the circuit pattern permanently into the wafer. This is one of several techniques used in the etching process. The wafer is returned to the furnace and given another coating on which to etch another circuit layer. The procedure is repeated for each circuit layer until the wafer is complete.

7. The result of the coating/etching process is a silicon wafer that contains from 100 to 400 integrated circuits.

8. It takes only a second for this instrument to drill 1440 tiny holes in a wafer. The holes enable the interconnection of the layers of circuits. Each

layer must be perfectly aligned (within a millionth of a meter) with the others.

TESTING

9. The chips are tested while they are still part of the wafer. Each integrated circuit on the wafer is powered up and given a series of tests. Fine needles make the connection for the computer-controlled tests. The precision demands are so great that as many as half the chips are found to be defective. A drop of ink is deposited on defective chips.

PACKAGING

10. A diamond saw separates the wafer into individual chips in a process called *dicing*.

11. The chips are packaged in protective ceramic or metal carriers. The carriers have standard-sized electrical pin connectors that permit the chip to be conveniently plugged into circuit boards. Because the pins tend to corrode, the pin connectors are the most vulnerable part of a computer system. To avoid corrosion and a bad connection, the pins on some carriers are made of gold.

12. The completed circuit boards are installed in computers and thousands of other computer-controlled devices.

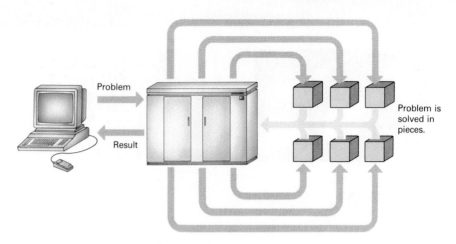

FIGURE 4–8 Parallel Processing
In parallel processing, auxiliary processors address pieces of a problem to enhance system throughput.

In parallel processing, one main processor (for example, a mini or a host mainframe) examines the programming problem and determines what portions, if any, of the problem can be solved in pieces (see Figure 4–8). Those pieces that can be solved separately are routed to other processors and solved. The individual pieces are then reassembled in the main processor for further computation, output, or storage. The net result of parallel processing is better throughput. Many people feel that parallel processing may be the wave of the future. However, much is yet to be done. Research and design in this area, which some say characterizes a fifth generation of computers, is still in the formative stages.

4–6 Computer Operation: What Happens Inside

Some automobiles have the engine in the front, some have it in the rear, and a few have it in the middle. It's the same with computers. Computer architecture—the way in which they are designed—varies considerably. For example, one vendor's computers might have separate primary storage areas for data and programs. In some microcomputers the *motherboard*, a circuit board, holds the electronic circuitry for the processor, memory, and the input/output interface with the peripheral devices. A knowledge of these idiosyncrasies is not required of the user; therefore, the following example focuses on the *essentials* of computer operation.

The BASIC program in Figure 4–9 computes and displays the sum of any two numbers. BASIC is a popular programming language. Figure 4–10 illustrates how a processor works by showing the interaction between primary storage, the control unit, and the arithmetic and logic unit during the execution of the BASIC program in Figure 4–9. Primary storage in Figure 4–10 has only 10 primary storage locations, and these are used only for data. In practice, both program

FIGURE 4–9   A BASIC Program

This program, written in the BASIC programming language, adds any two numbers and displays the sum. The execution of this program is illustrated in Figure 4–10.

```
10   INPUT "INPUT NO."; X
20   INPUT "INPUT NO."; Y
30   LET SUM=X+Y
40   PRINT "THE SUM IS"; SUM
50   END
```

FIGURE 4–10   Internal Computer Operation

This figure, which is explained in the text, illustrates what happens inside the computer when the BASIC program of Figure 4–9 is executed. Primary storage is shown with 10 numbered storage locations.

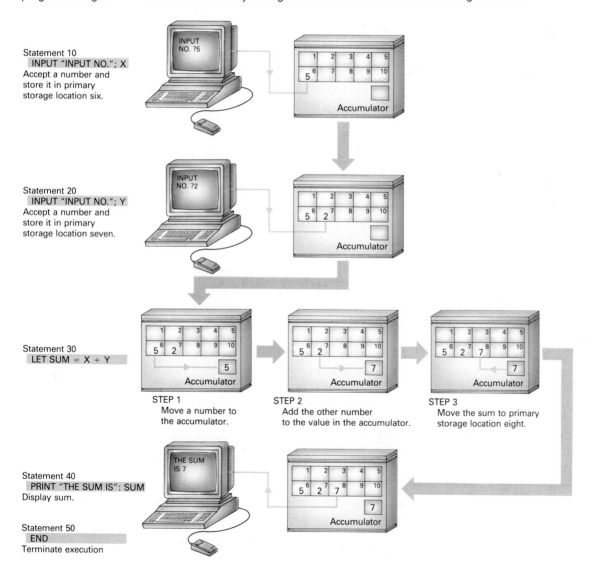

Statement 10
INPUT "INPUT NO."; X
Accept a number and store it in primary storage location six.

Statement 20
INPUT "INPUT NO."; Y
Accept a number and store it in primary storage location seven.

Statement 30
LET SUM = X + Y

STEP 1
Move a number to the accumulator.

STEP 2
Add the other number to the value in the accumulator.

STEP 3
Move the sum to primary storage location eight.

Statement 40
PRINT "THE SUM IS": SUM
Display sum.

Statement 50
END
Terminate execution

and data would be stored in primary storage, which usually has a minimum of 640,000 storage locations.

During execution of the BASIC program, one of the numbers (5 in the example) is loaded to the accumulator. The other number in primary storage (2 in the example) is added to the 5 in the accumulator, and the value in the accumulator becomes 7. The following statement-by-statement discussion of the BASIC program of Figure 4–9 illustrates exactly what happens as each instruction is executed.

- *Statement 10* (INPUT "INPUT NO."; X) permits the terminal operator to enter any numeric value. The control unit arbitrarily assigns the value to primary storage location *six*. In Figure 4–10, the value entered is 5. Future program references to *X* recall the content of the storage location whose address is *six*.
- *Statement 20* (INPUT "INPUT NO."; Y) permits the terminal operator to enter any numeric value. The control unit arbitrarily assigns the value to primary storage location *seven*. In the figure, the value entered is 2.
- *Statement 30* (LET SUM = X + Y) adds the content of location *six* to that of location *seven*. The sum is then stored in location *eight*. This addition is accomplished in three steps.

  STEP 1. The 5 in location *six* is copied to the *accumulator*. The 5 remains in location *six*, and the value of the *accumulator* becomes 5.

  STEP 2. The content of location *seven* (value = 2) is added to the content of the *accumulator* (value = 5). The addition changes the content of the *accumulator* to 7.

  STEP 3. The 7 cannot be output directly from the *accumulator*; therefore, the content of the *accumulator* (value = 7) is copied arbitrarily to location *eight*. The value of the *accumulator* is unchanged.
- *Statement 40* (PRINT "THE SUM IS"; SUM) displays, on the terminal screen, "THE SUM IS" and the result of the addition (content of location *eight*), or 7 in the figure.
- *Statement 50* (END) signals the end of the program.

More complex arithmetic and I/O tasks involve further repetitions of these fundamental operations. Logic operations are similar, with values being compared between primary storage locations, the accumulator, and registers.

4–7 Describing the Processor: Distinguishing Characteristics

People are people, and computers are computers, but how do we distinguish one from the other? We describe people in terms of height, build, age, and so on. We describe computers or processors in terms of *speed*, the *capacity* of their associated primary storage, and the

This supercomputer, which looks something like a space-age sofa, helps an oil company process mountains of data into pictures of the underground. It has a word size of 64 bits and offers up to 1024 megabytes of primary storage.

word length. For example, a computer might be described as a 20 MHz, 1 Mb, 32-bit micro. Let's see what this means.

Processor Speed: Minis, Mainframes, and Supercomputers

Processor speed is often measured in **MIPS**, or millions of instructions per second. The processing speed of today's minis, mainframes, and supercomputers is in the range of 20 to 1000 MIPS. We even have 1-MIPS micros.

The timed intervals of the machine cycle also provide a measure of processor speed (see Section 4–5). The shorter the machine cycle, the faster the processor. Machine cycles are measured in milliseconds, microseconds, and nanoseconds—or thousandths, millionths, and billionths of a second. As technology advances, machine cycles eventually will be measured in picoseconds—or trillionths of a second.

Processor Speed: Micros

A *crystal oscillator* paces the execution of instructions within the processor of a microcomputer. A micro's processor speed is rated by its frequency of oscillation, or the number of clock cycles per second. Most personal computers are rated between 5 and 20 megahertz or

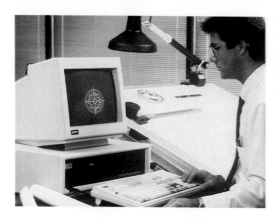

The COMPAQ DESKPRO 386™ being used by this city planner has a processor speed of 16 MHz, a RAM capacity of 10 megabytes, and word length of 32 bits.

✓

Memory Bits

**PROCESSOR
DESCRIPTION**
- *Speed* (*mainframes*): MIPS and machine cycle
- *Speed* (*micros*): MHz (clock cycles)
- *RAM Capacity*: Kb or Mb
- *Word length*: bits handled as a unit

MHz (clock cycles). The elapsed time for one clock cycle is 1/frequency (one divided by the frequency). For example, the elapsed time to complete one cycle on a 20 MHz processor is 1/20,000,000, or 0.00000005 seconds, or 50 nanoseconds. Normally, several clock cycles are required to retrieve, decode, and execute a single program instruction. The shorter the clock cycle, the faster the processor.

We seldom think in time units smaller than a second; consequently, it is almost impossible for us to think in terms of computer speeds. Imagine, today's microcomputers can execute more instructions in a minute than you have had heartbeats since the day you were born!

Capacity of Primary Storage   The capacity of primary storage, or RAM, is stated in terms of the number of bytes that it can store. As we learned earlier in this chapter, a byte is roughly equivalent to a character (such as A, 1, &).

The memory capacity of microcomputers is usually stated in terms of **kilobytes**, or **Kb**, a convenient designation for 1024 (2^{10}) bytes of storage. The memory capacity of mainframe computers is stated in terms of millions of bytes (**megabytes**, or **Mb**). Memory capacities range from 640 Kb in small micros to 8000 Mb in supercomputers.

Word Length   A **word** is the number of bits that are handled as a unit for a particular computer system. The word size of modern microcomputers is normally 16 bits or 32 bits. Supercomputers have 64-bit words. Other common word lengths are 8 and 36 bits.

Now if anyone ever asks you what a 20 MHz, 1 Mb, 32-bit micro is, you've got the answer!

Summary Outline and Important Terms

4–1   DATA STORAGE: DATA IN THE COMPUTER.   Data, not information, are stored in a computer system. Data are stored temporarily during processing in **primary storage**, or **main memory**, and permanently on **secondary storage** devices, such as magnetic tape and disk drives.

4–2   A BIT ABOUT THE BIT.   The two electronic states of the computer are represented by a **bit**, short for *binary digit*. Letters and decimal numbers are translated into bits for storage and processing on computer systems.

4–3   ENCODING SYSTEMS: COMBINING BITS TO FORM BYTES. **Alphanumeric** characters are represented in computer storage by combining strings of bits to form unique bit configurations for each character. Characters are translated into these bit configurations, also called **bytes**, according to a particular coding scheme, called an **encoding system**. Popular encoding systems include **EBCDIC**, **ASCII**, and **ASCII-8**.

Parity-checking procedures ensure that data transmission between hardware devices is complete and accurate.

4–4 NUMBERING SYSTEMS AND COMPUTERS. The two primary numbering systems used in conjunction with computers are binary and **decimal**. Decimal is translated into binary on input and binary is translated into decimal on output. The **hexadecimal** numbering system is used primarily as a programmer convenience in reading and reviewing binary output.

4–5 COMPONENTS OF A COMPUTER SYSTEM: A CLOSER LOOK AT THE PROCESSOR AND PRIMARY STORAGE. The processor is the "intelligence" of a computer system. A processor, which is also called the **central processing unit** or **CPU**, has only two fundamental sections, the **control unit** and the **arithmetic and logic unit**, which work together with primary storage to execute programs. The control unit interprets instructions and directs the arithmetic and logic unit to perform computation and logic operations.

Primary storage, or RAM (random-access memory), provides the processor with temporary storage for programs and data. Most of today's computers use CMOS technology for primary storage. However, with CMOS, the data are lost when the electrical current is turned off or interrupted. In contrast, **bubble memory** provides nonvolatile memory. All input/output, including programs, must enter and exit primary storage. Other variations of internal storage are **ROM**, **PROM**, and **EPROM**.

Some computers employ **cache memory** to increase throughput. Like RAM, cache is a high-speed holding area for program instructions and data. However, cache memory holds only those instructions and data that are likely to be needed next by the processor. During execution, instructions and data are passed between very high-speed **registers** (for example, the **instruction register** and the **accumulator**) in the control unit and the arithmetic and logic unit.

Every machine language has a predefined format for each type of instruction. Each instruction has an **operation code** and an **operand**. During one **machine cycle**, an instruction is "fetched" from RAM, decoded in the control unit, executed, and the results are placed in memory. The machine cycle time is the summation of the **instruction time** and the **execution time**.

In **parallel processing**, one main processor examines the programming problem and determines what portions, if any, of the problem can be solved in pieces. Those pieces that can be solved separately are routed to other processors, solved, then recombined in the main processor to produce the result.

4–6 COMPUTER OPERATION: WHAT HAPPENS INSIDE. Data are passed between primary storage and the accumulator of the arithmetic and logic unit for both computation and logic operations.

4–7 DESCRIBING THE PROCESSOR: DISTINGUISHING CHARACTERISTICS. A processor is described in terms of its speed, primary storage capacity, and word length. Mainframe speed is measured in **MIPS** and by the timed intervals that make up the machine cycle. Microcomputer speed is measured in megahertz. Memory capacity is measured in **kilobytes** (**Kb**) or **megabytes** (**Mb**). The **word** (the number of bits that are handled as a unit) length of computers ranges from 16 bits for the smaller micros to 64 bits for supercomputers.

Review Exercises

Concepts

1. Distinguish between RAM, ROM, PROM, and EPROM.
2. How many EBCDIC bytes can be stored in a 32-bit word?
3. Which two functions are performed by the arithmetic and logic unit?
4. List examples of alpha, numeric, and alphanumeric characters.
5. Write your first name as an ASCII bit configuration.
6. What are the functions of the control unit?
7. What advantage does the use of a nibble offer when using the ASCII-8 or EBCDIC encoding system?
8. We describe computers in terms of what three characteristics?
9. What are the binary and hexadecimal equivalents of a decimal 12?
10. What is the basic difference between CMOS technology and nonvolatile technology, such as bubble memory?
11. For a given computer, which type of memory would have the greatest capacity to store data and programs: cache or RAM? RAM or registers? Registers or cache?
12. Name three type of registers.
13. Which portion of the fundamental computer instruction designates the operation to be performed?

Discussion

14. The letter *K* is used to represent 1024 bytes of storage. Would it not have been much easier to let *K* represent 1000 bytes? Explain.
15. Millions of bytes of data are transferred routinely between computing hardware devices without any errors in transmission. Very seldom is a parity error detected. In your opinion, is it worth all the trouble to add and check parity bits every time a byte is transmitted from one device to another? Why?

16. Create a five-bit encoding system that is used for storing uppercase alpha characters, punctuation symbols, and the apostrophe. Discuss the advantages and disadvantages of your encoding system in relation to the ASCII encoding system.

Self-Test (by section)

4–1 Data are stored permanently on secondary storage devices, such as magnetic tape. (T/F)

4–2 **a.** Bit is the singular of *byte*. (T/F)

    b. The base of the binary number system is: (a) 2, (b) 8, or (c) 16.

4–3 **a.** The combination of bits used to represent a character is called a _____.

    b. The procedure that ensures complete and accurate transmission of data is called ASCII checking. (T/F)

4–4 **a.** A _____ is a snapshot of the contents of primary storage at a given moment in time.

    b. When you count in hexadecimal, you carry to the next position in groups of _____.

4–5 **a.** Data are loaded from secondary to primary storage in a nondestructive read process. (T/F)

    b. The _____ is that part of the processor that reads and interprets program instructions.

    c. The arithmetic and logic unit controls the flow of programs and data in and out of main memory. (T/F)

    d. Order the following memories based on speed: cache, registers, and RAM.

    e. The timed interval that comprises the machine cycle is the summation of the _____ time and the _____ time.

4–6 A single BASIC program instruction can cause several internal operations to take place. (T/F)

4–7 **a.** The word length of most microcomputers is 64 bits. (T/F)

    b. MIPS is an acronym for "millions of instructions per second." (T/F)

    c. The elapsed time to complete one cycle on a 10 MHz processor is _____ nanoseconds.

Self-test answers. **4–1** T. **4–2** (a) F; (b) a. **4–3** (a) byte. (b) F. **4–4** (a) dump; (b) 16. **4–5** (a) T; (b) control unit; (c) F; (d) from the slowest memory: RAM, cache, registers; (e) instruction, execution. **4–6** T. **4–7** (a) F; (b) T; (c) 100.

5
Input/Output Devices

STUDENT LEARNING OBJECTIVES

- To describe the use and characteristics of the different types of terminals.
- To explain alternative approaches to and devices for data entry.
- To describe the operation and application of common output devices.

5-1 I/O Devices: Our Interface with the Computer

Data are created in many places and many ways. Before data can be processed and stored, they must be translated into a form that the computer can interpret. For this, we need *input* devices. Once the data have been processed, they must be translated back into a form that *we* can understand. For this, we need *output* devices. These input/output (I/O) devices, also called **peripheral devices**, enable communication between us and the computer.

The diversity of computer applications has encouraged manufacturers to develop and market a variety of I/O methods and hardware. Innovative I/O devices are being introduced continuously into the marketplace. For example, voice recognition devices accept data (input) through simple verbal communication. Speech synthesizers permit verbal communication in the other direction (as output).

This chapter is divided into three parts. The first part focuses on the variety of terminals available, most of which are used for both input and output. The second part presents devices for entering data using *source-data automation*—devices that permit data to be entered into the computer directly from the source, without the the need for manual data entry. The last part describes devices that are used strictly for output.

5-2 Terminals and Workstations

A *video display terminal*, or *VDT*, is a device that allows us to interact with a computer from just about anywhere. VDTs, or simply *terminals*, were first introduced in Chapter 1. A VDT's primary input mechanism is usually a *keyboard*, and the output is usually displayed on a televisionlike screen called a *monitor*. Terminals come in all shapes and sizes and have a variety of input/output capabilities.

Even the telephone can be used as a terminal. You can enter alphanumeric data on the keypad of a touch-tone telephone (keyboard)

Data entry terminals in the factory are becoming as common as steel-toed shoes. This one is designed to withstand the heat, humidity, and dust that accompany shop activity.

This department provides administrative support to three regional insurance claims offices. Because each of these knowledge workers routinely deals with computer-generated information, each person needs a terminal to interact with the computer.

or by speaking into the receiver (voice input). You would then receive computer-generated voice output. Salespeople use telephones as terminals for entering orders and inquiries about the availability of certain products into their company's mainframe computer.

Although telephones are the most familiar terminals, the VDT and the microcomputer are those most commonly used for remote interaction with a computer system. The VDT is affectionately known as "the tube," short for **cathode-ray tube**. From our past discussions (Chapter 3, "Microcomputers"), we know that a microcomputer can serve as a stand-alone computer or as a terminal linked to a mainframe.

The Keyboard

Just about all terminals and micros come equipped with a keyboard for input. The typical keyboard will have a standard *alphanumeric keyboard* with an optional numeric keyboard, called a *10-key pad*. Some keyboards will also have *special-function keys*, which can be used to instruct the computer to perform a specific operation that may otherwise require several keystrokes. Keyboards are described in detail in Chapter 3, in the context of interacting with a micro.

Some keyboards are designed for specific applications. The cash-register-like terminals at most fast-food restaurants have special-purpose keyboards. Rather than type in the name and price of an order of french fries, attendants need only press the key marked "french fries" to record the sale.

Other Input Devices

The keyboard is too cumbersome for some applications. A computer artist may want to enter curved lines to create an image. An engineer might need to "draw" a line to connect two points on a graph. A physician may have to outline the exact shape of a tumor. Such ap-

This laboratory technician uses the keyboard's 10-key pad to expedite the entry of numeric data into the computer for analysis.

plications call for devices that go beyond the capabilities of keyboards—devices that permit random movement of the cursor to create the image. The cursor, or blinking character, always indicates the location of the next input on the screen. The light pen, joy stick, track ball, digitizing tablet and pen, and mouse are among the most popular cursor movement and input mechanisms.

The *light pen* detects light from the cathode-ray tube when it is moved close to the screen. The cursor automatically locks onto the position of the pen and tracks its movement over the screen. An engineer may create or modify images directly on the screen with a light pen. A city planner can select from a menu of possible computer functions by simply pointing the light pen to the desired function.

Video arcade wizards are no doubt familiar with the *joy stick* and *track ball*. The joy stick is a vertical stick that moves the cursor in the direction the stick is pushed. The track ball is a ball inset in the work table in front of the screen. The ball is "rolled" to move the cursor. The *digitizing tablet and pen* are a pen and a pressure-sensitive tablet with the same *X–Y* coordinates as the screen. The outline of an image drawn on a tablet is reproduced on the display screen.

The *mouse*, sometimes called the "pet peripheral," is now standard equipment for some terminals and most micros. Attached to the computer by a cable, the mouse is a small device that, when moved across a desktop, moves the cursor accordingly. The mouse positions the cursor on the screen more quickly and easily than the arrow keys on the keyboard. The action is initiated when a button on the mouse is pushed. You can also move objects on the screen by holding down the button and moving the mouse. The mouse is also discussed in Chapter 3, in the context of interacting with a micro.

The Monitor

Alphanumeric and graphic output are displayed on the terminal's monitor. The three primary attributes of monitors are the *size* of the

This microcomputer is configured for desktop publishing applications. It has three input devices and a desktop laser printer (right). In addition to the keyboard and the mouse, the configuration includes a digital scanner (left) that permits images of photos and charts to be digitized and stored on disk. Once on disk, the images can be recalled for inclusion in an output document.

display screen; whether the display is *color* or *monochrome*; and the *resolution,* or detail, of the display. The size of the screen varies, the most common being one that displays up to 25 lines of 80 characters each. Other common screen sizes are 32 × 80 and 25 × 132. The diagonal dimension of the display screen varies from 5 to 25 inches.

FINGER-TANGLING QWERTY VS. USER-FRIENDLY DVORAK

The QWERTY keyboard design that you see on most typewriters and keyboards derived its name from the first six letters in the top row. Patented in the 1890s, it was designed to slow down fast typists who would otherwise get slow-moving type bars entangled.

The Dvorak keyboard layout, named after its inventor, August Dvorak, places the most frequently used characters in the center. You can enter nearly 4000 different words from the "home row" on the Dvorak keyboard, as opposed to 100 with the traditional QWERTY layout.

Professor Dvorak invented this keyboard arrangement in 1932. Through ergonomic studies of typists, he noticed that the QWERTY layout forces the majority of the work to be done by the weakest fingers—the fourth and fifth fingers of the left hand. The stronger, quicker right hand and middle fingers are used only for the least frequently typed characters.

On Dvorak's keyboard, the most frequently used keys are on the home row (the vowels plus *d, h, t, n,* and *s*). The next most frequently used characters are placed up one row because it is easier to reach up than down. Because this layout distributes the typing workload among the fingers according to their strengths,

This is the Dvorak keyboard. Notice how the letter *E*, the most frequently used character, is positioned directly under the left hand's most powerful finger.

awkward strokes are reduced by 90%. Word processing operators who have switched to Dvorak are experiencing as much as a 75% improvement in productivity.

The QWERTY keyboard can be changed electronically into a Dvorak keyboard and back again to QWERTY simply by pressing a couple of keys. With the widespread availability of the Dvorak keyboard, look for it to grow in popularity in the coming years.

Output on a monitor is *soft copy*; that is, it is temporary and is available to the end user only until another display is requested, as opposed to the permanent *hard copy* output of printers.

Monitors are either monochrome or color. Monochrome monitors display images in a single color, usually white, green, or amber. Color monitors add the dimension of other colors, which draw attention to various aspects of the output. For example, an engineer designing pipelines for an oil refinery can use colors to highlight such things as the direction and type of fluid flow, the size of the pipes, and so on.

Terminals and micros with color monitors can also be used to present alphanumeric information efficiently and effectively. For example, problem cases for a social worker can be highlighted—red for those needing immediate attention and yellow for those with less serious problems. At a glance, the social worker can evaluate the situation and make workload adjustments as appropriate.

Some monitors have a much higher **resolution**, or quality of output. Resolution refers to the number of addressable points on the screen—the number of points to which light can be directed under program control. A strictly alphanumeric terminal has about 65,000 such points. A terminal used primarily for computer graphics and computer-aided design may have over 16 million points. The high-resolution monitors project extremely clear images that almost look like photographs. (See the chapter-opening photographs of computer graphics images.)

Some space-saving monitors are flat. Most **flat panel monitors** use *liquid crystal* technology, the technology commonly used in digital wristwatches. Since liquid crystal monitors display the image by reflecting light, you must have some light in order to read the display.

The two monitors being used by these engineers highlight screen resolution differences between monitors used primarily for the display of alphanumeric information (left) and those that are used for computer-aided design (CAD). Typically, detailed engineering designs demand large screen high-resolution monitors. The mouse (between the monitors) is the primary input device for this CAD system.

The laptop computer, centered above the instrument panel of this space shuttle, has a flat-panel monitor that can be folded down to cover the keyboard when it is not being used. The astronauts use the computer to plot their flight over ground stations.

Those flat panel monitors that use *gas plasma* technology are easier to read with poor lighting.

Graphics Workstations

Video display terminals of every size and shape are used by secretaries for word processing, by programmers for interactive program development, by clerks for recording transactions, by commercial artists for creating ad pieces, by management for making decisions, by computer operators for communicating with the computer (via the **operator console**), by shop supervisors for line scheduling, and by thousands of other people for hundreds of applications.

The class of video display terminals designed especially for the sophisticated user is the **graphics workstation**. All are **intelligent workstations**; that is, they are endowed with their own processing capability as well as the ability to interface with a mainframe. Typically, a minimum configuration for a graphics workstation would include a medium-sized high-resolution graphics monitor, a keyboard, and at least two more modes of input (for example, a mouse, joystick, track ball, and/or digitizing tablet). Some graphics workstations have two monitors, a large one for graphics output and a small one for alphanumeric output. The graphics monitor may be monochrome or color. Often users elect to configure their graphics workstations with some kind of hard copy device, such as a printer/plotter (discussed later in this chapter).

The applications for these sophisticated workstations are endless. For the most part, graphics workstations help in the design process. Different types of engineers use them for computer-aided design (CAD) applications. For example, electrical engineers use them to design the logic for silicon chips. Industrial engineers use them to design the layout of manufacturing plants. Civil engineers use them

This advertising illustrator is using a graphics workstation with a keyboard and digitizing tablet for input to create colorful ad pieces.

to design bridges. Of course, people other than engineers use graphics workstations. Architects use them to design buildings. Systems analysts rely on graphics workstations to depict the work and information flow within an information system.

Portable Terminals: Computers to Go

A *portable* terminal has a built-in **modem** (discussed in Chapter 7, "Connectivity and Data Communications") that permits the use of a regular telephone line to transmit and receive data from the host computer. The same features and combinations of I/O found on regular desktop terminals or microcomputers are available on portable terminals. Input is usually done on a keyboard, and output is either printed or displayed on a small screen. Portable terminals weigh from 5 to 12 pounds and are packaged in containers that look like briefcases.

To use a portable terminal, you simply dial the number of the computer on a telephone. Upon hearing the computer's high whistle "greeting," you insert the telephone handset into the modem. This connects the terminal to the mainframe computer.

Portable terminals are used at home by programmers to take advantage of computer time on second and third shifts. Salespeople use portable terminals to make inquiries or to log a sale while in a customer's office. Executives use portable terminals to have corporate information resources available to them wherever they may travel.

Since most portable terminals are microcomputers, programmers, salespeople, executives, and others can do spreadsheet analysis, word processing, and many other applications while in stand-alone mode. An executive might compose several memos on a flight then, upon landing, upload the memos to the headquarter's mainframe for distribution via electronic mail.

Terminal and Workstation Summary

The trend in terminals and workstations is to provide processing as well as I/O capability. In the not-too-distant future, virtually all terminals will be microcomputers with stand-alone processing capability. Microcomputers are becoming so powerful that users are no longer completely dependent on mainframe capabilities for complex processing jobs. With these intelligent terminals and workstations, users can interact with mainframe computers or download data for stand-alone processing. Data processed in a stand-alone mode can also be uploaded to the mainframe so that the data can be shared with users at other terminals.

The computer is playing an ever-increasing role in how we do our jobs. Since the terminal is the means by which we communicate with the computer, it is fast becoming a companion to workers in most fields of endeavor.

5–3 Source Data Automation: Getting Data into the Computer System

Trends in Data Entry

The trend in data entry has been toward decreasing the number of transcription steps. This is accomplished by entering the data as close to the source as possible. For example, in sales departments, salespeople input orders directly to the system. In accounting departments,

Memory Bits

TERMINALS

- Also called
  Video display terminal
  VDT
  Cathode-ray tube
  The tube
- Input
  Keyboard
  Light pen
  Joystick
  Track ball
  Digitizing tablet and pen
  Mouse
- Output
  Monitor
  Diagonal size of 5 to 25
  inches
  Monochrome (white, green,
  or amber) or color
  Low or high resolution

Throughout this hospital, data are captured as close to the source as possible to help curb the rising cost of health care services. In this medical laboratory, data generated by the analytical equipment are fed directly into the computer system that analyzes the data and reports the results. Other related data (such as patient number) are entered via keyboard.

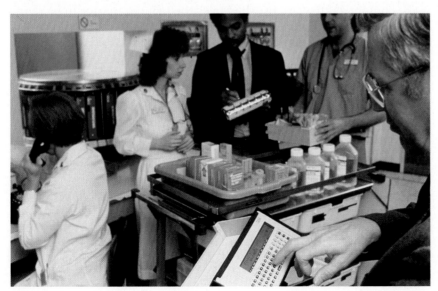

"I've sewn my name tag onto all of my clothes for computer camp."

bookkeepers and accountants record and enter financial transactions into the system. However, whenever possible, the need for key entry transcription of data is eliminated altogether. This is known as **source data automation**.

Until recently, data entry has been synonymous with *keystrokes*. The keystroke will continue to be the basic mode of data entry for the foreseeable future, but recent innovations have eliminated the need for key-driven data entry in many applications. For example, you have probably noticed the preprinted **bar codes** on grocery products. At some supermarket checkout counters these bar codes have eliminated the need for most key entry. Checkers need only pass the product over the *laser scanner* and the price is entered—and the shelf inventory is updated as well.

Data entry is an area in which enormous potential exists for increases in productivity. The technology of data entry devices is constantly changing. New and improved methods of transcribing raw data are being invented and put on the market each month. These data entry methods and associated devices are discussed next.

Optical Scanning

Optical character recognition (OCR) provides a way to encode (write) certain data in machine-readable format on the original source document. For example, the International Standard Book Number (ISBN) on the back cover of this book is written in machine-readable OCR. This eliminates the need for publishers and bookstore clerks to key these data manually. OCR equipment consists of a family of devices that encode and read OCR data.

OCR Scanners   OCR characters are identified through light-sensitive devices called **OCR scanners**. Both scanner technologies, *contact* and *laser*, bounce a beam of light off an image, then measure the reflected light to determine the value of the image. Hand-held *wand scanners* make contact as they are brushed over the printed matter to be read. Stationary *laser scanners* are more versatile and can read data passed near the scanning area. Both can recognize printed characters and various types of codes.

OCR devices can "learn" to read almost any typeface, including this book! The "learning" takes place when the structure of the character set is described to the OCR device. Special OCR devices can even read hand-printed letters if they are recorded on a standard form and written according to specific rules.

OCR scanners can be classified into the following five categories:

- *Label scanners*. These devices read data on price tags, shipping labels, and the like. A hand-held wand scanner is a label scanner.
- *Page scanners*. These devices scan and interpret the alphanumeric characters on regular typewritten pages.
- *Document scanners*. Document scanners are capable of scanning documents of varying sizes (for example, utility-bill invoice stubs and sales slips from credit card transactions).

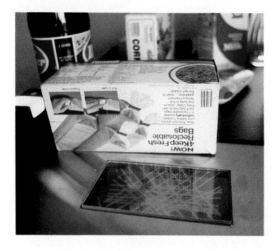

Supermarket checkout systems are now an established cost-saving technology. The automated systems use stationary laser scanners to read the bar codes that identify each item. Price and product descriptions are retrieved from a data base and recorded on the sales slip.

- *Continuous-form scanners*. These devices read data printed on continuous forms, such as cash register tapes.
- *Optical mark scanners*. Optical mark scanners scan preprinted forms, such as multiple-choice test answer forms. The position of the "sense mark" indicates a particular response or character.

Applications of Optical Scanners

Bar codes. Stationary scanners, such as those in supermarkets, use lasers to interpret the bar codes printed on products. Bar codes represent alphanumeric data by varying the width and combination of adjacent vertical lines. Just as there are a variety of internal bit encoding systems, there are a variety of bar-coding systems (see Figure 5–1). One of the most visible of these systems is the Universal Product

FIGURE 5–1 Various Codes That Can Be Interpreted by OCR Scanners

Dental groups use this OCR system for centralized record keeping and billing. Following each patient visit, a dental assistant scans the patient's account number and enters preset codes for each service provided.

Code (UPC). The UPC, originally used for supermarket items, is gaining popularity and is now being printed on other consumer goods. The advantage of bar codes over characters is that the position or orientation of the code being read is not as critical to the scanner. In a supermarket, for example, the data can be recorded even if a bottle of ketchup is rolled over the laser scanner!

The U.S. Postal Service has special-purpose computer systems that employ OCR technology to process all metered mail (bank statements and utility bills, for example). Bulk mailers deliver the mail to Post Offices in trays, then it is fed into multifont document scanners capable of reading many different type styles. The OCR scanner first locates the address on the envelope. It then reads the last line, containing the city, state, and ZIP code. To verify that the ZIP code in the address matches the city and state, it is compared to a ZIP code retrieved from a city/state master file. The OCR scanner then reads the next line up, usually the delivery address. The delivery address (for example, 1701 El Camino) is converted into a four-digit code (such as 5483) and combined with the five-digit ZIP (74604 for Ponca City, OK) to make up the nine-digit ZIP (74604-5483). An ink-jet printer inscribes the "ZIP+4" code in the form of a POSTNET bar code in the lower right corner of the envelope. Mail is processed by these special-purpose computer systems at the rate of 700 pieces per minute. Postal Service incentives encourage mass mailers to inscribe their own POSTNET bar codes, enabling mail to bypass the OCR scanner/inscriber. Once inscribed with bar codes, the mail can be sorted automatically at all mail distribution centers.

Wand scanners. The hand-held wand scanner is now common in point-of-sale (POS) systems in retail stores throughout the world. Clerks need only brush the wand over the price tag to record the sale. Since the POS terminal is on-line, the inventory is also updated as each item is sold.

Wand scanners are also used to read package labels in shipping and receiving and in inventory management. Passport inspection is even being automated with the use of wand scanners. Customs officials enter passport numbers via wand scanners to help speed the processing of international travelers.

OCR turnaround documents. OCR devices are custom-made for situations where data can be encoded by the computer system on a **turnaround document** when visual recognition is important. A turnaround document is *computer-produced output* that is ultimately returned as *machine-readable input* to a computer system. The billing system of an electric utility company is a good example of this OCR application.

The utility billing system procedures illustrated in Figure 5–2 are described below.

1. The invoices (turnaround documents) shown in Figure 5–3 are generated from the customer master file and the electricity us-

FIGURE 5–2   Electricity Utility Billing System

This system invoices customers with OCR turnaround documents, thereby minimizing the amount of key entry required. The five steps are discussed in the text.

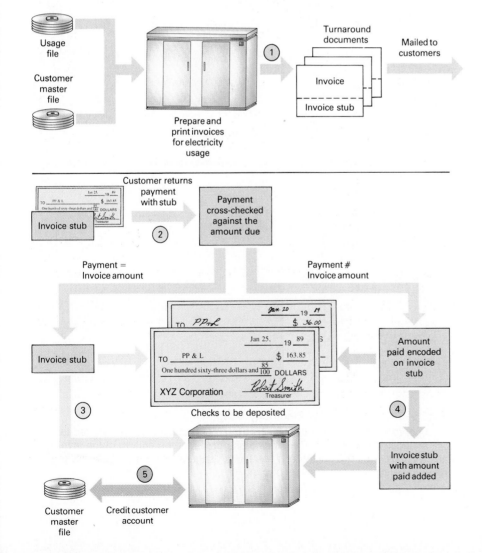

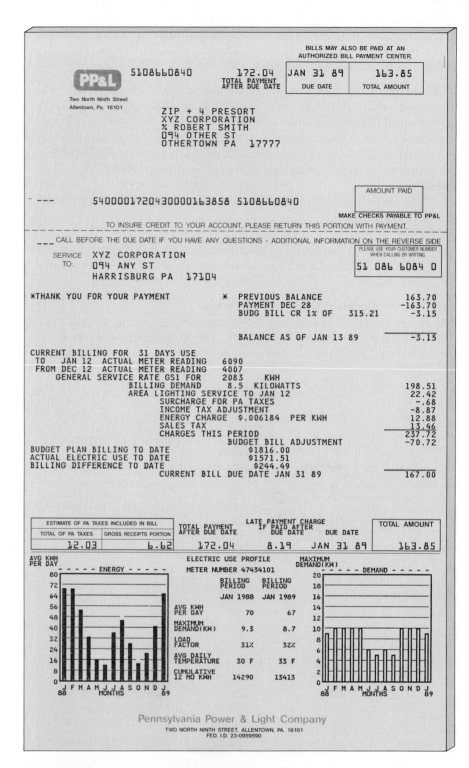

FIGURE 5–3   An Invoice for Electricity Usage

The top portion of this invoice is an OCR turnaround document that is used to record an incoming payment. The electric use profile at the bottom of the invoice graphically illustrates the customer's electricity usage over the past year. Notice the three different sizes and styles of print.

age file. Data on the invoice are printed in a format that can be read by an OCR document scanner. Therefore, no data entry is required unless the payment is less than the amount due.

2. The customers return the OCR-readable invoice stubs (turnaround documents) with the payment. Clerks cross-check the payment against the amount due. Partial payments are separated from full payments.

3. An OCR scanner reads the original turnaround document of full-payment customers to acknowledge receipt of payment.

4. The only data entry required is on partial payments. The amount of the payment is encoded on the partial-payment invoice stubs, and these are read by the OCR device.

5. The customer's account is credited by the amount of the payment.

In an attempt to cut costs and speed tax-return processing, the Internal Revenue Service is already distributing the short form as a turnaround document. The long form will be next!

Original-source data collection. Optical character recognition is also used for original-source data collection. An example is data collection for gasoline credit card purchases. When you make a credit card purchase, your card, a multicopy form, and a portable imprint device are used to record the sales data in machine-readable OCR format. On the form, the data recorded for most gasoline credit card purchases include the *account number of the buyer* (imprinted from the customer's credit card), the *account number of the service station* (imprinted from a permanently installed merchant card in the portable imprint device), and the *amount of the purchase* (entered by the attendant). One copy of the form is given to the customer as a record of purchase, one copy is retained by the service station, and the third copy, a stiffer card, is sent to the oil company that issued the credit card. With the data already in OCR format, no further data entry is required. During processing, the charged amount is recorded as a debit to the buyer's account and a credit to the service station's account.

Magnetic Ink Character Recognition

Magnetic ink character recognition (MICR) is similar to optical character recognition and is used exclusively by the banking industry. MICR readers are used to read and sort checks and deposits. You have probably noticed the *account number* and *bank number* encoded on all your checks and personalized deposit slips. The *date* of the transaction is automatically recorded for all checks processed that day; therefore, only the *amount* must be keyed in (see Figure 5–4) on a **MICR inscriber**. A **MICR reader-sorter** reads the data on the checks and sorts the checks for distribution to other banks and customers, or for further processing.

Magnetic ink character recognition devices are used instead of OCR because of MICR's increased speed and accuracy. The special

FIGURE 5–4   A Magnetic Ink Character Recognition (MICR)
Encoded Check
Notice that the amount is entered on the check when it is received
by the bank.

magnetic characters permit the processing speeds that banks need to
sort and process over 500 million checks each day.

Automatic teller machines (ATM) and electronic funds transfer
(EFT) permit funds to be electronically transferred from one account
to another without the need to produce a hard copy source document
such as a check or a deposit slip. As EFT grows, look for a diminished
need for handwritten checks and, therefore, MICR equipment. With
the cost of processing a check or deposit slip now in excess of $1, the
banking industry will do everything possible to eliminate the need
for hard copy checks and deposits, including offering home banking
services to PC owners.

In the near future, OCR data entry for credit card transactions
may be replaced with electronic funds transfer. With EFT, your transactions are recorded on-line, thereby eliminating the need for mailings
and subsequent OCR processing operations.

Magnetic Stripes and Smart Cards

The **magnetic stripes** on the backs of charge cards and badges offer
another means of data entry. The magnetic stripes are encoded with
data appropriate for the application. For example, your account number and privacy code are encoded on a card for automatic teller machines.

Magnetic stripes contain much more data per unit of space than
do printed characters or bar codes. Moreover, since they cannot be
read visually, they are perfect for storing confidential data, such as
the privacy code. Employee cards and security badges often contain
authorization data for access to physically secured areas, such as the
computer center. To gain access, an employee inserts a card or badge
into a **badge reader**. The authorization code is read and checked

The card that you insert into an automatic teller machine (ATM) has a magnetic stripe containing information on the bank that issues the card as well as your personal account number and privacy code.

before the individual is permitted into the secured area. The badge reader may also be on-line to the computer. On-line badge readers maintain a chronological log of those persons entering or leaving secured areas.

The enhanced version of cards with a magnetic stripe is the **smart card**. The smart card, similar in appearance to other cards, contains a microprocessor that retains certain security and personal data in its memory at all times. Because the smart card can contain more information, has some processing capability, and is almost impossible to duplicate, in the future smart cards may replace cards with magnetic stripes.

Voice Data Entry

Computers are great talkers, but they are not very good listeners. It is not uncommon for a **speech recognition** device to misinterpret slamming a door for a spoken word. Nevertheless, speech recognition

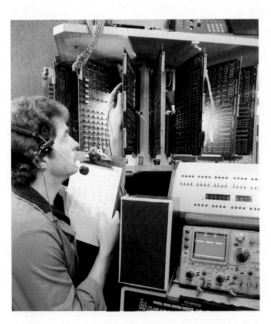

Quality-control inspectors in this circuit board assembly plant record defects through voice data entry. The system enables interactive communication with the computer and frees the inspector's hands for other activities.

systems can be used to enter limited kinds and quantities of information. Despite its limitations, speech recognition has a number of applications. Salespeople in the field can enter an order simply by calling the computer and stating the customer number, item number, and quantity. Quality control personnel, who must use their hands, call out defects as they are detected. Baggage handlers at airports simply state the three-letter destination identifier ("L-A-X" for Los Angeles International), and luggage is routed to the appropriate conveyer system. Physicians in the operating room can request certain information about a patient while operating. A computer-based audio response unit or a speech synthesizer makes the conversation two-way.

Figure 5–5 illustrates how it works. When you speak into a microphone, each sound is broken down and examined in several frequencies. The sounds in each frequency are **digitized** and are matched against similarly formed *templates* in the computer's electronic dictionary. The digitized template is a form that can be stored and interpreted by computers (in 1s and 0s). When a match is found, the word (*move* in Figure 5–5) is displayed on a VDT or, in some cases,

FIGURE 5–5 Speech Recognition
The sound waves created by the spoken word *move* are digitized by the computer. The digitized template is matched against templates of other words in the electronic dictionary. When a match is found, a written version of the word is displayed.

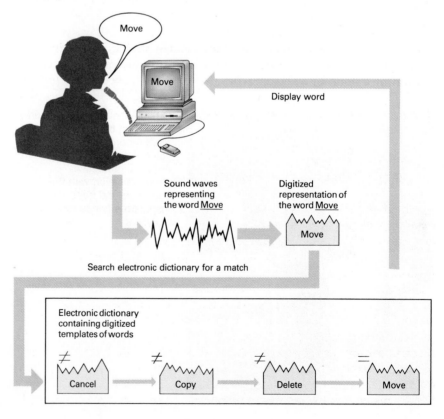

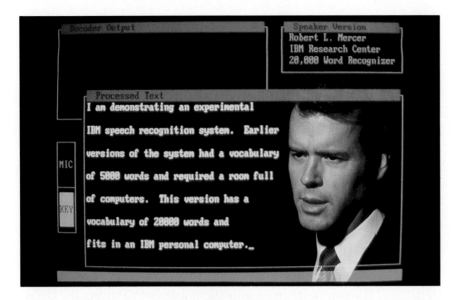

An experimental version of the speech recognition system being demonstrated here can interpret 20,000 spoken words. With this type of microcomputer-based capability, executives will be able to dictate most of their correspondence directly into a word processing system, occasionally inserting words that are not part of the system's vocabulary.

repeated by a speech synthesizer for confirmation. If no match is found, the speaker is asked to repeat the word.

In speech recognition, the creation of the data base is called *training*. Most speech recognition systems are *speaker dependent*; that is, they respond to the speech of a particular individual. Therefore, a data base of words must be created for each person using the system. To create this data base, each person using the system must repeat—as many as 20 times—every word to be interpreted by the system. This "training" is necessary because we seldom say a word the same way each time. There will probably be a different inflection or nasal quality even if we say the word twice in succession.

State-of-the-art *speaker-independent* systems have a limited vocabulary, perhaps *yes*, *no*, and the 10 numeric digits. Although the vocabulary is limited, speaker-independent systems do not require training and can be used by anyone. However, they do require a very large data base to accommodate anyone's voice pattern.

Voice inflections, grammatical exceptions, and words that have several meanings make speech interpretation difficult, but not impossible. For example, "I'm OK!" differs from "I'm OK?" For human beings, distinguishing these subtle differences is second nature. However, these subtleties have vastly complicated the plight of researchers working on simulating human sensory perception. Even so, researchers are developing speaker-independent data bases of several thousand words that enable the transcription of complete spoken sentences with a high degree of accuracy. It is only a matter of time before programmers can enter their programs in spoken English rather than through time-consuming keystrokes and before managers can dictate their correspondence directly to the computer. Today we must see and touch our workstations to interact with a computer, but in a few years we will be talking with computers as we move about our offices and homes.

Vision Input Systems

The simulation of human senses, especially vision, is extremely complex. For example, a computer does not actually see and interpret an image the way a human being does. To give computers "eyesight," a camera provides the input needed to create the data base. A vision system, complete with camera, digitizes the images of all objects to be interpreted. The digitized form of each image is then stored in the data base. When the system is placed in operation, a camera enters the image into a digitizer. The digitized image to be interpreted is then compared to the prerecorded digitized images in the computer's data base. The computer interprets the image by matching the structure of the input image with those in the data base. This process is illustrated by the digital vision inspection system in Figure 5–6.

As you can imagine, **vision input systems** are best suited to very specialized tasks where only a few images will be encountered. These tasks are usually simple, monotonous ones, such as inspection. For example, in Figure 5–6 a digital vision inspection system on an assembly line rejects those parts that do not meet certain quality control

FIGURE 5–6 Digital Vision Inspection System

In this digital vision inspection system, parts are examined by the system for defects. If the digitized image of the part does not match a standard digital image, the defective part is placed in a reject bin.

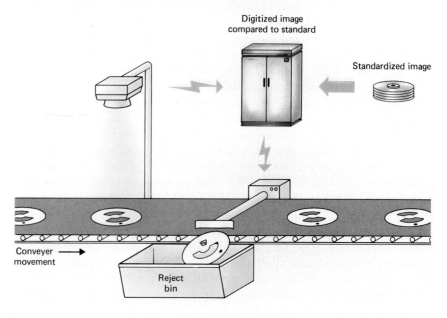

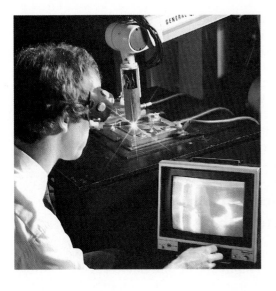

This robot has "eyes." The TV monitor in the foreground shows what it sees. This welding robot uses its vision system to steer itself along irregularly shaped joints as it makes the weld.

specifications. The vision system performs rudimentary gauging inspections and then signals the computer to take appropriate action.

Portable Data Entry

Portable data entry devices are hand-held and usually *off-line*; that is, the portable device is not linked to the main computer during data collection activities. The typical portable data entry device would have a limited keyboard and some kind of storage capability on which to capture the data, usually random access memory or magnetic cassette tape. After the data have been entered, the data entry device is

The equipment managers at this company use a portable data entry device to expedite checking out and logging in thousands of tools. This man enters data on the keyboard and with the OCR wand scanner. At the end of each day, the data gathered are transmitted via a telephone hookup to the company's host computer for processing.

linked with the host computer so that data can be *uploaded* (transmitted from the data entry device to host) for processing.

One portable data entry device combines a hand-held optical wand with a keyboard. Stock clerks in department stores routinely use such devices to collect and enter reorder data. As clerks check the inventory level visually, they identify the items to be restocked. First they scan the price tag with the wand, then they enter the number to be ordered on the keyboard.

Another portable data entry device contains a pressure-sensitive writing pad that recognizes hand-printed alphanumeric characters.

5–4 Output Devices: Computers Communicate with Us

Output devices translate bits and bytes into a form that we can understand. Terminals are both input and output devices. The monitors of terminals and workstations provide soft copy, or temporary output. The most common "output only" devices are discussed in this section. These include printers, plotters, desktop film recorders, screen image projectors, computer-output microform, and voice response units.

Printers

Printers produce hard copy output, such as management reports, memos, payroll checks, and program listings. Printers are generally classified as **serial printers**, **line printers**, or **page printers**. Printers are rated by their print speed. Print speeds for serial printers are measured in *characters per second* (*cps*), and for line and page printers they are measured in *lines per minute* (*lpm*). The print-speed ranges for the three types of printers are 40–450 cps, 1000–3600 lpm, and 500–40,000 lpm, respectively.

Printers are further categorized as impact or nonimpact. An impact printer uses some type of hammer or hammers to hit the ribbon and the paper, much as a typewriter does. Nonimpact printers use chemicals, lasers, and heat to form the images on the paper. Only nonimpact printers can achieve print speeds in excess of 3600 lpm.

Serial Printers   Most serial printers are configured with microcomputer systems. They are also used in support of terminal clusters to give users the flexibility to obtain hard copy output. Impact serial printers rely on **dot-matrix** and **daisy-wheel** technology. Nonimpact serial printers employ **ink-jet** and **thermal** technology. Regardless of the technology, the images are formed *one character at a time* as the print head moves across the paper.

The dot-matrix printer.   The dot-matrix printer arranges printed dots to form characters and all kinds of images in much the same way as lights display time and temperature on bank signs. One or several vertical columns of small print hammers are contained in a rectangular "print head." The hammers are activated independently

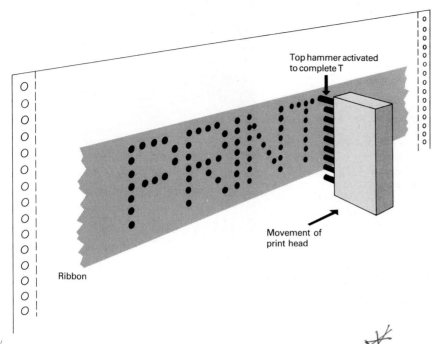

Top hammer activated
to complete T

Movement of
print head

Ribbon

FIGURE 5–7   Dot-Matrix Printer Character Formation
Each character is formed in a 7 x 5 matrix as the nine-hammer print head
moves across the paper. The two bottom hammers are used for lowercase
letters that extend below the line (for example, *g* and *p*).

to form a dot character image as the print head moves horizontally
across the paper. The characters in Figure 5–7 are formed within a
matrix that is seven dots high and five dots wide (7 × 5). The number
of dots within the matrix varies from one printer to the next.

The quality of the printed output is directly proportional to the
density of the dots in the matrix. High quality dot-matrix printers
form characters that appear solid, and they can be used for business
letters as well as for routine data processing output. Figure 5–8 illustrates how the dots can be overlapped to create a *near-letter-quality*
(NLQ) appearance. These printers are called *dual-mode* because of
their dual-function capabilities.

Dot-matrix printers are more flexible than printers of fully
formed characters (printers that use an embossed rendering of a char-

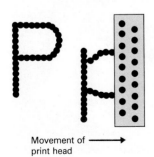

**FIGURE 5–8   Near-Letter-Quality Dot-Matrix
Character Formation**
The 18-hammer print head permits dots to be overlapped to increase the density and, therefore, the
quality of the image.

Movement of
print head

The daisy-wheel printer is so named because its print mechanism resembles the shape of a daisy. Each of the "petals" of the daisy wheel contains a fully formed impression of a character. The interchangeable daisy wheels are available in a wide variety of character sets.

acter to reproduce the image on paper). Depending on the model, dot-matrix printers can print a variety of sizes and types of characters (even old English and script characters), print in colors, print graphics, and print bar codes.

The daisy-wheel printer. The daisy-wheel printer produces *letter-quality* (*LQ*) output for word processing applications. An interchangeable daisy wheel containing a set of fully formed characters is spun to the desired character. A print hammer strikes the embossed character on the print wheel to form the image. The print quality is at least equal to that of the best electric typewriters.

Although daisy-wheel printers have the highest quality text output of serial printers, they are the slowest and cannot produce graphic output.

The ink-jet printer. Ink-jet printers squirt dots of ink on paper to form images in much the same way dot-matrix printers do. The big

The nozzles on the print head of a color ink-jet printer expel thousands of droplets per second to produce many different colors. The principle of ink-jet printing is illustrated as high-speed photography catches airborne droplets in flight. The results speak for themselves.

This line printer uses an operator-changeable steel band and prints 1500 lines per minute. To load the continuous-feed paper, the acoustical enclosure is raised and the "gate" containing the band and ribbon is swung open.

advantage that ink-jet printers have over dot matrix printers is that they can produce *multicolor* output. Sales of color ink-jet printers are expected to increase substantially as users, accustomed to color output on their video monitors, come to want color on their hard copy outputs.

The thermal printer.   The thermal printer is an alternative to the other serial printers. Heat elements produce dot-matrix images on heat-sensitive paper. The major disadvantage is the cost of the heat-sensitive paper. The advantages include compactness, limited noise, and low purchase price. Some thermal printers are capable of color output.

Line Printers   Line printers are impact printers that print *one line at a time*. The most popular types of line printers are the band printer, chain printer, and matrix line printer.

Band and chain printers.   Band and chain printers have a print hammer for each character position in the line of print (usually 132). On a band printer, several similar sets of fully formed characters are embossed on a horizontal band that is continuously moving in front of the print hammers. On a chain printer, the characters are embossed on each link of the print chain. On both types, the paper is momentarily stopped and, as the desired character passes over a given column, the hammer is activated, pressing the ribbon against the paper to form the image.

Band and chain printers are capable of printing on continuous-feed paper as well as on cards and on documents of varying sizes (even mailing labels). Interchangeable bands and chains make it easy for operators to change the style of print (the typeface).

The matrix line printer.   Matrix line printers print one line of *dots* at a time. Needlelike hammers are lined up across the width of the paper. Like serial matrix printers, the characters are formed in rectangular dot configurations as the paper passes the line of print hammers. Matrix printers are much more flexible than band printers are, and they can perform the same types of print operations as serial matrix printers do (see above), including graphic output and machine-readable bar codes.

Page Printers   Page printers are of the nonimpact type and use laser printing technology to achieve high-speed hard copy output by printing *a page at a time*. Operating at peak capacity during an eight-hour shift, the fastest page printer can produce almost a quarter of a million pages—that's 50 miles of output. This enormous output capability is normally directed to people outside an organization. For example, large banks use page printers to produce statements for checking and savings accounts; insurance companies print policies on page printers; and electric utility companies use them to bill their customers (see Figure 5–3).

Very high-speed laser printers used in the mainframe environment have the capability to superimpose preprinted forms on continuous-feed stock paper. This eliminates a company's need to purchase expensive preprinted forms. Page printers have the capability of printing graphs and charts, and they offer considerable flexibility in the size and style of print.

Until the mid-1980s, virtually all printers configured with microcomputers were serial printers. Now economically priced **desktop laser printers** are becoming the standard for office microcomputer systems. These printers, capable of print speeds in excess of eight pages per minute, have redefined the hard copy output potential of micros. Desktop laser printers have many inviting qualities: They are quiet (an important consideration in an office setting); they can print *near-typeset-quality* (*NTQ*) text and graphics; they can mix type styles and sizes on the same page; and they are much faster than serial printers. The emergence of desktop laser printers has fueled the

This graphics and text output shows the versatility of a desktop laser printer. A laser printer can produce hard copies of graphic images (as they would appear on a screen) just as easily as it prints letters and reports.

```
This sentence was printed on a 9-pin dot-matrix printer.
This sentence was printed in NLQ mode on a dot-matrix printer.
This sentence was printed on a daisy-wheel printer.
This sentence was printed on a desktop laser printer.
```

FIGURE 5–9   Printer Output Comparison

explosion of *desktop publishing* (discussed in detail in Chapter 14, "Word Processing, Desktop Publishing, and Communications Software").

Figure 5–9 contrasts the output of a dot-matrix printer, in both normal and near-letter-quality (NLQ) modes, a daisy-wheel printer (letter quality), and a desktop laser printer (near-typeset-quality).

Printer Summary   Hundreds of printers are produced by dozens of manufacturers. There is a printer manufactured to meet the hard copy output requirements of any company or individual, and almost any combination of features can be obtained. You can specify the speed, quality of output, color requirements, flexibility requirements, and even noise level. Printers sell for as little as a good pair of shoes or for as much as a small office building.

The trend in computer centers is toward producing less printed output. If a permanent hard copy is not needed, soft copy is less expensive and easier to obtain. Look for the requirements for printed output to diminish as more and more on-line terminals are installed. As an example, a computer center in a large Midwestern company delivered a truckload of printed output to the personnel department every Thursday night for almost 10 years. Now 20 on-line terminals allow people in the personnel department to interact directly with the computer and with the personnel data base.

In a few years, printers will be used almost exclusively for "external" output, such as bank statements and utility bills. In a few more years, even external output will be soft copy. Our utility bills will be delivered by *electronic mail* to our personal computers and paid by *electronic funds transfer* from our account to that of the utility company.

Plotters

Dot matrix, ink-jet, thermal, and laser printers are capable of producing graphic output, but they are limited in its quality and the size. **Pen plotters** are devices that convert computer-generated graphs, charts, and line drawings into high-precision hard copy output. The two basic types of pen plotters are the *drum plotter* and the *flatbed plotter*. Both types have one or more pens that move over the paper under computer control to produce an image. Several pens are required to vary the width and color of the lines, and the computer selects and manipulates them. On the drum plotter, the pens and the drum move concurrently in different axes to produce the image. Drum

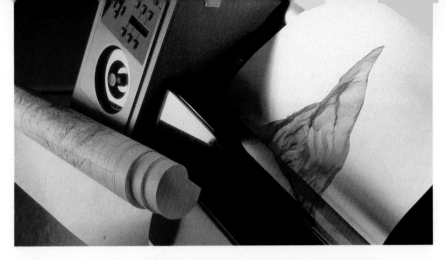

Cartographers use pen plotters to illustrate terrains in three dimensions.

plotters are used to produce continuous output, such as plotting earthquake activity, or for long graphic output, such as the structural view of a skyscraper.

On some flatbed plotters, the pen moves in both axes while the paper remains stationary. This is always true of very large flatbed plotters, some of which are larger than regulation pool tables. On smaller flatbed plotters, especially small desktop plotters, both paper and pen move concurrently in much the same way as drum plotters.

Electrostatic plotter/printers produce a "quick and dirty" hard copy of graphic images for plot previewing. The final plot is completed on the high-precision drum or flatbed plotter.

Presentation Graphics: Desktop Film Recorders and Screen Image Projectors

In business, people have found that sophisticated and colorful graphics add an aura of professionalism to any report or presentation. This demand for *presentation graphics* has created a need for corresponding

The output from this drum plotter is a circuit diagram for a hand calculator.

output devices. Computer-generated graphic images can be recreated on paper and transparency acetates with printers and plotters. Graphic images can also be captured on 35-mm slides, or they can be displayed on a monitor or projected onto a large screen.

Desktop film recorders reproduce a high-resolution graphic image on 35-mm film in either black and white or color. Some models allow users to process and mount their own slides. Others require outside processing. **Screen-image projectors** project the graphic image onto a large screen, similar to the way television programs are projected onto a large TV screen. Another device transfers the graphic image displayed on the monitor to a large screen with the use of an ordinary overhead projector.

Computer Output Microform

Computer output microform (COM) devices prepare microfilm and microfiche that can be read on microfilm viewers. Microfiche is hard copy output that becomes a permanent record that can be referenced over and over. Each COM device contains an image-to-film recorder and a duplicator for making multiple copies of a microfiche.

In the COM process (see Figure 5–10), the images (output) to be miniaturized are prepared, as if to be printed, on a computer system. This output is then sent to the COM device. Here the images are miniaturized for microform viewers.

In the miniaturization process, images are displayed on a small, high-resolution video display. A camera exposes a small segment of the microfilm for each display, thereby creating a grid pattern of images, or frames. The microfilm is then developed and cut into 4- by 6-inch sheets of microfiche, each containing up to 270 frames. The duplicator section makes multiple copies of the microfiche. Each sheet of microfiche is titled and indexed so that the appropriate frame, or "page," can be retrieved quickly on a viewer.

In an information center, end users employ graphics software to prepare professional-looking visuals for presentations. The device on the right, a film recorder, permits any of these users to capture a screen image on 35-mm film.

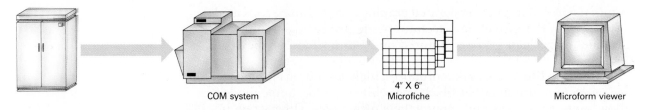

COM system   4″ X 6″   Microform viewer
Microfiche

FIGURE 5–10   The Computer Output Microfilm/Microfiche (COM) Process
In the on-line COM process, data are routed directly from the computer to the COM system.

COM is an alternative to an on-line computer-based system when up-to-the-minute information is not critical. COM is also used extensively instead of hard copy for archival storage (old income tax records, for example).

COM equipment can produce in minutes what may take hours to produce on a printer. But the real advantage of COM is the elimination of cumbersome volumes of printed output. Nevertheless, these advantages are overshadowed by the potential of on-line systems. As terminals and on-line systems become commonplace, a trend is emerging to replace COM applications with on-line systems. On-line systems offer the added advantages of direct access to and immediate update of the data base.

Voice Response Units

If you have ever called directory assistance, you have probably heard something like, "The number is eight-six-one-four-zero-three-eight." If you have not, you have probably been in a car that warned the driver to "fasten your seat belt." These are examples of talking machines—outputs from voice response units. There are two types of **voice response units**: One uses a *reproduction* of a human voice and other sounds, the other uses a *speech synthesizer*. Like monitors, voice response units provide a temporary, soft copy output.

The first type of voice response unit selects output from user-recorded words, phrases, music, alarms, or anything you might record on tape, just as a printer would select characters. In "recorded" voice response units, the actual analog recordings of sounds are converted into digital data, then permanently stored in a memory chip. When output, the selected sound is converted back into analog before being routed to a speaker. These chips are mass-produced for specific applications, such as output for automatic teller machines, microwave ovens, smoke detectors, elevators, alarm clocks, automobile warning systems, video games, and vending machines, to mention only a few.

Speech synthesizers convert raw data into electronically produced speech. To do this, these devices combine sounds resembling the phonemes (basic sound units) that make up speech. A speech synthesizer is capable of producing at least 64 unique sounds. The existing technology produces synthesized speech with only limited vocal inflections and phrasing. Still, the number of applications is growing. In one application, an optical character reader scans books

An interior view of this reading machine shows an optical scanner reading a typewritten letter. The scanner's output is automatically converted into computer signals which, in turn, are converted into full-word English speech, using a speech synthesizer. This machine can even read novels to blind people.

to retrieve the raw data. The speech synthesizer then translates the printed matter into spoken words for blind people. In another application, the use of speech synthesizers is opening a new world to speech-impaired children who were once placed in institutions because they could not communicate verbally. Speech synthesizers are also used in grocery checkout systems, alarm systems, and computer-based training. As the quality of the output improves, speech synthesizers will enjoy a broader base of applications. Speech synthesizers are relatively inexpensive and are becoming increasingly popular with many personal computer owners.

Summary Outline and Important Terms

5–1   I/O DEVICES: OUR INTERFACE WITH THE COMPUTER.   A variety of **peripheral devices** provide the interface between us and the computer system.

5–2   TERMINALS AND WORKSTATIONS.   We interact with a computer system through a video display terminal (also, VDT or, simply, terminal). The VDT is affectionately known as "the tube," short for **cathode-ray tube**. VDTs and micros are the most common terminals. The input mechanism is usually a keyboard, and the output is normally a display screen, called a monitor. Other input devices used with terminals include

Memory Bits

OUTPUT
- Terminal monitors
- Workstation monitors
- Printers
  Serial (40–450 cps)
    Impact
      Dot-matrix
      Daisy-wheel
    Nonimpact
      Ink-jet
      Thermal
  Line (500–3600 lpm)
    Band and chain
    Matrix
  Page (500–40,000 lpm)
    Desktop laser
    High-speed laser
- Plotters
  Pen plotters
    Drum
    Flatbed
  Electrostatic
- Presentation graphics
  Desktop film recorder
  Screen image projectors
- Computer output microform (COM)
- Voice response units
  Recorded voice
  Speech synthesizers

the light pen, the joy stick, the track ball, the digitizing tablet and pen, and the mouse. These devices permit random movement of the cursor to create an image.

A soft copy (as opposed to hard copy) of alphanumeric and graphic output is displayed on the monitor. The three attributes of monitors are size (diagonal dimension 5 to 25 inches), color (monochrome or color), and **resolution** (quality of output). Space-saving **flat panel monitors** use liquid crystal and gas plasma technologies.

Graphics workstations are **intelligent workstations** for sophisticated users. Typically, a minimum configuration for a graphics workstation would include a medium-sized high-resolution graphics monitor, a keyboard, and at least two more modes of input.

Portable terminals are packaged for ease of movement and handling and have built-in **modems** that enable connection to telephone lines for remote transmission of data.

Terminals and workstations are quickly becoming companions to workers in most fields of endeavor.

5–3 SOURCE DATA AUTOMATION: GETTING DATA INTO THE COMPUTER SYSTEM.   The trend in data entry has been toward **source data automation**, where the need for key entry transcription of data is eliminated altogether.

Optical character recognition reduces the need for manual data entry by encoding certain data in machine-readable format. **OCR scanners** (label, page, document, continuous-form, and optical mark) recognize printed characters and certain coded symbols, such as **bar codes**. OCR scanners are used for original-source data collection and with **turnaround documents**. **Magnetic ink character recognition (MICR)** devices, which are used almost exclusively in banking, are similar to OCR scanners in function but they are faster and more accurate.

Magnetic stripes and **smart cards** provide input to **badge readers**. **Speech recognition** devices can be used to enter limited kinds and quantities of data. They do this by matching **digitized** representations of words against similarly formed *templates* in the computer's electronic dictionary. **Vision input systems** are best suited for tasks that involve only a few images. **Portable data entry** devices are hand-held and normally are used to collect data off-line.

5–4 OUTPUT DEVICES: COMPUTERS COMMUNICATE WITH US.   Output devices translate data stored in binary to a form that can be interpreted by the end user. Terminals and workstations are both input and output devices. Printers prepare hard copy output at speeds of 40 characters per second to 40,000 lines per minute. **Serial printers** are both impact (**dot-**

matrix and **daisy-wheel**) and nonimpact (**ink-jet** and **thermal**). **Line printers** are impact only and **page printers** are nonimpact only. The emergence of **desktop laser printers** has fueled the explosion of desktop publishing. The technologies used to produce the image vary widely from one printer to the next. **Pen plotters** and **electrostatic plotter/printers** convert stored data into hard copy graphs, charts, and line drawings.

     Desktop film recorders reproduce a high-resolution graphic image on 35-mm film in either black and white or color. **Screen-image projectors** project the graphic image onto a large screen.

     Computer output microform (COM) devices prepare microfilm and microfiche as a space- and time-saving alternative to printed output. **Voice response units** provide recorded or synthesized voice output.

Review Exercises

Concepts

1. Which has greater precision, a pen plotter or an electrostatic plotter?
2. What is meant when someone says that speech recognition devices are "speaker-dependent"?
3. List devices, other than key-driven, that are used to input source data into a computer system.
4. What is the purpose of having an operator console?
5. Which types of printers print fully formed characters?
6. What is a turnaround document? Give two examples.
7. Identify all input and output methods used by an automatic teller machine.
8. What is a smart card?
9. What is the relationship between a light pen and a cursor?
10. Give two applications for bar codes.
11. Give three examples of how a police department would use computer output.
12. Why do banks use MICR rather than OCR for data entry?
13. What output device reproduces high-resolution graphic images on 35-mm film?
14. Name an output device, other than a monitor, that produces soft copy output.
15. What kind of printer can produce near-typeset-quality output?

Discussion

16. Describe the input/output characteristics of a workstation that would be used by engineers for computer-aided design.

17. Department stores use hand-held wands to interpret the bar codes imprinted on the price tags of merchandise. Why do they not use slot scanners as supermarkets do?

18. What input/output capabilities are available at your college?

19. Compare today's vision input systems with those portrayed in such films as *2001* and *2010*. Do you believe that we will have a comparable vision technology by the year 2001?

Self-Test (by section)

5–1 **a.** Input devices translate data into a form that can be interpreted by a computer. (T/F)

b. The primary function of I/O peripherals is to facilitate computer-to-computer data transmission. (T/F)

5–2 **a.** All keyboards have special-function keys. (T/F)

b. The quality of output on a terminal's monitor is determined by its _____.

c. A _____ is a blinking character that indicates the location of the next input on the screen.

d. The popularity of flat panel monitors can be attributed to the ease with which they can be read in poor lighting situations. (T/F)

e. VDTs designed especially for the sophisticated user are called _____.

5–3 **a.** Optical character recognition is a means of source data automation. (T/F)

b. The Universal Product Code (UPC) was originally used by which industry: (a) supermarket, (b) hardware, or (c) mail order merchandising.

c. Which technology is used by the U.S. Postal Service to facilitate the distribution of mail: (a) MICR, (b) OCR, or (c) COM?

d. In speech recognition, words are _____ and matched against similarly formed _____ in the computer's electronic dictionary.

e. Vision input systems are best suited to generalized tasks in which a wide variety of images will be encountered. (T/F)

5–4 **a.** Ink-jet printers are classified as impact printers. (T/F)

b. Dot-matrix printing technology is available in serial and line printers. (T/F)

c. What type of printers are becoming the standard for office microcomputer systems: (a) desktop laser printers, (b) daisy-wheel printers, or (c) thermal printers?

d. _____ convert raw data into electronically produced speech.

Self-test answers. **5–1** (a) T; (b) F. **5–2** (a) F; (b) resolution; (c) cursor; (d) F; (e) graphics workstations. **5–3** (a) T; (b) a; (c) b; (d) digitized templates; (e) F. **5–4** (a) F; (b) T; (c) a; (d) Speech synthesizers.

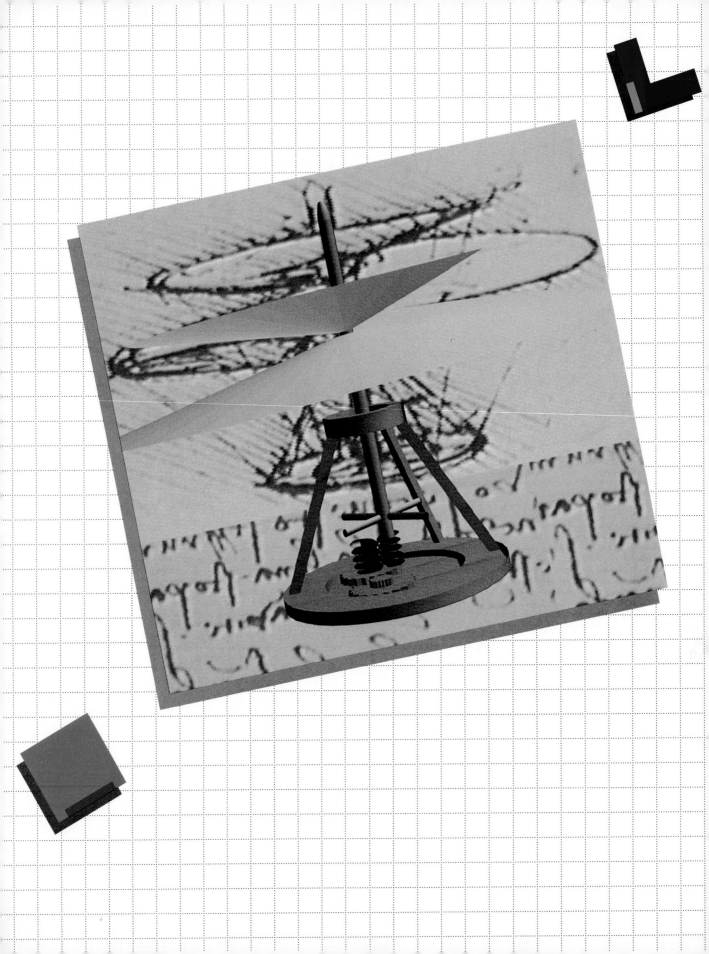

6

Data Storage Devices and Media

STUDENT LEARNING OBJECTIVES

- To distinguish between primary and secondary storage.
- To distinguish between secondary storage devices and secondary storage media.
- To describe the principles of operation, methods of data storage, and use of magnetic disk drives.
- To describe the principles of operation, methods of data storage, and use of magnetic tape drives.
- To discuss the applications and use of optical laser disk storage.

6–1 Secondary Storage: Permanent Data Storage

Within a computer system, programs and data are stored in *primary storage* and in *secondary storage* (see Figure 6–1). Programs and data are stored *permanently* for periodic retrieval in **secondary storage**, also called **auxiliary storage**. Programs and data are retrieved from secondary storage and stored *temporarily* in high-speed primary storage, also called random access memory, or RAM, for processing (see Chapter 4, "Inside the Computer").

"Why two types of storage?" you might ask. Remember from Chapter 4 that most primary storage is semiconductor memory, and the data are lost when the electricity is interrupted. Primary storage also is expensive and has a limited capacity. The RAM capacity of a large mainframe computer would not come close to meeting the data and program storage needs of even a small company. Secondary storage, however, is relatively inexpensive and has an enormous capacity.

Over the years, manufacturers have developed a variety of devices and media for the permanent storage of data and programs. *Paper tape*, *punched cards*, the *data cell*, and a variety of others have become obsolete. Today the various types of **magnetic disk drives** and their respective storage media are the state of the art for on-line storage of programs and data. **Magnetic tape drives** complement magnetic disk storage by providing inexpensive backup capability and off-line archival storage. In this chapter we focus on the terminology, principles, operation, and trade-offs of these secondary storage devices. We will also discuss the potential and applications of the emerging **optical laser disk** technology.

6–2 Sequential and Direct Access: New Terms for Old Concepts

An important consideration in both the design of an information system and the purchase of a computer system is the way that data are accessed. Magnetic tape is for **sequential access** only. Magnetic disks

FIGURE 6–1 Primary and Secondary Storage
Programs and data are stored permanently in secondary storage and temporarily in primary storage.

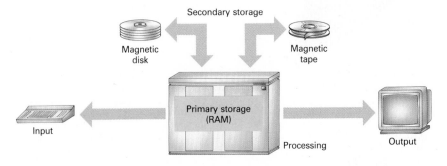

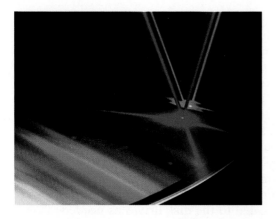

The most common secondary storage devices are the magnetic disk drive and magnetic tape drive. However, for certain applications, optical laser disk storage technology (shown here) is emerging as a viable alternative to disk and tape storage.

have **random-,** or **direct-, access** capabilities as well as sequential-access capabilities. You are quite familiar with these concepts, but you may not realize it. The magnetic tape is operationally the same as the one in home and automobile tape decks. The magnetic disk can be compared to a phonograph record.

Suppose you have the Beatles' classic record album *Sgt. Pepper's Lonely Hearts Club Band*. The first four songs on this record are: (1) "Sgt. Pepper's Lonely Hearts Club Band," (2) "With a Little Help from My Friends," (3) "Lucy in the Sky with Diamonds," and (4) "Getting Better." Now suppose you also have this Beatles' album on a tape cassette. To play the third song on the cassette, "Lucy in the Sky with Diamonds," you would wind the tape forward and search for it "sequentially." To play "Lucy in the Sky with Diamonds" on the phonograph record, all you would have to do is move the needle directly to the track containing the third song. This simple analogy demonstrates the two fundamental methods of storing and accessing data—*sequential* and *random*. Both methods are discussed in detail in the pages that follow.

6–3 Magnetic Disks: Rotating Storage Media

Hardware and Storage Media

Magnetic disk drives are secondary storage devices that provide a computer system with **random** *and* **sequential processing** capabilities. In random processing, the desired programs and data are accessed *directly* from the storage medium. In sequential processing, the computer system must search the storage medium to find the desired programs or data.

Since magnetic disk storage is used almost exclusively for direct access, random processing is discussed with magnetic disks in this section. Sequential processing is discussed with magnetic tape in the next section.

Because of its random and sequential processing capabilities, magnetic disk storage is the overwhelming choice of both micro and mainframe users. A variety of magnetic disk drives (the hardware device) and magnetic disks (the media) are manufactured for different

"Your toast might brown faster in something besides your portable computer."

business requirements. There are two fundamental types of magnetic disks: those that are interchangeable and those that are permanently installed or fixed. **Interchangeable magnetic disks** can be stored **off-line** (that is, not accessible to the computer system) and loaded to the magnetic disk drives as they are needed. Once inserted in the disk drives, the disks are said to be **on-line**, that is, the data and programs on the disks are accessible to the computer system.

The trend in magnetic storage media is to **fixed disks**, also called hard disks. All fixed disks are rigid, usually made of aluminum with a magnetic coating. Today's integrated software and data bases require all data and programs to be on-line at all times. In the past, interchangeable disks containing certain files and programs were taken from the shelf and loaded to the disk drives as needed. This is still true today, but to a much lesser extent.

The different types of interchangeable magnetic disks and fixed disks are shown in the accompanying photographs. As you can see, magnetic disks come in a wide variety of shapes and storage capacities. The type used would depend on the volume of data that you have and the frequency with which those data are accessed.

Magnetic Disks: The Microcomputer Environment

Microcomputer Disk Media The two most popular types of interchangeable magnetic disks for micros are the **diskette** and the **microdisk**.

- *Diskette*. The diskette is a thin, flexible disk that is permanently enclosed in a soft 5¼-inch square jacket. Because the magnetic coated mylar diskette and its jacket are flexible like a page in this book, the diskette is also called a **flexible disk** or a **floppy disk**. The storage capacity of diskettes ranges from about 360 Kb to 1.2 Mb.
- *Microdisk*. The 3½-inch flexible microdisk, also called a **microfloppy**, is enclosed in a rigid plastic jacket. The storage capacity of microdisks ranges from about 400 Kb to 1.4 Mb.

Several companies distribute their annual reports with supplemental software diskettes. The software on the 5¼-inch diskette provides stockholders with the opportunity to view interactively the financial data that are displayed in a variety of graphic formats.

Because of its convenient size and storage capacity, the 3½-inch microdisk is popular with users of both portable and desktop micros. This data-center manager is transferring data from his portable to his desktop computer via a microdisk.

The microcomputer hard disk is called the **Winchester disk**. The Winchester disk got its nickname from the 30-30 Winchester rifle. Early disk drives had two 30-megabyte disks—thus the nickname "Winchester." Most of the newer personal computers are configured with at least one diskette or microdisk drive and one hard disk. Having two disks facilitates system design and increases system throughput. The storage capacity of these 3½- and 5¼-inch hard disks ranges from about 20 Mb to 760 Mb, which is as much as 2300 times the capacity of a diskette.

A Winchester hard disk, which may have several disk platters, spins continuously at a high speed within a sealed enclosure. The

This Winchester disk has two read/write heads for each recording surface. The access arms move the read/write heads to the appropriate track to retrieve the data. Having two read/write heads saves precious milliseconds because a head will never have to transverse more than half the width of the disk's recording surface.

enclosure keeps the disk-face surfaces free from contaminants such as dust and cigarette smoke. This contaminant-free environment enables Winchester disks to achieve greater density in data storage than the interchangeable diskettes. In contrast to the Winchester disk, the floppy disk is set in motion only when a command is issued to read from or write to the disk. An indicator light near the disk drive is illuminated only when the diskette is spinning. The rotational movement of a magnetic disk passes all data under or over a **read/write head**, thereby making all data available for access on each revolution of the disk.

Micro Disk Organization   The manner in which data and programs are stored and accessed is similar for both hard and floppy disks. The disk storage medium has a thin film coating of cobalt, iron, or one of the other easily magnetized elements. The thin film coating on the disk can be electronically magnetized by the read/write head to represent the absence or presence of a bit (0 or 1). Data are stored in concentric circles called **tracks** by magnetizing the surface to represent bit configurations (see Figure 6–2). Bits are recorded using **serial representation**.

Microcomputer disk storage devices use **sector organization** to

FIGURE 6–2   Cutaway of a 5 $\frac{1}{4}$-Inch Diskette
Photoelectric cells sense light as it passes through the index hole. This feedback enables the computer to monitor which sector is under or over the read/write head at any given time. Data are read or written serially in tracks within a given sector.

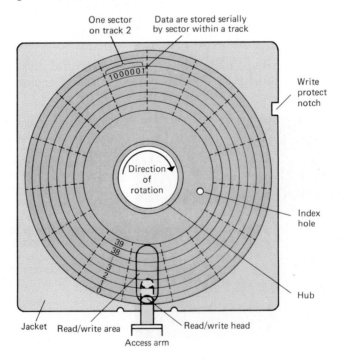

One sector on track 2

Data are stored serially by sector within a track

1 0 0 0 0 0 1

Write protect notch

Direction of rotation

Index hole

Hub

Jacket   Read/write area

Read/write head

Access arm

DON'T FOLD, SPINDLE, OR MUTILATE

Costing a little more than a large soft drink, a blank 5¼-inch flexible diskette has a very modest value. But once you begin to use it, its value increases greatly. Its value includes the many hours of work you have spent entering data, preparing spreadsheets, or writing programs. Such a valuable piece of property should be handled with care. The following are a few guidelines for diskette handling:

DO

■ *Do* label each diskette. Use a soft-tipped pen on the label.

■ *Do* cover the *write-protect notch* on all important diskettes intended for read-only use, such as the program diskettes for micro software packages.

■ *Do* store diskettes in their envelopes so the exposed surface is covered.

■ *Do* store diskettes vertically or, if stored flat, place no more than 10 in a stack.

■ *Do* store diskettes at temperatures ranging from 50 to 125 degrees Fahrenheit.

■ *Do* keep a backup of diskettes containing important data and programs.

■ *Do* remove diskettes from disk drives before you turn off the computer.

DON'T

■ *Don't* fold, spindle, or mutilate diskettes.

■ *Don't* force a diskette into the disk drive. It should slip in with little or no resistance.

■ *Don't* touch the diskette surface.

■ *Don't* place diskettes near a magnetic field, such as magnetic paper-clip holders, tape demagnetizers, or electric motors.

■ *Don't* expose diskettes to direct sunlight for a prolonged period of time.

■ *Don't* insert or remove a diskette from a disk drive if the red "drive active" light is on.

Although less vulnerable than the diskette, the 3½-inch microdisk should be treated with similar respect.

---

store and retrieve data. In sector organization, the recording surface is divided into from eight to 15 pie-shaped **sectors** (see Figure 6–2). Each sector is assigned a unique number; therefore, the *sector number* and *track number* are all that are needed to comprise a **disk address** (the physical location of data or a program). To read from or write to a disk, an **access arm** containing the read/write head is moved, under program control, to the appropriate *track*. When the sector containing the desired data passes under or over the read/write head, the data are read or written.

Magnetic Disks: The Mainframe Environment

Mainframe Disk Media   Magnetic disks are used for all information systems where the data must be on-line and accessed directly. An airline reservation system provides a good mainframe-oriented example of this need. Direct-access capability is required to retrieve the record for any flight at any time from any reservations office. The data must be current, or flights may be overbooked or underbooked. Because of the random nature of the reservations data, sequential-only magnetic tape cannot be used as a storage medium for this or any other system that requires random processing. File and data base organization for random processing, also called **direct processing**,

Sitting atop rows of disk drives are interchangeable magnetic disk packs that provide billions of characters of direct-access storage for this superminicomputer system.

and sequential processing are discussed in detail in Chapter 9, "Data Management."

In the mainframe environment, the most popular interchangeable disk storage media are the **disk cartridge** and the **disk pack** (see accompanying photos). Most disk cartridges have a single platter and are entirely encased in a hard plastic cover. When inserted into a disk drive, the disk-face surfaces are exposed to accommodate the movement of the read/write head. The 14-inch disk pack has been the disk media mainstay for the mainframe environment for the past three decades. Although its size has remained relatively stable, the density at which data can be written on the disk-face surfaces has increased dramatically. The larger disk packs have up to 12 platters stacked around a hollow core. Each of the finely machined aluminum platters has a magnetized coating about 40 millionths of an inch thick. Most mainframe computers and supercomputers use 14-inch disk packs with 11 platters and 20 usable disk-face surfaces. The current technology enables a single disk pack to store several *gigabytes* (billion bytes) of data. To mount a disk pack onto a disk drive, the disk is slipped over a shaft in the disk drive and the protective plastic coat is removed. The procedure is reversed to remove the disk pack for off-line storage.

Minis, mainframes, and supercomputers employ a wide variety of fixed disk media, also capable of storing several gigabytes of data. Fixed disk media come in 5¼-inch, 8-inch, and 14-inch formats. Generally speaking, the density at which data can be stored is greater for fixed than for interchangeable disks because the environment can be more carefully controlled. Some very high-density fixed disks can store over 30 million characters on one square inch of recording surface. That's the text of this and 20 other books on a space the size of a postage stamp!

Mainframe Disk Organization   The way data are organized on mainframe disk systems is similar to that of microcomputer disk systems.

Like microcomputer disks, data are recorded serially in concentric circles called tracks. The hard disks on mainframes spin continuously at a high speed, typically 3600 revolutions per minute.

To illustrate mainframe disk organization, we will use a fixed magnetic disk with four platters (see Figure 6–3). Data are stored on all *recording surfaces*. For a disk with four platters, there are eight recording surfaces on which data can be stored. A disk drive will have at least one read/write head for each recording surface. The heads are mounted on **access arms** that move together and literally float on a cushion of air over the spinning recording surfaces. The tolerance is so close that a particle of smoke from a cigarette will not fit between these "flying" heads and the recording surface. This is the primary reason why computer operators display "No Smoking" signs in the machine room.

Mainframe disk systems use either *sector* or **cylinder organization**. Sector organization is same as that described earlier in the section on micro disk systems. In the mainframe environment, each of the high-density disk-face surfaces can have up to 1600 tracks per inch; therefore, any disk-face surface may have several thousand tracks, numbered consecutively from outside to inside. A particular **cylinder** refers to every track with the same number on all recording surfaces. To read or write a record, the access arms are moved, under program control, to the appropriate *cylinder*. For example, each recording surface has a track numbered 0012, so the disk has a cylinder numbered 0012. If the record to be accessed is on recording surface 01, track 0012, then the access arm and the read/write heads for all eight recording surfaces are moved to cylinder 0012.

FIGURE 6–3 Fixed Hard Disk with Four Platters and Eight Recording Surfaces

In the illustration, the read/write heads are positioned over cylinder 0012. At this position, the data on any one of the eight tracks numbered 0012 are accessible to the computer on each revolution of the disk. The read/write head must be moved to another cylinder to access other data on the disk.

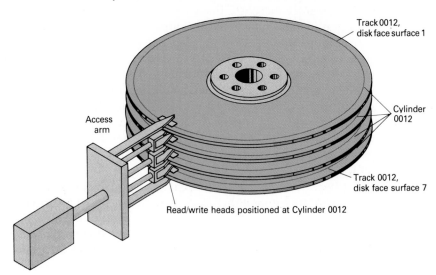

In Figure 6–3 the access arm is positioned over cylinder 0012. In this position, any record on any of the tracks in cylinder 0012 can be accessed without further movement of the access arm. If a record on surface 5, track 0145, is to be read, the access arm must be positioned over cylinder 0145 until the desired record passes under the read/write head.

Fortunately, software automatically monitors the location, or address, of our files and programs. We need only enter someone's name to retrieve his or her personnel record. The computer system locates the record and loads it to primary storage for processing. Although the addressing schemes vary considerably between disks, the address will normally include the *cylinder*, the *recording surface*, and the *relative position* of a record on a track (for example, the fourth record).

☑

Memory Bits

CHARACTERISTICS OF MAGNETIC DISK

Permanent media	Fixed (5¼″, 8″, and 14″)
Interchangeable media	For micros: diskette and microdisk
	For mainframes: disk cartridge and disk pac
Type access	Direct (random) or sequential
Data representation	Serial
Storage scheme	Cylinder, sector

Disk Access Time

The **access time** is the interval between the instant a computer makes a request for transfer of data from a secondary storage device to primary storage and the instant this operation is completed. The access of data from primary storage is performed at electronic speeds, or approximately the speed of light. But the access of data from secondary storage depends on mechanical apparatus. Any mechanical movement significantly increases the access time. The access time for hard disks is significantly less than for floppy disks because the hard disk is in continuous motion.

The *seek time*, which comprises the greatest amount of the total access time, is the time it takes the mechanical access arm to move the read/write head to the desired track or cylinder. Some disk drives have two access arms, one for reading and writing on the inside tracks and another for the outside tracks. The average seek time is significantly reduced with two access arms because they have a shorter distance to move and one can move while the other is reading or writing.

The *rotational delay time* is the time it takes for the appropriate record to be positioned under the read-write head. On the average, this would be half the time it takes for one revolution of the disk, or about 8 milliseconds for a hard disk spinning at 3600 rpm. The rotational delay time for a diskette spinning at 400 rpm is 75 millisec-

Memory Bits

DISK ACCESS TIME =

- Seek time +
- Rotational delay time +
- Transmission time

mitted to primary storage for processing. The next read transmits the next **block** of records to primary storage. When the computer is instructed to write to a tape, the data are transmitted from primary storage to the tape drive. Then a block of data and an IBG are written to the tape.

In Figure 6–4, the records have a blocking factor of 2 and are said to be "blocked two." Figure 6–5 shows how the same file would appear "blocked three" and unblocked. Notice how the tape blocked three contains more records per linear length of the tape.

To signal the beginning and end of a particular tape file, the computer adds a **header label** and a **trailer label**, respectively (see Figure 6–4). The header label contains the name of the file and the date it was created. The trailer label is written at the end of the data file and contains the number of records in the file.

Principles of Operation: Tape Cartridges

The ½-Inch Tape Cartridge   The operation of the ½-inch tape cartridge is more like that of the ½-inch mag tape reel than the ¼-inch tape cartridge that is so popular with micro and mini users. Besides the obvious differences in mechanical operation, the main difference lies in the number of tracks. The ½-inch tape cartridge has 18 tracks, as opposed to 9 for most mag tape reels. Like the 9-track mag tape reel, the *18-track tape cartridge* stores data using parallel representation; however, it stacks two bytes of data across the width of the tape. This enables more bytes of data to be stored per linear length of tape. Both ½-inch tapes block records for processing.

The ¼-Inch Tape Cartridge   In the past the simplicity and lower cost of magnetic tape processing often made it preferable to magnetic

FIGURE 6–5   Customer Records Blocked Three (top) and Unblocked (bottom)

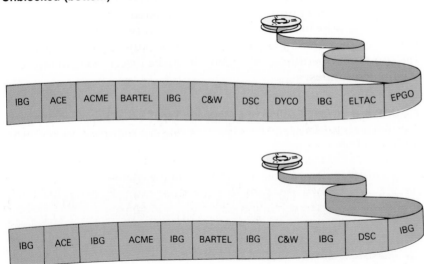

This is one of 10 aisles in a large magnetic tape library. The entire library is secured in a fireproof vault to protect the data stored on the tapes from theft and environmental disasters.

disk processing. This is no longer true, and today magnetic tape is used primarily for backup. During backup or recovery runs, backup tapes are processed continuously from beginning to end. Since there is seldom a need for selective access of records from magnetic tape, there is no reason to start and stop the tapes.

Most ¼-inch tape cartridges record data in a continuous stream, thereby eliminating the need for the start/stop operation of traditional tape drives. Drives for ¼-inch tape cartridges, often called **streamer tape drives**, store data in a **serpentine** manner (Figure 6–6). That is, data are recorded serially in tracks, as they are on mag disks. A data cartridge can have from four to 15 tracks, depending on the tape drive. The read/write head reads or writes data to one, two, or four tracks at a time. Figure 6–6 illustrates how data are written two tracks at a time. Data are written serially on the top two tracks for the entire length of the tape or until the data are exhausted. The tape is reversed, the read/write head is positioned over the next two tracks, and writing continues in a similar manner. If more backup capacity is needed, the computer operator is informed. He or she inserts a clean tape and writing continues.

FIGURE 6–6 Cross-Section of a Magnetic Tape: Serial Representation
Data are recorded serially on this eight-track tape in a serpentine manner, two tracks at a time.

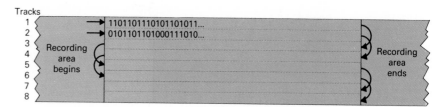

An alternative to disk and tape storage is the mass storage device. Mass storage devices are used when on-line access is required for very large data bases. A half-trillion characters of data can be stored in this mass storage device. Inside, data cartridges are retrieved from honeycomblike storage bins and loaded to the read/write station for processing. A modern disk pack can store about 2.5 billion characters of data, but the access time, about 16 milliseconds, is much faster. As the density of magnetic disks increases, look for the relatively slow mass storage devices to be replaced by magnetic disks.

Having no start/stop mechanisms, streamer tape drives can store data much more efficiently than the traditional tape drives that stop, then start the tape's movement over the read/write head at each IBG. Because streamer tape drives store IBGs on the fly (without stopping), an IBG occupies only 1/100 inch, as compared to over $\frac{1}{2}$ inch for start/stop tape drives. Streamer tape drives use that "extra" $\frac{1}{2}$ inch to store as many as 10,000 more characters of data. Streamer tape drives use 97% of the tape for data storage, whereas traditional start/stop tapes use only 35% to 70%, depending on the blocking factors.

Memory Bits

CHARACTERISTICS OF MAGNETIC TAPE

	$\frac{1}{2}''$ Reel	$\frac{1}{2}''$ Cartridge	$\frac{1}{4}''$ Cartridge
Tracks	9	18	4 to 15
Type access	Sequential	Sequential	Sequential
Data representation	Parallel	Parallel	Serial
Storage scheme	IBG separation	IBG separation	Serpentine

6–5 Optical Laser Disks: High-Density Storage

Some industry analysts have predicted that **optical laser disk** technology, now in its infant stage of development, may eventually make magnetic disk and tape storage obsolete. With this technology, the

On the Street

Ellen Strathy
Salon Owner

Have you ever shied away from trying a funky new hairstyle in a fashion magazine because you weren't sure how it would look on you? This is not an uncommon fear. Rather than have customers leave their shops in tears after changing to a radical new look, many salon owners are opting for *New Image Salon System*, a user-friendly computer, camera, and interactive video display. Developed by Los Angeles salon owner Kirk LaMar and physicist/computer-graphics expert John Halloran, it allows prospective clients to try different hairstyles and colors before any locks are snipped or dyes cast.

Based on the idea that it's easier to decide on a new look if you actually can see yourself in it, the *New Image Salon System* combines computer graphics and color videos to help bridge the gap between the client's fantasies and reality. (After all, you wouldn't buy a new outfit without first trying it on, or put a downpayment on a new car without first going for a test drive!)

Ellen Strathy, owner of Designing Image, read about this revolutionary system in magazines and saw one in use at a trade show. She was very impressed by is capabilities and decided to purchase one of the models for her shop. "It really helps when someone wants to do something extreme Ike cut off waist-length hair or become a platinum blonde. Instead of playing guessing games, the client actually can see what it will look like before making the commitment. It certainly saves a lot of tears. And, as it turns out, many do wind up making the change!"

Here's how it works: The stylist takes a "before" photo of the client, and stores it in the computer's memory. Together they choose from among the hundreds of hairstyle possibilites also on hand in the computer's memory. The stylist then superimposes the selected styles over the client's head on the videoscreen and uses a light pen to blend in the hairline and facial shape, and then contour and restyle if necessary. For a modest fee, the client can take home up to four computer-generated pictures to show family and friends before deciding to take the plunge.

But hairstyles aren't all the computer can show you. It also has the capability of performing makeovers and showing the results of cosmetic surgery. And it's not just for women. A bald man can see what he'd look like with a full head of hair!

So the next time you get the urge to try a new look, check with your local salon first. A picture truly can be worth a thousand words!

read/write head of magnetic storage is replaced by two lasers. One laser beam writes to the recording surface by scoring microscopic pits in the disk, and another laser reads the data from the light-sensitive recording surface. A light beam is easily deflected to the desired area of the optical disk, so an access arm is not needed.

Optical laser disks are becoming a very inviting option for users.

They are less sensitive to environmental fluctuations and they provide more direct-access storage at a cost that is much less per megabyte of storage than the magnetic disk alternative. Optical laser disk technology is still emerging and has yet to stabilize; however, at present, there are three main categories of optical laser disks. They are *CD-ROM*, *WORM disk*, and *magneto-optical disk*.

CD-ROM

Introduced in 1980, the extraordinarily successful CD, or compact disk, is an optical laser disk designed to enhance the reproduction of recorded music. To make a CD recording, the analog sounds of music are translated to their digital equivalents and stored on a 4.72-inch optical laser disk. Seventy-four minutes of music can be represented in digital format with 2 billion digital bits. With its tremendous storage potential, computer-industry entrepreneurs immediately recognized the potential of an optical laser disk technology. In effect, anything that can be digitized can be stored on an optical laser disk: data, text, voice, still pictures, music, graphics, and video.

CD-ROM (pronounced *cee-dee-rom*) is a spinoff of audio CD technology. CD-ROM stands for *compact disk–read only memory*. The name implies its application. CD-ROM disks, like long-playing record albums, are "pressed" at the factory and distributed with their prerecorded contents (for example, the complete works of Shakespeare or the first 30 minutes of *Gone With the Wind*). Once inserted in the disk drive, the text, video images, and so on, can be read into primary

We may be approaching the technological limits of magnetic data storage. When this happens, sophisticated optics and lasers (light amplification by stimulated emission of radiation) may help to take up the slack. A single CD-ROM disk can hold the equivalent of 13,000 images, 250,000 pages of text, or 1500 floppy disks. CD-ROM disks can be used with personal computers, minis, or mainframes because the manufacturing standard ensures that all CD-ROM readers will be compatible with all CD-ROM disks.

storage for processing or display; however, the data on the disk are fixed and cannot be altered. This is, of course, in contrast with the read/write capability of magnetic disks.

The tremendous amount of low-cost direct-access storage made possible by optical laser disks has opened the door to many applications. The capacity of a single CD-ROM is over 550Mb. To put this into perspective, the words in every book ever written could be stored on a hypothetical CD-ROM that is 7 feet in diameter. Currently, most of the hundred or so commercially produced CD-ROM disks contain reference material. A sampling of these disks follows: *The Groliers Electronic Encyclopedia*; *The Oxford English Dictionary*; *The Daily Oklahoman* (1981–86); the 1980 U.S. Census (county level); maps at the national, state, regional, and metro levels; a world history tutorial; and scientific writings for the Apple Macintosh. The cost of commercially produced CD-ROMs varies considerably, from as little as $50 to several thousand dollars.

WORM Disks

Write once, read many, or **WORM**, optical laser disks are used by end user companies to store their own, proprietary, information. Once the data have been written to the medium, they can be only read, not updated or changed.

WORM disks are a feasible alternative to magnetic tape for archival storage. For example, a company might wish to keep a permanent record of all financial transactions during the last year. Another popular application of WORM disks is in information systems that require the merging of text and images that do not change for a period of time. A good example is an electronic retail "catalog." A customer can peruse a retailer's electronic catalog on a VDT, or perhaps a PC, and see the item while reading about it. With a few keystrokes the customer can order the item as well. The Library of Congress is using WORM technology to alleviate a serious shelf-space problem.

Magneto-Optical Disk

A new technology called **magneto-optical disk** offers promise that optical laser disks will become commercially viable as a read-and-write storage technology. The $5\frac{1}{4}$-inch disks can store up to 1000Mb. However, the technology must be improved before they experience widespread acceptance. At present, magneto-optical disks are too expensive and do not offer anywhere close to the kind of reliability that users have come to expect with magnetic media. In addition, the access times are relatively slow, about that of a low-end Winchester disk.

As optical laser disk technology matures to reliable, cost-effective read/write operation, it may eventually dominate secondary storage in the future as magnetic disk and tape do today.

The Doomsday Program, a project of the British Broadcasting Corporation, uses a CD-ROM system to present a demographic profile of the United Kingdom. Fifty thousand photos, enough printed pages of text to stretch 50 miles, 24,000 maps, and millions of statistics are spread over two optical laser disks.

6–6 What's Next in Data Storage?

The growth in the number of on-line systems has established a need for devices that will permit the storage of more data that can be retrieved more quickly. Today the trade-off is between *speed of access* and *volume of storage*. Data access rates are thousands of times faster with primary storage, but the cost of state-of-the-art primary storage is prohibitive for high-volume storage.

We can expect at least one more leap in magnetic disk technology before it makes way for another technology, such as optical laser disks. The new magnetic disk technology will probably permit data to be stored vertically, or perpendicular to the disk-face surface, thereby increasing the density tenfold. Once read/write optical laser disks are perfected, look for the use of these high-density disks to soar.

Eventually a solid-state primary storage technology will be invented that will permit cost-effective temporary *and* permanent storage of data and programs, thus eliminating the need for rotating memory such as magnetic and optical laser disks. When this happens, primary and secondary storage will be one and the same. However, don't hold your breath. This may not happen until the end of the 1990s.

Summary Outline and Important Terms

6–1 SECONDARY STORAGE: PERMANENT DATA STORAGE. Data and programs are stored on **secondary**, or **auxiliary**, **storage** for permanent storage. **Magnetic disk drives** and

magnetic tape drives are the state of the art for both on-line and off-line storage. **Optical laser disk** technology is emerging as an alternative to magnetic disks and magnetic tapes.

6–2 SEQUENTIAL AND DIRECT ACCESS: NEW TERMS FOR OLD CONCEPTS.   Data are stored sequentially on magnetic tape; they are stored randomly on magnetic disks. **Sequential access** requires that the file be searched record by record until the desired record is found. **Random access** enables the desired record to be retrieved directly from its storage location.

6–3 MAGNETIC DISKS: ROTATING STORAGE MEDIA.   The different types of **interchangeable magnetic disks** are the **microdisk**, the **diskette**, the **disk cartridge**, and the **disk pack**. The trend is away from interchangeable disks to fixed disks.

Magnetic disk drives provide the computer system with direct-access and **random-processing** capabilities. Magnetic disks also support **sequential processing**. Data are stored via **serial representation** on each recording surface by **tracks**. Each record stored on a disk is assigned a **disk address** that designates the physical location of the record. An **access arm**, with **read/write heads** for each recording surface, is moved to the appropriate track to retrieve a record.

The two types of disk organization are **sector organization** and **cylinder organization**. In sector organization, the recording surface is divided into pie-shaped **sectors**, and each sector is assigned a number. In cylinder organization, a particular **cylinder** number refers to every track with the same number on all recording surfaces. To read or write a record, the access arms are moved, under program control, to the appropriate cylinder.

Interchangeable magnetic disks can be removed from the drive and stored **off-line**; **fixed disks** are permanently installed in the drive. When spinning in the drive, the disks are said to be **on-line**.

In the microcomputer environment, the two most popular types of interchangeable magnetic disks are the **diskette** (also called a **flexible disk**, or a **floppy disk**) and the **microdisk** (also called a **microfloppy**). The microcomputer hard disk is called the **Winchester disk**. In the mainframe environment, the most popular interchangeable disk storage media are the **disk cartridge** and the **disk pack**.

The **access time** for a magnetic disk is the sum of the seek time, the rotational delay time, and the transmission time.

6–4 MAGNETIC TAPE: RIBBONS OF DATA.   A thin polyester tape is spun on a **reel** or encased in a **cartridge**. This magnetic tape is loaded onto a tape drive, where data are read or written as the tape is passed under a read/write head. The physical nature of the magnetic tape results in data being stored and accessed sequentially. Data are stored using **parallel representation**, and they are **blocked** to minimize the start/stop movement of the tape. The standard nine-track 2400-foot tape reel stores data at a **density** of 6250 **bytes per inch** (**bpi**). Magnetic tape density and its speed over the read/write head combine to determine the **transfer rate**.

The operation of the $\frac{1}{2}$-inch **data cartridge** (tape cartridge) is more like that of the $\frac{1}{2}$-inch mag tape reel than the $\frac{1}{4}$-inch tape cartridge. Most $\frac{1}{4}$-inch tape cartridges record data in a continuous stream, eliminating the need for the start/stop operation of traditional tape drives. These cartridges use **streamer tape drives**, which store data in a **serpentine** manner.

6–5 OPTICAL LASER DISKS: HIGH-DENSITY STORAGE. **Optical laser disk** storage, now in its infant stage of development, has the capability to store vast amounts of data. The three main categories of optical laser disks are **CD-ROM**, **WORM**, and **magneto-optical**. Most of the commercially produced read-only CD-ROM disks contain reference material. The write once, read many (WORM) optical laser disks are used by end user companies to store their own, proprietary, information. The new magneto-optical disk offers promise that optical laser disks will become commercially viable as a read-and-write storage technology.

6–6 WHAT'S NEXT IN DATA STORAGE? The trade-off in data storage is between speed of access and volume of storage. Disk data-storage technology will continue to improve in the foreseeable future, but eventually disk technology will give way to solid-state high-volume data storage.

Review Exercises

Concepts

1. What are other names for flexible disks? Auxiliary storage? Direct processing?
2. Optical laser disks are a spinoff from what technology?
3. What is the purpose of the interblock gap?
4. What information is contained on a magnetic-tape header label?
5. How many megabytes does it take to make a gigabyte?
6. A program issues a "read" command for data to be retrieved from a magnetic tape. Describe the resulting movement of the data.
7. Use the initials of your name and the ASCII encoding system to contrast graphically parallel and serial data representation.
8. A company's employee master file contains 120,000 employee records. Each record is 1800 bytes in length. How many 2400-foot, 6250-bpi magnetic tapes (interblock gap = 0.6 inch) will

be required to store the file? Assume records are blocked five. Next, assume records are unblocked and perform the same calculations.

9. A disk pack has 20 recording surfaces and 400 cylinders. If a track can store 10,000 bytes of data, how much data can be stored on eight such disk packs?

10. What are the three main categories of optical laser disks?

11. What is the nickname of the hard disk used with microcomputers?

12. What are the most popular interchangeable disk storage media in the mainframe environment?

Discussion

13. If increasing the blocking factor for a magnetic tape file improves tape utilization, why not eliminate all IBGs and put all the records in one big block? Explain.

14. A floppy disk does not move until a read or write command is issued. Once it is issued, the floppy begins to spin. It stops spinning after the command is executed. Why is a disk pack not set in motion in the same manner? Why is a floppy not made to spin continuously?

15. Every Friday night a company makes backup copies of all master files and programs. Why is this necessary? The company has both tape and disk drives. What storage medium would you suggest for the backup? Why?

16. Describe the potential impact of optical laser disk technology on public and university libraries. On home libraries.

Self-Test (by section)

6–1 Data are retrieved from temporary auxiliary storage and stored permanently in RAM. (T/F)

6–2 Magnetic disks have both _____ and _____ access capabilities.

6–3 **a.** In a disk drive, the read/write heads are mounted on an access arm. (T/F)

b. Fixed disks cannot be removed and stored off-line. (T/F)

c. The diskette is _____ inches in diameter, and the microfloppy is _____ inches in diameter.

d. What percent of the data on a magnetic disk is made available to the system with each complete revolution of the disk: (a) 10%, (b) 50%, or (c) 100%?

e. The _____ denotes the physical location of data or a program on a magnetic disk.

6–4 **a.** Tape density is based on the linear distance between IBGs. (T/F)

    b. The ½-inch tape cartridge has more in common with the magnetic tape reel than it does with the ¼-inch tape cartridge. (T/F)

    c. Streamer tape drives store data in a _____ manner.

6–5 **a.** _____ technology permits on-line direct access of both still pictures and video.

    b. All optical laser disk technology is read-only. (T/F)

6–6 Rotating data storage devices will be obsolete by 1990. (T/F)

Self-test answers. **6–1** F. **6–2** direct, or random; sequential. **6–3** (a) T; (b) T; (c) 5¼, 3½; (d) c; (e) disk address. **6–4** (a) F; (b) T; (c) serpentine. **6–5** (a) Optical laser disk; (b) F. **6–6** F.

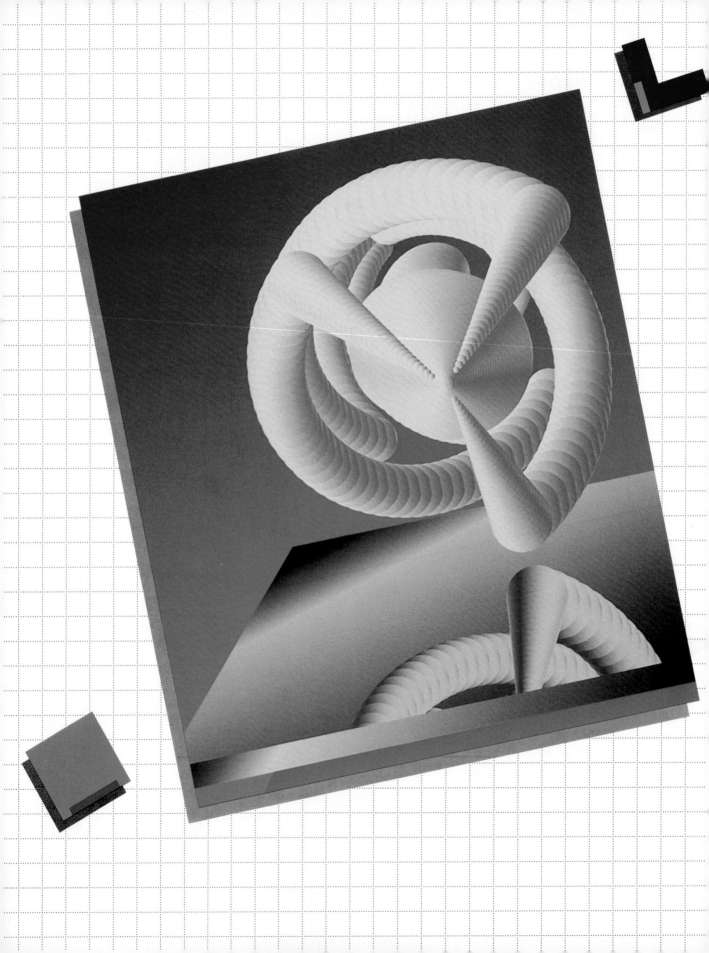

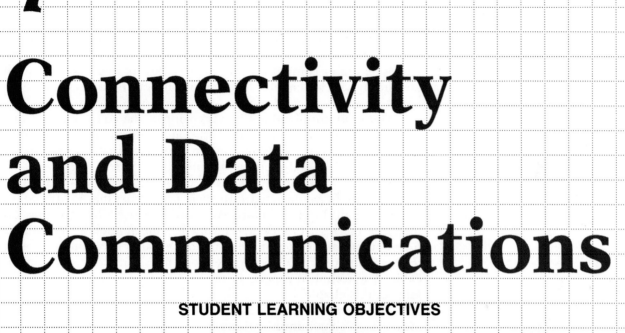

7

Connectivity and Data Communications

STUDENT LEARNING OBJECTIVES

- To describe the concept of connectivity and the challenges associated with its implementation.
- To demonstrate an understanding of data communications terminology and applications.
- To detail the function and operation of data communications hardware.
- To describe the alternatives for and sources of data transmission services.
- To illustrate the various types of computer networks.

In the 1960s computers numbered in the tens of thousands. Today they number in the tens of millions. Information is everywhere. Making this information more accessible to a greater number of people is the challenge of the next decade. To do this, the business and computer communities are seeking ways to interface, or connect, a diverse set of hardware, software, and data bases. **Connectivity**, as it is called, is necessary to facilitate the electronic communication between companies, end user computing, and the free flow of information within an enterprise. This chapter focuses on connectivity concepts and the base technology of connectivity—data communications.

Data communications is, very simply, the collection and distribution of the electronic representation of information from and to remote facilities. The information can appear in a variety of formats: data, text, voice, still pictures, graphics, and video. Prior to transmission, the raw information must be digitized. (For example, data and text might be encoded into their corresponding ASCII codes.) Ultimately, all forms of information are sent over the transmission media as a series of binary bits (1s and 0s). Information is transmitted from computers to terminals and other computers over land, through the air, and under the sea via telephone lines, satellites, and coaxial cable. The technical aspects of data communications are discussed later in this chapter.

Several other terms describe the general area of data communications. **Telecommunications** encompasses not only data communications but any type of remote communication, such as the transmission of a television signal. **Teleprocessing**, or **TP**, is the combination of *tele*communications and data *processing*; it is often used interchangeably with the term *data communications*. The inte-

This office is one of 15 regional customer support centers, each of which is part of a computer network. The terminals at this office are linked to a local minicomputer that is connected via a high-speed communications line to the company's headquarters office in Atlanta, Georgia. The regional minis are also used for local processing.

gration of computer systems, terminals, and communication links is referred to as a **computer network**.

Through the mid-1960s, a company's computing hardware was located in a single room called the machine room. The only people who had direct access to the computer were those who worked in the machine room. Since that time, microcomputers, terminals, and data communications have made it possible to move hardware and information systems "closer to the source"—to the people who use them. Before long, terminals will be as much a part of our work environment as desks and telephones are now.

7–2 The Beginning of an Era: Cooperative Computing

Intracompany Networking

This is the era of **cooperative computing**. Information is the password to success in today's business environment. To obtain meaningful, accurate, and timely information, businesses have decided that they must cooperate internally and externally to take full advantage of what is available. To promote internal cooperation, they are moving in the direction of *intracompany networking* (see Figure 7–1). For example, information maintained in the personnel department is made readily accessible to people throughout the company on a *need-to-know* basis. The same is true of information maintained by purchasing, engineering, or any other department. At the individual level, managers or knowledge workers create microcomputer-based systems and data bases to help them in the performance of their jobs. When these personalized systems and data bases have the potential

FIGURE 7–1 Intracompany and Intercompany Networking

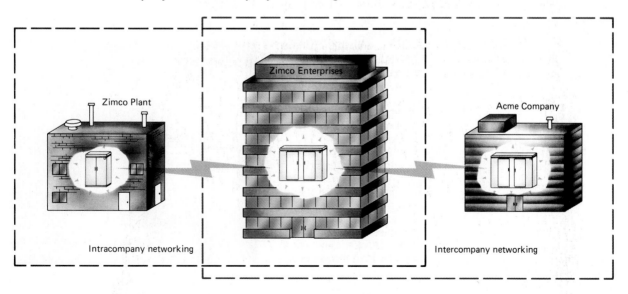

of benefiting other people in the company, they can be made a part of the company's computer network to permit the sharing of these information resources.

Intercompany Networking

Companies have recognized that they must cooperate with one another to compete effectively in a world market. They are doing this via *intercompany networking* (Figure 7–1) or, more specifically, **electronic data interchange** (**EDI**). EDI uses computers and data communications to transmit data electronically between companies. Invoices, orders, and many other intercompany transactions, including the exchange of information, can be transmitted from the computer of one company to the computer of another. For example, at General Foods, 50% of all shipments result from computer-to-computer order processing—customers submit their orders to General Foods via EDI. Figure 7–2 contrasts the traditional interaction between a customer and supplier company with interactions via EDI. EDI is a strategic advantage that some companies have over their competitors. It reduces paper processing costs and delays, it reduces errors and correction costs, it minimizes receivables and inventory disputes, and it improves relations between trading partners.

Executives are no longer debating whether or not to implement EDI; they are more concerned about the speed at which it can be put to work in their companies. Essentially, they have two choices. They can elect to create the hardware- and software-based EDI system in-house, or they can use a **third-party provider** of EDI services. A third-party provider is an intermediary who helps facilitate EDI between trading partners with incompatible hardware and software. By far the fastest way to take advantage of EDI is to contract for the services of a third-party provider. However, in-house development of EDI capabilities does not involve the expense of an intermediary, even though it may take longer.

Electronic data interchange (EDI), a technology that permits a computer at one company to interface with one at another company, is causing radical changes in traditional business practices. By establishing a communications link with a supplier's computer system, this inventory manager can determine the status of an order in seconds. Before EDI, the manager would submit the request by telephone and wait hours, even days, for a response from the supplier.

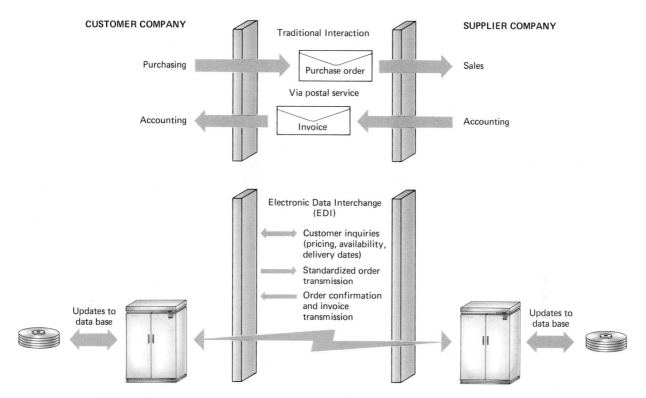

FIGURE 7–2   Interactions Between Customer and Supplier

In the figure, the traditional interaction between a customer company and a supplier company is contrasted with similar interactions via electronic data interchange.

External Computing Support

The phenomenal growth of the use of micros in the home is causing companies to expand their MIS capabilities to permit linkages with home and portable PCs. This form of cooperative computing increases system efficiency while lowering costs. For example, in over 100 banks, services have been extended to home micro owners in the form of home banking systems. Subscribers use their personal computers as terminals linked to the bank's mainframe computer system to pay bills, transfer funds, and inquire about account status.

The Internal Revenue Service (IRS) now permits tax returns to be filed from the tax preparer's home PC. The on-line system performs all the necessary table searches and computations, and it even cross-checks the accuracy and consistency of the input data. For the IRS, no further data entry or personal assistance is required. Brokerage firms now permit customers to access up-to-the-minute stock market quotations and to issue buy/sell orders directly through their personal computers. Several supermarkets are experimenting with "electronic shopping." In the 1990s, virtually every type of industry will provide the facility for external links to their mainframe computer systems.

BEAT THE TRAFFIC BY TELECOMMUTING

Just about every department in a business organization has at least one or more portable microcomputers. Most of these micros fold up to about the size of an attaché case and can be easily carried between the office and home. Some departments have the ultimate in computer portability—an IBM PC-compatible pocket PC that weighs less than a pound. Managers often take a portable micro home with them to take advantage of working in a different (often quieter) environment. These portable micros can be used as stand-alone computer systems, or they can serve as terminals linked to the company's mainframe computer system. The latter is known as *telecommuting*.

The ubiquitous microcomputer has made telecommuting very popular. Many people need a few hours or perhaps a day of uninterrupted time to accomplish a task that does not require direct personal interaction. These people are starting to telecommute to work. A recent survey indicated that about 75% of the workforce would elect to telecommute if given the the option to do so.

Everyone has a different reason for wanting to telecommute. A vice president of accounting and finance telecommutes to prepare the quarterly financial statements. He says: "All the information I need is at my fingertips. I finish in one day at home what used to take me a week at the office." The president of the same company stated emphatically: "I got sick and tired of spending nights up in my office. By telecommuting, at least I'm within earshot of my wife and kids. Also, I like to get into more comfortable clothes." At the same company, the director of MIS describes one of her many telecommuting applications: "Every Monday evening I write out the agenda for my Tuesday morning staff meeting. I then send a summary of the agenda via electronic mail to my managers so they will see it first thing Tuesday morning when they log in." Of course, there are

This programmer telecommutes via her PC and modem (under the telephone) at least one day a week.

differing opinions. A vice president of sales and marketing at the same company says: "I'm more productive working at the office, where household and family distractions fade into the distance."

Telecommuting may never catch on as an alternative to working in the office, but for some applications it has proven to be a boon to productivity. As the president of another company observed: "With the elimination of travel time, coffee breaks, idle conversations, and numerous office distractions, we have found that conscientious, self-motivated employees can be more productive at home when working on certain projects." The management at this company encourages workers to select their telecommuting activities carefully. Telecommuting is fine for interaction with the computer and the data base, but for interaction with other people, it has its limitations. Telecommuting does not permit the "pressing of the flesh" and the transmittal of the nonverbal cues that are so essential to personal interaction.

7–3 Connectivity: Linking Hardware, Software, and Data Bases

Connectivity refers to the degree to which hardware devices can be linked functionally to one another. Some people expand the scope of connectivity to include software and data bases. It has become such an important consideration that virtually all future decisions involving hardware, software, and data base management must be evaluated with respect to connectivity.

To get the most out of an information resource, it must be shared. To do this, the company must strive toward full connectivity.

- Connectivity means that a marketing manager can use a microcomputer to access information from a data base in the finance department's minicomputer.
- Connectivity means that a network of microcomputers can route output to the same laser printer.
- Connectivity means that a manufacturing company's mainframe computer can communicate with the mainframe computers of its suppliers.

Technologically, it is relatively easy to make an electronic connection between two computer systems, but realizing any meaningful transfer of information from the connection is another matter. Most computer systems and database software packages were not designed for efficient resource sharing by different types of computer systems and data bases. *Incompatible* computer systems differ, often dramatically, in architecture (basic design) and in the manner in which they store data. In essence, they do not speak the same language.

Connectivity is implemented in degrees. To achieve almost any level of connectivity, technical specialists must juggle communication protocols (rules), official and de facto standards, different approaches to data base design, different computer system architectures, and user information requirements. Each of these considerations poses formidable technological hurdles.

The ideal implementation of intracompany connectivity would be to make all corporate computer and information resources accessible from each worker's terminal. This ideal is referred to as **total connectivity**. Realistically, industry analysts are predicting that total connectivity is still a decade or more away. Nevertheless, almost every company has made a commitment to strive for a higher level of connectivity.

7–4 Data Communications Hardware

Data communications hardware is used to transmit data in a computer network between terminals and computers, and between computers. This hardware includes modems, down-line processors, front-end processors, and PBXs. The integration of these devices (except the PBX) with terminals and computer systems is illustrated in Figure 7–3 and discussed in the paragraphs that follow.

The Modem

If you have a micro, you have the capability to establish a communications link between your microcomputer and any remote computer system in the world. However, to do this you must have ready access

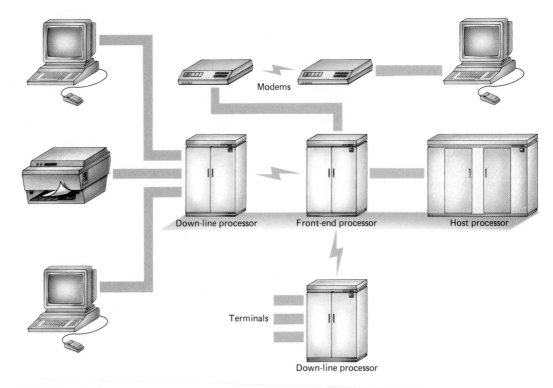

FIGURE 7–3 Hardware Components in Data Communications
Devices that handle the movement of data in a computer network are the modem, down-line processor, front-end processor, and host processor.

to a telephone line and your micro must be equipped with a *modem*. Telephone lines were designed for voice communication, not data communication. The **modem** (*mo*dulator-*dem*odulator) converts terminal-to-computer and micro-to-computer electrical *digital* signals to *analog* signals so that the data can be transmitted over telephone lines (see Figure 7–4). The digital electrical signals are modulated to make sounds similar to those you hear on a touch-tone telephone. Upon reaching their destination, these analog signals are demodulated by

FIGURE 7–4 The Modulation/Demodulation Process
Electrical digital signals are modulated to analog signals for transmission over telephone lines and then demodulated for processing at the destination.

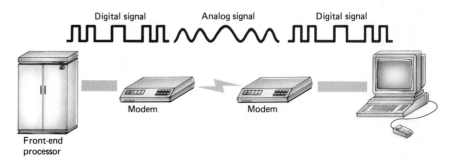

another modem to computer-compatible electrical signals for processing. The process is reversed for computer-to-terminal or computer-to-micro communication. A modem is always required when you dial up the computer on a telephone line. The modulation-demodulation process is not needed for transmission media other than telephone lines, so those media do not require modems.

Internal and External Modems   There are two types of modems for micros and terminals: *internal* and *external*. Most micros and terminals have internal modems; that is, the modem is on an optional add-on circuit board that is simply plugged into an empty expansion slot in the micro's processor unit or the terminal's housing. The external modem is a separate component, as illustrated in Figure 7–4, and is connected via an RS-232C serial interface port (see Chapter 3, "Microcomputers"). To make the connection with a telephone line and either type of modem, you simply plug the telephone line into the modem, just as you would when connecting the line to a telephone.

Smart Modems   Modems have varying degrees of "intelligence" due to embedded microprocessors. For instance, some modems can automatically dial up the computer (*auto-dial*), establish a link (*log on*), and even answer incoming calls from other computers (*auto-answer*). **Smart modems** have also made it possible to increase the rate at which data can be transmitted and received.

Acoustical Couplers   If you need a telephone hookup for voice conversations on the same telephone line used for data communication and do not want to disconnect the phone with each use, you can purchase a modem with an **acoustical coupler**. To make the connection, you mount the telephone handset directly on the acoustical coupler. Acoustical couplers are essential items for travelers who routinely make micro-mainframe connections from public telephones.

"I wish he'd use a modem like everyone else."

This advertising executive's portable computer is configured with an internal modem. He has only to establish a communications link via a telephone line to keep in touch with office activities and retrieve critical information wherever he travels.

The Down-Line Processor

The **down-line processor**, also called a **cluster controller**, is remote from the *host processor*. It collects data from a number of low-speed devices, such as terminals and serial printers. The down-line processor then transmits "concentrated" data over a single communications channel (see Figure 7–5).

The down-line processor, also called a **concentrator** or **multi-plexor**, is an economic necessity when several low-speed terminals are located at one remote site. One high-speed line connecting the down-line processor to the host is considerably less expensive than several low-speed lines connecting each terminal to the host. An airline reservations counter might have 10 terminals. Each terminal is connected to a common down-line processor, which in turn is connected to a central host computer. An airline might have one or several down-line processors at a given airport, depending on the volume of passenger traffic.

A microcomputer can be made to emulate the function of a down-line processor. This often occurs when a network of micros is linked to a mainframe computer.

The Front-End Processor

The terminal or computer sending a **message** is the *source*. The terminal or computer receiving the message is the *destination*. The **front-end processor** establishes the link between the source and destination in a process called **handshaking**.

FIGURE 7–5 "Concentrating" Data for Remote Transmission
The down-line processor "concentrates" the data from several low-speed devices for transmission over a single high-speed line. At the host site, the front-end processor separates the data for processing. Data received from a front-end processor are interpreted by the down-line processor and routed to the appropriate device.

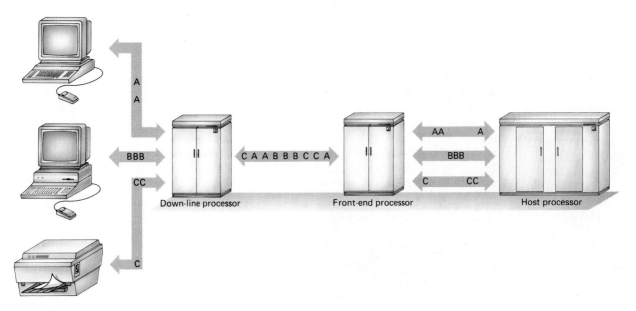

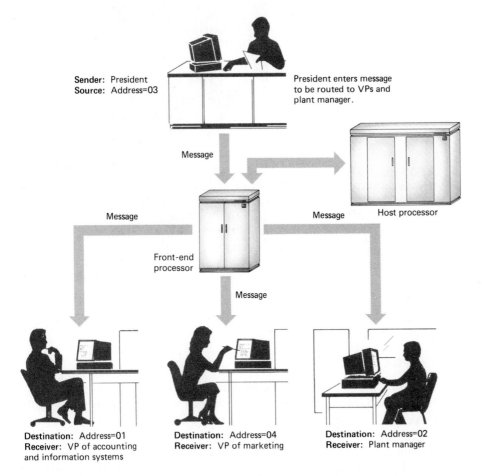

Sender: President
Source: Address=03

President enters message
to be routed to VPs and
plant manager.

Message

Message

Host processor

Front-end
processor

Message

Message

Destination: Address=01
Receiver: VP of accounting
and information systems

Destination: Address=04
Receiver: VP of marketing

Destination: Address=02
Receiver: Plant manager

FIGURE 7–6   Message Routing
In the illustration, the president sends a message to two vice presidents and the
plant manager. The front-end processor accepts the president's message for
processing and routes it to the appropriate addresses.

If you think of messages as mail to be delivered to various points
in a computer network, the front-end processor is the post office. Each
computer system and terminal is assigned an **address**. The front-end
processor uses these addresses to route messages to their destinations.
The content of a message could be a prompt to the user, a user inquiry,
a program instruction, an "electronic" memo, or any type of information that can be transmitted electronically, even the image of a
handwritten report. Figure 7–6 illustrates how a memo would be sent
from the president of a company to two vice presidents and the plant
manager. It is not uncommon for a front-end processor to control
communications between a dozen down-line processors and 100 or
more terminals.

The front-end processor relieves the host processor of communications-related tasks, such as message routing, parity checking, code
translation, editing, and cryptography (the encryption/decryption of
data). This processor specialization permits the host to operate more

A PBX connects computing devices for data communication in a manner similar to the way operators used to connect telephones for voice communication. However, with the modern voice and data PBX, it's all automatic.

efficiently and to devote more of its resources to processing applications programs.

The PBX

The old-time telephone **PBX** (private branch exchange) switchboard has evolved into a sophisticated device capable of switching not only voice but also digital electronic signals. The PBX is actually a computer that electronically connects computers and terminals much as telephone operators manually connected people on the old PBX switchboards. Approximately 70% of the traffic handled by a modern PBX is voice; the remainder consists of digital electronic signals.

As discussed earlier, there is definitely a trend toward making information systems more responsive to end users by "distributing" processing capabilities closer to the people who use them. Because of this trend, a single organization is likely to have at least one mainframe computer, several minis, and many micros and terminals. The PBX, serving as the hub of data activity, permits these computers and terminals to "talk" to one another. Figure 7–7 illustrates how several computer systems can be linked via a PBX.

7–5 The Data Communications Channel: Data Highways

Transmission Media

A **communications channel** is the facility by which electronic signals are transmitted between locations in a computer network. Data, text, and digitized images are transmitted as combinations of bits (0s and 1s). A *channel's capacity* is rated by the number of bits it can transmit per second. A regular telephone line can transmit up to 9600 **bits per**

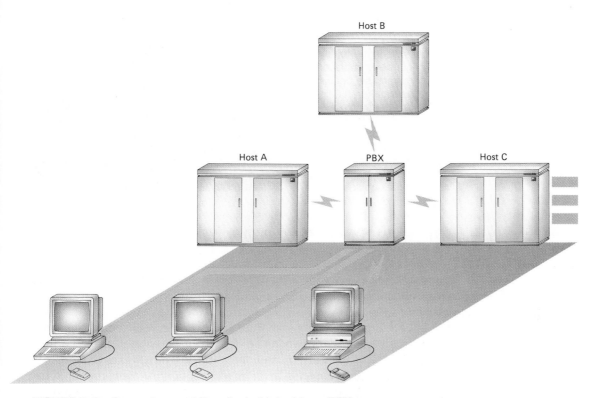

FIGURE 7–7   Computers and Terminals Linked by a PBX
Any two of the host computers or terminals can be linked together for data transmission by the PBX.

second (**bps**), or 9.6K bps (thousands of bits per second). Under normal circumstances, a 9.6K-bps line would fill the screen of a typical video monitor in one or two seconds.

In practice, the word **baud** is often used interchangeably with bits per second. In reality, they are quite different. Baud is a measure of the maximum number of electronic signals that can be transmitted via a communications channel. It is true that a 300-bps modem operates at 300 baud, but both 1200-bps and 2400-bps modems operate at 600 baud. A technical differentiation between baud and bits per second is beyond the scope of this book. Suffice it to say that when someone says *baud*, and he or she is talking about computer-based communications, that person probably means bits per second. The erroneous use of *baud* is so common that some software packages that facilitate data communication ask you to specify baud when they actually want bits per second.

Data rates of 1500K bps are available through common carriers, such as American Telephone & Telegraph (AT&T). The channel, also called a **line** or a **data link**, may comprise one or a combination of the transmission media discussed next.

Telephone Lines   The same transmission facilities we use for voice communication via telephones can also be used to transmit data. This

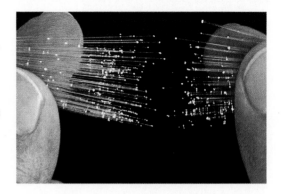

Copper wire in the telephone network is being replaced by the more versatile optical fiber. Laser-generated light pulses are transmitted through these ultra-thin glass fibers. A pair of optical fibers can simultaneously carry 1344 voice conversations and interactive data communications sessions.

capability is provided by communications companies throughout the country and the world.

Optical Fiber   Very thin transparent fibers have been developed that will eventually replace the copper wire traditionally used in the telephone system. These hairlike **optical fibers** carry data faster and are lighter and less expensive than their copper-wire counterparts.

The differences between the data transmission rates of copper wire and optical fiber are tremendous. In the time it takes to transmit a single page of Webster's *Unabridged Dictionary* over copper wire (about six seconds), the entire dictionary could be transmitted over a single optical fiber.

Another of the many advantages of optical fiber is its contribution to data security. It is much more difficult for a computer criminal to intercept a signal sent over optical fiber (via a beam of light) than it is over copper wire (an electrical signal).

Coaxial Cable   **Coaxial cable** contains electrical wire and is constructed to permit high-speed data transmission with a minimum of signal distortion. Coaxial cable is laid along the ocean floor for intercontinental voice and data transmission. It is also used to connect terminals and computers in a "local" area (from a few feet to a few miles).

Microwave   Communications channels do not have to be wires or fibers. Data can also be transmitted via microwave radio signals. Transmission of these signals is *line-of-sight*; that is, the radio signal travels in a direct line from one repeater station to the next until it reaches its destination. Because of the curvature of the earth, microwave repeater stations are placed on the tops of mountains and towers, usually about 30 miles apart.

Satellites have made it possible to overcome the line-of-sight problem. Satellites routinely are launched into orbit for the sole purpose of relaying data communications signals to and from earth stations. A satellite, which is essentially a repeater station, is launched and set in a **geosynchronous orbit** 22,300 miles above the earth. A geosynchronous orbit permits the communications satellite to main-

For intracity data communications, many companies are installing their own private microwave system. These miniature microwave stations provide an inexpensive alternative to the more costly coaxial cable systems.

tain a fixed position relative to the surface of the earth. Each satellite can receive and retransmit signals to slightly less than half of the earth's surface; therefore, three satellites are required to cover the earth effectively (see Figure 7–8). The big advantage of satellites is that data can be transmitted from one location to any number of other locations anywhere on (or near) our planet.

This communications satellite is being released from the space shuttle en route to a geosynchronous orbit 22,300 miles above the earth.

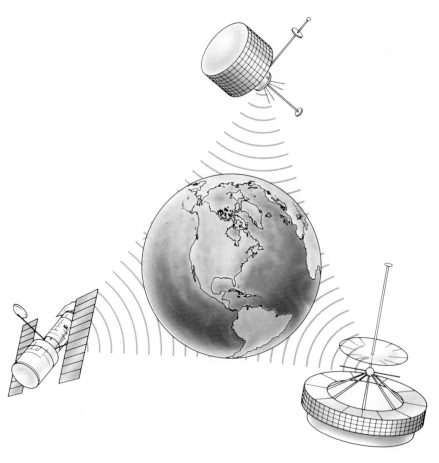

FIGURE 7–8   Satellite Data Transmission
Three satellites in geosynchronous orbit provide worldwide data transmission service.

Data Transmission in Practice

A communications channel from Computer A in Seattle, Washington, to Computer B in Orlando, Florida (see Figure 7–9), would usually consist of several different transmission media. The connection between Computer A and a terminal in the same building is probably coaxial cable. The Seattle company might use a communications com-

In satellite communications, data are first transmitted to an earth station, where giant antennae route signals to another earth station via a communications satellite. The signals are then transmitted to their destination over another type of communications channel.

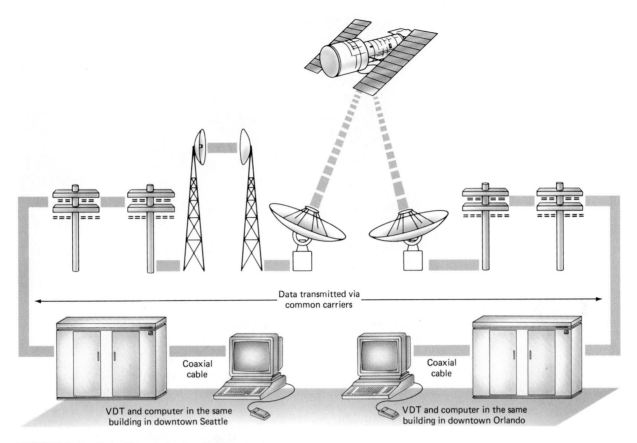

FIGURE 7–9 Data Transmission Path
It's more the rule than the exception that data are carried over several transmission media between source and destination.

pany such as AT&T to transmit the data. The company would then send the data through a combination of transmission facilities. These facilities might include copper wire, optical fiber, and microwave radio signals.

7–6 Data Transmission Services

Common Carriers

It is impractical, not to mention illegal, for companies to string their own coaxial cables between two locations, such as Philadelphia and New York City. It is also impractical for them to set their own satellites in orbit. Therefore, companies turn to **common carriers**, such as AT&T and Western Union, to provide communications channels. Communications common carriers, which are regulated by the Federal Communications Commission (FCC), offer two basic types of service: private lines and switched lines.

This common carrier's earth-station control console in New Jersey monitors video and data communications traffic between satellites and earth.

A **private line** (or **leased line**) provides a dedicated data communications channel between any two points in a computer network. The charge for a private line is based on channel capacity (bps) and distance (air miles).

A **switched line** (or **dial-up line**) is available strictly on a time-and-distance charge, similar to a long-distance telephone call. You make a connection by "dialing up" the computer; then a modem sends and receives data.

As a rule of thumb, a private line is the least expensive alternative if you expect to use the channel more than three hours a day and you do not need the flexibility to connect with several different computers.

Specialized Common Carriers

A **specialized common carrier**, such as a **value-added network (VAN)**, may or may not use the transmission facilities of a common carrier, but in each case it "adds value" to the transmission service. The value added over and above the standard services of the common carriers may include electronic mail, data encryption/decryption, access to commercial data bases, and code conversion for communication between incompatible computers. Not only do VANs such as Tymshares's Tymnet and GTE's Telenet offer expanded services but the basic communications service provided by the VAN may also be less expensive than the same service from a common carrier.

To illustrate how a VAN can offer the same or better service at a reduced rate, consider the following. The Ace Corporation wishes to lease a 9.6K bps private line between New York and Philadelphia from a common carrier. Ace is likely to use only 15% of the capacity

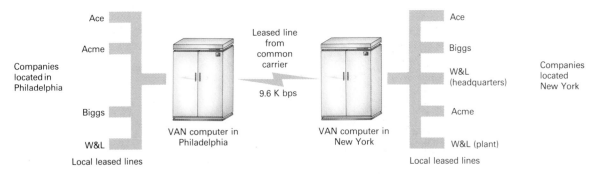

FIGURE 7–10 Part of a Value-Added Network (VAN)
A VAN uses transmission media more efficiently and therefore is able to offer transmission service at a reduced rate.

of the line. A VAN could lease the same line from the same common carrier (or use their own) and use the line to capacity by combining the New York/Philadelphia data transmission requirements of Ace Corporation with those of several other companies (see Figure 7–10). The VAN uses computers on each end of the line to collect the data and redistribute them to appropriate destinations. In effect, several corporations share the same line and its cost with little or no loss in performance.

7–7 Networks: Linking Computers and People

Network Topologies

Each time you use the telephone, you use the world's largest computer network—the telephone system. A telephone is an end point, or a **node**, connected to a network of computers that route your voice signals to any one of the 500 million telephones, or nodes, in the world. The node in a computer network can be a terminal or another computer. Computer networks are configured to meet the specific requirements of an organization. The basic computer **network topologies**—star, ring, and bus—are illustrated in Figure 7–11. A network topology is a description of the possible physical connections within a network. The topology is the configuration of the hardware and indicates which pairs of nodes are able to communicate.

The **star topology** involves a centralized host computer that is connected to a number of smaller computer systems. The smaller computer systems communicate with one another through the host and usually share the host computer's data base. Both the central computer and the distributed computer systems are connected to terminals (micros or video display terminals). Any terminal can communicate with any other terminal in the network. Banks usually have a large home-office computer system with a star network of mini-computer systems in the branch banks.

The **ring topology** involves computer systems that are approximately the same size, with no one computer system as the focal point

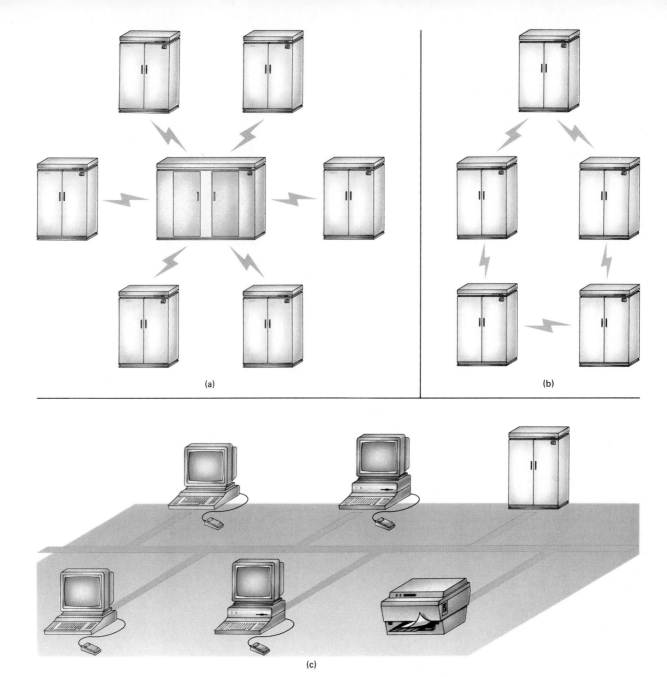

FIGURE 7–11   Network Topologies
(a) Star (b) ring (c) bus

of the network. When one system routes a message to another system, it is passed around the ring until it reaches its destination address.

The **bus topology** permits the connection of terminals, peripheral devices, and microcomputers along a central cable called a **transmission medium**. Devices can be easily added to or deleted from the network. Bus topologies are most appropriate when the devices linked are physically close to one another (see the discussion of local area networks that follows).

A pure form of any of these three topologies is seldom found in practice. Most computer networks are *hybrids*—combinations of topologies.

Three-Tier and Two-Tier Networks

The different types of networks are sometimes classified as **three-tier** or **two-tier networks**, referring to the number of layers of computers in the network. A three-tier network contains three layers of computers. At the top is the host mainframe that is linked to multiple minicomputers. Each mini is linked to multiple micros. The three-tier concept was the norm until the capabilities of micros began to approach that of the multiuser minis of the mid-1980s. The increased power of the microcomputer made three-tier networks redundant at the bottom two levels, thus prompting the concept of the two-tier network. A two-tier network has only two layers of computers, usually a mainframe computer that is linked directly to multiple minicomputers and/or microcomputers. The tier concept is most often associated with the star topology or a hybrid that is based on the star topology.

The Micro/Mainframe Link

Micros, initially designed for use by a single individual, have even greater potential when they can be linked with mainframe computers. To give micros this dual-function capability, vendors have developed the necessary hardware and software to enable some **micro/mainframe links**. There are three types of micro/mainframe links:

1. The microcomputer serves as a dumb terminal (that is, I/O only with no processing) linked to the mainframe.
2. Microcomputer users request that data be **downloaded** (mainframe-to-micro transmission of data) from the mainframe to their micros for processing. Upon completion of processing, user data may be **uploaded** from their microcomputers to the mainframe.
3. Both microcomputer and mainframe work together to process data and produce information.

Micro/mainframe links of the first two types are well within the state of the art, but achieving the third is more involved. The tremendous differences in the way computers and software are designed make complete integration of micro/mainframe activities difficult and, for some combinations of micros and mainframes, impossible.

Local Area Networks

A **local area network** (**LAN**), or **local net**, is a system of hardware, software, and communications channels that connects devices in close proximity, such as in a suite of offices. A local net permits the move-

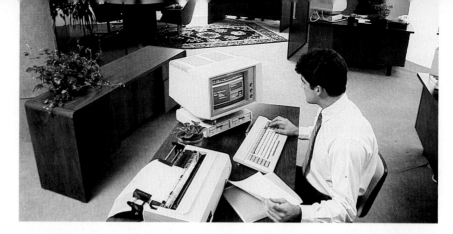

A local area network links microcomputers in this office so that managers and administrative staff can share hardware, software, and data base resources.

ment of data (including text, voice, and graphic images) between mainframe computers, personal computers, terminals, I/O devices, and PBXs. For example, your micro can be connected to another micro, to mainframes, and to shared resources, such as printers and disk storage. The distance separating devices in the local net may be a few feet to a few miles.

The unique feature of a local net is that a common carrier is not necessary for transmitting data between computers, terminals, and shared resources. Because of the proximity of devices in local nets, a company can install its own communications channels (such as co-axial cable or optical fiber).

Like computers, automobiles, and just about everything else, local nets can be built at various levels of sophistication. At the most basic level, they permit the interconnection of PCs in a department so that users can send messages to one another and share files and printers. The more sophisticated local nets permit the interconnection of mainframes, micros, and the gamut of peripheral devices throughout a large but geographically constrained area, such as a cluster of buildings.

In the near future you will be able to plug a terminal into a communications channel just as you would plug a telephone line into a telephone jack. This type of data communications capability is being installed in the new "smart" office buildings and even in some hotel rooms.

Local nets are often integrated with "long-haul" networks. For example, a bank will have home-office teller terminals linked to the central computer via a local net. But for long-haul data communication, the bank's branch offices must rely on common carriers.

7–8 Line Control: Rules for Data Transmission

Polling and Contention

When a terminal or a microcomputer is connected to a computer over a single communications channel, this is a **point-to-point connection**. When more than one terminal or micro is connected via a single communications channel, the channel is called a **multidrop line**. Terminals on a multidrop line must share the data communications channel. Because all terminals cannot use the same channel at once, line-control procedures are needed. The most common line-control procedures are **polling** and **contention**.

In polling, the front-end processor "polls" each terminal in rotation to determine whether a message is ready to be sent (see Figure 7–12). If a particular terminal has a message ready to be sent and the line is available, the front-end processor accepts the message and polls the next terminal.

Programmers can adjust the polling procedure so that some terminals are polled more often than others. For example, tellers in a bank are continuously interacting with the system. A loan officer, however, may average only two inquiries in an hour. In this case, the teller terminals might be polled four times for each poll of a loan officer's terminal.

In the contention line-control procedure, a terminal with a message to be sent automatically requests service from the host processor. A request might result in a "line busy" signal, in which case the terminal waits a fraction of a second and tries again, and again, until the line is free. Upon assuming control of the line, the terminal sends the message and then relinquishes control of the line to another terminal.

FIGURE 7–12 The Polling Process
Each terminal is polled in rotation to determine if a message is ready to be sent.

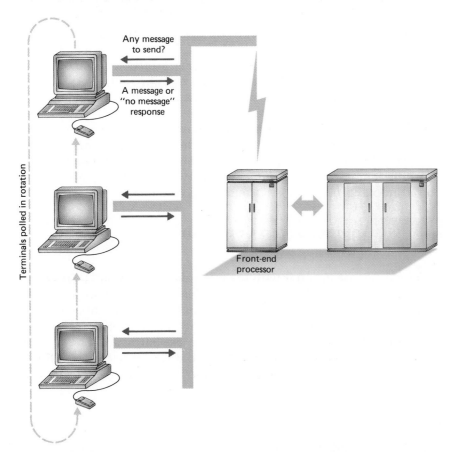

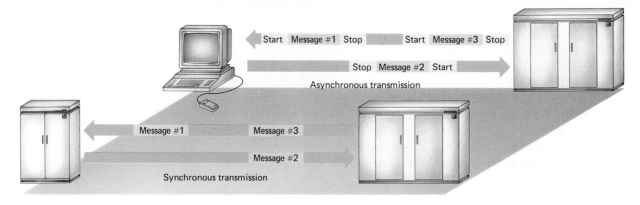

FIGURE 7–13 Asynchronous and Synchronous Transmission of Data
Asynchronous data transmission takes place at irregular intervals. Synchronous data transmission requires timed synchronization.

Communications Protocols

Communications protocols are rules established to govern the way data are transmitted in a computer network. A number of different protocols are in common use. For example, X12 is the standard for electronic data interchange (EDI); X.25 is used for packet switching; X.75 is used for interconnections between networks of different countries; XON/XOFF is the de facto standard for microcomputer data communications; and XMODEM is used for uploading and downloading files. Protocols fall into two general classifications, **asynchronous** and **synchronous** (see Figure 7–13).

In asynchronous data transmission, data are transferred at irregular intervals on an as-needed basis. *Start/stop bits* are appended to the beginning and end of each message. The start/stop bits signal the receiving terminal/computer at the beginning and end of the message. A message could be a single character or a short string of characters, depending on the communications protocol. Asynchronous transmission, sometimes called *start/stop transmission*, is best suited for data communication involving low-speed I/O devices, such as terminals and serial printers.

In synchronous transmission, the source and destination operate in timed synchronization to enable high-speed data transmission. Start/stop bits are not required in synchronous transmission. Data transmission between computers and between down-line processors and front-end processors is normally synchronous.

7–9 Approaches to Connectivity: Gateways and Bridges

Now that you are familiar with the technologies associated with data communications and have an appreciation of the technological challenges of connectivity, it is time to discuss approaches to achieving degrees of hardware connectivity. Perhaps the most effective way to overcome compatibility problems and achieve hardware connectivity within the confines of an organization is to stay with one vendor. Even then, purchases must be limited to those hardware devices that are compatible. This approach is feasible for very small companies and start-up companies. But for larger companies, this straightforward solution is not an option. These companies already use many different vendors, and the expense of a total conversion is prohibitive.

Companies with established operating environments use gateway and bridge technologies to achieve connectivity. **Gateways** help alleviate the problems of linking incompatible micros, minis, and mainframes. A gateway is a combination of hardware and software that permits networks using different communications protocols to "talk" to one another. The use of a gateway normally implies a requirement for a protocol conversion.

Most commercially available gateways connect microcomputer-based local area networks to mainframes. In the micro/mainframe link, discussed earlier in this chapter, the micro is linked to a down-line processor that in turn is connected to a front-end processor, which is linked to the mainframe. A LAN-to-mainframe gateway makes it possible for one of the micros in a LAN to emulate the function of a down-line processor. Although efficiency may suffer slightly, the company can actually save money because down-line processors are considerably more expensive than microcomputers.

Some companies have many small, departmental local area networks. Instead of integrating these microcomputer-based LANs into a large network, they use **bridges** to enable these LANs to continue operation in their present format with the added advantage of being able to "talk" to each other. Bridges, which are protocol-independent hardware devices, permit communication between devices in separate local area networks. Bridges provide a relatively straightforward solution to enable LANs to communicate with one another.

For the foreseeable future, many connectivity questions can be answered with planning, restrictive policies, gateways, and bridges. However, with total connectivity the goal of most progressive companies, the computer community will continue to focus its sights on overcoming the barriers to it.

Summary Outline and Important Terms

7–1 DATA COMMUNICATIONS: FROM ONE ROOM TO THE WORLD. **Connectivity** facilitates the electronic communication between companies, end user computing, and the free flow of information within an enterprise. Modern businesses use **data communications** to transmit data and information at high speeds from one location to the next. Data communications, or **teleprocessing (TP)**, makes an information system more accessible to the people who use it. The integration of computer systems via data communications is referred to as a **computer network**.

7–2 THE BEGINNING OF AN ERA: COOPERATIVE COMPUTING. This is the era of **cooperative computing**. To obtain meaningful, accurate, and timely information, businesses have decided that they must cooperate internally and externally to take full advantage of available information. To promote internal cooperation, they are promoting intracompany networking. To compete in a world market, they are encouraging intercompany networking, or **electronic data interchange** (**EDI**).

7–3 CONNECTIVITY: LINKING HARDWARE, SOFTWARE, AND DATA BASES. *Connectivity* refers to the degree to which hardware devices can be functionally linked to one another. Some people expand the scope of connectivity to include other aspects of MIS, such as software and data bases. Connectivity is viewed differently, depending on the perspective of the observer (user, vendor, computer specialist). The ideal implementation of connectivity is referred to as **total connectivity**.

7–4 DATA COMMUNICATIONS HARDWARE. The data communications hardware used to facilitate the transmission of data from one remote location to another includes **modems**, **down-line processors** (also called **cluster controllers**, **concentrators**, or **multiplexors**), **front-end processors**, and **PBXs**. Modems modulate and demodulate signals so that data can be transmitted over telephone lines. Down-line processors, front-end processors, and PBXs are special-function processors; they not only convert the signal to a format compatible with the transmission facility but also relieve the host processor of a number of processing tasks associated with data communications. One of the duties of the front-end processor is to establish the link between source and destination in a process called **handshaking**.

7–5 THE DATA COMMUNICATIONS CHANNEL: DATA HIGHWAYS. A **communications channel** (**line**, or **data link**) is the facility through which data are transmitted between locations in a computer network. A channel may be composed of one or more of the following transmission media: telephone lines, **optical fiber**, **coaxial cable**, and microwave radio signal. Satellites are essentially microwave repeater stations that maintain a **geosynchronous orbit** around the earth.

A channel's capacity is rated by the number of bits it can transmit per second (**bits per second** or **bps**). In practice, the word **baud** is often used interchangeably with bits per second; in reality, they are quite different.

7–6 DATA TRANSMISSION SERVICES. **Common carriers** provide communications channels to the public, and lines can be arranged to suit the application. A **private**, or **leased**, **line** provides a dedicated communications channel. A **switched**, or **dial-up**, **line** is available on a time-and-distance charge basis. **Specialized common carriers**, such as **value-added networks** (**VANs**), offer expanded transmission services.

7–7 NETWORKS: LINKING COMPUTERS AND PEOPLE. Computer systems are linked together to form a computer network.

The basic patterns for configuring computer systems within a computer network are **star topology**, **ring topology**, and **bus topology**. In practice, most networks are actually hybrids of these **network topologies**. Networks are sometimes classified as **three-tier** or **two-tier**.

The connection of microcomputers to a mainframe computer is called a **micro/mainframe link**. With this link, microcomputer users **download/upload** data from/to the mainframe as needed.

A **local area network (LAN)**, or **local net**, is a system of hardware, software, and communications channels that connects devices in close proximity and does not involve a common carrier. A local net permits the movement of data between mainframe computers, personal computers, terminals, I/O devices, and PBXs.

7–8 LINE CONTROL: RULES FOR DATA TRANSMISSION. A communications channel servicing a single workstation is a **point-to-point connection**. A communications channel servicing more than one workstation is called a **multidrop** line. The most common line-control procedures are called **polling** and **contention**.

Communications protocols are rules for transmitting data. The **asynchronous** protocol begins and ends each message with start/stop bits and is used primarily for low-speed data transmission. The **synchronous** protocol permits the source and destination to communicate in timed synchronization for high-speed data transmission.

7–9 APPROACHES TO CONNECTIVITY: GATEWAYS AND BRIDGES. Companies with established operating environments use **gateway** and **bridge** technologies to achieve connectivity. Gateways help alleviate the problems associated with incompatible hardware. A gateway permits networks using different communications protocols to "talk" to one another. Bridges enable LANs to continue operation in their present format with the added advantage of being able to "talk" to other LANs.

Review Exercises

Concepts

1. Would EDI be more closely associated with intercompany networking or intracompany networking?
2. What technologies do companies with established operating environments use to achieve connectivity?
3. What is meant by *geosynchronous orbit*, and how does it relate to data transmission via satellite?
4. What is the unit of measure for the capacity of a data communications channel?

5. Expand the following acronyms: TP, bps, VAN, and LAN.
6. What is the purpose of a multiplexor?
7. What is the relationship between teleprocessing and a computer network?
8. At what channel capacity is the bits per second equal to the baud?
9. What computerese term refers to the degree to which hardware devices can be functionally linked to one another?
10. What device converts digital signals into analog signals for transmission over telephone lines? Why is it necessary?
11. Why is it not advisable to increase the distance between microwave relay stations to 200 miles?
12. What is the ideal implementation of connectivity called?
13. Briefly describe the function of a PBX.
14. What is the purpose of the X12 communications protocol?
15. Describe circumstances in which a leased line would be preferred to a dial-up line.
16. Consider this situation: A remote line printer is capable of printing 800 lines per minute (70 characters-per-line average). Line capacity options are 2.4K, 4.8K, or 9.6K bps. Data are transmitted according to the ASCII encoding system (seven bits per character). What capacity would you recommend for a communications channel to permit the printer to operate at capacity?

Discussion

17. For the most part, *Fortune* 500 companies are relying primarily on gateways and bridges to achieve connectivity. What is the alternative?
18. What is the relationship between EDI, electronic funds transfer (EFT), and connectivity?
19. Discuss connectivity from the perspective of any non-IBM hardware vendor. From the perspective of IBM.
20. Describe how information can be made readily accessible, but only on a need-to-know basis.
21. List and discuss those characteristics that would typify a knowledge worker.
22. Corporate management is evaluating a proposal to allow employees to telecommute one day each week—that is, to work at home with a direct link to the company via a workstation. Argue for or against this proposal.
23. The five PCs in the purchasing department of a large consumer goods manufacturer are used primarily for word processing and database applications. What would be the benefits and burdens associated with connecting the PCs in a local area network?

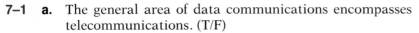

Self-Test (by section)

7–1 **a.** The general area of data communications encompasses telecommunications. (T/F)

    b. The integration of computer systems, terminals, and communication links is referred to as a _____.

7–2 Using computers and data communications to transmit data electronically between companies is called: (a) EDI, (b) DIE, or (c) DEI.

7–3 A company either has total connectivity or it has no connectivity. (T/F)

7–4 **a.** The modem converts computer-to-terminal electrical _____ (digital or analog) signals to _____ (digital or analog) signals so that the data can be transmitted over telephone lines.

    b. The terminal sending a message is the source and the computer receiving the message is the destination. (T/F)

    c. Another name for a front-end processor is multiplexor. (T/F)

7–5 **a.** It is more difficult for a computer criminal to tap into an optical fiber than a copper telephone line. (T/F)

    b. A 9600-bits-per-second channel is the same as a: (a) 9.6 kps line, (b) 9.6K bps line, or (c) dual 4800X2K bps line.

7–6 **a.** The two basic types of service offered by common carriers are a private line and a leased line. (T/F)

    b. A value-added network will always use the transmission facilities of a common carrier. (T/F)

7–7 **a.** A LAN is designed for "long-haul" data communications. (T/F)

    b. An end point in a network of computers is called a _____.

    c. The central cable called a transmission medium is most closely associated with which network topology: (a) ring, (b) star, or (c) bus?

7–8 **a.** In asynchronous data transmission, start/stop bits are appended to the beginning and end of each message. (T/F)

    b. The _____ communications protocol is the standard for electronic data interchange.

7–9 The use of a gateway normally implies a requirement for a protocol conversion. (T/F)

Self-test answers. **7–1** (a) F; (b) computer network. **7–2** a. **7–3** F. **7–4** (a) digital, analog; (b) T; (c) F. **7–5** (a) T; (b) b. **7–6** (a) F; (b) F. **7–7** (a) F; (b) node; (c) c. **7–8** (a) T; (b) X12. **7–9** T.

8

Programming Languages and Software Concepts

STUDENT LEARNING OBJECTIVES

- To discuss the terminology and concepts associated with programming languages and software.
- To distinguish between and give examples of applications software and systems software.
- To characterize programming languages.
- To describe the function of compilers and interpreters.
- To describe the capabilities and limitations of natural languages.
- To describe the function and purpose of application generators.
- To detail the purpose and objectives of an operating system.
- To demonstrate an understanding of common software concepts.

8–1 Programming and Software

In Chapters 2 through 7 we discussed the operation and application of computer systems and specific hardware devices. However, a computer system does nothing until directed to do so. A **program**, which consists of instructions to the computer, is the means by which we tell a computer to perform certain operations. These instructions are logically sequenced and assembled through the act of **programming**. **Programmers** use a variety of **programming languages**, such as COBOL and BASIC, to communicate instructions to the computer.

We use the term **software** to refer to the programs that direct the activities of the computer system. Software falls into two general categories: applications and systems. **Applications software** is designed and written to perform specific personal, business, or scientific processing tasks, such as payroll processing, order entry, or financial analysis.

Systems software is more general than applications software and is usually independent of any specific application area. Systems software programs support *all* applications software by directing the basic functions of the computer. For example, when the computer is turned on, an initialization program readies all devices for processing. Systems software also includes programs that help in the development of applications software (for example, programming languages such as COBOL and BASIC).

8–2 Generations of Programming Languages

We "talk" to computers within the framework of a particular programming language. Programming languages, such as FORTRAN and COBOL, fall within the systems software category. There are many

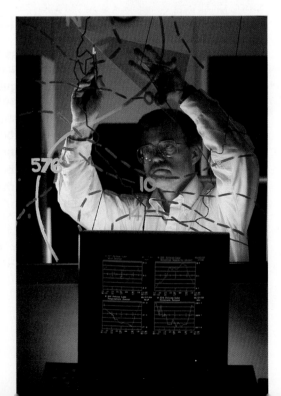

Programs written to address a specific processing task, such as helping the National Weather Service predict the possibility of flooding, are called applications software.

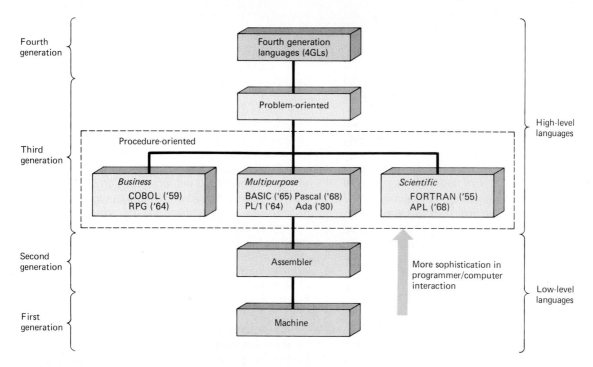

FIGURE 8–1 The Hierarchy of Programming Languages
As you progress from one generation of programming language to the next,
fewer instructions are required to perform a particular programming task.

different programming languages, most of which have highly structured sets of rules. The selection of a language depends on who is
involved and the nature of the "conversation." The president of a
company may prefer a different type of language than a professional
programmer; languages used for payroll processing may not be appropriate for ad hoc (one-time) inquiries. The application of the
more common programming languages is discussed later in this
chapter.

Like computers, programming languages have evolved in generations. (See Appendix A, "An Abbreviated History of Computers,"
for an overview of computer generations.) With each new generation,
fewer instructions are needed to tell the computer to perform a particular task. For example, a program written in a first-generation
language that computes the total sales for each sales representative,
then lists those over quota, may require 100 or more instructions; the
same program in a fourth-generation language may use fewer than
10 instructions.

The hierarchy in Figure 8–1 illustrates the relationships between
the various generations of programming languages. The later **high-
level languages** (third and later generations) do not necessarily provide us with greater programming capabilities, but they do provide
a *more sophisticated programmer/computer interaction*. In short, each
new generation is easier to understand and use. For example, in the
fourth-generation language you need only instruct the computer sys-

Prior to the invention of the electronic digital computers, companies relied on electromechanical accounting machines (EAM) for automated data processing. The EAM family consisted of about a dozen punched-card devices (sorter, accounting machine, collator). The act of programming these devices was referred to as "wiring the program." Early programmers, called *operators* during this era, literally created the circuitry for the devices by inserting wires into interchangeable removable control panels. A different panel was wired for each type of operation to be performed (merge the employee and name/address files, print payroll checks). A typical company might have 50 of the two-foot-square prewired control panels for use with an accounting machine, the central device in punched-card processing. The company would have scores of other prewired control panels for other devices. Each control panel might involve hundreds of wires. For example, to read and add the numbers in Columns 4 through 6 and 12 through 14 of a punched card and to print the results using Print Hammers 56 through 60, the operator would have to insert wires to accept the data, to add them, and to print the result. Punched-card devices were used by thousands of companies well into the third generation of computers (1964–71).

In 1946 Dr. John W. Mauchly and J. Presper Eckert, Jr., created the first large-scale fully operational electronic digital computer called the ENIAC (see Appendix A, "An Abbreviated History of Computers"). However, the quantum leap in technology brought about by the ENIAC was offset by the cumbersome method of programming the machine. Switches had to be set and wires inserted into a series of panels resembling those used by telephone operators of the period. Each time a different program was to be run, the switches had to be reset and the wires repositioned—a task often taking several hours. Not only did early programmers spend countless hours setting switches and wiring boards, but they hoped that the computer would run long enough to complete the program without breaking down!

Mauchly and Eckert realized that a better method of programming was necessary to make their computer truly a general-purpose machine. In 1949 they worked with a mathematician named John Von Neumann to develop a computer that would store a program the way it stored data. The introduction of the "stored-program" concept enabled computers to execute one program, then electronically load and ready another program for execution within a matter of minutes. All early programs were written in machine language that consisted entirely of 1s and 0s. Imagine the difficulty in keeping track of the sequence of program instructions made up entirely of 1s and 0s, not to mention the eyestrain!

Von Neumann reconceived one of Lady Augusta Lovelace's concepts 90 years after her death. Lady Lovelace had suggested the use of a conditional transfer instruction long before the existence of electronic computers. This type of instruction would permit the sequence in which the instructions were executed to be altered, based on certain criteria. For example, in a payroll processing program, the criterion might be type of pay. One set of instructions is executed for salaried personnel and a different set is executed for hourly personnel.

The conditional transfer instruction and the introduction of the stored-program concept made the general-purpose computer a reality. By the early 1950s the business and scientific communities had recognized the utility of these "giant brains." However, programmers had little relief from the tedium of writing programs in low-level languages until the introduction of the first high-level one in 1955, a scientific language called FORTRAN. COBOL, still the most frequently used business-oriented language, was introduced in 1959.

This EAM control panel was inserted in an accounting machine to provide it with the logic to calculate and print a payroll register.

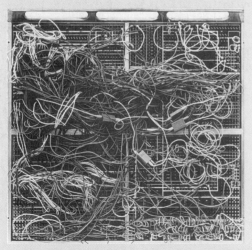

Early programmers had to set hundreds of switches manually to enter a program to the computer.

tem *what to do*, not necessarily *how to do it*. When programming in one of the first three generations of languages, you have to tell the computer what to do *and* how to do it.

The ease with which the later generations can be used is certainly appealing, but the earlier languages also have their advantages. All generations of languages are in use today. According to a recent survey of companies that use IBM mainframe computers, approximately three quarters of their applications programs are developed with third-generation languages. Fourth-generation languages account for 14% of the development effort, and first- and second-generation languages account for 6%. The remaining 4% falls in the "other" category. The trend, however, is to greater use of fourth-generation and other very high-level languages.

8–3 The First and Second Generations: Low-Level

Machine Language

Each computer has only *one* programming language that can be executed—the **machine language**. We talk of programming in COBOL, Pascal, and BASIC, but all these languages must be translated into the machine language of the computer on which the program is to be executed. These and other high-level languages are simply a convenience for the programmer.

Machine-language programs, the *first generation*, are written at the most basic level of computer operation. Because their instructions are directed at these fundamental operations, machine languages and assembler languages (see following) are called **low-level languages**. In machine language, instructions are coded as a series of 1s and 0s. As you might expect, machine-language programs are cumbersome and difficult to write. Early programmers had no alternative. Fortunately, we do.

Assembler Language

A set of instructions for an **assembler language** is essentially one to one with those of a machine language. Like machine languages, assembler languages are unique to a particular computer. The big difference between the two types is the way the instructions are represented by the programmer. Rather than a cumbersome series of 1s and 0s, assembler languages use easily recognized symbols, called **mnemonics**, to represent instructions (see Figure 8–2). For example, most assembler languages use the mnemonic *MUL* to represent a "multiply" instruction. The assembler languages became the *second generation* of programming languages.

```
COMP$PAY        PROC PUBLIC
;
;       COMP$PAY - procedure to compute gross pay (PAY = HOURS * RATE)
;
        MOV     AX,HOURS                    ;multiplicand
        MUL     RATE+2                      ;  times second word of multiplier
        MOV     PAY+2,AX                    ;store the product in PAY
;
        MOV     AX,HOURS                    ;multiplicand
        MUL     RATE                        ;  times first word of multiplier
        ADD     PAY+2,AX                    ;add the product to PAY
        ADC     PAY,DX                      ;add the carry, if any
        RET                                 ;end procedure
COMP$PAY        ENDP
```

FIGURE 8–2   An Assembler Program Procedure

These assembler instructions compute PAY by multiplying the number of HOURS times the RATE.

8–4   Compilers and Interpreters: Programs for Programs

No matter which high-level language (third and above) a program is written in, it must be translated into machine language before it can be executed. This conversion of high-level instructions into machine-level instructions is done by systems software programs called *compilers* and *interpreters*.

Compilers

The **compiler** program translates the instructions of a high-level language, such as COBOL, into machine-language instructions that the computer can interpret and execute. A separate compiler (or an interpreter, discussed in the next section) is required for each programming language intended for use on a particular computer system. That is, to execute both COBOL and Pascal programs, you must have a COBOL compiler and a Pascal compiler.

High-level programming languages are simply a programmer convenience; they cannot be executed in their source, or original, form. The actual high-level programming-language instructions, called the **source program**, are translated, or **compiled**, into machine-language instructions by a compiler. The circled numbers in Figure 8–3 cross-reference the following numbered discussion of the compilation process.

1. Suppose you want to write a COBOL program. You first enter the instructions into the computer system through an on-line terminal. Having done so, you identify the language (COBOL) in which you wrote the program and request that the program be compiled.

2. The COBOL compiler program is called from secondary storage and loaded to primary storage along with the COBOL source program. (*Note*: Step 3 will be attempted but not completed if the source program contains errors, or **bugs** [see Step 4].)

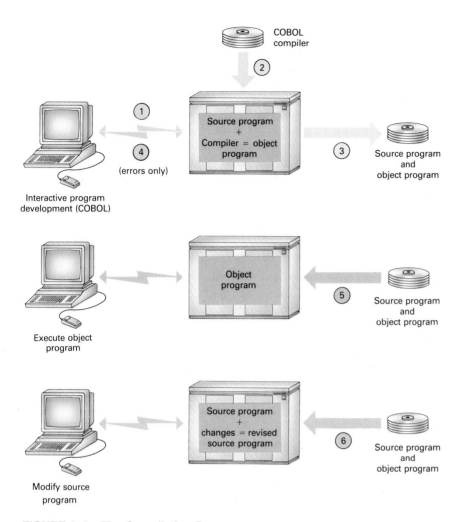

FIGURE 8–3 The Compilation Process
A source program is translated into an object program for execution. The steps
of the compilation process are discussed in the text.

3. The COBOL compiler translates the source program into a machine-language program called an **object program**. The object
   program is the output of the compilation process. At this point,
   the object program resides in primary storage and can be executed upon your command.

   The compilation process can be time-consuming, especially for
   large programs. Therefore, if you intend to execute the program
   at another time, perhaps during another session, you should store
   the object program on secondary storage for later recall. On most
   mainframe computer systems this is done automatically.

4. If the source program contains a **syntax error** (for example, an
   invalid instruction format), the compiler will display an error
   message on the terminal screen, then terminate the compilation
   process. An error message identifies the program statement or
   statements in error and the cause of the error. Syntax errors

usually involve invalid instructions. Consider the following COBOL statement: DISPLY "WHOOPS". The statement is invalid because DISPLAY is misspelled.

As a programmer, you will make the necessary corrections and attempt the compilation over, and over, and over again, until the program compiles and executes. Don't be discouraged. Very few programs compile on the first, second, or even third attempts. When your program finally compiles and executes, don't be surprised if the output is not what you expected. A "clean," or error-free, compilation is likely to surface undetected **logic errors**. For example, your program logic might result in an attempted division by zero; this is mathematically and logically impossible and will result in a program error. In most cases, you will need to remove a few such bugs in the program logic and in the I/O formats before the program is finished.

5. Suppose you come back the next day and wish to execute your COBOL program again. Instead of repeating the compilation process of Step 2, you simply call the object program from secondary storage and load it to primary storage for execution. Since the object program is already in machine language, no compilation is necessary.

6. If you want to make any changes in the original source programs, you will: Recall the original source program from secondary storage, make the changes, recompile the program, and create an updated object program (repeat Steps 1 through 4).

Programs that are run frequently are stored and executed as object programs. Recompilation is necessary only when the program is modified.

Interpreters

An **interpreter** is a systems software program that ultimately performs the same function as a compiler—but in a different manner. Instead of translating the entire source program in a single pass, an

Commodore Grace Murray Hopper (USNR, Ret.) helped to make life a lot easier for today's programmers. While a mathematician at Remington Rand in 1951, Dr. Hopper proposed an "automatic programming" technique that was later perfected by others and called a compiler.

On the Street

Denise Ward
Attorney

A s a partner in a small law firm that primarily represents real estate developers and appraisers, Denise Ward keeps her Zenith Z180 laptop and Sperry AT pretty busy. She finds that the computer skills she has acquired over the last six years as a practicing attorney have given her a definite negotiating edge with lenders as she helps her clients obtain loan financing on new property acquisitions.

"The computer has been extremely helpful, especially in terms of expediency. I use my word processing package (MultiMate Advantage II) extensively in contract negotiations. Before, I would begin by taking a lot of handwritten notes, then ask my secretary to decipher what I had scribbled—not always an easy task! Now I'm able to do a first draft directly on the computer, print it out, and send it out to the prospective purchaser. Any changes are then entered easily by myself or my secretary. Having the contract on disk also prevents my secretary from tedious retyping every time there is a slight alteration."

Denise has also become a proficient user of Lotus 1-2-3. She uses the program to prepare both cash flow analyses and spreadsheets for budgeting construction projects. "Using Lotus is great for me because I'm not mathematically inclined; I used to shy away from numbers. Now I simply plug them in, and my computer does the calculations for me."

She also recently purchased Time Slips II, software designed specifically for attorneys that breaks out time into billable hours. This program also saves her a lot of time. "Anything that does math for me, I love!"

But perhaps the greatest advantage of owning a portable laptop is the fact that it affords Denise the opportunity to do much of her work at home. Since becoming a mother not too long ago, Denise welcomes any chance she gets to spend time with her daughter—especially one that allows her to catch up on her paperwork, too.

interpreter translates *and* executes each source program instruction before translating and executing the next.

The obvious advantage of interpreters over compilers is that an error in instruction syntax is brought to the attention of the programmer immediately, thereby prompting the programmer to make corrections during program development. This is a tremendous help.

But, as we know, advantages are usually accompanied by disadvantages. The disadvantage of interpreters is that they do not use computing resources as efficiently as a program that has been compiled. Since the interpreter does not produce an object program, it must perform the translation process each time a program is executed.

Programmers take advantage of the strengths of both interpreters and compilers for programs that are to be run often. First they develop and debug their programs using an interpreter. Then they compile the finished program to create a more efficient object program that can be used for routine processing.

8–5 The Third Generation: For Programmer Convenience

The introduction of the *third generation* of programming languages produced a quantum leap in programmer convenience. A third-generation language belongs in one of two categories: **procedure-oriented languages** or **problem-oriented languages** (review Figure 8–1).

Procedure-Oriented Languages

The flexibility of procedure-oriented languages permits programmers to model almost any scientific or business procedure. Instructions are **coded**, or written, sequentially and processed according to program specifications.

Unless triggered by program logic to do otherwise, the processor selects and executes instructions in the sequence in which they are written. In a production payroll system, for example, a particular sequence of program instructions is executed for each salaried employee; another sequence is executed for each hourly employee.

Procedure-oriented languages are classified as *business*, *scientific*, or *multipurpose*. These are illustrated in Figure 8–1 and discussed below.

Business Languages   Business programming languages are designed for developing business information systems. The strength of business-oriented languages lies in their ability to store, retrieve, and manipulate alphanumeric data.

The arithmetic requirements of most business systems are minimal. Although sophisticated mathematical manipulation is possible, it is cumbersome to achieve, so it is best left to scientific languages.

COBOL.   COBOL, the first business programming language, was introduced in 1959, and it remains the most popular. Over half of all business programs are written in COBOL. The original intent of the developers of COBOL (*Common Business Oriented Language*) was to make its instructions approximate the English language. Here is a typical COBOL *sentence*:

> IF SALARY-CODE IS EQUAL TO "H" MULTIPLY SALARY BY HOURLY-RATE GIVING GROSS-PAY ELSE PERFORM SALARIED-EMPLOYEE-ROUTINE.

Note that the sentence contains several instructions and even a period.

The American National Standards (ANS) Institute has established standards for COBOL and other languages to make these pro-

```
0100 IDENTIFICATION DIVISION.
0200 PROGRAM-ID.              PAYPROG.
0300 REMARKS.                 PROGRAM TO COMPUTE GROSS PAY.
0400 ENVIRONMENT DIVISION.
0500 DATA DIVISION.
0600 WORKING-STORAGE SECTION.
0700 01 PAY-DATA.
0800        05 HOURS      PIC 99V99.
0900        05 RATE       PIC 99V99.
1000        05 PAY        PIC 9999V99.
1100 01 LINE-1.
1200        03 FILLER     PIC X(5)       VALUE SPACES.
1300        03 FILLER     PIC X(12)      VALUE "GROSS PAY IS  ".
1400        03 GROSS-PAY  PIC $$$$9.99.
1500 01 PRINT-LINE.        PIC X(27).
1600 PROCEDURE DIVISION.
1700 MAINLINE-PROCEDURE.
1800        PERFORM ENTER-PAY.
1900        PERFORM COMPUTE-PAY.
2000        PERFORM PRINT-PAY.
2100        STOP RUN.
2200 ENTER-PAY.
2300        DISPLAY "ENTER HOURS AND RATE OF PAY".
2400        ACCEPT HOURS, RATE.
2500 COMPUTE-PAY.
2600        MULTIPLY HOURS BY RATE GIVING PAY ROUNDED.
2700 PRINT-PAY.
2800        MOVE PAY TO GROSS-PAY.
2900        MOVE LINE-1 TO PRINT-LINE.
3000        DISPLAY PRINT-LINE.
```

```
Enter hours and rate of pay
43, 8.25
    Gross pay is $354.75
```

FIGURE 8–4 A COBOL Program

This COBOL program accepts the number of hours worked and the pay rate
for an hourly wage earner, then computes and displays the gross pay amount.
The interactive session shows the input prompt, the values entered by the
user, and the result.

grams *portable*. A program is said to be portable if it can be run on
a variety of computers. Unfortunately, the ANS standards are followed
only casually; it is unlikely that a COBOL program written for a
UNISYS computer, for example, can be executed on a DEC computer
without some modification.

Figure 8–4 illustrates a COBOL program that computes gross
pay for hourly wage earners. Notice that the program is separated
into four *divisions*: identification, environment, data, and procedure.
The procedure division contains the logic of the program—the sequence of instructions that tells the computer to accept, process, and
display data.

For the purpose of comparison, the COBOL program in Figure
8–4 and all other examples of third-generation programs (Figures
8–5 through 8–8) are written to perform the same input, processing,
and output activities: Compute gross pay for hourly wage earners.
The interactive session (see Figure 8–4) is the same for all these programs.

RPG.   RPG (*R*eport *P*rogram *G*enerator) was originally developed
in 1964 for IBM's entry-level punched-card business computers and
for the express purpose of generating reports. As punched cards went
the way of vacuum tubes, RPG remained—evolving from a special-

Programmers often work as a team on big projects. This COBOL programming team meets as a group at least once a week to coordinate efforts, discuss problems, and report on individual and team progress.

purpose, problem-oriented language to a general-purpose, procedure-oriented language. Its name has made RPG the most misunderstood of the programming languages. People who do not know RPG still associate it with report generation when, in fact, it has become a powerful programming language that matured with the demands of RPG users.

RPG has always differed somewhat from other procedure-oriented languages in that the programmer specifies certain processing requirements by selecting the desired programming options. That is, during a programming session, the programmer is presented with *prompting formats* at the bottom of the terminal screen. The programmer requests the prompts for a particular type of instruction, then responds with the desired programming specifications.

Scientific Languages   Scientific languages are algebraic/formula-type languages. These are specifically designed to meet typical scientific processing requirements, such as matrix manipulation, pre-

Scientists sometimes write FORTRAN programs to analyze the data they collect during their experiments.

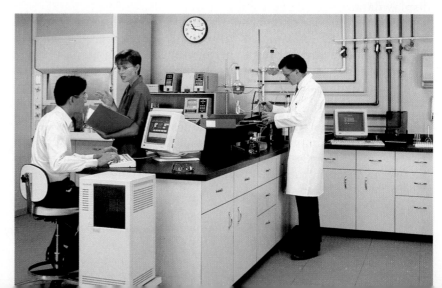

```
        program payprog
c
c       payprog      - Program to compute the pay for an employee,
c                      given hours worked and the employee's pay rate.
c
        real hours, rate, pay                    !define the variables
c
        write(6,1)                               !input prompt
1       format(1H,'Enter hours and rate of pay')
        read(5,*) hours, rate                    !accept hours & pay rate
        pay = hours * rate                       !compute pay
        write(6,2) pay                           !display gross pay
2       format(1H,5X,'Gross pay is $',F7.2)
        end
```

FIGURE 8–5   A FORTRAN Program
This FORTRAN program accepts the number of hours worked and the pay rate
for an hourly wage earner, then computes and displays the gross pay amount.
The resulting interactive session is the same as that of Figure 8–4.

cision calculations, iterative processing, the expression and resolution
of mathematical equations, and so on. Engineers and actuaries turn
to scientific languages when writing programs for statistical analysis.

FORTRAN.   **FORTRAN** (*For*mula *Tran*slator), the first procedure-
oriented language, was developed in 1955. It was, and it remains, the
most popular scientific language. The FORTRAN program in Figure
8–5 performs the same processing functions as the COBOL program
in Figure 8–4.

APL.   **APL** (*A* *P*rogramming *L*anguage), introduced in 1968, is a symbolic interactive programming language that is popular with engineers, mathematicians, and scientists. A special keyboard with "shorthand" symbols helps speed the coding process.

Multipurpose Languages   Multipurpose languages are equally effective in both business and scientific applications. These languages are
an outgrowth of the need to simplify the programming environment
by providing programmers with one language capable of addressing
all of a company's programming needs.

BASIC.   **BASIC**, developed in 1964, is the primary language supported by millions of personal computers. BASIC is also used extensively on mainframe computer systems, primarily for one-time
"quick-and-dirty" programs.
     BASIC is perhaps the easiest language to learn and use (see Figure
8–6). It is commonly used in both scientific and business applica-

FIGURE 8–6   A BASIC Program
This BASIC program accepts the number of hours worked and the pay rate for
an hourly wage earner, then computes and displays the gross pay amount. The
resulting interactive session is the same as that of Figure 8–4.

```
100 REM payprog          Program to compute the pay for an employee,
110 REM                  given hours worked and the employee's pay rate.
120 REM
130 PRINT "Enter hours and rate of pay"    'input prompt
140 INPUT HOURS, RATE                       'accept hours & pay rate
150 LET PAY = HOURS * RATE                  'compute pay
160 PRINT TAB(5);"Gross pay is $";PAY       'display gross pay
170 END
```

```
program payprog(input,output);
{        Program to compute the pay for an employee,
         given hours worked and the employee's pay rate. }

var      hours, rate, pay : real;                    (define the variables)

begin
  writeln(output,'Enter hours and rate of pay');     (input prompt)
  readln(input,hours,rate);                           (accept hours & pay rate)
  pay := hours * rate;                                (compute pay)
  writeln(output,'       Gross pay is $',pay:0:2)     (display gross pay)
end.
```

FIGURE 8–7   A Pascal Program
This Pascal program accepts the number of hours worked and the pay rate for an hourly wage earner, then computes and displays the gross pay amount. The resulting interactive session is the same as that of Figure 8–4.

tions—and even in developing video games. The widespread use of BASIC attests to the versatility of its features. In fact, it is the only programming language that is supported on virtually every computer.

Pascal.   Introduced in 1968, **Pascal**, named after the seventeenth-century French mathematician Blaise Pascal, has experienced tremendous growth. Pascal is considered the state of the art among widely used procedure-oriented languages (see Figure 8–7).

   Pascal's power, flexibility, and self-documenting structure have made it the language of choice in many computer science curriculums and for many developers of systems software. Currently, only 1% to 2% of the business-system programs are written in Pascal, but it is enjoying a growing acceptance in the business community.

C.   The results of a recent employment survey showed **C** programmers to be in the greatest demand. Developers of proprietary packaged software are very interested in C, introduced in 1972, because it is considered more transportable than other languages. In other words,

Pascal, a multipurpose programming language, is often used to develop software for computer image generation.

```
/*      payprog.c    - Program to compute the pay for an employee,
                       given hours worked and the employee's pay rate. */

main()
{
        float hours, rate, pay;                 /* define the
                                                   variables used */
        printf("Enter hours and rate of pay\n");  /* input prompt */
        scanf("%f %f", &hours, &rate);             /* accept hours
                                                   and pay rate */
        pay = hours * rate;                        /* compute pay */
        printf("\tGross pay is $%.2f\n",pay);      /* print gross pay */
}
```

FIGURE 8–8   A C-Language Program
This C program accepts the number of hours worked and the pay rate for an
hourly wage earner, then computes and displays the gross pay amount. The
resulting interactive session is the same as that of Figure 8–4.

it is relatively machine-independent: A C program written for one
type of computer (see Figure 8–8) can be run on another type with
little or no modification.

PL/I.   PL/I (*Programming Language/I*), introduced in 1964, was
hailed as the answer to many of the problems of existing languages
such as COBOL and FORTRAN. It has not, however, won the widespread acceptance originally anticipated, but it is widely used.

Ada.   Ada, introduced relatively recently (1980), is a very sophisticated, procedure-oriented language. It is a multipurpose language
developed for the U.S. Department of Defense. The language was
named in honor of the nineteenth-century pioneer, Lady Augusta Ada
Lovelace, considered by some to be the first programmer. Its developers are optimistic that as more people begin to study it, Ada will
gain widespread acceptance not only in the military but also in the
private sector as well.

Other Procedure-Oriented Languages   The foregoing coverage of
third-generation procedure-oriented languages is not intended to be
exhaustive. The languages were selected to provide you with an overview some of the languages you might encounter in practice. A dozen
other languages are commonly used in business and taught in academic institutions. These include the following.

- *ALGOL* (1958). A scientific language, like FORTRAN, but with a
  more structured approach to the presentation of the logic.
- *LISP* (1959). A list-processing language better at manipulating
  symbols than numbers (used in artificial intelligence).
- *LOGO* (1967). A language that uses a "turtle" to teach children
  geometry, mathematics, and programming.
- *FORTH* (1971). Used for device control applications.
- *Prolog* (1972). Can manipulate relationships between facts (used
  in the development of expert systems).
- *Modula-2* (1981). A general-purpose language that enables self-
  contained modules to be combined in a program.

Because English is the language of computers, programmers throughout the world prefer using English-language versions of programming languages. However, users in non-English–speaking countries prefer an interface that is more familiar. In China, they use a Chinese keyboard.

Problem-Oriented Languages

A problem-oriented language is designed to address a particular application area or to solve a particular set of problems. Problem-oriented languages do not require the programming detail of procedure-oriented ones. The emphasis of problem-oriented languages is more on *input* and *the desired output* than on the *procedures* or *mathematics involved*.

Problem-oriented languages have been designed for scores of applications: simulation (for example, GPSS, SLAM); programming machine tools (APT); and analysis of stress points in buildings and bridges (COGO).

8–6 The Fourth Generation: 4GLs

Types of 4GLs

The trend in software development is toward using high-level, user-friendly, **fourth-generation languages** (**4GLs**). There are two types of 4GLs.

- *Production-oriented 4GLs.* Production-oriented 4GLs are designed primarily for computer professionals and for the development of mainframe-based information systems. These products are usually, although not always, associated with a vendor's database management system software (discussed in Chapter 9, "Data Management"). Production-oriented 4GLs include ADR's Ideal, Software AG's Natural 2, and Cincom's Mantis.

- *User-oriented 4GLs*. The other type of 4GL is designed primarily for end users. Users write programs to query (extract information from) a database and to create function-based information systems. User-oriented 4GLs include Mathematica Products Group's RAMIS II and Application Builders' FOCUS.

Over the years, most companies have accumulated large quantities of computer-based data. Prior to fourth-generation languages (the mid-1970s), these data were not directly accessible to users. Users had to describe their information needs to a professional programmer, who would then write a program in a procedure-oriented language like COBOL to produce the desired results. Fulfilling a typical user request would take at least a couple of days and as long as two weeks. By then the desired information might no longer be needed. With fourth-generation languages, these same ad hoc requests, or queries, can be completed in minutes. When 4GLs are available, many users elect to handle their own information needs, without involving computer professionals at all!

With a day or so of training and practice, a computer-literate user can learn to write programs, make inquiries, and get reports in user-oriented 4GLs. Once they become familiar with user-oriented 4GLs, users often find it is easier and quicker to sit down at the nearest terminal and write a program than it is to relate inquiry or report specifications to a professional programmer. With 4GLs, managers can attend to their own seemingly endless ad hoc requests for information and even write their own production information systems. If the data base is already in place, about 75% of a typical user's information needs can be met with 4GLs. 4GLs benefit everyone concerned: Users quickly get the information that they need, and, because programmers have fewer ad hoc programming assignments, they can focus their efforts on the ever-increasing backlog of information systems projects. Of course, professional programmers use 4GLs to increase their productivity as well. Programmers claim productivity

These managers are being taught the use and application of fourth-generation query languages. After completing a one-day seminar, they will be able to make inquiries to the corporate data base without the assistance of a computer specialist.

improvements over third-generation procedure-oriented languages (COBOL, FORTRAN, BASIC, and so on) of 200% to 1000%.

Principles and Use

Fourth-generation languages use high-level English-like instructions to retrieve and format data for inquiries and reporting. Most of the procedure portion of a 4GL program is generated automatically by the computer and the language software. That is, for the most part the programmer specifies what to do, *not* how to do it. In contrast, a COBOL or FORTRAN programmer writes instructions for what to do *and* how to do it.

The features of a 4GL include English-like instructions, limited mathematical manipulation of data, automatic report formatting, sequencing (sorting), and record selection by criteria.

Using 4GLs The 4GL example presented here gives you a sense of the difference between a procedure-oriented language, such as COBOL, and a 4GL. About 20 4GLs are commercially available. The example shows how a representative 4GL program can be used to generate a management report. Suppose, for example, that a personnel manager wants to make the following request for information:

> List the employee ID, sex, net pay, and gross pay for all employees in Departments 911 and 914.

To obtain the report, the manager wrote the query-language program in Figure 8–9; the report generated by this program is shown in Figure 8–10.

- *Instruction 1* specifies that the payroll data are stored on a FILE called PAYROLL. The payroll file contains a record for each employee. Although the data of only one file are needed in this example, requests requiring data from several files are no more difficult.

FIGURE 8–9   A 4GL Program
This representative 4GL program generates the report shown in Figure 8–10. Each instruction is discussed in detail in the text.

```
1.  FILE IS PAYROLL
2.  LIST BY DEPARTMENT:    NAME ID SEX NET GROSS
3.  SELECT DEPARTMENT = 911, 914
4.  SUBTOTALS BY DEPARTMENT
5.  TITLE: "PAYROLL FOR DEPARTMENTS 911, 914"
6.  COLUMN HEADINGS:   "DEPARTMENT", "EMPLOYEE, NAME";
    "EMPLOYEE, NUMBER"; "SEX"; "NET, PAY"; "GROSS, PAY"
```

PAYROLL FOR DEPARTMENTS 911, 914

DEPARTMENT	EMPLOYEE NAME	EMPLOYEE NUMBER	SEX	NET PAY	GROSS PAY
911	ARNOLD	01963	1	356.87	445.50
911	LARSON	11357	2	215.47	283.92
911	POWELL	11710	1	167.96	243.20
911	POST	00445	1	206.60	292.00
911	KRUSE	03571	2	182.09	242.40
911	SMOTH	01730	1	202.43	315.20
911	GREEN	12829	1	238.04	365.60
911	ISAAC	12641	1	219.91	313.60
911	STRIDE	03890	1	272.53	386.40
911	REYNOLDS	05805	2	134.03	174.15
911	YOUNG	04589	1	229.69	313.60
911	HAFER	09764	2	96.64	121.95
DEPARTMENT TOTAL				2,522.26	3,497.52
914	MANHART	11602	1	250.89	344.80
914	VETTER	01895	1	189.06	279.36
914	GRECO	07231	1	685.23	1,004.00
914	CROCI	08262	1	215.95	376.00
914	RYAN	10961	1	291.70	399.20
DEPARTMENT TOTAL				1,632.83	2,403.36
FINAL TOTAL				4,155.09	5,900.88
17 RECORDS TOTALED					

FIGURE 8–10 A Payroll Report
This payroll report is the result of the execution of the 4GL program of Figure 8–9.

- *Instruction 2* specifies the basic format of the report. Employee records are *sorted* and LISTed BY DEPARTMENT. It also specifies which data elements within the file (NAME and ID, for example) are to be included in the report of Figure 8–10. If the instruction had been LIST BY DEPARTMENT BY NAME, then the employee names would be listed in alphabetical order for each department.
- *Instruction 3* specifies the criterion by which records are SELECTed. The personnel manager is interested only in those employees from Departments 911 and 914. Other criteria could be included for further record selections. For example, the criterion "GROSS > 400.00" could be added to select only those people (from Departments 911 and 914) whose gross pay is greater than $400.00.
- *Instruction 4* causes SUBTOTALS to be computed and displayed BY DEPARTMENT.
- *Instructions 5 and 6* allow the personnel manager to improve the appearance and readability of the report by including a title and labeling the columns. Instruction 5 produces the report title, and Instruction 6 specifies descriptive column headings.

The COBOL equivalent of this request would require over 150 lines of code!

Fourth-generation languages are effective tools for generating responses to a variety of requests for information. Short programs, similar to the one in Figure 8–9, are all that is needed to respond to the following typical management requests:

- Which employees have accumulated over 20 sick days since May 1?
- Are there going to be any deluxe single hospital rooms vacated by the end of the day?
- What is a particular student's average in all English courses?
- List departments that have exceeded their budget alphabetically by the department head's name.

Strengths and Weaknesses   The problem with 4GLs is that they are less efficient than third-generation languages. That is, 4GLs require more computer capacity to perform a particular operation. Proponents of 4GLs claim that the added cost of the hardware is more than offset by the time saved in creating the programs with 4GLs. Critics claim that 4GL capabilities are limited (when compared to third-generation languages) and that users end up fitting their problems to the capabilities of the software.

Entrepreneurial Innovation   Procedure-oriented languages, such as FORTRAN and COBOL, were designed by volunteer committees and individuals, primarily for the public domain. Then companies such as DEC, CDC, and IBM developed *compilers* and *interpreters* that could translate the FORTRAN and COBOL instructions into the type of instructions that could be executed by the computer. The 4GLs and higher level languages are products of entrepreneurial innovation. These languages (for example, Natural 2 and FOCUS) were developed to be marketed and sold. The demand for very high-level programming languages is so great that many software entrepreneurs have elected to compete in this highly competitive market.

8–7   Natural Languages: The Ultimate Programming Language

Natural languages refer to software that enables computer systems to accept, interpret, and execute instructions in the native, or "natural," language of the end user—typically, English. The premise for a natural language is that the programmer or user needs little or no training. He or she simply writes, or perhaps verbalizes, processing specifications without regard for instruction syntax (the rules by which instructions are formulated). In theory, people using natural languages are not constrained by the instruction syntax inherent in traditional programming languages. In practice, however, there are limitations.

"Is he well enough to program?"

When using a natural language, all you have to do is ask. To produce this graph, this product manager entered the following request: "Show me a bar graph of total sales by region for the past quarter." The graph and an optional tabular summary was generated automatically in response to the request.

The State of the Art of Natural Languages

The state of the art of natural languages is still somewhat primitive. To date, there are no pure natural languages. However, natural languages with certain syntax restrictions are available. Most commercial natural languages are designed to provide the *front end*, or the user interface, for a variety of domain-specific applications. These applications could involve an interface with the corporate data base, an expert system, or certain micro-based software products, such as electronic spreadsheets.

Researchers are currently working to develop pure natural languages that permit an unrestricted dialogue between us and a computer. Although the creation of such a language is difficult to comprehend, it is probably inevitable. In the interim, the complexities involved in translating one language into another are substantial. For example, a program designed to translate English into Russian and Russian into English was used to translate "The spirit is willing, but the flesh is weak" into Russian and then back into English. The result of the double translation was: "The vodka is good, but the meat is rotten." The result gives us some insight into the complexities involved in the creation of natural language programs. Similar subtleties must be considered when translating English into the language of computers, and vice versa.

Existing natural languages enable more people to take advantage of available information because even casual users can articulate their information needs in their native tongues. For limited information processing tasks, such as ad hoc inquiries and report generation for a specific application area (inventory management, purchasing, and so on), existing natural languages work quite well. Eventually, as natural languages mature, they will provide the front end for all categories of software, from word processing to operating systems.

Natural Language Concepts

Here is how a natural language works. Take, for example, the following request:

Let me see the average salaries by job category
in the marketing department.

The natural language software analyzes the sentence in much the same way that we used to diagram sentences during our studies of grammar. This process, known as **parsing**, results in a **parse tree** (see Figure 8–11). The components of the requests are translated into applications commands through a semantic analysis. In the semantic analysis, the components are matched, typically beginning with the verb, against key words in the user-created application dictionary. The dictionary is essentially a list of command synonyms for English words that might be used in a request for a particular applications environment (marketing, medical diagnosis, and so on).

In the example inquiry, the verb *see* would be translated into the applications command *display*. For example, at its most fundamental level, the request is interpreted as "[Let me] see . . . salaries" or, simply, "Display salaries." The *salaries* part of the request indicates that access to the salary field and, therefore, the employee record in the data base, is critical to the response. On closer examination, *average* specifies a function that is to be applied to the salary field. The phrase *by job category in the marketing department* identifies the user's selection criteria: Include in the response only those employees in the marketing department and compute the average salary

FIGURE 8–11   Interpreting a Natural-Language User Request
Following the parsing process, a natural-language user request is translated into applications commands through a semantic analysis.

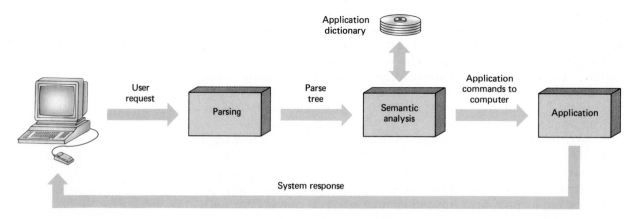

```
                    MARKETING DEPARTMENT

    Job Category            No. of Employees   Average Salary
    --------------------------------------------------------
    Director                      1               $ 71,000
    Administrative Assistant      4               $ 26,550
    Product Manager               4               $ 48,333
    Secretary                     3               $ 21,480
```

FIGURE 8–12   The Results of a Natural Language Inquiry
The inquiry: Let me see the average salaries by job category in the marketing department.

for each job category. The response to the example inquiry is shown in Figure 8–12.

The user would get the same results if he or she had entered the following request:

> What is the average salary in the marketing department for each job classification?

If your query is unclear, the natural language software might ask you questions that will clarify any ambiguities. For example, in the preceding request the system might respond, "I do not understand 'What is'. Do you mean 'Let me see' or 'display'?"

A natural language interprets many common words, but other words peculiar to a specific application or company would need to be added by the user. All common and user-supplied words comprise the **lexicon**, or the dictionary of words that can be interpreted by the natural language. The sophistication of the types of queries that can be accepted depend on the comprehensiveness of the lexicon. In the example inquiry, the words *Let*, *me*, and *see*; their meaning; and the context in which they are used would have to be entered into the lexicon before the phrase *Let me see* could be interpreted by the natural language software. In addition, references to job *category* and *classification* must be defined in the lexicon to mean the same thing.

Usually state-of-the-art natural language software can interpret no more than a one-sentence query at a time. Even so, much can be accomplished with a brief command. For example, instead of writing the 4GL program in Figure 8–9, the user could have entered this request directly to the natural language interface:

> List the employee ID, sex, net pay, and gross pay for all employees in Departments 911 and 914.

The natural language interface analyzes the request and translates it into instructions that can be interpreted by the 4GL. Other typical natural language queries might be:

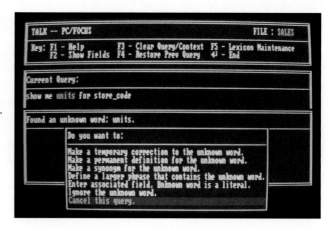

FOCUS, a popular 4GL/DBMS from Information Builders, Inc., provides a nonprocedural alternative to traditional programming languages such as COBOL and FORTRAN. One of the add-on capabilities to PC/FOCUS, the PC version of FOCUS, is EQL (English Query Language). EQL is a natural language interface that enables users to make inquiries to the data base in simple English sentences. EQL translates the sentence into FOCUS instructions. When the sentence is not understood by EQL, the system asks for clarification. In the example, EQL did not recognize the word *units*.

- Are there any managers between the ages of 30 and 40 with MBA degrees in the northwest region?
- Show me a pie graph that compares voter registrations for Alabama, Georgia, North Carolina, South Carolina, and Florida.
- What are the top 10 best-selling books of fiction in California?

8–8 Application Generators: Let the Computer Do It

Application generators are designed primarily for use by computer professionals. The concept of an application generator is not well defined, nor will it ever be, because entrepreneurs are continually working to provide better ways of creating information systems. In general, application generators are designed to assist in the development of full-scale information systems.

When using application generators, also called **code generators**, to develop information systems, programmers specify what information processing tasks are to be performed by engaging in an interactive dialogue with the system. This is essentially a fill-in-the-blank process. The code generator asks a question, and the programmer responds by filling in the blank. For example, the code generator might ask the user to categorize the proposed program as data entry, inquiry, report generation, or file maintenance. If the programmer responds "Inquiry," then the code generator will ask the programmer to identify appropriate data bases. Code generators interpret the programmer-supplied information and actually generate the program code or instructions, usually in the form of COBOL or PL/I programs. These instructions become commands to the computer to make a database inquiry, update a data base, and so on.

When using application generators to create an information system, systems analysts and programmers describe the data base, then specify screen layouts for file creation and maintenance, data entry, management reports, and menus. The application generator software consists of modules of **reusable code** that are pulled together and integrated automatically to complete the system.

Application generators are currently in the infant stage of development. Existing application generators do not have the flexibility of procedure-oriented languages; therefore, the generic reusable code of application generators must occasionally be supplemented with **custom code** to handle unique situations. Normally, about 10% to 15% of the code would be custom code. Application generators provide the framework in which to integrate custom code with generated code. When used for the purposes intended, application generators can quadruple the output of programmers and systems analysts. With this kind of contribution to productivity, application generators are sure to play an ever-increasing role in information systems development.

8–9 The Operating System: The Boss

Just as the processor is the nucleus of the computer system, the **operating system** is the nucleus of all software activity. The operating system is a family of *systems software* programs that are usually, although not always, supplied by the computer system vendor.

Mainframe Operating Systems

Design Objectives   All hardware and software, both systems and applications, are controlled by the operating system. You might even call the operating system "the boss." Some of the more popular mainframe operating systems include IBM's *MVS* and *VM*, DEC's *VMS*, and AT&T's *UNIX*. The logic, structure, and nomenclature of these and other operating systems vary considerably. However, each is designed with the same three objectives in mind:

1. Minimize turnaround time (elapsed time between submittal of a job [for example, print payroll checks] and receipt of output).
2. Maximize throughput (amount of processing per unit of time).
3. Optimize the use of the computer system resources (processor, primary storage, and peripheral devices).

The Supervisor   One of the operating system programs is always *resident* in primary storage (see Figure 8–13). This program, called the **supervisor**, loads other operating system and applications programs to primary storage as they are needed. For example, when you request a COBOL program compilation, the supervisor loads the COBOL compiler to primary storage and links your source program to the compiler to create an object program. In preparation for execution, another program—the **linkage editor**—assigns a primary storage address to each byte of the object program.

Allocating Computer Resources   In a typical computer system, several jobs will be executing at the same time. The operating system

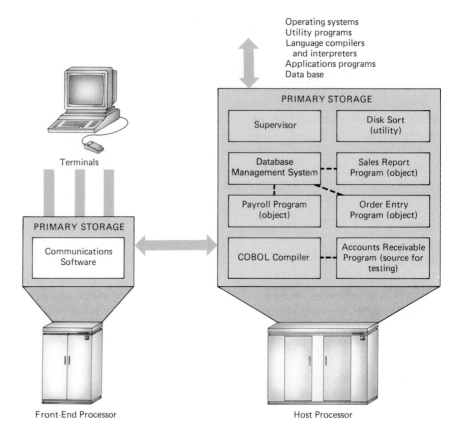

Operating systems
Utility programs
Language compilers
  and interpreters
Applications programs
Data base

PRIMARY STORAGE

Supervisor	Disk Sort (utility)
Database Management System	Sales Report Program (object)
Payroll Program (object)	Order Entry Program (object)
COBOL Compiler	Accounts Receivable Program (source for testing)

Terminals

PRIMARY STORAGE

Communications Software

Front-End Processor

Host Processor

FIGURE 8–13   Software, Storage, and Execution
The supervisor program is always resident in primary storage and calls other programs, as needed, from secondary storage. For example, applications programs rely on database management system software to assist in the retrieval of data from secondary storage. Software in the front-end processor handles data-communications-related tasks.

determines which computer system resources are allocated to which programs. As an example, suppose that a computer system with only one printer has three jobs whose output is ready to be printed. Obviously, two must wait. The operating system continuously resolves this type of resource conflict to optimize the allocation of computer resources.

Operator Interaction   The operating system is in continuous inter-action with computer operators. The incredible speed of a computer system dictates that resource-allocation decisions be made at com-puter speeds. Most of these decisions are made automatically by the operating system. For decisions requiring human input, the operating system interrogates the operators through the operator console (a VDT in the machine room). The operating system also sends messages to the operator. A common message is: "Printer no. 1 is out of paper."

Operators enter commands to direct the operating system to perform specific tasks. For example, operators request the execution of certain programs, reallocate computing resources, and perform system shutdowns.

Programmer Interaction Programmers can interact with the operating system within the context of their individual programs, or they can use **job control language (JCL)**. Programmers often use JCL to specify the **job stream**, the sequence in which their programs are to be executed. They also use JCL to tell the operating system what programming language they are using and where to find the data (for example, which disk drive).

Compatibility Considerations There are usually several operating system alternatives available for medium-sized and large computers. The choice of an operating system depends on the processing orientation of the company. Some operating systems are better for *time-sharing* (servicing multiple end users), others for *processor-intensive jobs*, and still others for *distributed processing*.

Applications programs are not as portable between operating systems as we would like. An information system is designed and coded for a specific *compiler*, *computer*, and *operating system*. This is true for both micros and mainframes. Therefore, programs that work well under one operating system may not be compatible with a different operating system.

To minimize compatibility problems, some mainframe operating systems create a **virtual machine (VM)** environment. A VM-type operating system enables a single mainframe computer to emulate other computers and their operating systems while executing programs in its own computing environment. That is, a program that was written to be run on Computer *A* with Operating System *X* can be executed on a VM computer. The specifications of the program designate that it is to be run on Computer *A* using Operating System *X*. Upon interpreting the specifications, the VM computer loads the program to that portion of main memory that contains the emulation software for Computer *A* and Operating System *X*. Another portion of memory might contain the emulation software for Computer *B* and Operating System *Y*.

Virtual machine operating systems are especially valuable when a company is in transition from one computing environment to another. Typically, the new VM computer emulates the old computing environment while applications programs are being modified to run in the new environment. Virtual machine operating systems provide the best of both worlds by using working programs from the past and by improving the price-performance of new technology.

Microcomputer Operating Systems

Objectives and Functions The objectives and functions of microcomputer operating systems are similar to those of mainframe operating systems. However, they differ markedly in orientation. In the main-

Although some personal computers can service several workstations, the operating systems for most personal computers are oriented to servicing a single user. This professor has arranged his computer system so that all components are within arm's reach.

frame environment, specially trained operators and programmers interact with the operating system so that end users can focus on their applications. In contrast, all micro users need a working knowledge of their micro's operating system because they must use it to interface their applications programs with the microcomputer hardware.

The four most popular micro operating systems based on number of installations are:

1. *MS-DOS* (Microsoft Corporation). MS-DOS is the operating system used with IBM PC–compatible computers. The version of MS-DOS used with the IBM PC and is called *PC-DOS*. In practice, MS-DOS is referred to simply as DOS (rhymes with *boss*), an acronym for *d*isk *o*perating *s*ystem. DOS is a disk operating system because the operating system is stored on disk.
2. *Macintosh DOS* (Apple Computer, Inc.). Macintosh DOS is the operating system for the Macintosh line of computers.
3. *Operating System/2* or *OS/2* (Microsoft/IBM). OS/2 is the operating system designed for IBM's Personal System/2 (PS/2) line of microcomputers.
4. *UNIX* (AT&T). Originally a mainframe operating system, UNIX and its spinoffs, such as *XENIX*, are frequently used with multiuser microcomputers.

Because these operating systems are so widely used, hundreds of software vendors have developed systems and applications software with which they are compatible.

Besides controlling the ongoing operation of the microcomputer systems, the micro operating system has two other important functions.

- *Input/output control.* DOS facilitates the movement of data between peripheral devices, the processor, RAM, and programs.
- *File and disk management.* The microcomputer operating system and its file and disk management utility programs enable users

to perform such tasks as making backup copies of work disks, erasing disk files that are no longer needed, making inquiries about the number and type of files on a particular diskette, and preparing new diskettes for use. It also handles many file- and disk-oriented tasks that do not involve the end user. For example, the operating system keeps track of the physical location of disk files so that we, as users, need only refer to them by name (for example, MYFILE) when loading them from disk to RAM for processing.

Booting the System   Before you can use a microcomputer, you must load the operating system, or **boot** the system. When you do this, the computer "pulls itself up by its own bootstraps" (without the assistance of humans). The procedure for booting the system on most micros is simply to load the operating system from disk storage into random access memory. In most micros this is no more difficult than inserting an operating system disk in a disk drive, closing the disk drive door, and flipping on the switch. On micros with hard disks, all you have to do is turn on the system and the operating system is automatically loaded from the hard disk to RAM.

Operating Environments   Most micro applications software packages would be considered more user friendly than the operating system. There are, however, programs that make micro operating systems as user friendly as any other applications program. These programs are sometimes called *DOS shells* or *DOS helpers* and provide users with a user-friendly interface between the operating system, applications software, and user files. The term **operating environment** is sometimes used to describe a user-friendly DOS interface. Instead of entering sometimes-cryptic operating system commands, you interact with DOS by selecting options from pull-down menus or by identifying the appropriate symbolic icon (a pictograph of a file cabinet representing file operations, for example).

These RAM-resident interface software packages are accompanied by a variety of helpful RAM-resident programs, including an on-line calendar, scratch pad, calculator, and clock. Since these programs

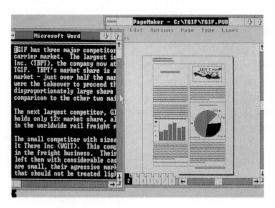

For occasional users, operating system commands can be difficult to learn and use. There are, however, programs that provide users with a user-friendly interface between the operating system, applications software, and user files. The term *operating environment* is sometimes used to describe the use of such an interface. Microsoft's Windows, shown here, permits an operating environment.

remain in RAM with the operating system, they can be called up at any time, even in the middle of a word processing session.

User-friendly operating system interfaces have effectively eliminated the need for users to memorize and enter cumbersome commands. This user-friendly concept is being applied to future enhancements of personal computer operating systems, Operating System/2, the successor to IBM's ubiquitous PC-DOS.

Other System Software Categories

In this chapter we have discussed two system software categories: *programming-language compiler/interpreters* and *operating systems*. Other system software categories are *utility programs*, *performance monitoring software*, *communications software*, and *database management system software*.

- **Utility programs** are service routines that make life easier for us. They eliminate the need for us to write a program every time we need to perform certain computer operations. For example, with the help of utility programs, an employee master file can be easily "dumped," or copied from magnetic disk to magnetic tape for backup, or the employee master file can be sorted by Social Security number.
- **Performance monitoring software** is used to monitor, analyze, and report on the performance of the overall computer system and the computer system components. This software provides such information as the percentage of processor utilization and the number of disk accesses during any given period of time. This type of information enables the scheduler to make the most efficient use of hardware resources, and it helps management plan for future hardware upgrades.
- **Communications software** controls the flow of traffic (data) to and from remote locations. Functions performed by communications software include: preparing data for transmission (inserting start/stop bits in messages), polling remote terminals for input, establishing the connection between two terminals, encoding and decoding data, and parity checking. In the mainframe environment, communications software is executed on the front-end processor, the down-line processor, and the host processor.
- **Database management system (DBMS)** software provides the interface between application programs and the data base. If you want to write a program to update employee records, the only instructions you will need to retrieve a record are those required to accept the employee's name at a VDT. Once the employee's name is entered, the database management system software does the rest. The employee record is retrieved from secondary storage and moved to primary storage for processing. Control is then returned to your application program to complete the update.

MEMORY BITS

SYSTEM SOFTWARE CATEGORIES
- Programming-language compiler/interpreters
- Operating systems
- Utility programs
- Performance monitoring software
- Communications software
- Database management system (DBMS) software

DBMS concepts are discussed in greater detail in Chapter 9, "Data Management."

8–10 Software Concepts

Multiprogramming

All computers except small micros have **multiprogramming** capability. Multiprogramming is the *seemingly simultaneous execution* of more than one program at a time. A computer can execute only one program at a time. But its internal processing speed is so fast that several programs can be allocated "slices" of computer time in rotation; this makes it appear that several programs are being executed at once.

The great difference in processor speed and the speeds of the peripheral devices makes multiprogramming possible. A 40,000-line-per-minute printer cannot even challenge the speed of an average mainframe processor. The processor is continually waiting for the peripheral devices to complete such tasks as retrieving a record from disk storage, printing a report, or copying a backup file onto magnetic tape. During these "wait" periods, the processor just continues processing other programs. In this way, computer system resources are used efficiently.

In a multiprogramming environment, it is not unusual for several programs to require the same I/O device. For example, two or more

The operating system of this large host computer system is the nerve center of a network of distributed computer systems. The system services hundreds of on-line users in a multiprogramming environment.

programs may be competing for the printer. Rather than hold up the processing of a program by waiting for the printer to become available, both programs are executed and the printer output for one is temporarily loaded to magnetic disk. As the printer becomes available, the output is called from magnetic disk and printed. This process is called **spooling**.

Virtual Memory

We learned in Chapter 4, "Inside the Computer," that all data and programs must be resident in primary storage in order to be processed. Therefore, primary storage is a critical factor in determining the throughput, or how much work can be done by a computer system per unit of time. Once primary storage is full, no more programs can be executed until a portion of primary storage is made available.

Virtual memory is a systems software addition to the operating system that effectively expands the capacity of primary storage through the use of software and secondary storage. This allows more data and programs to be resident in primary storage at any given time.

The principle behind virtual memory is quite simple. Remember, a program is executed sequentially—one instruction after another. Programs are segmented into **pages**, so only that portion of the program being executed (one or more pages) is resident in primary storage. The rest of the program is on disk storage. Appropriate pages are *rolled* (moved) into primary storage from disk storage as they are needed to continue execution of the program. The paging process and use of virtual memory is illustrated in Figure 8–14.

The advantage of virtual memory is that primary storage is effectively enlarged, giving programmers greater flexibility in what they can do. For example, some applications require several large programs to be resident in primary storage at the same time (see the order-processing and credit-checking programs illustrated in Figure 8–14). If the size of these programs exceeds the capacity of "real" primary storage, then virtual memory can be used as a supplement to complete the processing.

The disadvantage of virtual memory is the cost in efficiency during program execution. If the logic of a program causes frequent branching between pages, the program will execute more slowly because of the time required to roll pages from secondary to primary storage. Excessive page movement results in too much of the computer's time being devoted to page handling and not enough to processing. This excessive data movement is appropriately named *thrashing* and actually can be counterproductive.

Summary Outline and Important Terms

8–1 PROGRAMMING AND SOFTWARE. A **program** directs a computer to perform certain operations. The program is produced by a **programmer**, who uses any of a variety of **pro-**

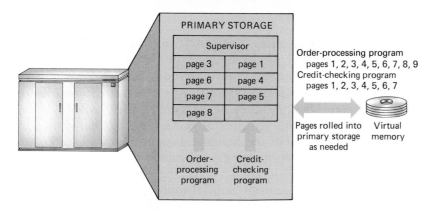

FIGURE 8–14   Virtual Memory
Pages of the order-processing and credit-checking programs are rolled from virtual memory on magnetic disk into "real" memory (primary storage) as they are needed.

gramming languages to communicate with the computer. Programs are referred to as **software**.

Software is classified as either **applications software** or **systems software**. Applications software is designed to perform certain personal, business, or scientific processing tasks. Systems software is more general and supports the basic functions of the computer.

8–2   GENERATIONS OF PROGRAMMING LANGUAGES.   Like computers, programming languages have evolved in generations. With each new one comes a **higher level language** and a more sophisticated programmer/computer interaction.

8–3   THE FIRST AND SECOND GENERATIONS: LOW-LEVEL.   The first two generations of programming languages are **low-level languages**; that is, the programmer must identify each fundamental operation the computer is to perform. The **machine language** is the only language that actually can be executed on a particular computer. High-level languages have surpassed machine language and **assembler language**, which uses easily recognized symbols to represent instructions, in terms of human efficiency.

8–4   COMPILERS AND INTERPRETERS: PROGRAMS FOR PROGRAMS.   High-level languages must be translated into machine language in order to be executed. They are a programmer convenience and facilitate the programmer/computer interaction. A **compiler** is needed to translate a **source program** in a high-level language into an **object program** in machine language for execution. An **interpreter** performs a function similar to a compiler, but it translates one instruction at a time.

8–5   THE THIRD GENERATION: FOR PROGRAMMER CONVENIENCE.   Third-generation languages are either **procedure-oriented languages** or **problem-oriented languages**. Procedure-oriented languages are classified as business (**COBOL** and **RPG**), scientific (**FORTRAN** and **APL**), or multipurpose (**BASIC**, **Pascal**, **C**, **PL/I**, and **Ada**). Problem-oriented languages are designed for particular applications.

8–6 THE FOURTH GENERATION: 4GLs. In **fourth-generation languages**, the programmer need only specify *what* to do, not *how* to do it. The features of **4GLs** include English-like instructions, limited mathematical manipulation of data, automatic report formatting, sequencing (sorting), and record selection by criteria. Higher level languages (fourth and above) are products of entrepreneurial innovation.

8–7 NATURAL LANGUAGES: THE ULTIMATE PROGRAMMING LANGUAGE. **Natural languages** are programs that permit a computer to accept instructions without regard to format or syntax in the native language of the end user. To date, there are no pure natural languages.

Natural languages provide the user interface for a variety of domain-specific applications. The natural language software **parses** a user inquiry into a **parse tree** that is translated into applications commands through a semantic analysis. All common and user-supplied words comprise the **lexicon**, or the dictionary of words that can be interpreted in the natural language.

8–8 APPLICATION GENERATORS: LET THE COMPUTER DO IT. When using **application generators**, or **code generators**, to develop information systems, programmers specify what information processing tasks are to be performed by engaging in an interactive dialogue with the system. Code generators interpret the programmer-supplied information and actually generate the program code.

Because existing application generators do not have the flexibility of procedure-oriented languages, the generic **reusable code** of application generators occasionally must be supplemented with **custom code** to handle unique situations.

8–9 THE OPERATING SYSTEM: THE BOSS. The design objectives of an **operating system**, the nucleus of all software activity, are to minimize turnaround time, maximize throughput, and optimize the use of computer resources. Operating systems are oriented to a particular type of processing environment, such as timesharing, processor-intensive jobs, or distributed processing.

The memory-resident **supervisor** program loads other operating system and applications programs to primary storage as they are needed. The **linkage editor** assigns a primary storage address to each byte of the object program.

Programmers can interact with the operating system within the context of their individual programs or they can use the **job control language (JCL)**. Programmers often use JCL to specify the **job stream**.

A **virtual machine (VM)** operating system enables a single mainframe computer to emulate other computers and their operating systems while executing programs in its own computing environment.

MS-DOS, Macintosh DOS, OS/2, and UNIX are popular operating systems for microcomputers. Until recently micro operating systems were oriented to servicing a single user. Today the more sophisticated micro operating systems support the multiuser multitasking environment. Besides controlling the ongoing operation of a microcomputer system, the micro operating system controls all input/output and handles the file and disk management duties.

Before you can use a microcomputer, you must **boot** the system; that is, load the operating system from disk storage into RAM.

DOS shells or *DOS helpers* provide a user-friendly interface between users, the operating system, applications software, and user files. The term **operating environment** is sometimes used to describe the user-friendly operating system interface.

Systems software categories include programming-language compilers/interpreters, operating systems, **utility programs**, **performance monitoring software**, **communications software**, and **database management systems**.

8–10 SOFTWARE CONCEPTS. **Multiprogramming** is the seemingly simultaneous execution of more than one program at a time on a single computer. **Virtual memory** effectively expands the capacity of primary storage through the use of software, the **paging** process, and secondary storage.

 Review Exercises

Concepts

1. Associate each of the following with a particular generation of languages: reusable code, mnemonics, and Ada.
2. What are the four divisions in a COBOL program? Which contains the program logic?
3. Name two types of program errors.
4. Name two procedure-oriented programming languages in each of the three classifications—business, scientific, and multipurpose.
5. What are the programs called that translate source programs into machine language? Which one does the translation on a single pass? Which one does it one statement at a time?
6. Contrast 4GLs with code generators.
7. Why is it necessary to spool output in a multiprogramming environment?
8. Give two examples each of applications and systems software.

9. Name the systems software category associated with: (a) a company's data base, (b) file backup, and (c) overall software and hardware control.

10. Who are the users of application generators?

11. What is meant by booting the system?

12. What is the lexicon of a natural language?

13. Briefly describe what is meant by an operating environment.

Discussion

14. Discuss the difference between a program and a programming language.

15. If each new generation of languages enhances interaction between programmers and the computer, why not write programs using the most recent generation of languages?

16. Which generation(s) of languages would a public relations manager be most likely to use? Why?

17. Suppose you are a programming manager and find that 12 of your 16 programmers would prefer to switch to COBOL from RPG. Would you support the switch, given that all 600 existing programs are written in RPG and only three programmers are proficient in COBOL? Why or why not?

18. Describe the circumstances in which the use of virtual memory would be counterproductive.

19. Explain in general terms what a natural language would do with the following command: "List all fixed inventory items in the purchasing department purchased prior to 1985." Give an example of what a response to the request might look like. Fixed inventory items would include items such as desks, chairs, lamps, and so on.

20. If code generators can produce functional COBOL and PL/I programs, why would anyone ever write a COBOL or PL/I program?

Self-Test (by section)

8–1 _____ software is more general than _____ software.

8–2 When programming in one of the first three generations of languages, you tell the computer *what* to do, not *how* to do it. (T/F)

8–3 Assembler languages use mnemonics to represent instructions. (T/F)

8–4 **a.** An object program is always free of logic errors. (T/F)

    b. What systems software program ultimately performs the same function as a compiler: (a) utility program, (b) DBMS, or (c) interpreter?

8–5 **a.** A COBOL program has _____ (how many) divisions.

b. FORTRAN is oriented to addressing what type of applications: (a) business, (b) scientific, or (c) multipurpose?

8–6 A fourth-generation program normally will have fewer instructions than the same program written in a third-generation language. (T/F)

8–7 **a.** An individual must undergo extensive training before he or she can write programs in a natural language. (T/F)

b. The dictionary of words that can be interpreted by the computer in a natural language is called the _____.

8–8 **a.** Application generators are used almost exclusively for ad hoc requests for information. (T/F)

b. The generic reusable code of application generators must occasionally be supplemented with _____ to handle unique situations.

8–9 **a.** The operating system program that is always resident in main memory is called the supervisor. (T/F)

b. A micro user must "kick the system" to load the operating system to RAM prior to processing. (T/F)

c. A user-friendly interface between the operating system, the applications program, and user files is called an operating environment. (T/F)

d. Programmers often use JCL to specify the _____, or the sequence in which their programs are to be executed.

e. What type of systems software provides information on processor utilization: (a) utility programs, (b) performance monitoring software, or (c) communications software?

8–10 **a.** Programs are segmented into pages before they are spooled. (T/F)

b. Virtual memory effectively expands the capacity of primary storage through the use of software and secondary storage. (T/F)

Self-test answers. **8–1** Systems, applications. **8–2** F. **8–3** T. **8–4** (a) F; (b) c. **8–5** (a) four; (b) b. **8–6** T. **8–7** (a) F; (b) lexicon. **8–8** (a) F; (b) custom code. **8–9** (a) T; (b) F; (c) T; (d) job stream; (e) b. **8–10** (a) F; (b) T.

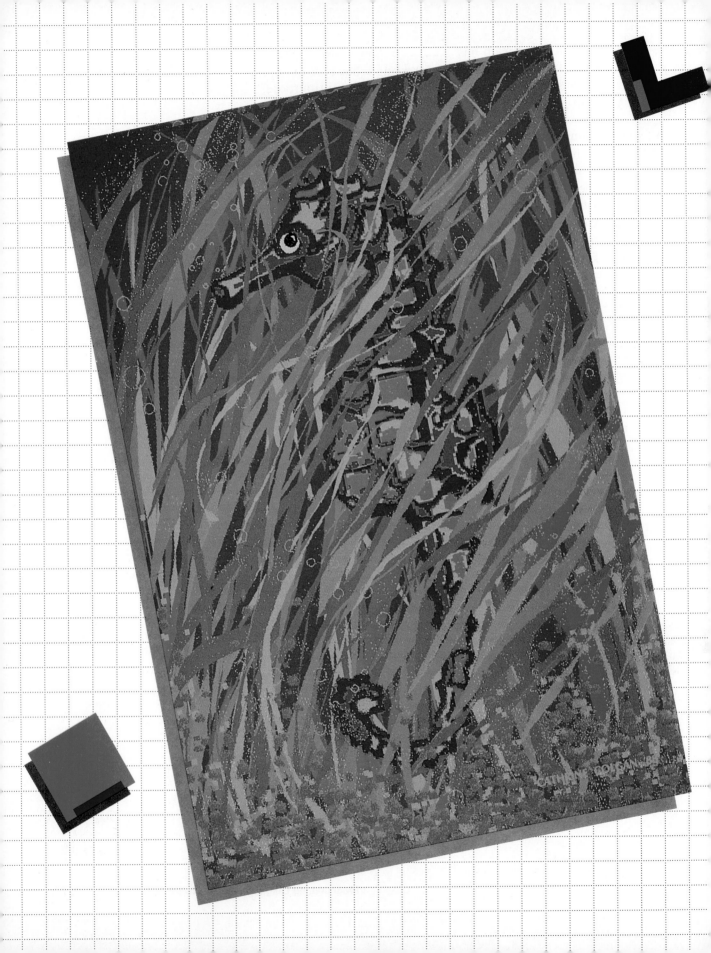

9
Data Management

STUDENT LEARNING OBJECTIVES

- To identify sources of data.
- To describe and illustrate the relationships between the levels of the hierarchy of data organization.
- To describe how data are stored, retrieved, and manipulated in computer systems.
- To demonstrate an understanding of the principles and use of sequential and random processing.
- To demonstrate an understanding of the principles and use of database management systems.
- To discuss the differences between file-oriented and data base organization.
- To distinguish between the data structures of hierarchical, network (CODASYL), and relational database management systems.

9–1 Data: Sources and Management

Sources of Data

This chapter is about organizing and managing data, but where do data come from? And how are data compiled?

Obtaining the data necessary to extract information and generate output is always one of the more challenging tasks in information processing. Data have many sources. They can be compiled as a result of a telephone call (telephone orders); received in the form of letters and turnaround documents (utility bills with returnable stubs); and collected on remote terminals, perhaps as part of a point-of-sale transaction. Some data are generated outside the company (when a customer submits an order specifying type and quantity of products). Most data, however, are generated internally—expenses, inventory activity, hours worked, and so on.

Data can come from strange places. For example, metal sensors in the streets relay data to a central computer that controls traffic. Long-distance telephone calls generate destination and duration data for billing purposes. Digitizing an image, perhaps in an X-ray, creates data. Even hardware errors provide a source of data.

The data we need are not always readily available. They are not usually in the proper format, or they are not complete or up-to-date. Once consistent and reliable sources of data have been identified for a particular application, procedures must be established to obtain them. To do this, users and MIS professionals work together to es-

The stock exchange is a source of thousands of pieces of data. An information system continually updates a securities data base so that stockbrokers in offices all over the country have access to up-to-the-minute quotations on stocks, bonds, and commodities.

tablish a scheme for collecting and organizing the data and a method by which to manage the data. This chapter will provide some insight into how this is done.

Data Management

Data management encompasses the storage, retrieval, and manipulation of data. This chapter includes discussions of the concepts and methods involved in computer-based data management. Traditional methods of data organization are presented first, then database management systems.

Your present or future employer will probably use both the traditional and the data base approaches to data management. Many existing information systems were designed using traditional approaches to data management, but the trend now is to use the data base approach to develop new information systems.

9-2 The Hierarchy of Data Organization: Bits to Data Bases

This section is devoted to discussing the *hierarchy of data organization*. Each information system has a hierarchy of data organization, and each succeeding level in the hierarchy is the result of combining the elements of the preceding level (see Figure 9–1). Data are logically combined in this fashion until a data base is achieved. The six levels of the hierarchy are *bit*, *character*, *data element* or *field*, *record*, *file*, and *data base*. Bits—the first level—are handled automatically, without action on the part of either the programmer or the end user. The other five levels are important design considerations for any information

FIGURE 9–1 The Hierarchy of Data Organization

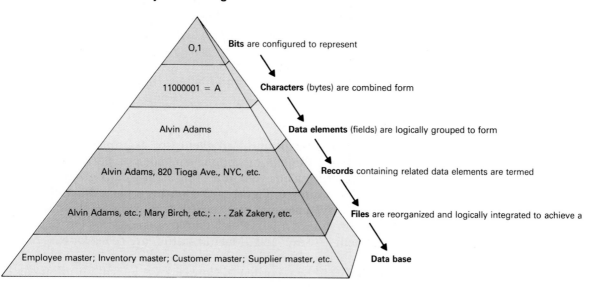

- **Bits** are configured to represent
- **Characters** (bytes) are combined form
- **Data elements** (fields) are logically grouped to form
- **Records** containing related data elements are termed
- **Files** are reorganized and logically integrated to achieve a
- **Data base**

0,1

11000001 = A

Alvin Adams

Alvin Adams, 820 Tioga Ave., NYC, etc.

Alvin Adams, etc.; Mary Birch, etc.; . . . Zak Zakery, etc.

Employee master; Inventory master; Customer master; Supplier master, etc.

processing activity. The following paragraphs explain each level of the hierarchy and how it relates to the succeeding level.

Bits and Characters

A **character** is represented by a group of **bits** that are configured according to an encoding system, such as ASCII or EBCDIC. Whereas the bit is the basic unit of primary and secondary storage, the character is the basic unit for human perception. When we enter a program instruction on a terminal, each character is automatically encoded into a bit configuration. The bit configurations are decoded on output so we can read and understand the output. In terms of data storage, a character is usually the same as a **byte**. (See Chapter 4, "Inside the Computer," for more on bits, bytes, and encoding systems.)

Data Elements, or Fields

The **data element**, or **field**, is the lowest level *logical* unit in the data hierarchy. For example, a single character (such as *A*) has little meaning out of context. But when characters are combined to form a name (for example, *Alicia* or *Alvin*), they form a logical unit. A data element is best described by example: Social Security number, first name, street address, marital status. These are all data elements.

An address is not one, but four data elements: street address, city, state, and ZIP code. If we treated the entire address as one data element, it would be cumbersome to print because the street address is normally placed on a separate line from the city, state, and ZIP code. Because name-and-address files are often sorted by ZIP code, it is also a good idea to store the ZIP code as a separate data element.

When it is stored in secondary storage, a data element is allocated a certain number of character positions. The number of these positions is called the field length. The field length of a telephone area code is 3. The field length of a telephone number is 7.

Whereas the data element, or field, is the general (or generic) reference, the specific content of a data element is called the **data item**. For example, a Social Security number is a data element, but *445487279* and *440214158* are data items. A street address is a data element, but *1701 El Camino* and *134 East Himes Street* are data items.

Records

A **record** is a description of an event (for example, a sale, a hotel reservation) or a thing (for example, a person or a part). Related data elements describing an event or a thing are logically grouped to form a record. For example, Figure 9–2 contains a partial list of data elements for a typical employee record. It also shows the data items for an *occurrence* of a particular employee record (Alvin E. Smith). "Department," "Sex," and "Marital status" are *coded* for ease of data entry and to save storage space.

In general, the record is the lowest level logical unit that can be

Data Elements	Data Items
Employee/social security number	445447279
Last name	SMITH
First name	ALVIN
Middle initial	E
Department (coded)	ACT
Sex (coded)	M
Marital status (coded)	S
Salary (per week)	800.00

FIGURE 9–2   A Portion of an Employee Record
The data elements listed are commonly found in employee records. Data items appear next to each data element.

accessed from a file. For instance, if the personnel manager needs to know only the marital status of Alvin E. Smith, he will have to retrieve Smith's entire record from secondary storage and transmit it to primary storage for processing.

Files

A **file** is a collection of related records. The employee master file contains a record for each employee. An inventory file contains a record for each inventory item. The accounts receivable file contains a record for each customer. The term *file* is also used to refer to a named area on a secondary storage device that contains a *program* or *textual material* (such as a letter).

Data Bases

The **data base** is the data resource for every computer-based information system. In essence, a data base is a collection of files that are in some way logically related to one another. In a data base, the data are integrated and related so that data redundancy is minimized. For example, if records are kept in a traditional file environment and an employee moves, his or her address must be changed in all files that maintain address data. In a data base, employee address data are stored only once and are made available to all departments. Therefore, only one update is needed.

The customer file on this sales representative's portable PC contains pertinent client information such as name, address, and product preference. The file also contains data for on-the-spot price quotations. To make inquiries involving product availability and delivery dates, the representative establishes a communications link with the company's centralized mainframe computer system and its data base. He can then use his portable PC as a remote terminal.

Memory Bits

**HIERARCHY OF DATA
ORGANIZATION**
- Bit
- Character (byte)
- Data element, or field
- Record
- File
- Data base

Database management system software, which is discussed later in this chapter, has enabled many organizations to move from traditional file organization to data base organization, thereby enjoying the benefits of a higher level of data management sophistication.

9-3 Traditional Approaches: Sequential and Random Processing

In traditional file processing, files are sorted, merged, and processed by a **key data element**. For example, in a payroll file the key might be *employee name*, and in an inventory file the key might be *part number*.

When you write programs based on the traditional approaches, data are manipulated and retrieved from secondary storage either *sequentially* or *randomly*. Typically, magnetic tape is used only for *sequential access*. Magnetic disks have *random-access*, or *direct-access*, capabilities as well as sequential-access capabilities. The function and operation of data storage devices, such as magnetic tape and disk, are covered in Chapter 6, "Data Storage Devices and Media." Sequential and random processing concepts are presented in detail in the sections that follow.

Sequential Processing

Sequential files, used for **sequential processing**, contain records that are ordered according to a key data element. The key, also called a **control field**, in an employee record might be Social Security number or employee name. If the key is Social Security number, the employee records are ordered and processed numerically by that number. If the key is employee name, the records are ordered and processed alphabetically by last name. A sequential file is processed from start to finish. The entire file must be processed, even if only one record is to be updated.

The principal storage medium for sequential files is magnetic tape. Direct-access storage devices (DASD), such as magnetic disks, also can be used for sequential processing.

Principles of Sequential Processing   Sequential-processing procedures for updating an inventory file are illustrated in Figures 9–3, 9–4, and 9–5. Figure 9–3 lists the contents of an inventory **master file**, which is the permanent source of inventory data, and a **transaction file**, which reflects the daily inventory activity.

Prior to processing, the records on both files are sorted and arranged in ascending sequence by part number (the key). A utility sort program takes a file of unsequenced records and creates a new file with the records sorted according to the values of the key. The sort process is illustrated in Figure 9–4.

Figure 9–5 shows both the inventory master and transaction files

Inventory master file (sorted by part number)

	Part no.	Price	No. used to date	No. in stock
One record →	2	25	40	200
	4	1.40	100 [106] *	100 [94]
	8	.80	500	450
	•	•	•	•
	•	•	•	•
	•	•	•	•
	20	4.60	60 [72]	14 [2]
	21	2.20	50	18

*[ ] reflects updated values

Transaction file (sorted by part number)

Part no.	No. used today
4	6
20	12

FIGURE 9–3 Inventory Master and Transaction Files
Both files are sorted by part number. The numbers in brackets [ ] reflect the inventory master file after the update. Figures 9–5 and 9–6 show the update process.

as input and the *new inventory master file* as output. Since the technology does not permit records to be "rewritten" on the master file, a new master file tape is created to reflect the updates to the master file. *A new master file is always created in sequential processing for master file updates.* The processing steps are illustrated in Figure 9–5 and explained as follows:

FIGURE 9–4 Sorting
Unsequenced inventory master and transaction files are sorted prior to sequential processing. Normally the master file would have been sorted as a result of prior processing.

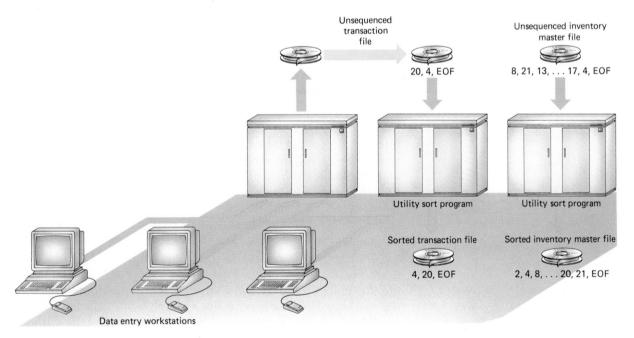

Unsequenced transaction file
20, 4, EOF

Unsequenced inventory master file
8, 21, 13, . . . 17, 4, EOF

Utility sort program

Utility sort program

Sorted transaction file
4, 20, EOF

Sorted inventory master file
2, 4, 8, . . . 20, 21, EOF

Data entry workstations

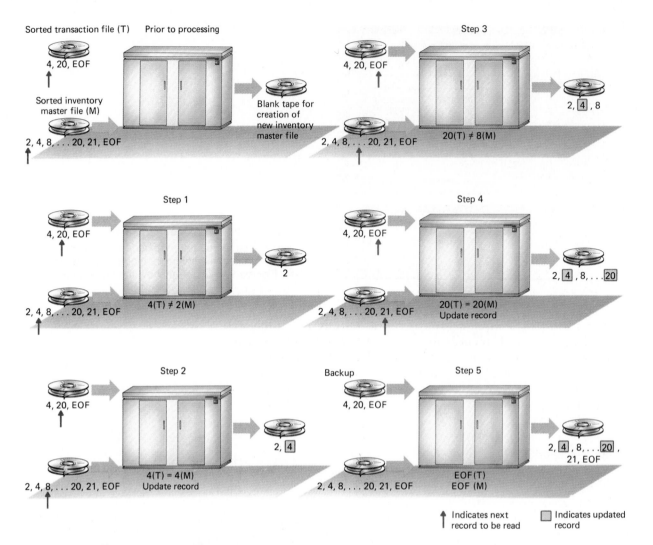

FIGURE 9–5 Sequential Processing
An inventory master file is updated using sequential processing and magnetic tapes. Processing steps are discussed in the text. Notice in Step 5 that the backup is a by-product of sequential processing.

■ *Prior to processing*. If the two input tapes are *not sorted* by part number, they must be sorted as shown in Figure 9–4. The sorted tapes are then mounted on the tape drives. A blank tape, mounted on a third tape drive, will ultimately contain the updated master file. The arrows under the part numbers in Figure 9–5 indicate which records are positioned before the read/write heads on the respective tape drives. These records are the *next* to be read. Each file has an **end-of-file marker** (**EOF**) that signals its end.

■ *Step 1*. The first record (4) on the transaction file (T) is read and loaded to primary storage. Then the first record (2) on the master file (M) is loaded to primary storage. A comparison is made of the two keys. Because there is not a match (4 ≠ 2), the first record on the master file is written to the new master file tape without being changed.

- *Step 2*. The next record (4) on the master file is read and loaded to primary storage. After a positive comparison (4 = 4), the record of Part Number 4 is updated (see Figure 9–3) to reflect the use of six items and then written to the new master file. In Figure 9–3 note that the "number in stock" data item is reduced from 100 to 94 and the "number used to date" is increased from 100 to 106. Updated records in Figure 9–5 are enclosed in boxes.

- *Step 3*. The next record from the transaction file (20) and the next record from the master file (8) are read and loaded to primary storage. A comparison is made. Because the comparison is negative (20 ≠ 8), the record for Part 8 is written to the new master file without being changed.

- *Step 4*. Records from the master file are individually read and loaded, and the part number is compared to that of the transaction record (20). With each negative comparison (for example, 20 ≠ 17), the record from the old master file is written, without change, to the new master file. The read-and-compare process continues until a match is made (20 = 20). Record 20 is then updated and written to the new master file.

- *Step 5*. A "read" is issued to the transaction file and an end-of-file marker is found. All records on the master file following the record for Part Number 20 are written to the new master file, and the end-of-file marker is recorded on it. All tapes are then automatically rewound and removed from the tape drives for off-line storage and processing at a later time.

Backup The transaction file and old master file are retained as **backup files** to the new master file. Fortunately, backup is a by-product of sequential processing. After the new master file is created, the old master file and the transaction file comprise the backup. If the new master is destroyed, the transaction file can simply be run against the old master file to re-create the new master file.

Backup files are handled and maintained by *generation*, the up-to-date master file being the current generation. This tape cycling procedure is called the **grandfather-father-son method** of file backup. The "son" file is the up-to-date master file. The "father" generation of backup is noted in Step 5 of Figure 9–5. Most computer centers maintain a "grandfather" file (from the last update run) as a backup for the most recent backup.

Random or Direct-Access Processing

A **direct-access file**, or a **random file**, is a collection of records that can be processed randomly (in any order). This is called **random processing**. Only the value of the record's key field is needed in order for a record to be retrieved or updated. More often than not, magnetic disks are the primary storage medium for random processing.

You can access records on a direct-access file by more than one key. For example, a salesperson inquiring about the availability of a particular product could inquire by *product number* and, if the product

Federal Express couriers use the SuperTracker (left), a hand-held OCR data collection device, to track the progress of packages from source to destination. Package status information, such as pickup or delivery times, is transmitted directly to the company's centralized data base through the DADS (Digitally Assisted Dispatch System) units in the courier vans. The customer service agents at this and other information pods (right) access the up-to-the-minute data base for package status information when responding to customer inquiries.

number is not known, by *product name*. The file, however, must be created with the intent of having multiple keys.

Principles of Random Processing   In Figure 9–6 the inventory master file of Figure 9–3 is updated from an on-line terminal to illustrate the principles of random processing. The following activities take place during the update:

- *Step 1*. The first transaction (for Part Number 20) is entered into primary storage from an on-line terminal. The computer issues a "read" for the record of Part Number 20 on the inventory mas-

FIGURE 9–6   Random Processing
An inventory master file is updated using random processing and magnetic disks. Processing steps are discussed in the text.

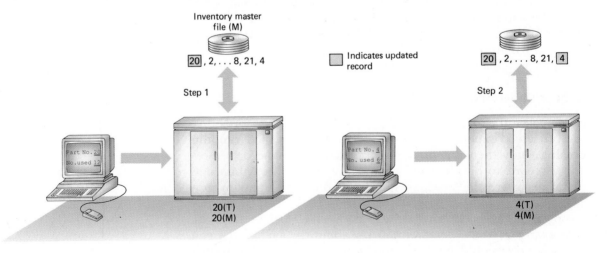

FIGURE 9–7 Backup Procedure for Random Processing
Unlike sequential processing, a separate run is required to create
the backup for random processing.

ter file. The record is retrieved and transmitted to primary storage for processing. The record is updated and written back to
the *same* location on the master file. The updated record is
simply written over the old record.

- *Step 2*. A second transaction (for Part Number 4) is entered into
  primary storage. The computer issues a "read" for the record of
  Part Number 4 on the inventory master file. The record is retrieved and transmitted to primary storage for processing. The
  record is then updated.

Because only two updates are made to the inventory master file,
processing is complete. However, unlike sequential processing where
the backup is built-in, random processing requires a special run to
provide backup for the inventory master file. In the backup activity
illustrated in Figure 9–7, the master file is "dumped" from disk to
tape at frequent intervals, usually daily. If the inventory master file
is destroyed, it can be re-created by dumping the backup file (on tape)
to disk (the reverse of Figure 9–7).

As you can see, random processing is more straightforward than
sequential processing, and it has those advantages associated with
on-line, interactive processing. Figure 9–8 summarizes the differences
between sequential and random processing.

**FIGURE 9–8 Differences Between Sequential
and Random Processing**

	Sequential Processing	Random Processing
Primary storage medium		
Preprocessing	Files must be sorted	None required
File updating	Requires complete processing of file and creation of new master file	Only active records are processed, then rewritten to the same storage area
Data currency	Batch (at best, data are a day old)	On-line (up-to-the-minute)
Backup	Built-in (old master file and transaction file)	Requires special provisions

Random-Access Methods

Indexed-sequential organization. The way a particular record is accessed directly is, for the most part, transparent to users, and even to programmers. That is, users and programmers are not involved in the mechanics of accessing data from disk storage. However, some familiarity will help you understand the capabilities and limitations of direct-access methods. The **indexed-sequential method** of file organization is a popular method that permits both sequential and random processing.

When accessing a record from magnetic disk, the disk access arm—and therefore the read/write head—must be positioned over the track containing the desired record. In indexed-sequential organization, the access of any given record is, in effect, a series of sequential searches through several levels of indices. These indices minimize the search time for locating the record to be processed. Figure 9–9 illustrates how indices are used to locate a particular record using the indexed-sequential method.

When an indexed-sequential file is created, several data records are grouped together, or *blocked*, and an **index file** is created. The index file is also blocked, but in a hierarchical manner. The number of levels of index blocks varies with the size of the file. Each index block contains *index records*. Extra index records are included in each block to allow records to be added in the future.

Each index record contains a value of a key and a **pointer** (see Figure 9–9). The pointer indicates whether to go to the next level of

FIGURE 9–9 Retrieving a Record from an Indexed-Sequential File
The figure illustrates how the record for Part Number 6173 would be located and retrieved using the indexed-sequential method of file organization. Processing steps are discussed in the text.

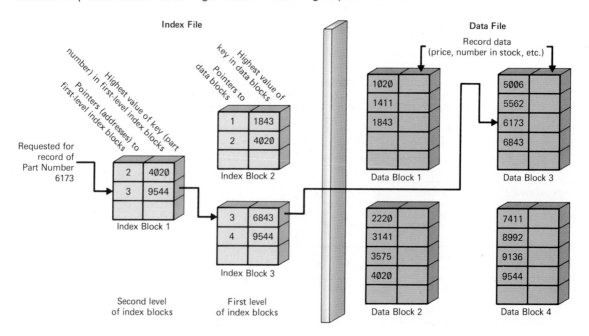

index blocks or directly to a data block. The pointer is a *physical address* indicating the disk location (that is, the disk pack, disk face surface and/or sector, track, and record number) of the first index record in an index block or the first data record in a data block. To simplify the example in Figure 9–9, the actual disk addresses are omitted and are replaced with the numbers of the index blocks (2 and 3) and data blocks (1, 2, 3, and 4).

The key value in each index record is the *highest value key* contained in the next level index block or the data block. For example, the first record in Index Block 1 (the second and highest level of index blocks) contains a pointer to Index Block 2 (in the first level of index blocks); therefore, the highest key value (4020) in Index Block 2 is included in the first record of Index Block 1. The second record in Index Block 1 contains a pointer to Index Block 3 and the highest key value (9544) in Index Block 3.

As you read through the following example, you should get a basic understanding of how an indexed-sequential file works. Suppose you would like to retrieve the record for Part Number 6173 in Figure 9–9.

- *Begin the search with Index Block 1*. The search begins with the first record of Index Block 1, the highest level index block. Each index block is searched sequentially, beginning with the first index record to determine which block to search at the next level. Because 6173 is greater than the highest key value in Index Block 2 (4020), the search proceeds to the next index record in Index Block 1. Since 6173 is less than 9544, the search is directed to Index Block 3 (in the first level of index blocks).

- *Continue the search at the next level of index blocks*. The search always begins with the highest level index block (second level in the example) and progresses through each successive level in the index file and eventually to the data file. Because the search is directed to Index Block 3, the records of Index Block 3 are searched sequentially until the search is directed to the next index level or, in the example, a data block. Since 6173 is less than 6843, there is no need to search any more records in Index Block 3. In the example, the search is directed to Data Block 3.

- *Search the data block for the desired record*. Data Block 3 is searched sequentially until the record for Part Number 6173 is located. The third record of Data Block 3 contains the record for Part Number 6173.

- *Read the desired record*. The record is read and transmitted to main memory for processing.

It should be emphasized again that the search and retrieval process is transparent to the programmer. The programmer has only to issue a "read" for Part Number 6173. The computer and indexed-sequential software do the rest.

Direct access. Another method of accessing records randomly applies a formula, called a *hashing algorithm*, to the record key. The disk address is arithmetically calculated from the key. The advantage of this method, sometimes called **hashing**, is that usually only one disk access is needed to retrieve a record. In contrast, the indexed-sequential method requires several disk accesses.

The address of a record is derived from the key field. For example, to obtain the record of Part Number 6173 in an inventory master file, the key value (6173) is input to a formula that yields a disk address (cylinder, recording surface, and record). A wide variety of hashing algorithms are used for directly accessing records.

The limited number of disk accesses permits records to be retrieved more quickly with direct access than with the indexed-sequential method. The latter, however, permits records to be accessed sequentially as well as randomly. These are the basic trade-offs between the two random-access methods.

9-4 The Data Base: Solving the Data Puzzle

Data Integration

The traditional sequential and random files discussed earlier in this chapter typically are designed to meet the specific information and data processing requirements of a particular functional area department such as accounting, sales, or purchasing. Different files are created to support these functions, but many of the data elements on each of these files are the same. For example, each of these functional areas needs to maintain customer data, such as customer name, customer address, and the contact person at the customer location. When the name of the contact person changes in a traditional file environment, each file must be updated separately.

Through the early 1980s, most installed information systems were implemented in a crisis environment with a single functional objective in mind. The integration of information systems was not a priority. As result, many companies are saddled with massive system, procedural, and data redundancies. These redundancies promote in-

The data base supporting the air traffic control system contains the location, altitude, and flight path of all aircraft. The system gives controllers a visual and audible warning when adequate aircraft separation is violated.

efficiencies and result in unnecessary expenses. Today companies are using **database management system** (**DBMS**) software as a tool to integrate data management and information flow within an organization.

Costly data redundancy can be minimized by designing an *integrated data base* to serve the organization as a whole, not just one specific department. The integrated data base is made possible by database management system software. Notice that *database* is one word when it refers to the software that manages the data base. *Data base* is two words when it refers to the highest level of the hierarchy of data organization (see Figure 9–1).

Benefits of a Data Base Environment

There are many reasons why a company would begin with or convert to a data base environment.

Greater Access to Information   Most organizations have accumulated a wealth of data, but translating these data into meaningful information has, at times, proved difficult, especially in a traditional file environment. The structure of an integrated data base provides enormous flexibility in the types of reports that can be generated and the types of on-line inquiries that can be made.

Better Control   A database management system allows data to be centralized for improved security. Also, by centralizing data, advanced data structures can be used to control data redundancy. The term *data structures* refers to the manner in which the data elements and records are related to one another.

More Efficient Software Development   The programming task is simplified with a database management system because data are more readily available. In addition, data in a data base are *independent* of the applications programs. That is, data elements can be added, changed, and deleted from the data base without affecting existing programs. Adding a data element to a record of a traditional file may require the modification and testing of dozens and sometimes hundreds of programs.

Approaches to Data Base Management

Database management systems software has overcome the processing constraints of traditional files. To do this, such systems rely on sophisticated data structures. The data structures vary considerably from one commercially available DBMS software package to another. However, there are three fundamental approaches to the design of DBMS software:

- The **hierarchical DBMS**
- The **network DBMS**, or **CODASYL DBMS** (The *C*onference for *Da*ta *Sy*stems *L*anguages, or CODASYL, is an industry-funded

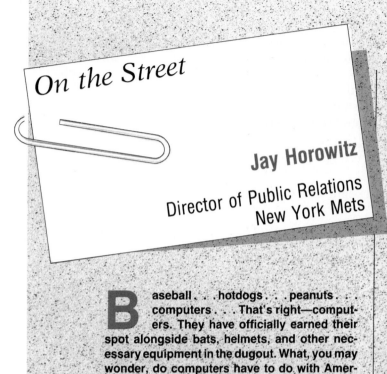

association in which volunteers from different organizations cooperate to develop and recommend standards for database management systems, programming languages, and other computer-related activities.)

■ The **relational DBMS**

The examples presented in the following sections should help you better understand the principles and advantages of the three types of database management systems.

Hierarchical DBMS

Background. Although network and relational DBMS technologies are considered superior to hierarchical DBMS technology, the hierarchical approach remains the most commonly used. This is more a result of momentum than choice. In 1968 IBM announced its *Infor-*

mation Management Systems (*IMS*), a hierarchical DBMS product. At the time it was the only database management system available and became enormously popular. *IMS* was designed to be run on the hardware of the day. A large mainframe in 1968 had approximately the same speed and capacity as today's top-of-the-line desktop micro. With limited hardware capabilities, *IMS* designers opted for the simplicity of the hierarchical design. Although *IMS* has been upgraded many times, it is still a hierarchical system and does not have the scope of features of the more sophisticated network and relational DBMSs. It does, however, have two decades of momentum, and *IMS* users are reluctant to scrap their sizable investments and start over with a network or relational DBMS. Nevertheless, virtually all new development in the area of database management systems uses network and/or relational technologies.

A hierarchical DBMS example. Hierarchical DBMSs are based on the tree data structure, actually an uprooted tree turned upside down. Hierarchies are easy to understand and conceptualize. A company's organizational chart is a good example of the tree structure. At the top of the chart is the president, with the vice presidents in the second level, subordinate to the president. Those people reporting to the vice presidents occupy the third level.

Hierarchical structures are equally appropriate for data management. Consider the employee data base in Figure 9–10. In the example, an information center in a large company has several full-time in-house instructors, each of whom gives courses on a variety of subjects. The data base includes the skill areas and associated skill levels for each instructor. For example, an instructor might have skills in word processing and local area networks at Skill Levels 4 and 3, respectively. A particular course (word processing) may be given sev-

FIGURE 9–10   A Structure for a Hierarchical Data Base
The data base records for instructor, [instructor] skills, course, [course] offering, and [course] attendees are linked to the root in a hierarchical manner to form the structure of a hierarchical data base.

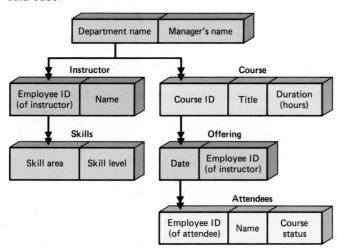

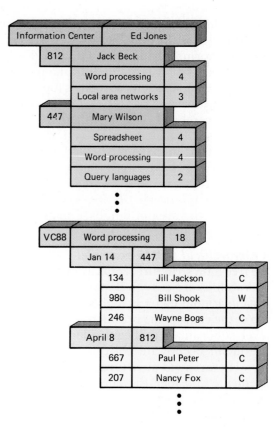

FIGURE 9–11 A Partial Occurrence of the Hierarchical Data Base Structure of Figure 9–10

Mary Wilson (employee ID 447) taught the January 14 offering of the word processing course.

eral times a year, possibly by different instructors. Each offering of a course is attended by at least one employee who either completes (C) the course or withdraws (W), thereby prompting a C or W to be entered in the course status field (see Figures 9–10 and 9–11).

Figure 9–11 shows a partial *occurrence* of the information center's hierarchical data base structure. The hierarchical structure of the data base and the occurrence are analogous to the data element and the data item (for example, employee name, Jack Beck). One is the definition—the category, or abstract—and the other is the actual value, or content.

In hierarchical DBMSs, a group of fields is called a **segment** and can be likened to the record in a traditional file. The segment, or **data base record**, is similar to the record of a traditional file in that it is a collection of related data elements and is read from, or written to, the data base as a unit. The relationship between a segment at a higher level to one connected by a line at a lower level is that of a *parent* and *child* or *children*. In Figure 9–10, the instructor segment is the parent of the skills segment. The possibility of "children" (for example, instructors with multiple skills) is denoted by a double arrow on the connector line. In a hierarchical data base, no segment has more than one parent. The *root*, or highest level, does not have a parent.

The information center tree illustrated in Figure 9–10 could be linked with other trees, perhaps the employee tree, to create informative reports. For example, the employee ID data items in the at-

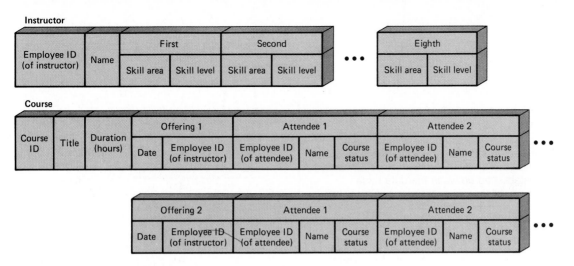

FIGURE 9–12 Record Layouts
These record layouts for a course file and an instructor file are traditional file alternatives to the hierarchical data base structure of Figure 9–10.

tendees' segments could be used to "point" to more detailed information about a particular attendee (department affiliation, extension number, and so on).

If this application were designed using traditional approaches to data management, there would probably be two files, the course file and the instructor file. The record layout for these two files might appear as shown in Figure 9–12.

Network, or CODASYL, DBMS The network approach to data management carries the hierarchical approach to the next level of sophistication by permitting "children" to have more than one "parent."

A network DBMS example. Consider the following situation. A library currently maintains a file that contains the following data elements on each record:

- Title
- Author(s)
- Publisher
- Publisher's address
- Classification
- Publication year

The head librarian wants more flexibility in obtaining decision-making information. Many of the librarian's requests would be impractical with the existing traditional file (see Figure 9–13). A data

FIGURE 9–13 Record Layout
This record layout is for a traditional book inventory file in a library.

Title	ISBN	Publication year	Publisher	Publisher's address	Author 1	Author 2	Author 3	Author 4

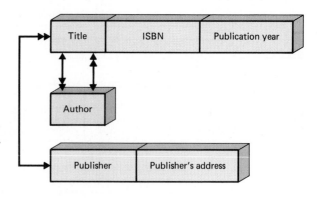

FIGURE 9–14   A Network, or CODASYL, Data Base Schema

The record layout of the traditional book inventory file in Figure 9–13 is reorganized into data base records and integrated into a data base schema to minimize redundancy. Relationships are established between the data base records so that authors, titles, and publishers can be linked as appropriate.

base administrator recommends restructuring the file as a network database management system. The data base administrator is an MIS specialist who designs and maintains the data base.

Not surprisingly, the data base administrator finds certain data redundancies in the existing file. Because each book or title has a separate record, the *name* of an author who has written several books is repeated for each book written. A given publisher may have hundreds, even thousands, of books in the library—but in the present file, the *publisher* and *publisher's address* are repeated for each title. To eliminate these data redundancies, the data base administrator suggests the records, or segments, shown in Figure 9–14.

Next, the data base administrator establishes the relationships between the records. There is a *one-to-many* relationship between the publisher and title records. That is, one publisher may publish any number of titles. The publisher–title relationship is represented in Figure 9–14 by a connecting line between the two records. A double arrow toward the title record represents the possibility of more than one title per publisher. The publisher–title combination is called a **set**. Other sets defined by the data base administrator are title–author and author–title. Figure 9–14 is a graphic representation of the logical structure of the data base, called a **schema** (pronounced *SKEE-muh*).

In the data base schema of Figure 9–14, a particular author's name appears only once. It is then linked to the title records of those books he or she has written. The publisher record is linked to all the titles it publishes. When accessing a record in a program, you simply request the record of a particular title, author, or publisher. Once you have the author's record, you can use the links between records to retrieve the titles of the books written by that author. Similarly, if you request the record of a particular publisher, you can obtain a list of all titles it has published.

Figure 9–14 is a representation of the schema and Figure 9–15 shows an occurrence of the data base structure.

Queries to the data base.   This data base design eliminates, or at least minimizes, data redundancy and permits the head librarian to make a wide range of inquiries. For example:

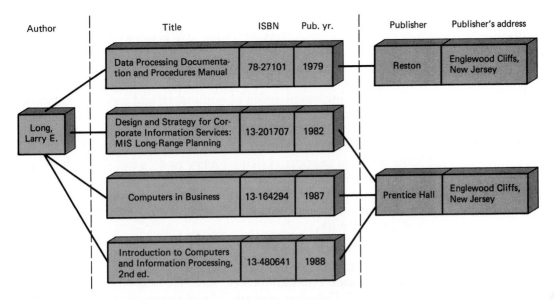

FIGURE 9–15   An Occurrence of the Network Data Base Structure of Figure 9–14
Notice that publishers can be linked to authors via the title record, and vice versa.

- What titles were written by Mark Twain?
- List those titles published by Prentice Hall in 1986 (alphabetically by title).

Responses to these and similar inquiries are relatively easy to obtain with a database management system. Similar inquiries of the library's existing traditional file (Figure 9–13) would require not only the complete processing of the file but perhaps several data-preparation computer runs for sorting and merging.

If the head librarian decides after a year to add, for example, the Library of Congress number to the title record, the data base administrator can make the revision without affecting existing programs.

Relational DBMS

Relational versus network DBMSs.   The relational approach to database management systems has been gaining momentum through the 1980s. In contrast to the network DBMS, data are accessed by *content* rather than by *address*. That is, the relational approach uses the computer to search the data base for the desired data rather than accessing data through a series of indices and physical addresses, as with both the hierarchical and network DBMSs. In relational DBMSs, the data structures, or relationships between data, are defined in *logical* rather than *physical* terms. That is, the relational data base has no predetermined relationship between the data, such as the one-to-many sets in the network schemas (see Figure 9–14). In this way, data can be accessed at the *data element* level. In network structures, the entire data base record must be retrieved in order to examine a single data element.

Until recently, relational DBMSs have been to slow to be effective in the real world, especially in transaction-oriented environments. Even with the increased speed of computers and innovations in relational technology, network data base management systems outperform relational DBMSs for transaction processing. However, for applications in which the transaction volume is low and the need for flexible decision support systems (query and "what if") is high, relational DBMSs outperform network DBMSs. Because relational structures provide greater flexibility in accessing information, relational DBMSs provide companies with greater opportunities to increase productivity.

A relational DBMS example. Let's stay with library applications for our relational DBMS example, but let's shift emphasis from book inventory to book circulation. The objective of a circulation system is to keep track of who borrows which books, then monitor their timely return. In the traditional file environment, the record layout might appear as shown in Figure 9–16. In the record shown, a library patron can borrow from one to four books. Precious storage space is wasted for patrons who borrow infrequently, and the four-book limit may force prolific readers to make more trips to the library.

The data base administrator recommended the relational DBMS organization shown in Figure 9–17. The data base contains two *tables*, each containing rows and columns of data. A *row*, or **tuple**, in a table is roughly equivalent to an occurrence of a data base record in a hierarchical or network data base. The column headings, called **attributes**, are analogous to fields (data elements) of the hierarchical and network data bases.

The first table contains patron data, and the second table contains data relating to books on loan. Each new patron is assigned a number and issued a library card with a number that can be read with an optical wand scanner. The patron's card number, name, and address are added to the data base. When the patron borrows a book, the librarian at the circulation desk uses a wand scanner to enter the card number and the book's ISBN (International Standard Book Number). These data and the due date, which are entered on a keyboard, become a row in the Book on Loan table. Notice that by using a relational DBMS, there is no limit to the number of borrowed books the system can handle for a particular patron.

FIGURE 9–16 Record Layout
This record layout is for a traditional book circulation file in a library.

Card No.	First Name	Last Name	Address				Book #1 (ISBN)	Due Date	Book #2 (ISBN)	Due Date	Book #3 (ISBN)	Due Date	Book #4 (ISBN)	Due Date
			Street	City	ST	ZIP								

			Patron Data							Books-on-Loan Data	

Patron Data

Card No.	First Name	Last Name	Address				
			Street	City	ST	ZIP
1243	Jason	Jones	18 W. Oak	Ponca City	OK	74601
1618	Kay	Smith	108 10th St.	Newkirk	OK	74647
2380	Heather	Hall	2215 Pine Dr.	Ponca City	OK	74604
2644	Brett	Brown	1700 Sunset	Ponca City	OK	74604
3012	Melody	Beck	145 N. Brook	Ark. City	KS	67005
3376	Butch	Danner	RD#7	Tonkawa	OK	74653
3859	Abe	Michaels	333 Paul Ave.	Kaw City	OK	74641

Books-on-Loan Data

Card No.	Book No. (ISBN)	Due Date
1618	89303-530	4/7
1243	12-201702	4/20
3859	13-48049	4/9
2644	18-23614	4/14
2644	71606-214	4/14
2644	22-68111	4/3
1618	27-21675	4/12

FIGURE 9–17   A Relational Data Base Organization
The record layout of the traditional book circulation file of Figure 9–16 is reorganized and integrated into a relational data base with a Patron Data table and a Books-on-Loan Data table.

Queries to the data base.   Suppose the circulation librarian wanted a report of overdue books as of April 8 (4/8). The query would be: "List all books overdue" (query date is 4/8). The search criterion of "due date < [before] 4/8" is applied to the Due Date column in the Books on Loan table (see Figure 9–18). The search surfaces two overdue books, then the system uses the card numbers to cross-reference delinquent patrons in the Patron table to obtain their names and addresses. The report at the bottom of Figure 9–18 is produced in response to the librarian's query. Data on each book, including publisher, author, and ISBN, might be maintained in another table in the relational data base.

Commercial Database Management Systems

There are well over 200 commercially available DBMS software packages. Each year some prove to be unprofitable and are removed from the market, but the gap is soon filled with innovative new products. Some microcomputer DBMSs sell for under $50 and some mainframe versions sell for over $250,000. Industry giant IBM dominates the minicomputer and mainframe DBMS market with the two-decade-old *IMS*, a hierarchical DBMS, and the recently introduced *DB2*, a relational DBMS. With *IMS* and *DB2*, IBM holds 50% of the DBMS

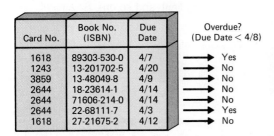

Card No.	Book No. (ISBN)	Due Date	Overdue? (Due Date < 4/8)
1618	89303-530-0	4/7	Yes
1243	13-201702-5	4/20	No
3859	13-48049-8	4/9	No
2644	18-23614-1	4/14	No
2644	71606-214-0	4/14	No
2644	22-68111-7	4/3	Yes
1618	27-21675-2	4/12	No

Overdue Books (4/8)			
Card No.	Name	Due Date	ISBN
1618	Kay Smith	4/7	89303-530-0
2644	Brett Brown	4/3	22-68111-7

FIGURE 9–18   Queries to a Relational Data Base
The figure illustrates the resolution and output of an April 8 query to the data base: "List all books overdue."

The emergence of high-density optical laser disk technology has made it economically feasible to store images as well as text in a data base. In this application, optical laser technology is used to store maps of British Telecom underground telephone lines and equipment. All maps are stored in the form of still pictures at different scales and can be retrieved with a microcomputer-based data management system.

market. *DB2*, announced in 1985, is far from the market leader, but all indicators say that it will lead the market in the early 1990s, if not sooner. Cullinet Software is a distant but solid second with *IDMS*, *IDMS/R*, and *IDMS/SQL*. Other major players include Applied Data Research's *Datacom*, Software AG of North America's *ADABAS*, Cincom Systems' *Total* and *Supra*, Oracle Corporation's *Oracle*, On-Line Software International's *RAMIS*, and Relational Technology's *Ingress*.

The runaway market leader among microcomputer DBMS products has been the dBASE series (*dBASE II, III, III PLUS*, and *IV*).

This realtor uses relational data management software to maintain a data base that contains pertinent client information, such as current address and various preferences (location, style of house, spending limit, and so on). Relational DBMSs are popular with micro users.

These Ashton-Tate products hold over one third of the market. Other commercially successful products include Borland International's *Paradox* and *Reflex*, Microrim's *R:base System V*, Micro Data Base Systems' *Knowledgeman*, and Condor Computer Corporation's *Condor 3*.

It is not always possible to pigeonhole a commercial DBMS as hierarchical, network, or relational. In practice, there are as many approaches to developing database management system software as there are DBMS products. To achieve the flexibility of relational technology and the transaction processing capabilities of network technology, a vendor might create a DBMS software package that embodies the best of both. Cullinet's *IDMS/R* is a good example of such a package. In fact, some commercial DBMSs are hybrids of all DBMS technologies, and others even make use of traditional file organization.

The application development tools that accompany commercial DBMS packages help differentiate them. A DBMS package can be purchased with none or all of the following development tools: fourth-generation query language, application or code generator, data dictionary, report generator, screen generator, prototyping tool, and others. They are discussed in Chapter 12, "System Analysis and Design."

Memory Bits

APPROACHES TO DATA MANAGEMENT

- Sequential processing
- Random (or direct) processing
  Indexed sequential
    organization
  Direct access
- Database management systems (DBMS)
  Hierarchical
  Network, or CODASYL
  Relational

Standards for Database Management Systems

For the most part, the 200-plus DBMS products on the market differ markedly in approach and the manner in which they store and retrieve data. Moreover, vendors have created their own proprietary data base query languages for data definition, retrieval, manipulation, and control. Typically, to respond to the query "List all books overdue" in the relational DBMS example, a query language program would have to be written (or generated automatically). The existence of a plethora of query languages has made it difficult, although not impossible, for data in one data base to be combined logically with that of another. However, this hurdle will be less of a concern in the coming years.

IBM's **SQL** (**Structured Query Language**), pronounced *sequel*, has been the de facto standard data access query language for relational data bases for several years. Recently, *SQL* was made the official standard by both ANSI (American National Standards Institute) and ISO (International Standards Organization). This means that in the future, vendors of relational DBMS software will design their packages so that they can interpret *SQL* commands. It also means that *SQL* can be used to permit the sharing of data by dissimilar software packages and DBMSs. This should spur the growth of both intercompany and intracompany networking.

Most industry observers, even skeptics, are predicting that IBM's *DB2* will be the de facto industry standard and may someday garner as much as two thirds of the DBMS market. In fact, *DB2* is already a market itself: Software vendors are developing productivity tools designed specifically for the *DB2* environment.

With *SQL* and *DB2* becoming industry standards, human skills (programming, data base administration) and software will have

DATA BASES CAN ENHANCE COLLEGE KNOWLEDGE

At some time or another, just about everybody is faced with resolving critical questions about college. Do I attend college? If so, where? College graduates must answer similar questions. Do I go on to graduate school? If so, where? To some prospective students, the answers are clear: Continue the family tradition at State U., or perhaps attend the local college. Others are faced with the awesome task of evaluating several thousand options. Certainly a well-informed decision maker is more likely to make the right decision than one who is not.

In the past, prospective students have sought information from a variety of sources, including "how to" books, books that summarize information about colleges, and thousands of college catalogs. Scanning through this information can be cumbersome, time-consuming, and expensive. Today's computer-based data bases offer an easier, faster, and less expensive way to choose a college. There are two ways of accessing these data bases. You can use your microcomputer to tap into a commercial information service that supports a college data base, or you can purchase the data base software on a diskette.

Peterson's College Database is one of a hundred databases made available to subscribers of CompuServe, the on-line information service with the most subscribers. Subscribers search its data base by identifying the features they desire in a college. The features include level of study, location, size, campus setting, housing, costs, majors, ethnic/geographic mix,

admissions requirements, entrance difficulty, type of student body, and 10 other categories. Options are selected for each feature. For example, for level of study, the user would choose:

1. Two-year college
2. Four-year college with no graduate work
3. University or four-year college with graduate work
4. Upper-level institution (starts at the junior year)

The data base is searched and only those colleges that meet the selection criteria are listed. The user can then request a display of an in-depth profile of any of the colleges on the list.

College Explorer is a software/data base product available for IBM PC compatibles and for the Apple II series. The interface with this program is similar to the on-line Peterson's College Database in that the prospective student must establish his or her search criteria. A search of the College Explorer data base results in two lists—one of colleges that meet all required and preferred conditions and the other consisting of colleges that meet all required conditions but not all the preferred conditions.

A criteria search of an on-line or diskette-based college data base can be completed in seconds. The advantages of computer-based data bases become vividly apparent when you consider that a similar but less rigorous search through printed college literature might take weeks, even months!

greater portability. That is, both humans and software can move easily from one computing environment to the next. When they do, humans will need little or no training and the software will need little or no modification. The overwhelming majority of people who have *SQL* programming skills and/or *DB2* design skills are MIS specialists.

DBMS Summary

The days of the centralized data base may be numbered. Emerging DBMS standards may enable MIS specialists to overcome the hurdle of data base connectivity. The ideal data storage scheme would optimize the use of available resources. Such a scheme would store data in the most convenient places within a computer network, depending on data entry requirements, storage capacity availability, processing load requirements, and so on. To implement this ideal data storage scheme, MIS specialists must use a **distributed DBMS**. A distributed

DBMS permits the interfacing of data bases located in various places throughout a computer network (departmental minicomputers, micro-based local nets, the corporate mainframe, and so on). The distributed DBMS functions as if it were centralized. The fact that it is distributed is transparent to the end user. That is, a user making a request would not be concerned about the source of the data or how they are retrieved. Unfortunately, the software for distributed DBMSs is still on the drawing board. However, talk of functionally distributed DBMSs will intensify as we move into the 1990s.

We all keep data, both at our place of business and at home. DBMS software and the availability of computing hardware make it easier for us to extract meaningful information from these data. In time, working with data bases will be as familiar to us as reaching in a desk drawer file for a manila folder.

Summary Outline and Important Terms

9–1 **DATA: SOURCES AND MANAGEMENT.** Data come from many sources. The source and method of data entry are important considerations in information processing. Some data are generated outside the organization, but most are generated as a result of internal operations. Most organizations use both the traditional and data base approaches to data management. The trend is toward the data base approach.

9–2 **THE HIERARCHY OF DATA ORGANIZATION: BITS TO DATA BASES.** The six levels of the hierarchy of data organization are **bit**, **character** (or **byte**), **data element** (or **field**), **record**, **file**, and **data base**. The first level is transparent to the programmer and end user, but the other five are integral to the design of any information processing activity. A string of bits is combined to form a character. Characters are combined to represent the content of data elements—**data items**. Related data elements are combined to form records. Records with the same data elements combine to form a file. The data base is the company's data resource for all information systems.

9–3 **TRADITIONAL APPROACHES: SEQUENTIAL AND RANDOM PROCESSING.** In traditional file processing, files are sorted, merged, and processed by a **key data element**. Data are retrieved and manipulated either sequentially or randomly.

Sequential files, used for **sequential processing**, contain records that are ordered according to a key, also called a **control field**. A sequential file is processed from start to finish, and a particular record cannot be updated without processing the entire file.

In sequential processing, the records on both the **transaction** and the **master file** must be sorted prior to processing. A new master file is created for each computer run in which records are added or changed. The transaction file and old master file are retained as **backup files** to the new master file.

The **direct-access**, or **random**, **file** permits **random**

processing of records. The primary storage medium for direct-access files is magnetic disk.

The **indexed-sequential method** is one of several access methods that permit a programmer random access to any record on the file. In indexed-sequential organization, the access to any given record is, in effect, a series of sequential searches through several levels of an **index file**. This search results in the disk address of the data block in question.

Direct access to a particular record also can be achieved using a **hashing** algorithm. With this method of random access, the disk address is arithmetically calculated from the key.

In random processing, the unsorted transaction file is run against a random master file. Only the records needed to complete the transaction are retrieved from secondary storage.

9–4 THE DATA BASE: SOLVING THE DATA PUZZLE.   A traditional file is usually designed to meet the specific requirements of a particular functional area department. This approach to file design results in the same data being stored and maintained in several separate files. Data redundancy is costly and can be minimized by designing an integrated data base to serve the organization as a whole, not any specific department. The integrated data base is made possible by **database management system**, or **DBMS**, software.

The benefits of a data base environment have encouraged many organizations to convert information systems that use traditional file organization into systems that use an integrated data base. Database management systems permit greater access to information, enable greater control of data, minimize data redundancy, and allow programmers more flexibility in the design and maintenance of information systems.

Database management systems rely on sophisticated data structures to overcome the processing constraints of traditional files. Three common types of DBMSs are the **hierarchical DBMS**; the **network**, or **CODASYL**, **DBMS**; and the **relational DBMS**.

Because of the tremendous momentum of IBM's *IMS* DBMS, the hierarchical approach to data base management remains the most commonly used. Hierarchical DBMSs are based on the tree data structure. In hierarchical DBMSs, the **segment**, or **data base record**, is similar to the record of a traditional file in that it is a collection of related data elements and is read from, or written to, the data base as a unit. The relationship between segments is that of a parent to a child or children. In a hierarchical data base, no segment has more than one parent. The root, or highest level, does not have a parent.

In network DBMSs, data links are established between

data base records. One-to-one and one-to-many relationships between data base records are combined to form **sets**. The data base **schema** is a graphic representation of the logical structure of these sets.

In relational DBMSs, data are accessed by content rather than by address. There is no predetermined relationship between the data; therefore, the data can be accessed at the data element level. The data are organized in tables in which each row, or **tuple**, is roughly equivalent to an occurrence of a segment in a hierarchical or network DBMS.

There are well over 200 commercially available DBMS software packages. IBM dominates the minicomputer and mainframe DBMS market with the two-decade-old *IMS* and the recently introduced *DB2*. Other popular DBMSs include *IDMS, IDMS/R, IDMS/SQL, Datacom, ADABAS, Total, Supra, Oracle, RAMIS,* and *Ingress*. The market leaders among microcomputer DBMS products are *dBASE III PLUS* and its successor, *dBASE IV*. Other popular micro DBMSs are *Paradox, Reflex, R:base System V, Knowledgeman,* and *Condor 3*.

To achieve the flexibility of relational DBMS technology and the transaction processing capabilities of network DBMS technology, some software vendors are creating DBMS software packages that embody the best of both technologies.

IBM's **SQL** was recently made the official standard data access query language for relational data bases by both ANSI and ISO. Industry observers are predicting that IBM's *DB2* will soon emerge as the de facto industry standard DBMS.

The ideal data storage scheme, which will eventually be made possible by **distributed DBMSs**, would optimize the use of available resources. A distributed DBMS will permit the interfacing of data bases located in various places throughout a computer network so that the location of the data is transparent to the user.

Review Exercises

Concepts

1. Which approach to data base management is based on the tree data structure?
2. Name four commercially available DBMSs for mainframes and minicomputers. For microcomputers.
3. What are the six levels of the hierarchy of data organization?
4. What is the official ANSI and ISO standard for data access query languages for relational data bases?
5. What is the lowest level logical unit in the hierarchy of data organization?
6. What is the logical structure of a CODASYL data base called?

7. Which level in a hierarchical data base does not have a parent?

8. Name two possible key data elements for a personnel file. Name two for an inventory file.

9. In the grandfather-father-son method of file backup, which of the three files is the most current?

10. What is the purpose of an end-of-file marker?

11. Under what circumstances is a new master file created in sequential processing?

12. What is meant when someone says that data are program independent?

13. Describe the search procedure for locating and retrieving the record for Part Number 3575 in the indexed-sequential file of Figure 9–9.

14. Use the technique of Figure 9–5 to illustrate graphically the sequential-processing steps required to update the inventory master file of Figure 9–3. The transaction file contains activity for Part Numbers 8 and 21. Assume that the transaction file is unsequenced.

15. Use the technique of Figure 9–6 to illustrate graphically the random-processing steps required to update the inventory master file of Figure 9–3. The transaction file contains activity for Part Numbers 8 and 21. Provide for backup.

16. The attribute of a relational DBMS is analogous to which level of the hierarchy of data organization?

Discussion

17. Even though network and relational DBMS technologies are considered superior to hierarchical DBMS technology, the use of the latter remains strong because of the momentum of IBM's *IMS*. Why are *IMS* users reluctant to convert their data bases to a more technologically advanced DBMS?

18. Identify the data elements that would provide the links between these four categories of data in an integrated data base: manufacturing/inventory, customer/sales, personnel, and general accounting. (For example, the customer account number data element is common to all data categories except personnel.)

19. Prior to the implementation of an integrated data base in 1981, a midwestern company maintained 113 separate computer-based files. Most of these files supported autonomous, departmental information systems and contained many instances of redundant data. Discuss the impact that redundant data have on the integrity and accuracy of data.

20. *SQL* and *DB2* are well on their way to becoming industry standards. How will this have an impact on the software industry in general and consumers of computer hardware and software in particular?

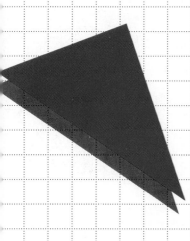

10

The MIS and Decision Support Systems

STUDENT LEARNING OBJECTIVES

- To describe how information needs vary at each level of organizational activity.
- To distinguish between programmed decisions and nonprogrammed decisions.
- To describe the circumstances appropriate for batch and transaction-oriented data entry.
- To identify the elements, scope, and capabilities of an information system.
- To define *data processing system, management information system, decision support system,* and *expert system.*
- To identify characteristics associated with data processing systems, management information systems, decision support systems, and expert systems.

The Decision-Making Environment

The four levels of activity within a company are strategic, tactical, operational, and clerical. Computer-based information systems process data at the clerical level and provide information for managerial decision making at the operational, tactical, and strategic levels.

- Strategic-level managers determine long-term strategies and set corporate objectives and policy consistent with these objectives.
- Tactical-level managers are charged with the responsibility of implementing the objectives and policies set forth at the stra-

FIGURE 10–1   A Business System Model

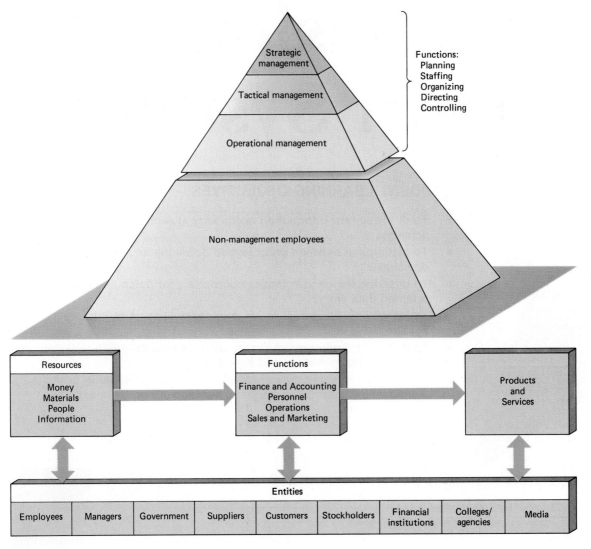

In years past, this executive would fill his attache case with reports, documents, and other work-related papers. Now he carries his portable personal computer and with it the information and computing resources of his company. From an airplane (or anywhere there is a telephone) he can establish a communications link with his company and make inquiries to the data base, check on his electronic mail, enter data, or send a memo to the managers in his department.

tegic level of management. To do this, managers identify specific tasks that need to be accomplished.

■ Operational-level managers complete specific tasks as directed by tactical-level managers.

The business system model shown in Figure 10–1 helps place the decision-making environment in its proper perspective. Information is critical in that it is necessary for managers to use the resources at their disposal more effectively, meet corporate objectives, and perform the management functions of *planning, staffing, organizing, directing,* and *controlling*.

Figure 10–1 illustrates how the corporate resources of *money, materials* (including facilities and equipment), *people,* and *information* become "input" to the various functional units, such as operations, sales, and accounting. People use their talent and knowledge, together with these resources, to produce products and services.

The business system acts in concert with several *entities,* such as employees, customers, and suppliers (see Figure 10–1). An entity is the source or destination of information flow. An entity also can be the source or destination of materials or product flow. For example, suppliers are a source of both information and materials. They are also the destination of payments for materials. The customer entity is the destination of products and the source of orders.

Filtering Information

The quality of an information system is judged by its output. A system that generates the same 20-page report for personnel at both the clerical and strategic levels is defeating the purpose of an information system. The information needs at these two levels of activity are substantially different: A secretary has no need or desire for such a comprehensive report; the president of the company would never use the report because it would take too long to extract the few pieces of information important to him or her.

The key to developing quality information systems is to filter information so that people at the various levels of activity receive just the information they need to accomplish their job functions—no more, no less. **Filtering** information results in the *right information* reaching the *right decision maker* at the *right time* in the *right form*.

Clerical Level   Clerical-level personnel, those involved in repetitive tasks, are concerned primarily with transaction handling. You might say that they process data. For example, in a sales information system, order-entry clerks key in customer orders on their terminals. In an airline reservation system, ticket agents confirm and make flight reservations.

Operational Level   Personnel at the operational level have well-defined tasks that might span a day, a week, or as long as three months, but their tasks are essentially short-term. Their information requirements often consist of operational feedback. In the sales information system, for example, the manager of the Eastern Regional Sales Department might want an end-of-quarter sales summary report. The report, illustrated in Figure 10–2, shows dollar-volume sales by salesperson for each of the company's four products: Alphas, Betas,

FIGURE 10–2   An Operational-Level Sales Summary and Exception Report
These sales reports are prepared in response to inquiries from an operational-level manager. Contrast the reports in this figure with those in Figures 10–3 and 10–4.

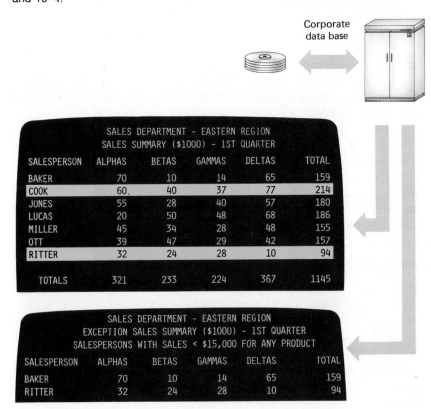

Corporate data base

SALES DEPARTMENT - EASTERN REGION SALES SUMMARY ($1000) - 1ST QUARTER					
SALESPERSON	ALPHAS	BETAS	GAMMAS	DELTAS	TOTAL
BAKER	70	10	14	65	159
COOK	60.	40	37	77	214
JONES	55	28	40	57	180
LUCAS	20	50	48	68	186
MILLER	45	34	28	48	155
OTT	39	47	29	42	157
RITTER	32	24	28	10	94
TOTALS	321	233	224	367	1145

SALES DEPARTMENT - EASTERN REGION EXCEPTION SALES SUMMARY ($1000) - 1ST QUARTER SALESPERSONS WITH SALES < $15,000 FOR ANY PRODUCT					
SALESPERSON	ALPHAS	BETAS	GAMMAS	DELTAS	TOTAL
BAKER	70	10	14	65	159
RITTER	32	24	28	10	94

On the Street

Eddie Neizard
Senior Citizen

Eddie Neizard, an 81-year-old enjoying retired life in Miami Beach, thought the computer age had passed him by. But now the very same mysterious machines that he felt were beyond his comprehension are providing him and millions like him with valuable consumer information on close to 5000 medicines, both prescription and over-the-counter. It's all available through a new in-store touch-screen computer system called *Pharmacy Information Center (PIC)* developed by Medical Strategies, Inc., in Cambridge, Massachusetts, and derived from the U.S. Pharmacopeial Convention's database—considered to be the definitive source on drugs and their effects.

For example, Eddie's cardiologist has prescribed both Procardia and Enderol for his angina. When Eddie goes to his local pharmacy to get the prescriptions filled, he can use the *PIC* to find out about proper use, drug/food interactions, precautions to take, possible side effects, and what to do if he accidentally misses a dose. This no-fee computer system (programmed with a printout option in both regular and large-sized type) is a lifesaver for senior citizens, who often take many different medications and may forget exactly what their doctors told them about each.

In addition to drug information, *PIC* also offers consumers current health news on such "hot topics" as cholesterol, heart disease, and high blood pressue. And it's as easy to use as an automated teller machine. Computer phobics like Eddie simply touch the screen and the *PIC* directs them to the information they want, all in easy-to understand language and colorful graphics.

At first Eddie shied away from the *PIC* because he thought it would be too confusing. However, once he gave it a try, he became an instant fan. "It's really something, and especially helpful when the pharmacist is too busy to answer my questions. I can't wait to tell my grandson about this experience; maybe I can learn what he does with his Apple next!"

Gammas, and Deltas. In the report, the sales records of the top (Cook) and bottom (Ritter) performers are highlighted so that managers can use this range as a basis for comparing the performance of the other salespeople.

Managers at the operational, tactical, and strategic levels often request **exception reports** that highlight critical information. They can make such requests through the information services department, or managers can make inquiries directly to the system using a query language. For example, the eastern regional sales manager used a fourth-generation language to produce the exception report in Figure 10–2. The manager's request was: "Display a list of all eastern region salespeople who had sales of less than $15,000 for any product in this quarter." The report highlights the subpar performances of Baker and Ritter.

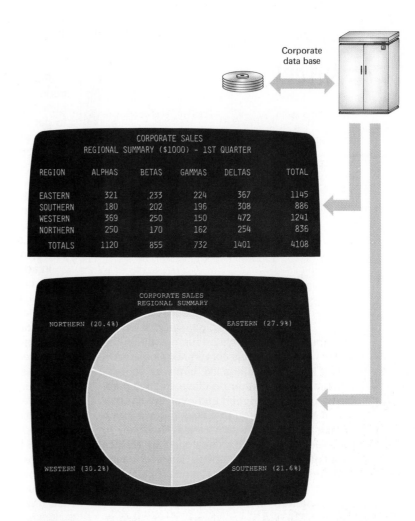

Corporate
data base

```
              CORPORATE SALES
     REGIONAL SUMMARY ($1000) - 1ST QUARTER

REGION    ALPHAS   BETAS   GAMMAS   DELTAS    TOTAL

EASTERN     321     233     224      367      1145
SOUTHERN    180     202     196      308       886
WESTERN     369     250     150      472      1241
NORTHERN    250     170     162      254       836

   TOTALS  1120     855     732     1401      4108
```

```
              CORPORATE SALES
             REGIONAL SUMMARY

NORTHERN (20.4%)                EASTERN (27.9%)




WESTERN (30.2%)                SOUTHERN (21.6%)
```

FIGURE 10–3 A Tactical-Level Sales Summary Report Shown in Tabular and Graphic Formats

The sales summary report and pie graph are prepared in response to inquiries from a tactical-level manager. Contrast the reports in this figure with those in Figures 10–2 and 10–4.

The information available for an operational-level decision is often conclusive. That is, the most acceptable alternative can be clearly identified based on information available to the decision maker. At this level, personal judgment and intuition play a reduced role in the decision-making process.

Tactical Level   At the tactical level, managers concentrate on achieving a series of goals required to meet the objectives set at the strategic level. The information requirements are usually periodic, but on occasion managers require one-time and "what if" reports. "What if" reports are generated in response to inquiries that depict what-if scenarios ("What if sales increase by 15% next quarter?"). Tactical managers are concerned primarily with operations and budgets from year to year. In the sales information system, the national sales manager, who is at the tactical level, might want the corporate sales report of Figure 10–3. The report presents dollar-volume sales by region for each of the company's four products. To get a better feeling for the relative sales contribution of each of the four regional offices during the first quarter, the national sales manager requested that the total sales for each region be presented in a pie graph (Figure 10–3).

FIGURE 10–4   A Strategic-Level Sales-Trend-by-Product Report Shown in Tabular and Graphic Formats

The sales trend report and bar graph are prepared in response to inquiries from a strategic-level manager. Contrast the reports in this figure with those in Figures 10–2 and 10–3.

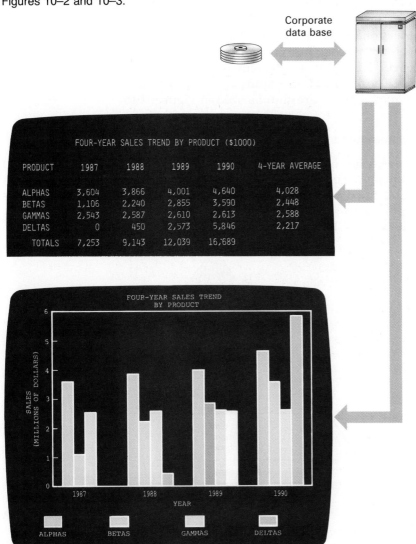

The information available for a tactical-level decision is seldom conclusive. That is, the most acceptable alternative cannot be identified from information alone. At this level, most decisions are made by using personal judgment and intuition in conjunction with available information.

Strategic Level   Managers at the strategic level are objective-oriented. Their information system requirements are often one-time reports, "what if" reports, and trend analyses. For example, the president of the company might ask for a report that shows the four-year sales trend for each of the company's four products and overall (Figure 10–4). Knowing that it is easier to detect trends in a graphic format than in a tabular one, the president requests that the trends be summarized in a bar graph (Figure 10–4). From the bar graph, he or she easily can see that the sales of Alphas and Gammas are experiencing modest growth while the sales of Betas and Deltas are better.

The information available for a strategic-level decision is almost never conclusive. To be sure, information is critical to strategic-level decision making, but virtually all decision makers at this level rely heavily on personal judgment and intuition.

The information requirements at the various levels of organizational activity are summarized in Figure 10–5.

Programmed and Nonprogrammed Decisions

The two basic types of decisions are **programmed decisions** and **nonprogrammed decisions**. Purely programmed decisions address well-defined problems. The decision maker has no judgmental flexi-

FIGURE 10–5   Information Requirement Profile by Level of Activity

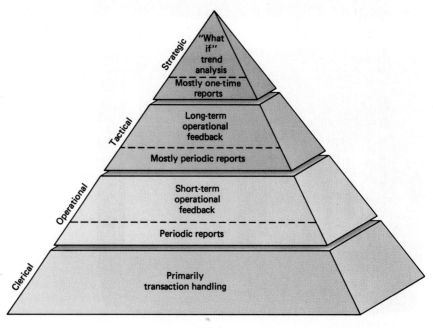

Through the mid-1980s, virtually all decisions made by sales clerks were programmed decisions. Now the greater availability of information made possible through on-line point-of-sale (POS) systems has enabled more of the decisions to be made at the clerical level. This is the case in virtually all types of industry.

bility because the actual decision is determined by existing policies or procedures. In fact, many such decisions can be accomplished by a computer without human intervention! For example, the decision required to restock inventory levels of raw materials is often a programmed decision that can be made by an individual or by a computer-based information system. When the inventory level of a particular item drops below the reorder point, perhaps two months' supply, a decision is made to replenish the inventory by submitting an order to the supplier.

Nonprogrammed decisions involve ill-defined and unstructured problems. Such decisions are also called **information-based decisions** because the decision maker needs information in order to make a rational decision. The information requirement implies the need for managers to use judgment and intuition in the decision-making process. Corporate policies, procedures, standards, and guidelines provide substantial direction for nonprogrammed decisions made at the operational level, less direction at the tactical level, and little or no direction at the strategic level. The greater the programmability of a decision, the greater the confidence of the decision maker that the most acceptable alternative has been selected.

10–2 Information System Concepts

The Information System Defined

The concept of an information system is introduced and briefly described in Chapter 1. *Hardware, software, people, procedures*, and *data* are combined to create an **information system** (see Figure 10–6). The term *information system* is a generic reference to a computer-based system that provides the following:

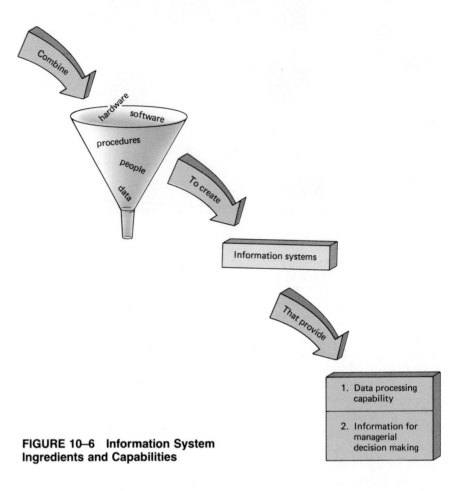

FIGURE 10–6   Information System Ingredients and Capabilities

- *Data processing* capabilities for a department or, perhaps, an entire company
- *Information* that people need to make better, more informed decisions

The data processing capability refers to the system's ability to handle and process data. The more sophisticated information systems provide decision makers with *on-demand reports* and *inquiry capabilities* as well as *routine periodic reports*.

Four types of information systems are discussed in this chapter: *data processing systems*, *management information systems*, *decision support systems*, and *expert systems*. Each is described in detail later in this chapter. The remainder of this section addresses important concepts that relate to information systems in general.

Information System Capabilities

Not surprisingly, an information system has the same four capabilities as a computer system: *input*, *processing*, *storage*, and *output*).

Input   The information system input capability can accept:

- *Source data*. Usually the recording of a transaction or an event.
- *An inquiry*. A request for information.
- *A response to a prompt*. For example, a *Y* or *N*.
- *An instruction*. For example, "Store file" or "Print record."
- *A message to another user on the system*.
- *A change*. For instance, editing a word processing document.

Processing   The information system processing capability encompasses:

- *Sorting*. Arranging data or records in some order (for example, alphabetizing a customer file by last name).
- *Accessing, recording, and updating data in storage*. For example, retrieving a customer record from a data base for processing, entering expense data into an accounting system's data base, and changing a customer's address on a marketing data base, respectively.
- *Summarizing*. Presenting information in a condensed format, often to reflect totals and subtotals.
- *Selecting*. Selecting records by criteria (for example, "Select all employees with 25 or more years of service in the company").
- *Manipulating*. Performing arithmetic operations (addition, multiplication, and so on) and logic operations (comparing an employee's years of service to 25 to determine if they are greater than, equal to, or less than 25).

Storage   The information system storage capability permits them to store *data, text, images* (graphs, pictures), and *other digital information* (voice messages) so that they can be recalled easily for further processing.

Output   The information system output capability allows them to produce output in a variety of formats:

- *Hard copy*. For example, printed reports, documents, and messages.
- *Soft copy*. Temporary displays on terminal screens, for instance.
- *Control*. For example, instructions to industrial robots or automated processes.

Manual Systems versus Computer-Based Information Systems

When someone speaks of an information system today, he or she implies an automated system. The elements of an information system are hardware, software, people, procedures, and data. The automated elements (the hardware and software) do not play a part in manual systems. Manual systems consist of people, procedures, and data. In terms of numbers, the overwhelming majority of systems in industry, government, and education are still manual. This is true of large organizations with hundreds of computers and of two-person companies. Tens of thousands of manual systems have been targeted to be upgraded to computer-based information systems. Ten times that many are awaiting tomorrow's creative users and MIS professionals to identify their potential for computerization.

Both manual systems and computer-based information systems have an established pattern for work and information flow. In a manual payroll system, for example, a payroll clerk receives time sheets from supervisors; then he or she retrieves each employee's records from folders stored alphabetically in a file cabinet. The clerk uses a calculator to compute gross and net pay, then manually types the payroll check and stub. Finally, the payroll clerk compiles the payroll register, which is a listing of the amount paid and the deductions for each employee, on a tally sheet with column totals. About the only way to find and extract information in a manual payroll system is to thumb through employee folders painstakingly.

Today most payroll systems have been automated. But look in any office in almost any company and you will find rooms full of filing cabinets, tabbed three-ring binders, circular address files, or drawers filled with 3-by-5-inch inventory cards. These manual systems are opportunities to improve a company's profitability and productivity through the application of MIS technologies.

Function-Based versus Integrated Information Systems

An information system can be either function-based or integrated. A **function-based information system** is designed for the exclusive support of a specific application area, such as inventory management or accounting. Its data base and procedures are, for the most part, independent of any other system. The data bases of function-based information systems invariably contain data that are maintained in other function-based systems within the same company. For example, much of the data needed for an accounting system would be duplicated in an inventory management system. It is not unusual for companies with a number of autonomous function-based systems to maintain customer data in five to 10 different data bases. When a customer moves, the address must be updated in several data bases (accounting,

An integrated information system links people throughout the company through a common data base. When someone on the sixth floor updates the data base, it is reflected in any subsequent information requested by people on the fifth floor.

sales, distribution, and so on). This kind of data redundancy is an unnecessary financial burden to a company.

During the past decade, great strides have been made in the integration of function-based systems. The resulting **integrated information systems** share a common data base. The common data base helps minimize data redundancy and allows departments to coordinate their activities more efficiently. Integrated data bases are discussed in detail in Chapter 9, "Data Management."

On-Line versus Off-Line

The four fundamental components of a computer system are input, processing, output, and storage. In a computer system, the input, output, and data storage components receive data from and transmit data to the processor over electrical cables, or lines. These hardware components are said to be **on-line** to the processor. Hardware devices that are not accessible to or under the control of a processor are said to be **off-line**. The concepts of on-line and off-line also apply to data. Data are said to be *on-line* if they can be accessed and manipulated by the processor. All other data are *off-line*.

On-line and off-line are important information system concepts. Consider the payroll example in Figure 10–7. In an *off-line* operation,

FIGURE 10–7 On-Line and Off-Line Operations
Those processing activities, hardware, and files that are not controlled by or accessible to the computer are referred to as off-line.

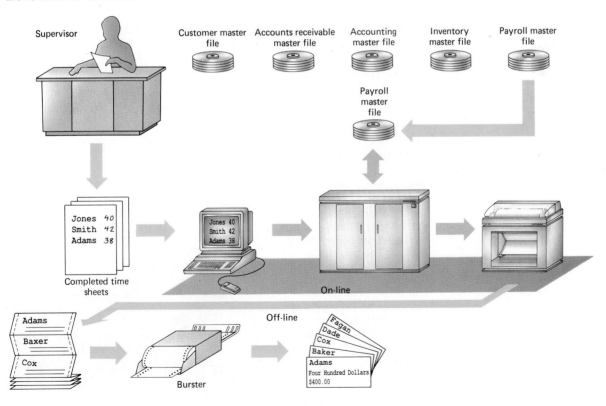

all supervisors complete the weekly time sheets. The time sheets are then collected and *batched* for input to the computer system. When transactions are grouped together for processing, it is called **batch processing**.

Before the data can be entered and the payroll checks printed, the payroll master file must be placed on-line, if it is not already. To do this, it is retrieved manually from a library of interchangeable disks and loaded to a storage component called a disk drive. Once loaded, the payroll master file is on-line. The process is analogous to selecting the phonograph record you wish to play and mounting it on the turntable. (Many computer-based files and data bases are stored on permanently installed fixed disks. These files and data bases are on-line whenever the computer system is operational.)

An operator at a terminal enters the data on the time sheets directly into the computer system in an *on-line* operation. Employee data, such as name, Social Security number, pay rate, and deductions, are retrieved from the payroll master file and combined with the number of hours worked to produce the payroll checks. The payroll checks are produced on a printer, which is an output device.

Because the payroll checks are printed on continuous preprinted forms, they must be separated before they can be distributed to the employees. In an *off-line* operation, a machine called a burster separates and stacks the payroll checks.

Data Entry Concepts

Source Data Most data do not exist in a form that can be "read" by the computer. In the example of Figure 10–7, the supervisor uses a pencil and paper to record manually the hours worked by the staff on the time sheet. Before the payroll checks can be computed and printed, the data on these time sheets must be *transcribed* (converted) into a *machine-readable format* that can be interpreted by a computer. This is done in an *on-line* operation by someone at a terminal. The time sheet is known as the **source document** and, as you might expect, the data on the time sheet are the **source data**.

Whenever possible, data are collected in machine-readable format. Shown here is the Videx TimeWand, an intelligent bar code reading system. The two-ounce TimeWand enables the off-line collection of up to 16,000 characters of machine-readable, time-stamped data. Once data have been collected, they are uploaded to the host computer for processing.

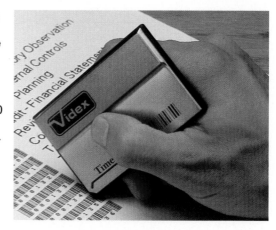

Not all source data have to be transcribed. For example, the numbers printed at the bottom of your bank checks are your individual account number and bank number. They are already machine readable, so they can be read directly by an input device. Other approaches to *source data automation* are discussed in Chapter 5, "Input/Output Devices."

Approaches to Data Entry   The term **data entry** is used to describe the process of entering data into an information system. Information systems are designed to provide users with display-screen prompts to make on-line data entry easier. The display on the operator's screen, for example, may be the image of the source document (such as a time sheet). A **prompt** is a brief message to the operator that describes what should be entered (for example, "INPUT HOURS WORKED ____").

Data can be entered on a terminal in the following ways:

- *Batch processing*, in which transactions are grouped, or batched, and entered consecutively, one after the other.
- **Transaction-oriented processing**, in which transactions are recorded and entered as they occur.

To illustrate the difference between batch and transaction-oriented processing, consider an order-processing system for a mail-order merchandiser (see Figure 10–8). The system accepts orders by both mail and phone. The orders received by mail are accumulated, or batched, for data entry—usually at night. There are no handwritten source documents for phone orders; people taking the phone orders interact with the computer via terminals and enter the order data on-line while talking with the customer.

FIGURE 10–8   Batch and Transaction-Oriented Processing
Mail-order merchandisers accept orders by mail and by phone.

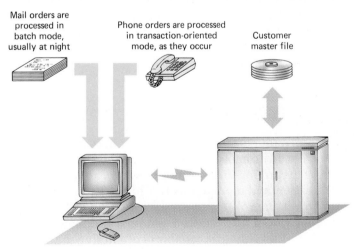

Mail orders are processed in batch mode, usually at night

Phone orders are processed in transaction-oriented mode, as they occur

Customer master file

All airline reservation systems are transaction-oriented. The workstations at ticket counters in airports are on-line to a centralized computer facility. Each time an agent writes a ticket and assigns a passenger a seat, the master record for that flight is immediately updated to reflect the addition of one more passenger.

On-Line Data Entry Most data entered into mainframe computer systems, both batch and transaction-oriented, is done on-line. Terminal operators enter data *directly* into the host computer system for processing as shown in Figure 10–8. The primary advantage of transaction-oriented data entry is that records on the data base are updated immediately, as the transaction occurs. This is quite different from batch data entry, where records are batched periodically. Another advantage of transaction-oriented data entry is that operators can make inquiries to the system. In the example of Figure 10–8, a salesperson can check the availability of an item and tell the customer when to expect delivery.

10–3 Data Processing Systems

The focus of **data processing systems** (**DP**) is transaction handling and record keeping, usually for a particular functional area. Data are entered and stored in a file format, and stored files are updated during routine processing. Periodic outputs include action documents (invoices) and scheduled reports, primarily for operational-level managers. In essence, data processing systems are inflexible and cannot accommodate data processing or information needs that are not already built into the system. Most enterprises have transcended the scope of DP systems and now have systems with the flexibility of providing management with information in support of an ever-changing decision-making environment.

10–4 Management Information Systems

In the not-too-distant past, most payroll systems were data processing systems that did little more than process time sheets, print payroll checks, and keep running totals of annual wages and deductions. Managers began to demand more and better information about their personnel. As a result, payroll *data processing systems* evolved into human resource **management information systems**. A human resource management information system is capable of predicting the average number of worker sick days, monitoring salary equality between minority

The trend is to develop information systems that provide on-line access to information. In our fast-paced society, having access to timely information is critical to staying competitive. This executive knows how to retrieve needed information from an MIS; those who do not must wait for others to do it for them. For the latter, the quality of the information they receive is diminished because it is less timely.

groups, making more effective use of available skills, and providing other information needed at all three levels of management—operational, tactical, and strategic.

The Management Information System Defined

If you were to ask any five executives or computer professionals to define a management information system, or **MIS**, the only agreement you would find in their responses is that there is no agreement on its definition. An MIS has been called a method, a function, an approach, a process, an organization, a system, and a subsystem. The following working definition of a management information system will be used in this book:

> An MIS is an integrated structure of data bases and information flow that optimizes the collection, transfer, and presentation of information throughout a multilevel organization whose component groups perform a variety of tasks to accomplish a united objective.

The concept of information flow in a multilevel organization (strategic, tactical, and so on) with component parts (finance, accounting, and so forth) is illustrated in Figure 10–9. The foregoing

FIGURE 10–9   Information Flow in a Multilevel Organization
An MIS is the mechanism that enables information to flow throughout all levels and components of a multilevel organization.

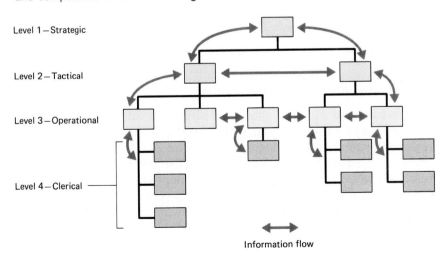

Level 1—Strategic

Level 2—Tactical

Level 3—Operational

Level 4—Clerical

Information flow

definition was formulated to represent the ideal. In reality, an organization can only strive for optimization and total integration. But even if the finished product falls short of the ideal, user and computer personnel are aiming for the same target.

Characteristics of Management Information Systems

The following are *desirable* characteristics of an MIS:

- An MIS supports the data processing functions of transaction handling and record keeping.
- An MIS uses an integrated data base and supports a variety of functional areas.
- An MIS provides operational-, tactical-, and strategic-level managers with easy access to timely but, for the most part, structured information.
- An MIS is somewhat flexible and can be adapted to meet changing information needs of the organization.
- An MIS provides an envelope of system security that limits access to authorized personnel.

The MIS versus the DP System

The basic distinctions between an MIS and a DP system are summarized as follows:

- The integrated data base of an MIS enables greater flexibility in meeting the information needs of management than the traditional file environment of DP systems.
- An MIS integrates the information flow between functional areas where DP systems tend to support a single functional area.
- An MIS caters to the information needs of all levels of management where DP systems focus on operational-level support.
- Management's information needs are supported on a more timely basis with an MIS (on-line inquiry capability) than with a DP system (usually scheduled reports).

10-5 Decision Support Systems

The Decision Support System Defined

Managers spend much of their day obtaining and analyzing information before making a decision. **Decision support systems** are interactive information systems that rely on an integrated set of user-friendly hardware and software tools to produce and present information targeted to support management in the decision-making process. On many occasions, decisions makers can rely on their experience to make a quality decision, or they need look no further than the information that is readily available from the integrated corporate

MIS. However, decision makers, especially at the tactical and strategic levels, are often confronted with complex decisions whose factors are beyond their human abilities to synthesize properly. These types of decisions are "made to order" for decision support systems.

A decision support system, or **DSS**, can help close the information gap so that managers can improve the quality of their decisions. To do this, DSS hardware and software employ the latest technological innovations (for example, color graphics and database management systems), planning and forecasting models, user-oriented query languages, and even artificial intelligence.

In many cases, the DSS facilitates the decision-making process. For example, a DSS can help a decision maker choose between alternatives. Some DSSs have the capability of automatically ranking alternatives based on the decision maker's criteria. Decision support systems also help remove the tedium of gathering and analyzing data. For example, managers are no longer strapped with such laborious tasks as manually entering and extending numbers (totaling rows and columns of numbers) on spreadsheet paper. Graphics software enables managers to generate illustrative bar and pie graphs in a matter of minutes. And, with the availability of a variety of user-oriented DSSs, managers can get the information they need without having to depend on direct technical assistance from an MIS professional.

The DSS versus the MIS

Management information systems are oriented to supporting decisions that involve *structured* problems, such as when to replenish raw

In the construction business, the accuracy of cost estimates may mean the difference between making or losing money. This engineer relies on a decision support system that uses historical data and updated cost data to produce reliable estimates of project costs.

materials inventory and how much to order. This type of routine operational-level decision is based on production demands, the cost of holding the inventory, and other variables that depend on the use of the inventory item. The MIS integrates these variables into an inventory model and presents specific order information (for example, order quantity and order date) to the manager in charge of inventory management.

In contrast to the MIS, decision support systems are designed to support decision-making processes involving *semistructured* and *unstructured* problems. A semistructured problem might be the need to improve the delivery performance of suppliers. The problem is partially structured in that information comparing the on-time delivery performance of suppliers during the past two years can be obtained either from hard-copy records or directly from the integrated data base supporting the MIS. The unstructured facets of the problem, such as extenuating circumstances, rush-order policy and pricing, and so on, make this problem a candidate for a DSS.

An example of an entirely unstructured problem would be the evaluation and selection of an alternative to the raw material currently used. A decision maker might enlist the aid of a DSS to provide information on whether it would be advisable to replace a steel component with a plastic or aluminum one. The information requirements for such a decision are diverse and typically beyond the scope of an MIS.

Another distinction that should be made between an MIS and a DSS is that an MIS is designed and created to support a specific application (accounting, inventory control) or set of applications (an integrated MIS). A DSS is a set of decision support tools that can be adapted to any decision environment.

Characteristics of Decision Support Systems

The following are *desirable* characteristics of a DSS:

- A DSS helps the decision maker in the decision-making process.
- A DSS is designed to address semistructured and unstructured problems.
- A DSS supports decision makers at all levels, but it is most effective at the tactical and strategic levels.
- A DSS makes general-purpose models, simulation capabilities, and other analytical tools available to the decision maker.
- A DSS is an interactive, user-friendly system that can be used by the decision maker with little or no assistance from an MIS professional.
- A DSS can be readily adapted to meet the information requirements of any decision environment.
- A DSS provides the mechanisms to enable a rapid response to a decision maker's request for information.
- A DSS has the capability of interfacing with the corporate data base.

- A DSS is not executed in accordance with a pre-established production schedule.
- A DSS is flexible enough to accommodate a variety of management styles.
- A DSS facilitates communication between levels of decision making (for example, graphic presentation of operational-level information for review by top management).

The DSS Tool Box

A decision support system is made up of a set of decision support tools that can be adapted to any decision environment (see Figure 10–10). These tools can be categorized as *software tools* and *hardware tools*.

FIGURE 10–10 The Decision Support System
A decision support system is a set of software and hardware tools that can be adapted to any decision environment.

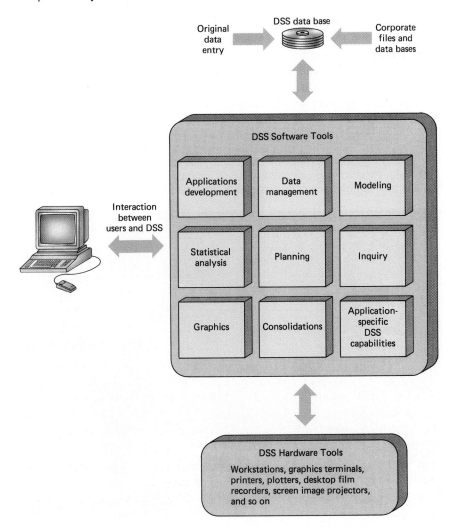

The combination of these general-purpose tools helps managers address decision-making tasks in specific application areas (the evaluation and promotion of personnel, the acquisition of companies, and so on). Any input/output device that facilitates interaction with or makes use of the system would be considered a DSS hardware tool. Software DSS tools include the following:

■ *Applications development.* Some decision support systems provide end users with the capability of developing computer-based systems to support the decision-making process. These applications typically involve the input, processing, and storing of data and the output of information. The ease with which DSS applications can be created has spawned a new term—**throwaway systems**. Often DSS applications are developed to support a one-time decision and are then discarded.

■ *Data management.* Each DSS software package has its own unique approach to data base management—that is, the software mechanisms for the storage, maintenance, and retrieval of data. This DSS tool is necessary to ensure compatibility of a DSS data base and an integrated set of DSS software tools.

■ *Modeling.* Decision support systems enable managers to use mathematical modeling techniques to re-create the functional aspects of a system within the confines of a computer. Models are appropriate when decisions involve a number of factors. For

The SAS System, a decision support system, consists of several components including SAS/Graph, SAS/QC (quality control), SAS/ETS (planning and forecasting), SAS/OR (project management), SAS/STAT (statistical analysis), and more. Plant managers use the SAS/QC component to signal unusual variations in the production process (at hours 4 and 8 in the display).

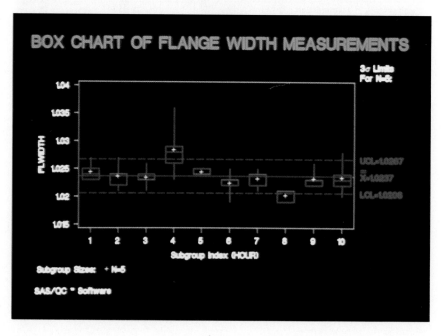

example, models are often used when uncertainty and risk are introduced, when several decision makers are involved, and when multiple outcomes are anticipated. In these cases, each decision needs to be evaluated on its own merit.

- *Statistical analysis*. The DSS statistical analysis capability includes everything from statistics such as average, median, and standard deviation to analytical techniques such as regression analysis, exponential smoothing, and discriminate analysis to complex procedures such as multivariate analysis. Risk analysis and trend analysis are common applications of DSS statistical tools.

- *Planning*. End user managers are often faced with making decisions that will be implemented at some time in the future. To help them get a glimpse into the future, they rely on DSS software that permits forecasting, "what if" analysis, and goal seeking (for example, "How much do we need to increase the advertising budget to achieve a goal of $120 million sales for next year?").

- *Inquiry*. DSS software enables managers to make on-line inquiries to the DSS data base using English-like commands (for example, a natural language interface with a 4GL). End users who query corporate data bases are able to communicate with computers in much the same language that they would use to communicate with their colleagues.

- *Graphics*. With the graphics DSS software tool, managers can create a variety of presentation graphics based on data in the DSS data base, including bar graphs, pie graphs, and line graphs.

- *Consolidations*. DSS software tools are available that enable the consolidation of like data from different sources (for example, the consolidation of financial statements from subsidiary companies into a single corporate financial statement).

- *Application-specific DSS capabilities*. DSS software that supports a particular decision environment, such as financial analysis and quality control, is being introduced routinely into the marketplace.

10–6 Expert Systems

What Is an Expert System?

The most recent addition to the circle of information systems is the **expert system**. Expert systems are associated with an area of research known as **artificial intelligence**. Artificial intelligence is the ability of a computer to reason, to learn, to strive for self-improvement, and to simulate human sensory capabilities. The scope of artificial intelligence research is discussed in Chapter 17, "Computers in Society: Today and Tomorrow." Like the DSS, expert systems are computer-based systems that help managers resolve problems or make better decisions. However, an expert system does this with a decidedly

These financial analysts rely on historical and predictive data as well as up-to-the-second stock trading information. They sometimes request a second opinion from an expert system before advising their clients.

different twist. It is an interactive computer-based system that responds to questions, asks for clarification, makes recommendations, and generally helps in the decision-making process. In effect, working with an expert system is much like working directly with a human expert to solve a problem because the system mirrors the human thought process. It even uses information supplied by a real expert in a particular field such as medicine, taxes, or geology.

An expert system is a computer-based system to which preset IF–THEN rules are applied to solve a particular problem, such as determining a patient's illness. Like management information systems and decision support systems, expert systems rely on factual knowledge, but expert systems also rely on *heuristic knowledge* such as intuition, judgment, and inferences. Both the factual knowledge and the heuristic rules of thumb are acquired from a *domain expert*, an expert in a particular field. The expert system uses this human-supplied knowledge to model the human thought process within a particular area of expertise. Once completed, a knowledge-based system can approximate the logic of a well-informed human decision maker.

Technically speaking, an *expert system* is the highest form of a **knowledge-based system**. In practice, the terms *expert system* and *knowledge-based system* are used interchangeably. The less sophisticated knowledge-based systems are called **assistant systems**. An assistant system helps users make relatively straightforward decisions. Assistant systems are usually implemented to reduce the possibility that the end user will make an error in judgment rather than to resolve a particular problem.

In effect, expert systems simulate the human thought process. To varying degrees, they can reason, draw inferences, and make judgments. Here is how an expert system works. Let's use a medical diagnosis system as an example. Upon examining a patient, a physician might interact with an expert diagnosis system to get help in diagnosing the patient's illness or, perhaps, to get a second opinion. First the doctor would relate the symptoms to the expert system: male, age

10, temperature of 103°, and swollen glands about the neck. Needing more information, the expert system might ask the doctor to examine the parotid gland for swelling. Upon receiving an affirmative answer, the system might ask a few more questions and even ask for lab reports before giving a diagnosis. A final question put to the physician might be whether the patient had been previously afflicted with or immunized for parotitis. If not, the expert system would diagnose the illness as parotitis, otherwise known as the mumps.

In recent years expert systems have been developed to support decision makers in a broad range of disciplines, including medical diagnosis, oil exploration, financial planning, tax preparation, chemical analysis, surgery, locomotive repair, weather prediction, computer repair, troubleshooting satellites, computer systems configuration, nuclear-power plant operation, newspaper layout, interpreting government regulations, and many others.

Benefits of Expert Systems

The benefits of an expert system are somewhat different from those of other decision support systems and of management information systems.

- *An expert system enables the knowledge of experts to be "canned,"
so to speak.* The specialized knowledge of human experts can be captured in the form of an expert system. For example, at Campbell's Soup Company, Aldo Cimino was the only expert troubleshooter for Campbell's giant cookers. He and his 43 years of experience were about to retire, so Campbell's executives decided to "drain his brain" into an expert system. Mr. Cimino may be retired, but Campbell's Soup Company continues to benefit from his years of experience.

This 4-megabit (a storage capacity of about 500,000 characters) chip is the state of the art in chip technology. When you consider that the 4-kilobit (about 500 characters) chip was the standard only two decades ago, you realize that scientists are making phenomenal progress in the microminiaturization of electronic circuitry. However, the human brain has 10 trillion circuit elements, about 2.5 million times as many as this state-of-the-art silicon chip. This comparison helps put the field of artificial intelligence into its proper perspective.

- *A single expert system can expand the decision-making capabilities of many people.* In effect, an expert's knowledge can be distributed to and used by anyone associated with a specific decision environment. For example, a number of loan officers at a bank can enlist the aid of an expert system for guidance in approving and rejecting loan applications.

- *An expert system can improve the productivity and performance of decision makers.* By having ready access to an electronic partner with vast expertise in a particular area, decision makers can progress more rapidly to the most acceptable solution.

- *An expert system can provide stability and consistency to a particular area of decision making.* Unlike human beings, an expert system responds with exactly the same information to each instance of the same decision situation. When people in similar decision-making situations have access to the advice and guidance of an expert system, the decisions they make tend to be consistent with one another.

- *An expert system reduces dependencies on critical personnel.* Human beings retire, get sick, take vacations, and only a few of them ever attain the status of expert. Computers do not take coffee breaks. Expert systems can "drain the brains" of the very limited supply of experts so that others can benefit from their expertise, immediately and after they retire.

- *An expert system is an excellent training tool.* Companies are using expert systems to train decision makers in a way similar to airlines' use of flight simulators to train pilots. During training, individuals work through a particular decision with an expert system. After making the decision, they review the documentation of the decision rationale generated by the expert system. From this documentation, they learn how decisions are made within the context of a particular environment.

Selecting an Expert System Application

Not every company has a decision-making environment appropriate for expert systems. The situation has to be just right, or the cost of developing an expert system cannot be justified. Typically, the development and implementation of even the most basic expert systems will involve a minimum of one workyear of effort and a substantial monetary outlay for the purchase of software and hardware. Before a decision is made to create an expert system, top management should be made aware of what decision environments are appropriate for its implementation.

Those decision environments most conducive to expert systems share the following characteristics:

- *A number of people will use the expert system frequently as part of their work routine.*
- *Decisions are complex.*
- *The decision logic can be translated to a hierarchy of rules.*

WHAT IS *ASK DAN*?

Ask DAN About Your Taxes is a commercially available knowledge-based system designed to assist people in the preparation of their annual tax returns. The system contains on-line facsimiles of the official IRS tax forms onto which users enter their data. The system automatically performs all needed calculations based on the data entered. Official IRS tax schedules can be printed directly by the system for submission to the Internal Revenue Service. Of course, *Ask DAN* is updated each year to reflect revisions in the tax laws.

What sets this system apart from some other tax preparation programs are the "Ask DAN" and "Checklist" facilities available to the user. The "Ask DAN" facility is an assistant system that enables users to have a question-and-answer session with DAN, a computerized version of a tax expert. (A human named Dan served as the domain expert on federal taxes for the creation of the knowledge base.) DAN asks the user questions and, based on the answers provided, asks more detailed questions.

The "Checklist" facility asks questions of the user to determine such things as what income should be declared, what deductions can be taken, and what tax schedules should be submitted. The result includes a checklist of tax items the user should consider and a list of the IRS forms and line numbers to use to report or declare each item.

A TYPICAL *ASK DAN* SESSION

Let's look at a typical application scenario for *Ask DAN*. James Mitchell, a 22-year-old draftsperson from Pueblo, Colorado, purchased *Ask DAN* to help him prepare his income tax return. James already owns an IBM PC AT. The assistant system runs on IBM PCs and compatibles.

Compile "Checklist." First James selects the "Checklist" facility. By asking questions about James's income, expenditures, and investments, the system produces a checklist of tax items that James should consider and indicates which forms need to be completed. In James's case, he needs only to file Form 1040.

"Prepare Tax Return." Now that James knows which form he needs to complete, he selects the "Prepare Tax Return" option from the assistant system's main menu and, interactively, completes Form 1040. James progresses normally until he gets to Line 7, "Wages, salaries, tips, etc." Unsure of what figures to enter on this line, James presses the appropriate keys and asks DAN, the intelligent tax consultant!

"Ask DAN." Any questions addressed to DAN are context-sensitive; that is, DAN responds to requests for assistance based on the position of the cursor (for example, Line 7 of Form 1040). In this case, the screen

This screen appears when James asks DAN for help on Line 7 (wages, salaries, tips, etc.).

shown in the photo above appears. Now James knows he must enter the income amount from his employer-supplied W-2 form. James enters his income ($22,000) at the prompt, and the assistant system returns him to the updated on-line Form 1040.

As James continues filling out the on-line Form 1040, he becomes puzzled at Line 54, "Federal income tax withheld." Again, he calls on DAN for help, and the screen shown in the photo below is displayed. Again, DAN directs James to his W-2 form to obtain the amount for tax withheld. After entering the correct amount ($2,850), James is returned to the on-line Form 1040. Thanks to DAN, James has no further problems.

Print Tax Return. Now, James can print the tax information on preprinted IRS-approved forms. James Mitchell's return is relatively straightforward; however, the "Ask DAN" assistant system is equally as helpful to people with complex, multiform returns.

This screen appears when James asks DAN for assistance on Line 54 (Federal income tax withheld).

- *Applications typically focus on advice, classification, diagnosis, interpretation, explanation, selection of alternatives, evaluation of situations, or forecasting.*

The number and variety of expert system applications has increased dramatically with the advent of powerful, cost-effective microcomputers. Expert systems advise financial analysts on the best mix of investments; help taxpayers interpret the tax laws; help computer repairpersons diagnose the problems of a malfunctioning computer; and help independent insurance agents select the best overall coverage for their business clients. For early versions of expert systems, the minimum hardware configuration was an expensive dedicated superminicomputer. Today expert systems can run on everything from micros to supercomputers.

The Expert System Shell

When someone talks about expert systems, he or she is usually talking about systems that can help decision makers working in a particular *domain of expertise*, such as the configuration of computer systems or commercial lending. As mentioned earlier, these expert systems are the result of substantial development efforts. The software that enables the development of these expert systems has no "intelligence" and is known as the **expert system shell**.

Expert system shells are usually domain-independent proprietary software packages that have no applications "knowledge." An expert system shell contains the generic parts that are needed to create an expert system for a specific application. For example, the expert system shell provides companies with the capabilities needed to construct a knowledge base and the facility by which the user interacts with the knowledge base. The primary components of the expert system shell are the *knowledge acquisition facility*, the *knowledge base*, the *inference engine*, and the *user interface* (see Figure 10–11).

- *Knowledge acquisition facility*. The **knowledge acquisition facility** is that component of the expert system shell that permits the construction of the knowledge base. The knowledge base is created through the cooperative efforts of a **knowledge engineer** and one or more experts in a particular field, called **domain experts** (see Figure 10–11). The knowledge engineer translates the expert's knowledge into *factual knowledge* and *rules* to create the knowledge base.

- *Knowledge base*. Appropriate facts and rules are entered into the **knowledge base** during the acquisition phase. To complete the knowledge base, the knowledge engineer, in cooperation with the domain expert, enters the following: the identification of problem(s) to be solved; possible solutions to the problem(s); and how to progress from problem to solution (primarily through facts and rules of inference). Facts (employee name and so on) needed to articulate the solution to the user are retrieved from the corporate data base. (See Figure 10–11.)

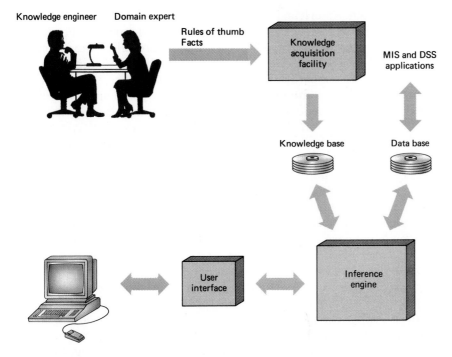

FIGURE 10–11   Components of an Expert System Shell

- *Inference engine.* The **inference engine** is the nucleus of an operational expert system (see Figure 10–11). It is the vehicle by which the facts and rules in the knowledge base are applied to a problem. The inference engine gives an expert system its ability to reason. It does this by leading the user through a logic path that results in a solution.

- *User interface.* Heuristic procedures are informal; that is, there are no formal algorithms available to solve the problem. An expert system problem is addressed by one strategy as long as it looks promising. The system always retains the option to switch to another strategy. This heuristic approach requires a flexible **user interface** (see Figure 10–11). This component of an expert system enables the type of interaction between end user and expert system that is needed for heuristic processing. The user interface permits the end user to describe the problem or goal. It permits both the end user and the expert system to structure questions and responses. Along with a response to a particular inquiry, an expert system usually explains and documents the rationale of why a particular course of action was recommended.

An Example of an Expert System

Credit card companies are using expert system technology to provide better service to their customers, increase productivity, and save money. A case in point is the American Express Authorizer's Assistant expert system. American Express retains 300 authorizers who provide around-the-clock service to cardholders and customers. For credit card purchases that exceed a preset amount, retailers must contact American Express to obtain authorization before completing the transaction. In cooperation with a human authorizer, the expert system ultimately recommends that a credit charge be approved or denied, or it recommends an alternative line of reasoning and the need for more information. The Authorizer's Assistant expert system was approved for development when the company realized that significant losses were resulting from bad authorization decisions made by the less experienced authorizers.

To create the Authorizer's Assistant expert system, several human expert authorizers related tried-and-true rules of thumb to a knowledge engineer. From them, a knowledge engineer constructed a knowledge base that contained 520 rules. During the testing phase the number of rules grew to 850. At the end of the test period, the system demonstrated that it could reduce bad authorization decisions by 76%. Authorizer's Assistant is one of American Express's success stories. The system resulted in more consistent decision making, improved authorizer productivity, reduced credit and fraud losses, reduced operating expenses, improved service to customers and cardholders, more accurate decisions, and reduced learning time for authorizers. The system was expensive and time consuming, but the benefits were so overwhelming that American Express recouped its entire investment during the first year of operation!

Expert System Summary

One of the myths surrounding expert systems is that they will replace human experts. Expert systems augment the capabilities of humans and make them more productive, but they will never replace them. Expert systems and humans complement one another in the decision-making process. The computer-based expert system can handle rou-

Locomotive mechanics get troubleshooting help with this computer-based expert system. The mechanic simply keys in responses to questions asked by the "expert" about the malfunction. Through interactive questioning, the expert system eventually identifies the cause of the malfunction and demonstrates repair procedures on the video monitor (screen at left).

tine situations with great accuracy, thereby relieving someone of the burden of a detailed manual analysis. Humans can combine the insight of an expert system with their flexible intuitive abilities to resolve complex problems.

In a short period of time, the track record of operational expert systems has been very convincing. The field is exploding. Decision makers in every environment are developing or contemplating developing an expert system. Attorneys will hold mock trials with expert systems to "pre-try" their cases. Doctors routinely will ask a second opinion. Architects will "discuss" the structural design of a building with an expert system. Military officers will "talk" with the "expert" to plan battlefield strategy. City planners will "ask" an expert system to suggest optimal locations for recreational facilities.

Some computer industry observers believe that expert systems are the wave of the future and that each of us will have "expert" help and guidance in our respective professions.

Memory Bits

INFORMATION SYSTEMS
- Data processing (DP) system
- Management information system (MIS)
- Decision support system (DSS)
- Expert system

Summary Outline and Important Terms

10–1 INFORMATION AND DECISION MAKING. Traditionally managers have been very adept at taking full advantage of the resources of money, materials, and people, but only recently have they begun to make effective use of information, the other resource. By **filtering** information, the right information reaches the right decision maker at the right time in the right form.

Information systems help process data at the clerical level and provide information for managerial decision making at the operational, tactical, and strategic levels. Managers at the operational, tactical, and strategic levels often request **exception reports** that highlight critical information. For decisions made at the tactical and strategic levels, information is often inconclusive, and managers also must rely on their experience, intuition, and common sense to make the right decision.

The two basic types of decisions are **programmed decisions** and **nonprogrammed decisions**. Purely programmed decisions address well-defined problems. Nonprogrammed decisions, also called **information-based decisions,** involve ill-defined and unstructured problems.

10–2 INFORMATION SYSTEM CONCEPTS. Hardware, software, people, procedures, and data are combined to create an **information system**. An information system provides companies with data processing capabilities and the company's people with information.

Commonly used systems terms are *information systems, data processing systems, management information systems, decision support systems*, and *expert systems*. All these are information systems.

An information system has the same four capabilities as

a computer system: input, processing, storage, and output. The processing capabilities include sorting; accessing, recording, and updating data in storage; summarizing; selecting; and manipulating.

An information system can be either function-based or integrated. A **function-based information system** is designed for the exclusive support of a specific application area. **Integrated information systems** share a common data base.

In a computer system, the input, output, and data storage components that receive data from and transmit data to the processor are said to be **on-line**. Hardware devices that are not accessible to or under the control of a processor are said to be **off-line**. **Source data** on **source documents** must be transcribed into a machine-readable format before they can be interpreted by a computer.

When transactions are grouped together for processing, it is called **batch processing**. In **transaction-oriented processing**, transactions are recorded and entered as they occur.

10–3 DATA PROCESSING SYSTEMS. **Data processing systems** (**DP**) are file-oriented, function-based systems that focus on transaction handling and record keeping and provide periodic output aimed primarily at operational-level management.

10–4 MANAGEMENT INFORMATION SYSTEMS. The author offers the following definition of a **management information system**, or **MIS**: An MIS is an integrated structure of data bases and information flow that optimizes the collection, transfer, and presentation of information throughout a multilevel organization whose component groups perform a variety of tasks to accomplish a united objective.

An MIS not only supports the traditional data processing functions, it also relies on an integrated data base to provide managers at all levels with easy access to timely but structured information. An MIS is flexible and can provide system security.

An MIS is oriented to supporting decisions that involve structured problems.

10–5 DECISION SUPPORT SYSTEMS. **Decision support systems** are interactive information systems that rely on an integrated set of user-friendly hardware and software tools to present information to support management in the decision-making process.

A **DSS** supports decision making at all levels by making general-purpose models, simulation capabilities, and other analytical tools available to the decision maker. A DSS can be readily adapted to meet the information requirements for any decision environment.

In contrast to the MIS, decision support systems are designed to support decision-making processes involving semistructured and unstructured problems.

A decision support system is made up of a set of software

and hardware tools. The categories of DSS software tools include applications development, data management, modeling, statistical analysis, planning, inquiry, graphics, consolidations, and application-specific DSS capabilities.

10–6 EXPERT SYSTEMS. **Expert systems**, which are associated with an area of research known as **artificial intelligence**, help managers resolve problems or make better decisions. They are interactive systems that respond to questions, ask for clarification, make recommendations, and generally help in the decision-making process. An expert system is the highest form of a **knowledge-based system**, but in practice the two terms are used interchangeably. The less sophisticated knowledge-based systems are called **assistant systems**.

The following are several of the more prominent benefits of expert systems: They enable the knowledge of experts to be "canned"; they can expand the decision-making capabilities of many people; they can improve the productivity and performance of decision makers; and they can provide stability and consistency to a particular area of decision making.

The **expert system shell** is a domain-independent proprietary software package that enables the development of expert systems. The primary components of the expert system shell are the knowledge acquisition facility, the knowledge base, the inference engine, and the user interface.

The **knowledge acquisition facility** of the expert system shell permits the construction of the **knowledge base**. The knowledge base is created through the cooperative efforts of a **knowledge engineer** and one or more **domain experts**.

The knowledge base of an expert system contains facts, rules of inference, identification of problem(s) to be solved, possible solutions, and how to progress from problem to solution.

An expert system's **inference engine** is the vehicle by which the facts and rules in the knowledge base are applied to a problem.

The **user interface** component of an expert system enables the interaction between end user and expert system needed for heuristic processing.

Review Exercises

Concepts

1. MIS is an abbreviation for what term?
2. What is the purpose of an exception report?
3. What elements are combined to create an information system?
4. What are the levels of organizational activity, from specific to general?
5. Which type of information system would most closely approximate working directly with a human expert to solve a problem?

6. Which of the following information systems can provide support for transaction handling and record keeping: expert systems, management information systems, DP systems, and decision support systems?

7. Which component of the expert system shell permits the construction of the knowledge base?

8. Name three DSS software aids to planning.

9. In which type of processing are transactions grouped together for processing?

10. What are the two basic types of decisions?

11. What is meant by filtering information?

12. List seven items in the DSS software tool box.

13. Distinguish between on-line operation and off-line operation.

14. What do expert systems and assistant systems have in common?

15. What are the primary components of an expert system shell?

Discussion

16. For each of the three levels of management illustrated in the business system model in Figure 10–1, what would the horizon (time span) be for planning decisions? Explain.

17. In general, top executives have always treated money, materials, and people as valuable resources, but only recently have they recognized that information is also a valuable resource. Why do you think they waited so long?

18. It is often said that "time is money." Would you say that "information is money"? Discuss.

19. Give examples of reports that might be requested by an operational-level manager in an insurance company. By a tactical-level manager. By a strategic-level manager.

20. Contrast a DP system with an MIS. Contrast an MIS with a DSS system.

21. Suppose the company you work for batches all sales data for data entry each night. You have been asked to present a convincing argument to top management why funds should be allocated to convert the current system to transaction-oriented data entry. What would you say?

22. The American Express Authorizer's Assistant, discussed in this chapter, paid for itself in one year. Explain briefly how you think the system was able to:
    a. Provide more consistent decision making.
    b. Improve authorizer productivity.
    c. Reduce credit and fraud losses.
    d. Reduce operating expenses.
    e. Improve service to customers and cardholders.
    f. Enable more accurate decision making.
    g. Reduce learning time for authorizers.

23. Describe a specific decision environment that would be appropriate for the implementation of an expert system.

Self-Test (by section)

10–1 **a.** Tactical-level managers are charged with the responsibility of implementing the objectives and policies set forth at the _____ level of management.

b. It is easier for a manager to detect trends presented in a graphic format than in a tabular format. (T/F)

c. Nonprogrammed decisions are also called: (a) computer-oriented decisions, (b) information-based decisions, or (c) human decisions.

10–2 **a.** The summarizing activity would be associated with which capability of a information system: (a) input, (b) output, or (c) processing?

b. An integrated information system is designed for the exclusive support of a specific application area. (T/F)

c. A burster separates and stacks the payroll checks in an _____ (on-line or off-line) operation.

10–3 The focus of data processing systems is _____ and _____.

10–4 **a.** An MIS has been called a method, a function, an approach, a process, an organization, a system, and a subsystem. (T/F)

b. Which type of information system integrates the information flow between functional areas: (a) DP system, (b) MIS, or (c) DSS?

10–5 **a.** Decision support systems are designed to support decision-making processes involving semistructured and unstructured problems. (T/F)

b. A DSS is most effective at which two levels of management: (a) clerical and operational, (b) operational and tactical, or (c) tactical and strategic?

c. DSS applications that are discarded after providing information support for a one-time decision are called _____.

10–6 **a.** An assistant system is the highest form of a knowledge-based system. (T/F)

b. Which type of information system has the greatest potential to reduce dependencies on critical personnel: (a) MIS, (b) expert system, or (c) DP system?

c. The software that enables the development of an expert system is known as the expert system _____.

d. During the creation of an expert system's knowledge base, the _____ translates the domain expert's knowledge into facts and rules.

Self-test answers. **10–1** (a) strategic; (b) T; (c) b. **10–2** (a) c; (b) F; (c) off-line. **10–3** transaction handling, record keeping. **10–4** (a) T; (b) b. **10–5** (a) T; (b) c; (c) throwaway systems. **10–6** (a) F; (b) b; (c) shell; (d) knowledge engineer.

Chapter 10/The MIS and Decision Support Systems   **305**

11

Applications of Information Technology

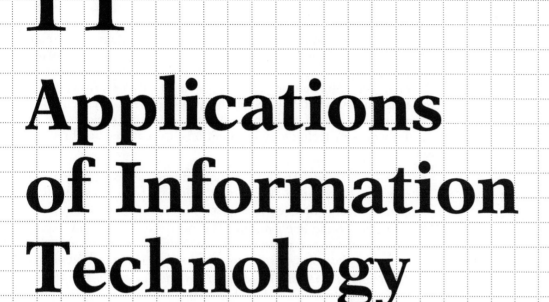

STUDENT LEARNING OBJECTIVES

- To discuss computer and information system applications common to most organizations.
- To discuss computer and information system applications unique to a specific type of industry.
- To discuss computer and information system applications that have the potential of giving organizations a competitive advantage.

11-1 The Uses of Information Technology

New and innovative uses of computers and information systems are being implemented every day in every type of organization. Even so, organizations are still in the early stages of automation. Each company has a seemingly endless number of opportunities to use information technology to operate more efficiently and, perhaps, achieve a *competitive edge*.

This chapter contains an overview of the applications of computers and information systems, sometimes referred to as **information technology**. This overview is not intended to be an exhaustive treatment of information technology applications. However, it can acquaint you with a few of the ways information technology is contributing to and, in many instances, changing society.

Information technology applications are covered in three sections.

- *Common systems.* The first section addresses those applications *common to just about any organization* that employs people to produce goods and services (payroll processing, for example).
- *Industry-specific applications.* The next section presents applications *unique to a particular type of industry or organization* (for example, the point-of-sale systems used in the retail industry).
- *Applications that result in a competitive advantage.* The last section presents several ways in which organizations have employed information technology to achieve a **competitive advantage**.

11-2 Applications of Information Technology Common to Most Organizations

Certain computer applications and information systems are universal and equally appropriate for a manufacturing company, a university, a hospital, or even a cottage industry (where people work out of their

The information system is fast becoming the ultimate strategic weapon in the business world. For example, an automobile manufacturer wanted to lower the cost of producing automobiles while retaining maximum flexibility in what is made. To do this, a computer-based information system was installed to control the assembly line and enable the communication and implementation of last-minute order changes.

With the advent of microcomputers, most small businesses have automated basic monetary accounting systems. This dry cleaning shop owner is examining monthly revenues for each of the various articles of clothing (shirts, pants, coats) that is processed.

homes). These applications normally involve *personnel* and *monetary accounting,* but they also include several other common application areas, such as inventory control. Each of these areas can be, and usually is, integrated to some extent with one or more of the other application areas.

Payroll

Having already read several payroll-related examples earlier in the text, you should be somewhat familiar with payroll systems. The two primary outputs of a payroll system are the payroll check and stub distributed to the employees and the payroll register, which is a summary report of payroll transactions.

Accounts Receivable

The accounts receivable system keeps track of money owed the company on charges for goods sold or services rendered. When a customer purchases goods or services, the customer record is updated to reflect the charge. An invoice, bill, or statement reflecting the balance due is periodically sent to active customers. Upon receipt of payment, the amount due is decreased by the amount of the payment.

Management relies on the accounts receivable system to identify overdue accounts. Reports are generated that "age" accounts to identify those customers whose accounts are overdue by more than 30, 60, or 90 days.

Accounts Payable

Organizations purchase everything from paper clips to bulldozers on credit. So the accounts payable system is the other side of the accounts receivable system. An invoice from a creditor company's accounts receivable system is input to the accounts payable system. When a company receives an invoice, the system generates a check and adjusts the balance. Most companies design their accounts payable system to take advantage of discounts for prompt payment.

General Ledger

Every monetary transaction that occurs within an organization must be properly recorded. Both payment of a bill and an interdepartmental transfer of funds are examples of monetary transactions. The general ledger system keeps track of these transactions and provides the input necessary to produce an organization's financial statement. A financial statement includes the *profit and loss statement* and the *balance sheet*.

The Securities & Exchange Commission (SEC) requires publicly held companies to file quarterly financial statements. In the past this requirement resulted in six million pages of reports being sent to the SEC every three months. Now each report is transmitted to the SEC electronically via data communications. With the current system, stockbrokers and investors can look through thousands of financial statements from their terminals, whereas in the past they had to wait several weeks before they could see reports.

In the not-too-distant past, accountants posted debits and credits for each account manually in a ledger book, thus the name *general ledger* for today's electronic system. Other "account" systems (accounts receivable, accounts payable, payroll, and so on) are sources of financial transactions and feed data into the general ledger system.

Inventory Management and Control

Walk into most organizations and you see desks, file cabinets, and even computers. These items are called *fixed assets*. A fixed-asset inventory record is maintained for each item and includes such data as date purchased, cost, and inventory item number. These records are maintained for asset-control and tax purposes.

Manufacturing companies must also manage in-process and finished-goods inventories. These inventory systems monitor the quantity on hand and the location of each inventory item. Figure 11–1 illustrates a few of the menus and input/output displays in a typical on-line inventory system.

Human Resource Development

Human resource development systems are essentially personnel accounting systems that maintain pertinent data on employees. Besides routine historical data (educational background, salary history, and so on), the system includes data on performance reviews, skills, and professional development.

Budgeting

Each year managers spend months preparing their departmental budgets for the coming fiscal year. To help in this task, the budget system provides each manager with information on past line-item expenditures (salaries, office equipment, office supplies, and so on). Based on this information and projected budget requirements,

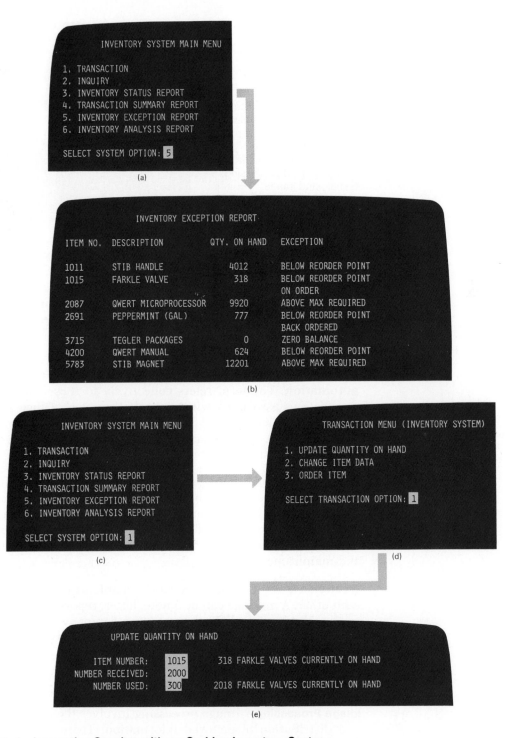

(a)

(b)

(c)

(d)

(e)

FIGURE 11–1   Interactive Session with an On-Line Inventory System

(a) The main menu presents the user with six processing options. The user enters Option 5 to obtain an inventory exception report. (b) This exception report is produced when Main Menu Option 5 is selected. Only those inventory items whose quantity on hand is too high or too low are listed. (c) From the main menu, the user selects Option 1 to get the transaction menu. (d) This screen is produced when Main Menu Option 1 is selected. Desiring to update quantity on hand, the user selects Transaction Option 1. (e) From this transaction display screen, the user enters *item number* (1015), *number received* (2000), and *number used* (300) to update quantity on hand for Farkle valves.

The micros in this office are part of a local area network (LAN) that provides support for a variety of office automation applications, including word processing. E-mail, and image processing. They system also has an on-line calendar and directory.

each manager can make budget requests for the next fiscal year. The budget system matches these requests against projected revenues and generates an exception report showing those budget line items that exceed projected funding levels. The budget items are reviewed, and the process is repeated until the coming year's budget is established.

Office Automation

During the last 15 years much has been said and written about **office automation**. The term refers collectively to those computer-based applications associated with general office work. Office automation applications include word processing (also considered a productivity tool), electronic mail, image processing, voice processing, and office information systems.

Word Processing Word processing, the cornerstone of office automation, concerns written communication and is found wherever there is an office with a computer. Word processing, which is discussed in detail in Chapter 14, "Word Processing, Desktop Publishing, and Communications Software," is available on virtually every micro, mini, and mainframe computer.

Electronic Mail Computer networks enable us to route messages to each other. A message can be a note, letter, report, chart, or even the manuscript for a book. Each person in a company can be assigned an *electronic mailbox* in which messages are received and held in secondary storage, usually magnetic disk. To "open" and "read" **electronic mail**, or **E-mail**, the user simply goes to the nearest terminal and recalls the message from storage.

Image Processing Image processing involves the creation, storage, and distribution of pictorial information. There are two levels of image processing sophistication. At the first level, **facsimile** equipment, which has been around since the 1960s, transfers images of hard-copy documents via telephone lines to another office. The process is similar to using a copying machine except that the original is inserted in a facsimile, or "fax," machine at one office and a hard copy is produced on another fax machine in another office.

Image processing has come a long way in the last few years. Some companies are beginning to digitize handwritten documents and store them on disk to facilitate their storage and recall. In this era of sophisticated information processing, it is just too inefficient to make frequent trips to the file cabinet.

Recent technological innovations have expanded the scope of image processing. An **image processor** uses a camera to scan and digitize an image and then stores the digitized image on a disk. The image can be handwritten notes, a photograph, a drawing—anything that can be digitized. In digitized form, the image can be retrieved, displayed, altered, merged with text, stored, and sent via data communications to one or several remote locations.

Voice Processing   Voice processing includes **voice message switching** and **teleconferencing**. The terminal for voice message switching (a store-and-forward "voice mailbox" system) is a touch-tone telephone. Voice message switching accomplishes the same function as electronic mail, except the hard copy is not available. When you send a message, your voice is digitized and stored on a magnetic disk for later retrieval. The message is routed to the destination(s) you designate using the telephone's keyboard; then it is heard upon request by the intended receiver(s). A voice store-and-forward system permits you to send one or many messages with just one telephone call.

Teleconferencing enables people in different locations to see and talk to each other and to share charts and other visual meeting materials. The voice and video of teleconferencing are supported by the telephone network. People who are geographically scattered can meet without the need for time-consuming and expensive travel.

Office Information Systems   Several small information systems address traditional office tasks. For example, one system allows people to keep their *personal calendars* on-line. As workers schedule activities, they block out times on their electronic calendars.

There are definite advantages to having a central data base of personal calendars. Let's say that a public relations manager wants to schedule a meeting to review the impact of some unexpected favorable publicity. To do this, the manager enters the names of the participants and the expected duration of the meeting. The *conference scheduling system* searches the calendars of people affected and suggests possible meeting times. The manager then selects a meeting

Memory Bits

COMMON INFORMATION SYSTEMS
- Payroll
- Accounts Receivable
- Accounts Payable
- General Ledger
- Inventory Management and Control
- Human Resource Development
- Budgeting
- Office Automation
    Word processing
    Electronic mail
    Image processing
    Voice processing
    Office information systems

APPLICATIONS OF COMPUTER GRAPHICS

1.

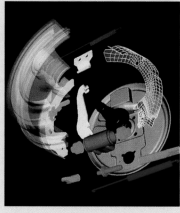

2.

3.

4.

1. Television has been the impetus behind some of the most artistic innovations in computer graphics. Sports events are often introduced by dynamic graphics. When viewed on television, this PGA (The Professional Golfers Association of America) logo almost seems to jump off the screen and into your living room.

2. With the prospect of increased productivity, manufacturing companies have been rushing to install more and more applications of computer-aided design (CAD). The photo illustrates how CAD enables engineers to explode an assembly to highlight its components. The components of this automobile brake assembly are highlighted in different colors.

3. Computer-aided design enables chemical engineers to see, test, and modify the design of a chemicals plant from any viewpoint. With this background work done in the office, the chance of on-site construction difficulties is lessened.

4. Is it real? No, this three-dimensional image of a Bell Helicopter aircraft cannot actually fly. It was created using Paint and Animation Software, a proprietary product of Symbolics, Inc. No longer do aircraft manufacturers have to build functional prototypes to see how they will look (or perform) in flight.

time, and the participants are notified by electronic mail. Of course, their calendars are automatically updated to reflect the meeting time.

Another common office application is the company *directory*. The directory contains basic personnel data: name, title, department, location, and phone number. To look up someone's telephone number, all you have to do is enter that person's name on your terminal, and the number is displayed. The beauty of the directory data base is that it is always up to date, unlike hard-copy directories, which never seem to have all the current titles or phone numbers.

Other systems permit users to organize *personal notes*, keep *diaries*, document ideas in a *preformatted outline*, and keep a *tickler file*. When users log on in the morning, the tickler file automatically reminds them of things to do for that day.

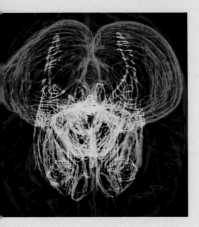
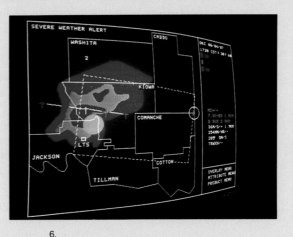
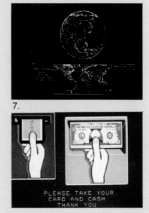

6.

7.

8.

5. This frontal perspective of the human brain graphically illustrates the relationship between the cerebellum, brain stem, cerebral cortex, ventricles, and basal ganglia.

6. The Next Generation Weather Radar System (Nexrad) is being developed by the U.S. Department of Commerce. The graphics display improves severe weather forecasting by color-coding varying weather conditions in a geographical area (southern Oklahoma in photo).

7. This satellite tracking application presents information regarding the position of satellites relative to the earth. The top portion of the screen shows the earth as it would be viewed from the current position of a particular satellite as well as the relative position of other satellites. The bottom portion superimposes the track of the satellite in question and several other satellites on a flat map of the world.

8. Computer graphics is being used to enhance the user interface and, therefore, the user-friendliness of all kinds of computer-based systems. The display on this automatic teller machine (ATM) provides the user with both visual cues and written instructions.

11–3 Industry-Specific Applications of Information Technology

Many applications of information technology are unique to a particular type of industry or organization. For example, fire incident reporting systems are unique to local governments. The use of automatic teller machines is unique to the banking industry. These and other industry-specific applications are briefly discussed in the remainder of this section.

Manufacturing

Traditional Manufacturing Information Systems   In a manufacturing company, the *order entry and processing system* accepts and processes customer orders. The system then feeds data to the warehouse or plant, depending on whether the order is for stock items or special order, and to the *accounts receivable system* for billing. The order entry and processing system also tracks orders and provides status information from the time the order is received until the product is delivered to the customer.

Production scheduling systems allocate manufacturing resources in an optimal manner. A well-designed system will minimize idle time for both workers and machines and ensure that materials are at the right place at the right time.

Market analysis systems rely on historical and current data to identify fast- and slow-moving products, to pinpoint areas with high sales potential, to make forecasts of production requirements, and to plan marketing strategy. For example, in Figure 11–2, the scatter plot of regional sales over the last four quarters demonstrates clearly that fourth-quarter sales in the northeast region did not keep pace with the others. Based on this finding, management might elect to focus more attention on the northeast region during the coming quarter.

Project management and control systems provide management with the information necessary to keep projects within budget and on time. Periodic reports present actual versus anticipated project costs and the number of days ahead of or behind schedule.

Other information systems commonly found in manufacturing companies include *standard costing* and *manufacturing resource planning (MRP)*.

Robotics

Rudimentary robotics. **Robotics**, the integration of computers and **industrial robots**, is more often than not associated with manufacturing. By 1990 the "steel-collar" workforce throughout the world will be made up of over 250,000 industrial robots. The most common industrial robot is a single mechanical arm controlled by a computer. The arm, called a *manipulator*, has a shoulder, forearm, and wrist and is capable of performing the motions of a human arm. The manipula-

FIGURE 11–2 Scatter Plot of Regional Sales
Quarterly sales figures from four regions are plotted to help in market analysis.

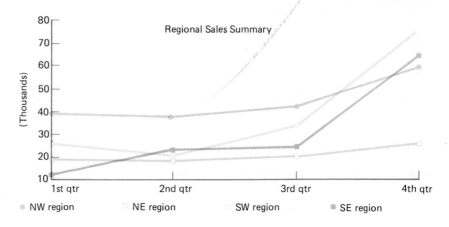

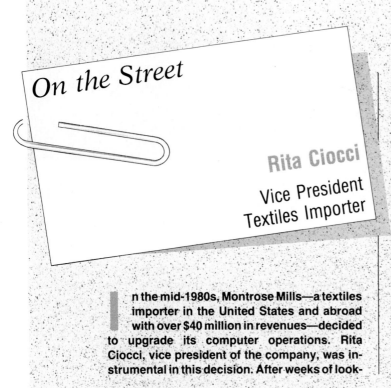

tor is fitted with a hand designed to accomplish a specific task, such as painting, welding, picking and placing, and so on.

An industrial robot is best at tasks that are repetitive and tasks that require precision movements, moving heavy loads, and working in hazardous areas. Such tasks are not unique to manufacturing; they exist in virtually every kind of industry, from hospitals to cannery row. The automotive industry is the largest user of robots (painting, welding), and the electronics industry (circuit testing, connecting chips to circuit boards) is second. Even surgeons are using robots to help in brain surgery. They can be set up to manipulate the surgical drill and biopsy needle with great accuracy, thereby making brain surgery faster, more accurate, and safer.

Teaching robots to do their jobs. A computer program is written to control the robot just as one is written to print payroll checks. It includes such commands as when to reach, in which direction to reach, how far to reach, when to grasp, and so on. Once programmed, robots do not need much attention. One plant manufactures vacuum cleaners 24 hours a day, seven days a week, in total darkness!

Outfitting robots with intelligence and human sensory capabilities. Most robots are programmed to reach to a particular location, find a particular item, and then place it somewhere else. This

Industrial robots help assure quality in the assembly of everything from electrical components to automobiles. Here a robot applies spotwelds to auto bodies in this automobile assembly plant. They then paint every nook and cranny of the body.

simple application of robotics is called *pick and place*. Instead of a grasping mechanism, other robots are equipped with a variety of industrial tools such as drills, paint guns, welding torches, and so on. Of course, it will be a very long time before our companions and workmates are robots. However, industrial robots are being equipped with rudimentary sensory capabilities, such as vision, that enable them to simulate human behavior. A robot with the added dimension of vision can be given some intelligence. (Robots without intelligence simply repeat preprogrammed motions.) Even though the state of the art of vision systems is low, a robot can be "taught" to distinguish between dissimilar objects under controlled conditions. With the addition of this sensory subsystem, the robot has the capability of making crude but important decisions. For example, a robot equipped with a vision subsystem can distinguish between two boxes approaching on the conveyor. It can be programmed to place a box of particular dimensions on an adjacent conveyer and let all other boxes pass.

If vision system technology continues to improve, more and more robots will have navigational capabilities. Now most robots are stationary; those that are not can only detect the presence of an object in their path or are programmed to operate within a well-defined work area where the positions of all obstacles are known. Within the decade of the 1990s, robots will be able to move about the work area just as people do.

Computer-Integrated Manufacturing   Manufacturing companies are using information technologies to streamline their operations. The integration of computers and manufacturing is called **computer-integrated manufacturing (CIM)**. The computer is used at every stage of the manufacturing process, from the time a part is conceived until it is shipped. In computer-integrated manufacturing, the various computer systems are linked together via data communications, and they feed data to one another. CIM uses an integrated network of computers to design the product, to operate and monitor production equipment, to facilitate communication and information flow throughout the plant and the company, and to interface with the company's administrative information systems: An engineer uses a **computer-aided**

In the textile industry, computer-aided design (CAD) allows manufacturers to create and view cloth patterns in a fraction of the time it would have taken to prepare a preproduction sample for customer inspection.

design (**CAD**) system to design the part. The design specifications are produced and stored on a magnetic disk. The specifications, now in an electronic data base, become input to another computer system that generates programs to control the robots and machine tools that handle and make the part. These computer-driven tools are even linked to the company's MIS computers to provide data for order processing, inventory management, shop-floor scheduling, and general accounting. Some CIM systems go one step further and provide a link between the manufacturer and the customer via EDI.

Several companies in each industry are working feverishly toward the implementation of total CIM. Few, if any, have achieved it, but many have achieved at least a degree of CIM.

Financial Services

The financial services industries, which include banking, savings and loan institutions, and brokerage firms, are entering an exciting era. The computer is the impetus for some radical and progressive changes in the way these money brokers do business. For example, financial services organizations serve as a "money buffer" between buyer and

Computer-aided design (CAD) has revolutionized the way in which engineers and scientists design, draft, and document a product. With CAD, most of the "bugs" can be worked out of a design before a prototype is built. Take the design of an automobile as an example. At the stage where it is no more than an idea in an electronic data base, an automobile design can be put through the paces in a simulated wind tunnel and on a simulated test track. It can even be crashed into a brick wall!

The banking industry would prefer that its customers use ATMs for banking transactions rather than tellers. This bank gives customers who come in the bank the option of selecting a teller or an ATM. The average ATM transaction takes less time, but most important, it costs less than half that of a teller-aided transaction. The more customers use ATMS, the more banks can reduce the cost of their services.

seller. The traditional approach to money exchange has been for the seller to bill the buyer, the buyer to write a check for the amount of the bill, the seller to deposit the check, and the bank to transfer the funds from the buyer's to the seller's account. This approach is not only time-consuming, but expensive for all concerned. Throughout the remainder of the 1980s we can expect to see this traditional approach give way more and more to *electronic funds transfer* (*EFT*).

In electronic funds transfer, the amount owed is transferred electronically from one account to another in a bank, savings and loan, or brokerage firm. For example, rather than sending out thousands of statements that require each customer to pay the bill in his or her own way, some utility companies are cooperating with customers and banks so that payments are transferred electronically at the end of each billing period. As another example, some employers are bypassing printing payroll checks. Based on data supplied to the banks, pay is electronically transferred from employer to employee accounts.

Automatic teller machines (*ATMs*) are the most visible symbol of EFT (see Chapter 1, "The World of Computers"). In over 100 banks, however, EFT has been extended to the home in the form of *home banking systems*. Subscribers to a home banking service use their personal computers as terminals to pay bills, transfer funds, and inquire about account status. Some systems also provide subscribers with other services, such as "electronic shopping," electronic mail, and up-to-the-minute stock market quotations. For example, several brokerage firms permit clients to use their PCs to tap into a data base that contains their account data as well as timely information about the securities market.

All financial institutions offer *financial planning services*. Part of the service involves a computer-based analysis of a customer's investment portfolio. Input to the system includes current and anticipated income, amount and type of investments, assets and liabilities, and financial objectives (such as: minimize taxes; desired pension at age 65). The output from the analysis consists of recommendations aimed at optimizing the effectiveness of a particular person's investment portfolio.

Futurists are predicting that the current system of currency exchange gradually will be replaced by EFT. More and more point-of-sale systems are being integrated with EFT systems so that what is now a *credit* transaction will be a *cash-transfer* transaction. That is, when a customer purchases an item, the amount of the sale is debited, via EFT, from the customer's checking account and credited to the account of the retail store. No further funds transfer is needed. Of course, the option of making a credit purchase will remain.

Publishing

Word processing, computerized *typesetting*, computer-aided *graphics design*, and *page formatting* have revolutionized the way newspapers, books, and magazines are produced. Reporters and writers enter and edit their stories on their portable micros or on-line terminals. Once all copy is on-line, pages are automatically formatted according to type and spacing specifications. Traditionally, a manually produced document prepared with pencils, paper, and typewriters went on to the editing, retyping, composing, proofreading, cutting, pasting, and photographing of the final page format before plates could be made for the presswork.

Eventually, *customized printing on demand* will be available at bookstores. Instead of choosing from books on hand, you will make a selection from a list of virtually any current book. It will then be printed (figures and all) and bound while you wait. This approach will provide a greater selection for the customer and vastly reduce costly inventory for both bookstore and publisher.

Although customized printing on demand is a few years away, *magazines on a disk* are here today. These magazines are distributed in diskette format for display on microcomputers. Dictionaries, encyclopedias, and other reference materials already are being sold in the form of high-density optical laser disks.

Insurance

The information systems of an insurance company have more external interaction, or communication with people outside the company, than most other businesses. Most of this external communication is with

Computer and information technology has enabled USAA, an insurance company, to eliminate the intermediary. Because it does not have a field sales force, it enjoys a competitive advantage and is able to offer insurance to its customers at very competitive rates.

customers. The volume of such transactions makes computer-based *policy administration* and *claims processing systems* a necessity. Insurance agents hook up to computers at headquarters so they can quote, write, and deliver insurance policies while customers wait.

An insurance company makes or loses money according to the accuracy of its *actuarial accounting system*. This system maintains countless statistics that serve as the basis for the rate structure. An actuarial system provides the following kinds of information: the probability that a 20-year-old Kansas City resident with no automobile accident history will have an accident or the life expectancy of a 68-year-old female whose parents died of natural causes.

Entertainment

The computer is now an integral part of the entertainment industry. *Pro football* coaches rely heavily on feedback from their computer systems to call plays and set defenses during a game. The system predicts what the opposing team is expected to do, based on statistics of what they have done in the past. In fact, the computer is becoming the deciding factor between evenly matched opponents in many sports.

Computers have had quite an impact on the *film industry*. Many *special effects* and even the sets for some movies are generated with computer graphics. *Animation* for cartoons and movies is no longer drawn one frame at a time. The scenes and characters are drawn, by hand or with a computer, then manipulated with computer graphics to create the illusion of motion.

Computer graphics has even made it possible to revive old black-and-white movies—in color! Imagine Laurel and Hardy in living color! Now, through an innovative use of computer technology called *colorization*, it is possible to change the old black-and-white films to color.

Coaches in many sports, including tennis, have turned to computers to help provide them with better information about the performance of their athletes. This tennis teaching professional observes his students during matches and enters data to his portable micro on each point played. After the match, the data can be summarized and printed for evaluation and critique. The statistics highlight a player's strengths, weaknesses, and patterns of play.

Laurel and Hardy in living color! This photo shows a colorized version of a black-and-white Laurel and Hardy movie.

In the *theater*, playwrights use word processing systems especially designed for the theater environment. Besides the obvious value of word processing, there are additional benefits to having the script on-line. Actors can learn their lines by interacting with a computer that "reads" the lines of other actors; that is, only the lines of other actors are displayed on the screen unless the actor requests that all lines be displayed.

Then, of course, there are *video*—or should we say "computer"—*games*. Interest in video games seems to be lessening as people realize what they have is a computer with a seemingly infinite number of practical applications. The computer games industry, however, is anticipating a resurgence of interest with the introduction of videodisk technology. With videodisk-based games (for example, "Dragon's Lair"), the images are lifelike color motion pictures instead of computer graphics.

Health Care

Hospitals   The computer is a constant companion to both patients and medical personnel. This is especially so in hospitals where, at the beginning of each day, the status of each room is updated in the *room census* data base. The *patient accounting system* updates patient records to reflect lab tests, drugs administered, and visits by a physician. This system also handles patient billing.

In the *operating room*, surgeons have on-line access to the patient's medical records. Some of these interactive systems are even voice-activated to free the surgeon's hands for more critical tasks. Computers have taken some of the risk out of complex surgical procedures by warning surgeons of life-threatening situations: During brain surgery, for example, a computer monitors the patient's blood flow to the brain. Once a patient is moved to an *intensive care unit*,

Data obtained during scanning by magnetic resonance (MR) diagnostic equipment are computer-reconstructed to form cross-sectional images of the body's tissues and organs. This technology enables doctors to distinguish between benign and malignant tumors, and to detect conditions that could lead to heart attacks.

computers continue to monitor vital signs and alert attending personnel of dangerous situations. Most life-support systems (such as artificial lungs) are also computer controlled.

Computer-controlled devices provide physicians and surgeons with information that simply was not available a few years ago. Because surgeons can "see" more clearly into a person's body with *CT*, or *CAT* (computer tomography), *scanners* and *MR* (magnetic resonance) *scanners*, medical procedures may be less drastic because better information is available. For example, a surgeon may not have to amputate an entire limb to stop the spread of bone cancer if an MR scan detects the cancer only in a limb's extremities. CAT scanners permit the results of several scans to be combined and forged into three-dimensional images. MR scanners, the most recent technology for viewing inside the body, combine computers and a large doughnut-shaped magnet to produce video images of a cross-section of a body. Before MR scanners, exploratory surgery was necessary to produce such internal "pictures." Physicians see and analyze the images from CAT and MR scanners on color graphics monitors.

Expert diagnosis systems (see Chapter 10, "The MIS and Decision Support Systems") help physicians identify diseases and isolate problems. The physician enters the patient's symptoms, and the system queries an expert system data base to match the symptoms with possible illnesses. If the illness cannot be diagnosed with existing information, the system requests more information.

In recent years the cost of a hospital room has soared, and some hospitals still operate in the red. To get back in the black, they are implementing procedures to help control costs. For the first time, they are using systems that optimize their resources while maximizing revenue. A *physician's accounting system* provides hospital administrators with information about how each physician is using hospital facilities. For example, such systems identify physicians who tend to admit patients who could just as well be treated on an outpatient basis. These patients typically generate less revenue for the hospital and take up beds that could best be used by seriously ill patients.

Medical Research The microprocessor has opened new vistas for *medical research*. Our body is an electrical system that is very com-

Computers open up new horizons in communication for people with special needs due to a disability such as cerebral palsy.

patible with these tiny computers. Researchers have made it possible for paraplegics to pedal bicycles and take crude steps under the control of external computers: Various muscle groups are electronically stimulated to cause the legs to perform a walking motion. The system has given new hope to paraplegics who thought they would never walk again. Much remains to be done, but researchers insist that someday computer implants will enable paraplegics to walk.

Government

Local Government　Local governments use a wide variety of information systems. Most cities supply and bill citizens for at least one of the three major utility services—water, refuse, and electricity. Besides these *utility billing systems*, a *tax collection system* periodically assesses citizens for income, school, and real estate taxes.

Cities also have *police systems* that are used for incident reporting, inquiry, and dispatching. Many police departments even have terminals mounted in their cruisers. On these terminals, officers can see the arrest record of an individual, request a "rundown" on an auto's license number, or check on what other officers are doing. Police detectives can search data bases for suspects by matching modi operandi, nicknames, body marks, physical deformities, locations, times of day, and even footwear.

The local fire and police departments fight crime and fires and attend to other emergencies with the help of an information system. In seconds, dispatchers can select which squad car or fire station would be the most responsive to a given emergency.

✔

Memory Bits

INDUSTRY-SPECIFIC INFORMATION SYSTEMS

- Manufacturing
  Order-entry and processing
  Production scheduling
  Market analysis
  Project management and control
  Standard costing
  Manufacturing resource planning (MRP)
  Robotics
  Computer-integrated manufacturing (CIM)
  Computer-aided design (CAD)
- Financial services
  Electronic funds transfer (EFT)
  Automatic teller machines (ATM)
  Home banking
  Financial planning
- Publishing
  Word processing
  Typesetting
  Graphics design
  Page formatting
  Customized printing on demand
  Magazines on a disk
- Insurance
  Policy administration
  Claims processing
  Actuarial accounting
- Entertainment
  Professional sports systems
  Film industry
      Special effects
      Animation
      Colorization
  Theater (on-line scripts)
  Video games   *(cont.)*

Some fire departments are electronically informed of the location of a fire by a *fire incident reporting system*. Here's how it works: Someone at the site of the fire calls a three-digit "fire-reporting" number. In a split second a computer system searches its data base for the address of the phone (and the location of the fire), then automatically dispatches vehicles from the nearest fire station.

Local governments also install and support the *automated traffic-control systems* that coordinate traffic signals to minimize delays and optimize traffic flow (see Chapter 1, "The World of Computers").

State Government   At the state level of government, each major agency has its own information services department. *Welfare, employment security, highway patrol, revenue,* and *education* are only a few of the many state agencies that have such departments. In some states one of the most visible systems is the *lottery* agency. A bet is registered immediately at any of thousands of on-line terminals located in stores and restaurants throughout the state. The on-line lottery systems have made it possible for people to be "instant" winners (or losers).

Several state *crime bureaus* are using computers for fingerprint identification. Once the millions of fingerprints have been converted into digital data and stored on magnetic disk, the system can check up to 650 prints per second. In a manual search, an investigator would take hours to do what a computer can do in a single second. This new technology doesn't give criminals much of a head start!

Federal Government   The federal government has thousands of computer systems scattered throughout the world. The Federal Bureau of Investigation (FBI) uses its *national crime information system* (*NCIS*) to help track down criminals. The Internal Revenue Service (IRS) now permits qualified accountants to *file tax returns* on-line. This service saves us and the IRS a lot of time and money. The on-line system performs all the necessary table searches and computations, and it even cross-checks the accuracy and consistency of the input data. For the IRS, no further data entry or personal assistance is required.

In the past a manual search through a fingerprint file could take a detective months—often without success. Today computers take only a few minutes to check fingerprints from the scene of a crime against a large data base of fingerprints—often with great success!

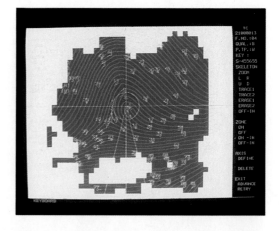

NASA's Mission Control Center tracks space shuttle flights with the help of two large mainframe computers. Tracking stations around the world gather data directly from the computers on board the space shuttle. These data are transmitted via satellite to the Mission Control Center, where a host mainframe computer provides position reports and makes trajectory predictions. This breathtaking view of the space shuttle as it is about to release a communications satellite contrasts the black of deep space with our watery planet.

Computer technology has given Congress a new look. Senators and representatives have terminals in their offices that allow them to scan proposed legislation, send electronic mail, vote on legislation from their offices, do research, and correspond with constituents. The system also allows lobbyists, reporters, and other interested people to monitor voting records, session attendance, and other matters of public interest. Another benefit of the *congressional computer network* is that it lets congressional committees poll members of Congress for their feedback while legislation is still in draft form, instead of waiting until the legislation is put to a vote.

The most sophisticated government computer systems are associated with *NASA* and the space program. A mind-boggling network of ground and on-board computers must work together, without malfunction, to take people to and from the moon and shuttle people between the earth and orbit around the earth.

11–4 Gaining the Competitive Advantage with Information Technology

The days are gone when good management and hard work would invariably result in success and profits. Now that these organizational qualities have become prerequisites for survival, managers are seeking strategies that can give their companies the *competitive advantage*, especially those strategies that involve information technology.

In this highly competitive era, the judicious use of information technology can make the difference between profitability and failure in just about every type of organization. This section provides examples of how organizations are employing information technology to realize a competitive advantage.

Making Strategic Alliances with Customers

Electronic data interchange (EDI) (introduced in Chapter 7, "Connectivity and Data Communications") has altered the basic constructs of the wholesale drug distribution industry, and it is likely to do the

INDUSTRY-SPECIFIC INFORMATION SYSTEMS

- Health care
  - Hospitals
    - Room census
    - Patient accounting
    - Operating room
    - Intensive care unit
    - Diagnostic equipment
    - Expert diagnosis systems
    - Physicians' accounting
    - Source data automation
  - Medical research
- Pharmaceutical
  - Electronic data interchange
  - Drug interaction data base
- Retail grocery
  - Automated checkout system
  - Personalized shopping lists
- Transportation
  - Reservations
  - Fleet maintenance
- Retail sales
  - Point of sale (POS)
- Government
  - Local
    - Utility billings
    - Tax collection
    - Police systems
    - Fire incident reporting
    - Traffic control
  - State
    - Welfare
    - Employment security
    - Highway patrol
    - Revenue
    - Education
    - Lottery
    - Crime bureau
  - Federal
    - National crime information system
    - Filing taxes
    - Congressional computer network
    - Space programs (NASA)

This pharmacist has a direct link to the distributor's central computer system via EDI. Using his workstation, he can request up-to-the minute pricing information and enter orders. Such systems benefit both the customer and the supplier.

same with other industries as well. EDI is using computers and data communications to transmit data (for example, invoices and orders) electronically between companies. In the drug industry it is a win–win situation. *Strategic alliances* involving EDI ultimately benefit all parties involved.

Traditionally pharmacists at over 50,000 drugstores devote many hours each week to taking inventory and creating handwritten lists of the items they need to restock. Those who have computer systems usually enter order data into their own local systems. The system prints the purchase orders, often in triplicate, and they are sent by mail to one or more wholesale distributors. It is not unusual for a single order to contain hundreds, even thousands of items. When the wholesaler receives the hard-copy order, key entry operators enter the orders into their computer system.

The trend today is toward drug wholesalers providing EDI capabilities to their customers as an incentive to do business with them. Those who provide this capability are realizing a competitive advantage and substantial increases in market share. Those who do not provide EDI capabilities are struggling or going out of business.

Pharmacists use distributor-supplied, hand-held bar-code scanners to expedite the order entry process. The only datum keyed in by the druggist is the quantity. Order data are loaded from the portable data entry device directly to the pharmacist's computer system, and an electronic order is transmitted from the retailer to the distributor via data communications. This approach eliminates the need for hard-copy orders and redundant key data entry.

Besides expediting the order entry process, the wholesaler provides the pharmacist with other information-based incentives as well. For example, pharmacists have only to ask for sales reports by department and product, and products are even shipped with price labels that include the customer-designated profit margin. In an ongoing effort to provide the best customer incentives and gain the competitive advantage, drug wholesalers are continuing to "up the ante." One distributor provides computer-generated suggestions for the most effective visual presentation of products. Another processes insurance forms and provides records needed for preparing income tax returns.

Taking Full Advantage of Available Technology

Perhaps the most price-sensitive market of all is the grocery business. A company can lure customers from a competitor by lowering prices by a few pennies on selected items. Supermarket managers are continually seeking ways to lower prices and reap the competitive advantage. Thousands of supermarkets have installed automated checkout systems to take advantage of the machine-readable Universal Product Code (UPC) imprinted on each item. The automated checkout systems not only speed the checkout process but they also save money that can be passed on to customers in the form of lower prices. Supermarkets experience gains in checker productivity from 20% to 50%. Besides those gains, the system electronically tallies purchases, speeds cash flow, updates the inventory, and alerts store personnel when bad checks are presented. Even though thousands of automated checkout systems have been installed, five times as many supermarkets do not have them. These supermarkets are at a disadvantage because their operating costs are higher, their checkout process is slower, and management is unable to monitor inventory levels on a timely basis.

Within a few years all supermarkets will have automated checkout systems—and what then? Some supermarkets are not waiting. They are seeking new competitive strategies involving information systems. Several have installed terminals in the stores so that customers can inquire about the location of an item. Other stores give each customer a personalized shopping list and coupons based on the customer's shopping history. These strategies focus on improving customer service.

This grocery store has an automated checkout system and the capability of operating without cash transfers. The customer swipes her bank card (containing account number and authorization data) through a badge reader and enters a personal identification number on the keyboard, both of which are connected to a network of banking computers. The customer then enters the amount of the purchase. This amount is deducted from her bank account and credited to that of the grocery store.

Computer-Based Training: Optimizing the Effectiveness of the People Resource

Not all uses of information technology involve information systems. Computers can make significant contributions in all phases of a business endeavor, including the education of its employees. The most valuable resource that any company has is its people, and time and time again education has proved to be one of the most cost-effective investments that a company can make. There are many sources of education: on-the-job training (OJT), college courses, seminars, professional conferences, and independent study, to mention a few. Some companies feel that the judicious use of **computer-based training** (**CBT**) has enabled them to be more effective in their use of people resources, the net result of which has been a competitive advantage. CBT, which has added a new dimension to education, has many benefits:

- A CBT system can give "individual attention" to a student.
- CBT is interactive and is quick to respond to a student's input.
- CBT is capable of multidimensional communication (sound, print, graphics, and color).
- CBT can demonstrate and present material, provide opportunities for drill and practice, test for understanding of the material, evaluate the test results, and provide follow-up instruction based on test results.
- CBT systems can interact with students to enhance the learning process. Through interactive computer graphics, a CBT system can demonstrate certain concepts more effectively than books, manuals, or even teachers can.
- CBT is self-paced so the student controls the speed of learning.

Educational software packages have been developed that reinforce and complement virtually every business-related topic, from word processing to project management. Companies using CBT are

Lloyd Bank, a financial institution in Britain, employs an interactive videodisc system to train its employees in teller and customer service techniques. Lloyd's notes the system has reduced training time by as much as 30% for its 48,000 employees in some 1500 branches. Each program begins with a display of the bank's logo.

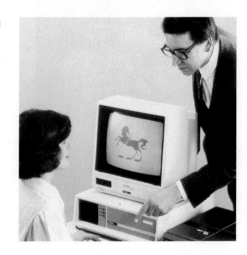

Hospitals use hand-held wand scanners to collect data at the source. Nurses update patient records by scanning preprinted labels on medicines and supplies that are to be used by patients. By collecting data at the source, hospitals simplify record keeping while maintaining tight control over inventory.

saving money and getting the most out of their people. This, they feel, gives them a slight competitive edge.

Source Data Automation: Collecting Data at the Source

In recent years, health care has become a competitive industry. Overcapacity and the emergence of for-profit hospitals have forced hospital administrators to pursue the competitive advantage aggressively. The best way to do this is to offer better service at a better price. This means improving the quality of health care and increasing productivity. Hospital administrators are turning to information systems to do this.

If a hospital can use management information systems to improve productivity to the point where they can offer services that are priced less than the competition, they will enjoy a competitive advantage. A cost-reduction program involving information systems would normally encompass several facets of hospital operation. A study at one hospital revealed that nurses devoted over 40% of their time to recording what they do. For example, nurses must log every prescription they deliver and every time they respond to a patient call. A computer-based data collection system was developed and installed at that hospital that enables data to be captured in machine-readable format (for example, bar codes) from bedside terminals at the point of care. By reducing the time nurses spend recording data about their activities from 40% to 5%, the source data automation system enabled more time to be devoted to direct patient care. In this case, the implementation of an MIS resulted in both cost reduction and improved services.

 Summary Outline and Important Terms

11–1 THE USES OF INFORMATION TECHNOLOGY. New and innovative uses of computers and information systems are being implemented every day in every type of organization. The general area of computers and information systems is sometimes referred to as **information technology**.

11–2 APPLICATIONS OF INFORMATION TECHNOLOGY COMMON TO MOST ORGANIZATIONS. Certain computer applications and information systems are universal and equally appropriate in any business environment. Computer applications found in most organizations include payroll, accounts receivable, accounts payable, general ledger, inventory management and control, human resource development, budgeting, and **office automation**.

Office automation refers collectively to computer-based applications associated with general office work. These include word processing, **electronic mail**, image processing (**facsimile** and **image processor**), voice processing (**voice message switching** and **teleconferencing**), and office information systems.

11–3 INDUSTRY-SPECIFIC APPLICATIONS OF INFORMATION TECHNOLOGY. Some computer applications are unique to a particular type of business, such as production scheduling (manufacturing), electronic funds transfer (financial services), typesetting (publishing), actuarial accounting (insurance), and special effects in movies and on-line theater scripts (entertainment).

Robotics (the integration of computers and **industrial robots**), **computer-integrated manufacturing** (**CIM**), and **computer-aided design** (**CAD**) are three of the more prominent applications of information technology commonly found in manufacturing.

In health care, computers help hospital administrative personnel with billing and help doctors diagnose illnesses. The computer has enabled medical research advance in leaps and bounds.

Some of the computer applications found in local government include utility billing, tax collection, and police and fire incident reporting. State governments use computers for everything from fingerprint analysis to running statewide lotteries. The federal government has thousands of computer systems throughout the world that are used in a wide variety of applications.

11–4 GAINING THE COMPETITIVE ADVANTAGE WITH INFORMATION TECHNOLOGY. Corporate America is beginning to use computers and information systems to improve profitability and achieve a competitive advantage.

The strategic alliances established between the wholesale drug distribution industry and drug retailers via EDI has altered the basic constructs of the industry. The trend today is for the drug wholesalers to provide EDI capabilities to their customers as an incentive to do business with them.

Supermarkets are using automated checkout systems to speed the process and offer products at a lower price. These systems enable supermarkets to take full advantage of the automation opportunities afforded by the availability of the UPC imprinted on all packaged grocery items.

Computer-based training (CBT) has enabled some companies to be more effective in their use of people resources, the net result of which has been a competitive advantage.

At one hospital a computer-based data collection system was developed and installed that enables data to be captured in machine-readable format from bedside terminals. By emphasizing source data automation, the hospital has achieved a competitive advantage.

Review Exercises

Concepts

1. Electronic funds transfer is associated with what industry?
2. Information systems common to most businesses usually involve accounting for what two corporate resources?
3. How do computers help surgeons in operating rooms?
4. Name four applications of the computer in a municipal government.
5. CAD and robotics are usually associated with what industry?
6. What computer-based applications are unique to hospitals?
7. Which common information system produces invoices? Purchase orders? Balance sheets?
8. Name three office information systems.
9. List three advantages of computer-based training.
10. Briefly describe the CIM concept.
11. What machine-readable code provides the basis for automated checkout systems in supermarkets?
12. What term is used to describe the linking of computers of different companies?

Discussion

13. Movie purists abhor the thought of great black-and-white classics, such as *Casablanca*, being changed to color with the help of computer technology. What do you think?

14. Has the application of computer technology in the theater in any way stifled artistic creativity? Has it enhanced creativity? Explain.

15. Discuss the emerging role of personal computers in electronic funds transfer.

16. Physicians' accounting systems have been implemented under a cloud of controversy. Why?

17. Would you buy a "magazine on a disk"? Why or why not?

18. Describe MIS strategies that companies in the construction industry could employ to achieve a competitive advantage.

19. The hospital data collection system that was discussed in the chapter reduced the time that nurses spend recording data about their activities from 40% to 5%. Assuming that the number of nurses on staff remained the same after system implementation, how do you think the cost of the system was justified?

Self-Test (by section)

11-1 The general area of computers and information systems is sometimes referred to as _____.

11-2 **a.** The balance sheet is a by-product of a general ledger system. (T/F)

   b. Accounts payable is generally associated with office automation applications. (T/F)

   c. Management relies on which common information system to identify overdue customer accounts: (a) accounts receivable, (b) accounts payable, or (c) budgeting?

   d. Voice message switching is associated with the office automation application of _____.

11-3 **a.** The integration of the computer with manufacturing is called CIM, or _____.

   b. Automatic teller machines are an implementation of EFT. (T/F)

   c. Actuarial accounting systems are associated with the _____ industry.

   d. Computer-based traffic control systems are implemented at the _____ level of government.

   e. Among financial institutions, only brokerage firms offer computer-based financial planning services. (T/F)

   f. The Internal Revenue Service is investigating the feasibility of allowing people to file tax returns from their personal computers, but such a service is not yet available. (T/F)

11–4 **a.** The trend today is for the drug wholesalers to provide _____ capabilities to their customers.

b. CBT is self-paced so that the student controls the speed of learning. (T/F)

Self-test answers. **11–1** information technology. **11–2** (a) T; (b) F; (c) a; (d) voice processing. **11–3** (a) computer-integrated manufacturing; (b) T; (c) insurance; (d) local; (e) F; (f) F. **11–4** (a) EDI; (b) T.

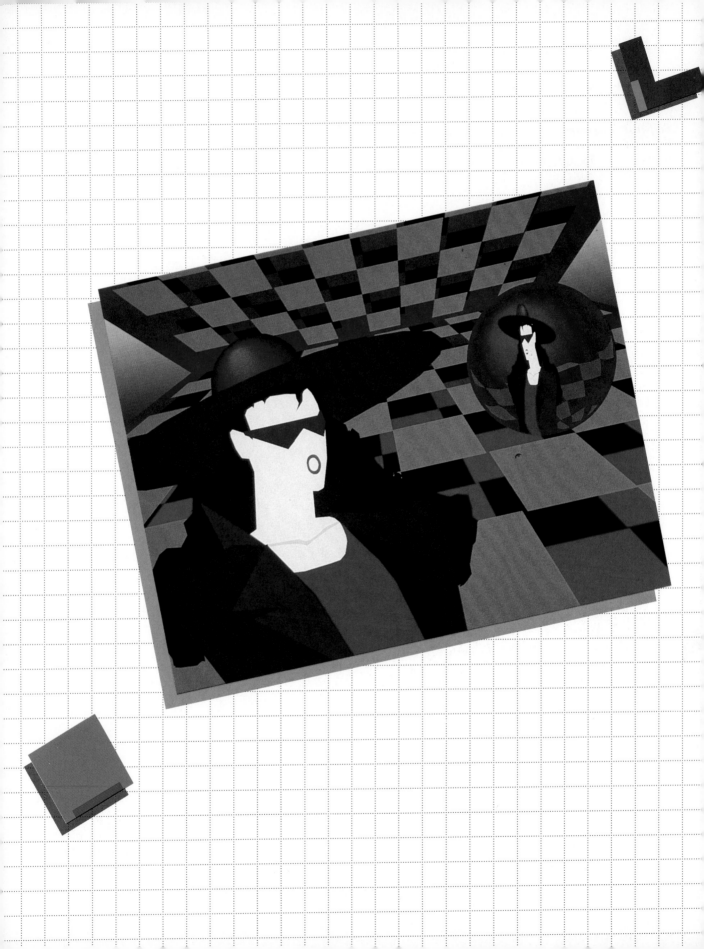

12

Systems Analysis and Design

STUDENT LEARNING OBJECTIVES

- To describe the four stages of the system life cycle.
- To discuss two basic approaches to satisfying an organization's information processing needs.
- To distinguish between the prespecification and prototyping approaches to systems development.
- To describe and order the major activities that take place during the systems analysis phase of system development.
- To describe and order the major activities that take place during the systems design phase of system development.
- To describe the scope and capabilities of CASE tools.
- To explain the concept of prototyping.

12-1 The System Life Cycle

An information system is analogous to the human life form. It is born, it grows, it matures, and it eventually dies. The **system life cycle** has four stages, as shown in Figure 12–1.

Birth Stage   In the *birth stage* of the system life cycle, someone has an idea about how the computer can help provide better and more timely information.

Development Stage   The idea becomes a reality during the *development stage* of the system life cycle. During this stage, systems analysts, programmers, and users work together to analyze a company's information processing needs and design an information system. The design specifications are then translated into programs, and the system is implemented.

Production Stage   Upon implementation, the information system enters the *production stage* and becomes operational, serving the information needs of the company. The production stage is the longest of the four stages and will normally last from four to seven years. During this stage, information systems are continuously modified, or maintained, to keep up with the changing needs of the company.

Death Stage   The accumulation of system modifications to a dynamic information system eventually takes its toll on system efficiency. The *death stage* arrives when an information system becomes so cumbersome to maintain that it is no longer economically or operationally effective. At this time, it is discarded, and the system life cycle is repeated.

12-2 In-House versus Proprietary Software: Whether to Make or Buy

There are two basic approaches to satisfying an organization's information processing needs. The first is to use employees and/or out-

FIGURE 12–1   The System Life Cycle

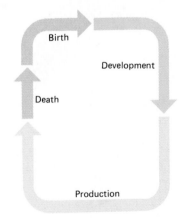

An idea often signals the birth of an information system. These architects are discussing the possibility of designing a system that will help them to better coordinate the work of contractors.

side consultants to create an information system that is customized to meet specifications. The alternative is to purchase and install a **proprietary software package**. Proprietary software is developed by a software vendor to sell to a number of potential buyers. With these two options, managers are faced with a classic "make-versus-buy" decision. Some systems should be created in-house and others should be purchased. Each approach has its advantages and disadvantages. The best *application portfolios* contain an optimal mix of the two.

In-House Development of Information Systems

Most organizations have the capability of developing information systems using in-house personnel. Because they have limited personnel resources, decisions regarding in-house–developed information systems must be made carefully. As a rule of thumb, the efforts of programmers, systems analysts, and users should be channeled to develop only systems whose characteristics are unique to that particular company.

There are as many ways to design an information system as there are systems analysts and end users. Invariably, each person involved has his or her ideas about how to proceed with the design.

Using Proprietary Software

Most proprietary software packages fit into one of these six categories:

- Applications software (for example, inventory control, accounts payable)
- Systems software (operating systems, programming languages)
- Personal productivity software (electronic spreadsheet, word processing)
- Data management software (for example, DBMS)
- Hardware-related software (performance measurement)
- Software engineering tools (tools that provide automated support during the development of information systems)

These accountants are interacting with a proprietary software package called a financial information system. The accounts payable subsystem, shown here, enables the accounts payable staff to respond quickly and effectively to management and vendor inquiries.

Virtually all installed software in the last five categories is proprietary, and there are literally thousands of proprietary applications software packages on the market, from billing systems for veterinarians to general ledger accounting systems for billion-dollar multinational companies. If there is a market for a software product, chances are that some entrepreneur has developed a package to meet the need.

When a company purchases a proprietary applications software package, it will usually receive the programs (on magnetic tape, diskettes, or microdisks) and associated documentation. Depending on the scope and complexity of the software, on-site education, on-site consultation, and the use of a hotline may be included in the price.

12–3 The Systems Development Process

The systems development process is a cooperative effort of users and computer professionals. On one hand, computer professionals are familiar with the technology and how it can be applied to meet a business's information processing needs. On the other, users have in-depth familiarity with their respective functional areas and the information processing needs of the organization. The skills and knowledge of these two groups complement each other and can be combined to create any type of information system during the systems development process.

There are two fundamental approaches to the development of in-house information systems:

1. The prespecification approach
2. The prototyping approach

This chapter contains an overview of both approaches.

The Prespecification Approach to Systems Development

Because systems development is a team effort, most companies have adopted a standardized **systems development methodology** that provides the framework for cooperation. This step-by-step approach to systems development is essentially the same be it for an airline reservation system or an inventory management system. As members of a project team progress through the procedures outlined in a systems development methodology, the results of one step provide the input for the next step and/or subsequent steps.

The methodological approach to systems development is a tool that information services and user-managers can employ to coordinate the efforts of a variety of people engaged in a complex process. One of the major premises of a systems development methodology is that users must relate their information processing needs to the project team during the early stages of the project and then make a commitment to stick to these **system specifications** through system implementation. These **specs** include everything from the functionality of the system to the format of the system's output screens and reports. Because of this premise, this approach to systems development is called the **prespecification** approach.

The major advantage of the prespecification approach is that it provides a framework within which those involved can coordinate their activities. The major disadvantage is that it leaves little room for flexibility in design.

The activities of the traditional approach to systems development are typically grouped in phases, often labeled *systems analysis, systems design, programming, conversion,* and *implementation.* Systems analysis and systems design are presented in this chapter along with prototyping, the alternative approach to systems development. The other phases of the traditional approach to systems development are presented in Chapter 13, "System Implementation."

Prototyping

In recent years the technology has finally begun to have a positive impact on the systems development process. Sophisticated hardware and software are now available that enable the project team to work with users to develop a **prototype system**, a model of a full-scale system. This approach, called **prototyping**, is discussed later in this chapter.

12–4 Systems Analysis: Understanding the System

The systems analysis phase of the systems development process produces the following results:

- Existing system review
- System objectives
- Design constraints
- Requirements definition

Each of these results defines an activity that is to take place.

Existing System Review

Before designing a new or enhanced MIS, the members of the project team must have a good grasp of the existing work and information flow, be it manual or computer-based. If the existing system is computer-based, it is usually accompanied by some type of documentation. If the existing system is manual, the project team may need to compile a basic documentation package that includes a list of and examples of all reports and documents, system data elements and files, and a graphic illustration of the current work and information flow.

The work and information flow of the present system is documented by reducing the system to its basic component parts: *input*, *processing*, and *output*. A variety of design techniques can be used to depict graphically the logical relationships between these parts. Perhaps the most popular, although not necessarily the best for all situations, is **flowcharting**. Other more "structured" techniques include **data flow diagrams** and **hierarchical plus input-processing-output (HIPO)**. Data flow diagrams are introduced later in the systems design portion of this chapter. Flowcharting, HIPO, and other design techniques are discussed in in Appendix C, "Design Techniques."

System Objectives

Once the existing system is documented, the project team can begin to identify the obvious and not-so-obvious problem areas, including procedural bottlenecks, inefficiencies in information flow and storage, duplication of effort, deficiencies in information dissemination, worker discontent, problems with customer interaction, inaccuracy of operational data, and so on. Once these are identified, project team members can concentrate their energies on identifying opportunities for the coordination of effort, the integration of systems, and the use of information.

By this time the project team should know what can be achieved with the judicious application of information. However, this knowledge needs to be formalized as system objectives. The project team arrives at general system objectives by engaging in discussions with all end user managers who will ultimately be affected by the target system. In the end, everyone should be satisfied that the system objectives are consistent with business needs. And everyone concerned should have a clear picture of the direction in which the project is heading.

Design Constraints

The target system will be developed subject to specific constraints. The purpose of this activity is to detail, at the onset of the systems development process, any costs, hardware, schedule, procedural, software, data base, and operating constraints that may limit the definition and design of the target system. For example, cost constraints include any limits on developmental, operational, or maintenance

Just as an author begins with a blank page and an idea, the members of the project team begin with empty RAM (random-access memory) and the information requirements definitions. From here, they must create what can sometimes be a very complex information system. The number of ways in which a particular information system can be designed is limited only by the imaginations of the project team members.

Completing the General System Design   The project team analyzes the existing system, assesses information processing requirements, and then develops a **general system design** for the target system. The general system design, and later the detailed design, involves continuous communication between members of the project team and all levels of users (clerical through strategic), as appropriate. After evaluating several alternative approaches, the project team translates the system specifications into a general system design.

At a minimum, the documentation of the general design of the target system includes the following:

- A graphic illustration that depicts the fundamental operation of the target system (for example, data flow diagrams).
- A written explanation of the graphic illustration.
- General descriptions of the outputs to be produced by the system, including display screens and hard-copy reports and documents. (The actual layout—for example, spacing on the page or screen—is not completed until the detailed system design.)

Data Base Design

The data base is the common denominator of any system. It contains the raw material (data) necessary to produce the output (information). In manufacturing, for example, you decide what you are going to make, then you order the raw material. In the process of developing an information system, you decide what your output requirements

Software packages are available that enable project team members to design systems interactively at their workstations. Automated design tools, such as Teamwork/SA from Cadre Technologies, have helped programmers and systems analysts to make significant strides in productivity improvement. With Teamwork/SA, systems analysts can depict the work and information flow in a system that uses any of a variety of structured design techniques.

are, then you determine which data are needed to produce the output. In a sense, output requirements can be thought of as input to data base design.

With the trend to integrated on-line systems and DBMS technology, at least part and perhaps all of the data base may already exist; its creation may not be necessary. However, it is likely that data elements will need to be added to the data base.

The first step in data base design is to compile a **data dictionary**. A data dictionary, illustrated in Figure 12–2 is simply a listing of all data elements in the data base. An existing data base will already have a data dictionary. The data elements, together with certain descriptive information, are listed along the left-hand side of the data dictionary form in Figure 12–2. The data dictionary provides the bases for the creation or modification of a data base. Data base management systems and structures (hierarchical, network, and relational) are discussed and illustrated in Chapter 9, "Data Management."

The remainder of the data dictionary form in Figure 12–2 is completed *after* the data base organization has been determined and *after* the reports and input screens are designed. The data elements are then cross-referenced to reflect their occurrence in data base records, reports, and input screens.

Detailed System Design

The **detailed system design**—the detailed input/output, processing, and control requirements—is the result of the analysis of user feedback on the general system design. The general system design depicts

FIGURE 12–2 Data Dictionary

Companies maintain an up-to-date data dictionary with descriptive information for all data elements. The use or occurrence of these data elements is cross-referenced to appropriate files, reports, and source documents. The entry in the Format column describes the data element's length and whether it is numeric (9) or alphanumeric (X).

| | | | | | | Report (R) | | | Data base (D) | | Display screen (S) | | |
| | | | | | | Best-seller list (R) | Overdue report (R) | On-loan report (R) | Patron data base (D) | Book data base (D) | Checkout display (S) | Acq. data entry (S) | Data base update (S) |
No.	Name	Description	Format	Coded	Responsibility								
1	TITLE	Complete title of book	X(150)	No	Acquisitions	X	X	X		X	X	X	X
2	ISBN	Int'l Std. Book No.	9(13)	No	Acquisitions				X	X	X	X	X
3	PUBYR	Year of publication	9(2)	No	Acquisitions	X				X		X	X
4	AUTHOR	Name of author	X(25)	No	Acquisitions	X				X		X	X
5	PUBL	Name of publisher	X(25)	No	Acquisitions					X		X	X
6	DUE	Due date of book	9(6)	No	Circulation		X		X		X		
7	CARDNO	Patron card number	9(4)	Yes	Circulation				X		X		
8	FNAME	First name of patron	X(10)	No	Circulation		X		X		X		

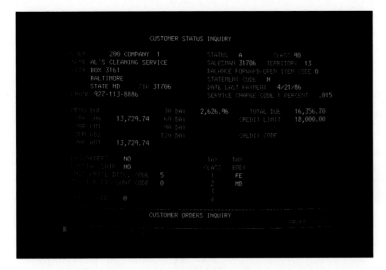

During detailed system design, the project team creates the detailed specifications for all input and output from the system. Typically, analysts and users experiment with several alternatives before selecting the one that displays the information in the most effective manner. Project team members worked closely with users, primarily customer service personnel and salespeople, to create the layout for the "Customer Status Inquiry" in the photo.

the relationship between major processing activities and is detailed enough for users to determine whether or not that is what they want. The detailed design includes *all* processing activities and the input/output associated with them.

The detailed design is the cornerstone of the systems development process. It is here that the relationships between the various components of the system are defined. The system specifications are transformed by the project team's imagination and skill into an information system. The detailed system design is the culmination of all previous work. Moreover, it is the *blueprint* for all project team activities that follow.

A number of techniques help programmers and analysts in the design process. Each of these techniques permits the system design to be illustrated graphically. One of these techniques, data flow diagrams, is briefly discussed here. Flowcharting, HIPO, and other design techniques are discussed in Appendix C, "Design Techniques."

Structured System Design It is much easier to address a complex design problem in small, manageable modules than as one big task. This is done using the principles of **structured system design**. The structured approach to system design encourages the top-down design technique. That is, the project team divides the system into independent modules for ease of understanding and design. The HIPO **structure chart** in Figure 12–3 illustrates how a payroll system can be conceptualized as a hierarchy of modules. In the hierarchy, the system is broken down into modules at finer levels of detail until a

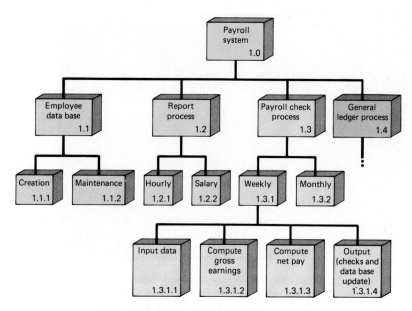

FIGURE 12–3   HIPO Structure Chart
This structure chart breaks a payroll system down into a hierarchy of modules.

particular module can best be portrayed in terms of procedural logic. Eventually the logic for each of the lowest level modules is represented in detail in step-by-step diagrams that illustrate the interactions between input, processing, output, and storage activities for a particular module.

Data Flow Diagrams   Data flow diagrams, or **DFD**s, enable analysts to design and document systems using the structured approach to systems development. Only four symbols are needed for data flow diagrams: entity, process, flow line, and data store. The symbols are summarized in Figure 12–4 and their use is illustrated in Figure 12–5.

- *Entity symbol*. The entity symbol, a square with a darkened "shadow," is the source or destination of data or information flow. An entity can be a person, a group of people (for example, customers or employees), a department, or even a place (such as

FIGURE 12–4   Data Flow Diagram Symbols

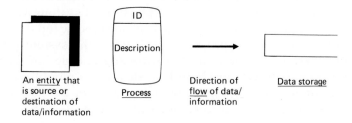

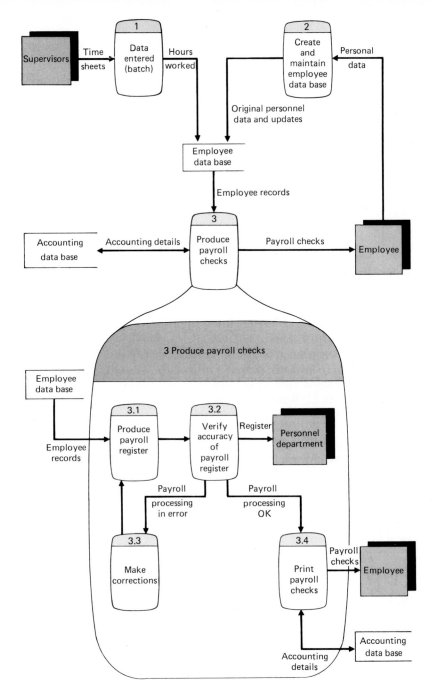

FIGURE 12–5 Data Flow Diagram

In this data flow diagram of a payroll system, Process 3 is exploded to show greater detail.

a warehouse). The interactions between the various entities in a typical business system are illustrated in Figure 10–1 in Chapter 10, "The MIS and Decision Support Systems."

■ *Process symbol.* Each process symbol, a rectangle with rounded corners, contains a description of a function to be performed.

Process symbols also can be depicted as circles. Typical processes include *enter data*, *calculate*, *store*, *create*, *produce*, and *verify*. Process-symbol identification numbers are assigned in levels. (For example, Processes 1.1 and 1.2 are subordinate to Process 1.)

- *Flow line*. The flow lines indicate the flow and direction of data or information.
- *Data store*. These symbols, open-ended rectangles, identify storage locations for data, which could be a file drawer, a shelf, a data base on magnetic disk, and so on.

In Figure 12–5, a data flow diagram documents that portion of a personnel system that produces payroll checks. Processes 1 and 2 deal with the employee data base, but in Process 3 the actual payroll checks are produced. In the bottom portion of Figure 12–5, Process 3 is *exploded* to show greater detail. Notice that the second-level processes within the explosion of Process 3 are numbered 3.1, 3.2, 3.3, and 3.4. Process 3.1 could be exploded to a third level of processes to show even greater detail (for example, 3.1.1, 3.1.2, and so on).

There is no one best analytical or design technique. If you elect to take a course on systems analysis and design, you will gain a deeper understanding of data flow diagrams and the other techniques discussed in Appendix C. Remember, however, that design techniques are just tools. It's your skill and imagination that make an information system a reality.

The Presentation of Information   Within the context of an information system, information can be presented in many ways. During the systems design process, members of the project team work in close cooperation with users to describe each output that will be generated from the target system. An output could be a hard-copy report, a display of information, or a transaction document (an invoice). Transaction documents are typically periodic (monthly invoices). Reports, or generally the presentation of information in either hard-copy or soft-copy format, can be either *periodic* or *ad hoc* (see Figure 12–6).

Both periodic and ad hoc reports can be classified as to *content* and *time* (see Figure 12–6). The content-based classifications are:

- *Comprehensive reports.* The comprehensive report presents all pertinent information about a particular subject.
- *Summary reports.* The summary report presents a summary of information about a particular subject.

FIGURE 12–6   Summary of Types of Reports
Periodic and ad hoc reports can be classified with respect to content and time.

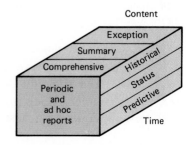

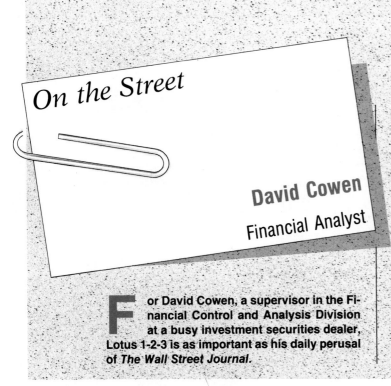

- *Exception reports.* Exception reports highlight critical information (see Chapter 10).

Not surprisingly, time-based classifications deal with the past, the present, and the future.

- *Historical reports.* Historical reports are generated from data gathered in the past and do not reflect the current status.
- *Status reports.* Status reports reflect the current status.
- *Predictive reports.* Predictive reports are often the output of models based on current and historical data.

Of course, not all reports contain numbers and text. Some of the most effective ways of presenting information involve the use of graphics.

12–6 Computer-Aided Software Engineering: The CASE Tool Kit

For years most people thought the best way to improve productivity in systems development was to make it easier for programmers to create programs. *Fourth-generation languages* and *application gener-*

In a manufacturing company, the finance and account-ing, sales and marketing, operations, and personnel divisions work together to accomplish the goals of the corporation. Each division is dependent on information derived from the others. For example, the finance and accounting division receives purchase orders from the operations division, accounts receivable data from the sales and marketing division, and pay and benefits data from the personnel division. In turn, the finance and accounting division provides information to the other divisions.

To facilitate the work and information flow within this company, its computer and information services division implemented and supports an integrated management information system (MIS). The accompanying data flow diagrams (DFDs) illustrate the information flow at two levels. (Data flow diagram techniques are described in the chapter material.) The first DFD provides a general overview of the integrated MIS. This first-level DFD shows interactions between the four divisions, nine en-tities, and the integrated data base. The four major com-ponents of the integrated MIS share a common data base, thereby eliminating much of the data redundancy that plagues other nonintegrated companies.

These interactions shown in the overview DFD are further expanded, or "exploded," in four tactical- and operational-level DFDs, each of which corresponds to a functional area. The second-level DFD, shown here, is an explosion of the finance and accounting compo-nent of the MIS. Notice in the overview DFD that the

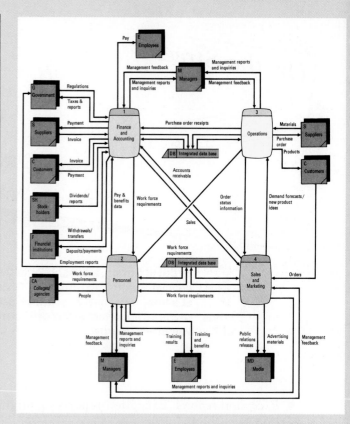

four components of the MIS are numbered 1, 2, 3, and 4. The numbering scheme is used in data flow diagrams to identify subordinate processes. Because the finance

ators, both covered in Chapter 8, "Programming Languages and Soft-ware Concepts," are an outgrowth of this quest for better produc-tivity. In essence, these languages were designed to let the computer do much of the programming. In the early 1980s people began asking the question "Why can't the power of the computer be applied to analysis and design work as well?" Now we know that it can. Many of the time-consuming manual tasks, such as creating a data dic-tionary and documenting information flow, can be automated. This general family of software development productivity tools falls under the umbrella of **computer-aided software engineering**, or **CASE**, tools. The term **software engineering** was coined to emphasize an approach to software development that combines automation and the rigors of the engineering discipline.

CASE tools, which are also referred to as **workbench technol-**

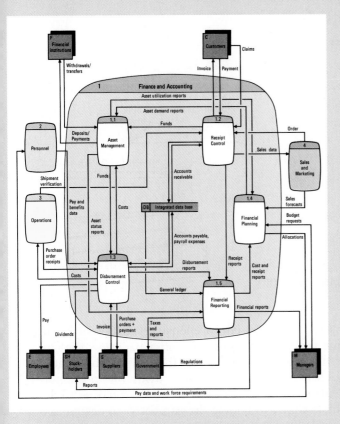

1.1 Asset Management
1.2 Receipt Control
1.3 Disbursement Control
1.4 Financial Planning
1.5 Financial Reporting

The second-level DFDs for the other three components are not shown. The personnel component is divided into three subsystems:

2.1 Recruiting
2.2 Pay and Benefits Administration
2.3 Training and Education

The operations component is divided into five subsystems:

3.1 Production
3.2 Research and Development
3.3 Schedule and Monitor Production
3.4 Acquire and Manage Materials
3.5 Shipping

The sales and marketing component is divided into five subsystems:

4.1 Market Research
4.2 Advertising and Promotion
4.3 Customer Services
4.4 Sales and Order Processing
4.5 Sales Forecasting and Analysis

and accounting component is numbered 1, the first-level subordinate systems are identified as 1.1, 1.2, 1.3, and so on. The five finance and accounting subsystems are:

ogies, provide automated support throughout the entire system life cycle. The CASE tool kit is made up of these tools (see Figure 12–7):

- Design tools
- Prototyping tools
- Information repository tools
- Program development tools
- Methodology tools

Throughout this section, photographs illustrate the use and application of a variety of commercially available CASE tools. Each tool is discussed in more detail in the following sections. Note that there is some overlap in the functions of the various CASE tools.

CASE tools are in their infancy. To some extent, each tool is

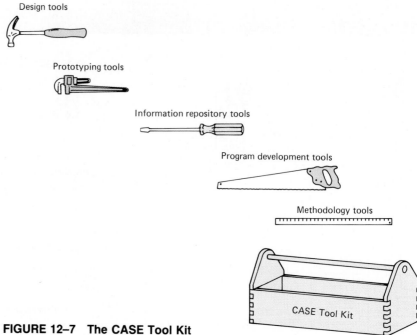

Design tools

Prototyping tools

Information repository tools

Program development tools

Methodology tools

CASE Tool Kit

FIGURE 12–7　The CASE Tool Kit

available commercially. While no comprehensive CASE tool kit to date integrates all the tools, some companies offer packages that integrate two or three. It is reasonable to expect that very sophisticated integrated CASE tool kits will be commercially available in the not-too-distant future. **Software engineers** are working overtime to develop software products that will bridge the gap between design and executable program code. In a two-step process, these tool kits would enable project teams to use automated software packages to help them complete the logic design (information flow, I/O), then the CASE software would translate the logical design into the physical implementation of the system (executable program code). In fact, several existing CASE products are bordering on this level of sophistication.

Design Tools

Prior to the introduction of CASE technologies, the tool kit for the systems analyst and programmer consisted of flowcharting and data flow diagram templates, lettering templates, rulers, scissors, glue, pencils, pens, and plenty of erasers and "white-out." The CASE *design tool* provides an automated alternative. It helps analysts and programmers prepare the schematics that graphically depict the logic of a system or program (for example, data flow diagrams, structure charts). They do this in much the same way word processing software helps a writer prepare an article for publication. They also help designers prepare screen and report layouts.

All CASE design tools use structured design techniques, such as data flow diagrams, to model the work flow, information flow, and program interactions within a system. Automated design tools enable an analyst or programmer to select and position symbols, such as the DFD process and entity symbols, and to connect these symbols with flow lines. Both symbols and flow lines can be labeled. For example, an analyst might label a process symbol "enter order data." Flow lines can be clarified with arrows to indicate the direction of flow and with descriptions of what is being transferred. Because all the design techniques supported by CASE products are structured design techniques, systems ultimately are depicted in several levels of generality. For example, at the highest level, the entire system might be represented by four process symbols of a data flow diagram. However, at the second level, each of these processes might be broken down into finer detail and presented as a more detailed data flow diagram. The processes at the second level can be broken down into finer detail, and so on.

Programmers and analysts can change the size of symbols to fit the diagram on the screen and/or change the color of a symbol or flow line to indicate special significance (a control procedure, for example). They can also help clarify the diagram by adding explanatory notations, both visible and hidden (that is, they can be called up in pop-up windows). A diagram can be exploded to the next level of generality by positioning the cursor over the appropriate symbol. The next screen would show an *explosion* (the next level of detail) of the desired process. Of course, levels of generality can be explored in both directions.

KnowledgeWare, Inc., provides an integrated CASE environment for the planning, analysis, design, and construction of information systems. The KnowledgeWare tools function as an integrated set and independently as stand-alone products. The windows in the screen illustrate the capabilities of the Analysis Workstation, an integrated set of diagrammatic tools for requirements analysis. The techniques incorporated into the software include decomposition diagrams (top left), data flow diagrams (top right), entity relationship diagrams (middle), and action diagrams (bottom left).

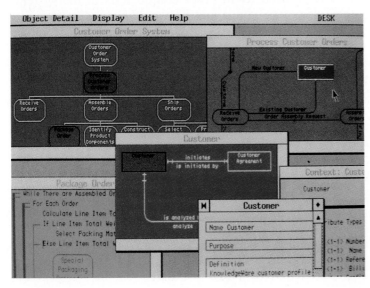

Prototyping Tools

CASE *prototyping tools* are used by project team members to create a physical representation of a target system at one of the three levels of sophistication—a nonfunctional, partially functional, or fully functional prototype system.

The basic components of prototyping tools are:

- *The user interface.* This capability enables the project team to design and create the user interface. Typically the user interface consists of a hierarchy of menus, which may be displayed in windows superimposed over the current display.
- *Screen generators.* **Screen generators**, also called **screen formatters**, provide systems analysts with the capability of generating a mockup, or layout, of a screen while in direct consultation with the user. The layout is a detailed output and/or input specification that graphically illustrates exactly where information should be placed, or entered, on a terminal display screen or on a printer output.
- *Report generators.* **Report generators** are similar to screen generators, with one exception. Report generators permit the calculation of summary totals by criteria and overall totals, and the editing of output. For example, a report generator can produce a sales report that includes summary totals for each sales region and overall totals. The output could be edited so that sales amounts are displayed in currency notation ($23,462.50).

Information Repository Tools

The *information repository* is analogous to the data dictionary in the traditional approach to systems design. However, the information repository contains everything the data dictionary includes and much more. It is a central computer-based storage facility for all design information. For example, in an information repository, each data element is cross-referenced to all other components in the system. That is, the data element *customer number* would be cross-referenced to every screen, report, graph, record/file, data base, program, or any other design element in which it occurred. Cross-references are also made to processes in data flow diagrams. Once the company has had the information repository in place for a while, cross-references can be extended between information systems. Besides the data dictionary component, the information repository permits all system documentation to be packaged electronically. That is, any part of the system—layouts, data dictionary, notes, pseudocode (nonexecutable program code), project schedules, and so on—can be recalled and displayed for review or modification. In effect, the information repository is the "data base" for the system development project.

Program Development Tools

Program development tools focus on the back-end, or the latter stages, of the systems development effort (see Chapter 13, "System Imple-

This programmer and systems analyst work in an information services department for a medical instruments manufacturer. Their current project is a human resources information system that will help managers use the skills of their workers more effectively. The system will match the tasks with the skills of the individual workers.

mentation." CASE program development tools fall into four categories:

- *Program structure charts.* The program structure chart enables programmers to create a graphic hierarchical representation of all the programs in a system. The resulting chart is similar to the one illustrated in Figure 12–3.
- *Code generators.* Code generators, which are also called application generators (see Chapter 8 for a detailed discussion) are perhaps the most valuable program development tool. Instead of actually coding programs, programmers use code generators to describe the structure of a data base and to create screens and report layouts in what is essentially a fill-in-the-blank process.
- *Program preprocessors.* This tool preprocesses programmer-written programs of high-level programming languages, such as COBOL and PL/I, to point out potential problems in the program logic and syntax and to generate the documentation for the program.
- *Test data generators.* One of the more laborious tasks associated with programming is the generation of test data. Programmers using CASE tools rely on test data generators to compile test data. The programmer describes the parameters of the desired data (format, ranges, distributions, and so on), and the test data generator does the rest.

Methodology Tools

Systems development methodologies are usually presented in a hardcopy manual, but they are being automated and presented as on-line, interactive systems with increasing frequency. The *methodology tool* is a computer-based version of the traditional systems development methodology manual. Both describe phased procedures and responsibilities, and both provide forms and formats for documenting the system.

12–7 Prototyping: Creating a Model of the Target System

Throughout the twentieth century, manufacturers have built prototypes of everything from toasters to airplanes. Automobile manufacturers routinely build prototypes according to design specifications. Scaled-down clay models are made to evaluate aesthetics and aerodynamics. Ultimately, a full-size, fully functional prototype is created that enables the driver and passengers to test all aspects of the car's functionality. If engineers see possibilities for improvement, the prototypes are modified and retested until they meet or exceed all specifications. Today over three quarters of all new mainframe-based information systems emerge from a prototype system, and the percentage is increasing each year.

Prototyping is one of the two fundamental approaches to systems development. The other approach, *prespecification*, involves the up-front specification of user information processing requirements and the use of a systems development methodology.

The Prototype System

The three objectives of prototyping are:

1. To analyze the current situation
2. To identify information needs
3. To develop a scaled-down model of the target system

The scaled-down model, called a *prototype system*, would normally handle the main transaction-oriented procedures, produce the critical reports, and permit rudimentary inquiries. The prototype system gives users an opportunity to actually work with the functional aspect of the target system long before the system is implemented. Once users gain hands-on familiarity with the prototype system, they are in a position to be more precise when they relate their information processing needs to the project team.

For years automobile manufacturers have built prototype models that could be tested for aerodynamics, aesthetics, and functionality. Only recently has prototyping become popular with information systems development. Now over 70% of all new information systems emerge from a prototype system, and the percentage is increasing each year.

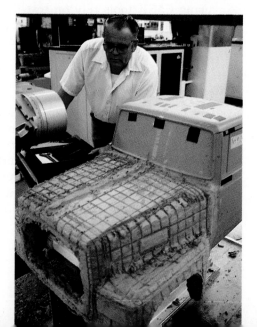

A prototype system can be anything from a nonfunctional demonstration of the input/output of a target information system to a full-scale operational system. Both the prespecification and prototype approaches can result in an information system but, in practice, most prototype systems are merely models. These models are tested and refined until the users are confident that what they see is what they want. In some cases, the software that was developed to create an initial prototype system is expanded to create a fully operational information system. However, in most cases, the prototype system provides an alternate vehicle for completing the functional specifications activity of a systems development methodology. Incomplete and/or inaccurate user specifications have been the curse of the prespecification approach to systems development. Many companies have exorcised this curse by the integration of prototyping into their methodologies.

Creating the Prototype System

To create a prototype system, project team members rough out the logic of the system and how the elements fit together with a CASE design tool. Then they work with the user to define the I/O interfaces (the system interaction with the user). During interactive sessions, project team members and users create whatever interactive display screens are required to meet the user's information processing needs. To do this, project team members use the applications development tools discussed earlier in this chapter to create the screen images (menus, reports, inquiries, and so on) and to generate much of the programming code. In some cases, an existing data base can be modified to service the target system. In other cases, a new data base must be created.

Users can actually sit down at a terminal and evaluate portions of and, eventually, all of the prototype system. Invariably, they have suggestions for improving the user interfaces and/or the format of the I/O. And, without fail, their examination reveals new needs for information. In effect, the prototype system is the beginning. From here, the system is expanded and refined to meet the users' total information needs. Prototyping software tools are limited in what they can do, so the typical system may require a considerable amount of custom coding, probably written in third- and fourth-generation languages.

Prototyping Summary

Prototyping has two great advantages over the prespecification approach to system development. First, an information system can be produced in considerably less time. And second, errors in judgment and oversights can be remedied quickly without costly redesigning or reprogramming. The greatest disadvantage of prototyping is that it assumes full cooperation on the part of users who will ultimately be affected by the information system. If the users fail to meet their obligations, the advantages of prototyping are negated.

In practice, information services divisions are realizing the best of both worlds by integrating prototyping into their systems development methodologies. By doing this, they can simultaneously enjoy the flexibility of prototyping and the structured framework of a systems development methodology. In this integrated environment, prototyping becomes the vehicle by which system specifications are determined. From these specs, an information system is created that is capable of handling the required volume of work.

Summary Outline and Important Terms

12–1 THE SYSTEM LIFE CYCLE. The four stages of a computer-based information system comprise the **system life cycle**. They are birth, development, production, and death.

12–2 IN-HOUSE VERSUS PROPRIETARY SOFTWARE: WHETHER TO MAKE OR BUY. There are two basic approaches to satisfying a company's information processing needs. The first is to use company employees and/or outside consultants to create an information system customized to meet user specifications. The alternative is to purchase and install a **proprietary software package**. Most proprietary software packages fit into one of six categories: applications software, systems software, personal productivity software, data management software, hardware-related software, and software engineering tools.

12–3 THE SYSTEMS DEVELOPMENT PROCESS. The systems development process is a cooperative undertaking by users who know the functional areas and MIS professionals who know the technology. The two fundamental approaches to the in-house development of information systems are the prespecification and prototyping approaches.

The step-by-step **systems development methodology** provides the framework for **prespecification** approach to system development. In this approach, users commit to **system specifications**, or **specs**, early in development.

In **prototyping**, project team members create a **prototype system**, or model, of a full-scale system.

12–4 SYSTEMS ANALYSIS: UNDERSTANDING THE SYSTEM. During the systems analysis phase of the systems development process, the following activities take place: existing system review, system objectives, design constraints, and requirements definition.

The work and information flow of the present system is documented by reducing the system to its basic component parts—input, processing, and output. System design techniques include **flowcharting** and other more "structured" techniques, such as **data flow diagrams** and **hierarchical plus input-processing-output (HIPO)**.

The project team arrives at general system objectives by engaging in discussions with all end user managers ultimately affected by the target system. The target information system must be developed within the boundaries of any applicable hardware, costs, schedule, procedural, software, data base, and operating constraints.

User feedback provides the basis for the **functional specifications** for system input, processing, and output requirements. These specs describe the logic of the system from the perspective of the user. The **user sign-off** indicates that he or she has examined the work, that the work and specs meet the objectives, and that the user is committed to the specs.

12–5 SYSTEMS DESIGN: A SCIENCE OR AN ART?   During the systems design phase of the systems development process, the following activities are completed: **general system design**, data base design, and **detailed system design**.

At a minimum, the documentation of the general system design includes a graphic illustration and explanation of the fundamental operation of the target system and general descriptions of the outputs to be produced by the system.

During systems development, designers describe the output requirements and determine which data are needed to produce the output. Data elements are documented in the **data dictionary**.

The detailed design includes all processing activities and the input/output associated with them. When adhering to **structured system design**, designers divide the system into independent modules for ease of understanding and design.

Data flow diagrams enable analysts to design and document systems using the structured approach to systems development. The four symbols used in **DFDs** are entity, process, flow line, and data store.

Reports, or the general presentation of information, can be either periodic or ad hoc. Based on content, reports are classified as comprehensive, summary, or exception. Based on time, reports are classified as historical, status, or predictive.

12–6 COMPUTER-AIDED SOFTWARE ENGINEERING: THE CASE TOOL KIT.   The general family of automated software development tools falls under the umbrella of **computer-aided software engineering**, or **CASE,** tools. The term **software engineering** was coined to emphasize an approach to software development that combines automation and the rigors of the engineering discipline.

The CASE tool kit, also called **workbench technologies**, consists of design tools, prototyping tools, information repository tools, program development tools, and methodology tools.

CASE design tools help analysts and programmers prepare schematics that graphically depict the logic of a system or program, and they help designers in the preparation of screen and report layouts.

CASE prototyping tools are used by project team members to create a physical representation of a target information system. The basic components of prototyping tools are the user interface, **screen generators**, and **report generators**.

In the CASE information repository tool, each data element is cross-referenced to all other components in the system.

The CASE program development tool includes program structure charts, code generators, program preprocessors, and test data generators.

The CASE methodology tool is a computer-based version of the traditional systems development methodology manual.

12–7 PROTOTYPING: CREATING A MODEL OF THE TARGET SYSTEM. The three objectives of prototyping are to analyze the current situation, to identify information needs, and to develop a scaled-down model of the target system. A prototype system normally would handle the main transaction-oriented procedures, produce the critical reports, and permit rudimentary inquiries.

Ideally, users should experiment and familiarize themselves with the operation of a target system as early in the development process as possible. The prototyping process enables users to relate accurate information processing needs to the project team during the early phases of the project and throughout the project.

In practice, the MIS community is enjoying the best of both worlds by using systems development methodologies that include prototyping.

 Review Exercises

Concepts

1. In which stage of the information system life cycle are systems "conceived"? "Maintained"?
2. What are the two basic approaches to satisfying a company's information processing needs?
3. Associate each of the following types of software with a particular category of proprietary software: DBMS, marketing information system, and presentation graphics.
4. Name the four symbols used in data flow diagrams.

5. Classify the following outputs with respect to content and time: payroll register, third-quarter sales forecast, and delinquent accounts report.

6. The functional specifications describe the logic of a proposed system from whose perspective?

7. Describe the relationship between the data dictionary and the data base.

8. What is the design philosophy called that enables complex design problems to be addressed in small, manageable modules?

9. Name three system design techniques.

10. What is a structure chart, and how is it used?

11. Custom code written to augment a prototype system is probably written in what type of programming language?

12. What is the purpose of the CASE design tool?

13. Besides producing critical reports and permitting rudimentary inquiries, what else does a prototype system typically do?

14. Briefly describe the function of program preprocessors, one of the CASE program development tools.

15. Name the tools in the CASE tool kit.

16. What is another name for CASE tools?

17. What is the objective of prototyping?

Discussion

18. In general, is it better to change internal procedures to fit a particular proprietary software package or modify the software to fit existing procedures? Discuss.

19. Would it be possible for a company with 600 employees to maintain a skeleton information services division of about five MIS professionals and use commercially available packaged software for all their computer application needs? Explain.

20. Corporate management is routinely confronted with "make-versus-buy" decisions regarding software. Discuss the advantages and disadvantages of each alternative.

21. Why is the user sign-off a controversial procedure?

22. Give examples of schedule, procedural, and hardware constraints that might limit the definition and design of a proposed marketing information system for a pharmaceutical company.

23. Design a screen layout for an on-line hospital admittance system. Design only that screen with which the hospital clerk would interact to enter basic patient data. Distinguish between input and output by underlining the input.

24. How does adhering to a systems development methodology help a project team "do it right the first time"?

25. One of the objectives of prototyping is to develop a scaled-down model of the proposed system. However, some prototype systems are fully functional. Describe how such a prototype system is scaled down.

Self-Test (by section)

12–1 The information system becomes operational in the _____ stage of the system life cycle.

12–2 **a.** The best corporate application portfolios contain only proprietary software packages. (T/F)

12–2 **b.** Virtually all installed DBMS software is developed in-house. (T/F)

12–3 **a.** A _____ system is a model of a full-scale information system.

b. A standardized _____ provides the framework for cooperation during the systems development process.

c. The prespecification approach to systems development leaves little room for flexibility in design during the latter stages of the project. (T/F)

12–4 **a.** Which of the following is not a design technique: (a) HIPO, (b) data flow diagrams, or (c) SAD?

b. In the systems development process, the project team begins with the desired input and works backward to determine output and processing requirements. (T/F)

c. Functional specifications include system input, output, and _____ requirements.

12–5 **a.** Which results are realized during the systems design stage of the systems development process: (a) data base design, (b) existing system review, or (c) design constraints?

b. The _____ (general/detailed) system design includes all processing activities and the input/output associated with them.

c. If DFD Process 3.4 were exploded to two third-level processes, the numerical labels of the new processes would be 3.4.1 and 3.4.2. (T/F)

12–6 **a.** Which CASE tool is analogous to the data dictionary in the traditional manual approach to systems design: (a) design tool, (b) information repository tool, or (c) methodology tool?

b. Another name for CASE tools is _____.

c. What component of the CASE prototyping tool provides systems analysts with the capability of generating a mockup of a screen: (a) screen formatter, (b) report generator, or (c), user interface?

12–7 **a.** A prototype system is essentially a complete information system, but without the data base. (T/F)

b. A prototype system normally would permit rudimentary inquiries. (T/F)

Self-test answers. **12–1** production. **12–2** (a) F; (b) F. **12–3** (a) prototype; (b) systems development methodology; (c) T. **12–4** (a) c; (b) F; (c) processing. **12–5** (a) a; (b) detailed; (c) T. **12–6** (a) b; (b) workbench technologies; (c) a. **12–7** (a) F; (b) T.

13

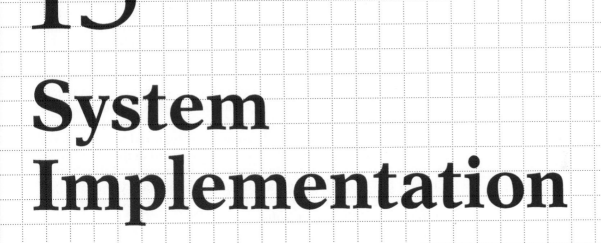

System Implementation

STUDENT LEARNING OBJECTIVES

- To describe and order the major activities that take place during the programming phase of system development.
- To describe systems testing procedures and considerations.
- To distinguish between the different approaches to system conversion.
- To know what to look for during post-implementation system evaluations.
- To describe system controls that can be employed to ensure the accuracy, reliability, and integrity of an information system.
- To identify points of security vulnerability for the computer center and for information systems.

13–1 Programming: Ideas Become Reality

The preceding chapter discusses approaches and techniques that can be used to design and create the specifications for an information system. This chapter is concerned with the implementation of a newly created information system and its ongoing operation. The first challenge in system implementation is to translate the system design and specifications into instructions that can be interpreted and executed by the computer. This, of course, is the programming phase of the systems development process.

Programming languages have improved continually during the past four decades. Early, or first-generation, programming languages, required the programmer to write many complex instructions to accomplish simple tasks. Each new generation of programming languages reduced the number of instructions required to perform tasks and made the instructions easier to comprehend and code. (The generations of programming languages are discussed and illustrated in Chapter 8, "Programming Languages and Software Concepts.")

The programming phase of the systems development process produces the following results:

- System specifications review
- Program identification and description
- Program coding, testing, and documentation

Each of these results defines an activity that is to be accomplished. With detailed specifications in hand, programmers are now ready to write the programs needed to make the target system operational.

System Specifications Review

During the programming phase, programming becomes the dominant activity. The system specifications completed during the system analysis and design phase are all that is necessary for programmers to write, or *code*, the programs to implement the information system. But before getting started, programmers should review

In programming, two heads are sometimes better than one. A programmer can become so close to a program that he or she may overlook obvious errors in logic. These errors often shine as bright as a neon light when the program design is discussed with a colleague.

the system specifications created during system analysis and design. These include:

- Printer output layouts of reports and transactions
- Terminal input/output screen layouts
- Data dictionary
- Files and data base design
- Controls and validation procedures
- Data entry specifications
- General system design
- Detailed system design

Once programmers have reviewed and understand the specs, the programming task begins. A superior programming effort will be wasted if the system specifications are incomplete and poorly written. As the saying goes, "Garbage in, garbage out."

Program Identification and Description

An information system needs an array of programs to create and update the data base, print reports, permit on-line inquiry, and so on. Depending on the scope of the system and how many programs can be generated using application development tools, as few as three or four or as many as several hundred programs may need to be written before the system can be implemented. At this point, all programs necessary to make the system operational are identified and described. A typical program description would include:

- Type of programming language (COBOL, BASIC, FOCUS, Ideal, and so on)
- A narrative of the program, describing the tasks to be performed
- Frequency of processing (for example, daily, weekly, on-line)
- Input to the program (data and their source)
- Output produced by the program
- Limitations and restrictions (for example, sequence of input data, response-time maximums, and so on)
- Detailed specifications (for example, specific computations and logical manipulations, tables)

Program Coding, Testing, and Documentation

Armed with system specifications and program descriptions, programmers can begin the actual coding of programs. The development of a program is actually a project within a project. Just as there are certain steps the project team takes to develop an information system, there are certain steps a programmer takes to write a program (see Figure 13–1).

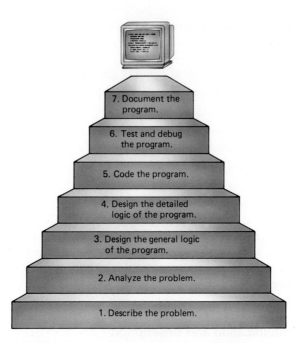

FIGURE 13–1 Steps in Writing a Program

Step 1. Describe the problem.
Step 2. Analyze the problem.
Step 3. Design the general logic of the program.
Step 4. Design the detailed logic of the program.
Step 5. Code the program.
Step 6. Test and debug the program.
Step 7. Document the program.

These steps are described in more detail in the following sections.

Not all programs are developed by professional programmers. These corporate recruiters created the software for a department-based information system that helps them expedite the candidate screening process. More and more users are learning to write programs, especially in high-level fourth-generation languages. Of course, users follow the same seven basic steps that professional programmers follow.

Step 1. Describe the Problem   The problem is presented in the program descriptions. For example, a problem might be to write a program that accepts numeric quiz scores and assigns a letter grade. Another problem might be to write a program that identifies and prints the names of customers whose accounts are delinquent.

Step 2. Analyze the Problem   In this step the programmer breaks down the problem into its basic components for analysis. "Divide and conquer" is one of the key strategies for both systems analysts and programmers. Although different programs have different components, a good place to start with most programs is to analyze the *output*, *input*, *processing*, and *file-interaction* components. The programmer would then identify important considerations in the design of the program logic. By the end of the problem-analysis stage, the programmer should have a complete understanding of what needs to be done and a good idea of how to do it.

Step 3. Design the General Logic of the Program   Next, the programmer has to put the pieces together in the form of a logical program design. Any of the systems design techniques, such as data flow diagrams, are applicable to program design as well. (Data flow diagrams are introduced in Chapter 12, "Systems Analysis and Design." Other popular design techniques, such as flowcharting and HIPO, are illustrated and discussed in Appendix C, "Design Techniques.") As in the information system, the program is also designed in a hierarchical manner, or from the general to the specific. For example, Figure 13–2 illustrates a structure chart of a program for printing weekly payroll checks. (Hourly and commission employees are processed weekly.) The structure chart permits a programming problem to be broken down into a hierarchy of tasks. A task can be broken down

FIGURE 13–2   Program Structure Chart
The logic of a payroll program for printing weekly payroll checks can be broken down into modules for ease of understanding, coding, and maintenance.

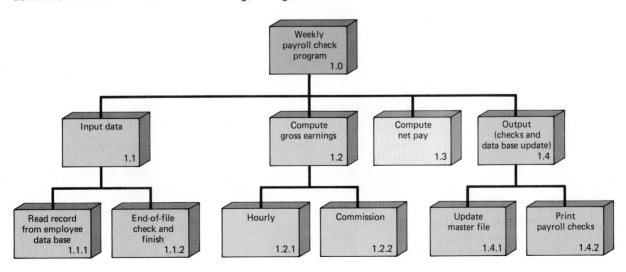

into subtasks if a finer level of detail is desired. The most effective programs are designed so they can be written in **modules**, or independent tasks. It is much easier to address a complex programming problem in small, more manageable modules than as one big task. This is done using the principles of **structured programming**.

In structured programming, the logic of the program is addressed hierarchically in logical modules (see Figure 13–2). In the end, the logic of each module is translated into a sequence of program instructions. The modules interact with one another by passing data back and forth. By dividing the program into modules, the structured approach to programming reduces the complexity of the programming task. Some programs are so complex that if taken as a single task, they would be almost impossible to conceptualize, design, and code.

In the general design of a particular program, the programmer creates a logic diagram for the overall program and for each module. These diagrams depict the major processing activities and the relationships between these activities. By first completing a general flow diagram, the programmer makes it easier to investigate alternative design approaches. The program flowchart in Figure 13–3 illustrates the general design of Task 1.3, "Compute net pay," from the structure chart of Figure 13–2. Once the programmer is confident that he or she has identified the best approach, a more detailed flow diagram can be completed.

Step 4. Design the Detailed Logic of the Program   This level of detail includes the graphic representation of all processing activities and their relationships, calculations, data manipulations, logic operations, and all input/output.

The flowchart in Figure 13–4 is a more detailed representation of the logic presented in the general flowchart in Figure 13–3. In programming, the level of detail portrayed in the graphic representation of the logic is a matter of personal preference. The flowcharts in Figures 13–3 and 13–4 illustrate the difference between general and detailed logic diagrams. Other programmers might prefer to have more or less detail.

Step 5. Code the Program   Whether a programmer *writes* or *codes* a program is a matter of personal preference. In this context, the terms are the same. In Step 5, the graphic and narrative design of Program Development Steps 1 through 4 is translated into machine-readable instructions, or programs. If the logic is sound and the design documentation (flowcharts, data flow diagram, and so on) is thorough, the coding process is relatively straightforward.

The best way to write a program is to work directly from the design documentation and compose the program interactively at a

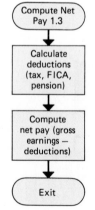

FIGURE 13–3   General Flowchart
The logic of Module 1.3, "Compute Net Pay," of Figure 13–2 is depicted in a general flowchart.

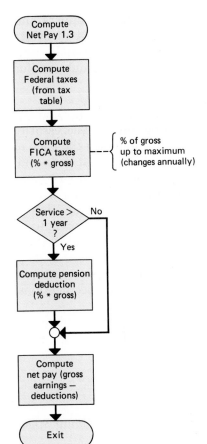

FIGURE 13–4 **Detailed Flowchart**
The logic of the general flowchart in Figure 13–3 is depicted in a detailed flowchart.

terminal or PC. Programs are much easier to write when broken down into several small, more manageable modules. Time and time again programmers have shown that it takes less time to code ten 50-line modules than it does to code a single 500-line program.

Not every programming task requires programmers to create code "from scratch." Many organizations maintain libraries of frequently used program modules, called *reusable code*. For example, several programmers might use the same reusable code as the basis for their input modules.

Step 6. Test and Debug the Program Once the program has been entered into the system, it is likely that the programmer will encounter at least one of those cantankerous **bugs**. A bug is an error in program syntax, logic, or input/output. Ridding a program of bugs is the process of **debugging**.

Syntax errors. Debugging a program is a repetitive process whereby each successive attempt gets the programmer one step closer to a working program. The first step is to eliminate **syntax errors**; the programmer gets a syntax error when one of the rules for writing instructions (for example, placement of parentheses, spelling of commands, and so on) is violated. The errors on the first run are mostly typos (for example, REED instead of READ). Most compilers and interpreters display an **error message**. The error message identifies the number of the statement causing the error, and it usually provides the programmer with an idea of what the error might be (for example, "unidentified variable").

Logic and I/O errors. Once the syntax errors have been removed, the program can be executed. An error-free program is not necessarily a working program. The programmer now has to debug the *logic of the program* and the *input/output formats*. To do this, **test data** and, perhaps, a **test data base** must be created so that the programmer knows what to expect as output. For example, suppose you write a program to average three grades and assign a letter grade. If your test data are 85, 95, and 75, then you would expect the average to be 85 and the letter grade to be B. If the output is not 85 and B, there is a bug in the program logic.

A program whose logic is sound might have input or output formats that need to be "cleaned up" to meet layout specifications. Suppose your output looked like this:

THE LETTER GRADE ISB.

and the layout specs called for this:

THE LETTER GRADE IS B.

You would need to modify the output format to include a blank space between *IS* and the letter grade.

Step 7. Document the Program In the business environment, a program may be used every day—for years! Procedures and information requirements change over the life of the system. For example, because the Social Security tax rate is revised each year, certain payroll programs must be modified accordingly. To keep up with these changes, programs must be updated periodically, or maintained. Program maintenance can be difficult if the program documentation is not complete and up to date. A good program documentation package includes the following items:

- *Program title.* A brief descriptive title (for example, PRINT_PAY-ROLL_CHECKS)
- *Language.* The language in which the program is written (for example, COBOL, BASIC, FOCUS, Ideal)
- *Narrative description.* A written description of the functions performed
- *Variables list.* A list containing the name and description of each variable used in the program (for example, FIRST-NAME or PART-NO)
- *Source listing.* A hard-copy listing of the source code

THOSE COSTLY LITTLE BUGS

We trust computers with our money and our lives. Did you know that most money exchanged is not from hand to hand, but between computers? Were you aware that computers monitor airport traffic to establish altitude and direction for aircraft flying in the "soup" (a dense fog) around airports? These computers are responsible for our money and our lives, but are they given proper instructions? We hope so, but such is not always the case.

A computer does exactly what a program tells it to do, nothing less and nothing more. Unfortunately, some programs have bugs that remain undetected, even after rigorous testing and extensive use. Some bugs are relatively harmless, but others can cause the loss of millions of dollars and even lives.

■ The Mariner 1 spacecraft was en route to deep space when it suddenly "turned left, and nosed down." An investigation into the multimillion-dollar crash surfaced one of those costly little bugs. Apparently a programmer had omitted one character from an equation in the guidance program—the same program that had been used successfully in other Atlas missions! A curious set of circumstances caused the program to take branches not tested or taken in previous missions. Fortunately, a similar calamity was avoided in a later manned space flight. A serious bug in the space shuttle's software lay dormant for two years, even after thousands of hours of testing. It was discovered 20 minutes before an April 1981 launch!

■ Program design flaws can have an adverse effect on the bottom line. A software error in American Airlines's Sabre reservation system gave travel and ticket agents the impression that reduced-fair tickets were not available. Thousand of potential customers were turned away while flights departed with empty seats. The company lost $50 million before the error was detected.

■ The components of virtually all new medical diagnosis and treatment machines are controlled by computers. Machines that provide radiation therapy for cancer patients depend on exact programming to deliver the proper dosage to the malignant area. A bug in the software of one of these machines resulted in an overdose of radiation and the loss of a man's life.

■ A software bug can affect governments, too. A state government erroneously sent bondholders millions of dollars worth of interest checks. The interest, however, was not due them.

■ A large bank was forced to borrow over $20 billion overnight because it was unable to complete transactions involving large amounts of government securities—all because of a bug in the software. Had the software worked properly, the loan and a $5 million interest charge would have been unnecessary.

■ Most new automobiles are equipped with at least one microprocessor. An apparent bug in the software for the computerized fuel delivery system of a European luxury sedan caused the automobile to accelerate out of control. The design flaw resulted in intense negative publicity for the company and subsequent loss of sales. However, the importance of a decline in profits pales when you consider the serious injuries and loss of life that have been attributed to the defective system.

These examples serve to highlight the importance of comprehensive testing. But can extremely complex systems ever be fully tested? Very large information systems, such as those for major insurance companies, may consist of millions of lines of program code and be written by hundreds of programmers. Thousands of complex systems are currently in operation. Are these systems error-free or will an unusual set of circumstances trigger the execution of defective code and throw the system into disarray?

Star Wars, the Pentagon's Strategic Defense Initiative (SDI), is an easy choice for the most complex computer-based system ever conceived. The objective of SDI is to seek out and destroy hostile nuclear missiles, possibly thousands of them. This unbelievably complex system must work perfectly the first time, and it can never be fully tested. When and if Star Wars is completed, what are the chances of having bugs in the system?

Memory Bits

RESULTS OF PROGRAMMING PHASE
- System specifications review
- Program identification and description
- Program coding, testing, and documentation

- *Detailed program design.* The structure charts, flowcharts, and so on
- *Input/output layouts.* The printer and terminal display layouts, examples of hard-copy output (for example, a payroll check)
- *Frequency of processing.* How often the program is run (daily, weekly, on-line)
- *Detailed specifications.* The arithmetic computations, sorting and editing criteria, tables, control totals, and so on
- *Test data.* A test package that includes test data and expected results (The test data are used to test and debug the program after each program change.)

Some of these documentation items can be included in the actual program as *internal documentation*. Descriptive remarks throughout the program make it easier to follow and to understand. Typically, the program title, a narrative description, and the variables list would also be included as internal documentation. The program examples in Chapter 8, "Programming Languages and Software Concepts," illustrate internal documentation.

13–2 System and Acceptance Testing

Whether the information system is created by using the traditional prespecification approach, prototyping, or a combination of these two, the final step before system conversion and implementation is system and acceptance testing. This testing encompasses everything that makes up the information system—the hardware, the software, the end users, the procedures (for example, user manuals), and the data. If needed, the interfaces between the system and other systems are tested as well.

The importance of system testing cannot be overemphasized. In 1988 the American Airlines reservation system, the Sabre System, lost an estimated $50 million because the system stopped selling dis-

At IBM's Software Usability Laboratory, engineers monitor subjects while they learn and use software packages that may some day be released as commercial software products. The objective of this phase of testing is to gather feedback that enables system designers to fine-tune the user interface before the software is released for beta testing (prerelease testing by potential users of the software product).

During system testing, systems analysts are constantly gathering feedback from users. Analysts are especially interested in hearing about errors and parts of the system where interaction is cumbersome or slow.

count fares while discount seats were still available. According to an American Airlines' spokesperson, a modification to the existing system, which was designed to provide an optimum mix of regular and discount seats on a given flight, "was not fully tested."

Testing with Test Data

During the programming phase of systems development, programs are written according to system specifications and individually tested. Although the programs that comprise the software for the system have undergone **unit testing** (individual testing) and have been debugged, there is no guarantee that the programs will work as a system. To ensure that the software can be combined into an operational information system, the project team performs integrated **systems testing**. An information system for inventory management and control may have a hundred programs and a comprehensive data base; all must be tested together to ensure harmony of operation. The purpose of the system test is to validate all software, input/output, procedures, and the data base. It is a safe bet that a few design errors, programming errors, procedural errors, or oversights will surface during system testing. Minor modifications in design and programming may be required to complete the system test to the satisfaction of the users.

To conduct the system test, the project team compiles and thoroughly tests the system with test data. In this first stage of system testing, tests are run for each subsystem (one of the functional aspects of the system) or cycle (weekly or monthly activities). The test data are judiciously compiled so that all program and system options and all error and validation routines are tested. The tests are repeated and modifications are made until all subsystems or cycles function properly. At this point the entire system is tested as a unit. Testing and modifications continue until the components of the system work as they should and all input/output is validated.

Testing with Live Data

The second stage of system testing is done with *live data* by several of the people who will eventually use the system. Live data are data that have already been processed through the existing system. Testing

✓

Memory Bits

TESTING
- Unit testing
- System testing
  With test data
  With live data
- User acceptance testing

with live data provides an extra level of assurance that the system will work properly when implemented. Testing and modifications are continued until the project team and participating users are satisfied with the results.

User Acceptance Testing

The system is now subjected to the scrutiny of the user managers whose departments will ultimately use the system. The purpose of this last test, called **user-acceptance testing**, is to get the user's stamp of approval. User managers examine and test the operation of the system (using live data) until they are satisfied that it meets the original system objectives. Modification and testing continues until it does.

13–3 System Conversion and Implementation

Approaches to System Conversion

Once acceptance testing is complete, the project team can begin to integrate people, software, hardware, procedures, and data into an operational information system. This normally involves a conversion from the existing system to the new one. An organization's approach to system conversion depends on its *willingness to accept risk* and the *amount of time available* for the conversion. Four common approaches are parallel conversion, direct conversion, phased conversion, and pilot conversion. These approaches are illustrated in Figure 13–5 and discussed in the paragraphs that follow.

Parallel Conversion   In **parallel conversion**, the existing system and the new system operate simultaneously, or in parallel, until the project team is confident that the new system is working properly. Parallel conversion has two important advantages. First, the existing system

FIGURE 13–5   Common Approaches to System Conversion

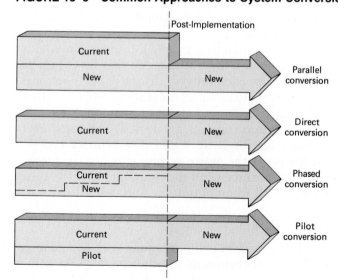

In preparation for in-house user training sessions, instructors devise operational scenarios complete with test data to give users an opportunity to familiarize themselves with the system. During the sessions, instructors provide insight into how to make the most effective use of the system. The conversion and implementation process progresses smoothly when users feel comfortable with a system.

serves as a backup if the new system fails to operate as expected. Second, the results of the new system can be compared to the results of the existing system.

There is less risk with this strategy because the present system provides backup, but it also doubles the workload of personnel and hardware resources during the conversion. Parallel conversion usually takes one month or a major system cycle. For a public utility company, this might be one complete billing cycle, which is usually a month.

Direct Conversion   As companies improve their system testing procedures, they begin to gain confidence in their ability to implement a working system. Some companies forego parallel conversion in favor of a **direct conversion.** Direct conversion involves a greater risk because there is no backup in case the system fails.

Companies select this "cold turkey" approach when there is no existing system or when the existing system is substantially different. For example, all on-line hotel reservations systems are implemented "cold turkey."

Phased Conversion   In **phased conversion**, an information system is implemented one module at a time by either parallel or direct conversion. For example, in a point-of-sale system, the first phase might be to convert the sales accounting module. The second phase could involve the inventory management module. The third might be the credit-check module.

Phased conversion has the advantage of spreading the demand for resources to avoid an intense demand. The disadvantages are that the conversion takes longer and an interface must be developed between the existing system and the new one.

Pilot Conversion   In **pilot conversion**, the new system is implemented by parallel, direct, or phased conversion as a pilot system in only one of the several areas for which it is targeted. For example, suppose a company wants to implement a manufacturing resources planning system in its eight plants. One plant would be selected as a pilot, and the new system would be implemented there first.

The advantage of pilot conversion is that the inevitable bugs in a system can be removed before the system is implemented at the other locations. The disadvantage is that the implementation time for the total system takes longer than if the entire system were implemented at one time.

The System Becomes Operational

Once the conversion has been completed, the information system enters the production stage of the system life cycle (see Figure 12–1 in Chapter 12). During the production stage the system becomes operational and is turned over to the users. The operations function of the information services division provides operational support for the system. This function encompasses everything associated with running an information system including all interaction with the hardware that supports the system. The scope of operations support would typically include these major areas:

- Data entry and transaction processing, both batch and on-line
- Interactive inquiry, both built-in and ad hoc
- Maintenance of the data base
- Output, including reports (summary, exception, historical, graphic, and so on) and documents (for example, utility bills, mailing labels, authorizations to build, air travel tickets)
- Transition or preprocessing (massaging data to put them in the proper format for processing, a common activity for electronic data interchange applications)

13–4 Post-Implementation Activities

Just as a new automobile will need some screws tightened after a few hundred miles, an information system will need some fine-tuning just after implementation. Thereafter and throughout the production stage of the system life cycle, the system will be modified many times to meet the changing needs of the company.

Post-Implementation Review

The **post-implementation review** is a critical examination of the system three to six months after it has been put into production. This waiting period allows several factors to stabilize: the resistance to change, the anxieties associated with change, and the learning curve. It also allows time for unanticipated problems to surface.

The post-implementation review focuses on the following:

- A comparison of the system's actual performance versus the anticipated performance objectives
- An assessment of each facet of the system with respect to preset criteria

Three to six months after the hardware, software, people, procedures, and data have been integrated into an operational material requirements planning system, key members of the project team conduct a post-implementation evaluation to assess the overall effectiveness of an inventory management system.

- Mistakes made during system development
- Unexpected benefits and problems

System Maintenance

Once an information system is implemented and "goes on-line," the emphasis switches from *development* to *operations*. In a payroll system, supervisors begin to enter hours worked on their terminals, and the computer center produces and issues payroll checks. Once operational, an information system becomes a cooperative effort between the users and the information services division.

An information system is dynamic and must be responsive to the changing needs of the company and those who use it. The process of modifying an information system to meet changing needs is known as **system maintenance**.

An information system cannot live forever. The accumulation of modifications and enhancements will eventually make any information system cumbersome and inefficient. Minor modifications are known as **patches**. Depending on the number of patches and enhancements, an information system will remain operational—that is, be in the production stage—from four to seven years.

Toward the end of the useful life of an information system, it is more trouble to continue patching the system than it is to redesign the system completely. The end of the production stage signals the death stage of the information system life cycle (see Figure 12–1 in Chapter 12). A new system is then "born" of need, and the system development process is repeated.

13–5 System Controls and Backup

An information system should run smoothly under normal circumstances. But as Murphy has taught us, "If anything can go wrong, it will." Users, programmers, and operators make oversights and errors in judgment. Computers sometimes fail to work as planned, and sometimes they simply cease to function. There is always the threat of computer crime. Malicious hackers have vandalized thousands of systems. System controls help ensure that the system runs as planned and that errors, inappropriate procedures, or unauthorized accesses are detected before the system is affected.

System Controls

Because of the ever-present potential for human and hardware errors coupled with the threat of computer crime, it is important that an organization build in controls to ensure the accuracy, reliability, and integrity of an information system. Without controls, an enterprising computer criminal might be able to supplement his or her checking account without making a deposit. An erroneous data entry error could result in the delivery of a red car instead of a blue one. Someone expecting a monthly paycheck of $2500 might receive $250,000. A computer operator could cause chaos by forgetting to do the daily audit run. System controls are introduced to prevent these and any of a thousand other undesirable events from happening.

Information system controls minimize or eliminate errors before, during, and after processing so that the data entered and the information produced are complete and accurate. Controls also minimize

FIGURE 13–6 System Controls

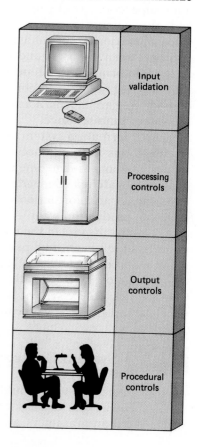

At this insurance company, much of the data is entered to the system by the customer service agents who update existing policies, write new policies, and process claims. A variety of techniques are used to validate the input. For example, written text and names are checked for spelling errors; policy numbers are validated; claim amounts are matched against those with similar circumstances; and city/zip code combinations are matched against a master zip code directory.

the possibility of computer fraud. There are four types of controls: *input validation*, *processing controls*, *output controls*, and *procedural controls* (see Figure 13–6).

Input Validation   Data are checked for accuracy when they are entered into the system. In on-line data entry, the data entry operator verifies the data by sight checks. In addition, a variety of checking procedures are designed into the software. Two of these software-control procedures are as follows:

- *Reasonableness check.* Suppose that a customer's maximum order to date is for 250 widgets and an order is entered for 2000 widgets. Because an order for 2000 is much greater than the maximum order to date for 250, the entry is historically unreasonable, and the probable error is brought to the attention of the data entry operator.
- *Limits check.* A limits check assesses whether the value of an entry is out of line with that expected. For example, a company's policy guarantees 40 hours of work per week for each employee and limits overtime to 15 hours per week. A limits check on the "hours-worked" entry guarantees that a value between 40 and 55, inclusive, is entered.

Processing Controls   Systems analysts and programmers employ a variety of techniques to validate the fact that processing is complete and accurate. Control totals and consistency checks are two of the many techniques that can be built into the software:

- *Control total.* A control total, or hash total, is a value known to be the accumulated sum of a particular data element. Control totals are used primarily to verify that processing is complete.

For example, when a company's payroll checks are printed, the employee numbers are added together and compared to a known value. If the accumulated control total is not equal to the known value, the computer operator knows immediately that some checks were not processed or that some checks were processed that should not have been.

- *Consistency check.* The consistency check compares like data items for consistency of value. For example, if a company's electric bill for March is 300% higher than the bill for March of last year, the invoice would not be processed. Management would then ask the electric company to check the accuracy of the meter reading.

Output Controls   Some people take for granted that any computer-produced output is accurate. This is not always the case. There are too many things that can go wrong. One of many methods of output control is *crossfoot checking*. This technique is used in reports, such as the one in Figure 13–7, that have column and row totals with some arithmetic relationship to one another. In Figure 13–7, the column totals for each beverage type should equal the total for all delivery routes.

Procedural Controls   In an information system, the work is done either by the computer system or by people. Programs tell the computer what to do. Procedures guide people. Some procedures are built into the system for control purposes. For example, many companies subscribe to the *separation-of-duties* procedure. The theory behind this procedure is that if responsibilities for input, processing, and output are assigned to different people, most attempts to defraud the system will be foiled. It is unlikely that would-be computer criminals could solicit that much cooperation.

A corporation is vulnerable when one operator has sole respon-

FIGURE 13–7   Crossfoot Checking
The sum of the row totals equals the sum of the column totals.

ROUTE NO.	COLA	FIZZ	BURP	ROUTE TOTAL
1	41	68	32	141
2	29	18	64	111
3	71	65	48	184
4	67	58	56	181
TOTAL	208	209	200	617

QUERY: Let me see the daily delivery report.

On the Street

Marilyn Farrar-Wagner
Office Manager
Veterinary Hospital

Marilyn Farrar-Wagner combines a love of animals with outstanding organizational skills in her job as office manager at the Ridgewood Veterinary Hospital. Her responsibilities in this capacity are varied, but they have been made much easier since the purchase in late 1986 of five Northstar computers and the AniMed software program, a package designed specifically for veterinarians that includes Easy Writer II, a word processing program.

"In addition to helping me do the books [accounts payable and accounts receivable] at the end of each day and month and printing out pharmacy labels, the computer automatically generates personalized, ready-to-mail postcards reminding our clients of when their pets are due for vaccinations. We used to write these cards by hand, and since we have close to 10,000 patients, this was a very tedious (not to mention time-consuming) task!"

The computer also comes in handy by keeping an exact inventory of all the surgical supplies and medications the hospital has at any given time. "Before, we would reorder a particular drug only when it looked like we were getting low. Now the computer can provide us with more accurate information."

Besides helping Marilyn with the day-to-day operations of running an animal hospital, the computer system also provides a valuable servce for the clients—the ability to help track lost pets through identification numbers on the dogs' rabies tags, which are kept on file in the system. (Ridgewood's phone numbers also appears on the tag.) For a family searching for a missing furry member, this special function is truly a lifesaver.

sibility for running a particular information system. Because of this, many companies have a mandatory vacation policy requiring programmers, operators, and others in sensitive positions to take their vacations in blocks of no less than two weeks.

System Backup

Occasionally the worst case scenario comes to pass—total system failure. To avoid catastrophe during system failure, **backup** and **checkpoint/restart** procedures are defined during the systems development process. These procedures describe the extra processes included in the system that cope with system failures. During the chronology of system processing, operators periodically establish a checkpoint so that any processing up to that point in time is saved and cannot be destroyed. When a system fails, backup files or data bases and/or backup transaction logs (see Chapter 9, "Data Management") are used to re-create processing from the last checkpoint. The system is "restarted" at the last checkpoint and normal operation is resumed.

All the backup files and procedures in the world are worthless if there is no hardware on which to run them. Any of a number of disasters, from fire to malicious vandalism, could render a company's computer system useless. As a backup, many companies have agreements with one another to share their computing resources in case of disaster. When this happens, both companies would operate only critical systems until a new computer system could be installed. Other companies contract with a commercial disaster recovery service. These services make a fully configured computer system available to clients in case of a disaster.

13–6 Computer-Center and System Security

Security is certainly one of the most important considerations in the development and ongoing operation of an information system. As more and more systems go on-line, more people have access to the overall system. A company must be extremely careful not to compromise the integrity of its system. It must be equally careful with the "engine" of the information system—the computer.

There are too many points of vulnerability and too much is at stake to overlook the threats to the security of an information system and a computer center. These threats take many forms—white-collar crime, natural disasters (earthquakes, floods), vandalism, and carelessness.

White-collar crime exists undetected in some of the most unlikely places. It is sophisticated crime with sophisticated criminals. Most computer crimes are undetected, others are unreported, so it is more widespread than estimates would lead us to believe. A bank may prefer to write off a $100,000 embezzlement rather than publicly announce to its depositors that its computer system is vulnerable.

This section is devoted to discussing the measures needed to neutralize security threats to an information system or to a computer center.

Computer Center Security

A company's computer center has a number of points of vulnerability; these are *hardware*, *software*, *files/data bases*, *data communications*, and *personnel*. Each is discussed separately in the following sections and illustrated in Figure 13–8.

Hardware If the hardware fails, the information system fails. The threat of failure can be minimized by implementing security precautions that prevent access by unauthorized personnel and by taking steps to keep all hardware operational.

Common approaches to securing the premises from unauthorized entry include closed-circuit TV monitors, alarm systems, and com-

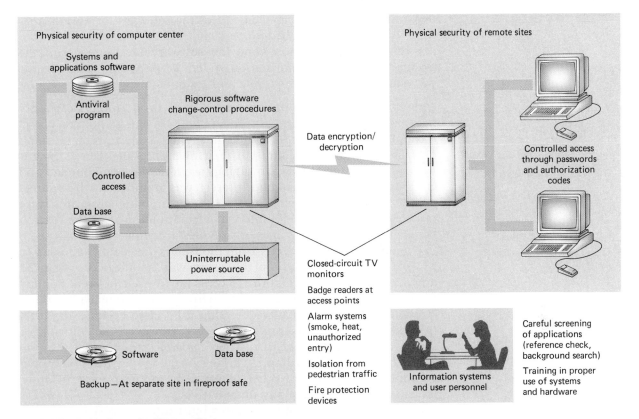

FIGURE 13–8 Security Precautions
Some or all of the security measures noted in the figure are in force in most computer centers. Each precaution helps minimize the risk of an information system or a computer system's vulnerability to crime, disasters, and failure.

puter-controlled devices that check employee badges, fingerprints, or voice prints before unlocking doors at access points. Computer centers also should be isolated from pedestrian traffic. And machine-room fires should be extinguished by a special chemical that douses the fire but does not destroy the files or equipment.

Computers, especially mainframe computers, must have a "clean," continuous source of power. To minimize the effects of "dirty" power or power outages, many computer centers have installed an **uninterruptible power source (UPS)**. Dirty power, with sags and surges in power output or brownouts (low power), causes data transmission errors and program execution errors. A UPS system serves as a buffer between the external power source and the computer system. In a UPS system, the computer is powered by batteries that deliver clean power, which in turn are regenerated by an external power source. If the external power source fails, the UPS system permits operation to continue for a period of time after an outage. This allows operators to either "power down" normally or switch to a backup power source, usually a diesel generator. Until recently UPS systems were associated only with mainframe computer systems. Now they are economically feasible for microcomputer systems.

Software Unless properly controlled, the software for an information system can be modified for personal gain, or it can be vandalized and rendered useless. Close control of software development and the documentation of an information system is needed to minimize the opportunity for computer crime and vandalism.

Unlawful modification of software. Bank programmers certainly have opportunities to modify software for personal gain. In one case, a couple of programmers modified a savings system to make small deposits from other accounts to their own accounts. Here's how it worked: The interest for each savings account was compounded and credited daily; the calculated interest was rounded to the nearest penny before being credited to the savings account; programs were modified to round down all interest calculations and put the "extra" penny in one of the programmer's savings accounts. It may not seem like much, but a penny a day from thousands of accounts adds up to a lot of money. The "beauty" of the system was that the books balanced and depositors did not miss the 15 cents (an average of $\frac{1}{2}$ cent per day for 30 days) that judiciously was taken from each account each month. Even auditors had difficulty detecting this crime because the total interest paid on all accounts was correct. However, the culprits got greedy and were apprehended when someone noticed that they repeatedly withdrew inordinately large sums of money from their own accounts. Unfortunately, other enterprising programmers in other industries have been equally imaginative.

Operational control procedures built into the design of an information system will constantly monitor processing accuracy. These controls are discussed earlier in this section. Unfortunately, cagey programmers have been known to get around some of them. Perhaps the best way to safeguard programs from unlawful tampering is to use rigorous change-control procedures. Such procedures make it difficult to modify a program for purposes of personal gain.

Viruses. The growing threat of viruses has resulted in tightening software controls. A **virus** is a program that literally "infects" other programs and data bases. Viral programs are written with malicious intent and are loaded to the computer system of an unsuspecting victim. Viruses have been found at all levels of computing, from PCs to large mainframe computers. The end user computing environment is particularly susceptible to virus infiltration because of its lack of system controls.

The virus is so named because it can spread from one system to another like a biological virus. There are many types of viruses. Some act quickly by erasing user programs and data bases. Others grow like a cancer, destroying small parts of a data base each day. Some viruses act like a time bomb: They lay dormant for days or months but eventually are activated and wreak havoc on any software in the system. Some viruses attack hardware and have been known to throw the mechanical components of a computer system, such as disk access arms, into costly spasms. Viruses can spread from one computer network to another through data communications. A Cornell graduate

"Boss, our security problems are over. You won't see another unauthorized report leave this computer."

The university environment is conducive to the origination and propagation of viruses. One virus wreaked havoc at several universities. It infected the operating systems of IBM-compatible microcomputers, specifically the DOS COMMAND.COM file. When booted, the infected disk would replicate itself to an uninfected COMMAND.COM file. After repeating the replication four times, the original software virus would destroy itself—and all the files on its diskette. The other infected disk would continue to reproduce.

student created a costly virus that infected over 6000 computers throughout the world. Viruses also spread from one system to another via common diskettes.

Since first appearing in the mid-1980s, viruses have erased bank records, damaged hospital records, destroyed the programs in thousands of microcomputers, and even infected part of the systems at NORAD (strategic defense) and NASA. Disgruntled employees have inserted viruses in disks that were distributed to customers. The motives of those who would infect a system with a virus run from electronic vandalism to revenge to terrorism. There is no monetary reward, only the "satisfaction" of knowing that their efforts have been very costly to individuals, companies, governments, and so on.

Viruses are a serious problem. They have the potential to affect an individual's career and even destroy companies. For example, a company that loses its accounts receivable records could be a candidate for bankruptcy. Antiviral programs, which are sometimes called *vaccines*, exist, but they can be circumvented by a persistent (and malicious) hacker. The best way to cope with viruses is to recognize that they exist and take precautionary measures. For example, one company requires micro users to turn off their micros and reload their personal copy of the operating system before each use. In the mainframe environment, systems programmers must continually search for suspicious-looking programs and be particularly wary of downloading programs from computer systems outside the company.

Files/Data Bases   The data base contains the raw material for information. Often the files/data bases are the lifeblood of a company. For example, how many companies can afford to lose their accounts receivable file, which documents who owes what? Having several *generations of backups* (backups to backups) to all files is not sufficient insurance against loss of files/data bases. The backup and master files should be stored in fireproof safes in separate rooms, preferably in separate buildings.

Data Communications The mere existence of data communications capabilities, where data are transmitted via communications links from one computer to another, poses a threat to security. A knowledgeable criminal can tap into the system from a remote location and use it for personal gain. In a well-designed system, this is not an easy task. But it can be and has been done! When one criminal broke a company's security code and tapped into the network of computers, he was able to order certain products without being billed. He filled a warehouse before he eventually was caught. Another tapped into an international banking exchange system to reroute funds to an account of his own in a Swiss bank. In another case, an oil company consistently was able to outbid a competitor by "listening in" on the latter's data transmissions. On several occasions, overzealous young hackers have tapped into sensitive defense computer systems; fortunately, no harm was done.

Some companies use **cryptography** to scramble messages sent over data communications channels. Someone who unlawfully intercepts such a message would find meaningless strings of characters. Cryptography is analogous to the code book used by intelligence people during the "cloak-and-dagger" days. Instead of a code book, however, a key is used in conjunction with **encryption/decryption** hardware to unscramble the message. Both sender and receiver must have the key, which is actually an algorithm that rearranges the bit structure of a message. Companies that routinely transmit sensitive data over communications channels are moving to data encryption as a means by which to limit access to their information systems and their data bases.

Personnel The biggest threat to a company's security system is the dishonesty and/or incompetence of its own employees. Managers are paying close attention to who gets hired for positions with access to computer-based information systems and sensitive data. Many companies flash a message on each terminal display such as: "All information on this system is confidential and proprietary." It's not very user friendly, but it gets the message across to employees that they may be fired if they abuse the system. Someone who is grossly incompetent can cause just as much harm as someone who is inherently dishonest.

PCs are everywhere and, as such, are particularly vulnerable to unauthorized use or malicious tampering. As an alternative to passwords or as an added layer of security, many companies use a magnetic card reader in the user sign-on procedure. The card reader reads common credit cards, door-opener cards, telephone cards, and so on. When used with authorization codes, a PC can have the same level of security as an automatic teller machine.

Information Systems Security

Information systems security is classified as physical or logical. **Physical security** refers to hardware, facilities, magnetic disks, and other items that could be illegally accessed, stolen, or destroyed.

Logical security is built into the software by permitting only authorized persons to access and use the system. Logical security for on-line systems is achieved primarily by using **passwords** and **authorization codes**. Only those people with a need to know are told the password and given authorization codes. On occasion, however, these security codes fall into the wrong hands. When this happens, an unauthorized person can gain access to programs and sensitive files by simply dialing up the computer and entering the codes.

Keeping passwords and authorization codes from the computer criminal is not easy. One criminal took advantage of the fact that a bank's automatic teller machine (ATM) did not "time out" for several minutes. That is, the authorization code could be entered without reinserting the card to initiate another transaction. Using high-powered binoculars, he watched from across the street as the numeric code was being entered. He then ran over to the ATM and waited until the customer left. He quickly entered the code and made withdrawals before the machine timed out. Needless to say, this design flaw has been eliminated in existing ATM systems.

Level of Risk   No combination of security measures will completely remove the vulnerability of a computer center or an information system. Security systems are implemented in degrees. That is, an information system can be made marginally secure or very secure, but never totally secure. Each company must determine the level of risk that it is willing to accept. Unfortunately, some corporations are willing to accept an enormous risk and hope that those rare instances of crime and disaster do not occur. Some of them have found out too late that *rarely* is not the same as *never*!

Summary Outline and Important Terms

13–1   PROGRAMMING: IDEAS BECOME REALITY.   During the programming phase of the systems development process, programs are written to create the software necessary to make the information system operational. The following activities take place: system specifications review; program identification and description; and program coding, testing, and documentation.

A typical program description would include the type of programming language, a narrative description, frequency of processing, input/output, limitations and restrictions, and detailed specifications.

For each program, the programmer describes the problem; analyzes the problem; designs the general, then the detailed logic; and codes, tests, and documents the program. When a programmer analyzes the problem, he or she breaks down the problem into its basic components (output, input, processing, and file-interaction) for analysis. In **structured programming**, a programming problem is broken down into a hierarchy of tasks called **modules**.

The graphic display of the program logic at the detailed level of design includes all processing activities and their relationships, calculations, data manipulations, logic operations, and all input/output.

Programmers must **debug** programs to rid them of **bugs** (**syntax errors**, logic errors, or I/O errors).

13-2 SYSTEM AND ACCEPTANCE TESTING. Although the programs that make up an information system have been debugged on an individual basis (**unit testing**), they must be combined and subjected to integrated **systems testing** prior to implementation.

After systems testing with live data comes **user-acceptance testing.** User managers examine and test the operation of the system until they are satisfied that it meets the original system objectives.

13-3 SYSTEM CONVERSION AND IMPLEMENTATION. The four common approaches to system conversion are **parallel conversion**, **direct conversion**, **phased conversion**, and **pilot conversion**. The approach that an organization selects depends on its willingness to accept risk and the amount of time available for the conversion.

Once the conversion has been completed, the information system enters the production stage of the system life cycle and is turned over to the users.

13-4 POST-IMPLEMENTATION ACTIVITIES. The **post-implementation review**, which is a critical examination of the system after it has been put into production, is conducted three to six months after implementation.

An information system is dynamic and must be responsive to the changing needs of the company and those who use it. The process of modifying, or **patching**, an information system to meet changing needs is known as **system maintenance**.

13-5 SYSTEM CONTROLS AND BACKUP. Companies build controls into their information systems to ensure system accuracy, reliability, and integrity. The four types of controls are input validation, processing controls, output controls, and procedural controls.

To avoid catastrophe during system failure, **backup** and **checkpoint/restart** procedures are defined during the systems development process.

13-6 COMPUTER-CENTER AND SYSTEM SECURITY. The threats to the security of computer centers and information systems call for precautionary measures. A computer center can be vulnerable in its hardware, software, files/data bases, data communications, and personnel. Organizations use a variety of approaches to secure the computer center, including the installation of an **uninterruptible power source (UPS)** and the use of **cryptography** to scramble messages sent over data communications channels.

Viruses are programs that infect other programs and data bases, and sometimes cause damage to hardware. Virus programs are written with malicious intent and are loaded to the computer system of an unsuspecting victim.

Information systems security is classified as **physical security** or **logical security**. Logical security for on-line systems is achieved primarily by using **passwords** and **authorization codes**. Security systems are implemented in degrees, and no computer center or system can be made totally secure.

 Review Exercises

Concepts

1. Which comes first during system testing, testing with live data or testing with test data?
2. List three areas addressed during a post-implementation review.
3. What is the purpose of transition or preprocessing?
4. Name two types of controls for validating input. Name two types of processing controls.
5. What is the purpose of a key in cryptography?
6. What precautions can be taken to minimize the effects of hardware failure?
7. The mere fact that a system uses data communications poses a threat to security. Why?
8. What advantage does direct conversion have over parallel conversion? Parallel over direct?
9. Give two examples of the uses of a control total.
10. Differentiate between a program syntax error and a program logic error.
11. Describe the contents of a program documentation package.
12. What are the first and last steps in the program development process?
13. What name is given to programs written with malicious intent then loaded to the computer system of an unsuspecting victim?

Discussion

14. Assuming that test data are designed and compiled to test all system options, why is it recommended to continue testing with live data?

15. Evaluate your college's (or your company's) computer center with respect to security. Identify areas where you think it is vulnerable and discuss ways to improve its security.

16. In the past, bank officers have been reluctant to report computer crimes. If you were a customer of a bank that made such a decision, how would you react?

17. As a security precaution, some MIS managers have initiated a policy that requires two programmers to be familiar with each program. Argue for or against this procedure.

18. A bank programmer developed an algorithm to determine the check digit for the bank's credit card numbers. The programmer sold the algorithm, one of the bank's control procedures, to an underground group that specialized in counterfeit credit cards. A year later the programmer was caught and pleaded guilty. What do you feel is a just sentence for this crime?

19. Some programmers are accused of producing "spaghetti code," so named because their indecipherable flowcharts resemble a bowl of spaghetti. What steps should their managers take to eliminate inefficient spaghetti code and improve program quality?

20. What is meant by the remark "Garbage in, garbage out" as applied to system specifications and programming?

Self-Test (by section)

13–1 **a.** Programming is the only phase of system development that can be completed out of sequence. (T/F)

 b. Before coding programs, programmers must review the _____ created during system analysis and design.

 c. A typical program description would *not* include which of the following: (a) the type of programming language, (b) the output produced by the program, or (c) the data base design?

 d. In structured programming, the logic of the program is addressed hierarchically in logical modules. (T/F)

13–2 **a.** Individual program testing is known as: (a) unit testing, (b) module testing, or (c) hierarchical testing.

 b. A newly developed information system is subjected to the scrutiny of the user managers during user acceptance testing. (T/F)

13–3 **a.** Greater risk is associated with direct conversion than with phased conversion. (T/F)

b. In the _____ approach to system conversion, the existing system and the new system operate simultaneously until the project team is confident the new system is working properly.

13–4 **a.** The post-implementation evaluation is normally conducted one year after system implementation. (T/F)

b. Once an information system is implemented, the emphasis is switched from development to: (a) testing, (b) operations, or (c) training.

13–5 **a.** The limits check is a procedural control. (T/F)

b. A hash total is: (a) an input control, (b) a output control, or (c) a processing control.

c. Checkpoint/restart procedures are most closely associated with: (a) backup, (b) input controls, or (c) system testing.

13–6 **a.** Logical security for on-line systems is achieved primarily by _____ and authorization codes.

b. Cryptography is the study of the assignment of security codes. (T/F)

Self-test answers. **13–1** (a) F; (b) system specifications; (c) c; (d) T. **13–2** (a) a; (b) T. **13–3** (a) T; (b) parallel. **13–4** (a) F; (b) b. **13–5** (a) F; (b) c; (c) a. **13–6** (a) passwords; (b) F.

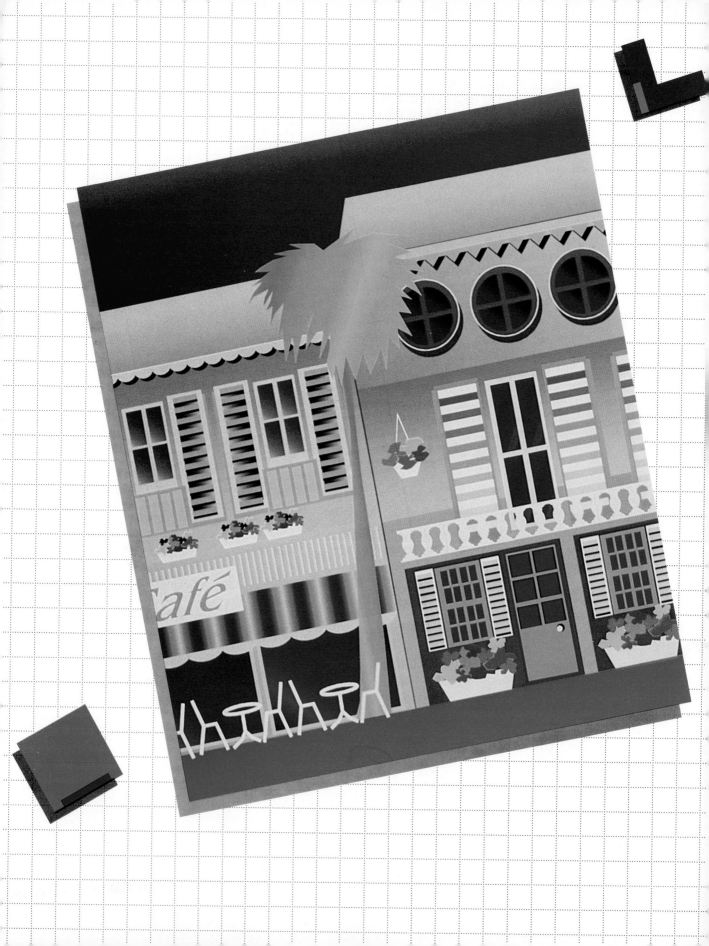

14

Word Processing, Desktop Publishing, and Communications Software

STUDENT LEARNING OBJECTIVES

- To describe the function, purpose, and applications of word processing software.
- To discuss common word processing concepts.
- To identify and describe add-on capabilities for word processing software packages.
- To describe the function, purpose, and applications of desktop publishing software.
- To describe the function, purpose, and applications of communications software.

14–1 The Microcomputer Family of Productivity Software

The office without a microcomputer is more the exception than the rule. The home without a microcomputer will be more the exception than the rule in the not-too-distant future. The growth of this kind of computing, called **personal computing**, has surpassed even the boldest forecasts of the mid-1970s.

Inexpensive microcomputers have made automation economically feasible for virtually any business environment. As a result, microcomputer software is available to support thousands of common and not-so-common business applications. There is, of course, an established need for applications such as payroll, accounting, sales analysis, project management, and inventory control. There are also hundreds of industry-specific software packages for thoroughbred breeding, medical laboratories, professional football, veterinary practices, art dealing, and just about anything else. Personal computers also provide managers with access to a variety of decision support systems (simulation, modeling, forecasting, "what if" analysis), many of which were available only on mainframe computers a few years ago. Most of the new commercially available expert systems (tax reporting, medical diagnosis, and so on) are being created for personal computers.

Microcomputer Productivity Tools

Thousands of commercially available software packages run on microcomputers, but the most popular business software is the family

Microcomputers and productivity software have become fixtures in every business environment. At this Texas bank, staffers use micros in combination with word processing, graphics, and desktop publishing software to turn out better looking sales proposals in less time.

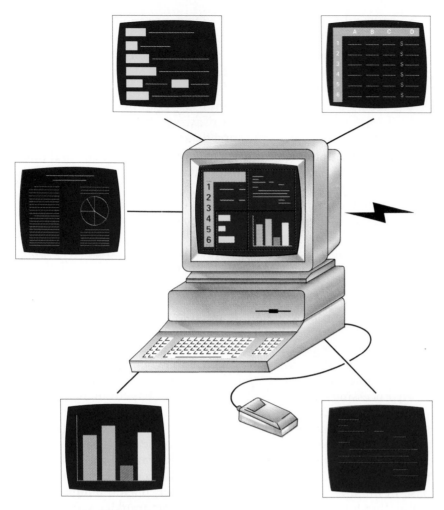

FIGURE 14–1 Microcomputer Productivity Software
Popular microcomputer productivity software packages include (clockwise from top left) database, electronic spreadsheet, communications, word processing, presentation graphics, and desktop publishing.

of productivity software packages (see Figure 14–1). In contrast to software designed for a specific application (such as sales analysis), these and other productivity software packages are general purpose, providing the framework for a great number of business and personal applications. These programs are the foundation of personal computing. The primary microcomputer productivity tools include:

- *Word processing.* **Word processing** software permits users to enter, store, manipulate, and print text.
- *Desktop publishing.* **Desktop publishing** software allows users to produce near-typeset-quality copy from the confines of a desktop.
- *Communications.* Communications software enables users to

send and receive transmissions of data to and from remote computers, and to process and store the data as well.

- *Electronic spreadsheet.* **Electronic spreadsheet** software permits users to work with the rows and columns of a matrix (or spreadsheet) of data.
- *Presentation graphics.* **Presentation graphics** software allows users to create charts and line drawings that graphically portray the data in an electronic spreadsheet or data base.
- *Database.* **Database** software permits users to create and maintain a data base and to extract information from the data base.

The *function*, *concepts*, and *use* of each of these micro software tools are the focus of the two chapters in Part V, "Personal Computing." This chapter covers word processing, desktop publishing, and communications software. Electronic spreadsheet, presentation graphics, and database are covered in Chapter 15. Concepts relating to the use of microcomputers are discussed in Chapter 3, "Microcomputers." You should be familiar with these general microcomputer concepts (for example, scrolling, RAM, function keys, ENTER key, windows, default options, and so on) before reading the chapters in Part V.

The software packages illustrated in Figure 14–1 often are characterized as productivity tools because they help relieve the tedium of many time-consuming manual tasks. No more retyping, thanks to word processing software. Desktop publishing has eliminated the need for expensive typesetting of many printed items. Communications software helps minimize redundant data entry by permitting the transfer of files between computers. Electronic spreadsheets permit us to perform certain arithmetic and logic operations without writing programs. With database software we can format and create a data base in minutes. Say goodbye to grid paper, plastic templates, and manually plotting data because presentation graphics software prepares bar, pie, and line graphs without our drawing a single line.

Developing Hands-on Skills with a Particular Productivity Tool

In each productivity tool category, there are dozens of commercially available software packages from which to choose. The software packages in each category accomplish essentially the same functions. They differ primarily in the scope and variety of the special features they have to offer and in their user friendliness.

The material in Part V, "Personal Computing," is intended to acquaint you with the capabilities of these six popular productivity software packages. For the most part, the discussions are generic and can be applied to any applicable commercially available software package in the respective categories. Should you wish to develop hands-on skills in the use of a particular package, *Microcomputer Software: Step by Step* by Ted Kalmon, Nancy Long, and Larry Long (Prentice Hall, 1990) provides instruction and tutorials for MS-DOS

√

Memory Bits

MICROCOMPUTER PRODUCTIVITY TOOLS
- Word processing
- Desktop publishing
- Communications
- Electronic spreadsheet
- Presentation graphics
- Data management

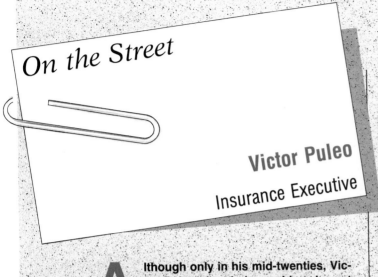

Although only in his mid-twenties, Victor Puleo already has achieved great success as president of The Bell Financial Group, a wholesale distributor of life insurance in Jacksonville, Florida. His company acts as an intermediary between over 30 insurance companies and in excess of 300 brokers.

As president, Victor has his hand in a variety of functions, including writing and designing marketing material, servicing existing accounts, and underwriting new business. His IBM PC and AT play an important role in all three of these areas.

He uses telecommunications software provided by the home offices of the companies he represents to access their mainframes for illustrations and quotes to give prospective insureds; to check pending underwriting files and applications; to find out the status of in-force policies; and to send and receive messages instantly to and from the companies.

He uses WordPerfect, a word processing package, to draft all correspondence and sales memos to brokers, and Lotus 1-2-3 and Multiplan, spreadsheet packages, to prepare cash flow statements and to analyze sales figures (weekly, monthly, and year-to-date). In this way, he can know in minutes how many of a particular product (term, universal life) were placed with Company A as compared to Company B, by which broker, and over what period of time.

"Computers have accelerated everything we do. What used to take days and weeks now takes a matter of hours or minutes. I used to do many of my calculations by hand. Now I can make changes and do refiguring so quickly. It's really amazing. I can't imagine running an agency without them. Now if I could only find software that would improve my golf swing and lower my handicap, my life would be perfect!"

(the operating system for the IBM PC and its compatibles), WordPerfect (the leading word processing package), Lotus 1-2-3 (the leading integrated electronic spreadsheet package: spreadsheet, graphics, and database), and dBASE IV (the leading database package). *Microcomputer Software: Step by Step*, which is designed to complement the material in this text, enables a beginning student to progress to the advanced level of competency in the most recent versions of MS-DOS, WordPerfect, Lotus 1-2-3, and dBASE IV. Microcomputer operating system concepts are discussed in Chapter 8 of this text, "Programming Languages and Software Concepts."

Throughout Part V, microcomputer software concepts are discussed and illustrated in the context of Zimco Enterprises, a fictitious medium-sized manufacturer of handy consumer products—the Stib, Farkle, Tegler, and Qwert.

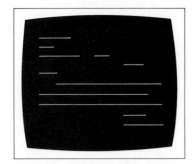

14–2 Word Processing

Function

Word processing is using the computer to enter, store, manipulate, and print text in letters, reports, books, and so on. Once you have used word processing, you will probably wonder (like a million others before you) how in the world you ever survived without it!

Word processing has virtually eliminated the need for opaque correction fluid and the need to rekey revised letters and reports. Revising a hard copy is time-consuming and cumbersome, but revising the same text in electronic format is quick and easy. You simply make corrections and revisions to the text on the computer before the document is displayed or printed in final form.

Concepts

Creating a Document

Formatting a document. Before you begin keying in the text of a word processing document, it is always a good idea to *format* the document. When you format a document, you describe the size of the print page and how you want the document to look when it is printed. As with the typewriter, you must set the left and right margins, the tab settings, line spacing (for example, lines/inch), and character spacing (for example, characters/inch). Depending on the software package, some or all of these specifications are made in a *layout line*. You can have as many layout lines as you want in a single document. Text is printed according to specifications in the most recent layout line until another layout line is defined. You must also specify the size of the output document, then set margins for the top and bottom of the text. The default document size is almost always $8\frac{1}{2}$ by 11 inches.

Entering text. Text is entered in either **replace mode** or **insert mode.** When in replace mode, the character you enter *overstrikes* the

At many companies, all office workers, including executives, are trained to use word processing. Executives at this company save time and money by using word processing to edit their reports. They find this approach more effective than having a secretary key in their red-pencil revisions from a hard copy.

```
To:      Field Sales Staff
From:    G. Brooks, Northern Sales Manager
Re:      Weekly Briefing Session

     The Sales Department's weekly briefing session will be
held at 9:00 a.m. this Thursday.  Last month's sales figures
and new sales strategies for the Tegler and Qwert will be
discussed.  We'll meet in the second floor conference room.
```

FIGURE 14–2   Word Processing: Memorandum
This first-draft memo is revised for illustrative purposes in Figures 14–3
through 14–7.

character at the cursor position. For example, suppose you typed the
word "the", but you wanted to type "and". To make the correction
in replace mode, you would position the cursor at the "t" and type
a-n-d, thereby replacing "the" with "and".

On most word processing systems you **toggle**, or switch, between
replace and insert mode by pressing a key. When in insert mode, you
can enter *additional* text. Let's use a memo written by George Brooks,
the northern regional sales manager for Zimco Enterprises, to illustrate insert mode data entry. George often uses word processing to
generate memos to his staff. The first draft of one of George's memos
is shown in Figure 14–2. George wanted to emphasize that an upcoming meeting was to be on Thursday, so he decided to insert "See
you Thursday! " just before the last sentence. To do this, he selected
the insert mode, placed the cursor on the "W" in "We'll", and entered
"See you Thursday! " (see Figure 14–3).

On most word processing packages, text that extends past the
defined margins is automatically *wrapped* to the next line. That is,
words that are pushed past the right margin are automatically moved
onto the next line, and so on, to the end of the paragraph. In Figures
14–2 and 14–3, notice how the words "conference room." (in the last
sentence) are wrapped around to the next line when "See you

FIGURE 14–3   Word Processing: Insert Mode
This memo is the result of the sentence "See you Thursday! " being inserted
before the last sentence of the memo of Figure 14–2.   Notice how the text
wraps around to make room for the addition of a sentence.

```
To:      Field Sales Staff
From:    G. Brooks, Northern Sales Manager
Re:      Weekly Briefing Session

     The Sales Department's weekly briefing session will be
held at 9:00 a.m. this Thursday.  Last month's sales figures
and new sales strategies for the Tegler and Qwert will be
discussed.  See you Thursday!  We'll meet in the second floor
conference room.
```

Thursday! " is inserted. On some packages, you must *reformat* the document if you wish to see the document within the predefined margins.

Word processing permits *full-screen editing*. That is, you can move the cursor to any position in the document to insert or replace text. You can browse through a multiscreen document by *scrolling* a line at a time or a "page" (a screen) at a time. You can edit any part of any screen.

When you enter text, you press the ENTER key only when you wish to begin a new line of text. As you enter text in replace mode, the computer automatically moves the cursor to the next line. In insert mode, the computer manipulates the text such that it wraps around. This type of text movement is called **word wrap**.

Block Operations   Features common to most word processing software packages are mentioned and discussed briefly in this section. The *block* operations are among the handiest word processing features. They are the block *move*, the block *copy*, and the block *delete* commands. These commands are the electronic equivalent of a "cut and paste" job. Let's discuss the move command first. With the move feature, you can select a block of text (for example, a word, a sentence, a paragraph, a section of a report, or as much contiguous text as you desire) and move it to another portion of the document. To do this, follow these steps:

1. Issue the move command (a main menu option or a function key).
2. Indicate the start and ending positions of the block of text to be moved (*mark* the text).
3. Move the cursor to the beginning of the destination location (where you wish the text to be moved).
4. Press the ENTER (or the appropriate function key) to complete the move operation.

At the end of the move procedure, the entire block of text you selected is moved to the location you designated and the original is deleted. The text is adjusted accordingly.

The following example demonstrates the procedure for marking and moving a block of text. After reading over the memo (Figure 14–3), George decided to edit his memo to the field staff to make it more readable. He did this by moving the last sentence from the end of the memo to just after the first sentence. To perform this operation, he first selected the move option (a function key on his word processing system) and marked the beginning ("W" in "We'll") and end (the position following the "." at the end of the paragraph) of the block. On most word processing systems, the portions of text marked for a block operation are usually displayed in **reverse video** (see Figure 14–4). After marking the block, George then positioned the cursor at the destination location (just after the first sentence) and pressed the

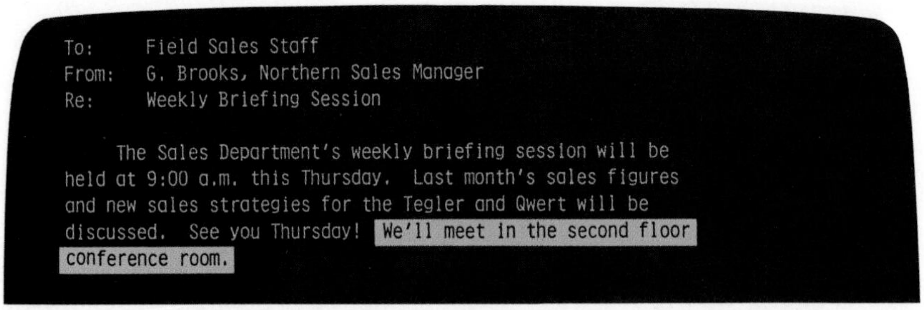

```
To:      Field Sales Staff
From:    G. Brooks, Northern Sales Manager
Re:      Weekly Briefing Session

     The Sales Department's weekly briefing session will be
held at 9:00 a.m. this Thursday.  Last month's sales figures
and new sales strategies for the Tegler and Qwert will be
discussed.  See you Thursday! We'll meet in the second floor
conference room.
```

FIGURE 14–4   Word Processing: Marking Text for a Block Operation
The last sentence of the memo is marked to be moved.

appropriate key (a function key) to complete the operation (see Figure 14–5).

The copy command works in a similar manner, except that the text block you select is copied to the location you designate. At the completion of the operation, two exact copies of the text block are present in the document. To delete a block of text, mark the block in the same manner, then select the delete block option.

The "Search" Features   Just as George Brooks was about to print his memo (Figure 14–5), he learned that an important client was coming to town on Thursday, so he decided to switch the meeting from Thursday to Friday. He can make the necessary revisions in the memo by using any of several word processing features. One option is to use the *search*, or *find*, feature. This feature permits George to search through the entire document and identify all occurrences of a particular character string. For example, if George wanted to search for all occurrences of "Thursday" in his memo of Figure 14–5, he would simply initiate the search command and type in the desired *search string*—"Thursday", in this example. The cursor is immediately positioned at the first occurrence of the character string "Thursday" so he easily can edit the text to reflect the new meeting day. From there, he can "find" other occurrences of "Thursday" by pressing the appropriate key.

FIGURE 14–5   Word Processing: Move Text
This memo is the result of the marked block in Figure 14–4 being moved to a position following the first sentence.

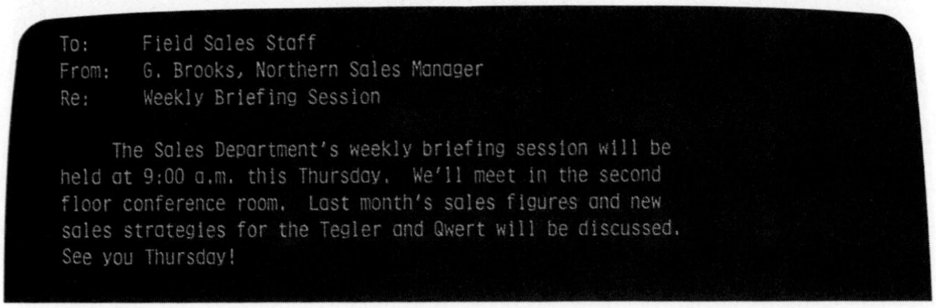

```
To:      Field Sales Staff
From:    G. Brooks, Northern Sales Manager
Re:      Weekly Briefing Session

     The Sales Department's weekly briefing session will be
held at 9:00 a.m. this Thursday.  We'll meet in the second
floor conference room.  Last month's sales figures and new
sales strategies for the Tegler and Qwert will be discussed.
See you Thursday!
```

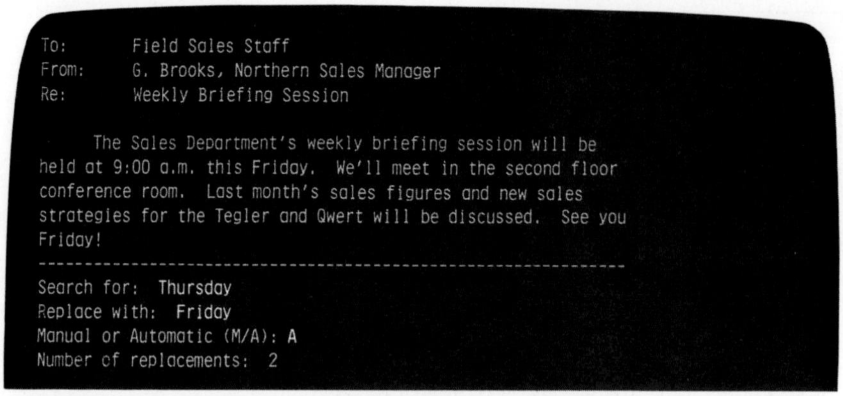

```
To:       Field Sales Staff
From:     G. Brooks, Northern Sales Manager
Re:       Weekly Briefing Session

    The Sales Department's weekly briefing session will be
held at 9:00 a.m. this Friday.  We'll meet in the second floor
conference room.  Last month's sales figures and new sales
strategies for the Tegler and Qwert will be discussed.  See you
Friday!
-----------------------------------------------------------------
Search for:  Thursday
Replace with:  Friday
Manual or Automatic (M/A): A
Number of replacements:  2
```

FIGURE 14–6   Word Processing: Search and Replace
With the search-and-replace command, the two occurrences of "Thursday" in
Figure 14–5 are located and replaced automatically (Option A) with "Friday".

As an alternative approach to making the Thursday-to-Friday
change, George could use the *search and replace* feature. This feature
enables George to selectively replace occurrences of "Thursday" in
his memo with "Friday". Because he knew that he wanted *all* occurrences of "Thursday" replaced by "Friday", he performed a *global
search and replace* (see Figure 14–6).

Features That Enhance Appearance and Readability   George used several other valuable word processing features to enhance the appearance and readability of his memo before distributing it to his staff.
First, he decided to enter the word "MEMORANDUM" at the top of
his memo and use the automatic *centering* feature to position it in the
middle of the page. On his word processing system, all he has to do
to center a particular line is move the cursor to that line and press
the *center* function key. The rest is automatic (see Figure 14–7).
    Word processing provides the facility to *boldface* and/or *under-*

FIGURE 14–7   Word Processing: Boldface and Underline
Text to be in boldface type or underlined is displayed differently, depending on
the word processing system and the color or resolution of the monitor. In the
figure, the white characters indicate boldfaced text and the blue characters
indicate underlined text.

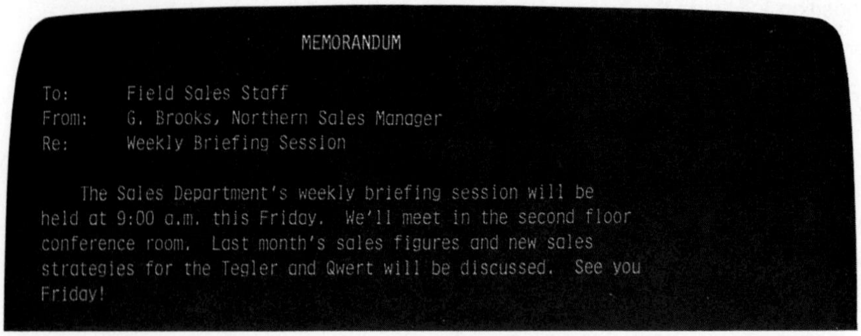

```
                        MEMORANDUM

To:       Field Sales Staff
From:     G. Brooks, Northern Sales Manager
Re:       Weekly Briefing Session

    The Sales Department's weekly briefing session will be
held at 9:00 a.m. this Friday.  We'll meet in the second floor
conference room.  Last month's sales figures and new sales
strategies for the Tegler and Qwert will be discussed.  See you
Friday!
```

MEMORANDUM

```
To:       Field Sales Staff
From:     G. Brooks, Northern Sales Manager
Re:       Weekly Briefing Session

    The Sales Department's weekly briefing session will be
held at 9:00 a.m. this Friday.  We'll meet in the second floor
conference room.  Last month's sales figures and new sales
strategies for the Tegler and Qwert will be discussed.  See you
Friday!
```

FIGURE 14–8 Word Processing: Printing Text
The memo of Figure 14–7 is printed on letterhead paper.

line parts of the text for emphasis. In the memo of Figure 14–7, highlighting the word "MEMORANDUM" as boldface causes it to appear in boldface print on output (see Figure 14–8). By highlighting the sentence "See you Friday!" as underlined text, it is underlined on output (see Figure 14–8). On color monitors, highlighted words usually appear on the screen in a different color (see Figure 14–7). Some word processing systems display text that is to be in boldface type or underlined on output in reverse video. Systems with high-resolution monitors permit text to be displayed in boldface and underlined directly on the display screen.

To enhance the appearance of a document, some people like to *justify* (line up) both the left and the right margins, like the print in newspapers and in this book. Word processing software is able to produce "clean" margins on both sides by adding small spaces between characters and words in a line. Traditionally, a *ragged right* margin is preferred for letters and memos, so George did not right-justify the memo (see Figure 14–8). Right and left justification is illustrated in Figure 14–9.

In creating the memo of Figure 14–8, George Brooks used many but not all the features available to enhance appearance and readability. He did not need the features that allow him to *indent* a block of text, to automatically print *header* and *trailer labels*, or to automatically number the pages (*pagination* feature). On long reports, George usually repeats the report title at the top of each page (header label) and numbers each page at the bottom (pagination). These and other word processing features are illustrated in Figure 14–9.

File Features   Certainly one of the most important features of a word processing package is the ability to store a document on disk for later recall. The stored version of a document is referred to as a *text file*. The *file* feature permits you to save, retrieve, and delete a text file. At a minimum, most word processing systems provide users with the *save*, *retrieve*, and *delete* file options. No matter which option you choose, you are asked by the system to identify the file (document). You then enter an arbitrary name that in some way identifies the

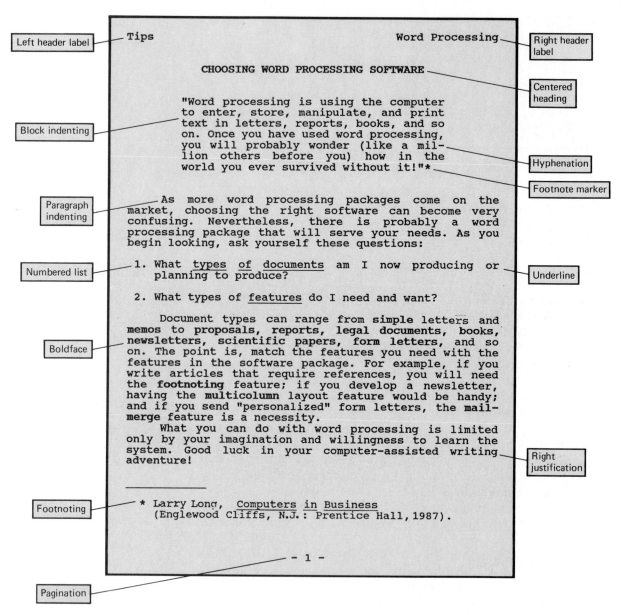

Left header label — Tips

Right header label — Word Processing

CHOOSING WORD PROCESSING SOFTWARE

Centered heading

"Word processing is using the computer to enter, store, manipulate, and print text in letters, reports, books, and so on. Once you have used word processing, you will probably wonder (like a million others before you) how in the world you ever survived without it!"*

Block indenting

Hyphenation

Footnote marker

Paragraph indenting — As more word processing packages come on the market, choosing the right software can become very confusing. Nevertheless, there is probably a word processing package that will serve your needs. As you begin looking, ask yourself these questions:

Numbered list

1. What <u>types</u> <u>of</u> <u>documents</u> am I now producing or planning to produce?

2. What types of <u>features</u> do I need and want?

Underline

Document types can range from **simple** letters and **memos** to **proposals, reports, legal documents, books, newsletters, scientific papers, form letters,** and so on. The point is, match the features you need with the features in the software package. For example, if you write articles that require references, you will need the **footnoting** feature; if you develop a newsletter, having the **multicolumn** layout feature would be handy; and if you send "personalized" form letters, the **mail-merge** feature is a necessity.

Boldface

What you can do with word processing is limited only by your imagination and willingness to learn the system. Good luck in your computer-assisted writing adventure!

Right justification

Footnoting — * Larry Long, <u>Computers</u> <u>in</u> <u>Business</u> (Englewood Cliffs, N.J.: Prentice Hall, 1987).

Pagination — - 1 -

FIGURE 14–9 Word Processing: Features Overview

Many of the more common capabilities of word processing software are illustrated in this printout of a text file.

document (for example, "MEMO"). To retrieve or delete an existing file, enter the file name of an existing file.

George Brooks "saved" his memo (stored it on disk) under the file name MEMO because he was planning a similar meeting next week at the same time and place to discuss sales and strategies for Farkles and Stibs. Because he already had prepared the memo of Figure 14–7, all he would have to do to prepare a memo to announce next week's meeting would be to retrieve the MEMO file and change the phrase "Tegler and Qwert" to "Farkle and Stib".

With a line of over 500 products, this manufacturing sales representative keeps product information handy in the form of word processing documents. He uses on-screen displays of product information during customer presentations.

Printing a Document   To print a document, all you have to do is ready the printer (turn it on and align the paper) and select the print option on the main menu. Some word processing systems present you with a few final options. For example, you can chose to print the document as single- or double-spaced, or you are given the option of printing specific pages or the whole document. Depending on the type of software and printer you have, you may even be able to mix the size and style of type fonts in a single document. For example, George could print the word "MEMORANDUM" in 48-point (about ½-inch high) old English print if he wanted to.

Most word processing packages are **WYSIWYG** (pronounced *WIZ-e-wig*), which is short for "What you see is what you get." That is, what you see on the screen is what the document will look like when it is printed. Other word processing packages use embedded commands within the text of the document (for example, *indent 5 spaces*). These packages usually have a *preview* feature that permits you to format and display the document as it would appear when printed.

Advanced Features   The features discussed in this section are available with the more sophisticated word processing packages. For example, some word processing software contains sophisticated features for writers. A simple command creates a *table of contents* with page references for the first-level headings. An alphabetical *index of key words* can be compiled that lists the page numbers for each occurrence of designated words. One of the most tedious typing chores, *footnoting*, is done automatically (see Figure 14–9). Footnote spacing is resolved electronically before anything is printed. Another feature permits a *multicolumn output* (for example, one or more columns of text on a single page). The *hyphenation* feature automatically breaks and hyphenates words that fall at the end of the line on output (see Figure 14–9).

Add-on Capabilities   A number of software programs are designed to enhance the functionality of word processing programs. These add-on capabilities are usually separate programs that can interface with a word processing package. They can be purchased separately or as part of a word processing package.

Have you ever been writing and been unable to put your finger on the right word? Some word processing packages have an **on-line thesaurus**! Suppose that you have just written: *The Grand Canyon certainly is beautiful*. But *beautiful* is not quite the right word. Your electronic thesaurus is always ready with suggestions: *pretty, elegant, exquisite, angelic, pulchritudinous, ravishing*, and so on.

If spelling is a problem, then word processing is the answer. Once you have entered the text and formatted the document the way you want it, you can call on the **spelling checker** capability. The spelling checker checks every word in the text against an **electronic dictionary** (usually from 75,000 to 150,000 words) and alerts you if a word is not in the dictionary. Upon finding an unidentified word, the spell function will normally give you several options.

1. You can correct the spelling.
2. You can ignore the word and continue scanning the text. Normally you do this when a word is spelled correctly but is not in the dictionary (for example, a company name such as Zimco).
3. You can ask for possible spellings. The spell function then gives you a list of words of similar spelling from which to choose. For example, upon finding the nonword *persors*, the spell function might suggest: *person, persona, persons, personal*, and *personnel*.
4. You can add the word to the dictionary and continue scanning. George Brooks would probably add the word *Zimco* to his dictionary.

Grammar and style checkers are the electronic version of a copy editor. A **grammar checker** highlights grammatical concerns and deviations from conventions. For example, it highlights split infinitives, phrases with redundant words (*very highest*), misuse of capital letters (*JOhn or MarY*), subject and verb mismatches (*they was*), double words (*and and*), and punctuation errors. A **style checker** alerts users to such writing concerns as sexist words or phrases (*chairman*), long or complex sentence structures, clichés (*the bottom line*), and sentences written in the passive rather than the active voice.

Like word processing software, an **idea processor** permits the manipulation of text, but with a different twist. It deals with one-line explanations of items: ideas, points, notes, things, and so on. Idea processors, which are also called **outliners**, can be used to organize

The display shows what happens when WordPerfect's spelling checker detects a misspelled word (*Sals* in the first line of the document). Alternative spellings are listed below the word processing document. The user simply enters option V (*sales*) to replace *Sals* with *Sales*.

```
                        MEMORANDUM

    To:       Field Sals Staff
    From:     G. Brooks, Northern Sales Manager
    Re:       Weekly Briefing Session

       The Sales Department's weekly briefing session will be
    held at 9:00 a.m. this Friday. We'll meet in the second floor
    conference room. Last month's sales figures and new sales
    =====================================================

    A. saes           B. sags           C. sails
    D. sale           E. sales          F. salk
    G. salsa          H. salt           I. salts
    J. sans           K. saps           L. sass
    M. sats           N. saws           O. says
    P. seals          Q. cellist        R. cellos
    S. cellose        T. cells          U. sails
    V. sales          W. sallies        X. seals

    Not Found!   Select Word or Menu Option (0=Continue); 0
    1 Skip Once; 2 Skip; 3 Add Word; 4 Edit; 5 Look Up; 6 Phonetic
```

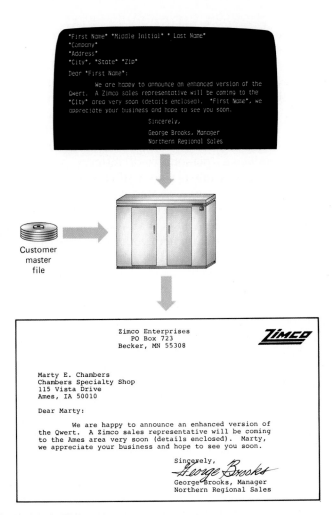

FIGURE 14–10   Merging Data with Word Processing
The names and addresses from a customer master file are retrieved
from secondary storage and are merged with the text of a letter. In the actual letter,
the appropriate data items are inserted for *First Name*, *Company*, *Address*,
City, and so on. In this way, a "personalized" letter can be sent to each customer.

these single-line items into an outline format. Some people have referred to the idea processor as an electronic version of the yellow
notepad. When you use it, you can focus your attention on the thought
process by letting the computer help document your ideas.

Use

You can create just about any kind of text-based document with word
processing: letters, reports, books, articles, forms, memos, tables, and
so on. The features of some word processing packages go beyond the
generation of text documents, however. For example, some word processing systems provide the capability of merging parts of the data
base with the text of the document. An example of this *mail merge*
application is illustrated in Figure 14–10. In the example, Zimco En-

terprises announced the enhanced version of its Qwert. Each regional sales manager sent a "personal" letter to every one of the thousands of Zimco customers in his or her respective region. Using word processing, a secretary can enter the letter once, store it on the disk, then simply merge the customer name-and-address file (also stored on the disk) with the letter. The letters can then print with the proper addresses and salutations. Figure 14–10 illustrates how the Qwert announcement letter could be merged with the customer name-and-address file to produce a "personalized" letter.

The mail merge example is a good illustration of the use of **boilerplate**. Boilerplate is existing text that can in some way be customized to be used in a variety of word processing applications. One of the beauties of word processing is that you can accumulate text on disk storage that will eventually help you meet other word processing needs. You can even *buy* boilerplate.

The legal profession offers some of the best examples of the use of boilerplate. Simple wills, uncontested divorces, individual bankruptcies, real estate transfers, and other straightforward legal documents may be as much as 95% boilerplate. Even more complex legal documents may be as much as 80% boilerplate. Once the appropriate boilerplate has been merged into a document, the lawyer edits the document to add transition sentences and the variables, such as the names of the litigants. Besides the obvious improvement in productivity, lawyers can be relatively confident that their documents are accurate and complete. Lawyers, of course, do not have a monopoly on boilerplate. Its use is common in all areas of business, education, government, and personal endeavor.

Word processing is the perfect example of how automation can be used to increase productivity and foster creativity. It minimizes the effort you must devote to the routine aspects of writing so you can focus your attention on its creative aspects. Most word processing users will agree that their writing styles have improved measurably. The finished product is less verbose, better organized, devoid of spelling errors, and of course, more visually appealing.

14–3 Desktop Publishing

Function

The ultimate extension of word processing is *desktop publishing*. In fact, some are calling desktop publishing software the next generation of word processing software. Desktop publishing refers to the capability of producing *near-typeset-quality copy* from the confines of a desktop. The concept of desktop publishing is changing the way companies, government agencies, and individuals approach printing newsletters, brochures, user manuals, pamphlets, restaurant menus, periodicals, greeting cards, and thousands of other items.

Desktop publishing software certainly has captured the attention of the business community. Not only can users bypass the expense of professional typesetting and page layout, they can drastically reduce the time needed to prepare a camera-ready document. In the photo, a designer is creating an ad piece. To do this, he is using a microcomputer with a keyboard and mouse for input and a laser printer in conjunction with PageMaker, a desktop publishing software package.

Concepts

Traditionally, drafts of documents to be printed are delivered to commercial printers to be typeset. Desktop publishing has made it possible to eliminate this expensive typesetting process for those documents that required only near-typeset quality. In practice, near-typeset-quality copy is acceptable for most printed documents. Relatively few need to be prepared using the expensive commercial phototypesetting process. The output of the desktop publishing process is called *camera-ready copy*. Duplicates of the camera-ready copy are reproduced by a variety of means, from duplicating machines to commercial offset printing.

The primary components required for desktop publishing are *desktop publishing software*, a *microcomputer*, and a *laser printer*. The more sophisticated desktop publishing environments include *image processors* (see Chapter 11, "Applications of Information Technology") that can be used to digitize images, such as photographs. Image processors, also called *scanners*, re-create a black-and-white version of text or an image (photograph or line drawing) in an electronic format that can be manipulated and reproduced under computer control. Desktop publishing software is essentially sophisticated word processing software (all the capabilities described in the previous section of this chapter) plus *page-composition software*. The page-composition software enables users to design and make up pages.

The page makeup process involves integrating graphics, photos, text, and other elements into a visually appealing *page layout*. Besides the positioning of the elements, the user must also select the desired mix of type sizes and fonts.

Use

Desktop publishing software is being employed to produce the copy for every conceivable type of printed matter, from graduation certificates to full-length books. One problem with desktop publishing is that the capability of producing camera-ready documents is now available to a large number of people, many of whom do not have the artistic skills needed to produce aesthetically pleasing and functionally readable copy. Recognizing this, many companies are adopting standards and policies that apply to all copy that contains the company logo and is released to the public.

14–4 Communications Software

Function

Communications software makes the microcomputer more than a small stand-alone computer. With it, a micro can transmit and receive data to and from a remote computer. Communications software automatically *dials up* a remote computer (another micro or a mainframe) and then *logs on* (establishes a link with a remote computer). Once on-line, you can communicate and share data with a remote computer.

After logging on, communications software allows you to download files; that is, you can request and receive data or program files transmitted from a remote computer. Once the files have been downloaded to your micro, you can select any of the microcomputer productivity tools to work with the files. Once processing is complete, you can use the communications software to upload the file to a remote computer.

Concepts

You can use communications software to link your microcomputer via telephone lines to another computer system anywhere in the world. To do this, however, your micro must be equipped with a *modem*. The

You can use your personal computer and an information network to send flowers. To do so, you would make a selection from available arrangements, enter the name and address of the receiving party, and enter your credit card number. The system uses the destination ZIP code to search a file for the nearest participating florist. Once identified, your request is routed via data communications directly to the florist.

Combine words, graphics, imagination, creativity, software, and hardware and what do you have? You have the makings of desktop publishing, one of the hottest applications of computer technology. People in virtually every business endeavor are designing, creating, and producing more and more of their printed materials in-house. Before desktop publishing, businesses submitted drafts of their ads, memos, manuals, brochures, and so on to professional typesetters as a matter of routine. Desktop publishing has eliminated this costly and time-consuming process for many printed items.

PageMaker, a product of Aldus Corporation, is one of today's popular desktop publishing software packages. With PageMaker, you can produce finished, professional-looking documents in four steps.

1. *Prepare text and graphics*. Use your word processing software to create and edit the text of your document. For illustrations and graphics you can use electronic clip art (prepackaged electronic images), computer-created graphics (such as a pie graph), or scanned images (photos).
2. *Develop a format*. By using PageMaker's master page feature, you can define margins, set the number of columns and column widths, and add design elements to design the format for each page of the document.
3. *Place graphics in text*. With PageMaker's "Place" command, you can adjust the position of the text and resize your graphics to fit your needs. The display is WYSIWYG, that is, "What you see is what you

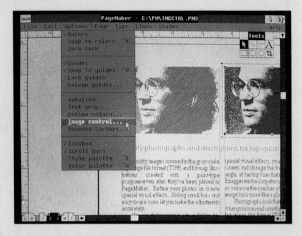

This display illustrates a representative screen that a user might encounter during a PageMaker session. Notice the contrast between the two images. The dot pattern in the images can be modified to achieve special visual effects. A pull-down menu is superimposed over the WYSIWYG display.

get" when the document is printed. If what you see is not what you want, then you can use the mouse to reposition text and graphics to the desired locations.
4. *Print the document*. Once the WYSIWYG display is as you would like it to appear, use a laser printer to produce the finished camera-ready copy.

modem links your micro with the telephone line that connects the two computers. On most microcomputers, the modem is an optional plug-in circuit board. You can purchase it with your micro, or you can add it later as the need arises. A modem can also be purchased as a separate unit and connected to the micro with an electrical cable.

In essence, communications software enables your micro to emulate any one of a number of popular terminals. To do this, you need to specify certain data communications parameters, such as the type of terminal you plan to emulate, whether or not parity bits are to be added, the number of stop bits used, the rate of data transmission (300 to 9600 baud), and so on. (Data communications concepts are discussed in Chapter 7, "Connectivity and Data Communications.")

Communications software can be set up so it automatically dials up and logs on to frequently accessed computer systems. It will even redial if a busy signal is detected. A micro with a modem and communications software can be on the receiving end as well—it can automatically answer "calls" from other computers.

One very handy feature of communications software is that it enables you to record on a disk file all input/output during an interactive session. At a later time you can recall the session from disk storage and browse through it at a more leisurely pace. The information gathered during an interactive session can be integrated into a word processing document, such as a letter or report.

Use

Information Networks   With a microcomputer and data communications software, users have a world of information at their fingertips. A growing trend among microcomputer users is to subscribe to the services of an **information network**. A few of the more popular commercial information networks are CompuServe, The Source, Dow Jones, Western Union, and NewsNet. These information networks consist of one or several large computer systems that offer a variety of information services from hotel reservations to daily horoscopes. The user normally pays a one-time fee. For it, the user gets an account number that will permit him or her to establish a link with the network. Billing is based on usage of network services.

The following list summarizes the types of entertainment, information, and services available through information networks:

Home banking.   Check account balances, transfer money, and pay bills in the comfort of the office or home.

News, weather, and sports.   Get the latest releases directly from the wire services.

Games.   Access hundreds of single and multiplayer games. Users can even play games with friends in other states!

Financial information.   Get up-to-the-minute quotes on stocks, bonds, options, and commodities.

As a subscriber to an information network, this scientist can use key words to scan the text of the most recent medical journals to see if anything has been written that might have some impact on the direction of his research. For example, he can ask the system to identify all articles published in the *New England Journal of Medicine* during the past year that reference epinephrine; then he can request the full text of the articles.

This prospective home buyer logged into an information network and asked to see homes in the northeast part of town that are no more than three blocks from school, have a double garage, are all-electric, and have an asking price between $150,000 and $250,000. A picture of the house and all pertinent data are displayed for all homes that meet her criteria.

Bulletin boards. Use special-interest electronic bulletin boards as a forum for the exchange of ideas and information. The largest information network, CompuServe, now has over 200,000 subscribers. Its closest rival is The Source. CompuServe has over 100 bulletin boards to choose from on topics ranging from graphics showing the FBI's most wanted fugitives to gardening, to astrology, to IBM personal computers. There are thousands of privately sponsored **bulletin board systems** (**BBSs**). One in Denver is devoted to parapsychology. Some senators sponsor BBSs to communicate with their constituents. Other BBSs are devoted to religion.

Electronic mail. Send and receive mail to and from other network users. Each subscriber is assigned an ID and an electronic mailbox. To retrieve mail, the subscriber must enter a secret password.

Shop at home. Select what you want from a list of thousands of items offered at discount prices. Payment is made via electronic funds transfer (EFT), and orders are delivered to your doorstep.

Reference. Look up items of interest in an electronic encyclopedia. Scan through various government publications. Recall articles on a particular subject.

Education. Choose from a variety of educational packages, from learning arithmetic to preparing for the Scholastic Aptitude Test. A user can even determine his or her IQ!

Real estate. Check out available real estate by scanning the listings for the city to which you may be moving.

Travel. Plan your own vacation or business trip by checking airline schedules and making your own reservations. You can even charter a yacht in the Caribbean or rent a lodge in the Rockies.

Local Electronic Bulletin Boards   Just about every city with a population of 25,000 or more has at least one *electronic bulletin board*, often sponsored by a local computer club. Members "post" messages, announcements, for-sale notices, and so on by transmitting them to a central computer, usually another micro. To scan the bulletin board, members again use communications software to link up to the central computer.

Telecommuting and Cottage Industries   In the coming years we'll probably see a shift to smaller briefcases. With communications software and an ever-growing number of home computers, people won't need to lug their paperwork between home and office every day. For a great many white-collar workers at all levels, much of their work is on computers. Continuing their work at home is simply a matter of establishing a link between their home and office computers. This is sometimes referred to as **telecommuting**. In the future, many white-collar workers will elect to telecommute at least one day a week.

The world has been made a little more compact with the computer revolution. The combination of microcomputers and communications software has fueled the growth of *cottage industries*. Stockbrokers, financial planners, writers, programmers, and people from a wide variety of professions may not need to "go to the office." They can live wherever they choose. Micros make it possible for them to access needed information, communicate with their clients, and even deliver products of their work (for example, programs, stories, or recommendations).

Summary Outline and Important Terms

14–1   THE MICROCOMPUTER FAMILY OF PRODUCTIVITY SOFTWARE.   The primary microcomputer productivity software tools include: **word processing**, **desktop publishing**, communications, **electronic spreadsheet**, **presentation graphics**, and **database** software. In contrast to software designed for a specific application, these and other productivity software packages are general purpose and provide the framework for a great number of business and personal applications.

14–2   WORD PROCESSING.   Word processing is using the computer to enter, store, manipulate, and print text in letters, reports, books, and so on.

When you format a document, you are describing the size of the print page and how you want the document to look when it is printed. Text is entered and edited in **replace mode** or **insert mode**. **Word wrap** is when text that extends past the defined margins automatically wraps around to the next line. Word processing permits full-screen editing.

The block move, the block copy, and the block delete commands are known collectively as block operations, the electronic equivalent of "cut and paste." The search, or find, feature permits the user to search through the entire word processing document and identify all occurrences of a particular character string.

Word processing has several features that enable users

to enhance the appearance and readability of their documents. These include automatic centering, boldface, underlining, right and left justification, indentation, header and trailer labels, pagination, and mixing type fonts.

All word processing packages permit users to save, retrieve, and delete files that contain word processing documents. The print function transforms your electronic document into a hard copy document.

The more sophisticated word processing packages have some or all of the following advanced features: footnoting, hyphenation, numbered lists, table of contents, indexing, and multicolumn output.

Several add-on programs are designed to enhance the functionality of word processing programs. An **on-line thesaurus** is always ready with synonyms for any word in a word processing document. The **spelling checker** program checks every word in the text against an **electronic dictionary** and alerts the user when a word is not in the dictionary. A **grammar checker** highlights grammatical concerns and deviations from conventions. A **style checker** alerts users to such writing concerns as sexist words and hackneyed cliches. **Idea processors**, or **outliners**, can be used to organize single-line items into an outline format.

Any kind of text-based document can be created with word processing software. **Boilerplate** is existing text that can in some way be customized so it can be used in a variety of word processing applications (for example, mail merge).

14–3 DESKTOP PUBLISHING. The ultimate extension of word processing is desktop publishing. Desktop publishing refers to the capability of producing near-typeset-quality copy from the confines of a desktop. The primary components required for desktop publishing are desktop publishing software, a microcomputer, and a laser printer. The more sophisticated desktop publishing environments include scanners that can be used to digitize images, such as photographs.

14–4 COMMUNICATIONS SOFTWARE. With communications software, a micro can transmit and receive data to and from a remote computer. Communications software provides the capability of automatically dialing up a remote computer and then logging on. Once on-line, the user can communicate and share data with a remote computer via the downloading and uploading of files. To use communications software, micros must be equipped with modems.

A growing trend among microcomputer users is to subscribe to the services of an **information network**. These information networks have large computer systems that offer a variety of information services.

By combining micros with communications software people can telecommute to their jobs or work in cottage industries.

Review Exercises

Concepts

1. What is the function of word processing software?
2. What must be specified when formatting a document?
3. What is meant when a document is formatted to be right and left justified?
4. Text is entered in either of what two modes? What mode would you select to change *the table* to *the long table*? What mode would you select to change *pick the choose* to *pick and choose*?
5. What causes text to wrap around?
6. Give an example of when you might issue a global search-and-replace command.
7. Name four of the six microcomputer productivity software tools that comprise the foundation of personal computing.
8. When running the spell function, what options does the system present when it encounters an unidentified word?
9. What productivity software package provides the capability of producing near-typeset-quality copy for printing jobs?
10. What are three primary components of desktop publishing?
11. What is the function of communications software?
12. Why is a modem needed to upload data via telephone lines?
13. Some communications software has automatic dial and redial capabilities. Describe these capabilities.

Discussion

14. Most word processing packages have a default document size. Discuss other defaults you might expect a word processing package to have.
15. The five PCs in the purchasing department of a large consumer goods manufacturer are used primarily for word processing and data base applications. What would be the benefits and burdens associated with connecting the PCs in a local area network?
16. Customer service representatives at Zimco Enterprises spend almost 70% of their day interacting directly with customers. Approximately one hour each day is spent preparing courtesy follow-up letters, primarily to enhance goodwill between Zimco and its customers. Do you think the "personalized" letters are a worthwhile effort? Why or why not?
17. Describe the relationship between word processing, presentation graphics, and desktop publishing software.
18. Discuss the emerging role of personal computers in electronic funds transfer.

19. Why would you download data? Upload data?

20. One popular information service is home banking. Describe an interactive session with at least one transaction involving both a checking and a savings account. Begin from the time you turn on your microcomputer.

Self-Test (by section)

14–1 Most of the new commercially available expert systems are being created for personal computers. (T/F)

14–2 **a.** The _____ line in a word processing document provides information on format specifications.

    b. To add a word in the middle of an existing sentence in a word processing document, you would use the insert mode. (T/F)

    c. Which word processing feature enables the automatic numbering of the pages of a document: (a) pagination, (b) page breaking, or (c) footers?

    d. The advanced word processing feature that automatically breaks long words that fall at the end of a line is called _____.

    e. An on-line thesaurus can be used to suggest synonyms for a word in a word processing document. (T/F)

14–3 **a.** The type of printer normally associated with desktop publishing is the daisy-wheel printer. (T/F)

    b. The output of the desktop publishing process is _____ copy.

    c. What device re-creates a black-and-white version of an image in an electronic format: (a) image processor, (b) image reduction aid, or (c) vision entry device?

14–4 **a.** Communications software enables a micro to emulate (a) a mainframe computer, (b) a color monitor, or (c) a terminal.

    b. The process of transmitting files from a host to a micro is called downloading. (T/F)

    c. A micro with a modem and communications software can make calls to other computers, but it cannot receive calls. (T/F)

    d. Microcomputers and communications software have helped spur the growth of cottage industries. (T/F)

Self-test answers. **14–1** T. **14–2** (a) layout; (b) T; (c) a; (d) hyphenation; (e) T. **14–3** (a) F; (b) camera-ready; (c) a. **14–4** (a) c; (b) T; (c) F; (d) T.

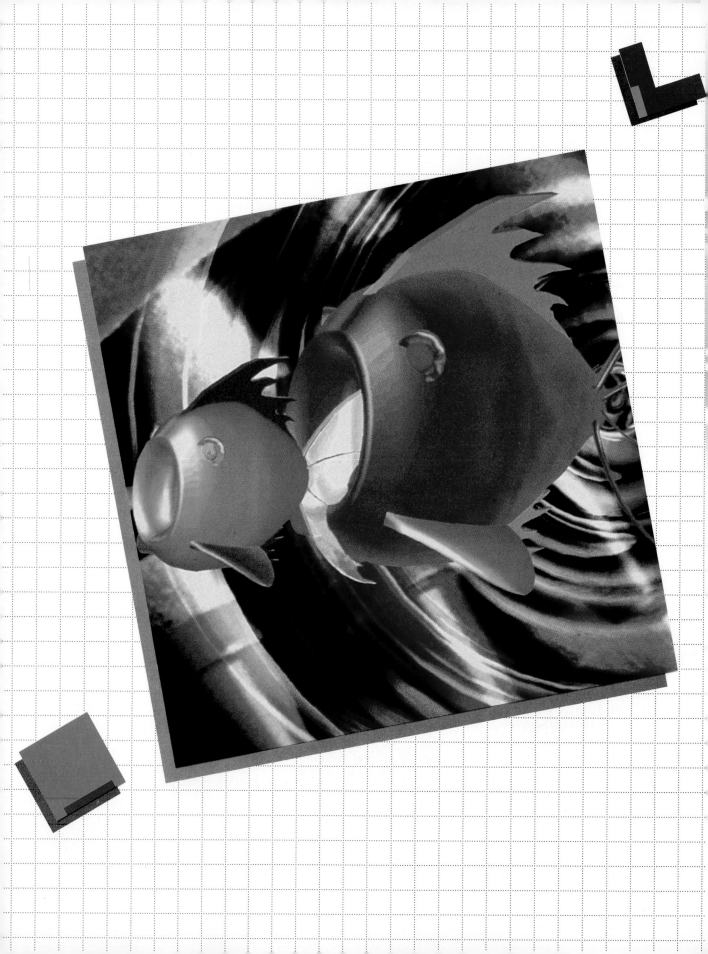

15

Electronic Spreadsheet, Presentation Graphics, and Database Software

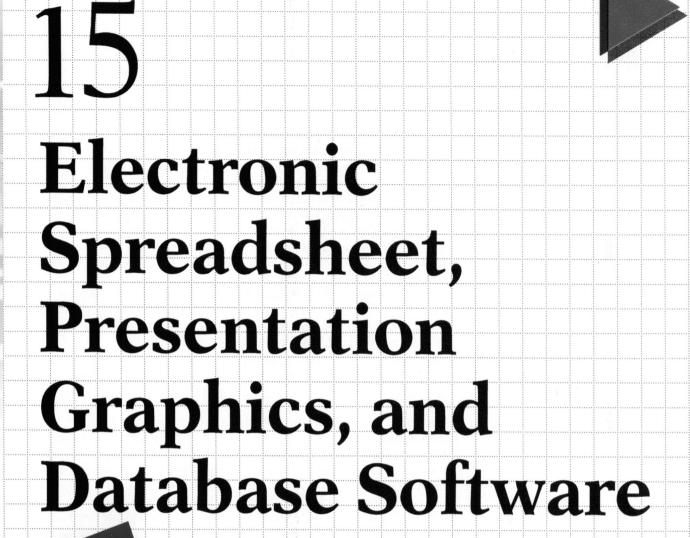

STUDENT LEARNING OBJECTIVES

- To describe the function, purpose, and applications of electronic spreadsheet software.
- To discuss common electronic spreadsheet concepts.
- To describe the function, purpose, and applications of presentation graphics software.
- To discuss common presentation graphics software concepts.
- To describe the function, purpose, and applications of database software.
- To discuss common database software concepts.

The Electronic Spreadsheet

Function

The name *electronic spreadsheet* describes this software's fundamental application. The spreadsheet has been a common business tool for centuries. Before computers, the ledger (a spreadsheet) was the accountant's primary tool for keeping the books. Professors' grade books are set up in spreadsheet format.

Electronic spreadsheets are simply an electronic alternative to thousands of what have been traditionally manual tasks. No longer are we confined to using pencils, erasers, and hand calculators to deal with rows and columns of data. Think of anything that has rows and columns of data and you have identified an application for spreadsheet software. For example, how about income (profit and loss) statements, personnel profiles, demographic data, and budget summaries—to mention a few? Because electronic spreadsheets so closely resemble many of our manual tasks, they are enjoying widespread acceptance.

All commercially available electronic spreadsheet packages provide the facility for manipulating rows and columns of data. However, the *user interface*, or the manner in which the user enters data and commands, differs from one package to the next. The conceptual coverage that follows is generic and applies to all electronic spreadsheets.

Concepts

The example we will use to illustrate and demonstrate electronic spreadsheet concepts is the Zimco Enterprises income statement. Monroe Green, the vice president of finance and accounting at Zimco, often uses an electronic spreadsheet **template** of Zimco's income statements for the past two years to do financial planning. The template, which is simply a spreadsheet model, contains a column that allows him to produce a pro rata income statement for next year (see Figure 15–1). In Figure 15–1, the actual income statement is shown on the first screen. The second screen displays the variables used to produce

For the last several years, this product manager spent one hour each week tallying regional sales figures. He finally spent five hours creating an electronic spreadsheet model to help with this task. Now his weekly sales reports take only 15 minutes, and they are more accurate. There are many applications for electronic spreadsheet software in every office.

```
C4: 153000
          A                    B          C          D
1 ==========================================================================
2 ZIMCO INCOME STATEMENT ($1000)  Next Year   This Year   Last Year
3 --------------------------------------------------------------------------
4 Net sales                   $183,600   $153,000   $144,780
5 Cost of sales & op. expenses
6    Cost of goods sold        116,413    115,260    117,345
7    Depreciation               4,125      4,125      1,500
8    Selling & admin. expenses 19,875     19,875     15,000
9                             ------------------------------
10      Operating profit       $43,187    $13,740    $10,935
11 Other income
12    Dividends and interest      405        405        300
13                             ------------------------------
14      TOTAL INCOME           $43,592    $14,145    $11,235
15 Less: interest on bonds      2,025      2,025      2,025
16                             ------------------------------
17 Income before tax           41,567     12,120      9,210
18 Provision for income tax    18,777      5,475      4,160
19                             ------------------------------
20    NET PROFIT FOR YEAR      $22,790     $6,645     $5,050
```

```
A34:  'FORECAST VARIABLES FOR NEXT YEAR'S PRO RATA INCOME STATEMENT
          A                    B          C          D
21 ==========================================================================
22
23
24
25
26
27
28
29
30
31
32
33 ==========================================================================
34 FORECAST VARIABLES FOR NEXT YEAR'S PRO RATA INCOME STATEMENT
35 --------------------------------------------------------------------------
36 Projected change in sales                        20.00%
37 Projected change in cost of goods sold            1.00%
38 Projected change in administrative expenses       0.00%
39 ==========================================================================
40
```

FIGURE 15–1   Electronic Spreadsheet: A Pro Rata Income Statement Template
This electronic spreadsheet template (both screens) is the basis for the explanation and demonstration of spreadsheet concepts. The "Next Year" pro rata income statement is extrapolated from the data in the "This Year" income statement and the values of forecast variables.

". . . and this computer monitor is designed especially for spreadsheets."

the pro rata income statement for next year. In Figure 15–1, Monroe projected sales, cost of goods sold, and administrative expenses to be 20%, 1%, and 0%, respectively.

Viewing Data in a Spreadsheet Scrolling through a spreadsheet is much like looking through a magnifying glass as you move it around a newspaper page. You scroll left and right (horizontal scrolling) and/ or up and down (vertical scrolling) to see different portions of a large spreadsheet. For example, because only 20 lines of the spreadsheet template in Figure 15–1 can be displayed at once, Monroe Green must *page up* or *page down* to see all of this spreadsheet.

What if the spreadsheet template in Figure 15–1 reflected data for the past five years? Because the screen on the monitor can display only a certain amount of information, Monroe would need to scroll horizontally through the spreadsheet to view the first three years.

Organization Electronic spreadsheets are organized in a *tabular structure* with **rows** and **columns**. The intersection of a particular row and column designates a **cell**. As you can see in Figure 15–1, the rows are *numbered* and the columns are *lettered*. Single letters identify the first 26 columns; double letters are used thereafter (A, B, . . . , Z, AA, AB, . . . , AZ, BA, BB, . . . , BZ). The number of rows or columns available to you depends on the size of your micro's RAM (random-access memory). Most spreadsheets permit hundreds of columns and thousands of rows.

Data are entered and stored in a cell, the intersection of a column and a row. During operations, data are referenced by their **cell address**. A cell address identifies the location of a cell in the spreadsheet by its column and row, with the column designator first. For example, in the income statement of Figure 15–1, C2 is the address of the column heading "This Year," and C4 is the address of net sales amount for this year ($153,000).

In the spreadsheet work area (the rows and columns), a movable highlighted area "points" to the *current cell*. This highlighted area, called the **pointer**, can be moved around the spreadsheet with the cursor control keys to any cell address. To add or edit an entry at a particular cell, the pointer must be moved to that cell. The address and content of the current cell (location of the pointer) are displayed in the user interface portion of the spreadsheet, the area above and/ or below the spreadsheet work area. Specifically, this information is displayed in a *cell status line* (C4 and A34 in Figure 15–1). The content or resultant value (for example, from a formula) of each cell is shown in the spreadsheet work area. The current cell is displayed in reverse video (black on white or, for color monitors, black on a color). Also notice in Figure 15–1 that when the pointer is positioned at C4, the actual numeric value (153000) is displayed as the cell contents in the user interface, and an optional *edited* version ($153,000) is displayed in Cell C4.

Cell Entries To make an entry in the spreadsheet, simply move the pointer with the cursor control keys to the appropriate cell and key in the data. To *edit* or replace an existing entry, you also move the pointer to the appropriate cell. Key in the new or revised entry in the user interface panel beside the cell address (see Figure 15–1). Once you have completed work on a particular entry, press the ENTER key or a cursor control key to insert the entry in the actual spreadsheet.

Spreadsheet packages allow the user to vary the column width to improve readability. The width for Column A in Figure 15–1 is set at 30 positions, and the width for Columns B, C, and D is set at 15 positions.

Ranges Many electronic spreadsheet operations ask you to designate a **range** of cells. The four types of ranges are highlighted in Figure 15–2:

1. A single cell. (Example range is B12.)
2. All or part of a column of adjacent cells. (Example range is A17..A20.)
3. All or part of a row of adjacent cells. (Example range is B2..D2.)
4. A rectangular block of cells. (Example range is B6..D8.)

A particular range is indicated by the addresses of the endpoint cells and separated by two periods. (Some packages use only one period or a colon, for example: C6.D8, C6:D8.) Any cell can comprise a single cell range. The range for the total income amounts in Figure 15–2 is

FIGURE 15–2 Electronic Spreadsheet: Ranges
The four types of ranges are highlighted: cell (B12), column (A17..A20), row (B2..D2), and block (B6..D8).

	A	B	C	D
1	===			
2	ZIMCO INCOME STATEMENT ($1000)	Next Year	This Year	Last Year
3	--			
4	Net sales	$183,600	$153,000	$144,780
5	Cost of sales & op. expenses			
6	Cost of goods sold	116,413	115,260	117,345
7	Depreciation	4,125	4,125	1,500
8	Selling & admin. expenses	19,875	19,875	15,000
9		----------------	----------------	----------------
10	Operating profit	$43,187	$13,740	$10,935
11	Other income			
12	Dividends and interest	405	405	300
13		----------------	----------------	----------------
14	TOTAL INCOME	$43,492	$14,145	$11,235
15	Less: interest on bonds	2,025	2,025	2,025
16		----------------	----------------	----------------
17	Income before tax	41,567	12,120	9,210
18	Provision for income tax	18,777	5,475	4,160
19		----------------	----------------	----------------
20	NET PROFIT FOR YEAR	$22,790	$6,645	$5,050

B14..D14, and the range for the row labels is A4..A20. The range of the dollar amounts in the three income statements for "Next Year", "This Year", and "Last Year" data is indicated by any two opposite corner cell addresses (for example, B4..D20 or D4..B20).

The copy operation requires users to define a "copy from" range and a "copy to" range. For example, when the operating profit formula in C10 of Figure 15–1 was copied to the adjacent cell in the "Last Year" column, C10 was defined as the "copy from" range, and D10 was the "copy to" range. When you want to move or erase a portion of the spreadsheet, you first define the range you wish to move or erase.

Text and Formula Entries   An entry to a cell is classified as either a *text* (also called *label*) entry, a *numeric* entry, or a *formula* entry. Strictly *numeric* entries fall under the formula heading in some spreadsheet programs. In Figure 15–1, the values in C4 and D4 are numeric. A text entry, or a label, is a word, phrase, or any string of alphanumeric text (spaces included) that occupies a particular cell. In Figure 15–1, "This Year" in Cell C2 is a text entry, as is "Net Sales" in A4 and "FORECAST VARIABLES FOR NEXT YEAR'S PRO RATA INCOME STATEMENT" in A34. Notice that the label in A34 extends across Columns B and C. If an entry were made in B34, only the first 30 positions, or the width of Column A, would be visible on the spreadsheet (for example, "FORECAST VARIABLES FOR NEXT YE").

Unless otherwise specified, numeric entries are right-justified (lined up on the right), and text entries are left-justified. However, you can specify that entries be left- or right-justified, or centered in the column.

Cells C10 and C14 contain formulas, but it is the numeric results (for example, $13,740 and $14,145) that are displayed in the spreadsheet. The formula value of C10 (see Figure 15–3) computes the operating profit (for example, net sales less the cost of sales and operating expenses or $+C4-C6-C7-C8$). With the pointer positioned at C10, the formula appears in the cell contents line in the user interface panel, and the actual numeric value appears in the spreadsheet work area (see Figure 15–3).

Spreadsheet formulas use standard notation for **arithmetic operators**: + (add), − (subtract), * (multiply), / (divide), ^ (raising to a power, or exponentiation). The formula contained in C10 (top of Figure 15–3) computes the operating profit for "This Year". Compare this formula:

$$+C4-C6-C7-C8$$

to the formula in Cell D10:

$$+D4-D6-D7-D8$$

The formulas are similar, but the first formula references those amounts in Column C, and the second formula references those amounts in Column D. Therefore, the formula contained in Cell D10 computes the operating profit for "Last Year".

```
C10: +C4-C6-C7-C8
```

	A	B	C	D
1	============================			
2	ZIMCO INCOME STATEMENT ($1000)	Next Year	This Year	Last Year
3	----------------------------			
4	Net sales	$183,600	$153,000	$144,780
5	Cost of sales & op. expenses			
6	Cost of goods sold	116,413	115,260	117,345
7	Depreciation	4,125	4,125	1,500
8	Selling & admin. expenses	19,875	19,875	15,000
9		----------	----------	----------
10	Operating profit	$43,187	$13,740	$10,935

FIGURE 15–3 Electronic Spreadsheet: Formulas
The actual content of C10 is the formula in the user interface panel in the upper left-hand part of the screen. The result of the formula appears in the spreadsheet at C10.

Relative and absolute cell addressing.   The distinction between the way the dollar amounts and the forecast variables are represented in the formulas highlights a very important concept concerning electronic spreadsheets, that of **relative cell addressing** and **absolute cell addressing**. *The relative cell address is based on its position relative to the cell containing the formula.* When you copy, or replicate, a formula to another cell, the relative cell addresses are revised to reflect their new positions in relation to the new location of the formula. The dollar signs ($), which preface both the column and row in an absolute cell address, distinguish it from a relative cell address. When a formula is copied, the absolute cell addresses in the formula remain unchanged.

The two types of cell addressing are illustrated in the spreadsheet in Figure 15–4. Suppose the formula B3∗$E$1 is in Cell A1. B3 is a relative cell address that is one column to the right of and two rows down from A1. If this formula is copied to C2, the formula in C2 is D4∗$E$1. Notice that D4 has the same relative position to the formula in cell C2 as B3 has to the formula in Cell A1: one column to the right

FIGURE 15–4 Electronic Spreadsheet: Relative and Absolute Cell Addressing
When the formula in A1 is copied to C2, the formula in C2 becomes D4∗$E$1.

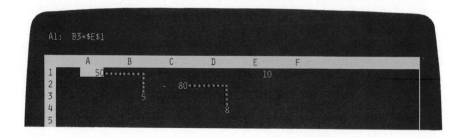

A buyer for a furniture store tracks actual versus planned sales for various classes of furniture with an electronic spreadsheet. This microcomputer permits voice as well as keyboard input.

and two rows down. The absolute cell address ($E$1) remains the same in both formulas.

Notice that Monroe Green used absolute cell addresses for the forecast values. The formulas that compute the "Next Year" values for net sales (B4), cost of goods sold (B6), and selling and administrative expenses (B8) are:

$$B4: \quad +C4*(1+\$C\$36)$$

$$B6: \quad +C6*(1+\$C\$37)$$

$$B8: \quad +C8*(1+\$C\$38)$$

Monroe was thinking ahead. The absolute cell reference would not be required if he did not intend to alter the current form of the spreadsheet template. But the absolute cell references will be needed later when Monroe adds an "After Next" year column. Through judicious use of absolute cell addressing, Monroe has added some flexibility to his spreadsheet template.

Copying formulas. In creating the spreadsheet template for the income statement of Figure 15–1, Monroe Green entered the operating profit formula only once—in C10 (see Figure 15–3). Then spreadsheet commands were selected that *copied*, or *replicated*, the formula into Cell D10. You can see from the results in Figure 15–1 that the exact formula was not copied. Instead, the formula in D10 ($+D4-D6-D7-D8$) manipulates the data in the cells for "Last Year", not "This Year" (as in the formula in C10: $+C4-C6-C7-C8$). The same is true of other formulas that were copied from the "This Year" column to the "Last Year" column.

The formula in C10 references cells that have a relative position to C10, the location of the formula. When the formula in C10 is copied to D10, the electronic spreadsheet software revises these *relative cell addresses* so they apply to a formula that is located in D10. As you can see, the formula in D10 references cells that contain the data for "Last Year".

Each of the three forecast variables (C36..C38) is assigned an absolute cell address. The absolute cell address does not change when a formula in which it appears is copied from row to row or from column to column. The formula in B4 will always reference the forecast variable in cell C36, even if copied to any other location in the spreadsheet.

Creating Spreadsheet Formulas   This section expands on the use and application of formulas—the essence of spreadsheet operations. A formula enables the spreadsheet software to perform numeric and/or string calculations and/or logic operations that result in a numeric value (for example, 13740) or an alphanumeric character string (for example, *ABOVE 25% LIMIT*). A formula may include one or all of the following: *arithmetic operations, functions, string operations,* and *logic operations.* The first two are discussed here in more detail. String operations (for example, joining, or concatenating, character strings) and logic operations (for example, formulas that involve relational and logic operators) are beyond the scope of this presentation.

When you design the spreadsheet, keep in mind where you want to place the formulas and what you want them to accomplish. Because formulas are based on relative position, you will need a knowledge of the layout and organization of the data in the spreadsheet. When you define a formula, you must first determine what you wish to achieve (for example, calculate net profit). Then select a cell location for the formula (for example, C20), and create the formula by connecting relative and absolute cell addresses with operators, as appropriate. In many instances, you will copy the formula to other locations (for example, in Figure 15–1, C20 was copied to D20).

Spreadsheet applications begin with a blank screen and an idea. The spreadsheet you create is a product of skill and imagination. What you get from it depends on how effectively you use formulas.

Arithmetic operations.   Formulas containing arithmetic operators are resolved according to a hierarchy of operations. That is, when more than one operator is included in a single formula, the spreadsheet software uses a set of rules to determine which operation to do first, second, and so on. In the hierarchy of operations, illustrated in Figure 15–5, exponentiation has the highest priority, followed by multiplication-division and addition-subtraction. In the case of a tie (for example, * and /, or + and −), the formula is evaluated from *left to right. Parentheses,* however, override the priority rules. Expressions placed in parentheses have priority and are evaluated innermost first, and left to right.

The formula that results in the value in B4 (183600) of Figure 15–1 is shown below:

$$+C4*(1+\$C\ \$36)$$

FIGURE 15–5   Hierarchy of Operations

The Hierarchy of Operations	
OPERATION	**OPERATOR**
Exponentiation	^
Multiplication-Division	* /
Addition-Subtraction	+ −

	A	B	C	D
1	===			
2	ZIMCO INCOME STATEMENT ($1000)	Next Year	This Year	Last Year
3	---			
4	Net sales	+C4*(1+$C$36)	153000	144780
5	Cost of sales & op. expenses			
6	Cost of goods sold	+C6*(1+$C$37)	115260	117345
7	Depreciation	+C7	4125	1500
8	Selling and admin. expenses	+C8*(1+$C$38)	19875	15000
9		-------------	-------------	-------------
10	Operating profit	+B4-B6-B7-B8	+C4-C6-C7-C8	+D4-D6-D7-D8
11	Other income			
12	Dividends and interest	+C12	405	300
13		-------------	-------------	-------------
14	TOTAL INCOME	+B10+B12	+C10+C12	+D10+D12
15	Less: interest on bonds	+C15	2025	2025
16		-------------	-------------	-------------
17	Income before tax	+B14-B15	+C14-C15	+D14-D15
18	Provision for income tax	(C18/C17)*B17	5475	4160
19		-------------	-------------	-------------
20	NET PROFIT FOR YEAR	+B17-B18	+C17-C18	+D17-D18
21	===			
22				
33	===			
34	FORECAST VARIABLES FOR NEXT YEAR'S PRO RATA INCOME STATEMENT			
35	---			
36	Projected change in sales		0.2	
37	Projected change in cost of goods sold		0.01	
38	Projected change in administrative expenses		0	
39	===			

FIGURE 15–6 Electronic Spreadsheet: Actual Content of Spreadsheet Cells
This figure illustrates the actual content of all cells in Figure 15–1. In an actual spreadsheet display, the formulas would be resolved when displayed (C10 would appear as $13,740), and the values would be displayed according to a preset format (C36 would appear as 20%).

The parentheses in the cell B4 formula cause the expression inside the parentheses to be evaluated first, then the value of the expression is multiplied by the value in Cell C4. All the formulas in the spreadsheet of Figure 15–1 are listed in Figure 15–6. Remember, once entered, these formulas can be copied so they apply to a different set of data.

Functions. Electronic spreadsheets offer users a wide variety of pre-defined operations called **functions**. These functions can be used to create formulas that perform mathematical, logical, statistical, financial, and character-string operations on spreadsheet data. To use a function, simply enter the desired function name (for example, AVG for "compute the average") and enter the **argument**. Some spreadsheet programs require the user to prefix the function with a symbol (for example, @; the symbol may vary between software packages). The argument, which is placed in parentheses, identifies the data to be operated on. The argument can be one or several numbers, character strings, or ranges that represent data.

In the spreadsheet in Figure 15–1, the operating profit (C10) can be calculated (see the formula in Figure 15–6) by subtracting the individual cell values under the "Cost of sales and operating expenses" heading (C6, C7, and C8) from the net sales (C4).

$$C10: \quad +C4-C6-C7-C8$$

Or the total of the "Cost of sales and operating expenses" items can be computed with a function and its argument:

$$C10: \quad +C4-@SUM(C6..C8)$$

The use of predefined functions can save a lot of time. What if the range to be summed was C6..C600? Other spreadsheet functions include trigonometric functions, square root, comparisons of values, manipulations of strings of data, computation of Julian dates, computation of net present value and internal rate of return, and a variety of techniques for statistical analysis. Vendors of spreadsheet software create slightly different names for their functions.

Formatting Data for Readability   The appearance of data in a spreadsheet can be modified to enhance readability. For example, the value .2 was entered as the projected change in sales in C36 (Figure 15–1), but it appears in the spreadsheet display as a percent (20.00%). This is because the range C36..C38 was *formatted* so that the values are automatically displayed as percents rather than fractions. The methods of formatting data vary considerably between spreadsheet software packages.

Currency amounts can be formatted so that commas and a dollar sign are inserted. For example, in Figure 15–1 the value for net sales for "This Year" is entered as 153000 in C4, which is formatted for currency. Notice that it is displayed as $153,000.

Numeric data can be defined so they are displayed with a fixed number of places to the right of the decimal point. In Figure 15–1, the format of the net sales data in the range B4..D4 is currency with the number of decimal places fixed at zero. Numbers with more decimal digits than specified in the format are rounded when displayed.

Use

Spreadsheet Templates   The electronic spreadsheet of Figure 15–1 is a *template*, or a model, of past years' income statements and a pro rata income statement. It can be used over and over for different

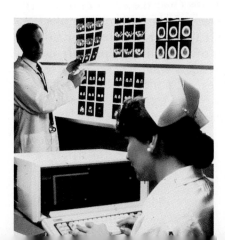

As this radiologist interprets X-rays, a nurse enters his verbal comments into a spreadsheet data base.

purposes by different financial analysts. Next year the data now in the "This Year" column will be moved to the "Last Year" column and a new set of data will be entered for "This Year".

With electronic spreadsheets, a template is modified easily to fit a variety of situations. Another analyst may wish to modify the template slightly to handle quarterly income statements (only the column headings would be changed).

"What If" Analysis   Monroe Green, Zimco's vice president of finance and accounting, uses the income-statement spreadsheet template of Figure 15–1 to create "what if" scenarios. For example, the vice president of the operations division has told Green that he is implementing a number of cost-cutting measures. He anticipates that the operations division can hold the cost of goods sold to a 1% increase, even though more products will be built and shipped. The vice president of sales and marketing has predicted that next year will be a "great year," and net sales will increase by 20%. The president of Zimco has asked all managers to "hold the line" on all selling and administrative expenses; therefore, these expenses are expected to remain about the same.

With spreadsheet software, Monroe was able to answer the question: "What if the cost of goods sold increases by 1%, sales increase by 20%, and everything else remains the same for the coming year?" After the financial data was entered, Monroe entered only the three forecast variables in C36, C37, and C38 (see Figure 15–1) to get the pro rata income statement (the "Next Year" column in Figure 15–1). All calculations (for example, sales with a 20% increase, net profit, taxes) are performed automatically because the appropriate formulas are built into the spreadsheet template.

Some of the entries in the "Next Year" column remain unchanged (for example, depreciation, dividends, and interest); however, if Monroe wanted to reflect a change in depreciation, he would simply change the value of the "Depreciation" entry in the "Next Year" column. The "Provision for income tax" entry is extrapolated from the "This Year" column data by a formula that assumes that the taxes will be paid at the same rate as the previous year, for example: B18: (C18/C17)*B17.

The real beauty of an electronic spreadsheet is that if you change the value of a cell, all other affected cells are revised accordingly. This capability makes spreadsheet software the perfect tool for "what if" analysis. For example, the spreadsheet template of Figure 15–1 reflects the projections of Zimco vice presidents. Over the years Zimco's president, Preston Smith, has learned to temper the optimistic projections of his vice presidents with a touch of reality, so he used the spreadsheet template of Figure 15–1 to create his own pessimistic pro rata income statement. This income statement reflects what he called the "worst case scenario": a 3% increase in sales, a 2% increase in cost of goods sold, and a 4% increase in administrative expenses. Preston Smith needed to change only the three forecast variables (C36..C38) to determine that a more realistic projected net profit for next year would be about one third ($7,462) of the the more optimistic projection.

Modifying a Spreadsheet Template   Modifying the appearance and/ or function of an existing spreadsheet to meet a different purpose is common practice among spreadsheet users. For example, Monroe Green modified the template of Figure 15–1 to include an "After Next" column (two years hence). When a new column is inserted at Column B, items in Columns B, C, and D are moved over one column to Columns C, D, and E. The "After Next" data would be in Column B. Of course, the spreadsheet software automatically adjusts the relative cell addresses to accommodate the new column.

After issuing the commands needed to insert a column at B, Monroe then copied the "Next Year" column (now in the range C4..C20) to the "After Next" column (range B4..B20). This copy operation highlights why Monroe used absolute cell addressing for all formula references to the forecast values in the original spreadsheet template in Figure 15–1. For example, the formula in B4 is +C4*(1 + $C $36). The absolute cell reference is needed because the relative position of the forecast values is different for both the "After Next" and the "Next Year" columns. Figure 15–7 illustrates how the income statement portion of the spreadsheet would appear after being modified to accommodate an "After Next" year column.

FIGURE 15–7   Electronic Spreadsheet: Inserting a Column
An "After Next" (two years hence) column is inserted at Column B in the income statement portion of the spreadsheet template of Figure 15–1.

```
A2:      'ZIMCO INCOME STATEMENT ($1000)
                A              B           C           D           E
1   =================================================================
2   ZIMCO INCOME STATEMENT ($1000) After Next  Next Year   This Year   Last Year
3   -----------------------------------------------------------------
4   Net sales                 $220,320    $183,600    $153,000    $144,780
5   Cost of sales & op. expenses
6     Cost of goods sold      117,577     116,413     115,260     117,345
7     Depreciation            4,125       4,125       4,125       1,500
8     Selling & admin. expenses 19,875    19,875      19,875      15,000
9                             ------------------------------------
10    Operating profit        $78,743     $43,187     $13,740     $10,935
11  Other income
12    Dividends and interest  405         405         405         300
13                            ------------------------------------
14    TOTAL INCOME            $79,148     $43,592     $14,145     $11,235
15  Less: interest on bonds   2,025       2,025       2,025       2,025
16                            ------------------------------------
17  Income before tax         77,123      41,567      12,120      9,210
18  Provision for income tax  34,839      18,777      5,475       4,160
19                            ------------------------------------
20    NET PROFIT FOR YEAR     $42,284     $22,790     $6,645      $5,050
```

Spreadsheet Summary

The possibilities of what Monroe Green, Preston Smith, you, and others can do with electronic spreadsheet software and micros are endless. For example, Monroe can add the Zimco balance sheets for the last two years to the spreadsheet in Figure 15–1 to create even more "what if" scenarios.

All major electronic spreadsheet software packages are *integrated packages* that offer spreadsheet, graphics, and database capabilities. The presentation graphics capability, which is discussed in the next section, enables graphs to be produced from spreadsheet data. When used as a database tool, electronic spreadsheet software organizes data elements, records, and files into columns, rows, and tables, respectively. For example, in a name-and-address file, each row in the spreadsheet would contain the data items for each individual record (for example, Jeffrey Bates, 1401 Oak St., Framingham, MA, 01710). All the records are combined in a table of rows (records) and columns (data elements) to make a file. Many of the capabilities of specialized database software (discussed later in this chapter) are also capabilities of electronic spreadsheet software. These include sorting records, extracting records that meet certain conditions (for example, STATE = "MA"), and generating reports.

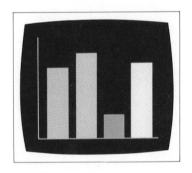

15–2 Presentation Graphics

Function

With presentation graphics software, you can create a variety of graphics from data in an electronic spreadsheet or a data base. Among the most popular presentation graphics are **bar graphs**, **pie graphs**, and **line graphs** (as seen in Figures 15–9, 15–11, and 15–12, respectively). Other types of graphs are also possible. Each of these graphs can be annotated with graph *titles*, *labels*, and *legends*.

The graphics component of an integrated software package is usually limited to producing bar, pie, and line graphs from the data in the associated spreadsheet or data base. However, dedicated, or stand-alone, presentation graphics packages offer an extensive array

With graphics software you can prepare professional-looking graphs for reports and presentations. Color ink-jet printers such as this one can draw graphic images on paper or directly on a blank acetate. The acetates can be used with an overhead projector to project the graph on a large screen.

of features. For example, dedicated graphics packages provide the ability to prepare *text charts* (such as lists of key points) and *organization charts* (such as block charts showing the hierarchical structure of an organization), and they provide users with the flexibility of customizing graphs. The functionality of graphs prepared by integrated packages and a dedicated graphics packages is about the same, but graphs produced by dedicated graphics packages are usually more visually appealing. (For example, pie and bar graphs are three-dimensional).

Besides offering the capability of preparing graphs from spreadsheet data, stand-alone graphics packages let you create and store original drawings. To do this, however, your personal computer must be equipped with a mouse, digitizing board, or some type of device that permits the input of curved and angular lines. To make drawing easier, such software even offers a data base filled with a variety of frequently used symbols, such as rectangles, circles, cats (yes, even cats), and so on. Some companies draw and store the image of their company logos so they can be inserted on memos, reports, and graphs.

Graphic representations of data have proved to be a very effective means of communication. It is easier to recognize problem areas and trends in a graph than it is in a tabular summary of the same data. For many years the tabular presentation of data was the preferred approach to communicating such information because it was simply too expensive and time consuming to produce presentation graphics manually. Prior to the introduction of graphics software, the turnaround time was at least a day and often a week. Today, you can use graphics software to produce perfectly proportioned, accurate, and visually appealing graphs in a matter of seconds.

Concepts

Usually the data needed to produce a graph already exist in a spreadsheet or data base. The graphics software leads you through a series of prompts, the first of which asks you what type of graph is to be produced—a bar graph, pie graph, line graph, and so on. You then select the data to be plotted. You can also enter names for the labels. Once you have identified the source of the data, have entered the labels and perhaps added a title, you can display, print, or plot the

Spice up a presentation with colorful graphics by using a microcomputer. Graphics software permits you to prepare a screen that can be produced instantly on a print for previewing or as a 35-mm slide for use in a presentation.

B1: 'ANNUAL SALES FOR ZIMCO BY REGION

	A	B	C	D	E	F
1		ANNUAL SALES FOR ZIMCO BY REGION				
2						
3	Region	Southern	Western	Northern	Eastern	Total
4						
5	Stibs	$7,140	$14,790	$13,260	$15,810	$51,000
6	Farkles	$5,460	$11,310	$10,140	$12,090	$39,000
7	Teglers	$3,150	$6,525	$5,850	$6,975	$22,500
8	Qwerts	$5,250	$11,875	$10,750	$12,625	$40,500
9						
10	Totals	$21,000	$44,500	$40,000	$47,500	$153,000
11						
12						
13						
14	Sales Summary by Region					
15	Product Sales Summary by Region					
16	Sales by Product					
17	Sales ($1000)					

FIGURE 15–8   Electronic Spreadsheet: Sales Data for Graphs
The bar, pie, and line graphs of Figures 15–9 through 15–12 are derived from these sales figures.

graph. Any changes made to data in a spreadsheet or data base are reflected in the graphs as well.

Use

Zimco Enterprise's vice president of sales and marketing is an avid user of spreadsheet and graphics software. The spreadsheet in Figure 15–8 is an annual summary of the sales for each of Zimco's four products by sales region. This spreadsheet is used in the following sections to demonstrate the compilation of bar, pie, and line graphs.

Bar Graphs   To prepare the bar graph in Figure 15–9, the vice president first had to specify appropriate ranges; that is, the values in the "Totals" row (range B10..E10 of Figure 15–8) are to be plotted, and the region names (range B3..E3 in Figure 15–8) are to be inserted as labels along the horizontal, or x, axis. The vice president also added a title for the graph ("Sales Summary by Region"), and titles for the x axis ("Region"), and the vertical, or y, axis ["Sales ($1,000)"].

The sales figures for each region in Figure 15–8 (range B5..E8) can be plotted in a *stacked-bar graph*. The resultant graph, shown in Figure 15–10, permits the vice president to understand better the regional distribution of sales. The *clustered-bar graph* is an alternative presentation to the stacked-bar graph in Figure 15–10. These graphs visually highlight the relative contribution each product made to the total sales for each region.

Pie Graphs   Pie graphs are the most basic of presentation graphics. A pie graph illustrates each "piece" of data in its proper relationship

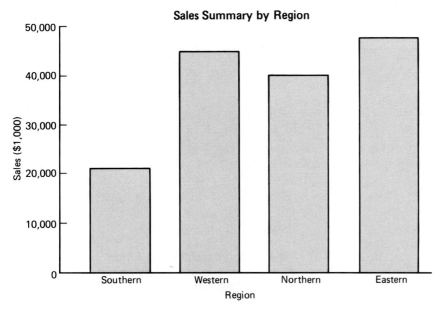

FIGURE 15-9 Presentation Graphics: Bar Graph
The total sales for each region in Figure 15–8 are represented in this bar graph.

to the whole "pie." To illustrate how a pie graph is constructed and used, refer again to the "annual sales" spreadsheet in Figure 15–8. The vice president of sales and marketing produced the sales-by-product pie graph in Figure 15–11 by specifying that the values in the

FIGURE 15-10 Presentation Graphics: Stacked-Bar Graph
Regional sales for each of the four products in Figure 15–8 are represented in this stacked-bar graph.

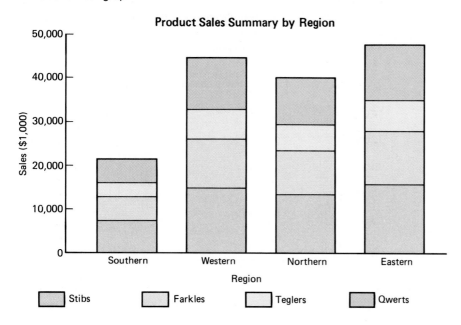

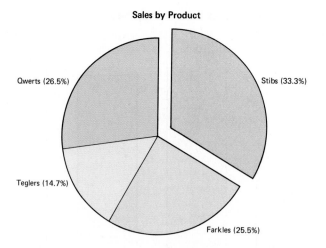

Sales by Product

Qwerts (26.5%)

Stibs (33.3%)

Teglers (14.7%)

Farkles (25.5%)

FIGURE 15–11   Presentation Graphics: Pie Graph
Total sales by product (for example, the "Totals" row,
B10..E10) in Figure 15–8 are represented in this pie graph.
The Stibs piece of the pie is exploded for emphasis.

"Total" column become the "pieces" of the pie. To emphasize the
product with the greatest contribution to total sales, she decided to
explode (or separate) the Stibs piece of the pie.

Line Graphs   A line graph connects similar points on a graph with
one or several lines. The Zimco vice president used the same data in
the spreadsheet of Figure 15–8 to generate the line graph in Figure
15–12. The line graph makes it easy for her to compare sales between
regions for a particular product.

FIGURE 15–12   Presentation Graphics: Line Graph
This line graph shows a plot of the data in Figure 15–8. A line connects
the sales for each product by region.

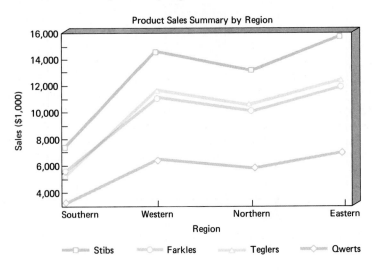

Computer-generated business graphics is one of the more recent applications of computers. With few exceptions, most computer-generated graphic outputs prior to 1980 were for engineers and researchers. Managers of business units who wanted a pie graph or a bar graph had it produced manually by the drafting department. This could take anywhere from a few days to weeks. Most managers were not willing to wait, so they continued preparing reports and presentations in the traditional tabular manner—rows and columns of data.

Today managers of business units have powerful microcomputers and user-friendly software packages that allow them to create a wide variety of visually appealing and informative presentation graphics in seconds. To capture and reproduce these graphic images, they use desktop plotters (for paper and transparency acetates), desktop film recorders (for 35mm slides), and screen-image projectors (to project an image onto a large screen).

During the past decade, the use of presentation graphics has become a business imperative. A progressive sales manager would never consider reporting a sales increase in tabular format. A successful year that may be otherwise obscured in rows and columns of sales figures will be vividly apparent in a colorful bar graph. Those in other areas of business also want to "put their best foot forward." To do so, they use computer-generated presentation graphics.

A number of studies confirm the power of presentation graphics. These studies uniformly support the following conclusions:

- People who use presentation graphics to get their message across are perceived as better prepared and more professional than those who do not.
- Presentation graphics can help persuade attendees or readers to adopt a particular point of view.
- Judicious use of presentation graphics tends to make meetings shorter. Perhaps it's true that a picture is worth a thousand words!

Whether you're preparing a report, a presentation, a newsletter, or any other form of business communication, it pays—immediately and over the long term—to take advantage of the capabilities of presentation graphics.

15–3 Database Software

Function

With database software, you can create and maintain a data base and extract information from it. To use database software, you first identify the format of the data, then design a display format that will permit interactive entry and revision of the data base. Once the data base is created, its *records* (related data about a particular event or thing) can be deleted or revised and other records can be added. Notice that *database* is one word when it refers to the software that manages the data base. *Data base* is two words when it refers to the highest level of the hierarchy of data organization (bit, character, data element or field, record, file, and data base).

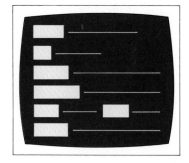

All database software packages have these fundamental capabilities:

1. To create and maintain (for example, add, delete, and revise records) a data base
2. To extract and list all records or only those records that meet certain conditions

3. To make an inquiry (for example, "What is average value of a particular field in a series of records?")
4. To sort records in ascending or descending sequence by primary, secondary, and tertiary fields
5. To generate formatted reports with subtotals and totals

The more sophisticated packages include a variety of other features, such as spreadsheet-type computations, graphics, and programming.

Concepts

Many similarities exist between commercially available word processing packages and commercially available electronic spreadsheet packages. With word processing, you see and manipulate lines of text. With electronic spreadsheets, you see and manipulate data in numbered rows and lettered columns. This is not the case with database packages. All commercial software packages permit the creation and manipulation of data bases, but what you see on the screen may be vastly different from one package to the next. However, the concepts behind these database packages are very similar. The conceptual coverage that follows is generic and can be applied to all database packages; however, the examples are oriented to the current market leader, *dBASE III PLUS* (a product of Ashton-Tate).

The organization of the data in a microcomputer data base is similar to the traditional hierarchy of data organization. Related fields, such as course identification number, course title, and course type, are grouped to form records (for example, the course record in the COURSE data base in Figure 15–13). A collection of related records make up a data file or a data base. (In database software terminology, *file* and *data base* are often used interchangeably.)

Students use database software to keep records relating to a wide range of activities: expenses (item, amount, date); friends (name, address, phone); intramural scores (opponent, score, date); courses (title, instructor, credit hours, term, grade); and so on.

```
Record#   ID     TITLE                  TYPE       SOURCE        DURATION
      1   100    MIS Orientation        in-house   Staff              24
      2   201    Micro Overview         in-house   Staff               8
      3   2535   Intro to Info. Proc.   media      Takdel Inc         40
      4   310    Programming Stds.      in-house   Staff               6
      5   3223   BASIC Programming      media      Takdel Inc         40
      6   7771   Data Base Systems      media      Takdel Inc         30
      7   CIS11  Business COBOL         college    St. Univ.          45
      8   EX15   Local Area Networks    vendor     HAL Inc            30
      9   MGT10  Mgt.Info.Systems       college    St. Univ.          45
     10   VC10   Elec. Spreadsheet      media      VidCourse          20
     11   VC44   4th Generation Lang.   media      VidCourse          30
     12   VC88   Word Processing        media      VidCourse          18
```

FIGURE 15–13   Database: The COURSE Data Base
The COURSE data base contains a record for each course that Zimco offers its employees.

The best way to illustrate and demonstrate the concepts of database software is by example. Zimco's education coordinator uses a micro-based database software package to help him with his record-keeping tasks. To do this, he created a COURSE data base (see Figure 15–13) that contains a record for each course Zimco offers its employees and for several courses at State University for which Zimco provides tuition reimbursement. Each record in the COURSE data base contains the following fields:

- Identification number (supplied by Zimco for in-house courses, by vendors, and by State University)
- Title of course
- Type of course (in-house seminar, multimedia, college or vendor seminar)
- Source of course (Zimco staff or supplier of course)
- Duration (number of hours required to complete course)

Creating a Data Base   To create a data base, the first thing you do is to set up a *screen format* that will enable you to enter the data for a record. The data entry screen format is analogous to a hard copy form that contains labels and blank lines (for example, a medical questionnaire or an employment application). Data are entered and edited (deleted or revised) one record at a time with database software, as they are on hard copy forms.

The structure of the data base.   To set up a data entry screen format, you must first specify the *structure* of the data base by identifying the characteristics of each field in the data base. This is done interactively,

```
Field      Field        Field      Field   Decimal
  no.      name         type      length   positions
---------------------------------------------------------
    1      ID           Character       5
    2      TITLE        Character      20
    3      TYPE         Character       8
    4      SOURCE       Character      10
    5      DURATION     Numeric         4           0
```

FIGURE 15–14   Database: Structure of the COURSE Data Base

with the system prompting you to enter the field name, field type, and so on (see Figure 15–14). For example, the ID field in Figure 15–14 is a five-character field. The *field name* is ID, the *field length* is five characters, and the *field type* is character. A character field type can be a single word or any alphanumeric (numbers, letters, and special characters) phrase up to several hundred characters in length. For numeric field types, you must specify the maximum number of digits (field length) and the number of decimal positions you wish to have displayed. Because the course durations are all defined in whole hours, the number of decimal positions for the DURATION field is set at zero (Figure 15–14).

FIGURE 15–15   Database: Data Entry Screen Format
The screen format for entering, editing, and adding records to the COURSE data base is illustrated. This screen is generated automatically from the specifications outlined in structure of the COURSE data base (see Figure 15–14).

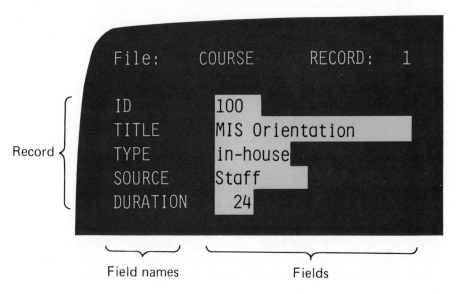

Entering and editing a data base. The screen format for entering, editing, and adding records to the COURSE data base is shown in Figure 15–15. This screen is generated automatically from the specifications outlined in the structure of the COURSE data base (see Figure 15–14). To create the COURSE data base, the education coordinator issued a command that called up the data entry screen in Figure 15–15; then he entered the data for first record, then the second record, and so on. On most database systems, the records are automatically assigned a number as they are entered. The reverse video portion of the screen in Figure 15–15 comprises the data for the five fields in Record 1. Records can, of course, be added to the data base and edited (deleted or revised).

Setting Conditions for Record Selection Database software also permits you to retrieve, view, and print records based on preset conditions. You set conditions for the selection of records by composing a *relational expression* that reflects the desired conditions. The relational expression normally compares one or more field names to numbers or character strings using the **relational operators** (= [equal to], > [greater than], < [less than], and combinations of these operators). Several expressions can be combined in a single condition with **logical operators** (*AND*, *OR*, and *NOT*). Commonly used relational and logical operators are summarized in Figure 15–16.

The education coordinator wanted a listing of all in-house seminars, so he issued commands to *locate* (*search* for), then *list* the records of all courses that are of TYPE "in-house" in the COURSE data base (see Figure 15–13). To retrieve these records, he set the condition to

TYPE = 'in-house'

Depending on the database package, the *search string* is enclosed in single or double quotes ("in-house"). Single quotes will be used here.

FIGURE 15–16 Relational and Logical Operators

Relational Operators	
COMPARISON	OPERATOR
Equal to	=
Less than	<
Greater than	>
Less than or equal to	< =
Greater than or equal to	> =
Not equal to	< >

Logical Operators AND and OR	
OPERATION	OPERATOR
For the condition to be true: Both subconditions must be true	AND
At least one subcondition must be true	OR

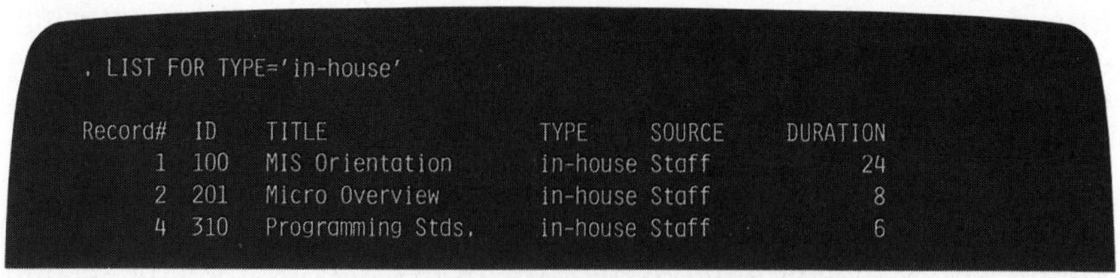

FIGURE 15–17 Database: Conditional Search and List

For the command LIST FOR TYPE = 'in-house', only the records from the COURSE data base (Figure 15–13) are displayed that meet the condition TYPE = 'in-house'.

To produce the output in Figure 15–17, the education coordinator keyed in the command

> LIST FOR TYPE = 'in-house'

Of course, one option is whether to route the output to a display screen or to a printer. If the education coordinator wanted only the ID and TITLE for those records that meet the condition TYPE = 'in-house', he would enter a command like this:

> LIST ID, TITLE FOR TYPE = 'in-house'

Figure 15–18 shows the output.

Data Base Inquiries Database software permits inquiries that involve parts of or all of one or more records. To extract then list (also display, print, or edit) selected records from a data base, you must first establish a condition or conditions. The following relational expressions establish conditions that will select or extract records (noted to the right of the expression) from the COURSE data base in Figure 15–13.

TYPE = 'in-house' .AND. DURATION < = 10	Records 2 and 4 (see Figure 15–19)
SOURCE = 'VidCourse' .OR. SOURCE = 'Takdel Inc'	Records 3, 5, 6, 10, 11, 12
DURATION>15 .AND. DURATION<25	Records 1, 10, 12
ID = 'CIS11'	Record 7

The process of selecting records by setting conditions is sometimes called *filtering*; that is, those records or fields that you don't want are "filtered" out of the display. The concept of filtering is introduced in Chapter 10, "The MIS and Decision Support Systems."

Sorting Records Data can also be sorted for display in a variety of formats. For example, Figure 15–20 illustrates how the COURSE data base in Figure 15–13 has been sorted by ID within SOURCE. This involves the selection of a *primary* and a *secondary key field*. The education coordinator selected SOURCE as the primary key field, but

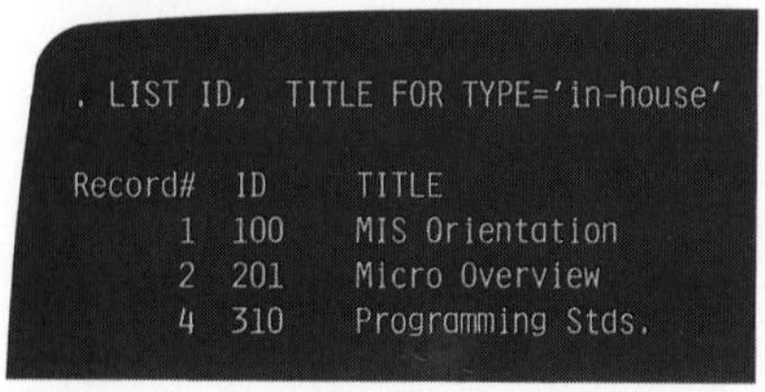

FIGURE 15–18 Database: Conditional Search and List, Specified Fields Only

For the command, LIST ID, TITLE FOR TYPE = 'in-house', only the ID and TITLE fields are displayed for the records from the COURSE data base (Figure 15–13) that meet the condition TYPE = 'in-house'.

```
. LIST FOR TYPE='in-house' .AND. DURATION<=10
Record# ID      TITLE                 TYPE      SOURCE      DURATION
      2 201    Micro Overview        in-house Staff             8
      4 310    Programming Stds.     in-house Staff             6
```

FIGURE 15–19 Database: Conditional Expression with AND Operator
For the command, TYPE = 'in-house' .AND. DURATION< = 10, only the records
from the COURSE data base (Figure 15–13) are displayed that meet the
conditions TYPE = 'in-house' and DURATION < = (less than or equal to) 10.

he wanted the courses offered by each source to be listed in ascending
order by ID. To achieve this record sequence, he selected ID as the
secondary key field. In most database packages, issuing a sort command results in the compilation of a temporary data base. After the
sort operation, the temporary data base contains the records in the
order described in the sort command (see Figure 15–20). Notice in
Figure 15–20 that the SOURCE field entries are in alphabetical order
and the three "Staff" records (Records 4, 5, and 6) are in sequence
by ID (100, 201, 310).

Customized Reports   Database software provides the capability of
creating customized, or formatted, reports. This capability allows you
to design the *layout* of the report. This means that you have some
flexibility in spacing and can include titles, subtitles, column headings, separation lines, and other elements that make a report more
readable. You describe the layout of the *customized* report interactively, then store it for later recall. The result of the description, called
a *report form*, is recalled from disk storage and merged with a data
base to create the customized report. Managers often use this capability to generate periodic reports (for example, weekly training status
reports).

**FIGURE 15–20 Data Management: COURSE Data Base Sorted by ID
Within SOURCE**
This display is the result of a sort operation on the COURSE data base
(Figure 15–13) with the SOURCE field as the primary key field and the ID
field as the secondary key field.

```
Record#  ID    TITLE                 TYPE      SOURCE      DURATION
      1  EX15  Local Area Networks   vendor    HAL Inc         30
      2  CIS11 Business COBOL        college   St. Univ.       45
      3  MGT11 Mgt. Info. Systems    college   St. Univ.       45
      4  100   MIS Orientation       in-house  Staff           24
      5  201   Micro Overview        in-house  Staff            8
      6  310   Programming Stds.     in-house  Staff            6
      7  2535  Intro to Info. Proc.  media     Takdel Inc      40
      8  3223  BASIC Programming     media     Takdel Inc      40
      9  7771  Data Base Systems     media     Takdel Inc      30
     10  VC10  Elec. Spreadsheet     media     VidCourse       20
     11  VC44  4th Generation Lang.  media     VidCourse       30
     12  VC88  Word Processing       media     VidCourse       18
```

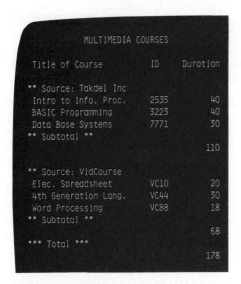

```
                 MULTIMEDIA COURSES

     Title of Course          ID       Duration

  ** Source: Takdel Inc
     Intro to Info. Proc.      2535         40
     BASIC Programming         3223         40
     Data Base Systems         7771         30
  ** Subtotal **
                                           110


  ** Source: VidCourse
     Elec. Spreadsheet         VC10         20
     4th Generation Lang.      VC44         30
     Word Processing           VC88         18
  ** Subtotal **
                                            68

 *** Total ***
                                           178
```

FIGURE 15–21   Database: Formatted Reports
This formatted report was compiled by merging a predefined report format with
the COURSE data base after it had been sorted by ID within SOURCE
(Figure 15–20).

Once a month, Zimco's education coordinator generates four
reports that summarize the offerings of each type of course: One report
summarizes Zimco's course offerings for TYPE = 'in-house', another
for TYPE = 'media' (multimedia), and so on. One of these formatted
reports is shown in Figure 15–21. This summary report of multimedia
courses was compiled by merging a predefined report format with
the temporary COURSE data base that was sorted by ID within
SOURCE (Figure 15–20).

You can bet that John Frank,
the president of Zenith Data
Systems, is a power user—a
person who takes full
advantage of the capabilities
of his computer and its
software. While en route to
Chicago's O'Hare Airport, he
is using his battery-powered
portable personal computer
to make a few inquiries to a
data base before a product
launch presentation.

Use

Database software earns the "productivity tool" label by providing users with the capability of organizing data into an electronic data base that can be maintained and queried (permit user inquiries) easily. The examples illustrated and discussed in the "Concepts" section merely "scratch the surface" of the potential of database software. With relative ease, you can generate some rather sophisticated reports that involve subtotals, calculations, and programming. You can even change the structure of a data base (for example, add another field). The programming capability enables users to create their own microcomputer-based information systems.

Summary Outline and Important Terms

15–1 **THE ELECTRONIC SPREADSHEET.** Electronic spreadsheets are simply an electronic alternative to thousands of manual tasks that involve rows and columns of data. The primary example used in this chapter to illustrate and demonstrate electronic spreadsheet concepts is an electronic spreadsheet **template** of a pro rata income statement.

Electronic spreadsheets are organized in a tabular structure with **rows** and **columns**. The intersection of a particular row and column designates a **cell**. During operations, data are referenced by their **cell addresses**. The **pointer** can be moved around the spreadsheet to any cell with the cursor control keys.

To make an entry or edit or replace an entry in a spreadsheet, move the pointer to the appropriate cell. When in edit mode, revise the entry in much the same way you would revise the text in a word processing document.

The four types of **ranges** are a single-cell, all or part of a column of adjacent cells, all or part of a row of adjacent cells, and a rectangular block of cells. A particular range is depicted by the addresses of the endpoint cells (for example, C6..D8).

An entry to a cell is classified as text (or label), numeric, or formula. A text entry is any string of alphanumeric text (spaces included) that occupies a particular cell. A numeric entry is any number. A cell may contain a formula, but it is the numeric results that are displayed in the spreadsheet. Spreadsheet formulas use standard programming notation for **arithmetic operators**.

The **relative cell address** is based on its position in relation to the cell containing the formula. When you copy, or replicate, a formula to another cell, the relative cell addresses in the formula are revised so that they retain the same position relative to the new location of the formula. When a formula is copied, the **absolute cell addresses** in the formula remain unchanged.

Predefined **functions** can be used to create formulas that perform mathematical, logical, statistical, financial, and character-string operations on spreadsheet data.

The appearance of data in a spreadsheet can be modified to enhance readability by adjusting the column width and formatting the individual numeric entries.

An electronic spreadsheet template can be used over and over for different purposes by different people. If you change the value of a cell in a spreadsheet, all other affected cells are revised accordingly. This capability makes spreadsheet software the perfect tool for "what if" analysis.

15–2 PRESENTATION GRAPHICS. With presentation graphics software, you can create a variety of graphics from data in an electronic spreadsheet or a data base. Among the most popular presentation graphics are **bar graphs** (including the stacked-bar and clustered-bar graphs), **pie graphs**, and **line graphs**. Each of these graphs can be annotated with titles, labels, and legends.

The variety of graphs that can be produced by an integrated software package is limited. However, dedicated, or stand-alone, graphics packages offer the user the capability of creating a more extensive array of graphs, such as text charts, organization charts, customized graphs, and even original drawings.

15–3 DATABASE SOFTWARE. Database software permits users to create and maintain a data base and extract information from it. Once the data base is created, its records can be deleted or revised, and other records can be added to it.

In database software, the user-defined structure of a data base identifies the characteristics of each field in the data base. The screen format for entering, editing, and adding records to a data base is generated automatically from the specifications outlined in the structure of the data base.

Database software permits users to retrieve, view, and print records based on preset conditions. To do this, users set conditions for the selection of records by composing a relational expression containing **relational operators** that reflects the desired conditions. Several expressions can be combined into a single condition with **logical operators**.

Records in a data base can be sorted for display in a variety of formats. To sort the records in a data base, select a primary key and, if needed, secondary and tertiary key fields. In most database packages, issuing a sort command results in the compilation of another data base.

Database software provides the capability of creating customized, or formatted, reports. The user describes the layout of the customized report interactively, then stores it for later recall.

 Review Exercises

Concepts

1. Describe the layout of an electronic spreadsheet.
2. Give an example of a cell address. Which portion of the address depicts the row and which portion depicts the column?
3. Give an example of each of the four types of ranges.
4. Give examples of the three types of entries that can be made in an electronic spreadsheet.
5. Write the equivalent formula for @ AVG(A1..D1) without the use of functions.
6. If the formula B2*$B$1 is copied from C1 to E3, what is the formula in E3? If the formula in E3 is copied to D45, what is the formula in D45?
7. List three alternative descriptors for the range A4..P12.
8. What formula would be entered in A5 to sum all numbers in the range A1..A4?
9. Name three types of charts commonly used for presentation graphics.
10. What is the source of the data needed to produce the charts?
11. Name and graphically illustrate (by hand) two variations on the bar chart.
12. What is meant when a portion of a pie chart is "exploded"?
13. What characteristics describe a field in a data base record?
14. What is the purpose of setting conditions for a data base?
15. What is the relationship between a field, a record, and the structure of a data base?
16. Give examples and descriptions of at least three other fields that might be added to the record for the COURSE data base.
17. What would the course ID be for the third record if the COURSE data base were sorted so that the primary and secondary key fields were TYPE and TITLE, respectively?

Discussion

18. All commercial electronic spreadsheet packages manipulate rows and columns of data in a similar manner. What makes one spreadsheet package more desirable than another?

19. If you were asked to create a micro-based inventory management system for a privately owned retail shoe store, would you use electronic spreadsheet software, database software, or both? Why?

20. In data base terminology, what is meant by *filtering*?

21. Describe two types of inquiries to a data base that involve calculations.

22. Under what circumstances is a graphic representation of data more effective than a tabular presentation of the same data?

23. Is it possible to present the same information in a stacked-bar and a line graph? How about stacked-bar and pie graphs?

Self-Test (by section)

15–1 **a.** The term *spreadsheet* was coined at the beginning of the personal computer boom. (T/F)

b. Data in an electronic spreadsheet are referenced by their cell _____.

c. The electronic spreadsheet pointer highlights the: (a) relative cell, (b) status cell, or (c) current cell.

d. D20..Z40 and Z20..D40 define the same electronic spreadsheet range. (T/F)

e. When the electronic spreadsheet formula H4∗$Z$18 is copied from A1 to A3, the formula in A3 is _____.

f. The electronic spreadsheet formula @ SUM(A1..A20) results in the computation of the sum of the values in the range A20..A1. (T/F)

g. A model of a spreadsheet designed for a particular application is sometimes called a _____.

15–2 **a.** Among the most popular presentation graphics are bar graphs, pie graphs, and _____ graphs.

b. An alternative presentation to the clustered-bar graph is the _____ graph.

c. Charts that contain a list of key points are called: (a) text charts, (b) organization charts, or (c) sequence charts.

15–3 **a.** If the COURSE data base in Figure 15–13 is to be sorted by ID within TYPE, the secondary key would be assigned to TYPE. (T/F)

b. The definition of the structure of a data base would not include which of the following: (a) field names, (b) selection conditions for fields, (c) field lengths?

c. The relational operator for greater than or equal to would be _____.

d. What record(s) would be selected from the COURSE data base in Figure 15–13 for the criteria SOURCE = "Staff" and DURATION > 20: (a) ID = 100, (b) ID = 8 and ID = 6, or (c) ID = VC10?

Self-test answers. **15–1** (a) F; (b) address; (c) c; (d) T; (e) + H6*$Z$18; (f) T; (g) template. **15–2** (a) line; (b) stacked-bar; (c) a. **15–3** (a) F; (b) b; (c) >=; (d) a.

16

Jobs and Career Opportunities

STUDENT LEARNING OBJECTIVES

- To identify computer specialist positions in information services departments and in user departments.
- To describe the functions, responsibilities, and organization of an information services department.
- To identify job opportunities in organizations that provide computer-related products or services.
- To discuss the issue of certification of computer professionals.
- To appreciate the scope and charge of computer-oriented professional societies.
- To explore ethical questions concerning the use of computers.
- To become aware of the relationship between career mobility and computer knowledge.

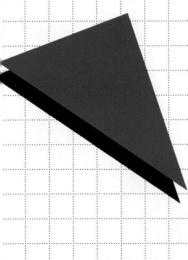

16–1 The Job Outlook

Whether you are seeking employment or perhaps a promotion as a teacher, an accountant, a writer, a fashion designer, a lawyer, (or in any of hundreds of other jobs), one question is frequently asked: "What do you know about computers?" Today interacting with a computer is part of the daily routine for millions of white-collar workers and is becoming increasingly common for blue-collar workers. No matter which career you choose, in all likelihood you will be a frequent user of computers.

Upon completion of this course, you will be part of the computer-literate minority, and you will be able to respond with confidence to any inquiry about your knowledge of computers. But what of that 95% of our society that must answer: "Nothing," or "Very little"? These people will find themselves at a disadvantage.

Opportunities for Computer Specialists

If you are planning a career as a computer specialist, opportunity abounds. Almost every company, no matter how small or large, employs computer specialists, and most of these companies are always looking for qualified people. For the last decade people with computer/

These programmer/analysts are in one of the top-rated professions. *The Jobs Rated Almanac* (1988) rated 250 common occupations based on six criteria: salary, stress, work environment, outlook, security, and physical demands. According to the rankings, the best occupation is actuary. (Actuaries compile and interpret statistics upon which insurance companies base their rate structures.) Job numbers two and three are computer programmer and computer systems analyst. Indeed, the future looks bright for the two mainstay computer-related occupations. As a basis for comparison, accountants are ranked 15; electrical engineers, 32; economists, 50; historians, 67; attorneys, 83; book authors, 137; mayors, 201; and NFL football players are 241!

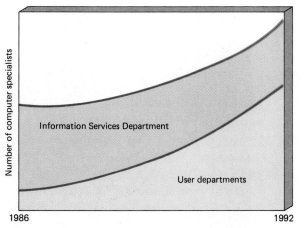

FIGURE 16–1
Computer Specialist Positions in Transition
The trend to end user computing has increased the number of computer specialists in the user areas.

information systems education have been at or near the top of the "most wanted" list. With millions (yes, millions!) of new computers being purchased and installed each year, it is likely that this trend will continue. Of course, the number of people attracted to the booming computer field is also increasing.

According to U.S. Department of Labor employment projections, the future is bright for computer specialists. For example, during the decade of the 1990s, the number of computer programmers is expected to increase from an estimated 575,000 to over 800,000. The number of computer systems analysts is expected to increase from an estimated 400,000 to over 580,000. The computer operator's career path is expected to follow a similar growth pattern.

This chapter should provide insight into career options and opportunities in the computer areas. Today the majority of computer specialist positions (such as operators, programmers, or systems analysts) are in a company's information services department. However, we are seeing a movement of computer specialists to the user departments with the trend toward distributed processing (see Figure 16–1). Notice that each year a growing percentage of a company's information processing needs is being met by computer specialists in user departments. Forecasters are predicting that as much as 90% of the computer specialist positions will be in the user areas by the year 2000. Even now, virtually every type of user group is vigorously recruiting people with computer expertise. Job opportunities in information services departments and in the user areas are discussed later in the chapter.

Career Opportunities for the Computer-Literate Minority

This chapter presents career opportunities in the computer specialist areas and in the computer services industry in general. However, opportunities abound for computer-literate people pursuing almost any career—from actuaries to zoologists. Every facet of automation is moving closer to the people who use it. In fact, most professions

The computer revolution has had a dramatic impact on people in hundreds of professions—the way they train and, ultimately, what they do in the work place. The field of nursing is one example. Here, computer-controlled critical care units provide nurses with a continuous graphic display of patient cardiac activity and other vital life signs. A warning is sounded when patient data exceed acceptable limits.

put you within arm's reach of a personal computer or a terminal. For example, the terminal has become standard equipment at hospital nursing stations and is often found in operating rooms. Draftspeople have traded their drawing tables for computer-aided design work-stations. Teachers are integrating the power of computer-based training into their courses. Economists would be lost without the predictive capabilities of their computer-based models. Truck dispatchers query their information systems before scheduling deliveries. Advertising executives use computers to help them plan ad campaigns. Construction contractors keep track of on-site inventory on portable laptop computers. The microcomputer is the secretary's constant companion. And stockbrokers often have terminals on both sides of their desks. In short, the capabilities of computers are being embraced by virtually all professionals. All things being equal, the person with the knowledge of and the will to work with computers will have a tremendous career advantage over those who think the age of information is a passing fad.

Automobile mechanics rely on automated diagnostic systems to help them service increasingly sophisticated automobiles. The typical automobile will have at least one computer for controlling fuel flow, ignition, security, braking, and other systems.

**The Centralized Information
Services Department:
Organization and Personnel**

If you are pursuing a career as a computer specialist, then the material in this section will familiarize you with some of the opportunities in a company's information services department. If you are pursuing a different career, then this section will give you some insight as to whom to contact when you have a computer-related question or request. It is not uncommon for computer users to have daily contact with people in the information services department. Besides helping to develop information systems, computer specialists in an information services department routinely respond to user inquiries about micro/mainframe links, hardware evaluation, and the use of software packages, to mention only a few.

The centralized information services department, which was introduced briefly in Chapter 1, "The World of Computers," is a company's primary source of information services. The typical department is charged with the support of the company's information processing requirements. Information services department responsibilities are:

1. Engaging in the development, the ongoing operation, and the maintenance of production information systems.
2. Acting as an advisor to users throughout the company on computer-related matters.
3. Serving as a catalyst for improving operations through system enhancements or new systems development.
4. Coordinating data and systems integration throughout the company.
5. Establishing standards, policies, and procedures relating to computers and information processing.
6. Evaluating and selecting hardware and software.
7. Conducting end user education programs.

Organizational Neutrality

Limited resources are available for the development and maintenance of information systems. Therefore, information services must maintain a balance between *being responsive* to user information needs and *being responsible* (see Figure 16–2). For example, an information services manager cannot divert previously committed resources from one project in an attempt to be responsive to another user. Unless extreme circumstances dictate this action, information services management cannot disregard its responsibility to keep approved projects on schedule. This is an almost daily conflict that information services and user managers must resolve. Because of this ever-present conflict, companies are opting for a structure that provides organizational neutrality for the information services department. Most solutions

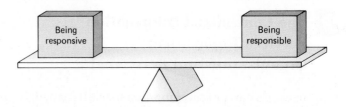

FIGURE 16–2　The Information Services Balancing Act
The information services department must maintain a
balance between being responsive to user information
needs and being responsible.

result in the director of information services reporting to the chief
executive officer (CEO) in either a line or staff capacity (see Figure
16–3). This type of structural organization allows projects to be pri-
oritized with the corporate good in mind.

Organization of an Information Services Department

In some information services departments, one person is the "chief
cook and bottle washer"—the entire staff. Other departments employ
several thousand people. Both small and large "shops" (a slang term
for information services departments) must perform the same functions of systems analysis, programming, technical support, data communications, operations, and so on. Differences in the way they are
staffed and organized are due primarily to the size and degree of
specialization.

Figure 16–4 illustrates how an information services department
in a medium- to large-sized corporation might be organized. It is a
representative organizational structure that could vary considerably,
depending on circumstances. The various components and specialist
positions shown in Figure 16–4 are discussed in the next section.

A typical organizational structure for a small company is illustrated in Figure 16–5. Some specialty areas are not noted in the chart

**FIGURE 16–3　Information Services Positioned for
Organizational Neutrality**
In the figure, the centralized information services department is shown as
subordinate to a high-level neutral office in both a line capacity (left) and a staff
capacity (right).

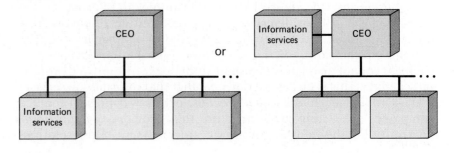

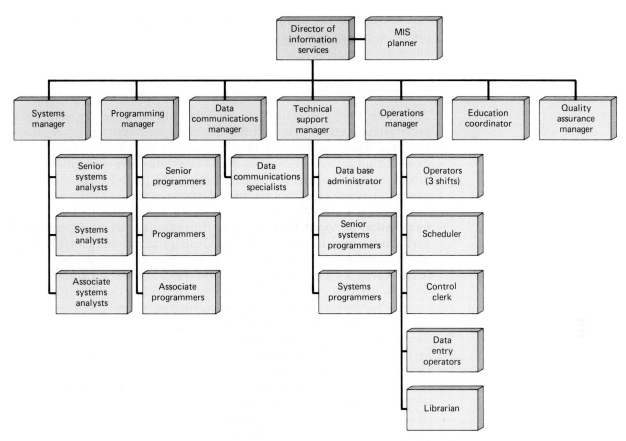

FIGURE 16–4 Organization Chart—Medium-Sized and Large Information Services Departments
No two information services departments are organized in the same way, but the example is, in general, representative.

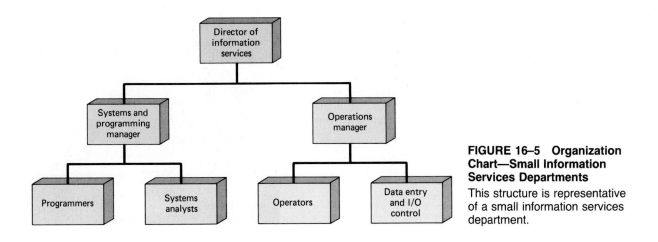

FIGURE 16–5 Organization Chart—Small Information Services Departments
This structure is representative of a small information services department.

because personnel in small companies double up on duties. For example, a programmer might also function as the data base administrator.

Information Services Functional Components and Specialists

This section will acquaint you with the functional components and professionals associated with the computer and information systems function. There is no "best" way to staff for the effective delivery of information services. However, each of the following components and job specialties is either implicitly or explicitly included in every company that employs computer specialists.

Information Services Management Information services managers perform the traditional management functions: planning, organizing, staffing, directing, and controlling. The **chief information officer (CIO)**, often a vice president, has responsibility for all information services activity in the company. Often the CIO is the director of the centralized information services department. At least half the CIO's time is spent interacting with user managers and executives. In this capacity, the CIO coordinates the integration of data and information systems and serves as the catalyst for new systems development. The remainder of the CIO's time is devoted to managing the information services department. The CIO must be somewhat futuristic, predicting what information technologies will become reality so the company can position itself to use them as a strategic weapon.

Systems Analysis The systems analysis group is composed of **systems analysts**. The systems analysts, or simply *analysts*, analyze, design, and implement information systems. They work closely with people in the user areas to design information systems that meet their data processing and information needs. These "problem solvers" are assigned a variety of tasks, including feasibility studies, system reviews, security assessments, long-range planning, and hardware/software selection.

The role of systems analysts is expanding with the technology.

Systems analysts work with users to ensure that they get the information they need in a format they can easily understand. This analyst recommended presenting quarterly sales data in the form of a color-coded line graph.

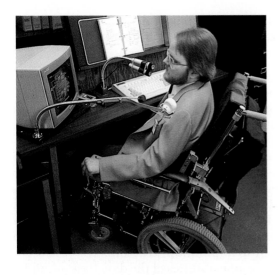

The nature of the work and the availability of specially designed workstations have made computer careers particularly inviting to the physically challenged. The man in the photo works as a data base administrator at a computer services company.

For example, with the recent trend to prototyping (see Chapter 12, "Systems Analysis and Design"), users and analysts can work together at a terminal to design *and* implement certain information systems—without programmer involvement!

Programming   The programming component of the information services department includes **applications programmers**, or simply *programmers*, who translate analyst-prepared system and input/output specifications into programs. Programmers design the logic, then code, debug, test, and document the programs. They write programs for a certain application, such as market analysis or inventory management.

Sometimes called "implementers" or "miracle workers," programmers are charged with turning system specifications into an information system. To do this, they must exhibit logical thinking and overlook nothing. A good programmer is *perceptive*, *patient*, *persistent*, *picky*, and *productive*—the "five Ps" of programming.

Some companies distinguish between *development* and *maintenance* programmers. Development programmers create *new* systems. Maintenance programmers *modify* existing programs to meet changing information processing needs. At a typical company, about 50% of the applications programming tasks are related to maintenance and 50% to new development.

A person holding a **programmer/analyst** position performs the functions of both a programmer and a systems analyst. The higher ranking people in the programming group are often programmer/analysts.

Data Communications   **Data communications specialists** design and maintain computer networks that link computers and terminals for data communications. This work involves selecting and installing appropriate hardware, such as modems, PBXs, and front-end processors, and selecting the transmission media (all discussed in Chapter 7, "Connectivity and Data Communications"). Data communications specialists also develop and implement the software that controls the flow of data between computing devices.

Technical Support The technical support group designs, develops, maintains, and implements *systems software*. Systems software is fundamental to the general operation of the computer; that is, it does not address a specific business or scientific problem.

The technical support group usually consists of systems programmers and the data base administrator. **Systems programmers** develop and maintain systems software. The **data base administrator (DBA)** position evolved with the need to integrate information systems. The data base administrator designs, creates, and maintains the integrated data base. The DBA coordinates discussions between user groups to determine the content and format of the data base so that data redundancy is kept to a minimum. The integrity and security of the data base are also responsibilities of the data base administrator.

Operations People in the operations group perform a variety of jobs that are described in the following paragraphs.

The **computer operator** performs those hardware-based activities that are needed to keep production information systems operational. An operator works in the machine room, initiating software routines and mounting the appropriate magnetic tapes, disks, and preprinted forms. The operator is in constant communication with the computer while monitoring the progress of a number of simultaneous production runs, initiating one-time jobs, and troubleshooting. If the computer system fails, the operator initiates restart procedures to "bring the system up."

The mainframe computer system run by these operators provides information processing support for over 2000 employees of an East Coast manufacturer of consumer goods.

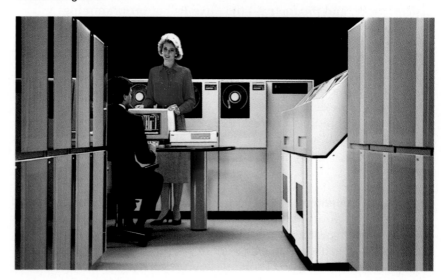

The **scheduler** strives to utilize the valuable hardware resources at optimum efficiency. Along with production information systems, the scheduler allocates and schedules computer time for program development and testing, system acceptance testing, data and file conversion, ad hoc jobs, preventive maintenance, general maintenance, and system downtime for hardware upgrades.

The **control clerk** accounts for all input to and output from the computer center. Control clerks follow standard procedures to validate the accuracy of the output before it is distributed to the user department.

Data entry operators, sometimes called the *key operators*, use key entry devices to transcribe data into machine-readable format. At most companies, only a small data entry group is attached to information services because the majority are distributed among the user areas.

The **librarian** selects the appropriate interchangeable magnetic tapes and disks and delivers them to the operator. The operator mounts the tapes and disks on the storage devices for processing and then returns them to the librarian for off-line storage. The librarian maintains a status log on each tape and disk. Medium-sized and large companies may have hundreds, even thousands, of tapes and disks. The librarian is also charged with maintaining a reference library filled with computer books, periodicals, and manuals as well as internal system and program documentation (logic diagrams, program listings, and so on).

Education   The **education coordinator** manages all computer-related educational activities. Anyone who works with computers or selects a computer-related career automatically adopts a life of continuing education. Computer technology is changing rapidly, so learning is an ongoing process. The education coordinator schedules users and computer specialists for technical update seminars, video training programs, computer-assisted instruction, and other training. The coordinator sometimes conducts the sessions.

Administration   Administration is the support function that handles the paperwork and administrative details associated with the operation of an information services department.

Planning   Although planning is a management function, the complexities of planning for the implementation of management information systems throughout a company demand that at least one **MIS planner** be dedicated to this function in medium-sized and large companies.

Quality Assurance   The quality assurance group encourages the "do it right the first time" approach to system development. **Quality assurance specialists** are assigned the task of monitoring the quality of every aspect of the design and operation of information systems, including system efficiency and documentation. They also ensure that computer specialists and users adhere to standards and procedures.

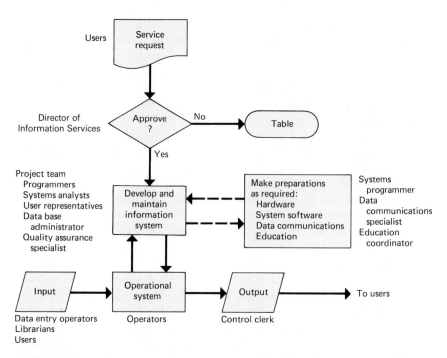

FIGURE 16–6   Position Functions and Information Systems
This chart summarizes the relationship between information services positions and user personnel in the development and operation of an information system.

Organization Summary

Figure 16–6 summarizes the relationships between computer specialty positions and users in the development and operation of an information system. A *user* request for a computer-related service, called a *service request*, is compiled and submitted to the information services department. Because resources are limited, not all requests are filled. The merits of service requests are evaluated by the *director of information services*. Major requests are incorporated into the MIS planning process by the *MIS planner* and assigned a priority.

A project team is formed to develop, implement, and maintain the information system. The project team typically is made up of *programmers*, *systems analysts*, *user representatives*, the *data base administrator*, and a *quality assurance specialist*, or some combination of the foregoing. *Systems programmers* and *data communications specialists* make changes in the hardware configuration, systems software, and data communications network, as required. The *education coordinator* schedules training sessions for both computer specialists and users. Once the system is implemented, operations people handle the routine input, processing, and output activities. *Data entry operators* transcribe the raw data to machine-readable format. The *librarian* readies magnetic storage media for processing. *Operators* initiate and monitor computer runs and distribute the output to *control clerks*, who then check the output for accuracy before delivering it to the *user*.

"I finally figured out an easy way to get the dust off of your computer."

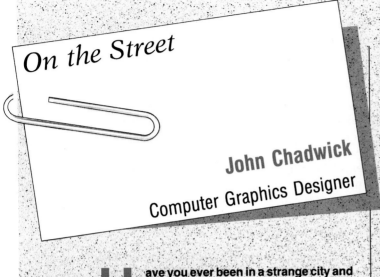

H ave you ever been in a strange city and wondered where you could go to fill your craving for good Chinese food? Or spent what seemed like hours looking up and down the aisles of your local supermarket, desperately searching for nacho-cheese sauce mix? Fortunately, many airports, highway rest stops, and stores now come equipped with public-access *kiosks*, computer systems whose sole purpose is to answer such questions.

One person who knows a lot about the ins and outs of kiosks is John Chadwick, a computer artist, who is one of the people responsible for designing the graphics you see. He does most of his work on PCs, using a variety of equipment, primarily True Vision's Targa 16 graphics board, and Tips imaging and painting software.

In addition to this work on kiosks, he uses his computer graphics expertise to create and manage design style for interactive video data bases (most recently for NYNEX and AT&T).

But of all the work he's done since receiving his Bachelor in Fine Arts degree in 1982, he probably had the most fun when he was given the opportunity to write and design animated story boards for new video-game ideas. After all, who wouldn't enjoy trying to design the perfect video game?

16–3 Departmental Computing: Users Take Control

Departmental computing is a generic reference to any type of computing done at the departmental level. The trend toward departmental computing is moving hardware, software, and processing closer to the people who use them. This concept has emerged because users are technically more sophisticated and better prepared to assume responsibility for their own computers and information systems.

Departmental computing could be as basic as using a micro-based electronic spreadsheet to do "what if" analysis. Or, at the other end of the spectrum, it could be as complex as using a supermini-computer with departmental terminals that support an on-line MIS. In the more sophisticated implementations of departmental computing, functional area managers find themselves managing their own miniature information services departments, often including programmers, analysts, operators, and other computer specialists. Departmental computing is also responsible for the emergence of several new computer specialist careers: user liaison, microcomputer specialist, and office automation specialist.

Opportunities for Traditional Computer Specialists in the User Areas

Because computer specialist careers have no geographical or industry boundaries, people pursuing careers as programmers, systems analysts, and operators always have had a plethora of options. A decade ago, a computer specialist could choose to work in Idaho in the potato industry, in Michigan in the automobile industry, in California in the entertainment industry, or in Texas in the oil industry. But, inevitably, his or her search would lead to an information services department. Today this is no longer the case. The emergence of departmental computing has expanded the career horizons for computer specialists. More and more are migrating to the user areas and departmental computing (see Figure 16–1). They now can seek employment in a medical research department, a consumer products marketing department, an internal auditing department, or virtually any area of business endeavor.

Emerging Computer Specialist Careers in the User Areas

User Liaisons   Computer and information processing activity is very intense in companies that seek to exploit the full potential of information technology. In this environment, someone who is attached to a particular functional area must be given the responsibility for taking full advantage of available computing resources. More often than not, this person is the **user liaison**. The user liaison is given a variety of titles, such as *internal consultant*, *functional specialist*, and *account executive*. The user liaison is a "live-in" computer specialist who coordinates all computer-related activities within a particular functional area. For example, you will often find user liaisons in finance departments and in manufacturing plants. User liaisons are intimately familiar with the functional areas to which they are assigned as well as the technical end of computers and information processing. They are often the impetus behind movements to upgrade existing information systems or to develop new information systems.

Within the business community, there are many cyberphobics (people who fear computers) and people with limited computer skills.

User liaisons foster improved communication between computer specialists and users. The better the communication, the better the resulting information systems.

A microcomputer specialist uses this six-pen plotter to create a color-coded stacked bar chart.

These people do not have the inclination, knowledge, or time to interface effectively with a computer specialist, so they relate what they want in general terms to the user liaison. The user liaison then does whatever is necessary to fulfill the user's request. This may involve anything from working with the computer specialist from the information services department to actually doing the programming for a department-based information system.

Microcomputer Specialists   From the growth of departmental computing and the popularity of microcomputers has emerged a new career, sometimes referred to as the **microcomputer specialist**. Micro specialists have been trained in the function and operation of microcomputers and related hardware (see Chapter 3, "Microcomputers"). They are proficient in the use and application of all common micro software packages such as word processing, desktop publishing, communications, electronic spreadsheet, presentation graphics, and database software. (See Chapters 14 and 15 in Part V, "Personal Computing.") Often, they have expertise in the installation and maintenance of micro-based local area networks and in establishing micro-mainframe links (see Chapter 7, "Connectivity and Data Communications").

A user does not always have the time to learn the details of using a microcomputer and its software. Rather than have each person in an office learn micros and micro software packages inside out, a firm can have a micro specialist help users over the rough spots as well as develop new systems. In this way, users can focus their attention on applying micros to their immediate information needs rather than on system quirks.

Microcomputer specialists keep abreast of the changes in technology, both in general and as these changes relate to their application area. Because microcomputer specialists are continuously attentive to an evolving technology, the departments in which they work are in a better position to take advantage of new innovations in microcomputer hardware and software.

Office Automation Specialists   Office automation encompasses those computer-based applications generally associated with office work. Traditionally, office automation applications encompass word processing, electronic mail, image processing, voice processing, and office information systems. These office automation applications are discussed in Chapter 11, "Applications of Information Technology." **Office automation specialists** are being hired to help with the growing demand for automating office activities. These specialists know the operation of the hardware and the use of the software associated with each of the office automation applications. They help employees make effective use of office systems.

16–4   Information Center Specialists

In Chapter 1 we learned that an *information center* is a "hands-on" facility in which computing resources and technical support are available to users. Information centers can provide personnel with the opportunity to learn to use computers and to be more productive with their time.

The availability of information centers has reduced the number of one-time user service requests received by the information services department by as much as 80%. With users literally taking matters into their own hands, programmers and analysts in the information services department have more time to devote to ongoing development projects.

Perhaps the most important component of an information center is the people who help users. These people, called **information center specialists**, conduct training sessions, answer questions, create sys-

Information center specialists routinely conduct in-house seminars to teach users how to apply available hardware and software to their business information processing needs. Here, managers from the personnel department are learning a fourth-generation language so they can do "what if" analysis.

tems that complement the information center function, and generally *help users to help themselves*. Because user computing needs run the gamut of computers and information processing, the information center specialist must be a generalist comfortable with micros, a wide variety of micro applications, and user-oriented mainframe software.

The theory behind an information center is that users have a place to go, not necessarily to request information services but to help themselves meet their own information needs. Besides providing access to user-oriented hardware and software, information centers and information center specialists provide three basic services: training, consulting, and software development.

- *Training*. The first step toward becoming a successful user of computing and information resources is learning how to use these resources. Recognizing this, information center specialists provide ongoing training in the use and application of available hardware and software resources.
- *Consulting*. The information center is a place where users go to get answers to their computer-related questions. The user might need help merging a spreadsheet graph into a word processing document, or debugging a query language program, or finding a cable to link a laser printer with a micro.
- *Software Development*. Although information centers are charged with helping users help themselves, some jobs are beyond users' capabilities. In these cases, information center specialists are called upon to develop small micro-based information systems for users.

16–5 Other Career Opportunities: Services, Hardware, Software, and Education

In the last two sections our discussion has focused on jobs typically found in an organization's information services department or in a user group. There are also a host of computer specialist career opportunities in organizations that provide computer-related products or services. For ease of discussion, let's divide these organizations into four groups: services, hardware vendors, software vendors, and education. But keep in mind that a particular organization may fit into two, three, or even all four of these groups. For example, Control Data Corporation markets computers and software, and it provides consulting and education services as well.

Commercial Information Services

The computer revolution is creating a tremendous demand for computer-related services. In response to this demand, a number of service organizations have emerged. These include *service bureaus, facilities management companies, turnkey companies, consulting firms, database services*, and *computer repair stores*, to mention a few.

Each year *Datamation*, one of the leading computer magazines, conducts a salary survey of computer/information systems jobs. The results are summarized in the first issue for October. The 1991 and 1992 salary projections in the accompanying table are based on the most recent (1988) *Datamation* salary survey prior to the publication of this book. An annual growth of 6% is assumed. This is consistent with historic and projected average annual raises for computer professionals.

The projected salaries are presented in 11 areas. When only one figure is presented, it represents the average salary for that position. When a salary range is presented, the lowest figure represents the average salary for the entry level position in that category (junior applications programmer, for example), and the highest figure represents the average salary for the highest level position in that category (lead applications programmer).

Projected average salary (in $)	1991	1992
Corporate Staff		
Vice president	80,546	101,710
Director of DP/MIS	64,540	81,480
Technical services manager	67,720	85,495
Information center/Data center manager	50,264	63,458
Director of security	48,684	61,462
Systems Analysis		
Manager	54,264	68,507
Systems analysts	32,871–49,449	41,499–62,428
Applications Programming		
Manager	54,288	68,537
Applications programmer	27,330–45,579	34,504–57,542
Systems Analysis/Programming		
Manager	61,118	77,160
Systems analysts/programmer	28,132–50,535	35,516–63,799

Service Bureaus   **Service bureaus** provide almost any kind of information processing services. These include but are not limited to developing and implementing information systems, providing computer time (timesharing), and transcribing source data. A service bureau is essentially a public computer center. Service bureau employees who work under contract to develop information systems for a client company are referred to as *contract programmers* and *contract systems analysts*.

Projected average salary (in $)	1991	1992
Operating Systems Programming		
Manager	68,306	86,235
Systems programmer	56,528–68,896	71,365–86,979
Data Base Administration		
Manager	49,605	62,625
Data base administrator	43,566	55,001
Data Communications/Telecommunications		
Manager	54,793	69,175
Analyst	40,492	51,120
Computer Operations		
Manager	44,153	55,743
Operator	25,423–36,715	32,096–46,352
Magnetic media librarian	24,877	31,406
Production and I/O Control		
Supervisor	34,559	43,629
Scheduler	29,172	36,828
Control clerk	25,163	31,767
Data Entry		
Supervisor	27,272	34,430
Operator	20,054	25,318
Office Automation		
Word processing supervisor	28,372	35,819
Word processing operator	21,355	26,960
Microcomputer specialist	29,840	37,672

Facilities Management Companies   **Facilities management companies** are the answer for firms that would like to have an internal information services department but do not want the responsibility of managing it. Employees of facilities management companies physically move into a client company's computer center and take over all facets of the center's operation. Facilities management companies are often engaged for turnaround situations—situations where the client company wants its information services function to make a

The jobs of consultants are not limited to implementation of hardware and software. One of their challenges is to design computer work areas that will be aesthetically pleasing while providing comfort and efficiency.

quantum leap in sophistication and capability that cannot be accomplished with existing staff.

Turnkey Companies   A **turnkey company** contracts with a client to install a complete system, both hardware and software. One of the major selling points of a turnkey company is that the hardware and/or software are installed with minimum involvement by personnel from the company purchasing them. Such companies are also called **system integrators** because they integrate various hardware and software products to provide a solution to a problem, such as setting up desktop publishing (for example, integrating PageMaker software, the Mac SE personal computer, and the Laserwriter laser printer).

Consulting Firms   The peaks and valleys of MIS requirements and the lack of internal expertise in specialty areas have made the use of outside consultants and contract programmers and analysts an economic necessity. Consulting firms give advice on using computers and the information resource. Consultants usually have specialized expertise that is otherwise not available to clients. Contract programmers, analysts, and other MIS specialists, on the other hand, are retained primarily for work-force augmentation, not because they have unique skills. For example, they may be hired to develop a high-priority information system for which internal resources are not available.

Data Base Services   A variety of applications-specific data bases are available commercially. Market researchers can obtain data bases that summarize sales by demographics for a particular type of product (such as shampoo or cough medicine). Pharmacists can purchase a data base that contains drug pairs that may result in an adverse reaction when taken together. Politicians can purchase data bases consisting of voter preferences. Entrepreneurs can purchase data bases that contain the names and addresses of the most likely buyers of their products.

Computer Repair Stores   One of the fastest growing service groups is computer repair stores. There weren't very many television repair shops in 1950, but look at them now. History is repeating itself with micros. Ten years ago, microcomputers were somewhat novel, not to mention expensive. Today they are a common consumer item, and they do "get sick" and need repair. One computer repair chain is even called the Computer Doctor. As a rule, microcomputers are very reliable and seldom need repair. However, a buyer usually has the option of paying for each service or buying a maintenance contract.

Hardware Vendors

Computer Systems Manufacturers   The most visible hardware vendors are the computer systems manufacturers, such as Digital Equipment Corporation (DEC), Apple, IBM, Unisys, and Hewlett-Packard (HP). Twenty-five years ago there were fewer than a dozen companies manufacturing computer systems; today there are hundreds. These companies manufacture the processor and usually some or all of the peripheral equipment (disk drives, printers, terminals, and so on).

The competition in the high-technology field of computer hardware is fierce. Manufacturers routinely purchase the competition's processors and peripheral equipment to disassemble them in search of technological innovations that can be applied to their own product line. This practice has become so widespread that the term *reverse engineering* was coined to describe it.

Leasing Companies   Most computers are available for purchase or for lease. The monthly charge for leasing a computer system is based roughly on what the monthly payments would be if the computer were purchased over a four-year period. Leasing companies purchase computers, often from manufacturers, then lease them for less than the manufacturer does. A leasing company, referred to as the *third party*, makes a profit by keeping its computers under contract for five years or more.

Manufacturers "burn in" microcomputers for several days before shipment to lower the probability that a system will fail on delivery.

Many companies specialize in the manufacture of peripheral devices. This clean-room worker is involved in the manufacture of CD-ROM disks and related hardware.

Plug-Compatible Manufacturers Plug-compatible manufacturers (**PCMs**) make peripheral devices that can be attached directly to another manufacturer's computer. A PCM might manufacture disk drives and tape drives that operate and sometimes look like those of the original computer system manufacturer. These devices are called *plug-compatible* because a PCM disk drive needs only to be plugged into the computer to become operational.

Value-Added Resellers **Value-added resellers**, or **VARs**, integrate the hardware and software of several vendors with their own software, then sell the entire package. They are called value-added resellers because they "add value" to each component of the system. For example, a VAR may integrate one vendor's microcomputer, another's electronic spreadsheet software, and yet another's voice input device to create a system on which spreadsheet applications can be run without a keyboard.

Computer Stores Until the late 1970s computer systems were sold exclusively in the customer's office. Computer retail outlets, such as Computerland, MicroAge Computer Stores, and Entre Computer Centers, have made it possible for customers to shop for computers in much the same way they would shop for stereo components. Because the price of a computer has been reduced so drastically, computer retail outlets and most department store chains now carry a wide variety of small computer systems, including minicomputers.

A used-computer market has given birth to a growing number of used-computer dealers. Individuals and companies are always "trading up" to computers with greater processing capabilities. This puts a lot of "pre-owned" computers on the market.

Jobs with Hardware Vendors Hardware vendors market and service hardware. To do so they need *marketing representatives* to sell the products and *systems engineers* to support them once they have been installed. Marketing representatives hold a technical sales position that requires a broad knowledge of the company's products and their capabilities. They normally spend time with customers assessing their information processing needs, then submit proposals for their review.

Hardware and software vendors employ technical experts to help customers diagnose and solve problems over the telephone.

(Marketing reps in retail outlets spend little time with customers and seldom prepare written proposals.) A systems engineer has more technical knowledge and is schooled in the details of the company's hardware and software operation. The systems engineer is the technical expert, often called on by customers for advice on technical matters. Behind the scenes, programmers and analysts develop software for the computer systems they sell.

Software Vendors

Software vendors that produce and market software are sometimes called **software houses**. What you buy from a software house is a *proprietary software package* for a particular computer-based system or application. The package contains the software on a magnetic tape or disk and includes its accompanying documentation. The software could be an expert system for archaeologists, an authoring system just for poets, a data base management system, or any of thousands of other applications. Software prices range from about $30 to hundreds of thousands of dollars.

Software vendors copyright proprietary software by registering their creations with the Copyright Office in Washington, D.C. Copyrighted software is protected from unlawful duplication and use. When you purchase or lease a software package, you receive a *license agree-*

Copyright laws protect literature, music, the design of a silicon chip, and software. Sophisticated computer-aided design software packages that would enable the creation of three-dimensional images, such as the one in the photo, may be the result of a multimillion-dollar research effort.

ment to use it. Typically, this agreement limits the use of the software to one computer system at a time. It is a violation of copyright law to duplicate proprietary software for use on several computer systems unless permission is granted by the vendor in a *site license agreement*.

Many stories are told about successful software entrepreneurs who turned an idea into millions of dollars. These opportunities still exist today, and thousands of aspiring entrepreneurs are creating companies and placing their software on the market each year. Some struggle to marginal success and some fail, but a few make it big— very big!

Education

The computer explosion in the last few years has created an insatiable demand for computer-related education. People in the workforce and those preparing to enter it need to be computer literate to be effective in this age of information. In essence, this means that every student and virtually every person in the workforce wants an opportunity to achieve computer literacy. Many of those taking computer-literacy courses are catching the "bug" and are pursuing advanced computer education in parallel with their chosen fields.

This demand for computer education is taxing the resources of our educational institutions and has given rise to a tremendous demand for *professors* and *instructors*. Over the past decade the fastest growing curriculums on most campuses are those in computer science and information systems. But the demand for computer-related education is so great that professors and instructors are being recruited

The growing demand for computer-related education has created more job opportunities in education than there are instructors to fill them. The demand for instructors in the computer areas is strong in industry as well as in colleges.

to teach computer applications in a variety of curriculums. Art professors teach computer graphics; physiology professors teach computer instrumentation for ergonomics experiments; sociology professors teach data base concepts as applied to the analysis of demographic trends; and music professors teach synthesized music and the use of the computer as a tool for composition.

Instructors are needed in industry as well. Programmers, analysts, and users are forever facing the announcement of a new technological innovation or the installation of a new system. In-house education is focused on the specific educational needs of the organization. Without instructors to direct this effort, a hundred new terminals may end up as bulky paperweights if people are not trained in how to use them.

The delivery of computer education can take many forms. Several firms specialize in the development of self-paced instructional videos and computer-based training (CBT) courses. Such courses cover everything from computer literacy to advanced data communications. The courses are normally accompanied by a support text and workbooks. Educators that develop these self-paced courses do not have the direct student contact that instructors have, but they need similar skills plus a sensitivity to the challenge of self-paced learning.

If you wish to pursue a career in the field of computer education, you will need a solid educational foundation and several years of field experience.

16–6 Professionalism and Ethics

Licensing and Certification

If your chosen career involves the use of computers, you may be in constant contact with sensitive data and may have the power to control events. An implied responsibility to maintain the integrity of the system and its data accompanies such a job. Failure to do so could have a disastrous effect on the lives of individuals and on the stability of the organization.

At present, licensing or certification is not a requirement for programmers, operators, or any other computer professional; nor is it required for users of computers. Licensing and certification are hotly debated issues. Many professions require demonstration of performance at a certain level of competence before permission is granted to practice. Through examination, the engineer becomes a registered professional engineer, the attorney becomes a member of the bar, and the accountant becomes a certified public accountant.

Within the computer community, there are several certifications. Recruiters may view certification as favorable, but not as a prerequisite of employment. The **Certificate in Data Processing (CDP)** is a general certification in the area of computers and information systems. The **Certificate in Computer Programming (CCP)** is specifically for programmers. The CDP and CCP are administered by the Institute for Certification of Computer Professionals. The **Certified System Professional (CSP)** is a general certification administered by the Association for Systems Management. The **Certified Information Systems Auditor (CISA)** is administered by the EDP Auditor's Association, and the **Certified Data Educator (CDE)** is administered by the Data Education Certification Council. The CDP, CCP, CSP, CISA, and CDE are awarded upon successful completion of an examination.

Professional Societies

Several hundred professional societies have emerged with the information revolution. These societies promote a common bond shared by professionals with similar interests. This unity of purpose instills a professional attitude among the membership. A few of the more prominent professional societies organized primarily for computer specialists include:

- Association for Computing Machinery (ACM)
- Data Processing Management Association (DPMA)
- Society for Information Management (SIM)
- Data Entry Management Association (DEMA)
- Independent Computer Consultants Association (ICCA)
- Association for Systems Managers (ASM)
- Association of Information Systems Professionals (AISP)
- EDP Auditor's Association (EDPAA)

Other professional societies are organized for special-interest groups—those interested in a particular application of the computer. Whatever your chosen profession or special interest, there is probably a computer society for you to join. The following are just a few of

Each month professional societies meet to discuss computer-related topics, issues, and trends. At this Data Processing Management Association meeting, the topic was "The Impact of Artificial Intelligence on Information Systems Development."

several hundred such organizations, and the list is growing each month.

- Association of Rehabilitation Programs in Data Processing (ARPDP)
- Association of Small Computer Users in Education (ASCUE)
- Black Data Processing Associates (BDPA)
- Health and Beauty Aids Computer Users Society (HABACUS)
- Hospital Information Systems Sharing Group (HISSG)
- Library and Information Technology Association (LITA)
- Life Insurance Systems Association (LISA)
- Society for Computer Applications in Engineering, Planning, and Architecture (CEPA)
- Society for Computer Medicine (SCM)
- Steel Industry Systems Association (SISA)
- Women in Information Processing (WIP)
- Computer Law Association

The American Federation of Information Processing Societies (AFIPS) is an umbrella organization that affords societies with similar goals an opportunity to join forces on certain issues and in certain activities.

The Question of Ethics

One of the largest professional societies adopted a code of ethics over 15 years ago. The code warns members that they can be expelled or censured if they violate it. To date, not one of the society's tens of thousands of members has been expelled or censured for violating the code. Other professional societies publish a code of ethics as well, and they too rarely or never take action against delinquent members. Does this mean there are no violations? Of course not. A carefully drafted code of ethics provides some guidelines for conduct, but professional societies cannot be expected to police the misdoings of their membership. In many instances, a code violation is also a violation of the law.

A code of ethics provides direction for computer professionals and users so that they act responsibly in their application of computer technology. The following code of ethics is in keeping with the spirit of those encouraged by computer societies.

1. Maintain the highest standard of professional behavior.
2. Avoid situations that create a conflict of interest.
3. Do not violate the confidentiality of your employer or those you service.
4. Continue to learn so your knowledge keeps pace with the technology.

5. Use information judiciously and maintain system integrity at all times.
6. Do not violate the rights or privacy of others.
7. Accomplish each task to the best of your ability.
8. Do not break the law.

If you follow this eight-point code, it is unlikely that anyone will question your ethics. Nevertheless, well-meaning people routinely violate this simple code because they are unaware of the tremendous detrimental impact of their actions. With the speed and power of computers, a minor code infraction easily can be magnified to a costly catastrophe. For this reason, the use of computers is raising new ethical questions. The three case studies that follow illustrate the ethical overtones surrounding the application of information technology.

Case 1 Let's take as an example the case of computerized dialers, a system that automatically dials a telephone number and plays a prerecorded message. Telephone numbers are entered into the system, then dialed one after another. If there is no answer, the number is redialed at a later time. Such systems are used for telemarketing a variety of products, not to mention politicians and ideologies. Is this an invasion of an individual's privacy?

Consider the company that, for a fee, will use its computerized dialing system to do telemarketing for local merchants. The system contains every telephone number in the city telephone directory. A message announcing a sale, a new service, or whatever is recorded for each client. Each day the system is activated and "the computer" makes calls from 8 A.M. to 10 P.M.

Is this application an ethical use of computers, or is it an invasion of privacy and an abuse of another person's time? During the course of a single day, the system can interrupt the lives of thousands of

It is more the rule than the exception that a computer professional will have ready access to a broad range of sensitive information, both personal and corporate. Because of the potential for the abuse of this information, some professional societies have adopted a code of ethics.

people. How many of us would welcome the opportunity to listen to a prerecorded commercial when we answer the phone? Is telemarketing in violation of the code of ethics just outlined? How about Item 6?

There are, of course, legitimate uses of computerized dialing systems. For example, the IRS uses them to notify delinquent taxpayers; school districts use them to notify parents of truant children; and retailers alert customers that they can pick up the items they ordered.

Case 2 The vice president of a sporting goods chain purchased a $500 electronic spreadsheet software package. The purchase agreement permits the use of the software on any micro at the office or at his home. However, the purchase agreement strictly prohibits the reproduction of this copyrighted software for purposes other than as a backup. After a week of transporting the software back and forth between his office and home, the vice president decided to make an extra copy so he would have one for home and one for the office. The VP knew that this act was in violation of the purchase agreement, but he rationalized his actions with the justification that he would be the only person to use the software.

The VP copied the software as a matter of personal convenience. After all, he could have continued transporting the software between home and work. Did he violate the code of ethics? What about Items 1 and 8?

Case 3 Members of the U.S. Congress have franking privileges, or free mail. Before computers, most letters were sent in response to constituent inquiries. Computers and high-speed printers have made it possible to crank out 30,000 "individualized" letters per hour. Some members of Congress have been known to send out millions of letters a year.

Is this massive amount of correspondence an attempt to better inform the constituents, or is it politically motivated and an abuse of the power of the computer? Is this application a violation of our code of ethics? How about Items 2 and 5?

16–7 Career Mobility and Computer Knowledge

Computer literacy is already a prerequisite of employment in many professions such as business and engineering. Within a few years computer literacy may well be a requirement for success in most professions. Career mobility is becoming forever intertwined with an individual's current and future knowledge of computers.

Just as advancing technology is creating new jobs, it is changing

Computers are changing the way virtually all of us do our jobs. Today career advancement depends on our ability to take advantage of computer and information technology, whether we work in the executive suite or on the shop floor.

old ones. Some traditional jobs will change or even disappear. For example, office automation is radically altering the function and role of secretaries and office managers. With computer-aided design (CAD), draftspersons are learning new ways to do their jobs.

Career advancement ultimately depends on your abilities, imagination, and performance, but understanding computers can only enhance your opportunities. If you cultivate your talents and you aspire to leave your mark on your chosen profession, the sky is the limit.

 Summary Outline and Important Terms

16–1 THE JOB OUTLOOK. People who include computer knowledge on their resumes will have an advantage over those who cannot. This is true in a great many professional disciplines.

Virtually every organization employs or is considering employing computer specialists. More and more of these computer specialist positions are being filled in user groups.

16–2 THE CENTRALIZED INFORMATION SERVICES DEPARTMENT: ORGANIZATION AND PERSONNEL. The information services department is the data and information "nerve center" of an organization. Its responsibilities include development, implementation, maintenance, and ongoing operation of information systems; acting as an advisor to users; serving as a catalyst; coordinating data and systems integration; establishing standards, policies, and procedures; evaluating hardware and software; and providing end user education.

An information services department must maintain a balance between being responsive to user information needs and being responsible. Because of this ever-present conflict, companies are opting for a structure that provides organizational neutrality for the information services department.

The actual organizational structure of an information services department will vary considerably from one organization to the next. Normally, individuals in smaller companies will perform several functions. Large companies have enough people to specialize.

The career fields in an information services department can be divided into 10 groups: management, systems analysis, programming, data communications, technical support, operations, education, administration, planning, and quality assurance.

The number and type of career paths open to someone entering the computer/information systems field is expanding each year. Some of the most visible career paths are **chief information officer (CIO)**, **systems analyst**, **programmer** (applications and systems), **programmer/analyst**, **data communications specialist**, **data base administrator (DBA)**, **computer operator**, **scheduler**, **control clerk**, **data entry operator**, **librarian**, **education coordinator**, **MIS planner**, and **quality assurance specialist**.

16-3 DEPARTMENTAL COMPUTING: USERS TAKE CONTROL. **Departmental computing** is any type of computing done at the departmental level. The trend to departmental computing is causing computing resources, including computer specialists, to be moved closer to the people who use them. Departmental computing is responsible for the emergence of several new computer specialist careers: **user liaisons, microcomputer specialists,** and **office automation specialists.**

The user liaison is a "live-in" computer specialist who coordinates all computer-related activities within a particular functional area served. The user liaison is familiar with computers and the functional area served. Office automation specialists help employees make effective use of office systems. The microcomputer specialist stays abreast of the latest micro hardware and software technology and helps implement this technology in user areas.

16-4 INFORMATION CENTER SPECIALISTS. An information center is a "hands-on" facility in which computing resources, including training, are made available to end users. **Infor-**

mation center specialists provide three basic services: training, consulting, and software development.

16–5 OTHER CAREER OPPORTUNITIES: SERVICES, HARDWARE, SOFTWARE, AND EDUCATION. There are a host of computer-related career opportunities in addition to those in an information services department or a user group. These opportunities are found with computer services, hardware vendors, software vendors, and in the area of computer education.

The computer revolution is creating a tremendous demand for computer-related services. In response to this demand, a number of service organizations have emerged including **service bureaus**, **facilities management companies**, **turnkey companies** (or **system integrators**), consulting firms, database services, and computer repair stores.

Computer system manufacturers produce the processor and usually some or all of the peripheral equipment. Leasing companies, referred to as the third party, buy computers and lease them for five or more years. **Plug-compatible manufacturers** (**PCMs**) make peripheral devices that can be attached directly to another manufacturer's computer. **Value-added resellers** (**VARs**) integrate the hardware and software of several vendors with their own software, then sell the entire package. Computer retail outlets have made it possible for customers to shop for computers as they would any other consumer product.

Hardware vendors that market and service hardware need marketing representatives to sell the products and systems engineers to support them once they have been installed.

Software houses produce and sell proprietary software packages. Such software is protected by copyright laws and is sold under a licensing agreement.

The demand for computer education has created a a tremendous need for professors and instructors.

16–6 PROFESSIONALISM AND ETHICS. People whose jobs put them in contact with sensitive data can actually control events. This places even greater pressure on these people to conduct themselves as professionals. Certification programs, such as the **CDP**, **CCP**, **CSP**, **CISA**, and **CDE**, and professional societies help encourage professionalism.

A code of ethics provides direction for computer professionals and users so that they act responsibly in their application of computer technology.

16–7 CAREER MOBILITY AND COMPUTER KNOWLEDGE. Computer literacy is a prerequisite of employment in many professions, and in a few more years it may well be a requirement in most professions.

Review Exercises

Concepts

1. What is the difference between the job functions of development and maintenance programmers?
2. People of what job function would be involved in the selection and implementation of PBXs and front-end processors?
3. What type of programmer is usually associated with the technical support group? With the programming group?
4. What is the function of a user liaison?
5. Which job function accounts for all input to and output from a computer center?
6. Name four positions in the operations area.
7. Would every company with an information services department have a data base administrator? Why or why not?
8. Describe the business of VARs.
9. Contrast the job of a systems engineer with that of a marketing representative. How do they complement each other?
10. What are the unabbreviated names for the following societies: SIM, DPMA, and EDPAA?
11. What are the uses of a computerized dialing system?
12. What are the three basic services provided by a typical information center?
13. What type of company contracts with a client to install a complete system, including both hardware and software?
14. What is the function of the chief information officer?

Discussion

15. Revise the organizational chart of Figure 16–4 so only four people report to the director of information services.
16. Of the job functions described in this chapter, which would you prefer? Why?
17. Some companies will have only one level of programmer or systems analyst, where other companies will have two, three, and even four levels. Discuss the advantages of having several levels for a particular position (Programmer I, Programmer II, and so on).
18. Do you feel that programmers and systems analysts should report to the same person, or should they be organized into separate groups? Defend your answer.
19. Discuss the merit of systems analysts having programming experience.

20. Select five positions from the classified ad section of *Computerworld*. Describe what you feel would be appropriate experience and education requirements for each of the positions.

21. Relatively few computer professionals have any kind of certification. Is it really necessary?

22. Many, perhaps most, of the information services divisions do not have the luxury of full-time quality-control specialists. In their absence, who do you think handles the quality-control function?

23. Discuss the similarities shared by a company's information services function and its finance function.

Self-Test (by section)

16–1 During the decade of the 1990s, the number of computer programmers is expected to increase to over: (a) 800,000, (b) 2 million, or (c) 4 million.

16–2 **a.** The librarian handles most of the training in an information services department. (T/F)

b. One of the responsibilities of an information services department is to act as an advisor to users regarding the interpretation of general corporate policy. (T/F)

c. Information services management must maintain a balance between being _____ to user information needs and being _____.

d. The _____ analyzes, designs, and implements information systems.

16–3 **a.** The trend to departmental computing is causing more and more computer specialists to move to the user departments. (T/F)

b. Office automation specialist is a fancy name for a word processor. (T/F)

c. What job function is also called internal consultant or functional specialist: (a) programmer/analyst, (b) user liaison, or (c) CIO?

d. _____ specialists are trained in the function and operation of microcomputers and related hardware.

16–4 The availability of information centers has increased the number of one-time user service requests received by the information services department by 80%. (T/F)

16–5 **a.** PCM stands for plug-compatible manufacturer. (T/F)

b. Turnkey companies are also called _____.

c. What law is violated when a company duplicates proprietary software without permission: (a) civil rights, (b) antitrust, or (c) copyright?

16–6 a. _____ is the umbrella organization for computer-oriented societies.

b. Professional societies are not legally obligated to expel members for code-of-ethics infractions. (T/F)

16–7 Computer literacy is not yet a prerequisite of employment in any profession. (T/F)

Self-test answers. **16–1** a. **16–2** (a) F; (b) F; (c) responsive, responsible; (d) systems analyst. **16–3** (a) T; (b) F; (c) b; (d) microcomputer. **16–4** F. **16–5** (a) T; (b) system integrators; (c) c. **16–6** (a) AFIPS; (b) T. **16–7** F.

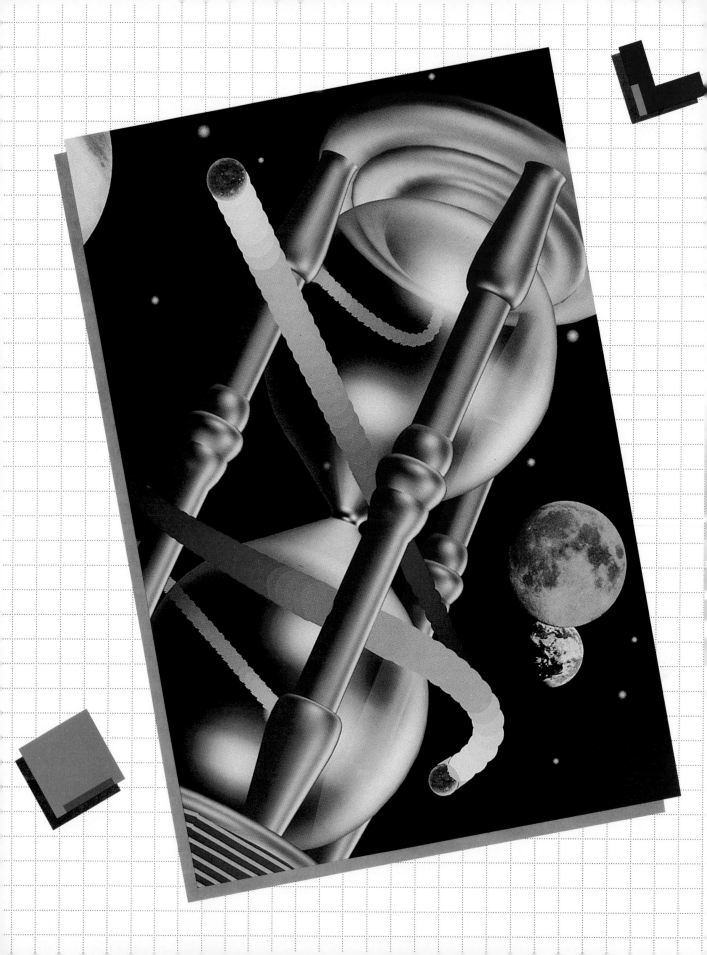

17

Computers in Society: Today and Tomorrow

STUDENT LEARNING OBJECTIVES

- To put society's dependence on computers in perspective.
- To identify and discuss controversial computer-related issues.
- To appreciate the scope and influence of computers in society.
- To identify causes of illegal information processing activity.
- To identify possible computer applications of the future.

Computers: Can We Live Without Them?

Reaching the Point of No Return

Albert Einstein said that "concern for man himself and his fate must always form the chief interest of all technical endeavors." There are those who believe that a rapidly advancing computer technology exhibits little regard for "man himself and his fate." They contend that computers are overused, misused, and generally detrimental to society. This group argues that the computer is dehumanizing and is slowly forcing society into a pattern of mass conformity. To be sure, the computer revolution is presenting society with difficult and complex problems, but they can be overcome.

Computers and information systems have enhanced our lifestyles to the point that most of us take them for granted. There is nothing wrong with this attitude, but we must recognize that society has made a very real commitment to computers. Whether it is good or bad, society has reached the point of no return in its dependence on computers. Stiff business competition means their continued and growing use. On the more personal level, we are reluctant to forfeit the everyday conveniences made possible by computers. More and more of us find that our personal computers are an integral part of our daily activities.

Society's dependence on computers is not always apparent. For example, today's automobile assembly line is as computer dependent as it is people dependent: An inventory-management system makes sure that parts are delivered to the right assembly point at the right time; computer-controlled robots do the welding and painting; and a process-control computer controls the movement of the assembly line.

Turn off the computer system for a day in almost any company, and observe the consequences. Most companies would cease to function. Turn off the computer system for several days, and many companies would cease to exist. A company that helps other companies recover from disasters, Sunguard Recovery Services, estimates that a large bank would be out of business in two days if its computer systems were down. It estimated that a distribution company would last three days, a manufacturing company would last five days, and

Crowded skies have resulted in a rash of "near misses" in recent years. Airlines and the Federal Aviation Administration are counting on sophisticated computer systems to eliminate or minimize the risk of mid-air collisions.

Some workers blame headaches, depression, anxiety, nausea, fatigue, and irritability on interacting with a video display terminal. These and other problems often associated with prolonged use of a VDT are collectively referred to as Video Operator's Distress Syndrome, or VODS. However, there is little evidence to link these problems with use of VDTs. The same problems occur in work environments that have no VDTs, from the executive suite to the assembly line.

an insurance company would last six days. A University of Minnesota study examined victims of disasters that disabled computing capabilities. The study concluded that the probability of a victim company's long-term survival was low if it was unable to recover critical operations within 30 hours. Recognizing their dependence on computers, most companies have made contingency plans that provide for backup computers in case of disaster.

Give Up My Computer? Never

Ask a secretary to trade a word processing system for a typewriter. Ask a physician for an alternative to a computer-controlled intensive care unit. Ask an airline executive how long the organization could continue to operate without its on-line reservation system. Ask yourself if you would give up the convenience of remote banking at automatic teller machines.

Our dependence on food has evolved into the joy of eating gourmet food—and so it is or can be with computers. Dependence is not necessarily bad as long as we keep it in perspective. We can't passively assume that computers will continue to enhance the quality of our lives. It is our obligation to learn to understand them so that we can better direct their application for society's benefit. Only through understanding can we control the misuse of computer technology. We, as a society, have a responsibility to weigh the benefits, burdens, and consequences of each successive level of automation.

17–2 Computers and the Law

Companies try to develop information systems and use the computer within the boundaries of any applicable law. Unfortunately, the laws are not always clear because many legal questions involving computers and information processing are being debated for the first time. To no one's surprise, computer law is the fastest growing type of law practice.

The inventory for most hospital blood banks is maintained on a computer. By mislabeling a quart of blood, a negligent employee could cause the wrong type blood to be administered to a patient. Negligence, one of the two kinds of illegal processing activity, is usually a result of poor input/output control.

Laws governing computer and information processing are few, and those that do exist are subject to a variety of interpretations. At present, two federal laws address computer crime. They are limited, however, because they apply only to those computer systems that in some way reflect a federal interest. These laws make it a felony to gain unauthorized access to any computer system with a federal interest with the intent to obtain anything of value, to defraud the system, or to cause more than $1000 in damage. Although most states have adopted computer crime laws, they are only the skeleton of what is needed to direct an orderly and controlled growth of automation. Only now are lawmakers beginning to recognize the impact of computers, and legislation is slow in coming. Critics say that the bottleneck is our lawmakers' reluctance to become computer literate.

Once we have definitive legislation, prosecution of computer crimes becomes another issue. Even when a computer crime is brought to the attention of the authorities, prosecutors lack sufficient technical knowledge to prepare a case. A judge and jury understand the concept of armed robbery and have a sense of the appropriate punishment, but what about computer crimes? Sophisticated computer crimes can be extremely complex and may be well beyond the understanding of most prosecutors, judges, and jurors. Legislation must be enacted and prosecution issues resolved before the criminal justice system can begin to cope with computer crime.

Illegal Information Processing

Negligence   The two main causes of illegal information processing are negligence and fraud. Negligence causes someone outside the organization to be unnecessarily inconvenienced, and it is usually a result of poor input/output control. For example, after she paid in full, a woman was sent dunning notices continually and visited by collection agencies for not making payments on her automobile. Although the records and procedures were in error, the company forcibly repossessed the automobile without thoroughly checking its procedures and the legal implications. The woman had to sue the company for the return of her automobile. The court ordered the automobile returned and the company to pay her a substantial sum as a penalty.

This is a clear case of a misinterpretation of a computer maxim—*GIGO* ("garbage in, garbage out"). GIGO does *not* stand for "garbage in, gospel out," as some people, who take the accuracy of computer output for granted, seem to think. The company blamed the incident on a mistake by the computer. The court stated that people enter data and interpret output and that the people affected should be treated differently from punched cards. *Trust in the infallibility of a computer does not constitute a defense in a court of law.* This incident points out the importance of careful system design and exhaustive testing.

Fraud The other area of illegal information processing is a premeditated or conscious effort to defraud the system. For example, a U.S. Customs official modified a program to print $160,000 worth of unauthorized federal payroll checks payable to himself and his co-conspirators. A 17-year-old high school student tapped into an AT&T computer and stole over $1 million worth of software. These are examples of fraud. Any illegal entry into a computer system for the purpose of personal gain is considered fraud. Over 50% of all computer frauds are internal; that is, they are committed by employees of the organization being defrauded. About 30% of those defrauding employees are MIS specialists who work in an information services department.

The Privacy of Personal Information

More media and legislative attention has been focused on the issue of an individual's privacy than on computer crimes involving negligence or fraud. The individual must be afforded certain rights regarding the privacy of data or of information relating to him or her.

The accumulation of personal data has become a matter of concern to our information society. Whether you realize it or not, you are continuously contributing data about yourself to some computer systems. For example, when you request a long-distance telephone number from an operator, your number and the requested number are recorded in a computer system. In this and most instances, personal data are collected as a matter of record, not for the purpose of abuse.

However, these rights have yet to be uniformly defined by our law-makers. In the absence of definitive legislative guidelines, the following principles are offered for consideration:

1. People should be made aware that data are being collected about them and made aware of how these data are to be used.
2. A person should be permitted to inspect his or her personal data and information.
3. A person should be permitted to supplement or clarify personal data and information.
4. Data and information found erroneous or irrelevant must be removed.
5. Disclosure of personal information should be limited to those with a need to know.
6. A log should be maintained of all people inspecting any individual's personal information.
7. Adequate safeguards must be in place to ensure the security of personal data and information (for example, locked doors, passwords).

17–3 Controversy: Another Word for Computer

Intense controversy is a by-product of the computer revolution. The emotions of both the general public and the computer community run high on computer-related issues. Some of the more heated are discussed here.

The Misuse of Personal Information

Sources of Personal Data The issue of greatest concern to the general public is the privacy of personal information. Some people fear that computer-based record keeping offers too much of an opportunity for the invasion of an individual's privacy. There is indeed reason for concern. For example, credit card users unknowingly leave a "trail" of activities and interests that, when examined and evaluated, can provide a rather comprehensive personal profile.

The date and location of all credit card transactions are recorded. In effect, when you charge a lunch, gasoline, or clothing, you are creating a chronological record of where you have been and your spending habits. From this information, a good analyst could compile a very accurate picture of your life-style. For example, the analyst could predict how you dress by knowing the type of clothing stores you patronize. On a more personal level, records are kept that detail the duration, time, and numbers of all your telephone calls. With computers, these numbers easily can be matched to people. So each time you make a phone call, you also leave a record of whom you call. Enormous amounts of personal data are maintained on everyone

This travel agent uses a computer-based reservation system to ensure that this couple gets the best value for their money. He also adds their name, address, and other personal information to the client data base. On average, each American is listed in about 40 government and 40 private-sector data bases. On a typical day, each person's name is passed between computers five times. People who are socially, economically, and politically active may be listed in hundreds of data bases.

by the IRS, your college, your employer, your creditors, your hospital, your insurance company, your broker, and on and on.

It is hoped that information about us is up-to-date and accurate. Unfortunately, much of it is not. Laws permit us to examine our records, but first we must find them. You cannot just write to the federal government and request to see your files. To be completely sure that you examine all your federal records for completeness and accuracy, you would have to write and probably visit each of the approximately 5800 agencies that maintain computer-based files on individuals. The same is true of computer-based personal data maintained in the private sector.

Violating the Privacy of Personal Information   Most will agree that the potential exists for abuse, but are these data being misused? Some say yes. Consider the states that sell lists of the addresses of and data on their licensed drivers. At the request of a manager of several petite women's clothing stores, a state provided the manager with a list of all licensed drivers in the state who were women between the ages of 21 and 40, less than 5 feet 3 inches tall, and under 120 pounds. You be the judge. Is the sale of such a list an abuse of personal information?

Personal information has become the product of a growing industry. Companies have been formed that do nothing but sell information about people. Not only are the people involved not asked for permission to use their data, they are seldom even told that their personal information is being sold! A great deal of personal data can be extracted from public records. For example, one company sends people to county courthouses all over the United States to gather publicly accessible data about people who have recently filed papers to purchase a home. Mailing lists are then sold to insurance companies, landscape companies, members of Congress seeking new votes, lawyers seeking new clients, and so on. Those placed on the mailing list eventually become targets of commerce and special-interest groups.

The use of personal information for profit and other purposes is growing at such a rapid rate that, for all practical purposes, the abuse of this information has slipped out from under the legislative umbrella. Antiquated laws, combined with judicial unfamiliarity with computers, make policing and prosecuting abuses of the privacy of personal information difficult and, in many cases, impossible. (See the "Computers and the Law" section earlier in this chapter.)

Computer Matching   Computer matching is a procedure whereby separate data bases are examined and individuals common to both are identified. Computer matching has been referred to as Orwellian by some, while auditors think it is a great help in their jobs.

The focus of most computer matching-applications is to identify people engaged in wrongdoing. Federal employees are being matched with those having delinquent student loans. Wages are then garnisheed to repay the loan. In another computer-matching case, a $30 million fraud was uncovered when questionable financial transactions were traced to common participants. The Internal Revenue Service also uses computer matching to identify tax cheaters. The IRS gathers descriptive data, such as neighborhood and automobile type, then uses sophisticated models to create life-style profiles. These profiles are matched against reported income on tax returns to predict whether people seem to be underpaying taxes. When the income and projected life-style do not match, the return is audited.

Securing the Integrity of Personal Information   Computer experts feel that the integrity of personal data can be more secure in computer data bases than in file cabinets. They contend that we can continue to be masters and not victims if we implement proper safeguards for the maintenance and release of this information and enact effective legislation to cope with the abuse of it.

Computer Monitoring

One of the newest and most controversial applications of information technology is computer monitoring. In computer monitoring, com-

Every minute, this antenna atop a skyscraper transmits and receives millions of pieces of data, much of which is personal or highly sensitive, to and from a satellite. Those who send information via data communications are responsible for ensuring that it is not intercepted by someone who could abuse it.

puters continuously gather and assimilate data on job activities to measure worker performance. Today computers monitor the job performance of over 7 million American workers. Most of these workers interact with a mainframe computer system via terminals or work on a micro that is part of a local area network. Others work with electronic or mechanical equipment that can be linked to a computer system.

Many clerical workers who use VDTs are evaluated by the number of documents they process per unit of time. At insurance companies, computer monitoring systems provide supervisors with information on the rate at which clerks process claims. Supervisors can request other information, such as time spent at the terminal and keying-error rate.

Computers monitor the activities of many jobs that demand frequent or constant use of the telephone. The number of inquiries handled by directory-assistance operators is logged by a computer. Some companies employ computers to monitor the use of telephones by all employees.

Although most computer monitoring is done at the clerical level, it is also being applied to higher level positions such as commodities brokers, programmers, loan officers, and plant managers. For example, CIM (computer integrated manufacturing) enables corporate executives to monitor the effectiveness of a plant manager on a real-time basis. At any given time executives can tap the system for productivity information, such as the rate of production for a particular assembly.

Workers complain that being constantly observed and analyzed by a computer adds unnecessary stress to their jobs. However, management is reluctant to give up computer monitoring because it has proved itself as a tool for increasing worker productivity. In general, affected workers are opposing any further intrusion into their professional privacy. On the other hand, management is equally vigilant in its quest for better information on worker performance.

Computer Crime

Computer crime is on the rise. There are many types of computer crimes, ranging from the use of an unauthorized password by a student to a billion-dollar insurance fraud. It is estimated that each year the total money lost from computer crime is greater than the sum total of that taken in all robberies. In fact, no one really knows the extent of computer crime because much of it is either undetected or unreported (most often the latter). In those cases involving banks, officers may elect to write off the loss rather than announce the crime and risk losing the goodwill of their customers.

Computer crime requires the cooperation of an experienced computer specialist. A common street thug does not have the knowledge or the opportunity to be successful at computer crime. The sophistication of the crime, however, makes it no less criminal.

The *The Computer Industry Almanac: 1989* by Egil Juliussen and Karen Juliussen (Brady, 1988, New York, New York) contains a plethora of interesting facts, figures, rankings, projections, trends, and sidelights on the computer industry. These summarized excerpts may give you added insight into this fascinating industry.

■ For every 1000 people in the United States there are 975 telephones, 889 televisions, and 167 computers.

■ The top five information systems companies (based on information systems revenues): IBM Corporation, Digital Equipment Corporation, Unisys Corporation, NCR Corporation, and Hewlett-Packard Company.

■ The top three mainframe manufacturers (based on value of installed systems in the United States): IBM Corporation, Unisys Corporation, and Amdahl Corporation.

■ The top three minicomputer manufacturers (based on total revenue): IBM Corporation, Digital Equipment Corporation, and Hewlett-Packard Company.

■ The top three microcomputer manufacturers (based on total revenue): IBM Corporation, Apple Computer Inc., and COMPAQ Computer Corporation.

■ The prices of RAM chips have declined an average of 20% per year over the last two decades. During the same period their storage capacity has quadrupled every $3\frac{1}{2}$ years.

■ The typical PC sold in 1993 will feature the following: price—$3000 to $3500; processor—Intel 80386 with 16Mb RAM; storage—160Mb hard disk, $3\frac{1}{2}$-inch microdisk, tape cassette backup; user interface—window software, mouse; printer—multifunction letter-quality, 500 cps; monitor—color, graphics coprocessor, VGA with 2Mb RAM; and connectivity—LAN interface, 9600-baud modem.

■ The top 10 general-purpose computer systems (based on value of installed systems): IBM 3090-400, IBM 3090-200, IBM 4381, IBM System/36, IBM 3090-IXX, IBM 3081, DEC VAX86XX, DEC VAX11/78X, IBM 3084, and IBM System/38.

■ The United States has over slightly more than half of the computer power in the world.

■ IBM employs over 400,000 people. Lotus Development Corporation employs about 0.5% of that number.

■ The top four career concerns for computer professionals: salaries, technical obsolescence, educational programs, and job market/security.

■ The top three vendors of DBMS software (based on market share): IBM Corporation, Cullinet Software, and Information Builders.

■ The U.S. electronic publishing market (the dissemination of information via electronic means) is expected to grow from $1.76 billion in 1988 to $6.84 billion in 1992.

■ By the turn of the century, the computer/electronics industry is expected to be a $900 billion industry, second only to agriculture.

■ CompuServe, Inc., the Ohio-based information network, has over 400,000 subscribers.

■ An experimental $3\frac{1}{2}$-inch microdisk produced at IBM's Almaden research lab stores 10 gigabits—more than 500 times the capacity of the current industry-standard microdisk.

■ Ed Roberts, the father of the first commercially successful personal computer (the Altair 8800), is now a physician in Georgia.

■ The Internal Revenue Service has ruled that you can deduct the cost of a personal computer as a business expense if, and only if, your employer requires you to have one.

■ You can subscribe to any one of approximately 20 diskette magazines for about $10 to $20 per month.

■ October is Computer Learning Month. (The first was in 1987.)

■ The top five independent microcomputer software publishers (based on total revenue): Microsoft Corporation, Lotus Development Corporation, Ashton-Tate Incorporated, WordPerfect Corporation, and Autodesk Incorporated.

Computer crime is a relatively recent phenomenon. Legislation, the criminal justice system, and industry are not yet adequately prepared to cope with it. (See the "Computer and the Law" section earlier in this chapter.) Only a few police and FBI agents in the entire country have been trained to handle cases involving computer crime. And when a case comes to court, few judges have the background necessary to understand the testimony.

Recognizing the potential severity of computer crime, the legal system and industry are trying to speed up precautionary measures. Some say we are still moving too slowly and that a Three Mile Island–level catastrophe is the only thing that will make industry and government believe how severe computer crime can be.

There is a growing concern that the media is glorifying the illegal entry and use of computer systems by overzealous hackers. These "electronic vandals" have tapped into everything from local credit agencies to top-secret defense systems. The evidence of unlawful entry, perhaps a revised record or access during nonoperating hours, is called a **footprint**. Some malicious hackers leave much more than a footprint—they infect the computer system with a *virus*. Viruses, which were discussed in Chapter 13, "System Implementation," can wreak havoc on a computer system's data bases and software, sometimes causing millions of dollars in damage.

A few hackers and computer professionals have chosen computer crime as a profession. But the threat of computer crime may be even greater from managers and consultants because they are in the best position to pull it off. They know how the systems operate, and they know the passwords needed to gain access to the systems.

The "Cashless Society"

The growing number of *automatic teller machines* (*ATM*) have made *electronic funds transfer* (*EFT*) very visible to the public. In EFT, money

The cashless society may someday become a reality, but not soon. Most banks are still doing everything they can to break the "wall"—the point at which more than 33% of their customers use ATMs. Some banks pay customers as much as $5 to give an ATM a try; other banks have begun to charge customers for teller transactions. Customers at this bank can complete their transactions at an ATM or with a real teller.

Very few jobs will be unchanged in the information society. Fast-food restaurants have used computers for over a decade to expedite the flow of food and people. Other types of restaurants are going high tech, too. Waiters enter orders on terminals like this by pressing keys corresponding to the appropriate menu item (New York strip) and options (medium) at terminals located throughout the restaurant. The order is routed to the kitchen staff, inventory is updated, and upon request, the customer's check is tallied and printed.

is transferred electronically from bank to bank, and from account to account, via computers. Each weekday the financial institutions of the world use EFT to transfer over one trillion dollars—that's $1,000,000,000,000! Applications of EFT are being implemented all around us. Automatic teller machines and automatic payroll transfer systems have become commonplace. Some banks offer *home banking* services that permit customers to pay bills and perform banking transactions via their personal computers without leaving home.

The debate rages on as we move closer to a cashless society. Is this a reasonable and prudent manner in which to handle financial transactions? It is well within the state of the art to just about eliminate money and make the transition to a cashless society.

Sometime in the future, the scope of EFT may be expanded because the buyer will be able to use a universal *smart card* (smart, because of the tiny embedded microprocessor) and perhaps a password to buy everything from candy bars to automobiles. Upon purchasing an item, a buyer would give the card, called a *debit card*, to the seller. The seller would use the purchaser's card to log the sale on a *point-of-sale* (*POS*) terminal linked to a network of banking computers. The amount of the sale would then be transferred from the buyer's account to the seller's account.

The advantages of an expanded use of EFT are noteworthy. EFT would eliminate the cumbersome administrative work associated with handling money and checks. It would also eliminate the need to carry money, eliminate rubber checks and counterfeit money, and minimize the possibility of error. It would provide a detailed record of all transactions. EFT would also eliminate the expense of making money. The cost of manufacturing a penny now exceeds the value of the coin!

The disadvantages are equally noteworthy. The critical issue is EFT's potential for the misuse of personal information. EFT generates a chronological record of all purchases. (See the discussion in the earlier section "The Misuse of Personal Information.") In effect, this type of system permits everything from a person's life-style to his or her location to be monitored. Opponents of EFT are also concerned about its vulnerability to crime.

Although there is a trend toward more electronic funds transfer, some experts feel that EFT is about to reach its peak of acceptance. Others think that total EFT is inevitable within the next 10 years.

The Affects of Automation on Jobs

Concern over the effects of automation began two hundred years ago with the industrial revolution, and the public is still concerned. To many people, computers mean automation, and automation means loss of jobs. Just as the industrial revolution created hundreds of new job opportunities, so will the information revolution.

There is no doubt that the emergence of computer technology has resulted in the elimination of jobs involving routine, monotonous, and sometimes hazardous tasks. However, the elimination of these jobs has been offset by the creation of more challenging jobs. For the most part, people whose jobs have been eliminated have been displaced to jobs carrying greater responsibilities and offering more opportunities. It is common for bookkeepers to become systems analysts, for draftpersons to advance to computer-aided design, and for secretaries to become specialists in a myriad of computer applications from word processing to data management. This pattern is repeated thousands of times each month.

Automation will continue to eliminate and create jobs. Historically, advancement in technology has increased overall productivity

As oil companies automate the distribution of gasoline and the handling of credit transactions, service station owners and attendants must familiarize themselves with computers.

"As a premium for my deposit I get a back rub? When do I collect?"

in certain areas, thereby cutting the number of workers needed. In addition, a new wave of jobs is created in the wake of cutbacks in traditional areas. With the cost of labor increasing and the cost of computers decreasing, the trend toward the automation of routine activities will probably continue. However, to realize a smooth transition to an automated environment, industry and government must recognize that they have a social responsibility to retrain those who will be displaced to other jobs.

The National Data Base

Like EFT, the technology is available to establish a national data base. Many have proposed a national data base as a central repository for all personal data. An individual would be assigned a unique identification number at birth. This ID number would replace the Social Security number, driver's license number, student identification number, and dozens of others.

A national data base would consolidate the personal data now stored on tens of thousands of manual and computer-based files. It could contain an individual's name, past and present addresses, dependent data, work history, medical history, marital history, tax data, criminal records, military history, credit rating and history, and so on. Proponents of the national data base recognize that the aforementioned data are currently maintained, but they are redundant and often inaccurate or out of date. Proponents' contention is that at least the national data base would be accurate and up-to-date.

Those who are in favor of a national data base list certain advantages. A national data base could provide the capability of monitoring the activities of criminal suspects; virtually eliminating welfare fraud; quickly identifying illegal aliens; making an individual's medical history available at any hospital in the country; taking the 10-year census almost automatically; and generating valuable information. Medical researchers could isolate geographical areas with inordinately high incidences of certain illnesses. The Bureau of Labor Statistics could monitor real, as opposed to reported, employment levels on a daily basis. The information possibilities are endless.

Those who oppose the national data base call it impersonal and an invasion of privacy. Their feelings are that any advantages are more than offset by the potential for abuse of such a data base.

The creation of a national data base is an extremely complex undertaking, the social implications notwithstanding. It is unlikely that we will see such a data base in this century. However, with the growing concern about welfare fraud, tax evasion, crime, and the influx of illegal aliens, it may be an increasingly appealing alternative.

17–4 Computer Applications of the Future

It seems as if the computer is everywhere—yet we are only scratching the surface of possible computer applications. At every level, our society is clamoring for more information and improvements in productivity through automation. The outlook for innovative, exciting, and beneficial computer applications is bright.

Expectations and Reality

The short-term expectations of the general public for computer technology are probably excessive. Intense media coverage has given the computer novice the impression that bedmaking, dishwashing, and domestic robots are just around the corner; that computer-controlled organ transplants are almost perfected; and that computers have all the answers! To be sure, we are making progress in leaps and bounds, but we have a long way to go before such applications are feasible. Nevertheless, these rising expectations are a challenge to computer professionals to deliver.

Of course, no one can see into the future, but we can extrapolate from trends and our knowledge of current research. This section paints a picture of some computer applications that are sociologically, economically, and technologically feasible within the next decade.

Information Networks

As the percentage of homes with micros increases, so does the potential for *information networks*. Information networks, a number of which exist today, provide certain services to an end user through a communications link to a microcomputer. Several currently available services provided by information networks are described

Although the state of the art of technology enables this tiny chip to hold 4 million bits, it's not enough. Our largest and fastest computers can simulate the wing, the fuselage, or the tail of an airplane in flight, but that's not enough. Aerospace engineers want the capability of simulating an entire airplane in flight. Their expectations are representative of people in other professions who already have plans for computers that are not yet developed.

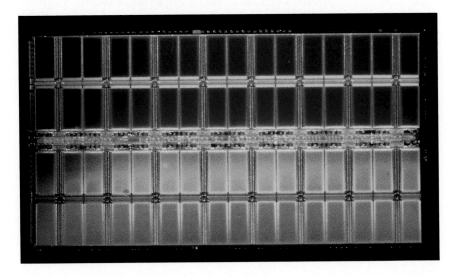

Because this real estate company subscribes to a regional on-line multilist service, it is enjoying a distinct advantage over its competitors. Real estate agents relying on traditional manual approaches are unable to offer the level of service made possible by the computer-based system. Some day, all realtors will have on-line access to a nationwide multilist service.

in Chapter 14, "Word Processing, Desktop Publishing, and Communications Software." The two-way system provides the end user with information (for example, airline flight schedules) and permits the end user to enter data (such as reservations for airline flights).

The four components of an information network are the central computer, the data base, the network, and the microcomputers. The central computer system is accessed by end users who desire a particular service. The data base contains data and screens of information (perhaps a graphic display of a refrigerator with price and delivery information) that are presented to users. As microcomputers proliferate, a greater variety of information networks will be made available to more and more people. Even now, microcomputers that can access these networks are available in many airplanes and hotel rooms.

Hotel guests can communicate with their homes, companies, or virtually anyone else through the use of computers in their rooms. They can obtain theater or airline tickets, shop or order gifts, scan restaurant menus, and even play video games. In a few years, all major hotels will provide their guests with access to microcomputers and information networks.

Commercially available information networks have an endless number of applications. Let's take real estate as an example. Suppose you live in Tuscon, Arizona, and have been transferred to Salt Lake City, Utah. It is only a matter of time before you will be able to gain access to a nationwide information network that maintains an up-to-date listing of every home in the country that is for sale. Here is how it will work: You will enter your purchase criteria: Salt Lake City, Utah; $120,000 to $180,000; no more than one mile from an elementary school; double garage; and so on. The system will then present pictures and specifications of those homes that meet your criteria.

Communications

The telephone as we know it will probably disappear. In the relatively near future, the function of the telephone will be incorporated into our home computers so we can not only hear but see the person on the other end of the line. Moreover, we will be able to pass data and information back and forth as if we were sitting at the same table.

Computers and data communications have turned our world into a "global village." This satellite is being launched into geosynchronous orbit above the Atlantic Ocean. It and a couple of earth stations will link North America with Europe.

Most of us will have ready access to microcomputers, whether at the office or on the road. From virtually anywhere, we will be able to use our microcomputers to read 50 different newspapers, turn on the heat at home, call a cab, order groceries, buy shares of stock, or make hotel reservations.

The television of the not-too-distant future will function as a terminal and enable limited two-way communication via a keyboard. You will be able to request that the stock market reports be subtitled across the screen while you continue to watch your favorite program. Newscasters will be able to sample the thinking of tens of thousands of people in a matter of minutes. After they ask the questions, we at home will respond on our keyboards. Our responses will be sent immediately to a central computer for analysis, and the results reported almost instantaneously. In this way, television news programs will keep us abreast of public opinion on critical issues and the feeling toward political candidates on a day-to-day basis.

In the Office

The traditional letter may never become obsolete, but electronic mail will become an increasingly popular alternative, especially because most of us will have our own microcomputers at home and at work. To prepare and send a letter, an executive will dictate—not to a secretary, but to a computer! The executive's words will be transcribed directly into text, without key entry. The letter will then be routed to appropriate destinations via electronic mail. The recipient of the letter can request that it be displayed at a microcomputer or read using synthesized speech.

With professionals spending a greater percentage of their working day interacting with the computer, look for the telecommuting and the electronic cottage concept to gain momentum (see Chapter 14, "Word Processing, Desktop Publishing, and Communications Software"). At least a part of the work of most professionals will be

As more companies increase their numbers of sophisticated workstations, look for an increase in the use hypertext systems. Such systems enable the on-line presentation of virtually any kind of document. With hypertext capabilities, companies can create on-line versions of sales manuals, training manuals, parts manuals, procedures, and policy statements—all complete with illustrations, diagrams, and icons. While interacting with a diagnostic expert system, this man was told that he would find the solution to his problem in the repair manual. The expert system then dispays the appropriate pages for the on-line manual.

done at home. For many professionals, their work is at their fingertips, whether at home or the office. Look for the emergence of telecommuting and cottage industries to alter the demographics of cities. Less frequent trips to the office will surely encourage urban spread.

A Peek at the Crystal Ball

Manufacturing Manufacturing companies, especially those that are labor intensive, are being faced with growing competition from international markets. In response to this challenge, James Baker, an executive vice president at General Electric, noted that American industry is confronted with three choices: ". . . automate, migrate, or evaporate." Companies can *automate*, thereby lowering costs and increasing productivity. They can *migrate* (move) to countries that offer less expensive labor. Or they can *evaporate*. Most have elected to automate, even with the blessing of organized labor. As one labor leader put it: "If we don't do it, I'm convinced we'll lose the jobs anyway."

With the trend toward greater use of automation, we can anticipate an increase in the number of industrial robots (see Chapter 11, "Applications of Information Technology"). As the smokestack industries become more "high-tech," the complexion of their workforce will change. There will be a shift of emphasis from brawn to brains. A few unmanned plants already exist, and this number will grow.

This man is shopping—via computer. The shift to the convenience of shopping at home is well underway with the phenomenal growth of the mail-order industry. However, shopping at home via computer is limited to those who subscribe to an information network. These people can comparison shop from the comfort of their own homes, select the best deal, pay via electronic funds transfer, and have any of hundreds of thousands of products delivered to their doors.

These radical changes are a by-product of our transition from an industrial society to an information society. Traditional jobs will change or be lost forever, but new and, it is hoped, more challenging jobs will emerge to replace them.

Retail Information networks will enable us to do our shopping electronically. Instead of walking down the aisle of a grocery store or thumbing through stacks of shirts, we will be able to use our personal computer in conjunction with an information network to select and purchase almost any retail item. The items selected will be automatically picked, packaged, and possibly delivered to our doorstep. This information service will help speed the completion of routine activities, such as grocery shopping, and leave us more time for leisure, travel, and the things we enjoy.

Time-consuming check authorizations at grocery stores may be a thing of the past with the introduction of cash dispensing systems. This customer uses his bank card (with magnetic stripe) and a keyboard to withdraw cash from his bank account.

Financial Services   The overwhelming acceptance of automatic teller machines has spurred the trend toward more electronic funds transfer (EFT). Over the next decade, transaction documents, such as checks and credit card purchase slips, will begin to disappear. Monies will be electronically transferred at the time of the purchase from the seller's account to the buyer's account. Total EFT will require an enormously complex communications network that links the computers of all financial institutions with virtually all businesses. Such a network is technologically and economically feasible today, but sociologically we are a few years away.

Publishing   Certainly books, magazines, newspapers, and the printed word in general will prevail for casual reading and study. However, it is not unreasonable to expect that publishers will offer *soft copy* publishing as an alternative to *hard copy* publishing. We'll be able to receive books, magazines, and newspapers in electronic format, perhaps via data communications on our home computer or on a disk. A few specialized computer trade magazines are available now on disks, but in a few years a wide variety of magazines will be distributed via data communications or disks.

Can you imagine a bookstore without books? It's possible! With customized printing on demand, you will be able to browse through virtually any current book from a terminal. Then, if you wish to purchase the book, it will be printed and bound while you wait!

In the short term, CD-ROM (see Chapter 6, "Data Storage Devices and Media") is expected have the greatest influence on the publishing industry. Publishers can offer over 250,000 pages of text in the form of a single CD-ROM disk. Libraries, already cramped for space, are considering the possibility of providing many reference materials, such as encyclopedias and journals, in the form of CD-ROM.

Transportation   Someday soon computer-based automobile navigation systems will be standard equipment on cars. There are already enough satellites in the sky for an on-board automobile navigation system to obtain a "fix" establishing the location of the car. You will be able to call up appropriate regional or city maps from on-board optical laser disk storage. The car's location will be noted on a video display of a road map, and you will be able to plot your course and track your progress.

Recent advances in superconductivity have opened the door for new applications of computer technology, especially in the area of transportation. In the photo, a magnet is floating above the surface of a superconducting material. Superconductors act as magnetic mirrors, causing magnets to repel themselves.

It's hard to find a more people-oriented entertainment facility than Walt Disney World's Epcot Center, yet much of the action is computer controlled. Its computer center controls your movement through the various exhibits, the movement of hundreds of lifelike animals and people, the sounds you hear, and even the temperature in the buildings.

By now you are probably saying that this Buck Rogers–type application is a bit farfetched. Well, prototypes of automobile navigation systems are now being tested—and they work!

Entertainment   How about interactive soap operas? Yes, because of the two-way communication capabilities of your television/terminal, you can be an active participant in how a story unfolds. The soaps will be shot so that they can be pieced together in a variety of ways. Imagine—you can decide whether Michelle marries Clifton or Patrick!

It won't be long before the rough drafts of television scripts are written by computers. Many weekly television shows have a formula plot. For instance, heroes are presented with a problem situation. They confront the problem, they get in trouble, they get out of trouble, stick the bad guys, and live to do it again next week. Formula plots lend themselves nicely to computer-produced rough-draft scripts. The computer system already will have the names of the key characters on file. The systems also will have dialogues for a variety of situations. The names of nonregulars (such as the bad guys) will be generated

Mathematicians, among the first users of computers, have recently discovered a new dimension of their use. While graphing complex equations, they created a new and intriguingly beautiful form of art called *fractal geometry*.

randomly by the computer. The script writers will enter a story-line sketch, then the computer will piece together dialogues and scenes within the restrictions of the show's formula plot and the story line. The script writers will then refine the draft script.

Sculptors may someday become more productive with the help of computers. For example, a sculptor will be able to create three-dimensional "sketches" on a computer, much the same way an engineer designs a part using computer-aided design (CAD). The computer will activate a robotlike sculpting tool that will rough out the general shape of the figure. The sculptor will then add the creative touches that turn a piece of clay into a work of art.

Health Care Expert systems have already benefited physicians by helping them diagnose physical illnesses (see Chapter 10, "The MIS and Decision Support Systems"). In the near future we can anticipate expert systems that help diagnose and treat mental illnesses and emotional problems as well. Psychologists and psychiatrists will continue to work with patients in the classical manner, but with the added advantage of a "partner." This "partner" will be able to tap a vast storehouse of knowledge and recommend everything from lines of questioning to diagnosis and treatment.

Encouraging research leads us to believe that the computer will play a vital role in tomorrow's medical "miracles." We are still a few steps away, but lifesaving computer implants are inevitable. These tiny computers will control mechanical devices that can replace organs that have ceased to function. Other medical research has given

A few years ago paraplegic Nan Davis shocked the world by walking to the podium to recieve her college diploma—with a little computer assistance. Here she is demonstrating an experimental outdoor tricycle that uses a computerized electrical stimulation-feedback system to stimulate paralyzed muscles to pedal the tricycle. Eventually researchers hope that paraplegics will be able to do much more than take a few crude steps or pedal tricycles. If research goes as planned, a pocket-sized computer will control sensors implanted in the skin that will give paraplegics the ability to walk forward and backward, sit, stand, and even climb stairs.

paraplegics renewed hope that they may someday walk again with the assistance of a computerized nervous system. The handicapped can look forward to improved mobility and independence. Sophisticated prostheses will be activated by voice, motion, muscle activity, breathing, and even the blinking of an eye.

Medical and technical researchers have dared to contemplate integrating computers and the brain. That is, eventually we may electronically connect tiny computer implants to the brain to enhance the brain's computational and factual-recall capabilities.

Government Computer-enhanced photography will enable us to break out the finer details in photographs. With computer-enhanced photography, the headlines in a newspaper can be read from a photograph taken 150 miles above the earth. Its immediate application is in the area of military intelligence.

Local, state, and federal elections might not require an army of volunteers. Politicians might not have to worry about rain on Election Day. We will eventually record our votes through home or business microcomputers. Such a system will encourage greater voter participation although, of course, security and voter authenticity will be a concern. One possible solution would be to ask voters to identify themselves with their Social Security number and a voter registration security code known only to the voter. A few years later we won't need to carry cards or remember numbers; each voter's identity will be validated when the system reads our fingerprint and our voiceprint. All we will have to do to identify ourselves will be to enter our voiceprint by speaking a few words and our fingerprint by placing our finger near an optical laser scanner.

Education Computer systems are revolutionizing the education process. For example, as students learn via computer-based instruction (CBT), they can request visual reinforcement from hundreds of

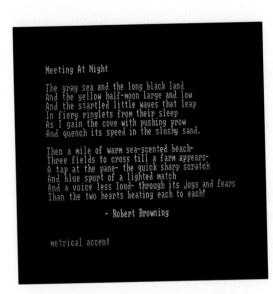

An authoring system can help writers bring their words alive on a computer screen with the use of color, animation, and interesting graphics. According to Edmund Skellings, a Florida poet laureate and developer of a system called The Electronic Poet, a professor can "show the intricate patterning and texturing of sound embedded in the work of the great poets of the past." This photo shows how Robert Browning's poem "Meeting at Night" can be highlighted to demonstrate metrical accent.

still and moving pictures stored on optical laser disks. There is truth to the old saying that "one picture is worth a thousand words."

Computers are beginning to play a more active role in the education of learning-disabled children. Current human-resource limitations do not permit the luxury of constant one-on-one attention for these children. However, in between group and one-on-one sessions, a computer system capable of responding to a wide variety of inputs can be dedicated to each child. For example, computers complement the kinesthetic (touch and feel) approach to dyslexia (impaired reading ability). Children with dyslexia can engage in interactive reading that offers immediate feedback and reinforcement. At present, we are only beginning to tap the computer as an educational tool.

Computers have the potential of enabling nationwide uniform testing for elementary and secondary students. With uniform learning standards for each subject at each level, it will be possible to advance students from one grade to the next on the basis of achievement rather than age.

Artificial Intelligence

We have access to artificial sweeteners, artificial grass, artificial flowers—why not artificial intelligence? To some extent, we do!

What Is Artificial Intelligence?   Today's computers can simulate many human capabilities, such as reaching, grasping, calculating, speaking, remembering, comparing numbers, and drawing. Researchers are working to expand these capabilities and, therefore, the power of computers by developing hardware and software that can imitate intelligent human behavior. For example, researchers are working on systems that have the ability to reason, to learn or accumulate knowledge, to strive for self-improvement, and to simulate human sensory and mechanical capabilities. This general area of research is known as *artificial intelligence,* or **AI**.

A number of expert systems are being created for the manufacturing environment. Here an engineer and an AI expert are planning an expert system that will help quality control personnel identify the source of problems that they encounter during testing.

Artificial intelligence? To some, the mere mention of artificial intelligence creates visions of electromechanical automatons replacing human beings. But as anyone involved in the area of artificial intelligence will tell you, there is a distinct difference between human beings and machines. Computers will never be capable of simulating the distinctly human qualities of creativity, humor, and emotions! However, computers can drive machines that mimic human movements (such as picking up objects and placing them in a prescribed location) and provide the "brains" for systems that simulate the human thought process within a particular area of expertise (tax preparation, medical diagnosis, and so on).

Even though significant strides have been made in the area of artificial intelligence, research is still at the embryonic level. Each year AI researchers come up with new discoveries and innovations that serve to redefine artificial intelligence. Some say that AI is such an abstract concept that it defies definition. It seems as if each new revelation in AI research raises more questions than it answers. "It's a moving horizon," as Marvin Minsky, a pioneer in AI research from MIT has put it.

The Future of Artificial Intelligence Research in the field of artificial intelligence can be divided into categories (see Figure 17–1):

- Knowledge-based and expert systems (discussed in Chapter 10, "The MIS and Decision Support Systems")
- Natural languages (discussed in Chapter 8, "Programming Languages and Software Concepts")

FIGURE 17–1 Categories of Artificial Intelligence

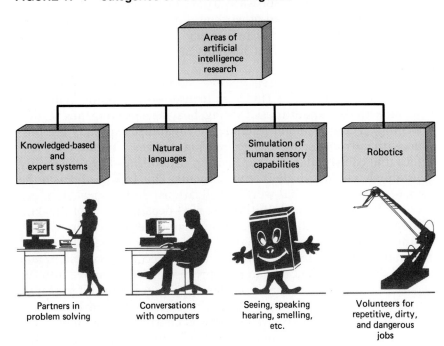

- Simulation of human sensory capabilities (discussed in Chapter 5, "Input/Output Devices")
- Robotics (discussed in Chapter 11, "Applications of Information Technology")

The concepts associated with each of these areas of AI research have been discussed in previous chapters, but where is AI headed in the future?

Expert systems already have begun to make a major impact on the way people in the business community make decisions. Today there are hundreds of expert systems, most of which were developed at great expenses to service a particular company. In a few years, there will be thousands of expert systems. In the professional environment, physicians in every specialty will have at least one expert system at their disposal. During the 1990s, it is not unreasonable to expect that some doctors will accept expert systems as a critical medical instrument and bring them into the examining room. Any person who routinely does some type of screening, such as a bank loan officer or a recruiter, will do so with the help of an expert system. At home we will be able to check an expert system out of the local library that will help us to decorate our homes.

Natural language software enables computer systems to accept, interpret, and execute instructions in the native language of the end user, typically English. At present, some relatively primitive natural languages enable a user-friendly interface of corporate data bases and expert systems. But with most other software, we must use programming and the selection of menu options to tell the computer what to do. In the future, look for natural language interfaces to accompany virtually all user-oriented software, from word processing to inventory modeling packages. Instead of working through a series of menus to specify the layout of a word processing document, the user might enter, "Set the left and right margins at $1\frac{1}{2}$ inches and 1 inch and double space the document."

One area of AI research involves computer simulation of human sensory capabilities. This area focuses on equipping computer systems with the capabilities of seeing, hearing, speaking, and feeling (touching). These artificial intelligence capabilities already are possible with current technology to varying degrees. "Intelligent" machines that can simulate human sensory capabilities have the ability to establish a link with their environments. This link has opened the door to a number of real-world applications. Today most data are keyed in from a keyboard. Within the next decade, much of the data will be entered verbally. For example, mail-order customers will be able to verbalize order information over the telephone. The verbal information will be interpreted by a speech recognition system and entered directly to the computer for processing. As we move into the twentieth century, keys may be replaced by voiceprints, fingerprints, veinprints, and other unique human attributes that easily can be interpreted by computers. AI research is continually enhancing the abilities of computers to simulate human sensory capabilities. In the near future, we will be able to have meaningful verbal conversations

With the prospect of increased productivity, manufacturing companies have been rushing to install more and more applications of robotics. In this photo, an industrial robot positions materials for assembly in a pick-and-place application.

with computers. These computers will be able to talk, listen, and even smell the roses!

Industrial robots can be "taught" to perform almost any repetitive manipulative task, such as painting a car, screwing on a bolt, moving material, and even complex tasks, such as inspecting a manufactured part for defects. However, most existing robots are stationary—they are programmed to operate within a well-defined work area. The inevitable advances in vision systems will enable robots to move about the work area just as people do, probably within the decade of the 1990s.

The Commercialization of Artificial Intelligence   Scientists have been working to build "thinking machines" for decades and, for the most part, paying little attention to the commercial viability of their work. For example, during the formative years of AI, hundreds of researchers were working to develop software that would enable humans to test their chess-playing skills against the skills of a computer. Early chess programs challenged the club player, but today's programs have proved to be formidable opponents of grand masters. Although of questionable commercial value, chess-related research has provided scientists with a greater understanding of the human thought process and how the process can be simulated by computers and software.

In the 1960s and 1970s, the power of multimillion-dollar computers was needed to support even simple commercial AI applications. By the mid-1980s computer technology had finally caught up to AI. Now relatively inexpensive but powerful microcomputers have the capabilities of supporting a wide variety of AI applications. For several years artificial intelligence was the darling of the computer and MIS industry. But after two or three years of heavy losses and no profits in sight, most of the companies folded. Reality had set in: People are not willing to buy products that do not contribute to profit. Executives at the surviving AI companies now have recognized that to be commercially viable, AI must be packaged in a manner that will increase productivity or help in the decision-making process. Today aggressive AI companies are marketing innovative products with the potential of having a positive impact on a company's bottom line.

17–5 Oversights: Are We Keeping Pace with the Technology?

For whatever reasons, business, government, and education have elected not to implement computer applications that are well within the state of the art of computer technology. Many cost-effective systems are working in the laboratory but have not been implemented in practice. The implementation of these potentially beneficial systems has lagged behind the state of the art of computer technology by five to 10 years. Some "oversights" are presented below.

Several experimental homes feature computer-controlled lighting, temperature, and security systems. Such systems would start the coffee maker so we could awaken to the aroma of freshly brewed coffee. They would even help with paying the bills. This technology is available today and is relatively inexpensive if properly designed and installed during construction. In any case, such a system would pay for itself in a couple of years through energy savings alone.

Although some sophisticated computer-controlled medical equipment is now being used, relatively few physicians take advantage of the information-producing potential of the computer to improve patient care. They have expert systems that can help them diagnose diseases, drug interaction data bases that can help them prescribe the right drug, and computer-assisted searches that can call up literature pertinent to a particular patient's illness. All the applications have the potential of saving lives.

A cashless society is technologically and economically possible. In a cashless society, the amount of a purchase would be transferred automatically from the purchaser's bank account to the vendor's bank account. Thus billing, payment, and collection problems would be eliminated, along with the need to write checks and to remember to mail them.

There are many reasons why these cost-effective and potentially beneficial computer applications have not been implemented. Among them are historical momentum, resistance to change, limited education, and lack of available resources. In the case of domestic-control

Some say that we are not tapping the full potential of computers in our system of education—these students being the exception rather than the rule. While doing research for a term paper, they are saving time by entering appropriate comments and citations directly into a word processing document.

Francis Bacon said, "Knowledge is power." You now have a base of computer knowledge. Combine this knowledge with your innate creative abilities and you are poised to make a significant impact on whatever field you choose to pursue, be it in the business world, health care, government, education, or the arts.

systems, it is probably a matter of education, both of the builder and the homeowner. In the case of computer diagnosis of illness, some physicians are reluctant to admit that the computer is a valuable diagnostic aid. In the case of the cashless society, the question of invasion of privacy is yet to be resolved.

These and hundreds of other "oversights" will not be implemented until enough people have enough knowledge to appreciate their potential. This is where you come in!

17-6 Your Challenge

Having mastered the contents of this book and this course, you are now poised to exploit the benefits of the computer in your personal and business lives. You should also have an appreciation of the scope and impact of computers on society, both now and in the future. This course, however, is only the beginning. The computer learning process is ongoing. The dynamics of a rapidly advancing computer technology demands a constant updating of skills and expertise. Perhaps the excitement of technological innovation and ever-changing opportunities for application is part of the lure of computers.

By their very nature, computers bring about change. With the total amount of computing capacity in the world doubling every two years, we can expect even more dramatic change in the future. The cumulative effects of these changes are altering the basic constructs of society and the way we live, work, and play. Terminals and microcomputers have replaced calculators and ledger books; electronic mail speeds communication; word processing has almost eliminated typewriters; computer-aided design has rendered the T-square and compass obsolete; computer-based training has become a part of the teaching process; EFT may eventually eliminate the need for money;

on-line shopping is affecting consumer buying habits . . . and the list goes on.

We as a society are, in effect, trading a certain level of computer dependence for an improvement in the quality of life. This improvement in the way we live is not a foregone conclusion. It is our challenge to harness the power of the computer and direct it toward the benefit of society. To be an active participant in this age of information, we as a society and as individuals must continue to learn about and understand computers. Charles Lecht, an outspoken advocate of computers, is fond of saying, "What the lever is to the arm, the computer is to the mind."

Never before has such opportunity presented itself so vividly. This generation, *your generation*, has the technological foundation and capability of changing dreams to reality.

Summary Outline and Important Terms

17–1 COMPUTERS: CAN WE LIVE WITHOUT THEM? Society has reached a point of no return with regard to dependence on computers. Business competition demands the use of computers. We are also reluctant to give up those personal conveniences made possible by the computer. Only through understanding can we control the misuse or abuse of computer technology.

17–2 COMPUTERS AND THE LAW. An information system should be developed to comply with any applicable law. At present the laws that govern the privacy of personal data and illegal computer-based activity are inadequate, but these laws are being revised and expanded. Therefore, the privacy of data and the possibility of fraud or negligence should be a consideration in the design of every information system.

17–3 CONTROVERSY: ANOTHER WORD FOR COMPUTER. The emotions of both the general public and the computer community run high on computer-related issues. The abuse of personal information is perhaps the issue of greatest concern. Other issues include the merits of computer monitoring, coping with computer crime, the growing use of electronic funds transfer, the effect of automation on jobs, and the implementation of a national data base.

17–4 COMPUTER APPLICATIONS OF THE FUTURE. The number and variety of computer applications is expected to grow rapidly in the coming years. In the near future, we can anticipate an even greater variety of services available through information networks; telephones integrated into terminals; the widespread acceptance and use of electronic mail; unmanned manufacturing facilities; electronic shopping; less use of cash; soft copy publishing; automobile navigation systems; create-your-own-story soaps on television; robot sculptors; computer-controlled artificial limbs; voting at home via microcomputers; nationwide uniform student testing; and **AI** (artificial intelligence), which encompasses expert systems, natural languages, simulation of human sensory capabilities, and robotics.

17–5 OVERSIGHTS: ARE WE KEEPING PACE WITH THE TECHNOLOGY? Although society has been the beneficiary of a wide variety of computer applications, much more can be done with existing technology. Historical momentum, resistance to change, limited education, and lack of resources have slowed the implementation of technologically feasible computer applications.

17–6 YOUR CHALLENGE. The computer offers us the opportunity to improve the quality of our lives. It is our challenge to harness the power of the computer and direct it to the benefit of society.

Review Exercises

Concepts

1. What are the four components of an information network?
2. Has society reached the point of no return with regard to its dependence on computers?
3. Most computer monitoring takes place at which level of activity: clerical, operational, tactical, or strategic?
4. Briefly describe how the business letter of the future will be composed and delivered.
5. What is the objective of computer matching?
6. What are the two main causes of illegal processing?
7. Name four human sensory capabilities that can be simulated by computers.
8. Describe two ways in which computers are contributing to the improved quality of health care.
9. What are the four categories of artificial intelligence research?

Discussion

10. Based on your knowledge of the capabilities of computers now and in the future, speculate on at least three applications that we can expect within the next 10 years.
11. Why would a judge sentence one person to 10 years in jail for an unarmed robbery of $25 from a convenience store and another to 18 months for computer fraud involving millions of dollars?

12. Some companies are experimenting with placing small microprocessors in charge cards as a means of thwarting theft and fraud. Describe how you think the computer would be used during the processing of a charge transaction. Speculate on the data that are input to, output from, permanently stored in, and processed by the charge card computer.

13. List and discuss applications, other than those mentioned in the text, of a national data base.

14. Do you feel society's dependence on computers is good or bad? What would you suggest be done to improve the situation?

15. Describe what yesterday would have been like if you had not used the capabilities of computers. Keep in mind that businesses with which you deal rely on computers and that many of your appliances are computer-based.

16. Why would a bank officer elect not to report a computer crime?

17. Argue for or against a cashless society.

18. Why do you suppose our laws governing computers and information processing are inadequate?

19. Discuss the kinds of personal information that can be obtained by analyzing a person's credit card transactions during the past year.

20. Describe problems that must be overcome to prosecute computer criminals in a court of law.

21. Describe ways in which you feel the privacy of your personal information has been abused.

22. Name two jobs and how computers can be used to measure worker performance.

23. Compare your perspective on computers today with what it was four months ago. How have your feelings and attitudes changed?

Self-Test (by section)

17–1 **a.** It would take at least a month to retool a typical automobile assembly line so it could function without computers. (T/F)

b. If the number of computer applications continues to grow at the present rate, our computer-independent society will be dependent on computers by the year 2000. (T/F)

17–2 **a.** Gaining unauthorized access to any computer system with a federal interest with the intent of defrauding the system is a: (a) violation of public ethics, (b) misdemeanor, or (c) felony.

b. Many legal questions involving computers and information processing are yet to be incorporated into the federal laws. (T/F)

   c. Trust in the infallibility of a computer does not constitute a defense in a court of law. (T/F)

17–3 **a.** It is estimated that each year the total monetary loss from computer crime is greater than the sum total of all robberies. (T/F)

   b. In _____, computers continuously gather and assimilate data on worker activities for the purpose of measuring worker performance.

   c. The number of federal government agencies that maintain computer-based files on individuals is between: (a) 50 and 100, (b) 500 and 1000, or (c) 5000 and 10,000.

   d. The evidence of unlawful entry to a computer system is called a _____.

17–4 **a.** The magazine-on-a-disk has been discussed but is beyond the state of the art. (T/F)

   b. Prototypes for on-board automobile navigation systems will be ready for testing by the turn of the century. (T/F)

   c. The abbreviation for artificial intelligence is: (a) artell, (b) AI, or (c) AIG.

   d. Most existing industrial robots are stationary or they are programmed to operate within a well-defined work area. (T/F)

17–5 A cashless society is technologically and economically possible. (T/F)

17–6 The total computing capacity in the world is increasing at slightly less than 25% per year. (T/F)

Self-test answers. **17–1** (a) F; (b) F. **17–2** (a) c; (b) T; (c) T. **17–3** (a) T; (b) computer monitoring; (c) c; (d) footprint. **17–4** (a) F; (b) F; (c) b; (d) T. **17–5** T. **17–6** F.

APPENDIX A

THE PASCALINE   Pascal's invention, the Pascaline, used gear-driven counting wheels to do addition. He built the Pascaline to help his father, a tax collector, calculate tax revenues. The numbers for each digit position were arranged on wheels so that a single revolution of one wheel resulted in one tenth of a revolution of the wheel to its immediate left.

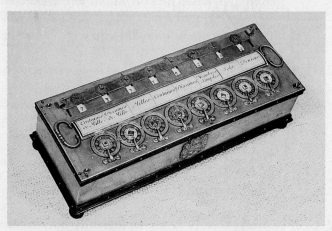

THE ABACUS   The abacus was probably the original mechanical counting device, and its effectiveness has withstood the test of time. It is still used to illustrate the principles of counting.

500 B.C.

1642

BLAISE PASCAL   French philosopher and mathematician Blaise Pascal (1623–62) invented and built the first mechanical adding machine. Pascal's early work with mechanical calculators is recognized today by the popular computer programming language that bears his name.

An Abbreviated History of Computers

JACQUARD'S LOOM The Jacquard weaving loom was invented by the Frenchman Joseph-Marie Jacquard (1753–1834) and is still in use today. It is controlled by cards in which holes are strategically punched. The punched cards are sequenced to indicate a particular weaving design.

CHARLES BABBAGE Concepts used in today's general-purpose computer were introduced over a century ago by Charles Babbage (1793–1871), an English visionary and Cambridge professor.

1805   **1822–33**

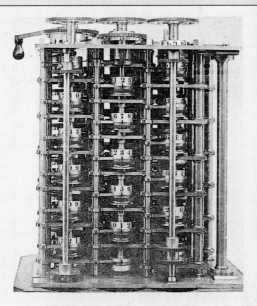

DIFFERENCE ENGINE Charles Babbage advanced the state of computational hardware by inventing a "difference engine" that was capable of computing mathematical tables. Unfortunately, he completed only a part of his difference engine (shown here). While working on it, Babbage conceived the idea of an "analytical engine." In essence, this was a general-purpose computer. As designed, his analytical engine would add, subtract, multiply, and divide in automatic sequence at a rate of 60 additions per minute. His 1833 design called for thousands of gears and drives that would cover the area of a football field and be powered by a locomotive engine. Babbage worked on his analytical engine until his death.

LADY ADA LOVELACE Lady Ada Augusta Lovelace suggested that punch cards could be prepared that would instruct Babbage's engine to repeat certain operations. Because of her suggestion, some people call Lady Lovelace the first programmer.

PUNCHED-CARD TABULATING MACHINE The U.S. Bureau of the Census did not complete the 1880 census until almost 1888. Bureau management concluded that before long, the 10-year census would take more than 10 years to complete! The Census Bureau commissioned Herman Hollerith to apply his expertise in the use of punched cards to the 1890 census. With punched-card processing and Hollerith's *punched-card tabulating machine* the census was completed in just three years and his process saved the bureau over $5,000,000. Thus began the emergence of automated data processing.

1843	1884	1890

DR. HERMAN HOLLERITH
Herman Hollerith, a statistician, applied for a patent for a punched-card tabulating machine. Hollerith's idea for the punched card came not from Jacquard or Babbage but from ''punch photography.'' Railroads of the day issued tickets with physical descriptions of the passengers. A conductor would punch holes in a ticket that noted a passenger's hair and eye color and the nose shape. Hollerith's daughter later said, ''This gave him the idea for making a punch photograph of every person to be tabulated,'' which he later applied to taking the 1890 census. The patent was issued in 1889.

THE EAM ERA For decades through the mid-1950s, punched-card technology improved with the addition of more punched-card devices and more sophisticated capabilities. The *electromechanical accounting machine* (*EAM*) family of punched-card devices includes the card punch, verifier, reproducer, summary punch, interpreter, sorter, collator, calculator, and the accounting machine. Most of the devices in this 1940s machine room were "programmed" to perform a particular operation by the insertion of a prewired control panel. A machine-room operator in a punched-card installation had a physically demanding job. Punched cards and printed output were moved from one device to the next on hand trucks.

IBM'S FIRST HEADQUARTERS BUILDING In 1896 Herman Hollerith founded the Tabulating Machine Company which, in 1911, merged with several other companies to form the Computing-Tabulating-Recording Company. In 1924 the company's general manager, Thomas J. Watson, changed its name to International Business Machines Corporation and moved into this building.

DR. JOHN V. ATANASOFF During the years 1935 to 1938, Dr. John V. Atanasoff, a professor at Iowa State University, had begun to think about a machine that could reduce the time it took for him and his physics students to make long, complicated mathematical calculations. The decisions he made about such concepts as an electronic medium with vacuum tubes, the base-2 numbering system, memory, and logic circuits set the direction for the development of the modern computer.

THE MARK I The first electromechanical computer, called the *Mark I*, was the result of IBM-sponsored research. Howard Aiken, a Harvard University professor, completed the Mark I in 1944. It was essentially a serial collection of electromechanical calculators and had many similarities to Babbage's analytical engine. (Aiken was unaware of Babbage's work.) The Mark I was a significant improvement in the state of the art, but IBM's management still felt that electromechanical computers would not replace punched-card equipment.

1935   **1942**   **1944**

THE ABC In 1939 Dr. Atanasoff and one of his graduate students, Clifford E. Berry, assembled a prototype of the *ABC* (Atanasoff Berry Computer), which by 1942 evolved into the working model shown here. However, Iowa State, the business world, and the scientific community showed little interest in the ABC. For example, when Dr. Atanasoff contacted IBM about what he called his "computing machine proper," the company responded that "IBM never will be interested in an electronic computing machine." A 1973 federal court ruling officially credited Atanasoff with the invention of the automatic electronic digital computer.

THE ENIAC Dr. John W. Mauchly (middle) collaborated with J. Presper Eckert, Jr.,(foreground) to develop a machine that would compute trajectory tables for the U.S. Army. The end product, a large-scale, fully operational electronic computer, was completed in 1946 and called the ENIAC (Electronic Numerical Integrator and Computer). The ENIAC (shown here), a thousand times faster than its electromechanical predecessors, signaled a major breakthrough in computer technology. It weighed 30 tons and occupied 1500 square feet of floor space. With over 18,000 vacuum tubes, the ENIAC needed a huge amount of electricity. Legend has it that the ENIAC, built at the University of Pennsylvania, dimmed the lights of Philadelphia whenever it was activated. Because of its imposing scale, electronic components, and wide applicability, the ENIAC is generally considered the first functional electronic digital computer.

THE UNIVAC I AND THE FIRST GENERATION OF COMPUTERS

The first generation of computers (1951–59), which is characterized by vacuum tubes, is generally thought to have started with the introduction of the first commercially viable electronic digital computer. The Universal Automatic Computer (*UNIVAC I* for short), developed by Mauchly and Eckert for the Remington-Rand Corporation, was installed in the U.S. Bureau of the Census in 1951. Later that year, CBS news gave the UNIVAC I national exposure when it correctly predicted Dwight Eisenhower's victory over Adlai Stevenson in the presidential election with only 5% of the votes counted. Shown here is Mr. Eckert instructing news anchor Walter Cronkite in the use of the UNIVAC I.

| 1946 | 1951 | 1954 |

THE IBM 650 Not until the success of the UNIVAC I did IBM make the decision and the commitment to develop and market computers. IBM's first entry into the commercial computer market was the *IBM 701* in 1953. However, the *IBM 650* (shown here), introduced in 1954, is probably the reason that IBM enjoys such a healthy share of today's computer market. Unlike some of its competitors, the IBM 650 was designed as a logical upgrade to existing punched-card machines. IBM management went out on a limb and estimated sales of 50, a figure that was greater than the number of installed computers in the United States at that time. IBM actually installed more than 1000. The rest is history.

THE IBM SYSTEM 360 AND THE THIRD GENERATION OF COMPUTERS What some computer historians consider the single most important event in the history of computers occurred when IBM announced its *System 360* line of computers on April 7, 1964. The System 360 ushered in the third generation of computers (1964–71). Integrated circuits did for the third generation of computers what transistors did for the second generation. *Business Week* reported IBM's announcement of its System 360 line of computers, saying that "In the annals of major product changes, it is like Ford's switch from the Model T to the Model A." The System 360s and the third-generation computers of other manufacturers made all previously installed computers obsolete.

1959   **1963**   **1964**

THE HONEYWELL 400 AND THE SECOND GENERATION OF COMPUTERS The invention of the transistor signaled the start of the second generation of computers (1959–64). The transistor meant more powerful, more reliable, and less expensive computers that would occupy less space and give off less heat than vacuum-tube-powered computers did. Honeywell (the *Honeywell 400* is shown here) established itself as a major player in the second generation of computers. Burroughs, Univac, NCR, CDC, and Honeywell—IBM's biggest competitors during the 1960s and early 1970s—became known as the BUNCH (the first initial of each name).

THE PDP-8 During the 1950s and early 1960s, only the largest companies could afford the six- and seven-digit price tags of mainframe computers. In 1963 Digital Equipment Corporation introduced the *PDP-8* (shown here). It is generally regarded as the first successful minicomputer. At $18,000, the transistor-based PDP-8 was an instant hit. It confirmed the tremendous demand for small computers for business and scientific applications. By 1971 over 25 firms were manufacturing minicomputers. Digital and Data General Corporation took an early lead in the sale and manufacture of minis.

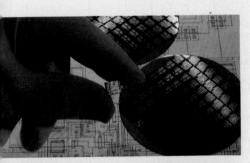

INTEGRATED CIRCUITS AND THE FOURTH GENERATION OF COMPUTERS Most computer vendors classify their computers as fourth generation. Some people prefer to pinpoint 1971 as the start of the fourth generation of computers, with the introduction of large-scale integration (more circuits per unit space) of electronic circuitry. The base technology of today's computers is still the integrated circuit. This is not to say that two decades have passed without any significant innovations. In truth, the computer industry has experienced a mind-boggling succession of advances in the further miniaturization of circuitry, data communications, the design of computer hardware and software, and input/output devices.

1971

1977

THE APPLE II Not until 1975 and the introduction of the *Altair 8800* personal computer was computing made available to individuals and very small companies. This event has forever changed how society perceives computers. Certainly the most prominent entrepreneurial venture during the early years of personal computers was the *Apple II* computer (shown here). Two young computer enthusiasts, Steven Jobs and Steve Wozniak (then 21 and 26 years of age, respectively), collaborated to create and build their Apple II computer on a makeshift production line in Jobs' garage. Seven years later, Apple Computer earned a spot on the Fortune 500, a list of the 500 largest corporations in the United States.

1981

THE IBM PC In 1981 IBM tossed its hat into the personal computer ring with the announcement of the *IBM PC*. In the first year, 35,000 were sold. In 1982, 800,000 were sold, and the IBM PC was well on its way to becoming the standard for the micro industry. When software vendors began to orient their products to the IBM PC, many microcomputer manufacturers created and sold *clones* of the IBM PC. These clones, called *IBM-PC compatibles*, run most or all the software designed for the IBM PC.

FIGURE A–1 Chronology of Computer History

Year	Historic Event	Processing	Input	Output	Storage (secondary)	Software	Systems Concepts	Information Systems Organization	Information Systems Personnel
1940	World War II begins	Electro-mechanical accounting machines / ABC computer	Punched card / Paper tape / Mark sense	Punched card / Paper tape / Printer	Punched card / Paper tape	Wired panels / Switches	Data processing (DP)	Centralized punched card departments	
	And ends	1st generation (vacuum tubes) / ENIAC							Programmer
						Machine language / Stored program / Assembler language			
1950		UNIVAC I (1st commercial)							
	Ike elected President			High-speed printers	Magnetic tape	Compilers	Artificial intelligence		Operator / Data entry / Systems analyst
	Sputnik launched	IBM 650 / 2nd generation (transistors)	Magnetic ink character recognition (MICR)	Plotters / MICR	Magnetic disk / Interchange-able disk	FORTRAN / APT / Virtual memory / COBOL / LISP			Proprietary software introduced
1960	J.F. Kennedy assassinated	PDP=8 / Minicomputer / 3rd generation (integrated circuits) / IBM 360 family / Computer networks	Optical character recognition (OCR) / Keyboard (on-line) / Light pen	OCR / Voice (recorded) / Soft copy (VDT) / Computer output microfilm (COM)	Mass storage devices	Propiatary software introduced / Multiprogram-ming / RPG / PL/I / BASIC / APL / LOGO	Management information systems (MIS)	Trend to large centralized information systems departments	Librarian / Programmer (systems and applications) / Control clerk
	Apollo II lands on moon								
1970	Watergate burglary	4th generation (large-scale integration) / Microprocessors / Microcomputers	Mouse / Hand print	Graphics (VDT) / Color graphics / High-speed laser printers	IK RAM chip / Floppy disk / Winchester disk	Pascal / Word processing / Fourth-generation languages		Trend to decentra-lization and distributed processing	Data base administrator / Project leader / Education coordinator / Documentalist
	USA's 200th birthday	Personal computers / Supercomputers / Word processors / Distributed processing / IBM PC	Voice / Vision input systems	Voice (synthesized) / Desktop laser printers	Video disk / Optical laser disk	UNIX operating system / Application generators / Electronic spreadsheet / Ada / Integrated micro software / Desktop publishing / User-friendly interfaces	Information resource management (IRM) / Decision support systems (DDS) / Expert systems	Information centers	Office automation specialist / Data communications specialist / MIS long-range planner / User-analyst / Information center specialist / User liaison / Microcomputer specialist
1980	Mt. St. Helens erupts / E.T. lands / Reagan begins second term / XXII Olympiad	Pocket computers / Multiuser micros / Apple Macintosh / IBM PS/2			1 megabit RAM chip / Magneto-optical disk / 4 megabit RAM chip			Departmental company	
1990									

FIGURE A–1 Chronology of Computer History
This chart summarizes important events in the history of computers and information processing. These events are discussed in this appendix and throughout the book.

Self-Test

1. John V. Atanasoff invented the electronic digital computer in 1931. (T/F)
2. Herman Hollerith used his tabulating machine for automated data processing at the U.S. Bureau of the Census. (T/F)
3. The first patent for an electronic digital computer was awarded to John V. Atanasoff for the: (a) ABC, (b) ENIAC, or (c) UNIVAC I.
4. The _____ was developed to compute trajectory tables for the U.S. Army.
5. The Mark I was IBM's first electronic digital computer. (T/F)
6. The _____ is considered the original mechanical computing device.
7. The devices used for data processing just prior to the emergence of electronic computers are known collectively as: (a) Pascal devices, (b) EAM equipment, or (c) micros.
8. The minicomputer was first introduced in the early 1970s. (T/F)
9. Electronic accounting machines used _____ as a storage medium.
10. The electrical component usually associated with the second generation of computers is the: (a) vacuum tube, (b) integrated circuit, or (c) transistor.
11. Jacquard's Loom was invented before the punched-card tabulating machine and after the: (a) ENIAC, (b) Pascaline, or (c) ABC.
12. The inventors of the ENIAC are _____ and _____.
13. Which of the following is not a microcomputer: (a) Apple II, (b) IBM PC, or (c) PDP-8?
14. Which came first: (a) UNIVAC I, (b) transistors in computers, or (c) personal computers?
15. In the early nineteenth century, a difference engine, capable of computing mathematical tables, was invented by J. Presper Eckert, Jr. (T/F)

Self-test answers. **1.** F. **2.** T. **3.** a. **4.** ENIAC. **5.** F. **6.** abacus. **7.** b. **8.** F. **9.** punched cards. **10.** c. **11.** b. **12.** Mauchly, Eckert. **13.** c. **14.** a. **15.** F.

APPENDIX B

Working with Numbering Systems

B–1 **Principles of Numbering Systems**
B–2 **Converting Numbers from One Base to Another**
B–3 **Arithmetic in Binary and Hexadecimal**

This appendix presents the principles of numbering systems, discusses numbering-system arithmetic, and illustrates how to convert a value in one numbering system to its equivalent in another. After studying this appendix you will be able to perform rudimentary arithmetic operations in the binary and hexadecimal numbering systems. The relationship between computers and the various numbering systems is discussed in Chapter 4, "Inside the Computer."

B-1 Principles of Numbering Systems
Binary

The binary, or base-2, numbering system is based on the same principles as the decimal, or base-10, numbering system, with which we are already familiar. The

FIGURE B–1
Numbering-System Equivalence Table

Binary (base a)	Decimal (base 10)	Hexadecimal (base 16)
0	0	0
1	1	1
10	2	2
11	3	3
100	4	4
101	5	5
110	6	6
111	7	7
1000	8	8
1001	9	9
1010	10	A
1011	11	B
1100	12	C
1101	13	D
1110	14	E
1111	15	F
10000	16	10

only difference between the two numbering systems is that binary uses only two digits, 0 and 1, and the decimal numbering system uses 10 digits, 0 through 9. The equivalents for binary, decimal, and hexadecimal numbers are shown in Figure B–1.

The value of a given digit is determined by its relative position in a sequence of digits. Consider the ex-

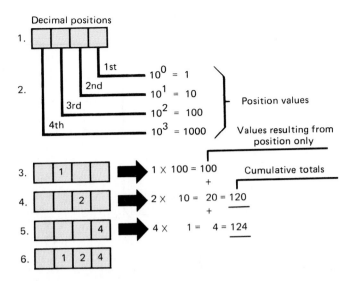

Decimal positions

1.

2.

1st — 10^0 = 1
2nd — 10^1 = 10   Position values
3rd — 10^2 = 100
4th — 10^3 = 1000   Values resulting from
                        position only

3. [ ][1][ ][ ] ➡ 1 × 100 = 100   Cumulative totals
                                +
4. [ ][ ][2][ ] ➡ 2 × 10 = 20 = 120
                              +
5. [ ][ ][ ][4] ➡ 4 × 1 = 4 = 124

6. [1][2][4]

FIGURE B–2 Numbering-System Fundamentals
Ralph, our two-fingered Martian who is used to counting in binary, might go through the thought process illustrated here when counting 124 marbles in decimal. Ralph's steps are discussed in the text.

ample in Figure B–2. If we want to write the number 124 in decimal, the interpretation is almost automatic because of our familiarity with the decimal numbering system. To illustrate the underlying concepts, let's give Ralph, a little green two-fingered Martian, a bag of 124 (decimal) marbles and ask him to express the number of marbles in decimal. Ralph, who is more familiar with binary, would go through the following thought process (see Figure B–2).

- *Step 1*. Ralph knows that the relative position of a digit within a string of digits determines its value, whether the numbering system is binary or decimal. Therefore, the first thing to do is determine the value represented by each digit position.

- *Step 2*. Ralph knows that as in any numbering system, the rightmost position has a value of the base to the zero power, or 1 ($10^0 = 1$). The second position is the base to the first power, or 10 ($10^1 = 10$). The third position is the base squared, or 100, and so on.

- *Step 3*. Because the largest of the decimal system's 10 digits is 9, the greatest number that can be represented in the *rightmost position* is 9 (9 × 1). The greatest number that can be represented in the *second position*, then, is 90 (9 × 10). In the *third position*, the greatest number is 900; and so on. Having placed the marbles in stacks of 10, Ralph knows immediately that there will be no need for a fourth-position digit (the thousands position). It is apparent, however, that a digit must be placed in the third position. Because placing a 2 in the third position would be too much (200 > 124), Ralph places a 1 in the third position to represent 100 marbles.

- *Step 4*. Ralph must continue to the second position

to represent the remaining 24 marbles. In each successive position, Ralph wants to represent as many marbles as possible. In this case, a 2 placed in the second position would represent 20 of the remaining marbles ($2 \times 10^1 = 20$).

- *Step 5*. There are still four marbles left to be represented. This can be done by inserting a 4 in the rightmost, or "1s," position.

- *Step 6*. The combination of the three numbers in their relative positions represents 124 (decimal).

Ralph would go through the same thought process if asked to represent the 124 (decimal) marbles using the binary numbering system (see Figure B–3). To make the binary conversion process easier to follow, the computations in Figure B–3 are done in the more familiar decimal numbering system. See if you can trace Ralph's steps as you work through Figure B–3.

Hexadecimal

Perhaps the biggest drawback to using the binary numbering system for computer operations is that programmers may have to deal with long and confusing strings of 1s and 0s. To reduce the confusion, the hexadecimal, or base-16, numbering system is used as a shorthand to display the binary contents of primary and secondary storage.

Notice that the bases of the binary and hexadecimal numbering systems are multiples of 2: 2 and 2^4, respectively. Because of this, there is a convenient relationship between these numbering systems. The numbering-system equivalence table shown in Figure B–1 illustrates that a single hexadecimal digit represents four binary digits ($0111_2 = 7_{16}, 1101_2 = D_{16}, 1010_2 = A_{16}$, where subscripts are used to indicate the base of the numbering system). Notice that in hexadecimal, or "hex," *letters* are used to represent the six higher order digits.

FIGURE B–3 Representing a Binary Number

To represent 124 marbles in binary, we would follow the same thought process as we would in decimal (see Figure B–2), but this time we have only two digits (0 and 1). For ease of understanding, the arithmetic is done in decimal.

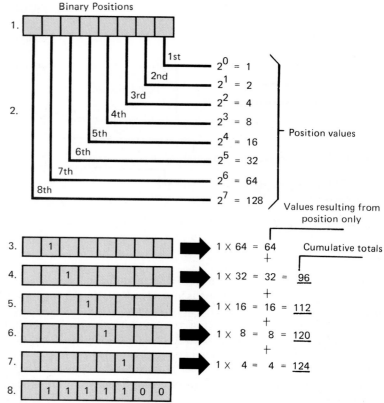

Two hexadecimal digits can be used to represent the eight-bit byte of an EBCDIC equals sign (=) (01111110_2 is the same as $7E_{16}$). Figure B–4 illustrates how a string of EBCDIC bits can be reduced to a more recognizable form using hexadecimal.

We will now examine how to convert one number in a numbering system to an equivalent number in another numbering system. For example, there are occasions when we might wish to convert a hexadecimal number to its binary equivalent. We shall also learn the fundamentals of numbering-system arithmetic.

B-2 Converting Numbers from One Base to Another

Decimal to Binary or Hexadecimal

A decimal number can be converted easily into an equivalent number of any base by the use of the *di-*

vision/remainder technique. This two-step technique is illustrated in Figure B–5. Follow these steps to convert *decimal to binary*.

- *Step 1.* Divide the number (19, in this example) repeatedly by 2, and record the remainder of each division. In the first division, 2 goes into 19 nine times with a remainder of 1. The remainder is always one of the binary digits—0 or 1. In the last division you divide 1 by the base (2) and the remainder is 1.

- *Step 2.* Rotate the remainders as shown in Figure B–5; the result (10011) is the binary equivalent of a decimal 19.

Figure B–6 illustrates how the same division/remainder technique is used to convert a decimal 453 to

Input/output (alphanumeric)	S		y		s		t		e		m	
Internal representation (binary)	1110	0010	1010	1000	1010	0010	1010	0011	1000	0101	1001	0100
Hexadecimal equivalent	E	2	A	8	A	2	A	3	8	5	9	4

FIGURE B–4 *System* Expressed in Different Ways

The word *System* is shown as it would appear in input/output, internal binary notation, and hexadecimal notation.

The problem: $19_{10} = \boxed{?}_2$

The procedure:

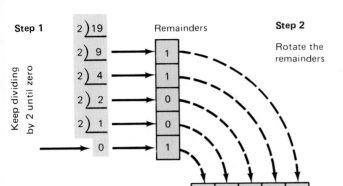

FIGURE B–5   Converting a Decimal Number to Its Binary Equivalent
Use the two-step division/remainder technique to convert a decimal number to an equivalent number of any base.

its hexadecimal equivalent (1C5). In a *decimal-to-hex* conversion, the remainder is one of the 16 hex digits.

Binary to Decimal and Hexadecimal

To convert from *binary to decimal*, multiply the 1s in a binary number by their position values, then sum

The problem: $11010_2 = \boxed{?}_{10}$

The procedure:

The problem: $453_{10} = \boxed{?}_{16}$

The procedure:

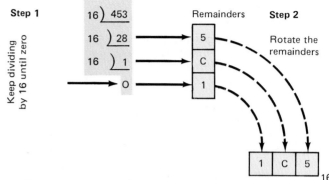

FIGURE B–6   Converting a Decimal Number to Its Hexadecimal Equivalent
The two-step division/remainder technique is used to convert a decimal number to its hex equivalent.

the products (see Figure B–7). In Figure B–7, for example, binary 11010 is converted to its decimal equivalent (26).

The easiest conversion is *binary to hex*. To convert binary to hex, simply begin with the 1s position on the right and segment the binary number into groups of

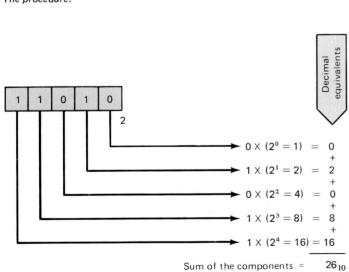

FIGURE B–7   Converting a Binary Number to Its Decimal Equivalent
Multiply the 1s in a binary number by their position values, then sum the products.

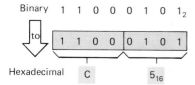

Binary 1 1 0 0 0 1 0 1₂

to → 1 1 0 0 | 0 1 0 1

Hexadecimal C 5₁₆

FIGURE B–8 Converting a Binary Number to Its Hexadecimal Equivalent
Place the binary digits in groups of four, then convert the binary number directly to hexadecimal.

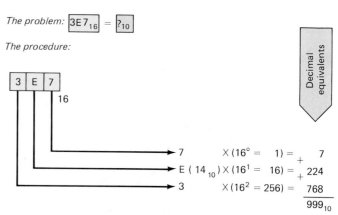

The problem: $3E7_{16} = ?_{10}$

The procedure:

3 E 7
16

7 × (16° = 1) = 7
E (14₁₀) × (16¹ = 16) = + 224
3 × (16² = 256) = + 768

999₁₀

Decimal equivalents

FIGURE B–9 Converting a Hexadecimal Number to Its Decimal Equivalent
Multiply the digits in a hexadecimal number by their position values.

four digits each (see Figure B–8). Refer to the equivalence table in Figure B–2, and assign each group of four binary digits a hex equivalent. Combine your result, and the conversion is complete.

Hexadecimal to Binary

To convert hex numbers to binary, perform the grouping procedure for converting binary to hex in reverse (see Figure B–8).

Hexadecimal to Decimal

Use the same procedure as that used for binary-to-decimal conversions (see Figure B–7) to convert *hex to decimal*. Figure B–9 demonstrates the conversion of a hex 3E7 to its decimal equivalent of 999.

B-3 Arithmetic in Binary and Hexadecimal

The essentials of decimal arithmetic operations have been drilled into us so that we do addition and subtraction almost by instinct. We do binary arithmetic, as well as that of other numbering systems, in the same way that we do decimal arithmetic. The only difference is that we have fewer (binary) or more (hexadecimal) digits to use. Figure B–10 illustrates and compares ad-

dition and subtraction in decimal with that in binary and hex. Notice in Figure B–10 that you carry to and borrow from adjacent positions, just as you do in decimal arithmetic.

	Binary	Decimal	Hexadecimal
Addition	1111100 + 10010 10001110	124 + 18 142	7C + 12 8E
Subtraction	1111100 − 10010 1101010	124 − 18 106	7C − 12 6A

FIGURE B–10 Binary, Decimal, and Hexadecimal Arithmetic Comparison
As you can see, the only difference in doing arithmetic in the various numbering systems is the number of digits used.

Self-Test (by section)

B–1 a. The hex numbering system has a base of _____, and the binary numbering system has a base of _____.
b. The value of a particular digit in a number is determined by its relative position in a sequence of digits. (T/F)
c. A single hexadecimal digit can represent how many binary digits: (a) two, (b) three, or (c) four?
d. The bases of the binary and decimal numbering systems are multiples of 2. (T/F)
B–2 a. The binary equivalent of a decimal 255 is _____.
b. The binary equivalent of a hexadecimal 1C is _____.
c. The decimal equivalent of a hexadecimal 1B6 is _____.
d. The hexadecimal equivalent of a decimal 129 is _____.
e. The decimal equivalent of a binary 110101 is _____.
f. The hexadecimal equivalent of a binary 1001 is _____.

g. The binary equivalent of a decimal 28 is _____.

h. The binary equivalent of a hexadecimal 35 is _____.

i. The decimal equivalent of a hexadecimal 7 is _____.

j. The hexadecimal equivalent of a decimal 49 is _____.

k. The decimal equivalent of a binary 110110110 is _____.

l. The hexadecimal equivalent of a binary 1110 is _____.

B–3 a. The result of $101_2 + 11_2$ is _____ (in binary).

b. The result of $A1_{16} + BC_{16} + 10_{16}$ is _____ (in hexadecimal).

c. The result of $60_{10} + F1_{16} - 1001001_2$ is _____ (in decimal).

d. The result of $11_2 + 27_8 + 93_{10} - B_{16}$ is _____ (in decimal).

Self-test answers. **B–1** (a) 16, 2; (b) T; (c) c; (d) F. **B–2** (a) 11111111; (b) 11100; (c) 438; (d) 81; (e) 53; (f) 9; (g) 11100; (h) 110101; (i) 7; (j) 31; (k) 438; (l) E. **B–3** (a) 1000_2; (b) $16D_{16}$; (c) 228_{10}; (d) 108_{10}.

APPENDIX C

Design Techniques

Systems analysts, programmers, and users employ a variety of techniques to help them design and document programs and information systems. This appendix introduces you to a representative sample of commonly used techniques. Included in the overview are *data flow diagrams, flowcharting, HIPO, SADT, pseudocode,* and *decision tables*.

Until recently, automated design tools were very expensive and limited to the mainframe environment. Only large companies could justify the cost of these proprietary software packages. Today sophisticated software for automated system design is reasonably priced and available for the microcomputer environment. Excelerator/RTS™ from Index Technology Corporation, a totally integrated PC-based package, offers all the capabilities needed to design and document even the most complex of systems.

C–1 Data Flow Diagrams

The use of **data flow diagrams**, or **DFDs**, encourages analysts and programmers to examine the system from the top down (general to the specific). The result is a more structured design. DFDs use the four symbols illustrated in Figure C–1 (entity, process, flow line, and

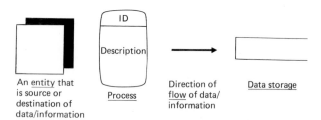

An <u>entity</u> that is source or destination of data/information

<u>Process</u>

Direction of <u>flow</u> of data/ information

Data storage

FIGURE C–1   Data Flow Diagram Symbols

data store) to document the system at several levels of generality. DFD concepts are discussed and illustrated in Chapter 12, "Systems Analysis and Design."

C–2 Flowcharting

In **flowcharting**, **flowcharts** are used to illustrate data, information, and work flow through the interconnection of *specialized symbols* with *flow lines*. The combination of symbols and flow lines portrays the logic of the program or system.

Flowcharting Symbols

Each symbol indicates the *type of operation to be performed*, and the flowchart illustrates the *sequence in which the operations are to be performed*. The more commonly used flowchart symbols are shown in Figure C–2 and discussed here.

- *Computer process* symbols (rectangles) signify some type of process. The process could be as specific as "Compute net pay" (in a program flowchart) or as general as "Produce payroll checks and register" (in a system flowchart).
- *Predefined process* symbols (rectangles with extra vertical lines) are a special use of the process symbol. The predefined process refers to a group of operations that may be detailed in a separate flowchart.

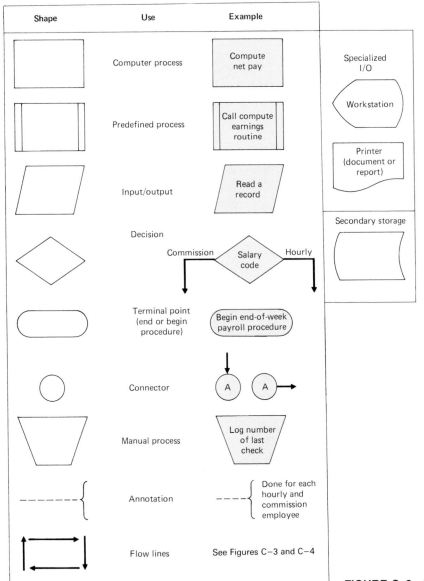

FIGURE C–2 Flowchart Symbols

- *Input/output* symbols (parallelograms) generally refer to any type of input to or output from the program or system.

- *Decision* symbols (diamond-shaped) mark the points at which decisions are to be made. In a program flowchart, a particular set of instructions is executed based on the outcome of a decision. For example, in a payroll program gross pay is computed differently for hourly and commission employees; therefore, for each employee processed, a decision is made as to which set of instructions is to be executed.

- *Terminal point* symbols (ovals) are used to indicate the beginning and the end of flowcharts.

- *Connector* symbols (small circles) are used to break and then link flow lines. The connector symbol is often used to avoid having to cross lines.

- *Manual process* symbols (trapezoids) indicate that a manual process is to be performed. Contrast this with a computer process represented by a rectangle.

- *Bracket* symbols permit descriptive notations to be added to flowcharts.

- *Workstation* symbols are used to indicate output to or input from a video display terminal.

- *Printer* symbols denote hard copy output.

- *On-line data storage* symbols are used to represent files or data bases on disk storage.

- *Flow lines* depict the sequential flow of the program or system logic.

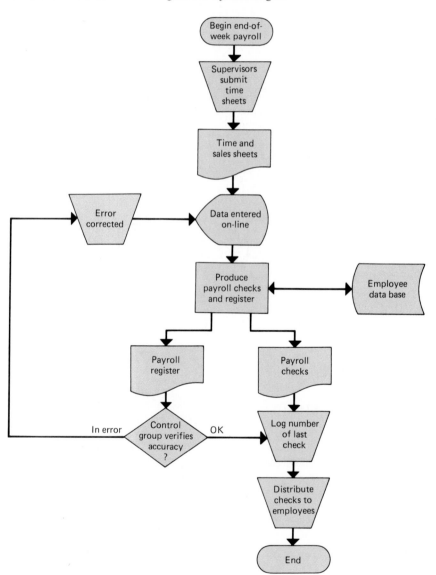

FIGURE C–3   General System Flowchart

This system flowchart illustrates the relationship between I/O and major processing activities in a payroll system.

These symbols are equally applicable to system and program flowcharting and can be used to develop and represent the logic for each.

System and Program Flowcharts

A **system flowchart** for a payroll system is illustrated in Figure C–3. This system flowchart illustrates the weekly payroll process for hourly and commission employees (salary employee checks are processed monthly). Gross earnings for hourly employees are computed by multiplying hours worked times the rate of pay. For salespeople on commission, gross earnings are computed as a percentage of sales.

Contrast the system flowchart in Figure C–3 with the **program flowchart** of Figure C–4. This program

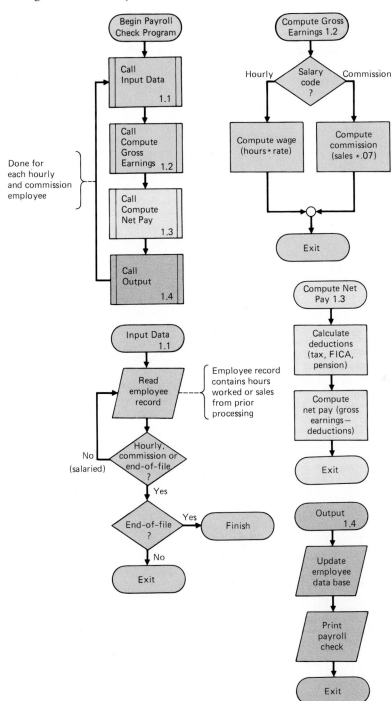

FIGURE C–4 Program Flowchart
This structured program flowchart portrays the logic of a program to compute and print payroll checks for commission and hourly employees. The logic is designed so that a driver module calls subroutines as they are needed to process each employee.

FIGURE C–5 HIPO Structure Chart

This structure chart breaks down a payroll system into a hierarchy of modules.

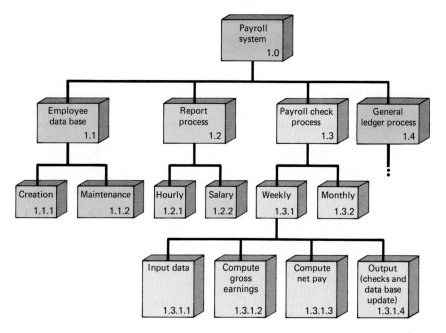

flowchart portrays the general logic of a program to compute and print payroll checks for commission and hourly employees. In structured programming, each program has a **driver module** that causes other program modules to be executed as they are needed. The example in Figure C–4 is expanded and discussed in more detail in Appendix D, "Programming Concepts."

C–3 Hierarchy plus Input-Processing-Output

Hierarchy plus input-processing-output, or **HIPO** (pronounced *HI-poe*), is a top-down design technique that permits the project team to divide the system into independent modules for ease of understanding and design. HIPO follows the "divide and conquer" line of reasoning.

HIPO has several standard forms. A *structure chart*

breaks a system down into a hierarchy of modules. For example, a structure chart for a payroll system is shown in Figure C–5. In the structure chart, the system is decomposed into modules at finer levels of detail until a particular module can be portrayed best in terms of procedural logic. Eventually, the logic for each of the lowest level modules is represented in detailed step-by-step *overview diagrams* that illustrate the interactions between input, processing, output, and storage activities for a particular module. Figure C–6 shows an overview diagram for Module 1.3.1 (weekly payroll processing) of Figure C–5.

Like DFDs, HIPO encourages top-down design. This advantage is, to some extent, offset by the cumbersome volume of paperwork required to document the system.

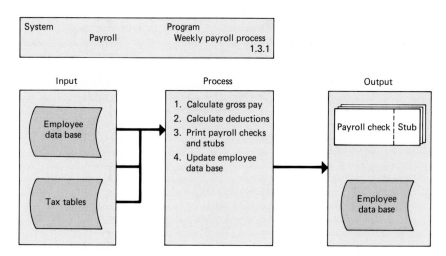

FIGURE C–6 HIPO Overview Diagram

This overview diagram illustrates the input, processing, and output components of Module 1.3.1 of Figure C–5.

FIGURE C-7
SADT Activity Box

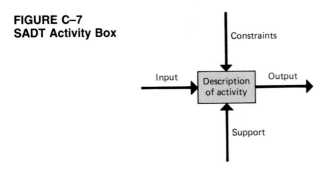

C-4 Structured Analysis and Design Technique

Structured Analysis and Design Technique, or **SADT**, is also a top-down design technique. Under SADT, a system is conceptualized as being composed of things and activities and the relationships between them. This conceptual view is described graphically using *actigrams* (activity diagrams) and *datagrams* (data diagrams).

Actigrams, which are models of the activities carried out by the system, consist of *activity boxes* (Figure C-7). Each activity box may have input and output data, constraints placed upon the activity, and sources of support for the activity. The activity within a system is described by creating an SADT activity box for each procedural function in the system and combining them into an actigram (Figure C-8).

Datagrams are models of the data relationships within the system. The *data box* (Figure C-9) is the foundation element in the datagram. The data box contains a description of the data and indicates which activity generates the data, which activity utilizes or receives the data, and what constraints are placed on the data. The data box may also show support activities or data storage areas. Data boxes for a system are com-

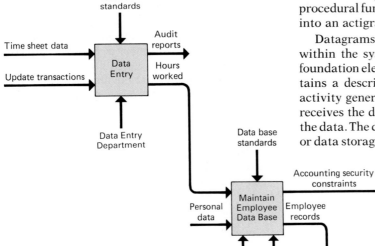

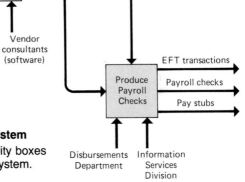

FIGURE C-8 SADT Actigram for a Payroll System
SADT actigrams are compiled by linking the activity boxes that depict the procedural functions of a payroll system.

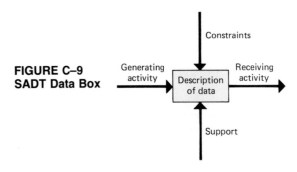

FIGURE C-9
SADT Data Box

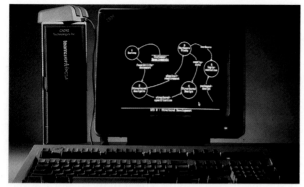

Teamwork/PCSA, a product of Cadre Technologies Inc., is a comprehensive computer-aided software engineering (CASE) tool that, among other things, enables system designers to create and edit flow diagrams.

bined into a datagram in a manner similar to the way activity boxes are combined to create an actigram.

C–5 Pseudocode

Another design technique that is used almost exclusively for program design is called **pseudocode**. While the other techniques represent the logic of the program graphically, pseudocode represents the logic in programlike statements written in plain English. Because pseudocode does not have any syntax guidelines (rules

for formulating instructions), you can concentrate totally on developing the logic of the program. Once you feel the logic is sound, the pseudocode is easily translated into a procedure-oriented language that can be executed. In Figure C–10, the logic of a simple program is represented in pseudocode and a flowchart.

C–6 Decision Tables

The **decision table** is a handy tool that analysts and programmers use to depict graphically what happens in a system or program for occurrences of various circumstances. The decision table is based on IF–THEN logic. *IF* this set of conditions is met, *THEN* take this action. Decision tables are divided into quadrants (see Figure C–11). Conditions that may occur are listed in the *condition stub* (the upper left quadrant). The possible occurrences for each condition are noted in the *condition entries* (the upper right quadrant). Each possible set of conditions, called a *rule*, is numbered at the top of each column. Actions that can result from various combinations of conditions, or rules, are listed in the *action stub* (the lower left quadrant). For each rule, an action-to-be-taken entry is made in the *action entries* (the lower right quadrant).

The decision table in Figure C–12 illustrates what action is taken for each of several sets of conditions. For example, *IF* the employees to be processed are salaried and it is the end of the month (Rule 1), *THEN*

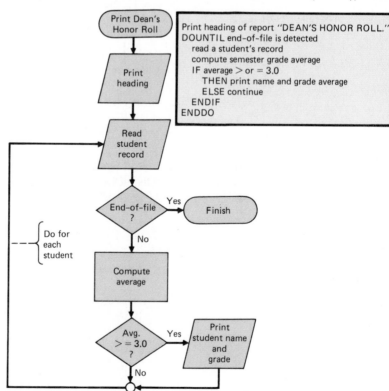

FIGURE C–10 Pseudocode with Flowchart

This pseudocode program depicts the logic of a program to compile a list of students who have qualified for the dean's honor roll. The same logic is shown in a flowchart.

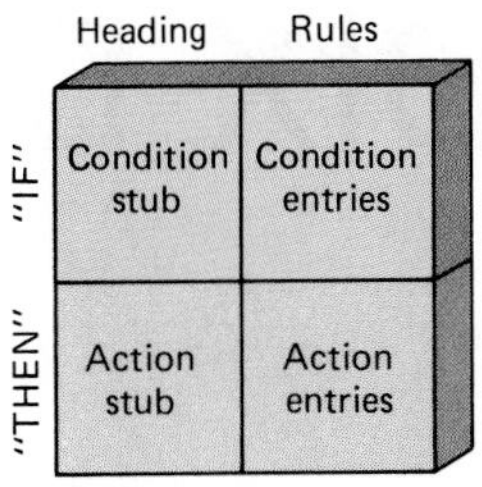

FIGURE C–11 Decision Table Format

Decision tables are divided into four quadrants: condition stub, condition entries, action stub, and action entries.

both paychecks and a payroll register are printed. *IF* the employees to be processed are on a commission and it is the end of the week (Rule 4), *THEN* only paychecks are printed.

The decision table is not a good technique for illustrating work flow. It is, however, very helpful when used in conjunction with the other techniques discussed in this appendix. The major advantage of decision tables is that a programmer or analyst must consider *all* alternatives, options, conditions, variables, and so on. With decision tables, the level of detail is dictated by the circumstances. With flowcharts and other design techniques, the level of detail is more a matter of personal preference.

Self-Test (by section)

C–1 The four symbols used in data flow diagrams are the entity, process, flow line, and _____.

C–2 a. Flowcharting is used primarily for program design and rarely for systems design. (T/F)

  b. The shape of a flowcharting decision symbol is: (a) an oval, (b) a diamond, or (c) a rectangle.

  c. In structured programming, the module that causes other program modules to be executed as they are needed is called a _____ module.

  d. The shape of a terminal point symbol is: (a) an oval, (b) a diamond, or (c) a rectangle.

C–3 a. The HIPO overview diagram illustrates the interactions between the input, _____, output, and storage activities for a particular module.

  b. A HIPO _____ breaks down a system into a hierarchy of modules.

C–4 a. Actigrams and datagrams are integral to the preparation of data flow diagrams. (T/F)

  b. SADT, HIPO, and DFD are all top-down design techniques. (T/F)

C–5 Pseudocode is a very flexible design technique, although it has rigid syntax guidelines. (T/F)

C–6 a. In a decision table, each possible set of conditions is called a _____.

  b. IF–THEN logic provides the foundation for: (a) DFDs, (b) SADT, or (c) decision tables.

  c. For each rule in a decision table, an action-to-be-taken entry is made in the action entries. (T/F)

Self-test answers. **C–1** data store. **C–2** (a) F; (b) b; (c) driver; (d) a. **C–3** (a) processing; (b) structure chart. **C–4** (a) F; (b) T. **C–5** F. **C–6** (a) rule; (b) c; (c) T.

Payroll type/output chart	Rules				
	1	2	3	4	5
Salaried employee	Y	N	N	N	N
Hourly employee	N	Y	Y	N	N
Commission employee	N	N	N	Y	Y
End of week	N	Y	N	Y	N
End of month	Y	N	Y	N	Y
Print paychecks	X	X		X	X
Print payroll register	X	X	X		X

FIGURE C–12 Decision Table

This decision table depicts what payroll outputs would be generated for various payroll types and conditions.

APPENDIX D

Programming Concepts

This appendix contains an overview of those programming concepts that should be understood prior to learning a particular programming language. After having studied the material, you should be able to identify approaches to solving a programming problem, describe the concept of structured programming, and classify the different types of programming instructions.

D–1 Programming in Perspective

A computer is not capable of performing calculations or manipulating data without exact, step-by-step instructions. These instructions take the form of a computer program. Five, fifty, or even several hundred programs may be required for an information system. Electronic spreadsheet software is made up of dozens of programs that work together so that you can perform spreadsheet tasks. The same is true of word processing software.

Most of the programs you develop while you are a student will be independent of those developed by your classmates and, more often than not, independent of one another. In a business environment, however, programs often complement one another. For example, you might write one program to collect the data and another program to analyze the data and print a report.

There is no such thing as an "easy" program. A programming task, whether it be in the classroom, in business, or at home, should challenge your intellect and logic capabilities. As soon as you develop competence at one level, your instructor will surely assign you a program that is more difficult than anything you have done in the past. Even when doing recreational programming on your personal computer, you won't be satisfied with an "easy" program. You will probably challenge yourself with increasingly complex programs.

A knowledge of programming will always be a plus, even if you don't plan to write programs at home or at work. The following are just a few of the many benefits of learning to program.

1. You will gain an appreciation for what the computer can and cannot do.
2. You will develop good logic skills.
3. You will be able to communicate more effectively with other programmers and systems analysts.
4. You will be able to write your own "custom" programs.

These insurance claims agents interact with mainframe-based information systems; however, a number of them also work with micro-based information systems. The techniques used in designing the computer programs for these systems are the same for both mainframes and micros.

If you wish to learn programming, ask your instructor about the availability of *BASIC for Introductory Computing* by Larry Long (Prentice Hall, 1990), a supplement to this book. This supplement is designed to provide you with the skills needed to achieve an intermediate level of competency in **BASIC** programming. **BASIC** is available on more computer systems than any other language and, not surprisingly, it is learned by more people than any other computer language.

D-2 Problem Solving and Programming Logic
The Power of Logic

A single program addresses a particular problem: to compute and assign grades, to permit an update of a data base, to monitor a patient's heart rate, to analyze marketing data, and so on. In effect, when you write a program, you are solving a *problem*. To solve the problem, you must derive a *solution*. And to do that, you must use your powers of *logic*.

A program is like the materials used to construct a building. Much of the brainwork involved in the construction of a building goes into the blueprint. The location, appearance, and function of a building are determined long before the first brick is laid. And so it is with programming. The design of a program, or its programming logic (the blueprint), is completed before the program is written (or the building is constructed).

Structured Program Design: Divide and Conquer

Figure D–1 illustrates a *structure chart* for a program to print weekly payroll checks. Hourly and commission employees are processed weekly. A structure chart for a program to print monthly payroll checks for salaried employees would look similar, except that Task 1.2, "Compute gross earnings," would not be required. The salary amount can be retrieved directly from the employee data base.

The structure chart permits a programming problem to be broken down into a hierarchy of tasks. A

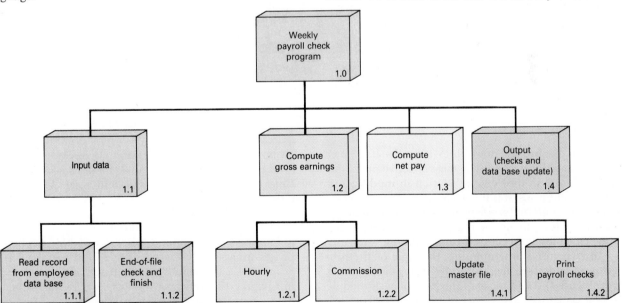

FIGURE D–1 Program Structure Chart
The logic of a payroll program to print weekly payroll checks can be broken down into modules for ease of understanding, coding, and maintenance.

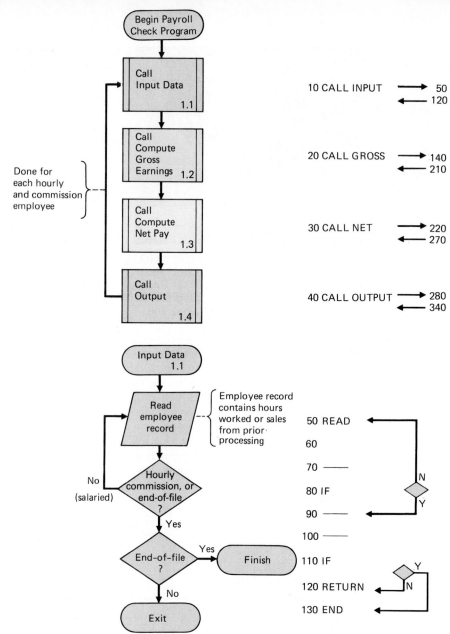

task can be broken down into subtasks if a finer level of detail is desired. The most effective programs are designed so they can be written in **modules**, or independent tasks. It is much easier to address a complex programming problem in small, more manageable modules than as one big task. This is done using the principles of **structured programming**.

In structured programming, the logic of the program is addressed hierarchically in logical modules (see Figure D–1). In the end, the logic of each module is translated into a sequence of program instructions that can be executed independently. By dividing the program into modules, the structured approach to programming reduces the complexity of the pro-

gramming task. Some programs are so complex that if taken as a single task, they would be almost impossible to conceptualize, design, and code. Again, we must "divide and conquer."

D–3 Program Design Techniques

A number of techniques are available to help programmers analyze a problem and design the program. These techniques are discussed and illustrated in Chapter 12, "Systems Analysis and Design" (data flow diagrams, or DFDs), and Appendix C, "Design Techniques" (flowcharting, HIPO, SADT, pseudocode, and decision tables). For decades flowcharting remained the design technique of choice for both systems

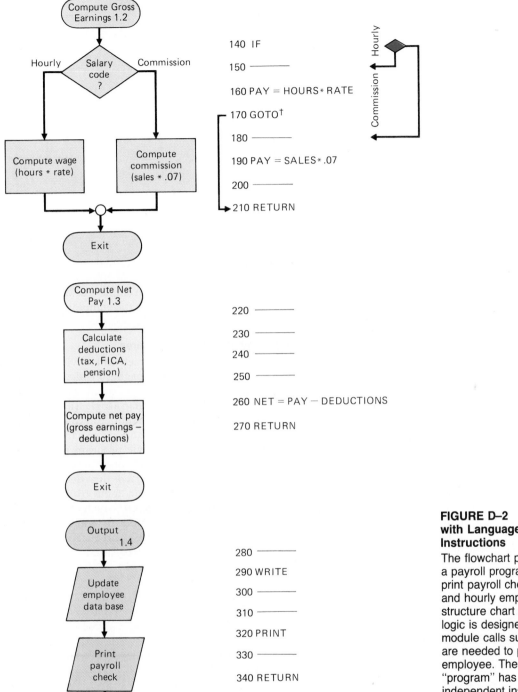

```
140 IF

150 ─────

160 PAY = HOURS * RATE

170 GOTO†

180 ─────

190 PAY = SALES * .07

200 ─────

210 RETURN
```

```
220 ─────

230 ─────

240 ─────

250 ─────

260 NET = PAY − DEDUCTIONS

270 RETURN
```

```
280 ─────

290 WRITE

300 ─────

310 ─────

320 PRINT

330 ─────

340 RETURN
```

†Included for demonstration purposes.
See "GOTO-less programming."

FIGURE D–2 Program Flowchart with Language-Independent Instructions

The flowchart presents the logic of a payroll program to compute and print payroll checks for commission and hourly employees (see the structure chart of Figure D–1). The logic is designed so that a driver module calls subroutines as they are needed to process each employee. The accompanying "program" has a few language-independent instructions to help illustrate the concepts and principles of programming. This figure is discussed in detail in the text.

analysts and programmers. Although analysts are opting for more structured techniques today, programmers continue to prefer flowcharting. The logic of the examples that follow is portrayed with flowcharts.

Program Flowcharts

Flowcharts illustrate data, information, and work flow through the interconnection of specialized symbols with flow lines. The combination of symbols and flow lines portrays the logic of the program. The program flowchart of Figure D–2 portrays the logic for the structure chart of Figure D–1. The flowchart symbols used in Figure D–2 are the computer process (rectangles), the predefined process (rectangles with extra vertical lines), the decision (diamond-shaped), and the terminal point (ovals). The use of these and other commonly used flowchart symbols is illustrated in Figure C–2 in Appendix C. The instructions in Figure D–2 adjacent to the flowchart symbols are discussed in the next section.

In the example of Figure D–2 the company processes hourly and commission employee checks each week (salary employee checks are processed monthly). Gross earnings for hourly employees are computed by multiplying hours worked times the rate of pay. For salespeople on commission, gross earnings are computed as a percentage of sales.

The Driver Module

In structured programming, each program has a *driver module* that causes other program modules to be executed as they are needed. The driver module for our example payroll program (see Figure D–2) is a **loop** that "calls" each of the subordinate modules, or **subroutines**, as they are needed to process each employee. The program is designed so that when the payroll program is initiated, the "input data" module (1.1) is executed, or "performed," first. After execution, control is then returned to the driver module unless there are

FIGURE D–3   Sequence Control Structures

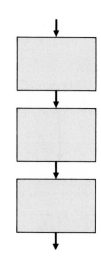

no more employees to be processed, in which case execution is terminated (the "Finish" terminal point). For each hourly or commission employee, Modules 1.2, 1.3, and 1.4 are performed. At the completion of each subroutine, control is passed back to the driver module.

Programming Control Structures

Through the 1970s, programmers unknowingly wrote what is now referred to as "spaghetti code." It was so named because their program flowcharts appeared more like a plate of spaghetti than a logical analysis of a programming problem. The redundant and unnecessary branching (jumps from one portion of the program to another) of a spaghetti-style program resulted in confusing logic, even to the person who wrote it.

Computer scientists thwarted this dead-end approach to developing program logic by identifying three basic *control structures* into which any program or subroutine can be segmented. By conceptualizing the logic of a program in these three structures—*sequence, selection,* and *loop*—programmers can avoid

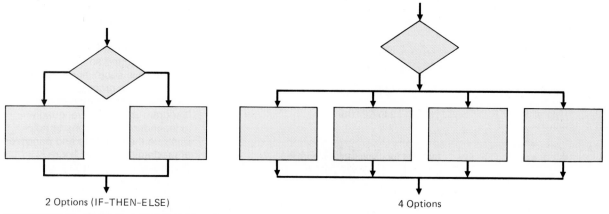

2 Options (IF–THEN–ELSE)   4 Options

FIGURE D–4   Selection Control Structures
Any number of options can result from a decision in a selection control structure.

writing spaghetti code and thus produce programs that can be understood and maintained more easily. The use of these three basic control structures has paved the way for a more rigorous and scientific approach to solving a programming problem. These three control structures are illustrated in Figures D–3, D–4, and D–5, and their use is demonstrated in the payroll example of Figure D–2.

Sequence Structure   In the sequence structure (Figure D–3), the processing steps are performed in sequence, one after another. Modules 1.3 and 1.4 in Figure D–2 are good examples of sequence structures.

Selection Structure   The selection structure (Figure D–4) depicts the logic for selecting the appropriate sequence of statements. In Figure D–2, our example payroll program, the selection structure is used to illustrate the logic for the computation of gross pay for hourly and commission employees (Module 1.2). In the selection structure, a decision is made as to which sequence of instructions is to be executed next.

The selection structure of Module 1.2 presents two decision options—hourly or commission. Other circumstances might call for three or more decision options.

Loop Structure   The loop structure (Figure D–5) is used to represent the program logic when a portion of the program is to be executed repeatedly until a particular condition is met. There are two variations of the loop structure (see Figure D–5): When the decision, or *test-on-condition*, is placed at the beginning of the statement sequence, it becomes a *DOWHILE loop*; when placed at the end, it becomes a *DOUNTIL loop* (pronounced *doo while* and *doo until*). Notice that the leading statements in a DOUNTIL structure are always executed at least once. In the example payroll flowchart of Figure D–2, that portion of the input data module (1.1) that reads an employee record is illustrated in a DOUNTIL loop. Employee records, containing hours worked and sales data, are read sequentially. Because only hourly or commission employees are processed weekly, the loop is repeated until the record of an hourly or commission employee is read, or until the end-of-file marker is reached. When an hourly or commission employee record is read, control is returned to the driver module, which in turn passes control to Module 1.2.

Level of Flowchart Detail   The example program flowchart of Figure D–2 is made somewhat general so that the concepts can be demonstrated more easily. A flowchart showing greater detail could be compiled, if desired. For example, Figure D–6 illustrates how Module 1.3, "Compute Net Pay," can be expanded to show more detail.

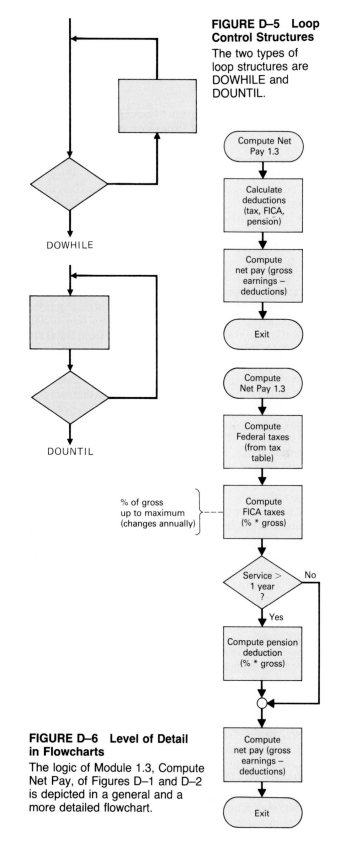

FIGURE D–5 Loop Control Structures
The two types of loop structures are DOWHILE and DOUNTIL.

DOWHILE

DOUNTIL

FIGURE D–6   Level of Detail in Flowcharts
The logic of Module 1.3, Compute Net Pay, of Figures D–1 and D–2 is depicted in a general and a more detailed flowchart.

In program flowcharting, the level of detail is a matter of personal preference. Some programmers complete a general flowchart that outlines the overall program logic, then develop a more detailed flowchart.

D–4 So What's a Program? Concepts and Principles of Programming

A computer program consists of a sequence of instructions that are executed one after another. These instructions, also called **statements**, are executed in sequence unless the order of execution is altered by a "test-on-condition" instruction or a "branch" instruction.

The flowchart of our example payroll program (Figure D–2) is accompanied by a sequence of language-independent instructions. Except for the computation of gross earnings, the processing steps are similar for both types of employees. Two sequences of instructions are needed to compute gross earnings for *hourly* and *commission* employees. We also can see from the flowchart that the sequence in which the instructions are executed may be altered at three places (decision symbols), depending on the results of the test-on-condition. In Module 1.2, for example, the sequence of instructions to be executed depends on whether the test-on-condition detects an hourly or a commission employee.

To the right of the flowchart in Figure D–2 is a representation of a sequence of language-independent instructions and the order in which they are executed. *Statement numbers* are included, as they are in most program listings. This program could be written in any procedure-oriented language. The purpose of the following discussion is to familiarize you with general types of programming instructions, not those of any particular programming language. Each language has an instruction set with at least one instruction in each of the following *instruction classifications:* input/output, computation, control, data transfer and assignment, and format.

Input/Output   Input/output instructions direct the computer to "read from" or "write to" a peripheral device (for example, printer, disk drive). *Statement 50* of Figure D–2 requests that an employee record, including pay data, be read from the data base. *Statement 320* causes a payroll check to be printed.

Computation   Computation instructions perform arithmetic operations (add, subtract, multiply, divide, and raise a number to a power). *Statement 160* (PAY = HOURS * RATE) computes gross earnings for hourly employees. *Statement 190* (PAY = SALES * .07) computes gross earnings for commission employees, where the commission is 7% of sales.

Control (Decision and/or Branch)   The two types of control instructions, *unconditional* and *conditional*, can alter the sequence of the program's execution. Unconditional and conditional instructions prompt a decision and, perhaps, a branch to another part of the program or to a subroutine. In Figure D–2, *Statements 10–40, 80, 110, 130, 140, 210, 270,* and *340* are control instructions.

Unconditional Instructions.   *Statements 10 through 40* are unconditional branch instructions. An unconditional branch instruction disrupts the normal sequence of execution by causing an unconditional branch to another part of the program or to a subroutine. In *Statements 10–40*, the branch is from the driver module to a subroutine. The CALL statement works in conjunction with the RETURN statement to branch to another location, then RETURN control back to the statement following the CALL. For example, the CALL at *Statement 10* passes control to the input data module (1.1) at *Statement 50*, then the RETURN at *Statement 120* passes control back to the driver module at *Statement 20*.

Another unconditional branch instruction, very popular before structured programming, is the GOTO (pronounced, *go to*) instruction. The GOTO statement causes control of execution to "go to" another portion of the program. A GOTO instruction is placed at *Statement 170* so that once the hourly pay is calculated, control is passed directly to the RETURN statement in order to bypass that portion of Module 1.2 that deals with commission employees.

The GOTO at *Statement 170* was included for demonstration purposes, but in an actual program it should have been avoided when possible. Programming gurus advocate that the GOTO statement be used sparingly. Excessive use of GOTOs destroys the logical flow of the program and makes it difficult to divide the program into modules. Some companies simply do not permit the use of GOTO statements at all, thus the term **GOTO-less programming**. The theory behind GOTO-less programming is that programmers tend to use GOTOs to get out of a programming corner instead of applying good sound logic. If GOTOs are not allowed, then programmers are encouraged to divide the program into modules and to make judicious use of the three control structures in Figures D–3, D–4, and D–5. For example, to avoid the GOTO statement (170) in the example, the "Compute Gross Earnings" module (1.2) could have been subdivided into Modules 1.2.1 (hourly computation) and Module 1.2.2 (commission computation).

The END instruction at *Statement 130* terminates program execution. Control is passed to the END instruction from *Statement 110* when the end-of-file marker is detected.

Programming is no longer limited to technical specialists. These product marketing managers have their own micros and have learned to program. For short programs, it may take less time for end users to write their own programs than to describe the problem to a professional programmer.

Conditional Instructions. Statements 80 and 110 are conditional branch instructions and are generally referred to as IF statements: If certain conditions are met, then a branch is made to a certain part of the program. The conditional branch at *Statement 80* causes the program to "loop" until the employee record read is for either an hourly or a commission employee, or the end-of-file marker is reached. The sequence of instructions, *Statements 50 through 80*, comprise a DOUNTIL loop. The IF at *Statement 110* causes the program to branch to an END instruction if there are no more employees to be processed.

Each programming language offers one or more specialized instructions for the express purpose of creating loops.

In *Statement 140*, the salary code is checked. IF the salary code is "commission," then a branch is made to *Statement 180* and processing is continued.

Data Transfer and Assignment Data can be transferred internally from one primary storage location to another. In procedure-oriented languages, data are transferred, or "moved," by *assignment instructions*. These instructions permit a *string constant*, also called a *literal value*, such as "The net pay is", or a *numeric value*, such as 234, to be assigned to a named primary storage location.

In a program, a primary storage location is represented by a **variable name** (for example, PAY, HOURS, NET). A variable name in a program statement refers to the *contents* of a particular primary storage location. For example, a programmer may use the variable name HOURS in a computation statement (*Statement 160*)

to refer to the numeric value of the *hours worked* by a particular employee.

Format Format instructions are used in conjunction with input and output instructions; they describe how the data are to be entered or outputted from primary storage. When the READ at *Statement 50* retrieves an employee's record from secondary storage, it is loaded to primary storage as a string of characters. The format instruction enables the program to distinguish which characters are to be associated with the variables EMPLOYEE-NAME, SALARY-CODE, and so on.

On output, format instructions print headings on reports and present data in a readable format. For example, PAY may be computed to be 324750; however, on output, you would want to "edit" 324750 and insert a dollar sign, a decimal point, and perhaps a comma for readability ($3,247.50). This is called *editing* the output.

With these few types of instructions, you can model almost any business or scientific procedure, whether it be sales forecasting or guiding rockets to the moon. Chapter 13, "System Implementation," contains a step-by-step description of the program development process.

Self-Test (by section)

D–1 a. The software for an electronic spreadsheet package is contained in a single program. (T/F)

   b. One of the benefits of learning how to write computer programs is that this knowledge will help you develop good logic skills. (T/F)

D–2 a. Programs can be written in _____, or independent tasks.

   b. In structured programming, the logic of the program is addressed in logical modules in a: (a) bottom-up manner, (b) hierarchical manner, or (c) horizontal manner.

   c. The design of a program is completed _____ (before/after) the program is written.

D–3 a. Flowcharting is the only design technique that is applicable only to programming. (T/F)

   b. In a flowchart, the combination of _____ and _____ portrays the logic of the program.

   c. Modules that are subordinate to the driver module in a computer program are called: (a) subroutines, (b) call segments, or (c) loop ends.

   d. The test-on-condition in a DOWHILE loop is placed at the _____ (beginning/end) of the loop.

e. Which of the following is not one of the three basic program control structures: (a) sequence, (b) selection, or (c) circle?

D–4 a. Instructions in a program are executed in sequence unless the order of execution is altered by a format instruction. (T/F)

b. "Subtotal Amount" is a _____ constant.

c. There is a direct relationship between the number of GOTO instructions in a program and how well the program's design is structured. (T/F)

d. _____ instructions direct the computer to "read from" or "write to" a peripheral device.

e. "PAY = SALES * .07" is an example of: (a) an I/O instruction, (b) a computation instruction, or (c) a control instruction.

f. Conditional branch instructions are generally referred to as _____ statements.

Self-test answers. **D–1** (a) F; (b) T. **D–2** (a) modules; (b) b; (c) before. **D–3** (a) F; (b) symbols, flow lines; (c) a; (d) end; (e) c. **D–4** (a) F; (b) string; (c) F; (d) Input/output; (e) b; (f) IF.

Glossary

Abacus Probably the original mechanical counting device, which can be traced back at least 5000 years. Beads are moved along parallel wires to count and perform arithmetic computations.

Absolute cell address A cell address in an electronic spreadsheet that always refers to the same cell.

Access arm The disk-drive mechanism used to position the read/write heads over the appropriate track.

Access time The time interval between the instant a computer makes a request for a transfer of data from a secondary storage device and the instant this operation is completed.

Accumulator The computer register in which the result of an arithmetic or logic operation is formed (related to *arithmetic and logic unit*).

Acoustical coupler A device on which a telephone handset is mounted for the purpose of transmitting data over telephone lines. Used with a modem.

Ada A multipurpose, procedure-oriented language.

Add-on boards Circuit boards that contain the electronic circuitry for a wide variety of computer-related functions (also called *add-on cards*).

Add-on cards See *add-on boards*.

Address (1) A name, numeral, or label that designates a particular location in primary or secondary storage. (2) A location identifier for terminals in a computer network.

ALGOL [*ALGO*rithmic *L*anguage] A high-level programming language designed primarily for scientific applications.

Algorithm A procedure that can be used to solve a particular problem.

Alpha A reference to the letters of the alphabet.

Alpha test The in-house testing of a software product by the vendor prior to its release for beta testing. (Contrast with *beta test*.)

Alphanumeric Pertaining to a character set that contains letters, digits, punctuation, and special symbols (related to *alpha* and *numeric*).

Analog computer A computer that operates on data expressed as a continuously changing representation of a physical variable, such as voltage. (Contrast with *digital computer*.)

Analog-to-digital (A–D) converter A device that translates an analog signal into a digital signal. (Contrast with *digital-to-analog converter*.)

ANSI [*A*merican *N*ational *S*tandards *I*nstitute] An organization that coordinates the setting of standards in the United States, including certain software standards.

APL [*A* Programming *L*anguage] An interactive symbolic programming language used primarily for mathematical applications.

Application A problem or task to which the computer can be applied.

Application generator A very high-level programming language in which programmers specify, through an interactive dialog with the system, which processing tasks are to be performed (also called *code generator*).

Applications portfolio The current mix of existing and proposed information systems in an organization.

Applications software Software that is designed and written to address a specific personal, business, or processing task.

APT [*A*utomatically *P*rogrammed *T*ools] A special-purpose programming language used to program machine tools.

Architecture The design of a computer system.

Arithmetic and logic unit That portion of the computer that performs arithmetic and logic operations (related to *accumulator*).

Arithmetic operators Mathematical operators (add [+], subtract [−], multiply [*], divide [÷], and exponentiation [ˆ]) used in electronic spreadsheet and database software for computations.

Array A programming concept that permits access to a list or table of values by the use of a single variable name.

Array processor A processor composed of several processors, all under the control of a single control unit.

Artificial intelligence (AI) The ability of a computer to reason, to learn, to strive for self-improvement, and to simulate human sensory capabilities.

ASCII [*American Standard Code for Information Interchange*] An encoding system.

ASCII file A generic text file that is stripped of program-specific control characters.

Assembler language A low-level symbolic language with an instruction set that is essentially one-to-one with machine language.

Assistant system A type of knowledge-based system that helps users make relatively straightforward decisions. (Contrast with *expert system.*)

Asynchronous transmission Data transmission at irregular intervals that is synchronized with start/stop bits. (Contrast with *synchronous transmission.*)

Attribute A data element in a relational data base.

Auto-answer A modem function that permits the automatic answering of a call from a remote computer.

Auto-dial A modem function that permits the automatic dialing of the number of a remote computer.

Automatic teller machine (ATM) An automated deposit/withdrawal device used in banking.

Automation The automatic control and operation of machines, processes, and procedures.

Auxiliary storage See *secondary storage.*

Back-end processor A host-subordinate processor that handles administrative tasks associated with retrieval and manipulation of data (same as *data base machine*).

Backup Pertaining to equipment, procedures, or data bases that can be used to restart the system in the event of system failure.

Backup file Duplicate of an existing production file.

Badge reader An input device that reads data on badges and cards (related to *magnetic stripe*).

Bar code A graphic encoding technique in which vertical bars of varying widths are used to represent data.

Bar graph A graph that contains vertical bars that represent specified numeric values.

Bar menu A menu in which the options are displayed across the screen.

BASIC A popular multipurpose programming language.

Batch file A disk file that contains a list of commands and/or programs that are to be executed immediately following the loading of the operating system to main memory.

Batch processing A technique in which transactions and/or jobs are collected into groups (batched) and processed together.

Baud (1) A measure of the maximum number of electronic signals that can be transmitted via a communications channel. (2) Bits per second (common-use definition).

Benchmark test A test for comparing the performance of several computer systems while running the same software, or comparing the performance of several programs that are run on the same computer.

Beta test Testing a software product in a live environment prior to its release to the public. (Contrast with *alpha test.*)

Binary notation Using the binary (base-2) numbering system (0, 1) for internal representation of alphanumeric data.

Bit A *bi*nary digi*t* (0 or 1).

Bits per second (bps) The number of bits that can be transmitted per second over a communications channel.

Block A group of data that is either read from or written to an I/O device in one operation.

Blocking Combining two or more records into one block.

Boilerplate Existing text in a word processing file that can in some way be customized so that it can be used in a variety of word processing applications.

Boot The procedure for loading the operating system to primary storage and readying a computer system for use.

BPI [*Bytes Per Inch*] A measure of data-recording density on secondary storage.

Bridge A protocol-independent hardware device that permits communication between devices on separate local area networks.

Bubble memory Nonvolatile solid-state memory.

Buffer Intermediate memory that temporarily holds data that are en route from main memory to another computer or an input/output device.

Bug A logic or syntax error in a program, a logic error in the design of a computer system, or a hardware fault. (See *debug.*)

Bulletin-board system (BBS) The electronic counterpart of a wall-mounted bulletin board that enables end users in a computer network to exchange ideas and information via a centralized data base.

Bus An electrical pathway through which the processor sends data and commands to RAM and all peripheral devices.

Bus architecture See *open architecture*.

Bus topology A computer network that permits the connection of terminals, peripheral devices, and microcomputers along an open-ended central cable.

Business Systems Planning (BSP) A structured process for MIS planning based on the premise that data are a corporate resource that must be evaluated carefully with respect to organizational needs.

Byte A group of adjacent bits configured to represent a character.

C A transportable programming language that can be used to develop both systems and applications software.

Cache memory High-speed solid-state memory for program instructions and data.

CAD See *computer-aided design*.

CAI See *computer-assisted instruction*.

Callback procedure A security procedure that results in a remote user being called back by the host computer system after the user password and authorization code have been verified.

CAM See *computer-aided manufacturing*.

Capacity planning The process by which MIS planners determine how much hardware resources are needed to meet anticipated demands.

Carrier Standard-sized pin connectors that permit chips to be attached to a circuit board.

Carrier, common [in data communications] A company that furnishes data communications services to the general public.

CASE [Computer-Aided Software Engineering] A collective reference to a family of software development productivity tools (also called *workbench technologies*).

Cathode ray tube See *CRT*.

CBT See *computer-based training*.

CD-ROM disk [Compact Disk Read-Only Memory disk] A type of optical laser storage medium.

Cell The intersection of a particular row and column in an electronic spreadsheet.

Cell address The location—column and row—of a cell in an electronic spreadsheet.

Central processing unit (CPU) See *processor*.

Certificate in Computer Programming (CCP) A certification for programmers.

Certificate in Data Processing (CDP) A general certification in the area of computers and information systems.

Certified Data Educator (CDE) A certification for educators in the general area of computers and information systems.

Certified Information Systems Auditor (CISA) A certification for information systems auditors.

Certified System Professional (CSP) A general certification in the area of computers and information systems.

Channel The facility by which data are transmitted between locations in a computer network (e.g., workstation to host, host to printer).

Channel capacity The number of bits that can be transmitted over a communications channel per second.

Character A unit of alphanumeric datum.

Chargeback system A system designed to allocate the cost of computer and information services to the end users.

Checkpoint/restart When a system fails, backup files/data bases and/or backup transaction logs are used to re-create processing from the last "checkpoint." The system is "restarted" at the last checkpoint, and normal operation is resumed.

Chief information officer (CIO) The individual responsible for all information services in a company.

CIM [Computer-Integrated Manufacturing] Using the computer at every stage of the manufacturing process, from the time a part is conceived until it is shipped.

Clone A hardware device or a software package that emulates a product with an established reputation and market acceptance.

Closed architecture Refers to micros with a fixed, unalterable configuration. (Contrast with *open architecture*.)

Cluster controller See *down-line processor*.

Clustered-bar graph A modified bar graph that can be used to represent a two-dimensional set of numeric data (for example, multiple product sales by region).

Coaxial cable A shielded wire used as a medium to transmit data between computers and between computers and peripheral devices.

COBOL [COmmon Business Oriented Language] A programming language used primarily for administrative information systems.

CODASYL [*CO*nference on *DA*ta *SY*stems Languages] An organization chartered to oversee and approve software tools and procedures, such as programming languages and database management systems.

Code (1) The rules used to translate a bit configuration into alphanumeric characters. (2) The process of compiling computer instructions in the form of a computer program. (3) The actual computer program.

Code generator See *application generator*.

Cold site A backup site equipped for housing a computer system. (Contrast with *hot site*.)

Collate To combine two or more files for processing.

Column A vertical block of cells that runs the length of a spreadsheet and is labeled by a letter.

COM [*C*omputer *O*utput *M*icrofilm/Microfiche] A device that produces a microform image of a computer output on microfilm or microfiche.

Command An instruction to a computer that invokes the execution of a preprogrammed sequence of instructions.

Command-driven Pertaining to software packages that respond to user directives entered as commands.

Common carrier [in data communications] See *carrier, common*.

Communications See *data communications*.

Communications channel The facility by which data are transmitted between locations in a computer network (same as *line* and *data link*).

Communications protocols Rules established to govern the way data are transmitted in a computer network.

Communications software Software that enables a microcomputer to emulate a terminal and to transfer files between a micro and another computer.

Compatibility (1) Pertaining to the ability of one computer to execute programs of, access the data base of, and communicate with another computer. (2) Pertaining to the ability of a particular hardware device to interface with a particular computer.

Competitive advantage A term used to describe a company's leveraging of computer and information technologies to realize an advantage over their competitors.

Compile To translate a high-level programming language, such as COBOL, into machine language in preparation for execution.

Compiler Systems software that performs the compilation process. (Compare with *interpreter*.)

Computer See *processor*.

Computer console The unit of a computer system that allows operator and computer to communicate.

Computer network An integration of computer systems, workstations, and communications links.

Computer system A collective reference to all interconnected computing hardware, including processors, storage devices, input/output devices, and communications equipment.

Computer-aided design (CAD) Use of computer graphics in design, drafting, and documentation in product and manufacturing engineering.

Computer-aided manufacturing (CAM) A term coined to highlight the use of computers in the manufacturing process.

Computer-assisted instruction (CAI) Use of the computer in the educational process. (Contrast with *computer-based training*.)

Computer-based training (CBT) Using computer technologies for training and education. (Contrast with *computer-assisted instruction*.)

Computerese A slang term that refers to the jargon associated with computers and information processing.

Concatenation The joining together of labels or fields and other character strings into a single character string in electronic spreadsheet or database software.

Concentrator See *down-line processor*.

Configuration The computer and its peripheral devices.

Connectivity Pertains to the degree to which hardware devices, software, and data bases can be functionally linked to one another.

Contention A line-control procedure in which each workstation "contends" with other workstations for service by sending requests for service to the host processor.

Contingency plan A plan that details what to do in case an event drastically disrupts the operation of a computer center (same as *disaster plan*).

Control clerk A person who accounts for all input to and output from a computer center.

Control field See *key data element*.

Control total An accumulated number that is checked against a known value for the purpose of output control.

Control unit The portion of the processor that interprets program instructions, directs internal operations, and directs the flow of input/output to or from main memory.

Conversion The transition process from one system (manual or computer-based) to a computer-based information system.

Cooperative computing An environment in which businesses cooperate internally and externally to take full advantage of available information and to obtain meaningful, accurate, and timely information (see also *intracompany networking*).

Coprocessor An extra processor under the control of the main processor that helps relieve it of certain tasks.

Core memory A main memory technology that was popular in the 1950s and 1960s.

Cottage industry People who do work-for-profit from their homes.

Counter One or several programming instructions used to tally processing events.

CPU The main processor in a computer system (see also *host processor*).

Critical Path Method (CPM) A network modeling technique that enables managers to show the relationships between the various activities involved in a project and to select the approach that optimizes the use of resources while meeting project deadlines (similar to *Project Evaluation and Review Technique*, or *PERT*).

Critical success factors (CSF) A procedure by which a manager identifies areas of business activity that are critical to the successful operation of the functions within his or her scope of responsibility.

CRT [*Cathode Ray Tube*] The video monitor component of a workstation.

Cryptography A communications crime-prevention technology that uses methods of data encryption and decryption to scramble codes sent over communications channels.

Cursor A blinking character that indicates the location of the next input on the display screen.

Cyberphobia The irrational fear of, and aversion to, computers.

Cylinder A disk storage concept. A cylinder is that portion of the disk that can be read in any given position of the access arm. (Contrast with *sector*.)

Daisy-wheel printer A letter-quality serial printer. Its interchangeable character set is located on a spoked print wheel.

DASD [*Direct-Access Storage Device*] A random-access secondary storage device.

Data Representations of facts. Raw material for information. (Plural of *datum*.)

Data base (1) An organization's data resource for all computer-based information processing in which the data are integrated and related to minimize data redundancy. (2) Same as a file in the context of microcomputer usage. (Contrast with *database*.)

Data base administrator (DBA) The individual responsible for the physical and logical maintenance of the data base.

Data base machine See *back-end processor*.

Data base management system (DBMS) A systems software package for the creation, manipulation, and maintenance of the data base.

Data base record Related data that are read from or written to the data base as a unit.

Data bits A data communications parameter that refers to the number of bits in a message.

Data communications The collection and distribution of the electronic representation of information from and to remote facilities.

Data communications specialist A person who designs and implements computer networks.

Data dictionary A listing and description of all data elements in the data base.

Data diddling The unauthorized revision of data upon being entered into a system or placed in storage.

Data element The smallest logical unit of data. Examples are employee number, first name, and price; same as *field*. (Compare with *data item*.)

Data entry The transcription of source data into machine-readable format.

Data entry operator A person who uses key entry devices to transcribe data into a machine-readable format.

Data flow diagram (DFD) A design technique that permits documentation of a system or a program at several levels of generality.

Data item The value of a data element. (Compare with *data element*.)

Data link See *communications channel*.

Data management software See *database software*.

Data processing (DP) Using the computer to perform operations on data.

Database An alternative term for microcomputer-based data management software. (Contrast with *data base*.)

Database software Software that permits users to create and maintain a data base and to extract information from the data base (also called *data management software*).

DB2 IBM's mainframe-based relational DBMS.

Debug To eliminate bugs in a program or system. (See *bug*.)

Decimal The base-10 numbering system.

Decision support system (DSS) An interactive information system that relies on an integrated set of user-friendly hardware and software tools to produce and present information targeted to support management decision making involving semistructured and unstructured problems. (Contrast with *executive support system* and *management information system*.)

Decision table A graphic technique used to illustrate possible occurrences and appropriate actions within a system.

Decode To reverse the encoding process. (Contrast with *encode*.)

Default options Preset software options that are assumed valid unless specified otherwise by the user.

Density The number of bytes per linear length of track of a recording medium. Usually measured in bytes per inch (bpi) and applied to magnetic tapes and disks.

Departmental computing Any type of computing done at the departmental level.

Departmental computing system Computer systems used both as stand-alone systems in support of a particular department and as part of a network of departmental minicomputers, all linked to a large centralized computer.

Desktop computer Any computer that can be placed conveniently on the top of a desk (same as *microcomputer*, *personal computer*, *PC*).

Desktop film recorders An output device that permits the reproduction of high-resolution computer-generated graphic images on 35-mm film.

Desktop laser printers A small printer that uses laser technology to print near-typeset-quality text and graphics one page at a time.

Desktop publishing Refers to the hardware and software capability of producing near-typeset-quality copy from the confines of a desktop.

Diagnostic The isolation and/or explanation of a program error.

Dial-up line See *switched line*.

Dictionary See *information repository*.

Digital computer A computer that operates on data that are expressed in a discrete format (such as an on-bit or off-bit). (Contrast with *analog computer*.)

Digital-to-analog (D–A) converter A device that translates a digital signal into an analog signal. (Contrast with *analog-to-digital converter*.)

Digitize To translate data or an image into a discrete format that can be interpreted by computers.

Digitizing tablet A pressure-sensitive tablet with the same *x-y* coordinates as a computer-generated screen. The outline of an image drawn on a tablet with a stylus or puck will be reproduced on the display.

DIP [*Dual Inline Package*] A toggle switch that is typically used to designate certain computer-system configuration specifications (such as the amount of RAM).

Direct access See *random access*.

Direct conversion An approach to system conversion whereby operational support by the new system is begun when the existing system is terminated.

Direct-access file See *random file*.

Direct-access processing See *random processing*.

Direct-access storage device See *DASD*.

Director of information services The person who has responsibility for computer and information systems in an organization.

Directory A list of the names of the files stored on a particular diskette or in a named area on a hard disk.

Disaster plan See *contingency plan*.

Disk, magnetic A secondary storage medium for random-access data storage. Available as microdisk, diskette, disk cartridge, or disk pack.

Disk drive, magnetic A magnetic storage device that records data on flat rotating disks. (Compare with *tape drive, magnetic*.)

Diskette A thin, flexible disk for secondary random-access data storage (same as *floppy disk* and *flexible disk*).

Distributed data processing Both a technological and an organizational concept based on the premise that information systems can be made more responsive to users by moving computer hardware and personnel physically closer to the people who use them.

Distributed DBMS Software that permits the interfacing of data bases located in various places throughout a computer network.

Distributed processor The nucleus of a small computer system linked to the host computer and physically located in the functional area departments.

Documentation Permanent and continuously updated written and graphic descriptions of information systems and programs.

Domain expert An expert in a particular field who

provides the factual knowledge and the heuristic rules for input to a knowledge base.

DOS [*D*isk *O*perating *S*ystem] A generic reference to a disk-based operating system.

Download The transmission of data from a mainframe computer to a workstation.

Downtime The time during which a computer system is not operational.

Down-line processor A computer that collects data from a number of low-speed devices, then transmits "concentrated" data over a single communications channel (also called a *concentrator* and *cluster controller*).

DP Abbreviation for *data processing*.

Driver module The program module that calls other subordinate program modules to be executed as they are needed.

Dump The duplication of the contents of a storage device to another storage device or to a printer.

E-mail See *electronic mail*.

Earth station An earth-based communications station that can transmit and receive data from communications satellites.

EBCDIC [*E*xtended *B*inary *C*oded *D*ecimal *I*nterchange *C*ode] An encoding system.

Education coordinator The person who coordinates all computer-related educational activities within an organization.

EDP Abbreviation for *electronic data processing*.

EFT [*E*lectronic *F*unds *T*ransfer] A computer-based system allowing electronic transfer of money from one account to another.

EGA [*E*nhanced *G*raphics *A*dapter] A circuit board that enables the interfacing of high-resolution monitors to microcomputers.

Electronic bulletin board A computer-based "bulletin board" that permits external users access to the system via data communication for the purpose of reading and sending messages.

Electronic data interchange (EDI) The use of computers and data communications to transmit data electronically between companies.

Electronic data processing Same as *data processing*.

Electronic dictionary A disk-based dictionary used in conjunction with a spelling-checker program to verify the spelling of words in a word processing document.

Electronic funds transfer See *EFT*.

Electronic mail A computer application whereby messages are transmitted via data communications to "electronic mailboxes." Also called *E-mail*. (Contrast with *voice message switching*.)

Electronic spreadsheet See *spreadsheet, electronic*.

Encode To apply the rules of a code. (Contrast with *decode*.)

Encoding system A system that permits alphanumeric characters to be coded in terms of bits.

Encyclopedia See *information repository*.

End user The individual providing input to the computer or using computer output (same as *user*).

End user computing A computing environment in which the end users handle both the technical and functional tasks of the information systems projects.

End-of-file (EOF) marker A marker placed at the end of a sequential file.

EPROM Erasable PROM [*P*rogrammable *R*ead-*O*nly *M*emory]. See *PROM*.

Exception report A report that has been filtered to highlight critical information.

Execution time The elapsed time it takes to execute a computer instruction and store the results.

Executive support system (ESS) A system designed specifically to support decision making at the strategic level. (Contrast with *decision support system* and *management information system*.)

Expansion slots Slots within the processing component of a microcomputer into which optional add-on circuit boards can be inserted.

Expert system An interactive knowledge-based system that responds to questions, asks for clarification, makes recommendations, and generally helps users make complex decisions. (Contrast with *assistant system*.)

Expert system shell The software that enables the development of expert systems.

Facilities management company For a fee, employees of facilities management companies physically move into a client company's computer center and take over all facets of the center's operation.

Facsimile Equipment that transfers images of hardcopy documents via telephone lines to another office.

Fault-tolerant system A computer system that can operate under adverse environmental conditions.

Feasibility study A study performed to determine the economic and procedural feasibility of a proposed information system.

Feedback loop In a process control environment, the

output of the process being controlled is input to the system.

Fetch instruction That part of the instruction cycle in which the control unit retrieves a program instruction from main memory and loads it to the processor.

Field See *data element*.

File (1) A collection of related records. (2) A named area on a secondary storage device that contains a program, data, or textual material.

Filtering The process of selecting and presenting only that information that is appropriate to support a particular decision.

Firmware Logic for performing certain computer functions that is built into a particular computer by the manufacturer, often in the form of ROM or PROM.

Fixed disk See *hard disk*.

Flat files A traditional file structure in which records are related to no other files.

Flat-panel monitor A monitor, thin from front to back, that uses liquid crystal and gas plasma technology.

Flexible disk See *diskette*.

Floppy disk See *diskette*.

Flops Floating point operations per second.

Flowchart A diagram that illustrates data, information, and work flow via specialized symbols which, when connected by flow lines, portray the logic of a system or program.

Footprint The evidence of unlawful entry or use of a computer system.

Format line See *layout line*.

FORTH A programming language particularly suited for microcomputers that enables users to tailor the language's set of commands to any application.

FORTRAN [*FOR*mula *TRAN*slator] A high-level programming language designed primarily for scientific applications.

Fourth-generation language (4GL) A programming language that uses high-level English-like instructions to retrieve and format data for inquiries and reporting.

Frequency division multiplexing A method of simultaneously transmitting several communications signals over a transmission medium by dividing its band width into narrower bands, each carrying a communications signal.

Front-end processor A processor used to offload certain data communications tasks from the host processor.

Frozen specifications System specifications that have been approved and are not to be changed during the system development process.

Full-duplex line A communications channel that transmits data in both directions at the same time.

Full-screen editing This word processing feature permits the user to move the cursor to any position in the document to insert or replace text.

Function A predefined operation that performs mathematical, logical, statistical, financial, and character-string operations on data in an electronic spreadsheet or a data base.

Function key A special-function key on the keyboard that can be used to instruct the computer to perform a specific operation (also called *soft key*).

Function-based information system An information system designed for the exclusive support of a specific application area, such as inventory management or accounting.

Functional specifications Specifications that describe the logic of an information system from the perspective of the user.

Functionally adjacent systems Information systems that feed each other, have functional overlap, and/or share all or part of a data base.

Gateway Software that permits computers of different architectures to communicate with one another.

Gateway computer A subordinate computer that translates communications protocols of remote computers to a protocol that is compatible with the host computer, thereby enabling the transmission of data from external sources.

General-purpose computer Computer systems that are designed with the flexibility to do a variety of tasks, such as CAI, payroll processing, climate control, and so on. (Contrast with *special-purpose computer*.)

Geostationary orbit See *geosynchronous orbit*.

Geosynchronous orbit An orbit that permits a communications satellite to maintain a fixed position relative to the surface of the earth (also known as *geostationary orbit*).

Gigabyte (G) Referring to one billion bytes of storage.

GIGO [*G*arbage *I*n, *G*arbage *O*ut] A euphemism implying that information is only as good as the data from which it is derived.

Global memory Pertaining to random-access memory that is shared by several processors.

Grammar checker An add-on program to word processing software that highlights grammatical concerns and deviations from conventions in a word processing document.

Grandfather-father-son method A secondary storage backup procedure that results in the master file having two generations of backup.

Graphics workstation A terminal with a high-resolution graphics monitor for the sophisticated user that is endowed with its own processing capability as well as the ability to interface with a mainframe.

Hacker A computer enthusiast who uses the computer as a source of recreation.

Half-duplex line A communications channel that transmits data in both directions, but not at the same time.

Handshaking The process by which both sending and receiving devices in a computer network maintain and coordinate data communications.

Hard carriage return In word processing, a special character that is inserted in the document when the carriage return is pressed. Typically, the character denotes the end of a paragraph or of a string of contiguous text.

Hard copy A readable printed copy of computer output. (Contrast with *soft copy*.)

Hard disk A permanently installed, continuously spinning magnetic storage medium made up of one or more rigid disk platters. (Same as *fixed disk*; contrast with *interchangeable magnetic disk*.) See also *Winchester disk*.

Hard-wired Logic that is designed into chips.

Hardware The physical devices that comprise a computer system. (Contrast with *software*.)

Hashing A method of random access in which the address is arithmetically calculated from the key data element.

Head crash A disk drive malfunction that causes the read/write head to touch the surface of the disk, thereby resulting in the loss of the disk head, the disk, and the data stored on the disk.

Help command A software feature that provides an on-line explanation of or instruction on how to proceed.

Help screen The display that results from initiating the help command.

Hertz One cycle per second.

Heuristic knowledge Rules of thumb that evolve from experience.

Hexadecimal A base-16 numbering system used as a programmer convenience in information processing to condense binary output and make it more easily readable.

Hierarchical data base A data base whose organization employs the tree data structure. (Contrast with *relational data base* and *network data base*.)

High-level programming language A language with instructions that combine several machine-level instructions into one instruction. (Compare with *machine language* or *low-level programming language*.)

HIPO [*H*ierarchical Plus *I*nput-Processing-Output] A design technique that encourages the top-down approach, dividing the system into easily manageable modules.

Historical reports Reports generated from data that were gathered in the past, and do not reflect the current status. Reports based solely on historical data are rare in practice. (Contrast with *status reports*.)

Host computer See *host processor*.

Host processor The processor responsible for the overall control of a computer system. The host processor is the focal point of a communications-based system (also called *host computer*).

Hot site A backup site equipped with a functioning computer system. (Contrast with *cold site*.)

I/O [*I*nput/Output] Input or output, or both.

Icons Pictographs used in place of words or phrases on screen displays.

Idea processor A software productivity tool that allows the user to organize and document thoughts and ideas (also called an *outliner*).

Identifier A name used in computer programs to recall a value, an array, a program, or a function from storage.

Image processor A device that uses a camera to scan and digitize an image that can be stored on a disk and manipulated by a computer.

Index file Within the context of database software, a file that contains logical pointers to records in a data base.

Index sequential access method A direct-access data storage scheme that uses an index to locate and access data stored on magnetic disk.

Inference engine The logic embodied in the software of an expert system.

Information Data that have been collected and processed into a meaningful form.

Information center A facility in which computing resources are made available to various user groups.

Information center specialist Someone who works with users in an information center.

Information engineering A term coined to emphasize using the rigors of the engineering discipline in the handling of the information resource.

Information management systems (IMS) IBM's mainframe-based hierarchical DBMS.

Information network Same as *information service*.

Information overload The circumstance that occurs when the volume of available information is so great that the decision maker cannot distinguish relevant from irrelevant information.

Information repository A central computer-based storage facility for all system design information (also called *dictionary* and *encyclopedia*).

Information resource management (IRM) A concept advocating that information be treated as a corporate resource.

Information service An on-line commercial network that provides remote users with access to a variety of information services (same as *information network*).

Information services auditor Someone who is responsible for ensuring the integrity of operational information systems.

Information services department The organizational entity that develops and maintains computer-based information systems.

Information society A society in which the generation and dissemination of information becomes the central focus of commerce.

Information system A computer-based system that provides both data processing capability and information for managerial decision making.

Information technology A collective reference to the combined fields of computers and information systems.

Information-based decision See *nonprogrammed decision*.

Input Data to be processed by a computer system.

Input/output-bound operation The amount of work that can be performed by the computer system is limited primarily by the speeds of the I/O devices.

Inquiry An on-line request for information.

Insert mode A data entry mode in which the character entered is inserted at the cursor position.

Instruction A programming language statement that specifies a particular computer operation to be performed.

Instruction cycle The cycle of operations performed by the processor to process a single program instruction: fetch, decode, execute, and prepare for the next instruction.

Instruction register The register that contains the instruction being executed.

Instruction time The elapsed time it takes to fetch and decode a computer instruction.

Integer Any positive or negative whole number and zero.

Integrated circuit (IC) Thousands of electronic components that are etched into a tiny silicon chip in the form of a special-function electronic circuit.

Integrated information system An information system that services two or more functional areas, all of which share a common data base.

Integrated software Two or more of the major microcomputer productivity tools integrated into a single commercial software package.

Intelligent Pertaining to computer aided.

Intelligent terminal A terminal with a built-in microprocessor.

Intelligent workstation A workstation endowed with its own sophisticated processing capability as well as the ability to interface with a mainframe.

Interactive Pertaining to on-line and immediate communication between the end user and computer.

Interactive computer system A computer system that permits users to communicate directly with the system.

Interblock gap (IBG) A physical space between record blocks on magnetic tapes.

Interchangeable magnetic disk A magnetic disk that can be stored off-line and loaded to the magnetic disk drive as it is needed. (Contrast with *hard disk*, or *fixed disk*.)

Intercompany networking See *electronic data interchange*.

Interpreter Systems software that translates and executes each program instruction before translating and executing the next. (Compare with *compiler*.)

Interrupt A signal that causes a program or a device to stop or pause temporarily.

Intracompany networking The use of computers and data communications to transmit data electronically within a company (see also *cooperative computing*).

ISAM See *indexed sequential access method*.

ISO [*International Standards Organization*] An organization that coordinates the setting of international standards.

Job   A unit of work for the computer system.

Job control language (JCL)   A language used to tell the computer the order in which programs are to be executed.

Job stream   The sequence in which programs are to be executed.

Joystick   A single vertical stick that moves the cursor on a screen in the direction in which the stick is pushed.

Kb   See *kilobyte*.

Kernel   An independent software module that is part of a larger program.

Key data element   The data element in a record that is used as an identifier for accessing, sorting, and collating records. (Same as *control field*.)

Keyboard   A device used for key data entry.

Keyboard templates   Typically, a plastic keyboard overlay that indicates which commands are assigned to particular function keys.

Keyword   See *reserved word*.

Kilobyte (Kb)   A computerese abbreviation for 2 to the 10th power, or 1024.

Knowledge acquisition facility   That component of the expert system shell that permits the construction of the knowledge base.

Knowledge base   The foundation of a knowledge-based system that contains facts, rules, inferences, and procedures.

Knowledge engineer   Someone trained in the use of expert system shells and in the interview techniques needed to extract information from a domain expert.

Knowledge worker   Someone whose job function revolves around the use, manipulation, and dissemination of information.

Knowledge-based system   A computer-based system that helps users make decisions by enabling them to interact with a knowledge base.

Large-scale integration (LSI)   An integrated circuit with a densely packed concentration of electronic components. (Contrast with *very large-scale integration*, or *VLSI*.)

Layout   A detailed output and/or input specification that graphically illustrates exactly where information should be placed/entered on a VDT display screen or placed on a printed output.

Layout line   A line on a word processing screen that graphically illustrates appropriate user settings (margins, tabs). Also called a *format line*.

Leased line   A permanent or semipermanent communications channel leased through a common carrier.

Lexicon   The dictionary of words that can be interpreted by a particular natural language.

Librarian   A person who functions to catalog, monitor, and control the distribution of disks, tapes, system documentation, and computer-related literature.

Light-emitting diode (LED)   A device that responds to electrical current by emitting light.

Limits check   A system check that assesses whether the value of an entry is out of line with that expected.

Line   See *communications channel*.

Line graph   A graph in which conceptually similar points are plotted and connected so they are represented by one or several lines.

Linkage editor   An operating system program that assigns a primary storage address to each byte of an object program.

Liquid crystal display (LCD)   An output device that displays characters and other images as composites of actuated liquid crystal.

LISP   [*LIS*t *Processing*]   A programming language particularly suited for the manipulation of words and phrases that is often used in applications of artificial intelligence.

Live data   Test data that have already been processed through an existing system.

Load   To transfer programs or data from secondary to primary storage.

Local area network (LAN or local net)   A system of hardware, software, and communications channels that connects devices on the local premises.

Local memory   Pertaining to the random access memory associated with a particular processor or peripheral device.

Log on procedure   The procedure by which a user establishes a communications link with a remote computer.

Logic bomb   A program, planted in a computer system by a malicious programmer, designed to destroy or alter programs or files when triggered by a particular sequence of events or the passage of a certain point in time.

Logic operations   Computer operations that make comparisons between numbers and between words, then perform appropriate functions, based on the result of the comparison.

Logical operators Used to combine relational expressions logically in electronic spreadsheet and database software (such as AND, OR). See also *relational operators*.

Logical record See *record*.

LOGO A programming language often used to teach children concepts in mathematics, geometry, and computer programming.

Loop A sequence of program instructions that are executed repeatedly until a particular condition is met.

Low-level programming language A language comprising the fundamental instruction set of a particular computer. (Compare with *high-level programming language*.)

Machine cycle The time it takes to retrieve, interpret, and execute a program instruction.

Machine independent Pertaining to programs that can be executed on computers of different designs.

Machine language The programming language that is interpreted and executed directly by the computer. (Contrast with *high-level programming language*.)

Macro A sequence of frequently used operations or keystrokes that can be recalled and invoked to help speed user interaction with microcomputer productivity software.

Magnetic disk See *disk, magnetic*.

Magnetic disk drive See *disk drive, magnetic*.

Magnetic ink character recognition (MICR) A data entry technique used primarily in banking. Magnetic characters are imprinted on checks and deposits, then scanned to retrieve the data.

Magnetic stripe A magnetic storage medium for low-volume storage of data on badges and cards (related to *badge reader*).

Magnetic tape See *tape, magnetic*.

Magnetic tape drive See *tape drive, magnetic*.

Magneto-optical disk An optical laser disk with read and write capabilities.

Mail merge A computer application in which text generated by word processing is merged with data from a data base (e.g., a form letter with an address).

Main memory See *primary storage*.

Main menu The highest level menu in a menu tree.

Mainframe computer A large computer that can service many users simultaneously.

Maintenance The ongoing process by which information systems (and software) are updated and enhanced to keep up with changing requirements.

Management information system (MIS) An integrated structure of data bases and information flow throughout all levels and components of an organization, whereby the collection, transfer, and presentation of information is optimized to meet the needs of the organization. (Contrast with *decision support system* and *executive support system*.)

Manipulator arm The movable part of an industrial robot to which special-function tools are attached.

MAP [*Manufacturing Automation Protocol*] A communications protocol, developed by General Motors, that enables the linking of robots, machine tools, automated carts, and other automated elements of manufacturing into an integrated network.

Master file The permanent source of data for a particular computer application area.

Maxicomputers That category of computers that falls between minicomputers and supercomputers.

Mb See *megabyte*.

Megabyte (Mb) Referring to one million bytes of primary or secondary storage capacity.

Memory See *primary storage*.

Memory-resident program A program, other than the operating system, that remains operational while another applications program is running.

Menu A workstation display with a list of processing choices an end user may select.

Menu driven Pertaining to software packages that respond to user directives that are entered via a hierarchy of menus.

Message A series of bits sent from a workstation to a computer, or vice versa.

Metal-oxide semiconductor (MOS) A technology for creating tiny integrated circuits in layers of conducting metal that are separated by silicon dioxide insulators.

Methodology A set of standardized procedures, including technical methods, management techniques, and documentation, that provides the framework for accomplishing a particular task (e.g., system development methodology).

MHz [megahertz] One million hertz.

MICR inscriber An output device that enables the printing of characters for magnetic ink character recognition on bank checks and deposit slips.

MICR reader-sorter An input device that reads the

magnetic ink character recognition data on bank documents and sorts them.

Micro/mainframe link Linking microcomputers and mainframes for the purpose of data communication.

Microchip An integrated circuit on a chip.

Microcomputer (or micro) A small computer (same as *desktop computer, personal computer, PC*).

Microcomputer specialist A specialist in the use and application of microcomputer hardware and software.

Microdisk A $3\frac{1}{2}$-inch flexible disk used for data storage.

Microframe A high-end microcomputer.

Microprocessor A computer on a single chip. The processing component of a microcomputer.

Microsecond One millionth of a second.

Milestone A significant point in the development of a system or program.

Millisecond One thousandth of a second.

Minicomputer (or mini) A midsized computer.

MIPS Millions of instructions per second.

MIS See *management information system.*

MIS planner The person in a company who has the responsibility for coordinating and preparing the MIS plans.

MIS steering committee A committee of top executives who are charged with providing long-range guidance and direction for computer and MIS activities.

Mnemonics Symbols that represent instructions in assembler languages.

Modem [*MO*dulator-*DEM*odulator] A device used to convert computer-compatible signals to signals suitable for data transmission facilities, and vice versa.

Modula-2 A general-purpose language that enables self-contained modules to be combined in a program.

Monitor A televisionlike display for soft-copy output in a computer system.

Motherboard A microcomputer circuit board that contains the microprocessor, electronic circuitry for handling such tasks as input/output signals from peripheral devices, and memory chips.

Mouse A small device that, when moved across a desktop a particular distance and direction, causes the same movement of the cursor on a screen.

MS-DOS [*MicroSoft Disk Operating System*] A microcomputer operating system.

Multicomputer A complex of interconnected computers that share memory while operating in concert or independently.

Multidrop The connection of more than one terminal to a single communications channel.

Multifunction add-on board An add-on circuit board that performs more than one function.

Multiplexing The simultaneous transmission of multiple transmissions of data over a single communications channel.

Multiprocessing Using two or more processors in the same computer system in the simultaneous execution of two or more programs.

Multiprogramming Pertaining to the concurrent execution of two or more programs by a single computer.

Multiuser microcomputer A microcomputer that can serve more than one user at any given time.

Nanosecond One billionth of a second.

Natural language A programming language in which the programmer writes specifications without regard to the computer's instruction format or syntax—essentially, using everyday human language to program.

Nested loop A programming situation where at least one loop is entirely within another loop.

Network, computer See *computer network.*

Network data base A data base organization that permits children in a tree data structure to have more than one parent. (Contrast with *relational data base* and *hierarchical data base*.)

Node An endpoint in a computer network.

Nonprocedural language A programming language that can automatically generate the instructions needed to create a programmer-described end result.

Nonprogrammed decision A decision that involves an ill-defined and unstructured problem (also called *information-based decision*).

Numeric A reference to any of the digits 0–9. (Compare with *alpha* and *alphanumeric*.)

Object program A machine-level program that results from the compilation of a source program. (Compare with *source program*.)

Object-oriented language A programming language structured to enable the interaction between user-defined concepts (such as a computer screen, a list of items) that contain data and operations to be performed on the data.

OCR scanner A light-sensitive input device that bounces a beam of light off an image to determine the value of the image.

Octal A base-8 numbering system used as a programmer convenience in information processing to condense binary output and make it easier to read.

Off-line Pertaining to data that are not accessible by, or hardware devices that are not connected to, a computer system. (Contrast with *on-line*.)

Office automation (OA) Pertaining collectively to those computer-based applications associated with general office work.

Office automation specialist A person who specializes in the use and application of office automation hardware and software (see *office automation*).

On-line Pertaining to data and/or hardware devices accessible to and under the control of a computer system. (Contrast with *off-line*.)

On-line thesaurus Software that enables a user to request synonyms interactively during a word processing session.

Opcode Pertaining to that portion of a computer machine-language instruction that designates the operation to be performed. Short for *operation code*. (Related to *operand*.)

Open architecture Refers to micros that give users the flexibility to configure the system with a variety of peripheral devices. (Contrast with *closed architecture*; also called *bus architecture*.)

Open systems interconnect (OSI) A standard for data communications within a computer network established by the International Standards Organization (ISO).

Operand Pertaining to that portion of a computer machine-language instruction that designates the address of the data to be operated on. (Related to *opcode*.)

Operating environment (1) A user-friendly DOS interface. (2) The conditions under which a computer system functions.

Operating system The software that controls the execution of all applications and systems software programs.

Operation code See *opcode*.

Operator The person who performs those hardware-based activities necessary to keep information systems operational.

Operator console The machine-room operator's workstation.

Optical character recognition (OCR) A data entry technique that permits original-source data entry. Coded symbols or characters are scanned to retrieve the data.

Optical fiber A data transmission medium that carries data in the form of light in very thin transparent fibers.

Optical laser disk A read-only secondary storage medium that uses laser technology.

Optical scanners Devices that provide input to computer systems by using a beam of light to interpret printed characters and various types of codes.

Orphan The first line of paragraph that is printed as the last line on a page in a word processing document.

Output Data transferred from primary storage to an output device.

Outliner See *idea processor*.

Packaged software Software that is generalized and "packaged" to be used with little or no modification in a variety of environments. (Compare with *proprietary software*.)

Packet switching A data communications process in which communications messages are divided into packets (subsets of the whole message), transmitted independent of one another in a communications network, then reassembled at the source.

Page A program segment that is loaded to primary storage only if it is needed for execution (related to *virtual memory*).

Page break In word processing, an in-line command or special character that causes the text that follows to be printed on a new page.

Page offset The distance between the left edge of the paper and the left margin in a word processing document.

Page-composition software The software component of desktop publishing software that enables users to design and make up pages.

Pagination The word processing feature that provides automatic numbering of the pages of a document.

Parallel Pertaining to processing data in groups of bits versus one bit at a time. (Contrast with *serial*.)

Parallel conversion An approach to system conversion whereby the existing system and the new system operate simultaneously until the project team is confident that the new system is working properly.

Parallel host processor A redundant host processor used for backup and supplemental processing.

Parallel port A direct link with the microcomputer's bus that facilitates the parallel transmission of data, usually one byte at a time.

Parallel processor A processor in which many, even millions, of processing elements simultaneously address parts of a processing problem.

Parity bit   A bit appended to a bit configuration (byte) that is used to check the accuracy of data transmission from one hardware device to another (related to *parity checking* and *parity error*).

Parity checking   A built-in checking procedure in a computer system to help ensure that the transmission of data is complete and accurate (related to *parity bit* and *parity error*).

Parity error   Occurs when a bit is dropped in the transmission of data from one hardware device to another (related to *parity bit* and *parity checking*).

Parsing   A process whereby user-written natural language commands are analyzed and translated to commands that can be interpreted by the computer.

Pascal   A multipurpose, procedure-oriented programming language.

Password   A word or phrase known only to the end user. When entered, it permits the end user to gain access to the system.

Patch   A modification of a program or an information system.

Path   The logical route that an operating system would follow when searching through a series of directories and subdirectories to locate a specific file on disk storage.

PBX   A computer that electronically connects computers and workstations for the purpose of data communication.

PC   [*Personal Computer*]   See *desktop computer* and *microcomputer*.

PC-DOS   [*PC Disk Operating System*]   A microcomputer operating system.

Performance monitoring software   System software used to monitor, analyze, and report on the performance of the overall computer system and the computer system components.

Peripheral equipment   Any hardware device other than the processor.

Personal computer (PC)   See *desktop computer* and *microcomputer*.

Personal computing   A computing environment in which individuals use microcomputers for both domestic and business applications.

Personal identification number (PIN)   A unique number that is assigned to and identifies a user of a computer network.

Phased conversion   An approach to system conversion whereby an information system is implemented one module at a time by either parallel or direct conversion.

Pick-and-place robot   An industrial robot that physically transfers material from one place to another.

Picosecond   One trillionth of a second.

Pie graph   A circular graph that illustrates each "piece" of data in its proper relationship to the whole "pie."

Pilferage   A special case of software piracy where a company purchases a software product without a site-usage license agreement, then copies and distributes it throughout the company.

Pilot conversion   An approach to system conversion whereby the new system is implemented by parallel, direct, or phased conversion as a pilot system in only one of the several areas for which it is targeted.

Pipe   Under the Unix operating system, the "connection" of two programs so that the output of one becomes the input of the other.

Pitch   Horizontal spacing (characters per inch) in printed output.

Pixel   An addressable point on a display screen to which light can be directed under program control.

PL/I   A multipurpose, procedure-oriented programming language.

Plotter   A device that produces hard copy graphic output.

Plug-Compatible Manufacturer (PCM)   A company that makes peripheral devices that can be attached directly to another manufacturer's computer.

Point-of-sale (POS) terminal   A cash-register-like terminal designed for key and/or scanner data entry.

Point-to-point connection   A single communications channel linking a workstation or a microcomputer to a computer.

Pointer   The highlighted area in an electronic spreadsheet display that indicates the current cell.

Polling   A line-control procedure in which each workstation is "polled" in rotation to determine whether a message is ready to be sent.

Pop-up menu   A menu that is superimposed in a window over whatever is currently being displayed on the monitor.

Port   An access point in a computer system that permits communication between the computer and a peripheral device.

Post-implementation evaluation   A critical examination of a computer-based system after it has been put into production.

Prespecification   An approach to information systems development where users determine their information processing needs during the early stages of the project, then commit to these specifications through system implementation.

Primary storage   The memory area in which all programs and data must reside before programs can be executed or data manipulated. (Same as *main memory*, *memory*, and *RAM*; compare with *secondary storage*.)

Printer   A device used to prepare hard copy output.

Printer spooler   A circuit board that enables data to be printed while a microcomputer user continues with other processing activities.

Private line   A dedicated communications channel between any two points in a computer network.

Problem-oriented language   A high-level language whose instruction set is designed to address a specific problem (such as process control of machine tools, simulation).

Procedure-oriented language   A high-level language whose general-purpose instruction set can be used to produce a sequence of instructions to model scientific and business procedures.

Process control   Using the computer to control an ongoing process in a continuous feedback loop.

Processor   The logical component of a computer system that interprets and executes program instructions (same as *computer*).

Processor-bound operation   The amount of work that can be performed by the computer system is limited primarily by the speed of the computer.

Program   (1) Computer instructions structured and ordered in a manner that, when executed, cause a computer to perform a particular function. (2) The act of producing computer software (related to *software*).

Program register   The register that contains the address of the next instruction to be executed.

Programmed decisions   Decisions that address well-defined problems with easily identifiable solutions.

Programmer   One who writes computer programs.

Programmer/analyst   The title of one who performs both the programming and systems analysis function.

Programming   The act of writing a computer program.

Programming language   A language programmers use to communicate instructions to a computer.

Project Evaluation and Review Technique (PERT)   A network modeling technique that enables managers to show the relationships between the various activities involved in the project and to select the approach that optimizes the use of resources while meeting project deadlines (similar to *Critical Path Method*, or *CPM*).

Project leader   The person in charge of organizing the efforts of a project team.

Prolog   A descriptive programming language often used in applications of artificial intelligence.

PROM [*Programmable Read-Only Memory*]   ROM in which the user can load read-only programs and data. (See *EPROM*.)

Prompt   A program-generated message describing what should be entered by the end user operator at a workstation.

Proportional spacing   A spacing option for word processing documents in which the spacing between characters remains relatively constant for any given line of output.

Proprietary software   Vendor-developed software that is marketed to the public. (Related to *packaged software*.)

Protocols   Rules established to govern the way data are transmitted in a computer network.

Prototype system   A model of a full-scale system.

Pseudocode   Nonexecutable program code used as an aid to develop and document structured programs.

Puck   A flat hand-held device with cross hairs used in conjunction with a digitizing tablet to translate an image into machine-readable format.

Pull-down menu   A menu that is "pulled down" and superimposed in a window over whatever is currently being displayed on a monitor.

Purging   The act of erasing unwanted data, files, or programs from RAM or magnetic memory.

Quality assurance   An area of specialty concerned with monitoring the quality of every aspect of the design and operation of information systems, including system efficiency and documentation.

RAM [*Random Access Memory*]   See *primary storage*.

Random access   Direct access to records, regardless of their physical location on the storage medium. (Contrast with *sequential access*.)

Random file   A collection of records that can be processed randomly. (Same as *direct-access file*.)

Random processing   Processing data and records randomly. (Same as *direct-access processing*; contrast with *sequential processing*.)

Range   A cell or a rectangular group of adjacent cells in an electronic spreadsheet.

Raster scan monitor   An electron beam forms the image by scanning the screen from left to right and from top to bottom. (Contrast with *vector scan monitor*.)

Read   The process by which a record or a portion of a record is accessed from the magnetic storage medium (tape or disk) of a secondary storage device and transferred to primary storage for processing. (Contrast with *write*.)

Read/write head   That component of a disk drive or tape drive that reads from and writes to its respective magnetic storage medium.

Real-time computing   The processing of events as they occur, usually in a continuous feedback loop.

Reasonableness check   A system checking procedure that determines whether entered or generated data is reasonable when compared to historical data.

Record   A collection of related data elements (such as an employee record). Also called *logical record*.

Recursion   Pertaining to the capability of a program to reference itself as a subroutine.

Register   A small high-speed storage area in which data pertaining to the execution of a particular instruction are stored. Data stored in a specific register have a special meaning to the logic of the computer.

Relational data base   A data base in which data are accessed by content rather than by address. (Contrast with *hierarchical data base* and *network data base*.)

Relational operators   Used in electronic spreadsheet and database formulas to show the equality relationship between two expressions (= [equal to], < [less than], > [greater than], ≤ [less than or equal to], ≥ [greater than or equal to], <> [not equal to]). See also *logical operators*.

Relative cell address   Refers to a cell's position in an electronic spreadsheet in relation to the cell containing the formula in which the address is used.

Replace mode   A data entry mode in which the character entered overstrikes the character at the cursor position.

Report generator   Software that produces reports automatically based on user specifications.

Request for information (RFI)   See *RFI*.

Request for proposal (RFP)   See *RFP*.

Reserved word   A word that has a special meaning to a software package. (Also called *keyword*.)

Resolution   Referring to the number of addressable points on a monitor's screen. The greater the number of points, the higher the resolution.

Response time   The elapsed time between when a data communications message is sent and when a response is received. (Compare with *turnaround time*.)

Responsibility matrix   A matrix that graphically illustrates when and to what extent individuals and groups are involved in each activity of a systems development process.

Reusable code   Modules of programming code that can be called and used as needed.

Reverse video   Characters on a video display terminal presented as black on a light background; used for highlighting.

RFI [*Request For Information*]   A request to a prospective vendor for information about a particular type of product.

RFP [*Request For Proposal*]   A formal request to a vendor for a proposal.

Ring topology   A computer network that involves computer systems connected in a closed loop, with no one computer system the focal point of the network.

Robot   A computer-controlled manipulator capable of locomotion and/or moving items through a variety of spatial motions.

Robotics   The integration of computers and industrial robots.

ROM [*Read-Only Memory*]   RAM that can only be read, not written to.

Root directory   The directory at the highest level of a hierarchy of directories.

Row   A horizontal block of cells that runs the width of a spreadsheet and is labeled by a number.

RPG   A programming language in which the programmer communicates instructions interactively by entering appropriate specifications in prompting formats.

RS-232-C   A "recommended standard" 25-pin plug that is used for the electronic interconnection of computers, modems, and other peripheral devices.

Run   The continuous execution of one or more logically related programs (such as printing payroll checks).

Scheduler   Someone who schedules the use of hardware resources to optimize system efficiency.

Schema   A graphical representation of the logical structure of a CODASYL data base.

Screen formatter   Same as *screen generator*.

Screen generator   A system design tool that enables a systems analyst to produce a mockup of a display while in direct consultation with the user. (Also called a *screen formatter*.)

Screen-image projector An output device that can project a computer-generated image onto a large screen.

Scrolling Using the cursor keys to view parts of a word processing document or an electronic spreadsheet that extends past the bottom or top or sides of the screen.

Secondary storage Permanent data storage on magnetic disk and/or tape. (Same as *auxiliary storage*; compare with *primary storage*.)

Sector A disk storage concept: a pie-shaped portion of a disk or diskette in which records are stored and subsequently retrieved. (Contrast with *cylinder*.)

Self-booting diskette A diskette that contains both the operating system and an applications software package.

Semiconductor A crystalline substance whose properties of electrical conductivity permit the manufacture of integrated circuits.

Sequential access Accessing records in the order in which they are stored. (Contrast with *random access*.)

Sequential files Files containing records that are ordered according to a key data element.

Sequential processing Processing of files that are ordered numerically or alphabetically by a key data element. (Contrast with *direct-access processing* or *random processing*.)

Serial Pertaining to processing data one bit at a time. (Contrast with *parallel*.)

Serial port A direct link with the microcomputer's bus that facilitates the serial transmission of data, one bit at a time.

Serial printer Printers that print one character at a time.

Serpentine A magnetic tape storage scheme in which data are recorded serially in tracks.

Service bureau A company that provides almost any kind of information processing service for a fee.

Service request A formal request from a user for some kind of computer- or MIS-related service.

Set A CODASYL data base concept that serves to define the relationship between two records.

Shelfware Software that was purchased but never used or implemented.

Simplex line A communications channel that transmits data in only one direction.

Situation assessment An MIS planning activity that results in a definition of where the information services division and the functional areas stand with respect to their use of computer and information technologies.

Skeletal code A partially complete program produced by a code generator.

Smalltalk An object-oriented language.

Smart card A card or badge with an embedded microprocessor.

Smart modems Modems that have embedded microprocessors.

SNA [*Systems Network Architecture*] IBM's scheme for networking its computers.

Soft carriage return In word processing, an invisible special character automatically inserted after the last full word within the right margin of entered text.

Soft copy Temporary output that can be interpreted visually, as on a workstation monitor. (Contrast with *hard copy*.)

Soft key See *function key*.

Software The programs used to direct the functions of a computer system. (Contrast with *hardware*; related to *program*.)

Software engineering A term coined to emphasize an approach to software development that embodies the rigors of the engineering discipline. (Also called *systems engineering*.)

Software package One or more programs designed to perform a particular processing task.

Software piracy The unlawful duplication of proprietary software (related to *pilferage*).

Sort The rearrangement of data elements or records in an ordered sequence by a key data element.

Source data automation Entering data directly to a computer system at the source without the need for key entry transcription.

Source code See *source program*.

Source document The original hard copy from which data are entered.

Source program The code of the original program. (Compare with *object program*.) Also called *source code*.

Special-purpose computer Computers designed for a specific application, such as CAD, video games, robots. (Contrast with *general-purpose computer*.)

Speech synthesizers Devices that convert raw data into electronically produced speech.

Spelling checker An add-on program to word processing that checks the spelling of every word in a word processing document against an electronic dictionary.

Spooling The process by which output (or input) is loaded temporarily to secondary storage. It is then output (or input) as appropriate devices become available.

Index

Acknowledgments
of Illustrations

COVER AND CHAPTER OPENINGS: The cover and chapter-opening photos feature works from the growing field of computer art. The **cover** and **chapters 1, 2, 4, 5, 7, 8, 10, 12, 14,** and **16**—Pansophic Graphics Systems and these artists: Robert Boyd (cover), Robert Beech (Ch. 2), Thomas Dahlin (Chs. 4, 5), Heather F. Graham (Ch. 14), Mike McCulley (Ch. 10), Thomas Olsson (Ch. 7), Steve Shepard (Chs. 1, 12), Glenn Simmons (Ch. 8), and Susan Wedeking (Ch. 16). **Chapter 3**—Melvin L. Prueitt, Los Alamos National Laboratory. **Chapters 6, 11, 15**—Genigraphics Corporation. **Chapters 9** and **17**—Wasatch Computer Technology. **Chapter 13**—Program of Computer Graphics, Cornell University.

CHAPTER 1: **2** NCR Corporation; **3** Compaq Computer Corporation, Genigraphics Corporation; **4** Compaq Computer Corporation; **7** courtesy of NEC Information Systems, Inc.; **9** courtesy of International Business Machines Corporation; **10** courtesy of Unisys Corporation; **13, 14** courtesy of International Business Machines Corporation; **18** Cromemco, Inc.; **21, 22** AT&T Technologies; **23** Genigraphics Corporation; **24** NCR Corporation, courtesy of Unisys Corporation; **25, 26** courtesy of International Business Machines Corporation.

CHAPTER 2: **35** Digital Equipment Corporation; **37, 38** courtesy of International Business Machines Corporation; **41** photo courtesy of Hewlett-Packard Company; **42** Boeing Computer Services; **43** Genigraphics Corporation; **44** courtesy of Iowa State University; **47, 48** NCR Corporation; **52** by permission of Bob Glueckstein.

CHAPTER 3: **59** courtesy of International Business Machines Corporation; **60** courtesy Intel Corporation, by permission of Brian Hansen; **61** Toshiba America, Inc., Information Systems Division; **62** photo courtesy of Hewlett-Packard Company; **63** courtesy of International Business Machines Corporation; **64** courtesy of Apple Computer, Inc.; **64** courtesy of International Business Machines Corporation; **66** AST Research Inc.; **69** courtesy of International Business Machines Corporation; **73** courtesy of Apple Computer, Inc.; **76** photo courtesy of Hewlett-Packard Company; **77** courtesy of Apple Computer, Inc.

CHAPTER 4: **86** NCR Corporation; **87** courtesy of International Business Machines Corporation; **92** courtesy of Unisys Corporation; **103** Phillips Petroleum Company, courtesy of Compaq Computer Corporation; **98–99** 1, 7, 8, 12—courtesy of International Business Machines Corporation, 2—courtesy of Unisys Corporation, 3, 4—© M/A-COM, Inc., 5, 11—courtesy Intel Corporation, 6—AT&T Technologies, 9—National Semiconductor Corporation, 10—Cray Research, Inc.

CHAPTER 5: **110, 111** courtesy of Unisys Corporation; **112** photo courtesy of Hewlett-Packard Company; **113** AST Research Inc., Key Tronic; **114** courtesy of Compaq Computer Corporation; **115** GRiD Systems Corporation; **116** Pansophic Graphics Systems; **117** courtesy of International Business Machines Corporation; **118** by permission of Brian Hansen; **119** courtesy of International Business Machines Corporation; **120** CAERE Corporation; **125** courtesy of International Business Machines Corporation, courtesy of Unisys Corporation; **127** courtesy of International Business Machines Corporation; **129** General Electric Company, photo courtesy of Hewlett-Packard Company; **132** Dataproducts Corporation, courtesy of International Business Machines Corporation, photo courtesy of Hewlett-Packard Company; **133** Storage Technology Corporation; **134** MicroAge Computer Stores, Inc.; **136** photo courtesy of Hewlett-Packard Company, CalComp; **137** Genigraphics Corporation; **139** Kurzweil Computer Products.

CHAPTER 6: **147** Storage Technology Corporation, by permission of Brian Hansen; **148** Intelligent Systems Corporation; **149** photo courtesy of Hewlett-Packard Company, courtesy of International Business Machines Corporation; **152** Copyright © Wang Laboratories, Inc. 1989; **155** Seagate Technology; **156** courtesy of International Business Machines Corporation; **157** AT&T Technologies; **160** Phillips Petroleum Company; **161** courtesy of International Business Machines Corporation; **163, 165** Philips and DuPont Optical Company.

CHAPTER 7: **172** NCR Corporation; **174** Zenith Data Systems; **179** photo courtesy of Hewlett-Packard Company, by permission of Fred Jackson III; **182, 184** AT&T Technologies; **185** © M/A-COM, Inc., NASA; **186** TRW Inc.; **188** RCA; **192** courtesy of Unisys Corporation.

CHAPTER 8: **202** courtesy of Compaq Computer Corporation; **204** courtesy of International Business Machines Corporation, Dahlgren Museum, Naval Surface Weapons Center; **208** courtesy of Unisys Corporation; **211** Management Science America, Inc. (MSA); **212** Digital Equipment Corporation; **214** Star Technologies, Inc., Graphicon Products Division; **216, 217** courtesy of International Business Machines Corporation; **220** by permission of Bob Glueckstein; **221** Digital Equipment Corporation; **224** Information Builders, Inc.; **228** courtesy of International Business Machines Corporation; **229** Microsoft Corporation; **231** Cullinet Software, Inc.

CHAPTER 9: **240** General Instrument Corporation; **243** photo courtesy of Hewlett-Packard Company; **248** courtesy of Federal Express Corporation, all rights reserved; **252** courtesy of International Business Machines Corporation; **253** by permission of Bob Glueckstein; **262** Philips and DuPont Optical Company, NEC Home Electronics [U.S.A.] Inc.

CHAPTER 10: **273** photo courtesy of Hewlett-Packard Company; **279** courtesy of International Business Machines Corporation; **282** courtesy of Compaq Computer Corporation; **284** Videx, Inc.; **286** courtesy of Unisys Corporation; **287** NCR Corporation; **289** courtesy of International Business Machines Corporation; **292** SAS Institute Inc., Cary, NC, USA; **294, 295** courtesy of International Business Machines Corporation; **297** Long and Associates; **300** General Electric Company.

CHAPTER 11: **308** courtesy of International Business Machines Corporation; **309** Texas Instruments, Inc.; **312** by permission of Fred Jackson III, courtesy of Apple Computer, Inc.; **313** Copyright © Wang Laboratories, Inc. 1989; **314** 1—Pansophic Graphics Systems, Mac Bright, artist, 2—courtesy of International Business Machines Corporation, 3—reprinted with permission from Computervision Corporation, Bedford, MA, 4—Symbolics, Inc.; **315** 5—Evans & Sutherland and the University of California at San Diego, 6—Sperry Corporation, 7—Star Technologies, Inc., Graphicon Products Division, 8—NCR Corporation; **318** GM Assembly Division, Warren, Michigan; **319, 320** courtesy of International Business Machines Corporation; **321** USAA; **322** Toshiba America, Inc., Information Systems Division; **323** Mobile Image Canada Limited; **324** General Electric Company; **325** courtesy of International Business Machines Corporation; **326** courtesy of NEC Information Systems, Inc.; **327** NASA; **328** photo courtesy of Hewlett-Packard Company; **329** NCR Corporation; **330** Philips and DuPont Optical Company; **331** CAERE Corporation.

CHAPTER 12: **339** courtesy of Compaq Computer Corporation; **340** NCR Corporation; **343, 344** photo courtesy of Hewlett-Packard Company; **345** Cadre Technologies Inc.; **347** courtesy of International Business Machines Corporation; **355** KnowledgeWare, Inc., Atlanta, GA, USA; **357** Symbolics, Inc.; **358** courtesy of Unisys Corporation.

CHAPTER 13: **368** reproduced with permission of AT&T; **370** NCR corporation; **376** courtesy of International Business Machines Corporation; **377, 379, 381** photo courtesy of Hewlett-Packard Company; **383** USAA; **388** by permission of Brian Hansen; **389** courtesy of International Business Machines Corporation; **390** Harcom Security Systems Corporation.

CHAPTER 14: **398** courtesy of Compaq Computer Corporation; **402, 409** photo courtesy of Hewlett-Packard Company; **410** Long and Associates; **413** Aldus Corporation; **414** photo courtesy of Hewlett-Packard Company; **415** courtesy of International Business Machines Corporation; **416** Zenith Data Systems; **417** courtesy of International Business Machines Corporation.

CHAPTER 15: **424** AST Research Inc.; **426** by permission of Fred Jackson III; **430** Texas Instruments, Inc.; **433** courtesy of Compaq Computer Corporation; **436** photo courtesy of Hewlett-Packard Company; **437** Digital Research Inc.; **442** Courtesy of Apple Computer, Inc.; **448** Zenith Data Systems.

CHAPTER 16: **456** Digital Equipment Corporation; **458, 462** courtesy of International Business Machines Corporation; **463** Boeing computer Services; **464** NCR Corporation; **466** by permission of Brian Hansen; **468** NCR Corporation; **469** photo courtesy of Hewlett-Packard Company; **470** NCR Corporation; **474** TRW Inc.; **475** Compaq Computer Corporation; **476** Philips and DuPont Optical Company; **477** photo courtesy of Hewlett-Packard Company; **478** Zenith Data Systems; **480** Long and Associates; **482** copyright © Wang Laboratories, Inc. 1989; **484** reproduced with the permission of AT&T.

CHAPTER 17: **492** reproduced with permission of AT&T; **493** courtesy of Xerox Corporation; **494** courtesy of International Business Machines Corporation; **495** reproduced with permission of AT&T; **497** courtesy of Unisys Corporation; **498** courtesy of International Business Machines Corporation; **501** NCR Corporation; **502** NCR Corporation; **503** Phillips Petroleum Company; **504** by permission of Brian Hansen; **505, 506** courtesy of International Business Machines Corporation; **507** NASA; **508** Symbolics, Inc.; **509** photo courtesy of Hewlett-Packard Company, Diebold, Incorporated; **510** courtesy of International Business Machines Corporation; **511** Long and Associates, courtesy of International Business Machines Corporation; **519** Wright State University, Dayton, Ohio; **513** Control Color Corporation; **514** Compaq Computer Corporation; **517** Calma Company; **518** Zenith Data Systems; **519** NCR Corporation

APPENDIX A: (*Note: credits read from left to right by date on the time line.*) **524** 500 B.C.—The Computer Museum, Boston, MA; 1642—courtesy of International Business Machines Corporation; **525** 1805, 1822–33 (top)—courtesy of International Business Machines Corporation; 1822–33 (bottom)—New York Public Library Picture Collection; **526** 1843—The Bettmann Archive/BBC Hulton; 1884, 1890—courtesy of International Business Machines Corporation; **527** 1924, 1920s–50s—courtesy of International Business Machines Corporation; **528** 1935, 1942—courtesy of Iowa State University; 1944—courtesy of International Business Machines Corporation; **529** 1946—United Press International Photo; 1951—courtesy of Unisys Corporation; 1954—courtesy of International Business Machines Corporation; **530** 1959—Honeywell, Inc.; 1963—Digital Equipment Corporation; 1964—courtesy of International Business Machines Corporation; **531** 1971—TRW Inc.; 1977—courtesy of Apple Computer, Inc.; 1981—courtesy of International Business Machines Corporation.

APPENDIX C: **540** Index Technology Corporation; **546** Cadre Technologies Inc.

APPENDIX D: **549** USAA; **555** photo courtesy of Hewlett-Packard Company.